FORDHAM UNIVERSITY SCHOOL OF LAW

FORDHAM UNIVERSITY PRESS

New York 2012

FORDHAM UNIVERSITY SCHOOL OF LAW *A History*

ROBERT J. KACZOROWSKI

Fordham University Press has no responsibility
for the persistence or accuracy of URLs for
external or third-party Internet websites referred
to in this publication and does not guarantee that
any content on such websites is, or will remain,
accurate or appropriate.

Fordham University Press also publishes its books
in a variety of electronic formats. Some content
that appears in print may not be available in
electronic books.

Library of Congress Cataloging-in-Publication
Data

Kaczorowski, Robert J.
    Fordham University School of Law : a history /
Robert J. Kaczorowski.
        p.   cm.
    Includes bibliographical references and index.
    ISBN 978-0-8232-3955-9 (hardback)
    1. Law schools—New York (State)—New
York—History.   2. Law—Study and
teaching—New York (State)—New
York—History.   I. Fordham University. School
of Law History.   II. Title.
KF292.F67K33   2012
340.071'17471—dc23

                                                2011040569

Printed in the United States of America
14 13 12   5 4 3 2 1
First edition

To the members of the

Fordham Law School

community:

past, present, and future

CONTENTS

Photographs follow pages 212 and 308

ACKNOWLEDGMENTS

I undertook to write this history in the summer of 2005 at the request of Dean William M. Treanor. His encouragement, suggestions, and support were indispensable to the successful completion of this undertaking.

Many people contributed their talents to this book, and I am deeply grateful for their contributions. Librarians were particularly helpful. Most of the materials that contain the history of Fordham University School of Law—or Fordham Law School as I shall refer to it—are housed in the Fordham University Archives and Special Collections Division of the Walsh Library. These materials are superbly organized, maintained, and indexed under the expert supervision of Patricia M. Kane. Ms. Kane greatly facilitated and expedited the research this book required. Members of the Fordham Law Library also performed extraordinary service. Kate McLeod solved seemingly unsolvable research issues. Deputy Director Mary McKee ensured that the Law Library acquired whatever materials I needed. When necessary materials were available only through interlibrary loan, Juan Fernandez expertly identified their location and acquired them with remarkable speed. I could not have done the statistical analyses in Chapter 2 without the aid of Professor Lorenz J. Finison of the Boston University School of Public Health and my colleague Professor John Pfaff. Larry and John generously gave their time and expertise in establishing the sampling strategy and statistical models we used to calculate the percentage of Fordham Law students who were immigrants and/or sons and daughters of immigrants, the students' ethnicity, and their religious affiliations. I was very fortunate to have had the research assistance of extraordinarily talented law students. I am deeply grateful to Annie Chen, Daniel Crockett, Christine Ford, Peter Handler, Marissa Marco, Gabrielle Markeson, Lauren Sasser McCulloch, Miles Plant Lauren Steele, and Chelsea Walsh. Alyssa L. Beaver, editor-in-chief of the *Fordham Law Review*, graciously made some of her staff available to cite-check two chapters of the manuscript and ensure the accuracy of the text. Mari Byrne, symposium editor of the *Law Review*, was very professional in supervising their work. The Law School's skilled administrative assistants were always available when I needed them, and they resolved every software problem I encountered. Christian Steriti's dedication and professionalism are incomparable. Christian, Kim Holder, and Emma Mercer generously gave their time and applied their exceptional skills in handling unusual and complex computer issues.

Many members of the Fordham Law community who were part of its history from the 1960s to the present read portions of the manuscript, and their comments and suggestions have greatly improved it. Professor Gail Hollister was especially helpful from the beginning of this project through the end. She read and offered valuable suggestions regarding the entire manuscript. Professors Robert Byrn, Hugh Hansen, Barry Hawk, Constantine Katsoris, Michael M. Martin, Joseph Perillo, Thomas Quinn, and Joseph Sweeney, Registrar Robert Hanlon, and Assistant Dean Robert Reilly made important contributions to the history that is recounted in this book. I also received valuable comments and recommendations from the participants of the Fordham Law School Faculty Workshop and the New York University School of Law Legal History Colloquium.

Two friends and colleagues read the manuscript in its entirety. William LaPiana offered many suggestions that helped me refine my discussions of the Fordham Law School's affiliation and administrative relationship with Fordham University and the Law School's natural law philosophy. William Nelson did more than read and comment on the manuscript—he helped me create it. Bill freely and frequently gave his precious time to discuss this history with me, and our discussions contributed to the overall conceptualization and interpretation of the history of Fordham Law School.

To each person who helped create this book, I say, thank you!

FORDHAM
UNIVERSITY
SCHOOL OF
LAW

CHAPTER ONE

THE FOUNDING OF

FORDHAM LAW SCHOOL

When Fordham University School of Law opened its doors on Thursday, September 28, 1905, profound changes were occurring in the United States. The agrarian, small-town America celebrated by Booth Tarkington and satirized by Mark Twain was becoming the industrial world power described and criticized by Frank Norris, Upton Sinclair, and John Dos Passos. The nature of the legal profession and the avenues of entry to the practice of law were undergoing comparable changes with the proliferation of law schools and their monopolization of entry to the bar. This evolution of law schools, in turn, was part of the transformation that was occurring in the nature and structure of higher education.[1]

Paul Fuller was chosen to be the first dean of Fordham Law School, and a good choice it was, because Fuller's humble origins and eventual success epitomized the lives and aspirations of many Fordham Law students. Fuller was as close to a character out of a Horatio Alger novel as one could get. He was born on January 26, 1847, on the clipper ship *Thomas E. Perkins* as it rounded Cape Horn en route to San Francisco. Paul's mother died two weeks after giving birth to him, and his father, who was in the army and traveling to a military post that did not have accommodations for the motherless baby, left Paul in the care of a Mexican family near San Francisco. By the time Paul was nine years of age, his father disappeared. Despairing of ever seeing his remaining parent again, Paul left his Mexican foster family and reportedly walked across the United States in search of his blood relatives in Vermont. Arriving there in 1856, he received such a cold reception from his aunt that he decided to walk a bit farther to New York City, and, at the age of ten, Paul Fuller became one of a legion of homeless boys living on the city's streets. One day, Charles Coudert Sr. happened upon the orphaned, homeless boy, who caught his attention with the perfect Spanish he was speaking, an extraordinary skill for a street waif. Coudert brought Paul home and into his family. Paul's childhood story in New York City paralleled that of the character Dick in Horatio Alger's novel *Ragged Dick, or, Street Life in New York.*[2]

Paul Fuller and the Couderts achieved social prominence within the Catholic community. Paul and his new family became members of New York City's Catholic social elite, whose activities were reported in the society pages of the local press along with those of the leading families of New York society memorialized in the novels of Edith Wharton and Henry James, such as the Astors, Rockefellers, Harrimans, and Roosevelts. Coudert's three sons, Frederic René (1832–1903), Charles Jr. (1833–97), and Louis Leonce (1836–83), became lawyers and founded in 1857 what would become the most important international law firm in New York City at the turn of the twentieth century: Coudert Brothers. This was a remarkable achievement in the face of discrimination against Catholics stemming from "an overwhelming social prejudice and the feeling on the part of many Protestants that Catholicism was somehow antidemocratic and, therefore, un-American." Anti-Catholic prejudice, for example, prevented Frederic René from running for public office and accepting judicial appointments. A prominent reform Democrat in the 1880s and 1890s, he turned down opportunities to run for governor or for the US Senate because he believed "his religion would constitute a crippling political disability outside the precincts of New York City." He said that "he realized that neither he nor any of his family for generations could aspire to any of the big public elective offices," and "unless I gave up my faith, I could never enter the White House except as a visitor." For other reasons, he turned down two separate appointments to the US Supreme Court and an appointment to serve as Minister to Russia offered to him by President Grover Cleveland, a close friend.[3]

Although he did not have the advantages of a college education or of a legal education, facts which he deplored, Paul Fuller became a partner in the Coudert Brothers law firm and "achieved a reputation in legal circles as one of the greatest authorities on international law in the country." He was essentially a self-taught " 'bibliophile of rare discernment and fanatic attachment, an omnivorous reader, a scholar of wide attainment,' who maintained a private library of some twenty-five thousand volumes." His memory was "prodigious"; his knowledge was "diversified" and extended to "all manner of subjects." Though self-taught, Fuller was described as a gifted scholar who possessed "the learning of the Jesuits." He was as fluent in French and Spanish as he was in English, and he read extensively the literature of each of these languages. His cultivation and scholarly bearing suited him perfectly for his practice in consular law, which brought him into contact with many nations' diplomats, who, like Fuller, were scholars and men of letters. The large number of foreign governments around the globe that Coudert Brothers counted as clients, such as France, Belgium, Italy, Venezuela, Russia and Turkey, was attributed by his law partner and nephew Frederic R. Coudert Jr. to Fuller's and the firm's scholarly expertise. Additionally, Fuller was a "'graceful and incisive speaker' and an effective litigator" and a superb brief writer.[4]

The eminence of Coudert Brothers is measurable by several standards. Founded in 1853, it was the "original multinational law firm," being the first American law firm to open a foreign office—in Paris, in 1879. By the founding of Fordham Law School in 1905, Coudert Brothers had additional offices in Manila, Havana, and Washington, DC. Its eminence in international and consular law led Coudert Brothers into important areas of public and private international law, constitutional law, and administrative law, and a number of its cases went to the US Supreme Court, for which Fuller often prepared the firm's arguments and briefs. Perhaps the most important cases it litigated, from a constitutional history standpoint, were the *Insular Cases*.[5]

Fuller's law partner and brother-in-law Frederic René Coudert Sr. was elected to the presidency of one of the nation's most prestigious and elite bar associations, the Association of the Bar of the City of New York, in 1890 and 1891. Fuller himself represented the United States in international arbitrations and was appointed by several American presidents to serve on international commissions. During the Mexican Revolution, he served as President Woodrow Wilson's personal representative to Mexico and reportedly was "the man who . . . had more to do with the adjustment of our relations with the several Mexican revolutionary Governments than even the officers of the State Department. Upon his advice Mr. Wilson has depended for the formulation of every step in the policy of the United States government."[6]

Fuller's dedication to public service and to representing clients who could not afford legal representation additionally suited him to be Fordham Law School's first dean, and it anticipated the school's strong commitment to public interest. Much of Fuller's and the Coudert firm's work was done *pro bono*. The firm's historian described Paul Fuller as having been especially prone to represent "those who had worthy cases but were without means to compensate an attorney for the necessary advice."[7]

Fuller and the Coudert brothers were active in philanthropic activities, public service, and political reform. Fuller served on and gave his time to a wide variety of charitable institutions, including the Catholic Church, orphan asylums, homes for the friendless, probation societies, the New York City School Board, and the Board of Trustees of Hunter College. He was also a political reformer involved in Progressive efforts to clean up government. A Progressive Democrat, Fuller supported anti–Tammany Hall political candidates and groups that attempted to reform New York City government, clean up city politics, and improve city services and city life. He was also a leader in New York City's professional law associations. He was elected vice president of the New York State Bar Association for the First District in January 1908 and served on the Nominating Committee of the New York Law Institute in 1914. For several years he was a member of the Committee on Character of the Association of the Bar of the City of New York, which tightened its requirements during his tenure. Fuller joined with leading members of the New York City Bar to select candidates of quality and integrity for the New York judicial system. The court system was rank with corruption as judicial positions were sold and distributed by Tammany Hall to reward party loyalists and to ensure that matters brought before the courts would be resolved in Tammany's favor. At the very moment he opened Fordham Law School in the fall of 1905, for example, Fuller, along with William D. Guthrie and John L. Cadwalader, supported the reelection of a reformer for district attorney, William Jerome. The following spring, Fuller served on a committee of "thirty-five of the best known lawyers of New York County," which included Alton J. Parker, Joseph Choate, Charles C. Burlingham, John G. Milburn, Elihu Root, Henry W. Taft, and Charles Evans Hughes, to make independent nominations for justices of the New York Supreme Court. Fuller also helped draw up a code of ethics as a member of a committee of the New York County Lawyers' Association, but it was not adopted.[8]

Fuller was a man whose deep religious faith reinforced his innate humility in shaping his character and professional bearing. He is said to have declined public honors but was "inclined . . . to do good unobserved." Unselfishness was his chief endowment, according to John Jay

Chapman, who described Fuller as one of the most unselfish men he ever knew. His selflessness "made him essentially a 'lawyer's lawyer'—an expert to whom others come for advice, but whose name is scarcely known to the public at large." He and the Coudert brothers could have had "the largest practice of any lawyer in New York" had they represented corporations "in doing things which were perverse" although within the letter of the law, but they reportedly refused to represent corporate clients in lucrative cases when the cause they had to argue conflicted with their personal and professional ethics. Frederic René Coudert Jr. thus lectured Columbia Law School students that, although as lawyers they had to make a living to support themselves and their families and would probably prefer wealthy clients to poor ones, he admonished that law "is a profession and not a trade." Business rules and ethics do not apply to lawyers, and a lawyer is not free to maximize his income "if [doing so] involves the slightest sacrifice of professional or personal honor. His self-respect cannot be measured in money."[9]

The founders and organizers of the Fordham University School of Law intended to provide an elite law school education suffused with Fuller's ethical values and scholarly perspective on law. This is evidenced by the first dean they selected to run the law school, from the first faculty they appointed, the curriculum and educational processes they established, and the standards they adopted. Fordham Law School was intended to raise Catholic immigrants and their sons into positions of leadership in professional, economic, and political life. As a leader of the bar, a partner in a preeminent law firm, a civic leader, and a scholar, Dean Fuller was a role model of the kind of lawyer Fordham Law School sought to produce.[10]

Although he had never attended law school (or college, or even high school), Paul Fuller was "a happy selection," as Judge William Hughes Mulligan observed decades later. A Fordham Law alumnus and former dean himself, Mulligan acknowledged that Fordham "was indeed fortunate in obtaining [Fuller's] services as the first Dean of its Law School," even though "this man had never spent a day in a classroom." The lack of a formal education and of a legal education did not hamper Fuller's efforts to make Fordham an outstanding law school, for he possessed in abundance all of the intellectual and professional qualities that the Jesuits at St. John's College (as Fordham was known before it became a university in 1907) could have hoped for.[11]

Dean Fuller and Fordham Law School's early faculty had a distinguished record of academic and scholarly achievements, public service, and professional accomplishments. Fuller published several articles in the *Columbia Law Review* before, during, and after his tenure as dean of Fordham Law School in which he critiqued the Supreme Court's decisions in the *Insular Cases*. He advanced a natural rights theory of constitutional rights and argued that the principles of self-government and individual liberty expressed in the Declaration of Independence and the text and structure of the Constitution followed the flag and that these principles must be extended to all peoples within the jurisdiction of the United States, including the inhabitants of the territories the United States acquired as a result of the Spanish-American War of 1898. He applied Chief Justice John Marshall's theory of broad constitutional construction expressed in *McCulloch v. Maryland* to the Bill of Rights and argued that the Constitution mandated a broad interpretation of the Bill of Rights' guarantees of personal rights and that these guarantees, along with a strict reading of the Constitution's Territorial Clauses, required the president, the Congress, and the federal courts to treat these possessions and their inhabitants in the same manner as the inhabitants of the nation's continental territories. Fuller also asserted a theory of popular constitutionalism that prohibited the government from curtailing constitutionally secured rights and relegated such decisions to the people through constitutional amendment. He maintained that there are constitutionally secured rights that not even a treaty can empower Congress to ignore, a doctrine that the Supreme Court has applied to US citizens in modern times. The status and constitutional rights of the territorial inhabitants went to the core of American democratic government, which required the federal government to guarantee that the inhabitants of the new territories be secure in their fundamental constitutional rights.[12]

Fuller interpreted the Constitution as a liberty-enhancing framework of government. His theory of constitutionalism assumed that the Constitution's "paramount purpose" was the "protection of all personal and civil rights." Its purpose made the Constitution "the greatest 'enabling act' of modern times whose protective scope should always be amplified and never restricted." Echoing the US Supreme Court's theory of constitutional construction expressed most eloquently by Justice Joseph Story before the Civil War, Fuller maintained that the Constitution's purpose of securing personal rights "should be put into execution by such an inter-pretation as will always aid and never hamper it."[13]

Given his view of the central importance of the Constitution to individ-ual liberty and American law, Fuller believed that constitutional law should be "an essential . . . Law School Course" and should "be made a part of any law curriculum." The broad historical and theoretical ap-proach Fuller took in analyzing the constitutional issues in his law practice was the way he thought the subject should be taught to law students: It should be presented as political science and as constitutional history and not as a body of technical legal rules derived from Supreme Court deci-sions. Fuller opined: "The historical background of the Constitution, the circumstances which made it necessary, the compromises which were unavoidable to insure its adoption and the application of its leading prin-ciples to changing conditions through the interpretation of the Courts—these are the things it seems to me that students of law should be thoroughly grounded in." Fuller believed that "the lack of this knowledge at the Bar, on the Bench and throughout the educated community [was] largely responsible for much of the political dissatisfaction and unrest of [his era]." Lawyers had an intellectual role to play in quelling political unrest.[14]

Fuller's commitment to an intellectual, scholarly approach to law; to excellence in lawyering; and to personal integrity, honor, and fairness was reflected in the school's standards, curriculum, and the faculty he and Fordham University President Father John J. Collins, S.J., assembled. While the faculty members continued their active law practices and were highly respected and sought-after lawyers, some were also prolific schol-ars. They also served in a variety of local, state, and federal governmental positions, agencies, and commissions, thus establishing Fordham's con-nection with state and local government. The school's standards for admission and its requirements for the law degree exceeded those of most of the nation's law schools as well as the requirements to be admitted to practice in the state of New York.[15]

At a time when academic prerequisites to entry into the legal profession were meager or nonexistent, Fordham Law School's faculty had substan-tial academic credentials. Of the five original full-time faculty, two held doctorates. One of the two, Reverend Terence J. Shealy, S.J., was a philoso-pher and not a lawyer, and he helped organize the Law School. Two others held the LLM degree. Dean Joseph McLaughlin characterized one of these, H. Gerald Chapin, as the Law School's "first full-time professor." His book *New York Code Pleading* "started a tradition of New York Practice experts at Fordham" that included Professors Francis X. Carmody, John F. X. Finn, and Edward Q. Carr, Dean McLaughlin observed in 1973. With typical McLaughlin humility, he added: "An excess of modesty prohibits my mentioning the name of the present encumbent [*sic*]." Chapin was affiliated with major legal periodicals in the northeastern United States. He served as editor-in-chief of *The American Lawyer* and as the law editor of *The American Banker*, and he wrote editorials on legal topics for the *New York World*. In addition to New York practice, Chapin was an expert in "branches of the law which affect newspapers" and negotiable paper. He also began teaching at New York University School of Law in 1913, although he remained on the Fordham faculty until his death in 1919.[16]

A prolific author who had "already achieved a deservedly high reputation" when he began his teaching career at Fordham, Chapin wrote ten books on banking law, a handbook and casebook on torts, a book on New York practice, and twenty-nine articles on a variety of legal and literary topics. A reviewer of his torts books in the *Fordham Law Review* was "certain" that the handbook would "prove of inestimable value both to the law student and to the practitioner." The reviewer praised Chapin's casebook for presenting "the necessary historical perspective, which," he noted, "is particularly important in the law of torts." The casebook was also very current and included the pathbreaking decision of the New York Court of Appeals in *McPherson v. Buick Motor Co.*, the case that inaugurated the law of products liability, which was decided while Chapin was compiling his casebook. In addition to his legal publications, Chapin wrote poetry and published several articles in the journals *American Lawyer*, *Greenbag*, *Medico-Legal Journal*, and *University Review*. These articles covered a variety of topics, including hypnotism, famous murder cases, preventing premature burial, religion, forgery, and the "Law and Lawyers of Dickens."[17]

Joseph A. Warren was the school's first registrar, and he was also a lecturer in law. He resigned in 1911 after he was elected to the New York Assembly. He subsequently became a partner in the law firm of MacIntyre and Downey, which was formed by Fordham Law professor and alumnus Francis J. MacIntyre. As a member of MacIntyre's law firm, Warren became associated with James J. Walker, who rented an office in the suite occupied by MacIntyre and Downey. MacIntyre and Warren became "intimate friends" of "Gentleman Jimmy" Walker and "protected Jim's interest whenever political duties interfered with his law practice." Walker "prevailed upon his old friend Warren" to accept the position of New York City police commissioner after Walker was elected New York City's mayor in 1926. Though Gentleman Jim's administration was riddled with corruption, Warren was described as "a man of excellent character and honest beyond doubt." This characterization of Warren is consistent with the strong stance he took on legal ethics when he was a member of the Fordham Law faculty. His upright character and honesty apparently contributed to ill health, because he became "a sick man. Nervously sick" over the corruption in Walker's administration. Warren resigned as police commissioner on December 13, 1928. He died eight months later of a paralytic stroke. Walker's critics claimed that "Jim's old friend died of a broken heart and from the 'strain as Commissioner.'" Indeed, Warren was reputed to be "an incorruptible police commissioner."[18]

In September 1906 Fordham Law School expanded its faculty to accommodate the second-year class. It added Dr. William J. O'Sullivan, who earned his medical and law degrees from Yale University, combining careers in law and medicine. The Law School also hired Joseph E. Corrigan, AB, LLB, and Ralph W. Gifford, AB, LLB. Corrigan received his AB degree from Seton Hall and his LLB from Columbia Law School, where he was a founding editor of the *Columbia Law Review*. At Fordham, Corrigan taught Criminal Law and Procedure, which was a good fit because he continued to serve as an assistant district attorney in Manhattan. Ralph W. Gifford became a revered professor at Fordham and Columbia law schools. He was a native of Massachusetts and received his AB degree *magna cum laude* from Harvard University in 1892. He entered Harvard Law School in 1898, tutored Harvard Law students, and taught in the night program at Boston High School in addition to teaching French at Harvard College. He was selected to serve as an editor of the *Harvard Law Review*. Gifford's law professors were among the most distinguished legal educators of the time and included Christopher Columbus Langdell, James Barr Ames, James Bradley Thayer, and Samuel Williston.[19]

Gifford, having been educated in the Langdellian method, introduced the case system of instruction to Fordham. In the 1907–8 academic year,

Gifford was appointed pro dean of the Law School, which is the name given to the position known today as an associate dean. The following year, Fuller appointed Michael F. Dee Pro Dean, a position Dee held until his resignation from the Law School in 1923. Yale Law School appointed Gifford the Lines Professor of Testamentary Law in 1912, but Gifford continued to teach Evidence at Fordham in addition to summer courses at Columbia Law School. Gifford left Yale and joined the Columbia Law faculty in 1914. His teaching was legendary, and he was particularly remembered for his "enormous gusto and wit . . . [and] a treasury of anecdotes." Teaching Criminal Law in the fall semester, he invariably got to the distinction between adultery and fornication just as his class was ending for the Christmas holidays. As the bell sounded, he was reputed to "gleefully rub his hands and deliver this farewell: 'And remember gentlemen, fornication is not a crime in the State of New York! Merry Christmas!' "[20]

In 1911 Fuller appointed William A. Keener to the faculty, one of the most distinguished faculty appointments Fordham Law School has ever made. Keener was one of the most important legal educators of his time and played a central role in shaping legal education in the late nineteenth and early twentieth centuries. Harvard President Charles W. Eliot appointed Keener to the Harvard Law faculty in 1883, and in 1888 Keener was appointed Story Professor of Law, the chair held by Oliver Wendell Holmes Jr. before he took his seat on the Massachusetts Supreme Judicial Court. Keener left Harvard and joined the faculty at Columbia Law School, which adamantly adhered to the older lecture and recitation method and rejected the Langdellian case method until after Keener's appointment in 1890. Keener left Columbia in 1902 and went into private practice, but he returned to law teaching in 1911 when he joined the Fordham Law faculty, and he ended his teaching career at Fordham Law School.[21]

Keener modified the Langdellian case method. He accepted the Langdellian assumptions that law was a science and that, under the case method, "the student must look upon the law as a science consisting of a body of principles to be found in adjudged cases" and that the case method would provide students with a "knowledge of what the law actually is." Under this method, Keener maintained, "the student is practically doing, under the guidance of the instructor what he will be required to do, without guidance, as a lawyer." Nevertheless, Keener recognized the inefficiencies of the case method and began a trend in legal education by writing a textbook to be used in conjunction with the casebook. Viewing law as more complex than did Langdell, Keener placed less reliance on the case method as a way of teaching substantive law and greater emphasis on its "unique ability" to instill in students the sense of law as process and to teach them "the skill of thinking like a lawyer."[22]

In 1912 Dean Fuller hired the first Fordham Law graduates, John T. Loughran and Ignatius M. Wilkinson. Both outstanding hires, Loughran and Wilkinson graduated *summa cum laude* in the class of 1911, with Wilkinson edging out Loughran for top "Honors of the Graduating Class." These men were two of only thirteen out of 10,603 graduates in the first sixty years of Fordham Law School's existence who graduated *summa cum laude*, with the last such graduate in the class of 1931. Only 229 students, or 2.066 percent, graduated with honors from 1908 to 1968.[23]

Wilkinson was born in New York City on January 8, 1887. He received his AB from St. Francis Xavier College in 1908 and entered Fordham Law School that year. He took and passed the bar exam and was admitted to practice in 1910, one year before he graduated with the highest honors of the class of 1911. On graduation, he immediately joined the Fordham Law faculty as an instructor, teaching Domestic Relations and Equity. Two years later he formed the law firm of King & Wilkinson. Wilkinson became dean in 1923, beginning a thirty-year tenure that is the longest in the school's history. In all, Wilkinson spent forty-four years at Fordham, as a student, professor, and dean. He was an active member of many law associations, including the Association of the Bar of the City of New York, the New York County Lawyers' Association, the New York State Bar Association, and the Guild of Catholic Lawyers. He was president of the New York County Lawyers' Association from 1944–46. In 1942 he was a member of the Executive Committee of the American Association of Law Schools. In 1943 Wilkinson served as chair of a committee Mayor Fiorello La Guardia appointed to study labor relations on the New York City transit system, and later he was appointed corporation counsel of the City of New York, a position he held until 1945. One of his last posts was as vice chairman of the New York State Crime Commission from 1951 until his death on June 22, 1953. He was remembered by generations of Fordham students and alumni for his "scrupulous fairness and impartiality" and "as one of [the school's] greatest teachers." "In his teaching and in his life, the Dean was absolutely uncompromising in any matter of principle, whatever the cost might be to him."[24]

Wilkinson was probably a Burkean conservative. He advised Fordham Law students not to "scorn our traditions and the great fabric of our common law as merely hampering survivals of a bygone age. Remember," he said, "that our political organization and the fundamental principles of our law are the fruit of the thinking of many great political and moral philosophers and great judges who built upon the accumulated wisdom of the centuries."[25]

Loughran was admitted to the New York bar the year he graduated, 1911. After one year of practice in his native city of Kingston, New York, he joined the Fordham Law faculty and taught Carriers, Contracts, Sales, and Common Law Pleading. Loughran taught at the Law School for eighteen years while maintaining a private practice in Kingston and, after 1922, in New York City. In the fall of 1930 he was elected a justice of the New York Supreme Court for the Third Judicial District, a position in which he served for over three years. In the spring of 1934, New York Governor Herbert Lehman appointed him a judge of the Court of Appeals to fill the vacancy created by the retirement of Judge Henry T. Kellogg. Loughran subsequently won the endorsement of all of the political parties in New York State, and he was elected to a full fourteen-year term. Although Loughran was a Democrat and identified with the liberal wing of the Court of Appeals, Republican Governor Thomas E. Dewey appointed Loughran Chief Judge of the Court of Appeals on the death of Chief Judge Irving Lehman in 1945. In 1952, on the recommendation of Governor Dewey, the state legislature increased Loughran's salary to $35,000, which was reportedly $10,000 higher than that of Chief Justice of the United States Fred M. Vinson and made Loughran the highest-paid public official in New York State. Loughran remained on the Court until his death on March 31, 1953. Fordham Law School conferred an honorary Doctor of Laws degree on Loughran in 1925, and it awarded him the school's first annual Gold Medal of Achievement in April 1952. The award committee described Judge Loughran as "a lawyer's lawyer and a judge's judge" and a man of "inspiring influence." St. John's and Syracuse Universities and Manhattan College also conferred honorary degrees on him.[26]

Fuller appointed another Fordham Law alumnus to the faculty in 1913, Francis J. MacIntyre. MacIntyre was originally from Philadelphia, where he received his BA and MA from St. Joseph's College. He taught the classics and English in Philadelphia and English at City College when he came to New York. MacIntyre received his LLB from Fordham Law School in 1909 and was appointed an Assistant US Attorney in Manhattan. Fuller hired him as a lecturer, and he was promoted to Associate Professor of Law in 1923. While on the faculty, MacIntyre formed the law firm of MacIntyre & Downey, and he practiced while he taught. He was also active in Democratic Party politics, serving as secretary of the National Democratic Club and as its president in 1945–46. Gentleman Jimmy Walker had his law office in MacIntyre's law firm until he was elected Mayor of New York City in 1926.[27]

Fuller made another significant appointment in his last year as dean, that of I. Maurice Wormser. Wormser enjoyed one of the longest careers on the Fordham faculty, teaching some seven thousand law students over his forty-two years there. A native New Yorker, Wormser earned his BA in 1906 and his LLB in 1909, both at Columbia University. He practiced law for two years and then entered legal academia at the University of Illinois Law School in 1911. He became the first Jewish professor at Fordham Law School when he joined the faculty two years later, and he remained at Fordham until his death on October 22, 1955. He conducted an active law practice at 60 Wall Street as a corporate lawyer and an appellate litigator. Notwithstanding his active law practice, Wormser was a prolific scholar. Judge William Hughes Mulligan, one of Wormser's former students and assistant dean of Fordham Law School when Wormser died, said, "Without a doubt, he was one of the greatest corporation lawyers. He pleaded more cases before the Court of Appeals than any other New York lawyer. He was often quoted before the Court of Appeals by other lawyers attempting to make a point." Wormser reflected the Fordham Law tradition of public service, accepting several government positions, including those of Special Assistant US Attorney and Government Appeal Agent in New York during World War I; special counsel to the New York Transit Commission in 1927; and consulting legal counsel to the Kings County Crime Investigation from 1938 to 1941.[28]

Fuller made some notable appointments of leading members of the New York Bar, public officials, and judges as special lecturers. The most significant of these appointments were three made in the 1906–7 academic year: Alton B. Parker, Morgan J. O'Brien, and Frederic R. Coudert Jr. Parker is perhaps best known as the Democratic candidate for president of the United States in the 1904 election, which he lost to the incumbent, Theodore Roosevelt. He was serving as Chief Judge of the New York Court of Appeals prior to his nomination in 1904. Another significant appointment was Fuller's putative nephew and law partner Frederic René Coudert Jr. Coudert possessed all of the virtues and professional qualities that Fuller himself possessed. In addition, he argued most of the Coudert Brothers' cases before the US Supreme Court. Coudert received his bachelor of law degree from Columbia University in 1890 and was admitted to the New York Bar in 1892, but he continued his studies at Columbia until he earned his PhD in 1894. At Fordham Law School, his title was Special Lecturer on Constitutional Law. He published his view of constitutional law and judicial review in books and articles in the *Yale Law Journal* and *Columbia Law Review*. Professor John W. Burgess, one of the nation's most distinguished constitutional law scholars at the time, recognized Coudert's eminence as a fellow constitutional law scholar when he was planning to retire as Ruggles Professor of Constitutional Law at Columbia University. Burgess picked Coudert to be his successor and tried mightily, but unsuccessfully, to persuade Coudert to accept the appointment.[29]

Fordham Law School's stated mission, educational objectives, course of study, method of instruction, and requirements for admission were comparable to those of the elite law schools of this era, although several aspects distinguished it from almost all other law programs. The school's mission statement made explicit its commitment to providing its students with a theoretical as well as a practical grounding in the law. Its stated objective reflected the idea that lawyers were public servants who dealt with issues of public policy in and out of government as well as private counselors who resolved private disputes in and out of courts. Fordham Law School sought to produce "efficient lawyers" qualified to conduct "public affairs."[30]

To achieve its educational objectives, the faculty taught "the historical and philosophical development, as well as the practical application of the subjects in the courses" it offered. Pedagogically, the school's design was "to afford a practical and scientific education in the principles" of "general jurisprudence," the common and statutory law of the United States, the English and American systems of equity jurisprudence, the public law of England and the United States, and civil and Roman law.[31]

Fordham Law students were required to take two courses that were not required at most other law schools. One was a "very comprehensive course of lectures on General Jurisprudence," which was described as relating "to the ethical meaning of the law, and the proper conduct of the lawyer in professional life." Columbia Law School did not require a course in Jurisprudence until 1938, and students did not take it until their third year. From its founding, Fordham's course in Jurisprudence was a required first-year course that dealt "with the fundamental ethical concepts [of the law], the general principles that form the basis of law, as well as its genesis and historical development." The other distinctive course was Legal Ethics, and it was taught by Dean Fuller while he served as dean. It addressed "some of the problems in legal ethics that confront the lawyer in actual practice." These two courses most likely represented the greatest presence of the Law School's affiliation with a Jesuit University.[32]

Dean Fuller's personal views reflected the Jesuit orientation toward professional education. Fordham President Father Collins, in a speech on the future of Fordham University, stated that "the professional schools were the mediums . . . for the uplifting of mankind." Fordham's "professional schools could best train young men in the science" of their life work and "preserve in them a belief in higher things than those which can be seen with the eye and touched with the hand." Fordham would prevent them from making the mistake of thinking that "the decision of the Court of Appeals [was] the highest norm of good and evil." Father Collins thus sought to train lawyers as public servants who should use their professional skills for the betterment of humankind and whose professional ethics derived from a higher authority than the common law. Dean Fuller undoubtedly shared this perspective and taught the Catholic perspective on ethics and morality on which it was based.[33]

Dean Fuller and Father Collins's emphasis on legal ethics was shared by the Fordham Law faculty. Joseph A. Warren, the school's registrar, proclaimed that ethics were an essential part of law. Elaborating, Warren said that law consists of rules "controlling man's outward relations with the state and with his fellow man. Ethics controls his inner relations with the state, with his fellow man and with his Creator. It is evident that the two cannot be divorced and hence it is essential that the student should bring to the study of law a mind well grounded and trained in the correct science of Ethics." Without ethics, Warren opined, the law student will lose himself "in the wilderness of later-day fancies—utilitarianism, socialism, 'might makes right,' and the like." Fordham offered the Ethics course "to ward off this danger" and "to prepare the lawyer to bear himself with all honesty and propriety in the pursuit of his profession." Warren reported that an article entitled "Boards of Legal Discipline," published in "a purely legal magazine," lauded Fordham Law School for being the first law school in the nation to offer a course in professional ethics. It also gave tribute to Dean Fuller "for his untiring efforts in upholding and advancing the standards of the profession."[34]

The school's course in Jurisprudence also had an ethics component. It was taught by Father Terence J. Shealy, S.J. That Father Shealy taught the Jurisprudence course from 1905 until 1921 was as distinctive in legal education as the course. It was not only that Father Shealy was a priest and a philosophical Thomist that made him distinctive. Rather, it was that Father Shealy was not a lawyer but a philosopher. Given the technical and vocational orientation of law schools in this period, even elite law schools did not allow nonlawyers to teach law students. Law schools refused to appoint nonlawyers to their faculties because they were thought to have nothing to contribute to the law schools' institutional missions. The appointment of a philosopher to the Fordham Law faculty thus set Fordham apart from other law schools, and the Jesuit community "hoped that [Father Shealy's Jurisprudence course] will inaugurate a movement which will place legal education in this country on a broader and more scientific basis." It did not at that time, but it did anticipate a trend that arose in the second half of the twentieth century of appointing to law faculties experts with formal graduate training in fields related to law, such as economics, history, philosophy, and political science.[35]

In addition, Dean William Hughes Mulligan thought that "Fordham was the first law school in the country to require Jurisprudence as a subject." His view is supported by a Jesuit publication that commented in the fall of 1907 that establishing "a chair in General Jurisprudence was thought by many of conservative mind to be too novel a thing to succeed in a modern law school." Nevertheless, it noted with pride that "Father Shealy has made the personal test, and his pupils praise his lectures as vehemently as he praises the response they made to them." The topics he discussed in his Jurisprudence course included the nature and importance of jurisprudence; the relationship between jurisprudence and ethics, philosophy, and religion; law as a science and as an art; the methods of legal science; the ultimate basis of law; natural law and jurisprudence; the nature and divisions of positive law; the sources of positive law; law and the sovereign power; law and liberty; law and justice; rights and duties; conflict of claims; and legal personality. Shealy was an extremely popular teacher, and his students lauded him for his eloquence and rhetorical skills, his infectious enthusiasm and versatile genius, and his high ideals. His course reportedly was "creating, perhaps, greater interest among the students and is certainly attracting more attention from the legal world than any other course offered at Fordham."[36]

Father Shealy taught his course from the perspective of the natural law philosophy of Thomistic Scholasticism, the philosophy associated primarily with the Catholic Church. He described his goal as studying social problems from a scientific perspective, applying the Aristotelian and Thomistic definition of science as "the knowledge of things in their causes" and "their principles of causation." Shealy's "science" assumed the existence of immutable metaphysical principles, and he attributed these principles of causation to God and the knowledge of these principles to "an infallible source," the Catholic Church. Shealy's understanding of "science" departed from the philosophical rationalism that arose in the late nineteenth century and pervaded American colleges and universities in the early twentieth century, which, although it acknowledged the existence of immutable metaphysical principles that explained reality, also assumed that these principles were discoverable through human reason. Shealy's thinking departed even more from another school of thought that was emerging in the early decades of the twentieth century, scientific naturalism, which rejected the notion of absolute principles governing the universe and embraced the idea that all knowledge derived from empirically verifiable scientific investigation. No notes from Shealy's course in Jurisprudence have survived, and, unlike the other courses listed in the school's catalog, his did not have a textbook. It is safe to assume that he taught the course within his philosophy of Thomistic Aristotelianism.[37]

Father Shealy believed that education must include "moral discipline." To teach without teaching morality gives "man only a greater capacity for crime," Shealy was quoted as saying. He admonished that "To know the

Constitution and the law is good, but without conscience it may be the shield of corruption in the hands of the pettifogger and the politician." Shealy maintained that "the practical effect of mere learning is to make the good man more powerful for good, and the bad man more powerful for evil." Shealy's view was echoed in the *Fordham Monthly*, which declared that the aim of every Catholic college must be more than mental training. "Mere mental training, though important, must be secondary to the inculcation of sound ethical, moral and political doctrine." It is only through a strong sense of ethics and morality that the individual will have "a greater influence and a nobler impulse" to contribute "to the advancement of Christian, Catholic and American ideals."[38]

In addition to teaching a philosophy of law and legal ethics, the purpose of Father Shealy's Jurisprudence course was to neutralize the Protestant orientation of higher education and its recurring hostility to Catholicism. Registrar Warren explained that Father Shealy's course was not to present a Catholic version of the historical development of the law. "It is neither necessary nor desirable that [Catholics] should look at history from a 'Catholic' standpoint," Warren opined, "but it is highly important that we do not on the other hand look at it from an anti-Catholic one." The course was intended to counteract "the malicious slanders of bigotry" against the Catholic Church found in the work of "unfair and biased" legal authorities such as Sir William Blackstone. Thus, the aim of Fordham's Jurisprudence course "is to examine fairly and impartially the history and philosophy of the law and to show the Church and all the other institutions which have influenced the growth of law in their true lights."[39]

A third-year student writing for the *Fordham Monthly* demonstrated the effectiveness of Fordham's approach to legal instruction. He asserted that "legal training must ever be a question of vital public interest" because the "status of the lawyer is, in a large measure, the ethical status of the public conscience." Expressing an awareness that "the palpable and almost universal defect in our law school system is the exaggerated technicalization of the law," he explained that "the reasons of law and government, their ultimate cause, their history and philosophy, are sacrificed for the practical and the technical" in most law schools, and the profession of law is reduced "to a trade, and the presumably scientific lawyer a skilful [*sic*] clerk." The "special feature of the Fordham system," he continued, is that the course in general jurisprudence supplements the case method by which students learn private law from the cases. This course teaches students "the history and theory of law, and the science of government," in addition to the "fundamental principles of law" and provides them with "knowledge of the law as an entire harmonious body of systematized rules." When he was a Fordham Law student in the mid-1930s, New York Governor Malcolm Wilson took the required Jurisprudence course with Father John Pyne, S.J., who taught that "civil law was based on natural law—moral law," and he urged "all students to become active in the law-making process and the administration of justice."[40]

Fifteen law schools offered a course in Jurisprudence in 1891. Nonetheless, Dean William Hughes Mulligan's claim that Father Shealy's Jurisprudence course "was probably the first ever given as a part of the regular curriculum in any law school in the United States" may have been correct if Dean Mulligan meant that Jurisprudence was a *required* course. In 1905, only a handful of law schools offered courses in jurisprudence and legal ethics or taught the history of law, but it is clear that such courses were not required. Leading legal educators, including Dean Langdell and President Eliot of Harvard, regarded such courses as inappropriate to a law school curriculum, which they argued should be restricted to practical, technical law courses. According to this pedagogical view, theoretical courses, such as jurisprudence, legal history, and ethics, should be taught in the academic departments of colleges and universities and should be taken before one entered law school. Although some law schools, such as Columbia, Yale, Georgetown, and Catholic University, included in their curricula theoretical courses, such as these and international law and legal ethics, law schools generally declined to offer such "academic" subjects, considering them "borderland" subjects. They instead focused their instruction on "the relatively narrow, though exceedingly important and difficult, field of judge-made technical law." Thus, the Carnegie Foundation for the Advancement of Teaching observed as late as 1925 that Legal Ethics was one of the "*new subjects* which are working their way" into the law school curriculum. The "theory" advanced by law schools such as Harvard, Columbia, Michigan, the University of Chicago, and Stanford for not offering a course in legal ethics, the Foundation reported, is that "it is a fallacy to assume that high ethical standards can be inculcated either by general exhortations or by case method drill in legal etiquette."

It is reasonable to conclude that Fordham Law School may have been more academically oriented in these respects than those elite law schools.[41]

Professional ethics were increasingly problematic at the school's founding, and the subject of ethics was a recurring theme in addresses given at Fordham Law School's commencements and other school events. Governor Charles Evans Hughes gave Fordham Law School's first commencement address in June 1908. This future Chief Justice of the United States warned the first graduating class against the "commercialism" that was infecting the legal profession. The governor admonished the graduates to honor the old ideals of the bar and to refuse to sell out by acting contrary to their convictions in order to earn a retainer. Acknowledging "the extraordinary temptations of a highly commercialized age," Hughes reminded them that they were "sworn ministers of justice" on whose professional ideals and public service depended the success of American government. Supreme Court Justice Peter A. Hendrick repeated some of these themes in the 1909 commencement, declaring that money could not be the motivation to practice law, for this motivation would produce bad lawyers. Rather, the graduates should "pursue the cause of justice and of right. And if you do that," Justice Hendrick urged, "do not fear about the money part. It will take care of itself." William McAdoo, former Assistant Secretary of the Navy, addressed the third graduating class in 1910 on "Legal Profession and the Public Conscience." He noted the central role the legal profession plays in American government and affirmed Tocqueville's observation that lawyers are America's intellectual elite. This meant that if the legal profession "becomes commercialized and corrupt it can do more injury to honest government than any other body of men in the country." McAdoo inveighed "against the prostitution of the profession" that was damaging the reputation of the legal profession and urged the graduates on "to the mountain top of Principle" as defenders of the "Public Conscience." He admonished the graduates to maintain high ideals and repeated the warning that, if they selected law to make money, they should recognize their mistake and seek some other field. The number of lawyers, "especially in New York City, who are utterly unfited [sic] for it, both by training, temperament and intellectual ability, strength and probity of character, is too great." Governor Martin H. Glynn was more succinct in his commencement address to the graduates of the class of 1914.

A graduate of Fordham College in the class of 1894, he told the law graduates, "Don't be slick lawyers, boys . . . and remember that your greatest asset will always be the confidence of your neighbors. There is no room in the temple of justice for the trickster or the knave." Commercialization not only affected practitioners, it evidently affected law schools as well. In 1922, the American Bar Association sponsored a meeting of state and local bar associations, known as the Conference of Bar Association Delegations, which, among other things, passed resolutions deploring the commercialization of legal education.[42]

In his address at the 1911 commencement, Judge Victor J. Dowling summarized and praised Fordham Law School for its philosophical and ethical approach to legal education. He complimented the school for "its individuality, commanding position and influence and the character and legal prestige of its faculty." He also praised the school's curriculum, congratulating New York "on having a Law School where the courses on the historical and philosophical aspects of the law, as well as the lectures on legal ethics, are made special features of the school," because it is only by this kind of training "that the student can acquire thoroughness in the scientific principles of the law, together with a definite training in their practical application." Judge Dowling thus emphasized the need for an understanding of the science, the history, and the theory of law and legal ethics as the best preparation for the practice of the law. Like other speakers at Fordham Law School functions, he proclaimed that this approach to legal education was essential, "especially at the present time, when there seems to be a great awakening of the public conscience which demands men of high moral character and learning in the different professions and especially in the administration of public duties."[43]

At its inception, Fordham Law School offered only a part-time program. Classes met in Collins Hall on the Rose Hill Campus in the Bronx every Monday through Friday from 4:15 to 6:15 in the afternoon, and on Saturday afternoons from 2:00 to 4:00. These hours were adopted to enable students, many of whom had full-time jobs as law clerks in Wall Street lawyers' offices, to attend classes at the end of their workdays. Part-time programs were important to enable Catholic children of immigrants to attend law school, because they had to support themselves. The annual tuition was $100, a considerable sum in those days.[44]

The school remained on the Bronx campus for only its first semester, moving at Dean Fuller's insistence to downtown Manhattan during the spring 1906 semester. The Bronx campus was too inconvenient for students and faculty, "as the transit is not yet rapid enough to make it convenient for them to go to Fordham." The move eliminated the inconvenient commute to the Bronx, bringing the school closer to the faculties' law offices and to the students who were working on Wall Street. The new location and the class hours enabled the students, most of whom were self-supporting young men, to walk from their day jobs to the school within minutes. It afforded the faculty the same convenience. The school leased the seventh floor of a two-year-old, twenty-one-story office building at 42 Broadway.[45]

Moving the school to lower Manhattan placed it in the center of a law student market. The *Fordham Monthly* foresaw this benefit when it observed that the school's new location "is peculiarly adapted to the furtherance of its end." Student enrollments quickly escalated. Thirty-five students entered Fordham Law School in September 1906, more than quadrupling the total enrollment to 42. The next entering class more than doubled the school's enrollment to 100 students for the 1907–8 academic year. By September 1914, the school's enrollment had risen to 400 students, representing almost a quarter of the entire Fordham University student population of 1,700, and the 92 LLB degrees Fordham Law School awarded to the graduating class of 1915 was almost double the number of other undergraduate degrees Fordham College awarded that year. The school's enrollment continued to increase dramatically until the United States entered World War I in 1917, peaking at 537 for the 1916–17 school year.[46]

The rapidly increasing student body forced the school to move three more times before it found a relatively lasting location. Each move was within the area of the city's concentration of law firms and to a building distinguished by its architecture. The school remained at 42 Broadway only two years. The need for library space and increasing enrollments forced the school to move over five days during the Easter Recess in April 1908 to more spacious quarters a few blocks north in the newly constructed New York *Evening Post* building at 20 Vesey Street. Expanding enrollment required another move in the fall of 1911, this time to the Morse Building, located at 140 Nassau Street, named after the inventor of the telegraph, Samuel F. B. Morse, who performed his early experiments with his revolutionary invention on this site. The Morse Building was located east of Broadway, convenient to public transportation used by commuters from New Jersey, upper Manhattan, Brooklyn, and the other boroughs, as well as to the courts and municipal buildings used by lawyers. In the fall of 1916, the school moved again to the location it would occupy until 1943, the magnificent Woolworth Building, located at 233 Broadway, across from City Hall and close to Manhattan's judicial and municipal centers. The school would move again during World War II, to 302 Broadway, from which it would make its last move in 1961 to its present location at Lincoln Center.[47]

Fordham Law School's course of studies and method of instruction were those of full-time law schools. Fordham satisfied the ABA's and the Association of American Law Schools' recommended standard course of studies for the degree of Bachelor of Laws, which was three years. All of the courses for each year were required; there were no electives. The first-year courses one hundred years ago are almost the same courses first-year students study today. The second- and third-year courses also bore some similarity to those of today, though less than those of the first year.[48]

After its first year, the school adopted the Langdellian case method of instruction, the method that was used in full-time programs at the most elite law schools of the nation, such as Harvard, Columbia, and Yale. Dean Mulligan attributed the introduction of the case method to Professor Ralph Gifford, who had been a student of Professor James Barr Ames at Harvard Law School. Fordham Law School informed prospective students that some of its faculty were trained in the case method and some were trained in the older textbook method, but the "unanimous verdict of both these classes of teachers is that the case system of instruction is the best existing method of studying and teaching the law." It was best suited to students who wanted to cultivate "the power to reason" rather than to acquire "a mere parrot-like use of the memory, and who wish to possess real knowledge and power as opposed to a mere appearance of knowledge without real power." Despite the belief that the case method required law students to be college educated and to devote their full time to the study of the law and that part-time programs were thus "debarred from using this method," Fordham Law School employed the case method successfully even though it was essentially a part-time law school for its first fifty years and has continued to operate a night school to the present day.[49]

The *Fordham University Bulletin of Information* informed prospective students of the nature of the *"case system,"* the school's reasons for using it, and its demands on students. The *Bulletin* explained that cases were the bases of instruction. A few cases were assigned each day for study, and students were required to summarize them, stating the facts of each case, the decision of the court, and the court's reasons for its decision. The class then discussed the decisions, explored whether the decisions were correct, and identified the principles of law they established. The instructor then presented the class with new and different hypothetical facts and required the class to apply the rule to them, "thus giv[ing] the students practice in the art of applying law to varying conditions of fact." The school's stated purpose for teaching law in this way reflected the Langdellian/Keener view of law as a science. The main objectives were "to teach the student to deduce legal principles from reported cases, and also to teach him to apply these principles to other cases, and thus to develop in him the power of legal reasoning through the use of the actual decisions of the courts." The *Bulletin* declared: "By this method the student learns from the very beginning to do the kind of work which every lawyer must do in actual practice, and thus receives the very best preparation for actual work at the bar."[50]

The *Bulletin* mentioned two additional justifications of the case method, reflecting a progressive view of the law. The case method *"stimulates the power of the student to investigate and reason*, instead of tending to make him rely on mere memory, which is the tendency where a textbook is used," and it *"is a far more interesting system of instruction*, both to student and teacher, than the text-book system." The case system did not teach law as a body of "abstract principles." Rather, it "teaches these principles in a vivid and realistic manner in connection with actual sets of facts. In this way alone," the *Bulletin* maintained, "can the student be made to realize from the start that the law is a living thing, *and not a dead mechanical set of rules."*[51]

Though it was a local law school, Fordham stated that it aimed to prepare its students to practice law in any common law jurisdiction. The casebooks Fordham faculty adopted in their law courses were those used in many of the elite law schools. For example, the Contracts course used Samuel Williston's casebook, which succeeded Langdell's Contracts casebook. Several law courses used casebooks compiled by James Barr Ames, the original academic law professor and, because he was a gifted teacher, the person who actually made Langdell's case method succeed in the classroom. However, the Law School anticipated that most of its graduates would practice in New York State and was careful to indicate "the peculiarities of the law of New York" in all of its courses. It also anticipated that most of its graduates would enter the most common form of law practice at the time, litigation. The *Bulletin* consequently gave special emphasis to courses in New York procedure and New York trial practice.[52]

Requirements for admission to an American law school at the turn of the twentieth century might strike one as curious today. Until the end of the nineteenth century, no law school in the nation required a college education for admission to its program. In 1896 only seven of seventy-six law schools even required a high school diploma. The major reform in the early years of the twentieth century was to raise admission standards to university-affiliated law schools to match those of other university undergraduate programs—that is, to require a high school diploma. Harvard Law School was the first to require a college degree in 1895, and it remained the only law school with that requirement until 1916, when it was joined by the University of Pennsylvania Law School. Columbia, Stanford, Yale, and Western Reserve law schools followed suit in 1921. By 1920, the requirement of a high school diploma was the norm for admission to law schools throughout the United States. Out of a total of 142 law schools in 1921, only 55 required any college education; 9 required three years of college; 24 required two years of college; and 22 required one year of college.[53]

Fordham Law School required a high school diploma from its very beginning even though no state enforced an educational prerequisite for admission to the practice of law until the 1920s. Although a high school diploma satisfied the educational prerequisite for admission, many students in the initial classes were college graduates. For example, the *Fordham Monthly* noted that seven of the nine members of the first entering class of Fordham Law School had college degrees. As more students were admitted to the school, the proportion of college graduates declined. Between 1910 and 1917, the proportion of Fordham Law students who were college graduates ranged between 32 and 40 percent. In the academic year in which the United States entered World War I, the percentage of college graduates dipped to 22 percent but rose to at least 25 percent for the rest of the decade.[54]

From its founding, Fordham Law School had stringent standards in administering examinations. A student's final grade was based primarily, but not exclusively, on the final examination. Class recitations also counted toward the final grade. Recitations consisted of the professor's calling on a student who would "get up and recite the case. You'd talk about the case," recalled Fordham Law alumnus Caesar Pitassy, "state the facts, and state what the holding was and then answer any questions that the Professor had." If the student was not prepared, he would say, "Not prepared." The professor would "make a note of it. If there were too many, you'd hear about it, but once in a while was no big deal." Remarkably, Professor Wormser was deaf, "but he could read your lips," Pitassy asserted. When a student recited a case, "he looked at you, and I'm sure he read your lips because he couldn't hear a word you said." Yet, Wormser's class format was the same as that of all of the other Fordham Law professors, "and he was an excellent Professor, excellent," Pitassy emphatically stated.[55]

Students who failed an examination were "conditioned" in the subject, that is, they failed, but they were "given the opportunity of [taking] an additional examination in the conditioned subjects." The faculty resolved on motion of the pro dean that "no member of the faculty should discuss with any student the result of any examination." Conditioned examinations were to be given within the first month of the following semester. Third-year students who failed an examination were denied their degree until they passed the conditioned subject's exam.[56]

Fordham Law School's attendance policy also prevented some students from taking final examinations or from graduating with their class. Rules regarding attendance were among the first rules the faculty adopted. The faculty resolved in September 1907 that "the attendance of students at lectures is to be recorded ten minutes after the beginning & ten minutes before the end of each lecture, and a student must be present both times to be duly recorded." Students were sometimes barred from taking final examinations or were denied their degrees because of excessive absences.[57]

The dropout rate was exceedingly high by today's standards. The percent of students who entered Fordham Law School between 1905 and 1913 who did not graduate in three years ranged between 28 and 54 percent, and the norm was between 40 and 50 percent. The reasons students failed to graduate in three years are impossible to determine, because there is no record explaining why they did not receive their degrees with their classes.[58]

The New York State educational requirements in these years allowed law students with college degrees to take the bar examination and, on passing the exam, to be admitted to practice after only two years of law school. Law students without a college degree had to attend law school for three years in order to sit for the bar exam. A number of Fordham Law students who were college graduates passed the bar examination and were admitted to practice before they graduated from the Law School. Two of the students in the school's first entering class passed the New York bar exam in 1907, and they were "full-fledged, bona-fide, dyed-in-the-wool lawyers" during their third year of law school. Several members of the third-year class and two members of the second year class passed the bar and became "full-fledged lawyers" in 1909, and ten members of the following year's third-year class took the bar exam, and all passed and were admitted to practice before they graduated.[59]

Systematic data relating to bar passage rates of Fordham alumni in this early period are not available. References to passage rates are sparse, and the data are erratic. But the information that is reported reveals that Fordham students and alumni who took the bar exam did extraordinarily well; it seems that the students who took the exam in their second year of law school all passed it. Most graduates who took the bar exam also passed it. In 1911, for example, the *Fordham Monthly* reported that only 70 of 600, or 11 percent of all those who took the "recent" New York bar exam, passed it, but 80 percent of the Fordham "applicants" passed, "a great triumph for Fordham," it boasted. The passage rate for the June 1912 bar exam for New York State was 48 percent, but 85 percent of Fordham Law graduates who took the exam passed. A Jesuit publication, the *Woodstock Letters*, reported the identical results for the 1913 "mid-term" bar exam. Fordham Law applicants to the bar enjoyed even greater success in the June 1913 bar exam. Father Thomas J. McCluskey, S.J., president of Fordham University, announced at the June 1913 commencement that 88 percent of the Fordham candidates had passed the June exam. The pass rate for all who took the "full-term" bar exam in June of that year was 48 percent, but the pass rate for Fordham alumni was a remarkable 85 percent. Fordham historian Raymond A. Schroth, S.J., writes that, by 1912, the school boasted that its students had achieved an 80 percent pass rate for the bar. However, this pass rate diminished after World War I. Approximately 89 of the 222 members of the 1922 graduating class took the bar examination in the month they graduated. The school announced that only 53 of the 89, or 60 percent, passed. In its view, the June 1922 exam was "one of the most difficult and most intricate examinations given to prospective advocates in recent years."[60]

The privilege New York State extended to law students with a college degree of being admitted to practice before they finished their law education ended in 1912, when the state raised the educational requirement to three years of law school for all law students to qualify for the bar. New Jersey continued to permit law students to be admitted before finishing law school, and as late as 1922 five male members of the graduating class of that year were admitted to practice in the state of New Jersey during their third year of law school. In New York, law school graduates who were also college graduates still enjoyed a privilege: They were exempted from an obligatory additional year of clerking in a law office before they were admitted to practice, a requirement that had been imposed in 1912 on law students who completed three years of law school but had only a high school diploma. In 1920 bar admission requirements changed again, as New York required that all who wished to be licensed to practice law satisfy the requirements of the Bar Character Committee.[61]

It must have been with a great deal of personal satisfaction for having established a first-rate law school that Paul Fuller decided to retire as its dean during the fall of 1913. Fuller continued his active schedule, however, practicing law, performing public service in New York City as a member of the New York Board of Education and as a trustee of Hunter College, and serving his nation. President Woodrow Wilson sent Fuller as his special emissary to negotiate with Pancho Villa, Venustiano Carranza, and Álvaro Obregón during the Mexican Revolution in 1914, and again as his personal emissary to a Five Power Conference in August 1915.[62]

Fuller died suddenly on the night of November 29, 1915. He was sixty-seven years old and his fragile health had been tested by his most important public service as President Wilson's emissary to Mexico. The law faculty wrote in their death notice that the school had "lost its earliest and greatest inspiration to legal ideals, its generous parent in the law, its pass-port to initial recognition by discerning members of the bar." Students, too, honored Fuller with a memorial notice in their law review, wherein they also took note of the "really sincere desire that possessed him to instill these high professional ideals in the minds of the students and the younger lawyers with whom he came in contact."[63]

CHAPTER TWO

WORLD WAR I AND ITS AFTERMATH

DEAN JOHN WHALEN AND THE GREAT WAR

John Whalen succeeded Paul Fuller as the dean of Fordham Law School in 1914. Whalen's humble beginnings, professional career, record of public service as a civic leader and public servant, and his philanthropy bore striking similarities to Fuller's, but they also had striking differences as well. Whalen was born in New York City to Irish immigrants, and he lost his father when he was just an infant. Like Fuller, he took advantage of the opportunities available to the ambitious in New York City and began his ascent from poverty "on the lowest imaginable rung of the legal ladder, that of errand boy in a law office." It was the law office of Charles O'Conor, one of the most prominent lawyers in New York City and the nation. The son of an Irish immigrant and a devout Roman Catholic, O'Conor served as US Attorney for New York in 1853–54, as Confederate President Jefferson Davis's senior counsel on his indictment for treason, and as lead prosecutor in the prosecution of William M. "Boss" Tweed and the "Tweed Ring" in the 1870s, for which he refused to accept a fee. On O'Conor's death, former New York Governor Samuel J. Tilden declared that "Mr. O'Conor was the greatest jurist among all the English-speaking races." Whalen clerked for O'Conor during these times of notable cases.[1]

After obtaining a law degree from New York University School of Law in 1877, Whalen built a successful practice in real estate law and served as legal counsel to the Lawyers' Title and Guarantee Company. He was active in New York public education, chairing the school board of the Twelfth Ward from 1881 to 1896, serving as Commissioner of Public Education from 1910 to 1913, and later as chairman of the Committee on High Schools of the New York Board of Education. Whalen's law practice and political connections led to his appointment as New York City Tax Commissioner (1893–96) and as the first Corporation Counsel (1898–1903) for the newly unified city. In this position, he strongly advocated for the development of the city's subway systems. Fordham University, Manhattan College, and the College of St. Francis Xavier recognized his professional achievements by conferring on Whalen their honorary Doctor of Law degrees.

Like Fuller, Whalen was a Democrat, but, unlike Fuller, Whalen was "a power in Tammany Hall." He "was a strong believer in party government" and condemned independent political movements as incapable of providing good and effective government because they lacked the discipline that political parties offered. Without "party organization the officials chosen when an independent movement is successful claimed to be free to do as [they] pleased," Whalen declared. Consequently, "There was no restraint upon them." He was a personal friend of Tammany Boss Richard Croker, whose organization Whalen assisted as "a tactician rather than a gladiator," declining offered offices and instead counseling behind the scenes and without compensation. Nor did Whalen accept payment for his services as president of the Bank of Washington Heights.[2]

A leading Roman Catholic layman, Whalen was a benefactor of Fordham University and the New York Archdiocese. He donated $100,000 to Fordham for a new chapel and additional funds for scholarships. A lifelong bachelor, he left half of his $3,000,000 estate to his friend Cardinal Patrick Joseph Hayes, of which the cardinal in 1930 applied $250,000 to acquire and install in St. Patrick's Cathedral "the Grand Gallery Organ, with one of the nation's most glorious wood facades adorned with angels and Latin inscriptions." This organ was renovated in the early 1990s and is still in use today.[3]

In February 1914 John Whalen took office as the second dean of Fordham Law School. Although not a scholar like Fuller, he presided over the school's continuing expansion and its move to more spacious quarters, and he successfully met the challenges presented to Fordham Law School by World War I. In the fall of 1916, Whalen oversaw the school's fourth relocation in its eleven-year history, this time to the magnificent Woolworth Building, located at 233 Broadway, just across from City Hall and a short walk to Manhattan's judicial and municipal centers. This terra cotta–tiled Gothic skyscraper was named for its builder, the 5 and 10 cent entrepreneur, F. W. Woolworth, who commissioned architect Cass Gilbert to design the tallest building in the world. Described at its dedication as a "cathedral of commerce," the Woolworth Building was 60 stories and 792 feet in height, the tallest building in the world when it was completed in 1913, a distinction it retained until the Chrysler Building surpassed it in

1930. The Woolworth Building served as the model for the skyscrapers that radically changed the Manhattan skyline after World War I. The law school occupied the twenty-eighth and twenty-ninth floors, affording law students glorious views of New York City. The move to the Woolworth Building was prompted not only by rapidly expanding enrollments but also by the university's decision to locate all of its graduate programs in one building in Manhattan. Fordham Law School shared the Woolworth Building with Fordham University's Graduate School of Arts and Sciences, the Teachers College, and the new School of Sociology and Social Service.[4]

The move to the Woolworth Building was accomplished while the Great War raged in Europe. The United States declared war on Germany on April 6, 1917. There were many graduates in uniform at the June 1917 commencement of Fordham University, particularly among the professional schools, reflecting the nation's rapid mobilization that had called up for service one in four men of military age. Some of Fordham Law School's graduating class were in military training at Plattsburgh, New York, and they obtained 24-hour furloughs to attend their commencements. President Woodrow Wilson appointed Fordham President Joseph A. Mulry, S.J., to a board with other educational leaders to mobilize the nation's colleges for war education, and Father Mulry turned the Rose Hill campus in the Bronx into a training center for several military services. Fordham College alumni raised funds to equip four ambulances that were sent to the battlefields of Europe. Fordham Law students subscribed $15,500 in Liberty Bonds toward the New York Federal Reserve District campaign to raise $1.5 billion of the national goal of $3.8 billion during the fall of 1917. More than 1,500 Fordham students and alumni made an even greater contribution when they went off to war as members of the armed forces.[5]

World War I "injuriously affected" legal education in the United States, the president of the Carnegie Foundation for the Advancement of Teaching reported. "Young men of spirit cannot give full attention to their books in an environment that resounds with preparation for war," he opined. Furthermore, voluntary enlistments and the Selective Service Act of May 1917, which drafted into military service men between the ages of twenty-one and thirty, sharply depleted the student populations of the nation's law schools. The Carnegie Foundation urged that, "For those who suspend their studies to follow the flag, concessions from the regulations applicable to normal times must be made."[6]

Fordham Law School complied with the Foundation's demand and suspended the normal degree requirements to accommodate those students who left school to serve in the military. In June 1918, the Law School faculty resolved that third-year students who entered military service "before the close of school, and who had successfully completed the first semester of the year 1917–1918, be awarded the degree of LL.B. with" the class of 1918. The following June, the faculty decided that students who withdrew to serve in the United States armed forces "either immediately preceding the close of their Second Year or with their Second Year completed, and who returned to the School in November and December, 1918, or in January 1919, and passed the mid-year examinations in Third Year, and successfully completed the Entire Second Semester of that year, be awarded their . . . degree of LL.B. with the class of 1919." The faculty extended this rule to "those students who, under above named conditions, were prevented from returning to their course prior to Feb 3, 1919, the beginning of Second Semester of their Third Year."[7]

World War I significantly diminished student bodies in law schools across the United States, including Fordham Law School. The 23,000 students enrolled in the nation's law schools in the 1915–16 academic year dropped to 7,000 in the 1918–19 academic year. Depleted student bodies forced a dozen law schools to close. New York Law School suspended operations.[8]

Fordham's enrollments dropped in two ways. Fewer individuals enrolled as first-year students, and dropout rates for enrolled students mushroomed between 1916 to 1918. The entering class of 1916 numbered 254, the largest entering class to date. The entering classes of 1917 and 1918 declined precipitously by 34.2 percent and 58.2 percent to 167 and 106 respectively. The dropout rate for these three entering classes was unusually high. Almost 62 percent of the entering class of 1916 left during the years the United States was fighting in World War I. About 30 percent of the entering class of 1917 and 33 percent of the entering class of 1918 left. Fordham's total enrollment during the war years declined by 40 percent, from 537 to 320. Georgetown Law Center's enrollment dropped by a third between October 1916 and October 1918. The decline in student enrollment at Columbia Law School was even more severe. The enrollment at Columbia in 1916 of 517 students dropped by almost 50 percent to 263 in 1918. Fortunately, Columbia University's endowment cushioned the impact of the radical reduction in law school revenues.[9]

The lack of an endowment handicapped Fordham Law School even before it felt the impact of World War I. This contributed to the school's later decline in academic distinction and reputation compared with other law schools, such as Yale, with which it was arguably on a par in its early years. Fordham lost its talented Professor Ralph W. Gifford to Yale in 1912 when the Yale Law School dean offered Gifford a higher salary. Fordham and other Catholic law schools were further disadvantaged by a rule adopted by the Carnegie Foundation, which created a program of pensions for academics at nonsectarian universities and explicitly excluded those at church-affiliated schools. Part of Yale's allure for Gifford was the offer of one of these pensions. Professor William A. Keener was offered a position at a western law school at twice his Fordham Law salary, but he turned it down, most likely because of his New York law practice and the absence of financial need. Nevertheless, Jesuits complained, "One of our most difficult problems both in Law and Medicine is to retain our professors, when other universities can offer them greater salaries on account of the enormous endowment which they possess." The Carnegie Foundation pensions increased this disparity.[10]

Being tuition driven, Fordham Law School suffered economic hardship when the war depleted the student body, and enrollments declined for the first time since its founding. The school reached its highest pre–World War I enrollment of 537 students, including 264 in the first year class, in the 1916–17 academic year. After the United States entered the war in April 1917, enrollments dropped 24 percent to 406 students, with only 167 first-year students, for the 1917–18 academic year. Enrollments at the opening of the 1918–19 academic year declined again, some 40 percent from their highest numbers in September 1916, to 320 students, and the entering class dropped to 94 students. The minutes of the faculty meeting of June 5, 1919, noted that, "owing to war conditions," there was only one session of classes during the first semester of the 1918–19 academic year. Apparently because of the depleted student body, classes met only in the evening, from 7:00 P.M. to 9:00 P.M.[11]

The decline in enrollments had a disastrous impact upon both the Law School and the university. Lacking an endowment, Fordham University was virtually dependent upon tuition and student fees to finance its operations. It was also dependent upon Law School revenues because surplus Law School funds subsidized other divisions of the university, including the financially struggling medical school. The shortfall in student tuition was probably offset somewhat by revenues from the federal government, which used the university's Rose Hill campus to train troops for action in the war. The military's takeover of Fordham' facilities itself triggered rumors of Fordham Law School's closing, prompting the university's president, Father Joseph A. Mulry, S.J., to issue a denial, declaring that there was no move to close the Law School.[12]

With the end of hostilities, the nation's law schools experienced a resurgence in their student populations. Student enrollments quickly returned to their prewar levels, and the schools enjoyed a decade-long expansion. As men returned from military service, enrollments doubled at Fordham in the fall of 1919 from 320 the preceding academic year to 687 students, making it the fifth-largest law school in the nation, after Georgetown (1,052), New York University (979), Harvard (883), and George Washington (752). Fordham Law School experienced a modest increase to 750 students the following year, but this represented not only an increase in the entering class of 1920 but also increases in the second- and third-year classes as students transferred in from other law schools. To meet rising demands for admission, the faculty decided in June 1921 that "a complete morning curriculum of the Law School be adopted commencing in September, 1921, with a First Year." Classes were scheduled to begin at 9:30 A.M. This decision resulted in a sharp spike in registration for the fall of 1921 as the morning class opened with 182 students, and the total entering class numbered 554, almost three-quarters of the previous year's total enrollment. More than 200 applicants were turned away. In the 1921–22 academic year, the school's student body doubled to 1,106, the largest number to date. This record was exceeded in the fall of 1922, when 1,291 students registered. Enrollments leveled off between 1,462 the following year and almost 1,500 in 1926, and registration gradually rose to its highest level of 1,513 in the 1927–28 academic year.[13]

Student enrollments greatly exceeded the regular capacity of the facilities at the Woolworth Building, which was designed for 700 to 800 students. The school introduced staggered sessions to accommodate the increased numbers of students. In the afternoon session, first-year students started their classes at 2:00 P.M, and the second- and third-year students reported at 4:30 P.M. In the evening session, first years began their classes at 6:00 P.M, and second- and third-year students began their classes at 7:00 P.M. The tight scheduling and crowded classes forced the school to change its rules governing student transfers from one division to another. Whereas students had been allowed to transfer between divisions during the school year "in case of necessity," they now had to remain in the division in which they were registered. If absent from class, students were no longer permitted to attend that class during another session.[14]

Even with these limitations, the three sessions offered people from all walks of life the opportunity to earn a law degree. Convenient hours and location and the relatively low tuition—compared with the cost of living and wage scales of the time—contributed to the steady increase in enrollment. From 1905 through 1914, tuition was $100 per year. However, Fordham steadily increased its annual tuition over the next few years to $110 in the fall of 1915, $125 in the fall of 1917, and $150 in the fall of 1920. The school's tuition was substantially lower than Columbia Law School's, which charged $150 in 1905, $180 in 1916, and $200 in 1922. But, Columbia instituted scholarships at the turn of the twentieth century, which replaced its "ancient practice" of lowering or waiving tuition fees to aid needy students. Fordham awarded a scholarship to only three students each year, the student in each class who attained "the highest average in recitations and examinations in their respective studies." Beginning in the 1913–14 academic year, this "scholarship" was described as "a prize of fifty dollars ($50) in gold." But Mary Knox Chapin, widow of Professor H. Gerald Chapin, bequeathed $2,000 to Fordham Law School as an endowment for a prize to be given "to that graduate of the School each year who shall have attained the highest average in his studies during his entire attendance at the School." The award was to be paid out of the income generated by the endowment. The first Chapin Prize, which was in the amount of $50, was awarded to Donald M. Dunn in June 1928. Thereafter, the prize consisted of a $100 award. But this was a prize awarded after the recipient had completed law school. The annual wages of non–farm workers were only $550 when the school was founded in 1905, and they remained under $700 to 1915. These wages steadily rose to $1,426 between 1915 and 1920. The average monthly wages of a clerical worker in New York City in 1923 were

$124.54 or just under $1,500 for the year. Women's wages throughout the period regardless of occupation were substantially lower. Consequently, Fordham Law students either had to rely on family assistance or personal earnings from jobs to pay tuition. Affordability as much as reputation was a consideration when students chose law schools.[15]

The academic prerequisites for admission to Fordham Law School were still satisfied by a high school diploma or its equivalent. Not surprisingly, the majority of its students were not college graduates. Although the proportion of law students with a Bachelor of Arts degree was high in the first few years of the school's existence, it dropped over the years as greater numbers of students were admitted. From 1905 to 1920, the proportion of Fordham Law students who had graduated from college varied between 20 and 40 percent. Many of the college graduates were educated at Catholic colleges, including Fordham University and other Catholic colleges in and around the city. Law students attended Catholic colleges and universities outside of the New York City area as well, schools such as Holy Cross and Boston College in Massachusetts; Georgetown in Washington, DC; and Notre Dame in Indiana. Increasingly, the Law School's college graduates had received degrees from Ivy League schools, such as Columbia, Cornell, Dartmouth, Harvard, Penn, and Yale; elite liberal arts colleges, such as Williams, Amherst, and Bowdoin; and large state universities, such as the University of Michigan. New York City schools such as New York University (NYU), Brooklyn College Polytechnic Institute, and City College of New York (CCNY) also were represented, with usually a half-dozen CCNY graduates in each class.[16]

Expanding enrollments after World War I included two new groups of students: women and African Americans. Like most law schools at the time of its founding, Fordham Law School did not permit women to enroll as students. The only concession to women the faculty made before World War I was in September 1908, when it decided that "ladies were to be admitted to the [school's] Public Lectures." However, "their presence . . . was not to be encouraged." Perhaps it was the decline in the 1917–18 Law School registration that inspired President Mulry to propose in May 1918 that women be admitted the following fall. The faculty apparently objected, and Father Mulry withdrew the suggestion. But that September, Father Mulry authorized the matriculation of women, and this change in policy was advertised in the local newspapers. In September 1918 the first women enrolled in Fordham Law School, eight women in all. The decision was made too late to be published in the *Law School Bulletin* for the 1918–19 school year, but the following year's *Bulletin* announced: "The University recognizes the growing movement in favor of equal social opportunities to both sexes, and has accordingly opened the Law School to women as fully as to men." Women were already enrolled at two of Fordham's downtown divisions, the Teachers College and the School of Sociology and Social Work, fields that had traditionally provided women with career opportunities. Women were also seeking advanced education through the university's Graduate School of Arts and Sciences. There were no women at Fordham College until 1964, when the university opened the all-female Thomas More College. This gender dichotomy between undergraduate and professional schools was not unusual at the time, and it was found at both secular and religiously affiliated universities. Yale, for example, welcomed women to its law school in 1919, the year after Fordham, but Yale College remained all-male until 1969.[17]

The admission of women to Fordham Law School was barely half a century after Belle Babb Mansfield became the first woman to be admitted by a state to the practice of law when Iowa admitted her in 1869. However, she never practiced law, choosing to become a history professor instead. Margaret Brent (ca. 1601–71) was the first woman to practice law in America, and she did so in the seventeenth-century colony of Maryland. After she arrived in the colony in 1638, she became executor for Maryland Governor Leonard Calvert, and she practiced in the provincial court. Karen Berger Morello described Brent as "a master negotiator, an accomplished litigator, and . . . a respected leader as well." In 1796 Luce Terry (1730–1823) became the first black woman to practice. However, women were generally refused admission to state bar associations. This exclusion began to change in the third quarter of the nineteenth century. For example, Lemma Barkaloo was admitted to practice law by the state of Missouri in 1870 without having completed law school. She began trying cases in St. Louis in the year she was admitted to practice. She, along with Phoebe Couzins, had been admitted to Washington University Law School in St. Louis in 1869, the first law school in the United States to accept students without regard to sex. The first woman to graduate from a US law school, Ada Kepley, received her degree in 1870 from Chicago's Union College of Law, which became Northwestern University Law School.[18]

Some states allowed women to practice law, but most required a special act of a court, of the legislature, or both. Thus, the Illinois Supreme Court had refused to admit a woman, Myra Bradwell, to the bar in 1869, the year that Iowa admitted the first woman lawyer. Bradwell was the editor of the *Chicago Legal News*, one of the best legal periodicals of its day, and she had satisfied all of the requirements for admission to the bar. She was also a married woman and consequently subject to the legal disabilities of the common law of coverture, that is, the common law relating to married women. Bradwell took her case to the US Supreme Court, claiming that, in refusing to admit her to the practice of law because she was a woman, Illinois had denied her one of the privileges and immunities of US citizenship secured by the Fourteenth Amendment. The court rejected her claim on the grounds that the right to practice law is not one of the privileges of US citizenship but of state citizenship, and that it was within the jurisdiction of the states to regulate. But Justice Joseph P. Bradley wrote a concurring opinion that elaborated the ideology preventing women from entering the professions as freely as men or at all. Known as the "cult of true womanhood," this ideology distinguished social roles and separate spheres of men and women based on their sex.[19]

It is worth examining Justice Bradley's opinion in some detail because it is so revealing of prevailing sexual attitudes that until the latter part of the twentieth century inhibited women from even attempting to achieve equality in the professions and impeded those who tried. Justice Bradley rejected the idea that women enjoyed the right to practice law based on his conception of natural law, the nature of "womanhood," divine ordinance, and social organization. His view of natural law and divine ordinance undoubtedly paralleled the ideas taught in Fordham Law School's Jurisprudence course.[20]

History demonstrated that no one had ever claimed that the right to practice law was "one of the fundamental privileges and immunities of the [female] sex," Bradley began. "On the contrary, the civil law, as well as nature herself, has always recognized a wide difference in the respective spheres and destinies of man and woman." Bradley then explained the separate spheres of men and women: "Man is, or should be, woman's protector and defender. The natural and proper timidity and delicacy which belongs to the female sex evidently unfits it for many of the occupations of civil life." Reinforcing the domestic nature of women is the divinely ordained organization of the basic unit of society, the family, Bradley opined. "The constitution of the family organization, which is founded in the divine ordinance, as well as in the nature of things, indicates the domestic sphere as that which properly belongs to the domain and functions of womanhood." This sexual division of spheres between a man and his wife was, according to Bradley's reasoning, essential to the harmonious functioning of their marriage and family: "The harmony, not to say identity, of interests and views which belong, or should belong, to the family institution is repugnant to the idea of a woman adopting a distinct and independent career from that of her husband." Bradley asserted that this divinely ordained division between a man and a woman which is found in nature was the basis of the common law of coverture. "So firmly fixed was this sentiment in the founders of the common law that it became a maxim of the system of jurisprudence that a woman had no legal existence separate from her husband, who was regarded as her head and representative in the social state." The common law of marriage, in other words, transformed a woman from an individual to a wife—that is, to a legally prescribed status encompassing rights and obligations in relation to her husband.

Acknowledging that a married woman was defined in terms of her "civil status," Bradley asserted that "many of the special rules flowing from and dependent upon this cardinal principle still exists [*sic*] in full force in most States." One of these rules of coverture is "that a married woman is incapable, without her husband's consent, of making contracts which shall be binding on him or her." This was undoubtedly one of the legal disabilities that led the Illinois Supreme Court to conclude that "a married woman [was] incompetent fully to perform the duties and trusts that belong to the office of an attorney and counselor." One might object that unmarried women were not subject to the "duties, complications, and incapacities arising out of the married state." Bradley acknowledged this point, but he dismissed it as an exception to the "general rule" governing women. Bradley appealed to nature and divine providence in explaining this general rule: "The paramount destiny and mission of women are to fulfill the noble and benign offices of wife and mother. This is the law of the Creator. And the rules of civil society must be adapted to the general constitution of things, and can not be based upon exceptional cases." Bradley then expressed a view of individual rights that subordinated the rights of the individual to the paramount needs of the community, a view that predominated in American legal culture until the 1960s: "In the nature of things it is not every citizen of every age, sex, and condition that is qualified for every calling and position." Access to callings and positions may be regulated by the legislature, Bradley wrote. "It is the prerogative of the legislator to prescribe regulations founded on nature, reason, and experience for the due admission of qualified persons to professions and callings demanding special skill and confidence." This kind of regulation was within the police power of the state, Bradley concluded, and, "in view of the peculiar characteristics, destiny and mission of woman, it is within the province of the Legislature to ordain what offices, positions and callings shall be filled and discharged by men and . . . are presumed to predominate in the sterner sex" to the exclusion of women.[21]

The "cult of true womanhood" notwithstanding, the Illinois legislature passed a statute in 1872 allowing all persons the freedom to select a calling without regard to sex. Myra Bradwell could have been admitted to the bar even as the US Supreme Court upheld her exclusion by the Illinois Supreme Court. But she did not apply again, even though the Illinois Supreme Court admitted her to the practice of law in 1890.

The first woman admitted to practice before the US Supreme Court itself also acquired this privilege by legislative action. In 1879 Belva Lockwood, an attorney in Washington, DC, was admitted to the Supreme Court Bar by an act of Congress. Seven years later, Kate Stoneman, an Albany, New York, teacher who had studied on her own and passed the bar exam, was denied admission to the New York State bar by a state court that found the Code of Civil Procedure restricted admission exclusively to "any male citizen." Following a concerted lobbying effort by men and women, the state legislature passed a bill to rectify this situation in 1886, and a few days later Stoneman became the first woman admitted to the bar in New York State. In 1901, the New York State Bar Association admitted its first female member, the first bar association in the state to take that step. But women did not gain membership in the American Bar Association (ABA) until 1918, and they were not admitted to the Association of the Bar of the City of New York until 1937.[22]

As a result of political action and litigation strategies that opened state bars to women, the number of female lawyers steadily increased over the closing decades of the nineteenth century, but the number remained quite small. The census of 1870 listed 5 female attorneys; the 1880 census listed 75; and that of 1900 identified 1,010 female attorneys. By World War I, women were admitted to practice in every state except Delaware and Rhode Island, which finally admitted women after the ratification of the Nineteenth Amendment in 1920. Women were admitted to 41 of the nation's 137 law schools by 1915–16, and 122 of 127 law schools by 1920. The war caused a sharp decline in male law students between 1916 and 1918, but women did not offset the drop in male enrollments. Whereas male enrollments fell by 5,034 students, from 7,477 in 1916 to 2,443 in 1918, or 67 percent, the number of female law students increased by only 106 students, from 397 to 503, or 26.7 percent. The greatest increase in female students occurred in night schools, where the number of enrolled female students increased 92.4 percent. The Carnegie Foundation concluded that females replaced male law students only slightly, principally in the night schools and mixed day and night schools in and around New York City. However, the number of female law students increased sharply to 1,171 in 1920.[23]

Fordham Law School might have been motivated to admit women, in part, because it competed for students with local law schools that did admit women. But this is unlikely. In the fall of 1918, the Law School offered classes only at night, from 7:00 to 9:00, "owing to war conditions." The Law School was forced to stop operations for the 1918–19 academic year, even with a large increase in women enrollments. The number of women enrolled at Brooklyn Law School also increased, from 44 out of 316 students (about 14 percent) in 1916 to 70 out of 379 students (18 percent) in 1918. The proportion of female students at Brooklyn Law and the increase in their numbers by 59 percent are unusually high. By 1910, the number of female attorneys had declined from more than 1,000 in 1900 to only 558 out of a total of 122,149 lawyers, or 0.46 percent. In 1915–16, there were only 687 female law students out of 22,993, or about 3 percent of law students nationwide. In 1918–19, the total number of female law students actually declined to 503, but the proportion of female students enrolled in law schools actually increased to 17 percent of total enrollments because the decline in male law students was so much more substantial.[24]

When one considers that women constituted no more than 1.4 percent of attorneys in any year prior to 1930, and then less than 2.5 percent through the 1940s, it is unlikely that law schools competed very hard for female students. Richard Abel maintains that, to the contrary, female enrollments remained low in the better law schools because of "hidden quotas and social and cultural barriers." Female enrollments were greatest in the less prestigious schools. During World War I, Abel notes, female enrollments actually declined in day law schools while they increased 31.5 percent in mixed day and night law schools and a whopping 92.4 percent in night schools. Women continued to be excluded from some of the elite law schools. Columbia Law School did not admit women until 1928, and Harvard began to admit women only in 1950. Of the three Catholic law schools founded before Fordham, at least two had no women in 1918. Georgetown did not enroll women until 1951 and Notre Dame until 1967.[25]

Like those of other law schools in the New York City area, Fordham Law School's graduating classes included significantly higher percentages of females than national percentages of female attorneys during the 1920s, but they were still relatively small. Table 2-1 shows that between 1921 (Fordham's first class of female law graduates) and 1930, the percent of females in each graduating class fluctuated from a low of 1.8 percent (7 of 371) in 1930 to a high of 7.9 percent (26 of 328) in 1927.

TABLE 2-1. FEMALE GRADUATES, 1921–30

Year	Total Number of Graduates	Number of Female Graduates	Percentage of Female Graduates
1921	119	4	3
1922	222	9	4
1923	252	15	5.9
1924	357	21	5.8
1925	382	30	7.8
1926	399	22	5.5
1927	328	26	7.9
1928	389	13	3.3
1929	451	14	3.1
1930	371	7	1.8

Source: Fordham Law School Registrar's Records.

Over these ten years, Fordham Law School graduated 3,270 students, of whom 161, or 4.9 percent, were women. Nationally, the average percent of female law graduates during the 1920s was 4.9. In New York City between 1925 and 1928, women constituted between 5.5 percent and 6.2 percent of law school enrollments. In sum, approximately 6.1 percent of Fordham Law graduates, 91 out of 1498, were women during these four years, numbers that compared favorably to those of other New York City law schools and that were significantly greater than those of law schools nationally. Nonetheless, the number of enrolled female law students and attorneys remained relatively low. It is likely that the ideology of "true womanhood" and ethnic cultural values kept down the numbers of women seeking entry into law. The feminist historian Joan Hoff attributed the failure of late nineteenth- and early twentieth-century feminists to achieve a genuine equality for women to their abandoning a radical theory of equal rights that would have achieved full citizenship rights for women, for failing to attack the multifarious discriminations that relegated women to second-class citizenship, and for pursuing a narrow "single-issue fight for suffrage."[26]

The women who were admitted to Fordham Law School participated fully in the school's community. They were elected class officers and leaders of student groups, won prizes for academic achievement, and became practicing attorneys along with their male classmates, whom they occasionally married. For example, in the 1920–21 academic year, Ella L. Ralston, AM, received the $50 prize for having the highest grade average in the third-year class of the evening division. Evelyn M. Maye and Rosemary C. Boylan, AM, were elected secretary and treasurer, respectively, of the second-year afternoon class. The second-year evening class elected Catherine P. O'Hale, AB, secretary and Marion F. McCaffrey, AB, vice president. The first-year morning class elected Virginia Bell treasurer, and the first-year afternoon class elected Virginia A. Reilly secretary. At the end of the academic year, Evelyn M. Maye was elected vice president of the Fordham Forum.[27]

Of the original eight women who enrolled in Fordham in 1918, two of the three women admitted to the day division, Patricia A. O'Connell and Mildred I. O'Connor, graduated in 1921, but none of the five women admitted to the evening division graduated that year. One other woman graduated with the class of 1921, Ella L. Ralston, who had transferred to the Fordham evening division in the fall of 1919 after one year at New York University Law School. Ralston was the first Fordham Law School–educated female attorney admitted to the New York Bar. That only one-third of the enrolled women graduated with their classes was unusual. Except for the years affected by students' leaving law school for military service during World War I and military veterans' returning to law school after the end of the Great War, the dropout rate between 1914 and 1924 ranged between 31.85 percent and 49.40 percent. Data that might explain why students did not graduate in three years are unavailable. Men and women probably left for a variety of reasons: because they were not academically prepared to do the work, because balancing work and school was too difficult, or because of the demands of family life.[28]

Within a few years of the admission of women, several African American students enrolled at the Law School. New York City's African American community was relatively small in 1920, about 152,000 in a city of five million, or 3 percent, but its visibility had been enhanced during the World War I period, a prelude to the great Harlem Renaissance of the 1920s. In 1917 Harlem had elected the first black member of the state assembly, Edward Johnson. In 1919 the 369th Regiment (known as the Harlem Hellfighters) paraded up Fifth Avenue to Lenox Avenue past a million spectators, feted for their valor and skill in battle and already recognized with numerous Croix de Guerre by the French government. In 1920 the gifted Paul Robeson, a Rutgers University football star and later singer, actor, and activist, enrolled at Columbia Law School. The first African American students at Fordham were not far behind, and still far in advance of their counterparts at a number of law schools, such as Georgetown Law, which did not admit African American students until after World War II.[29]

In the 1920s, racial prejudice was widespread in American education and American culture generally. "Separate but equal" reigned in the South, where violence against blacks lingered into the 1930s, including lynchings and riots, and unequal justice was the norm in the court system. Most African Americans who sought a legal education were limited to attending the unaccredited Howard University Law School, founded in 1868, or a handful of southern law schools established for "colored students" that did not survive very long. A few African Americans were admitted to the elite private law schools or the law schools at public universities in the North and the West, Robeson being one example. Another is Charles Hamilton Houston, future civil rights lawyer and an architect of *Brown v. Board of Education*, who graduated from Harvard Law School in 1922. The Association of the Bar of the City of New York admitted its first African American member in 1929, but the American Bar Association refused to admit African Americans to membership until 1943, yielding to pressure from such prominent New York attorneys as Samuel Seabury and Arthur Garfield Hays.[30]

The first two African Americans to graduate from Fordham Law School were Ruth Whitehead Whaley and Oliver D. Williams. They graduated in 1924, and Whaley graduated *cum laude*. Whaley was the first African American woman to be admitted to both the North Carolina and New York bars and the first to practice law in New York state on her admission in 1925. She went on to a distinguished career as an attorney, an activist, and a public servant. Whaley served as president of the National Council of Negro Women and was the first president of the Negro Professional and Business Club. A Tammany Hall Democrat, she served on the New York City Council during the 1940s and as secretary of the New York City Board of Estimate from 1951 to 1973. Williams was a veteran of World War I. He won a $200 scholarship given by the state of New York based on a competitive exam in academic subjects, open to former soldiers, sailors, Marines, and nurses. He went on to a career as a practicing attorney and jurist, serving as a judge of the Municipal Court (1954–62), a judge of the Civil Court (1962–63), and a justice of the state Supreme Court from the Second District (Brooklyn and Richmond), to which he was elected in 1963 with the endorsement of the Democratic, Republican, and Liberal parties. He served on the Supreme Court until his retirement in 1974.[31]

The presence of African Americans and women at the Law School represented an extension of one of Fordham University's educational missions: providing educational opportunities to disadvantaged and disparaged minorities. Until the 1970s, the number of African American students at Fordham Law School was negligible, and the number of female students was quite small. This was the norm at other law schools that admitted African Americans and women. Many law schools did not do so until after World War II. The admission of both African Americans and women may have gone relatively smoothly at Fordham because the student population was already religiously and ethnically diverse. Moreover, Catholics were subjected to discrimination with varying degrees of virulence through the first half of the twentieth century, as were white ethnic groups that were predominantly Catholic, such as the Irish and nationalities from southern, central, and eastern Europe, such as Italians, Germans, Slavs, and Poles. African Americans and women added two minority groups that were significant parts of the New York City population as a whole. New York's colleges and professional schools, like Fordham Law School, were in the vanguard of promoting the advancement of women and minorities.

Dean John Whalen had presided over the Law School's move to the Woolworth Building, the trying years of the Great War, and the admission of women. By the time of the armistice ending World War I, he decided to resign as dean. The university's president, Father Edward P. Tivnan, S.J., announced Whalen's resignation at the same time that he announced the appointment of Francis P. Garvan as Whalen's successor. Garvan assumed the office of Law School dean the very next day, April 7, 1919.[32]

DEAN FRANCIS P. GARVAN AND POSTWAR POLITICS

Francis P. Garvan's background set him apart from Paul Fuller and John Whalen. Although he was a staunch Roman Catholic like his predecessors, Garvan came from a relatively wealthy family in East Hartford, Connecticut. After graduating from Yale College in 1897, he came to New York and clerked in the law office of James, Schell & Elkus while he attended New York University Law School. He earned his LLB degree in 1899 and then spent a year of study at Catholic University in Washington, DC. Garvan practiced law briefly in small firms in Albany and New York City. His public career was launched when he was appointed Deputy Assistant District Attorney in New York County in January 1901 by District Attorney Eugene Philbin. When Judge William Travers Jerome became the District Attorney in 1902, he promoted Garvan to Assistant District Attorney, and Garvan became his chief aide. Jerome was an anti-Tammany Democrat, a highly regarded and popular reformer who reportedly "led a spectacular crusade against vice, crime and political corruption throughout [New York City]." He hired a group of "unusually able assistants," known as "the Jerome men," according to Mayor Fiorello La Guardia. As Jerome's chief aide, Garvan assisted in a number of high-profile murder cases, including the original trial of Harry Thaw for the murder of Stanford White and Thaw's subsequent attempts to be discharged from the Matawan Asylum to which he had been consigned after the trial jury found him guilty but insane. When Jerome left office in 1910, Garvan returned to private practice. He was a partner in two law firms, Garvan & Armstrong and Osborne, Lambe & Garvan.[33]

Garvan held an important office in the Woodrow Wilson administration when he accepted the appointment as Law School dean, but his wealth enabled him to donate his services to the federal government. His father was "one of Hartford's best-known paper manufacturers" and had been active in Connecticut Democratic Party politics. One sister was married to W. Babington Macaulay, the papal legate for the Irish Free State, and she became a Papal Duchess. Another sister entered the convent and became Mother Angeline, president of St. Joseph's College in West Hartford, Connecticut. Francis married into an even wealthier family in 1910. His marriage to Mabel Brady was the second union between the Garvans and the Bradys; Garvan's sister Genevieve married Mabel's brother Nicholas. Mabel Brady was the daughter of Anthony N. Brady, an Irish-Catholic businessman who had worked his way up from hotel clerk to a man of immense wealth whose fortune was compared to that of J. Pierpont Morgan. Brady built his fortune by investing in public service corporations that provided electric, gas, and water power and transportation systems to various cities, including Brooklyn, New York; Chicago; Philadelphia; and Washington, DC. He had substantial holdings in Consolidated Gas Company and its subsidiary, New York Edison Company, Commonwealth Edison Company of Chicago, and People's Gas, Light and Coke Company, also of Chicago. Having a substantial investment in the Brooklyn Rapid Transit System and being chairman of its board of directors, Brady reorganized it and later connected it with the Interboro Rapid Transit company in Manhattan. Though he was characterized as a "traction magnate," Brady also invested heavily in a number of other industries, including the rubber, oil, automobile, and tobacco industries. For example, he was the one of the largest stockholders in the American Tobacco Company, which yielded an income of $1,600,000 per year, before its dissolution. After the Tobacco Trust was broken up, Brady continued to be one of the largest stockholders in the companies that were created from the Trust, his shares being valued at $31,000,000. At Brady's death in 1913, his estate was estimated at between $70 million and $100 million, from which Francis and Mabel Garvan received a substantial inheritance of between $11 million and $12 million. In present-day dollars Brady's fortune would be approximately between $1.56 billion ($1,560,000,000) and $2.23 billion ($2,230,000,000), and the Garvans' inheritance would be between $246 million ($246,000,000) and $268 million ($268,000,000).[34]

The combined wealth of the Brady and Garvan families enabled Francis and Mabel Garvan to enjoy an opulent lifestyle. They had a Fifth Avenue townhouse in Manhattan, estates on Long Island and in the Adirondacks in upstate New York, stables with prizewinning show horses and thoroughbreds, memberships in the finest social clubs, and frequent mention in the society pages. The Garvans were among the foremost collectors of American art, specializing in eighteenth- and nineteenth-century silver, glass, pottery, furniture, and decorative metals; they also collected books and early American architecture and interiors. The couple made generous donations to Yale and Fordham universities and to numerous cultural, charitable, and scientific institutions, from the Metropolitan Museum of Art to the Roman Catholic Church. Just before Garvan was appointed dean of Fordham Law School, he and his wife gave several early American mantelpieces from a Pennsylvania house to the Metropolitan Museum of Art, which was developing its American collections for display in an anticipated new wing. In 1921, the Garvans gave $10,000 to the Greater Fordham Appeal Fund.[35]

Several factors predetermined Francis Garvan's appointment as the third dean of Fordham Law School. Among them were his distinguished legal career in the office of the Manhattan District Attorney and his work for the federal government during World War I. He was a leading Catholic layman who had known New York's Archbishop John Farley for many years, and he was a member of two prominent and devout Catholic families.

Garvan's generosity may have been a factor in his appointment. In his history of Fordham University, Father Robert Gannon, S.J., claims that Garvan agreed "to make good all deficits which might appear during the next five years—an offer unmatched by any Dean in the country before or since." Moreover, Garvin offered Fordham University $1,000,000 "if it would sell out and move to New Haven where it could be supervised by Yale." Apparently, had Father Gannon been Fordham's president in 1919 rather than decades later, he would have accepted Garvan's proposal, because he could not understand why this "this generous offer was not accepted." Father Gannon's reaction is understandable considering that Garvin's offer was worth $12,400,000 in present-day dollars.[36]

Garvan was often absent from the school because of the positions he held in the federal government while he was dean. In these positions, Garvan played two important roles in the nation's history. He contributed significantly to the development of the dye and chemical industries of the United States. He also was a central player in the federal government's response to the Red Scare of 1919. The actual administration of the school was performed by Pro Dean Michael F. Dee while Garvan was dean, much as it was during Dean Whalen's tenure.

When the United States entered World War I, Garvan volunteered his services to the federal government. In November 1917 President Wilson appointed Garvan director of the Bureau of Investigation of the Alien Property Custodian. The alien property custodian was A. Mitchell Palmer. Garvan's responsibilities as director were to uncover and investigate property owned and held by enemy aliens in the United States. Garvan is credited with having uncovered some $700,000,000 worth of enemy property in the United States, much of it owned by German aliens. This property consisted of 4,500 dye and chemical patents, processes, copyrights, and trademarks held by German firms. The Trading with the Enemy Act authorized Palmer, as the alien property custodian, to seize these properties, which he did. His goal was to break the pre–World War I German dye and chemical monopoly and to stimulate American production of dyes, medicines and chemicals. His plan was to make the German properties available to the American dye and chemical manufacturers in ways that ensured their widespread use in the United States.[37]

In March 1919 President Wilson elevated Palmer to the position of attorney general of the United States and appointed Garvan to replace Palmer as alien property custodian. At the request of President Wilson and Attorney General Palmer, and pursuant to the Trading with the Enemy Act, Garvan formed the American Chemical Foundation, Inc., to carry out Palmer's plan. By law, the foundation held these properties "as a trustee for American industry." The foundation's charter required that it grant nonexclusive licenses to use these patents, processes, copyrights, and trademarks on equal terms to all proper applicants, described as "any competent, equipped, and patriotic American individual firm, or corporation." As the alien property custodian, Garvan sold the German patents, processes, copyrights, and trademarks to the American Chemical Foundation. Garvan was then appointed to serve as the first president of the American Chemical Foundation, a post he held until his death in November 1937. The American Chemical Foundation sold these licenses and used the income to promote scientific research and to fund scholarships and grants to researchers in the field of chemistry. The American chemical industry benefited greatly from these actions.[38]

Republican opponents of the Wilson administration roundly attacked the purposes of the American Chemical Foundation and assailed Francis P. Garvan's assuming its presidency. They feared that Garvan, Palmer, and the foundation's board of directors were engaging in self-dealing and attempting to establish monopolistic control of the dye industry. In fact, Garvan and the others had no financial interest in the foundation and, as president, Garvan did not receive a single cent from it. Several lawsuits decided by federal District Judge Augustus Hand, his more distinguished cousin Judge Learned Hand, the U.S. Court of Appeals for the Third Circuit, and the U.S. Supreme Court vindicated Garvan and secured the American Chemical Foundation's ownership and distribution of the German property from legal challenges. Garvan used the German patents, processes, copyrights, and trademarks in developing the American dye and chemical industries.[39]

In May 1919, one month after Garvan became dean of Fordham Law School, President Wilson expanded his duties by appointing him assistant attorney general to oversee the investigation of "an organized campaign of anarchy and terrorism" attributed to bomb-throwing radicals, anarchists, and communists intent on overthrowing the government of the United States and the American capitalist system. Garvan played a central role in the federal government's response to the hysteria known as the post–World War I "Red Scare" of 1919–20. Economic dislocation produced by rapid military demobilization, which required American industry to reabsorb some four million returning American soldiers, and the conversion from wartime to peacetime production were accompanied by high unemployment and soaring inflation. Industrialists sought to cut back on the economic gains labor enjoyed during the war, and they especially sought to destroy the principle of collective bargaining that the federal government forced upon them in order to ensure wartime production. As economic conditions worsened after the armistice of November 1918, workers felt compelled to use their major economic weapon, the strike. Major strikes occurred so frequently that they became commonplace in 1919, when some four million workers left their jobs in 3,600 strikes across the country. The most significant strike occurred in Seattle, Washington, where the city's workers called a general strike that riveted the nation's frightened attention for almost a week in February 1919.[40]

Labor strife combined with bombs sent through the mails and placed in public buildings and private residences and rioting that occurred on May Day in 1919 caused the general public to believe the United States was threatened by imminent violent revolution. Parcels containing bombs were sent through the mails to thirty-six public officials and prominent industrialists who were earmarked for death, including Justice Oliver Wendell Holmes Jr.; Federal Judge Kenesaw Mountain Landis, who had given stiff prison sentences for violating the Espionage Act to William S. "Big Bill" Haywood, leader of the Wobblies and convert to the American Communist Party, and Victor Berger, leader of the Socialist Party; Postmaster General Albert S. Burleson, who had banned radical literature from the mails; Attorney General A. Mitchell Palmer; John D. Rockefeller; and J. P. Morgan. Other bombs were placed in public buildings and private homes.[41]

Newspapers across the country sensationalized reports of the "May Day bombs." They informed their horrified readers in large, bold headlines that "36 WERE MARKED AS VICTIMS BY BOMB CONSPIRATORS" and that "REDS PLANNED MAY DAY MURDERS." The conservative *Chicago Tribune* warned its readers that they, too, might be victims of the Communist bomb conspirators, warning them to "BEWARE BOX IF IT COMES THROUGH MAIL—Do not Open It—Call the police bomb squad." Some newspapers demanded that bomb makers and bomb throwers be summarily hanged and every anarchist be deported. Although some newspapers resisted the feeding frenzy, noting that the May Day bombs claimed only two victims and that the number of anarchists and communists was insufficient to pose a real danger of anarchy and revolution, their calming voices were virtually unheard in the growing hysteria that was gripping the nation.[42]

May Day was a significant international holiday for workers around the world. In the United States, socialists marked May Day 1919 as they had never done before. They staged rallies, mass meetings, and parades, sometimes without permits, prompting violent reactions by local police and bystanders who heckled and harassed them. Riots broke out in many cities, but the main disturbances occurred in Boston, Cleveland, and New York. Many people were injured, a few were killed, and hundreds of socialists were arrested and jailed, though not the nonsocialist rioters.[43]

On the evening of June 2, a month after the May Day bomb attempts and the May Day riots, explosions in eight cities that destroyed public and private buildings and killed two individuals appeared to vindicate those newspaper editors who had warned of further violence and called for summary action either to imprison or deport all radicals. Newspaper headlines screamed, "BOMB THROWERS RENEW TERRORISM" and "TERROR REIGNS IN MANY CITIES." These coordinated bombings in Cleveland; Newton, Massachusetts; Paterson, New Jersey; Boston; New York City; Pittsburgh; Philadelphia; and Washington, DC, seemed indiscriminate, further stoking the public's fear and confusion. The most sensational bombing was at the home of Attorney General Palmer in the nation's capital. The bomb demolished the front of Palmer's house and destroyed the windows of surrounding homes. Apparently, the bomb thrower tripped as he was walking up the stairs to the front porch and detonated the bomb, literally blowing himself to bits. Fragments of his clothes identified him as an Italian alien from Philadelphia, and an anarchist pamphlet found at the scene, which proclaimed a resolve to murder, kill, destroy, and do anything necessary to "suppress the capitalist class" and signed "The Anarchist Fighters," left little doubt as to his motivations. Franklin Delano Roosevelt, who was serving as Assistant Secretary of the Navy at the time, lived across the street and is credited with having called the police. The press coverage of and public officials' reactions to the June 2 bombings contributed to the shock and horror of ordinary Americans.[44]

In retrospect, it is clear that the number of genuine radicals was so small that no real danger of revolution or even serious threats to law and order existed after World War I. The Red Scare was created and held together by exaggerated, misreported, and misinterpreted facts that were manipulated by the news media and the federal government to support excessive claims of danger. They transformed in the minds of many

Americans what was only a theoretical possibility of revolution into a terrible reality.[45]

The Wilson administration responded to the mass hysteria with decisive governmental repression of radicals. Palmer appointed Garvan assistant attorney general to lead the government's war against radicals. William J. Flynn, who had been head of the Secret Service, was appointed chief of the Bureau of Investigation of the Department of Justice to spearhead discovery of these perceived dangerous terrorists and to work in conjunction with the Secret Service. He was to work under Garvan, who had "general charge of all investigation work and special criminal prosecutions of the Department of Justice."[46]

"Convinced that the nation faces an organized campaign of anarchy and terrorism which calls for heroic action," the New York Times announced, the Department of Justice and other federal departments "took steps which it is believed will effectively put an end to the plot." Palmer asked Garvan to reorganize the Bureau of Investigation and entrusted him with the "general supervision over this bureau," and he appointed the former head of the Secret Service, William J. Flynn, to take direct charge of investigations. Beginning on November 7, 1919 (the second anniversary of the Russian Revolution), a series of raids orchestrated by Garvan—later known as "Palmer raids"—netted the arrest of thousands of (perhaps as many as 10,000) suspected radicals in thirty cities. They were jailed without regard to whether they had actually been involved with bomb plots or had merely owned subversive literature or had just spoken out. Offices of unions and organizations of socialists and communists were destroyed. With little or no access to legal representation, hundreds of aliens were quickly deported. Garvan helped arrange the first ship, the Buford, to sail from New York harbor on December 22, 1919. The Buford carried 249 deportees to exile in the Soviet Union and a guard of 251 American soldiers. Among those on board were anarchist Alexander Berkman, who had attempted to kill Henry C. Frick; and Emma Goldman, anarchist, feminist, and proponent of free speech and birth control, who had been convicted of sedition for her opposition to conscription during the war and deprived of her citizenship in a secret government action. Of the thousands of suspected radicals who were arrested in the Palmer raids, most were eventually released after long detentions. Palmer's ability to stoke mass hysteria declined when he warned that there would be an uprising of communists on May Day 1920, and the uprising did not occur.[47]

World War I and its aftermath raised public policy questions that Fordham Law faculty, students, and guest lecturers had been discussing since before the war. The fundamental question was whether the nation's democratic ideals were being undermined by foreign ideas, variously labeled socialist, communist, or anarchist. The civility of these discussions at Fordham contrasted with the government's harsh approach to dealing with political differences. An antisocialist critique had long been present at public events at Fordham University, and at various graduations student and commencement speakers urged their audiences to understand how dangerous socialism could be to democracy and to religion. Speaking at an alumni association dinner in 1914, Fordham President Thomas McCluskey, S.J., attacked the growing presence of socialism on college and university campuses. "It is almost incredible," he admonished, "that the great universities of this country are centres of the teaching of false ideals, which may destroy the State, destroy the family, and enslave the individual, but which can never accomplish the Utopia which it promises."[48]

The Catholic Church condemned radical socialism because it perceived this movement as a threat to the autonomy of families and individuals in their relationships to the state, to the relationship of the churches to their members, and to the capitalist economic system. Yet the Church supported many of the social justice goals advocated by socialists, such as caring for and helping the poor, improving the wages and working conditions of laborers, and advocating a more equitable distribution of wealth. The Church's brand of social justice was closer to the homegrown brand of socialism that had emerged in late nineteenth-century America, drawing on the legacies of English and German thinkers and the ideas of Henry George, that also called for municipal ownership of utilities and strong unions to secure the economic rights of workers. In 1901 the Socialist Party of America was formed in New York City, attracting workers, artists, writers, and reformers to its membership. In 1914 a Socialist candidate, Meyer London, was elected to the US House of Representatives from the city. In 1917 the Socialists ran an unsuccessful candidate for mayor of New York, Morris Hillquit, but they succeeded in electing some of their own to the New York State Assembly and to the New York City Board of Aldermen. The State Assembly refused to seat the five assemblymen-elect.[49]

In the spring of 1920 the New York state legal academic community addressed issues relating to the rights of socialists at a meeting of the New York State Association of Legal Instructors, comprising faculty from the nine law schools of the state. Fordham Law School sent several law professors, including Pro-Dean Michael Dee and Professor I. Maurice Wormser. Attendees discussed a proposal to bar socialists from enrolling in law schools or getting a law degree. Dean Leslie J. Tompkins of New York University proposed excluding them, arguing that socialists who were "learned in the law" would be "doubly dangerous." Some speakers opposed Tompkins's proposal on pragmatic grounds, insisting that excluding them from "law schools would give the Socialists the opportunity to pose as martyrs and to further denounce lawyers, law professors and Judges as 'tools of the capitalist class.'" Dean Harlan F. Stone of Columbia suggested that law schools should not screen students because the legality of socialist discourse was a political question to be resolved at the ballot box. Wormser took a marketplace-of-ideas approach when he announced that "he was actively opposed to the teachings of Socialism, but that very fact caused him to want to give the Socialists an opportunity to have their doctrine repudiated, which he said would be done because it was wrong." The proposal was referred to the group's executive committee, and nothing further was heard about it.[50]

Dean Garvan and Father Terence C. Shealy, S.J., were two members of the Fordham Law School administration and faculty who were actively working against socialism and other forms of radical political ideologies. As already discussed, President Wilson and Attorney General Palmer delegated to Garvan responsibility for ferreting out and removing the radicals' threat to society. Father Shealy combined his academic career with social action, founding the Catholic Retreat Movement and establishing the Jesuit retreat house at Mt. Manresa in Staten Island and a School of Social Studies to educate Catholic men and women to serve as social workers, lecturers, and writers and to "bring Catholic principles to bear upon the social and economic life around them." The School of Social Studies' curriculum focused on social justice and social action from a Catholic perspective, identifying the dangers of socialism and elaborating Pope Leo XIII's encyclical *Rerum Novarum* on the rights of labor. Father Shealy's program followed the Church's teachings on the principles, tactics, and evils of socialism and socialist organizations, which he regarded as irreligious and immoral; relationship of the Church's teachings to economics, labor unions, and the schools; the Catholic Church's relationship to labor unions; and its teachings regarding a just wage and social reform. In 1916 Father Shealy organized Fordham University's School of Sociology and Social Service. An outgrowth of his School of Social Studies, its primary purpose was "to train Catholics as efficient social workers, fitting them to take the positions offered by the city." He affiliated his School of Social Studies with the Fordham University School of Sociology and Social Service and served as its dean from 1916 to 1918.[51]

Father Shealy was the most visible presence of the Law School's affiliation with a Jesuit University until he resigned in 1921. He was the only Jesuit at Fordham Law School for its first fifteen years, except when he was assisted in 1913 by Reverend Owen A. Hill, S.J., who taught Jurisprudence in the evening class that year, and when Reverend Matthew Fortier, S.J., replaced him for the 1918–19 academic year. In addition to holding the title of professor of jurisprudence, Father Shealy served as regent of the Law School. It was Jesuit practice to appoint a Jesuit representative to professional schools within its universities to ensure their connection to the university's central administration and to the Jesuit order, and to ensure that nothing was taught that was contrary to Catholic faith and morals. At some Jesuit institutions, such as the University of Detroit, the regent actually ran the law school. More typically, however, the administration of Jesuit law schools was in the hands of the dean and faculty, but administrative and academic decisions and policies were subject to the approval of the law school regent and the university's central administration.[52]

There were only a few situations in which students were likely to encounter reminders that Fordham Law School was part of a Catholic or Jesuit university. The Jurisprudence course was probably the most important expression of the school's Jesuit and Catholic affiliation, because it was undoubtedly taught from the Jesuits' Thomistic natural rights philosophical perspective. The Fordham University president, who was always a Jesuit, or another clerical representative of the university usually attended the opening convocation for each school year. Graduation was held at the Rose Hill campus, and the president of Fordham University was often joined by other local Church officials, such as the Archbishop of New York or a visiting prelate from abroad. Law students were encouraged to attend the Red Mass at St. Patrick's Cathedral. Many Catholic students belonged to the St. Thomas Aquinas Sodality, which met at Rose Hill.[53]

Catholic students organized the St. Thomas Aquinas Law School Sodality in 1921, with the help of Reverend Shealy and then his successor, Reverend Francis P. LeBuffe, S.J. The Sodality held its first meeting on December 4, 1921, at the Bronx campus. Eighty-nine men attended the 9:00 A.M. Mass and breakfast. The Sodality held its second Sunday Communion Breakfast on February 5, 1922. About eighty students were present. The guest speaker was Edward N. Glennon, Fordham University alumnus of 1905 and one of the students to matriculate through the Law School's first entering class. He was the current district attorney for the Bronx and a former justice of the New York State Supreme Court. He spoke about his experiences as a lawyer and "invited the sodalists to come to his office at any time and avail themselves of any practical information he or his associates might have." The Sodality meetings may have been what would be described in twenty-first-century terms as a "networking event." One of the students reported that Glennon spoke about "practical cases of interest to his hearers both as lawyers and as Catholics" and that the students "went away with the conviction that they had profited much both spiritually and legally."[54]

Perhaps that explains the sharp increase in attendance at the next meeting, as 120 students attended the Sodality's third Communion Breakfast on April 2, 1922. The university's president, Reverend Edward P. Tivnan, S.J., gave the sermon at Mass, and William F. K. Geoghan, a prominent lawyer, spoke about religious intolerance. Fifty-four members of the Sodality attended its first annual retreat at Mt. Manresa, Staten Island, that spring. Father LeBuffe was the moderator, and he was assisted by Reverend Francis Dore, S.J., of the Graduate School faculty. The *Fordham Monthly* reported that it was due to "the kind office of the former Regent of the Law School, Reverend Terence P. Shealy, S.J., that the historic Fox Hills Manor House, now the House of Retreats, with its twenty acres of garden land and its superb view of the city and the lower bay, was given over to the enjoyment of the Sodalists." The Sodality decided at its March 4, 1923, Communion Breakfast to meet every month rather than bimonthly, and in December 1923 the Sodalists set aside the first Sunday of each month for this event. Perhaps because of its founder, Father Shealy, the Sodality also engaged in Catholic social action. In February 1923 it made arrangements with the parole committee of Randall's Island to assist in promoting "the welfare of the boys released from that institution." The following academic year Sodality moderator Father LeBuffe, in a sermon to the Sodalists, "emphasized the need to instill Americanism into the children of New York's Chinatown." He intended "to commission certain Sodalists each week to perform this worthy work."[55]

When he was a student in the Bronx night division from 1933 to 1936, Governor Malcolm Wilson recalled, the St. Thomas Aquinas Sodality was the only schoolwide extracurricular activity at the Law School, except for the *Law Review*, which was a casualty of the Great War but was revived in 1935 and restricted to a limited number of students. Wilson was elected president of the Sodality, which required him to arrange speakers for the three Communion Breakfasts per year, to preside at the Communion Breakfasts, and to speak to students in all of the Law School's divisions, urging their support of the Communion Breakfasts.[56]

The Jesuit community may have wanted "to stamp the [law] school with a more Catholic character" with the appointment of more faculty "from the ranks of the Jesuit alumni," but this simply did not happen. During the tenures of Fordham Law School's first three deans, the faculty included only one Jesuit at any given time. The majority of the lay faculty were Catholic, but there is no evidence of an institutional policy restricting faculty recruitment to Catholics. To the contrary, some of the most eminent members of the faculty, such as Professors Keener and Wormser, were not Catholics.[57]

There is also no evidence that students were accepted or rejected because of their religion or ethnicity. At a time when elite universities and law schools discriminated against recent immigrants and their offspring because they were Catholics and Jews and because they were of Irish and southern and eastern European descent, Fordham Law School's student body, which initially was overwhelmingly Irish, quickly diversified. The Law School did not track the religious affiliations and nationalities of its students until the deanship of Ignatius Wilkinson. The first extant compilation of these data relating to students' religious affiliation was not made until the 1932–33 academic year. This compilation reveals that, of the students enrolled in that year, about 65 percent were Catholic, 20 percent were Jewish, and 15 percent were Protestant.[58]

Although the students and, apparently, the faculty of Fordham Law School were overwhelmingly Catholic, the school's culture evidently was inclusive and enabled non-Catholics to feel welcome. Louis Lefkowitz, an evening school graduate in the class of 1925, was probably representative of Jewish students when he later recalled: "I was of the Jewish faith. Most of the boys were of the Catholic faith. They didn't ask you what your faith was, but it was evident by your name. There was no trouble. None. . . . I'll say that is to Fordham's credit. A hundred percent." Although Lefkowitz acknowledged that the Law School "was Catholic oriented," he nevertheless maintained that "the comradeship was wonderful. No incident ever made me feel uncomfortable." Lefkowitz was proud of and grateful to Fordham for giving him the opportunity to embark upon his chosen career: "I'll tell you how proud I am of Fordham University. They gave me my start in life. I always referred to Fordham wherever I went." He manifested his appreciation to the Law School by recruiting many of its alumni. "I gave many students from Fordham Law School a position in my office when I served as [New York] Attorney General."[59]

Fordham Law School benefactor Louis Stein, an evening school graduate in the class of 1926, also recalled that he, too, never felt discriminated against in the school's "Catholic" atmosphere. Unable to afford medical school because classes were held during business hours and he needed to work, Stein was grateful that Fordham Law School's evening session made it possible for him to obtain a profession. "That was his opportunity into the middle class," noted a Fordham faculty member who knew Stein years later. "He always had an enormous gratitude to Fordham for that. That's why he was always such a wonderful benefactor to the school, what we enabled him to be."[60]

The tone of Fordham Law School during this era was set by its three deans, all urbane individuals who were used to interacting in a cosmopolitan setting with men (for the most part) of different faiths. Their professional and civic activities had required them to move beyond a separate Catholic sphere, and this was true of their faculty as well. The setting in lower Manhattan, where business was conducted in a decidedly secular manner, reinforced the disconnect between the more religiously oriented Bronx campus and the Law School's classrooms.

The Law School's portion of the *Fordham University Bulletin of Information* was essentially secular. Whereas the courses offered by Fordham

College and graduate divisions of Fordham University were informed by explicit Catholic social and ethical teachings, courses offered by the Law School were interchangeable with those offered at other New York law schools, with the possible exceptions of the courses in Jurisprudence and, when Paul Fuller was dean, Ethics. There were a few indications in the *Law School Bulletin* that the Law School was a sectarian institution. It listed both the president and the treasurer of Fordham University, each of whom was always a Jesuit. It explained the academic calendar, which included the days on which classes were not held. In addition to the secular legal holidays, the *Bulletin* identified Holy Days of Obligation, such as All Saints' Day; the Feast of the Immaculate Conception; Holy Thursday, Good Friday, and Easter Monday; and Ascension Day. There were no other references to religion in the *Law School Bulletin*.[61]

One of the important questions I sought to answer in researching the Fordham Law School history was whether this institution was established to serve the dispossessed: Catholic and other immigrant groups who were excluded from the elite law schools or who could not afford to attend them. There are no records that establish students' country of origin, ethnicity, and religion prior to 1925. As well as one can tell from students' surnames, most Fordham Law students in its early history were probably Irish. This conclusion is based on the assumption that most if not all British surnames were probably Irish. Because registration materials did not ask for the students' or their parents' country of origin or their religion, there is no empirical evidence of the ethnicity and religion of the student body. However, a review of students' names suggests that the proportion of students with Irish and British surnames fluctuated between 57 percent and 80 percent of the student body through 1923. Students with German surnames represented between 7 percent and 10 percent of the student body. Students with Jewish surnames first appeared in 1913 and fluctuated between 6.5 percent and 9 percent. Italian surnames also first appeared in 1913 and represented the next-largest group, ranging between 3 percent and 7 percent of the student body. In addition, there were smaller percentages of students with French, Swiss, Belgian, Austrian, Polish, Dutch, and Spanish surnames.[62]

Registration forms from 1925 through 1947 confirm these patterns of ethnicity. These records contain hard evidence of students' immigrant status, ethnicity, and religious affiliation. The Law School required entering students to fill out admission applications that asked for the applicants' place of birth, their fathers' and mothers' places of birth, and the students' religious affiliation, if any. These admission applications were randomly sampled to determine whether Fordham Law students were immigrants themselves and/or the children of immigrants, their ethnicity, and their religious affiliation. In 1948 the school stopped asking for the country of origin and immigrant status of students and their parents. It also changed the question relating to religious affiliation, asking only if the student was Roman Catholic. This question continued to be asked until 1968. These admission applications from each entering class between 1948 and 1968 were randomly sampled to determine the percentage of Catholic and non-Catholic students.[63]

Nearly all of the students admitted to Fordham Law School between 1925 and 1947 were born in the United States. The percentage of native-born students fell below 90 percent (to 89.5 percent) in only one year, 1943 (see Figure 2-1). In two years, 1940 and 1946, 100 percent of the entering class were native-born. When clustered in five-year periods, the percentage of native-born students remained quite consistent at about 95 percent (see Figure 2-2).

Approximately one-half of entering students were the children of immigrant parents through the 1920s. After 1930, one can discern a fairly steady rise in the proportion of students of US-born parents to 1935 and 1936, when the percentage of US-born parents reached its highest points at about 73 percent and 62 percent respectively. In a sudden and dramatic turnaround, children of immigrant parents spiked the next year (1937) to about 67 percent but declined in 1938 to just over one-half and then became a sizeable minority through the rest of the period except for 1944 and 1945, when 53 percent and 67 percent of both parents were foreign-born (see Figure 2-1). When one examines the data in five-year clusters, students whose parents were foreign-born became a minority after 1935, though a significant minority (see Figure 2-2).[64]

An analysis of students with foreign-born parents reveals the ethnicity of entering students and the correlation between their ethnicity and their religious affiliation. Not surprisingly, the largest number and percentage of students whose parents were born in "the old country" were Irish. Both parents of about 30 percent (31.61 percent) of the Irish students were

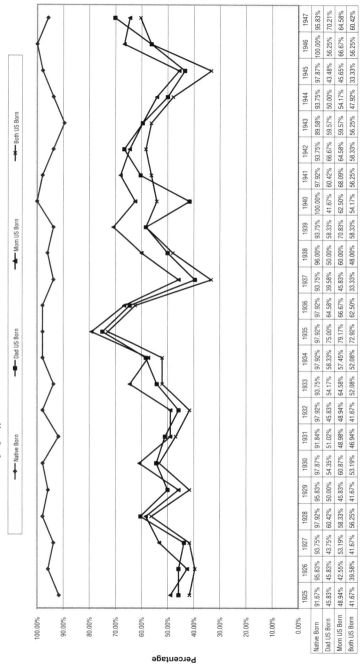

FIGURE 2-1. YEARLY IMMIGRATION 1925–47.

	1925	1926	1927	1928	1929	1930	1931	1932	1933	1934	1935	1936	1937	1938	1939	1940	1941	1942	1943	1944	1945	1946	1947
Native Born	91.67%	95.83%	93.75%	97.92%	95.83%	97.87%	91.84%	97.92%	93.75%	97.92%	97.92%	97.92%	93.75%	96.00%	93.75%	100.00%	97.92%	93.75%	89.58%	93.75%	97.87%	100.00%	95.83%
Dad US Born	45.83%	45.83%	43.75%	60.42%	50.00%	54.35%	51.02%	45.83%	54.17%	58.33%	75.00%	64.58%	39.58%	50.00%	58.33%	41.67%	60.42%	66.67%	59.57%	50.00%	43.48%	56.25%	70.21%
Mom US Born	48.94%	42.55%	53.19%	58.33%	45.83%	60.87%	48.98%	48.94%	64.58%	57.45%	79.17%	66.67%	45.83%	60.00%	70.83%	62.50%	68.09%	64.58%	59.57%	54.17%	45.65%	66.67%	64.58%
Both US Born	41.67%	39.58%	41.67%	56.25%	41.67%	53.19%	46.94%	41.67%	52.08%	52.08%	72.92%	62.50%	33.33%	48.00%	58.33%	54.17%	56.25%	58.33%	56.25%	47.92%	33.33%	56.25%	60.42%

Year

Percentage

Native Born   Dad US Born   Mom US Born   Both US Born

FIGURE 2-2. YEARLY IMMIGRATION 1925–47 (5-YEAR AGGREGATES).

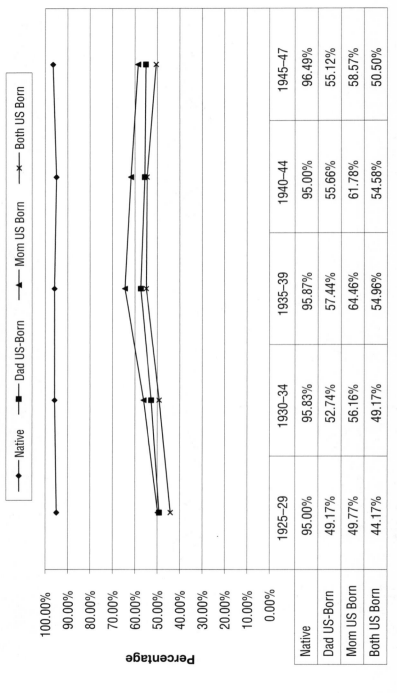

	1925–29	1930–34	1935–39	1940–44	1945–47
Native	95.00%	95.83%	95.87%	95.00%	96.49%
Dad US-Born	49.17%	52.74%	57.44%	55.66%	55.12%
Mom US Born	49.77%	56.16%	64.46%	61.78%	58.57%
Both US Born	44.17%	49.17%	54.96%	54.58%	50.50%

immigrants. Approximately the same percentages of fathers (28.30 percent) and mothers (29.93 percent) of these students were born in Ireland. Just under 99 percent of these parents were Roman Catholic. The second-largest ethnic group was Italian, and the children of Italian immigrants were virtually as numerous as those of the Irish. Both parents of about 30 percent (30.41 percent) of Italian students were born in Italy, but slightly more Italian fathers (27.88 percent) than Italian mothers (25.85 percent) were immigrants. Almost all of the Italian immigrant fathers (96.99 percent) and mothers (98.25 percent) were Roman Catholic.[65]

After the Irish and Italian students, there is a sharp drop in the percentage of students whose parents were born in specific countries. The third-largest ethnic group of students who were the children of immigrants was Russian. Both parents of about 10 percent (10.63 percent) of the Russian students were born in Russia. There was a slight variation in the percentage of fathers (10.69 percent) and mothers (9.98 percent) who were immigrants. Almost all of the fathers (96.09 percent) and mothers (97.73 percent) were Jewish. Students of Austrian and Polish heritage were the next-largest ethnic groups of children born of immigrants. Of these, both parents of about 6 percent of the Austrian (6.30 percent) and Polish (6.32 percent) students were born in their homelands. About the same percentages of Austrian fathers (6.92 percent) and mothers (6.58 percent) were born abroad, but there was a slight variation in the percentages of Polish fathers (5.66 percent) and mothers (6.35 percent) who were immigrants. Although Austria and Poland were predominantly Catholic countries, two-thirds of the Austrian-born fathers (66.67 percent) and mothers (65.52 percent) were Jewish, and only about a quarter of Austrian-born fathers (24.24 percent) and mothers (27.59 percent) were Catholic. The parents of greater percentages of the Polish students' immigrant fathers (37.04 percent) and mothers (39.29 percent) were Catholic, but the great majority of the fathers (62.96 percent) and mothers (60.71 percent) were Jewish.[66]

The next two largest ethnic groups of students who were the children of immigrants were Germans and English. About 5 percent (4.98 percent) of both parents of German students had emigrated from Germany. There was a slight variation in the percentages of fathers (5.66 percent) and mothers (4.99 percent) who were born in Germany. The religious affiliations of German-born parents were more diverse than those of the other ethnic groups discussed so far. About one-third of the fathers (33.33 percent) and mothers (36.36 percent) were Catholic. About two-fifths of the fathers (40.74 percent) but only about one-quarter of the mothers (27.27 percent) were Jewish. And, slightly more than one-fifth of the fathers (22.22 percent) and almost one-third of the mothers (31.82 percent) were Protestants. German-born fathers and mothers were more religiously diverse within their marriages as well as among their fellow immigrants. Parents who were born in England represented even greater religious diversity. About 1.5 percent of both parents had emigrated from England, and about the same percentage of fathers (2.31 percent) and mothers (2.72 percent) were immigrants. Although their numbers were relatively small, the spread across the three major religious groups was the greatest. Most of the fathers (63.64 percent) and mothers (58.33 percent) were Catholics. Slightly less than 20 percent of the fathers (18.18 percent) and almost 10 percent of the mothers (8.33 percent) were Protestants. About 9 percent (9.09 percent) of the fathers and 16 percent (16.67 percent) of the mothers were Jewish. Significant percentages of English-born fathers (9.09 percent) and mothers (16.67 percent) were "other." These data suggest that immigrants from Ireland, Italy, Russia, Austria, and Poland generally married within their faiths, but significant percentages of Jewish and Protestant immigrants from Germany and England married outside their faiths.

Not surprisingly, the religious affiliation of most of the students in the entering classes between 1925 and 1947 was overwhelmingly Catholic. With the exception of four years, the proportion of Catholic students varied between 68 percent and 75 percent. The proportion of Catholic students was greater than 75 percent in three of the four exceptional years: 1929 (79.1 percent), 1941 (85.4 percent), and 1946 (81.2 percent). In 1934 the proportion of Catholics fell to 60.4 percent (see Figure 2-3).

Non-Catholic students were overwhelmingly either Protestants or Jews. The percentage of each group fluctuated wildly in some years. For example, the lowest proportion of Protestants was 2.04 percent in 1931, and their highest percentage was 25 percent in 1939. The lowest percentage of Jewish students was 2.08 percent in 1939, and their highest was 22.4 percent in 1931 (see Figure 2-3). Notwithstanding these wide yearly variations, viewing the data in five-year clusters reveals that the percentage of Protestant students increased steadily from less than 10 percent in the late 1920s

FIGURE 2-3. YEARLY RELIGION 1925–47.

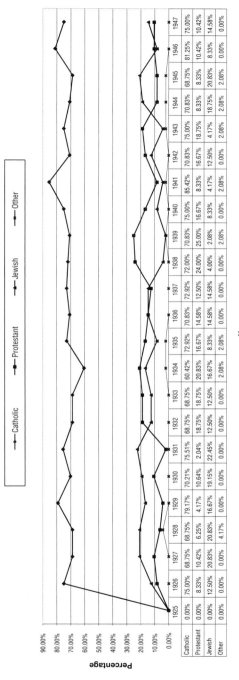

to between 15 percent and 20 percent in the 1930s. The number of Protestant students then receded in the 1940s to between 10 percent and 15 percent of the entering classes. The proportion of Jewish students was different. Representing just under 20 percent of students in the last half of the 1920s and between 15 percent and 20 percent in the first half of the 1930s, their percentages dropped to less than 10 percent for the remainder of the Great Depression and most of World War II (see Figure 2-4). However, the percentage of Jewish students rebounded, increasing to between 10 percent and 15 percent for the 1945–47 period (see Figure 2-4).

Data on the religious affiliation of students enrolled in each of the Law School's three divisions show variations in the percentages of enrolled Catholics, Protestants, and Jews within each division. Only the five-year aggregated data is presented because the sample size is so small that no generalizations can be made on a year-to-year basis. Even so, the data are approximations at best. That said, the proportion of Catholics in the morning and afternoon divisions steadily increased over the period 1925–47. In the morning division, the percentage of Catholic students tended to be higher than the average for all three divisions, and it increased in each five-year period from approximately 65 percent in 1925–29 to approximately 80 percent in 1945–47 (see Figure 2-5). The proportion of Catholics in the afternoon division was somewhat lower than that of the other divisions in the 1920s, approximately 56 percent, but it rose in a steady progression to about 80 percent in 1945–47 (see Figure 2-6). The evening division showed the opposite trend. The percentage of Catholic students in the evening division was highest in the period 1925–29, about 85 percent, and then it dropped to between 64 percent and 70 percent during the Depression, World War II, and the immediate postwar period (see Figure 2-7).[67]

The number of Protestant students in the morning division hovered around 10 percent, except for the second half of the 1930s when they peaked at about 15 percent (see Figure 2-5). They more consistently approximated 10 percent in the afternoon division, fluctuating between 10 percent and 15 percent through World War II and holding at about 6 percent from 1945 to 1947 (see Figure 2-6). Protestants were most numerous in the evening division, where they constituted between 15 percent and 20 percent for three of the five periods, and spiked to about 24 percent in the second half of the 1930s (see Figure 2-7).

FIGURE 2-4. YEARLY RELIGION 1925–47 (5-YEAR AGGREGATES).

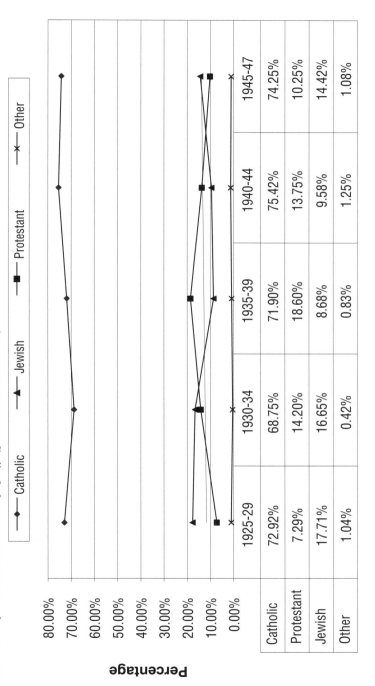

	1925-29	1930-34	1935-39	1940-44	1945-47
Catholic	72.92%	68.75%	71.90%	75.42%	74.25%
Protestant	7.29%	14.20%	18.60%	13.75%	10.25%
Jewish	17.71%	16.65%	8.68%	9.58%	14.42%
Other	1.04%	0.42%	0.83%	1.25%	1.08%

FIGURE 2-5. MORNING RELIGION 1925–47 (5-YEAR AGGREGATES).

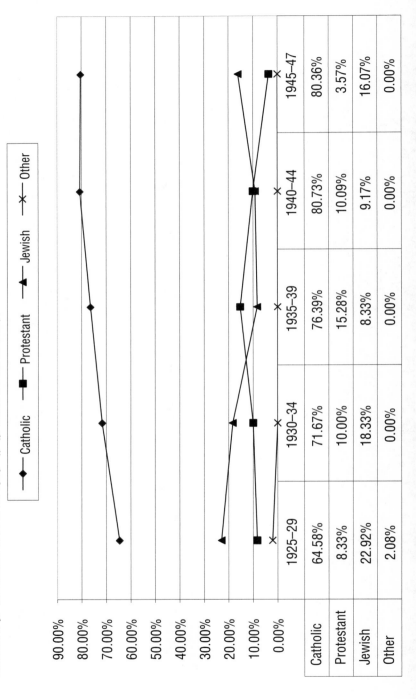

	1925–29	1930–34	1935–39	1940–44	1945–47
Catholic	64.58%	71.67%	76.39%	80.73%	80.36%
Protestant	8.33%	10.00%	15.28%	10.09%	3.57%
Jewish	22.92%	18.33%	8.33%	9.17%	16.07%
Other	2.08%	0.00%	0.00%	0.00%	0.00%

FIGURE 2-6. AFTERNOON RELIGION 1925–47 (5-YEAR AGGREGATES).

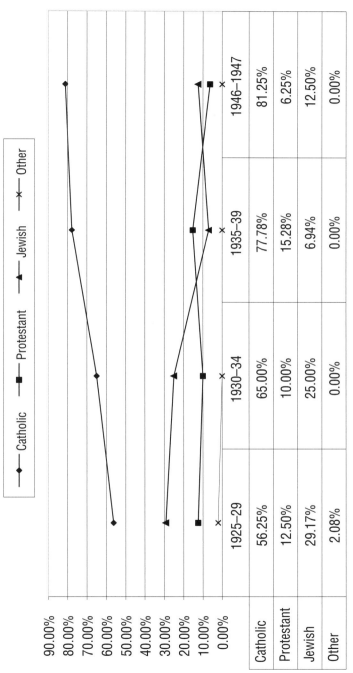

	1925–29	1930–34	1935–39	1946–1947
Catholic	56.25%	65.00%	77.78%	81.25%
Protestant	12.50%	10.00%	15.28%	6.25%
Jewish	29.17%	25.00%	6.94%	12.50%
Other	2.08%	0.00%	0.00%	0.00%

Year

FIGURE 2-7. EVENING RELIGION 1925–47.

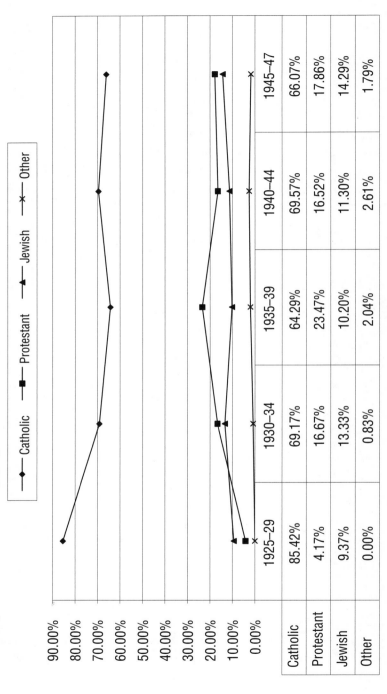

	Catholic	Protestant	Jewish	Other

Year	1925–29	1930–34	1935–39	1940–44	1945–47
Catholic	85.42%	69.17%	64.29%	69.57%	66.07%
Protestant	4.17%	16.67%	23.47%	16.52%	17.86%
Jewish	9.37%	13.33%	10.20%	11.30%	14.29%
Other	0.00%	0.83%	2.04%	2.61%	1.79%

Jewish students manifested the greatest fluctuations over the 1925–47 period. In the late 1920s, they represented over 20 percent of the morning division, declining slightly in the first half of the 1930s to below 20 percent. Their number dropped dramatically to below 10 percent of the student body during the second half of the 1930s and World War II, but they increased to about 15 percent after the war (see Figure 2-5). Jews constituted an even greater percentage of the afternoon division from 1925 to 1929, almost 30 percent. They again declined to about 25 percent in the period 1930–34 and, more dramatically, to under 10 percent from 1935 to 1939. But the percentage of Jewish students again increased to about 12 percent after World War II (see Figure 2-6). The proportion of Jewish students in the evening division was somewhat smaller than in the other divisions, but it was more consistent, fluctuating between 9 percent and 15 percent for the entire 1925–47 period (see Figure 2-7).

The admission application changed in 1948. From 1948 to 1968, entering students were asked their religious affiliation, but they were given only the choice of answering "Catholic" or "Non-Catholic." As a result, the Law School did not record the religious affiliation of non-Catholics. The data that follow show the proportion of the student body that was Catholic and non-Catholic from 1948 to 1968.[68]

The Catholic majority in the student body appears to have increased during the 1948–57 period but then began to fall from 1958 to 1968. Although it was on a downward trend, the Catholic majority remained greater than it was in the earlier decades. It remained above 70 percent except for two years, 1962 (58 percent) and 1967 (64 percent). The Catholic majority hit its highest point in 1953, when about 92 percent of the entering class was Roman Catholic (see Figure 2-8). Even when viewed in five-year clusters, the data show that the proportion of Catholic students increased sharply to about 80 percent from 1948 to 1957 and then steadily declined from 1958 to 1968 to around 75 percent and trending downward (see Figure 2-9). These data suggest that the proportion of non-Catholic students declined from 1948 to 1952 and then increased from 1953 to 1968 and probably beyond.

The main student extracurricular activity in the few years prior to the United States' entry into the Great War was the law review. Students started the *Fordham Law Review* in November 1914. Many of the elite law schools had law reviews with articles that were cited by leading jurists.

FIGURE 2-8. 1948–68 YEARLY CATHOLIC.

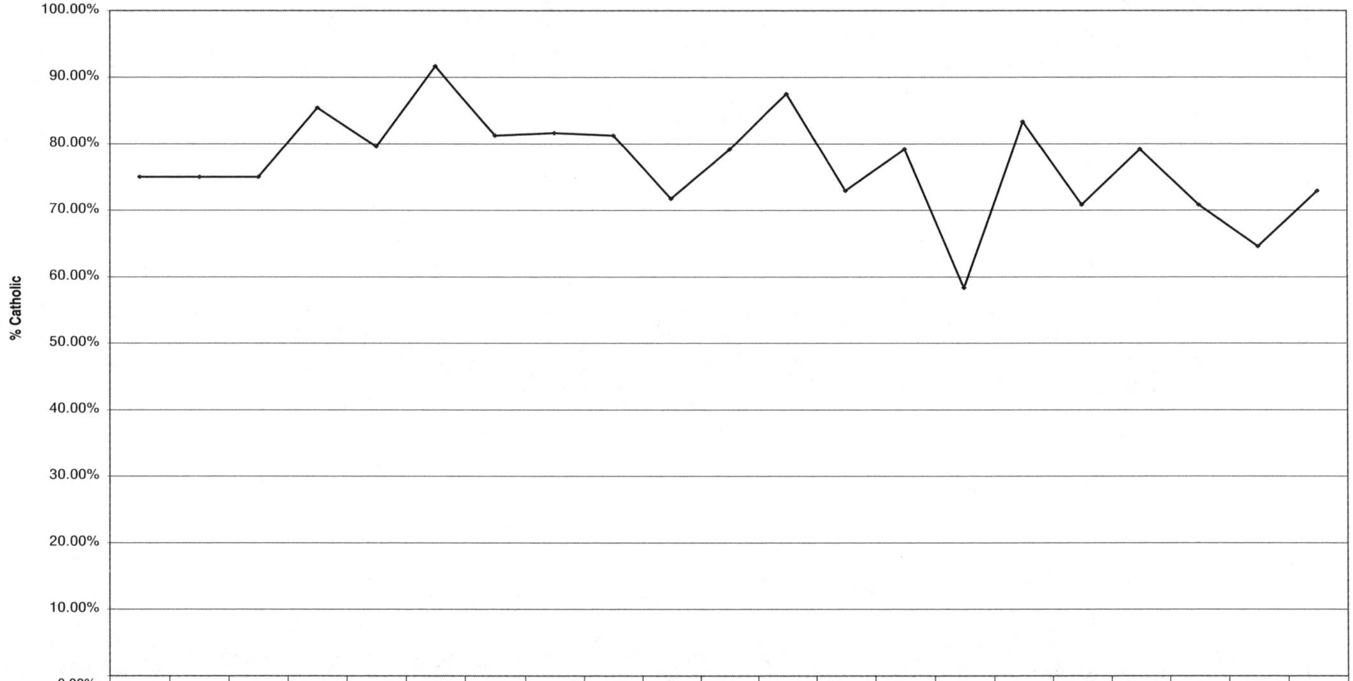

	1948	1949	1950	1951	1952	1953	1954	1955	1956	1957	1958	1959	1960	1961	1962	1963	1964	1965	1966	1967	1968
Catholic	75.00%	75.00%	75.00%	85.42%	79.59%	91.67%	81.25%	81.63%	81.25%	71.74%	79.17%	87.50%	72.92%	79.17%	58.33%	83.33%	70.83%	79.17%	70.83%	64.58%	72.92%

% Catholic

Year

FIGURE 2-9. 1948–68 YEARLY CATHOLIC (5-YEAR AGGREGATES).

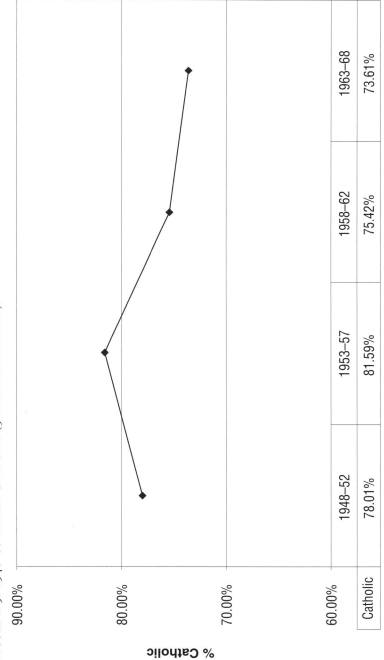

	1948–52	1953–57	1958–62	1963–68
Catholic	78.01%	81.59%	75.42%	73.61%

% Catholic

Year

Fordham's was among the first dozen law reviews in the country. The *University of Pennsylvania Law Review*, founded in 1852, is the oldest. The *Albany Law School Journal*, founded in 1875, was the second, followed by the *Harvard Law Review* in 1887, the *Yale Law Journal* in 1891, the *Columbia Law Review* in 1901, the *Michigan Law Review* in 1902, the *Northwestern University Law Review* (published as the *Illinois Law Review*) in 1906, and the *Georgetown Law Journal* and the *California Law Review* in 1912. Law reviews were and continue to be unique professional journals. They are student-run and provide students with valuable experience as editors, writers, and researchers, skills that enhance their appeal to potential employers. Students write notes, case summaries, and book reviews and edit articles submitted for publication by law professors, practicing attorneys, and judges. From the start, law reviews provided a venue for legal scholarship that influenced courts, legislatures, and government officials; promoted the individual law school; and strengthened ties to alumni. Their publication lent credibility to law schools as places of legal education as well as of professional training, paralleling the professional journals that had evolved during the last quarter of the nineteenth century in the sciences, social sciences, and humanities.[69]

The initial issues of the *Fordham Law Review*, which presented summaries of contemporary court decisions and a few book reviews, were actually published as part of the *Fordham Monthly*. The *Law Review*'s first editor-in-chief, Cornelius J. Smyth, graduated *summa cum laude* in June 1914 and accepted an appointment from the Law School in 1917 to teach Contracts. The student notes reported on decisions in the state and federal courts on a wide variety of topics, including whether fixtures were real property, whether a Christian Scientist had practiced medicine without a license, whether conviction for murder was dependent on death's being the immediate consequence of the injury, and whether a theater owner could exclude entrance to a newspaper drama critic "upon the grounds that his criticisms were offensive." The last of these, not surprisingly, was a New York case, and the decision was that the critic could not be excluded because the exclusion would cause irreparable harm to his livelihood. The first article appeared in the November 1915 issue, and it was written by faculty member John T. Loughran. Entitled

"The True Presumption of Death in New York," it considered the rule that permitted declaring persons to be dead after seven years absent evidence that they were alive.

In January 1916 the *Fordham Law Review* appeared as a separate publication of sixteen pages. It carried an article written by Professor Wormser entitled "Voting Rights and the Doctrine of Corporate Entity." Wormser, who had already published articles in the *Columbia Law Review* and the *Yale Law Journal*, joined other Fordham faculty, such as Loughran, Wilkinson, and Frederick Kane, in publishing articles in the young *Fordham Law Review*, thus helping it gain recognition. There were notes and articles by New York judges, too. Robert Ludlow Fowler, the powerful Surrogate of New York County, wrote about the history of probate law, the surrogate's court, and the 1914 revision of the New York surrogate law. He criticized the new law because, in his view, it did not meet the needs of New York City's Surrogate Court, which handled many large estates on a scale unknown elsewhere in the state and thus needed to be treated differently from the surrogate courts in other New York counties. Cuthbert W. Pound, judge on the New York Court of Appeals, contributed an article about an evolving area of tort law entitled "Are Automobiles Inherently Dangerous to Their Purchasers?" Members of the New York Bar also published in the *Review*'s pages on a variety of topics, thus helping the editors achieve one of their goals: to create a review that was "a handy and accurate means for a practicing lawyer to keep abreast of new professional developments." The students managed to start volume III but suspended publication with the June 1917 issue. The *Fordham Law Review* became a victim of the Great War, as members of the board of editors went into military training and left for active duty. Publication did not resume until 1935.[70]

Students inaugurated two activities in the early 1920s. At the suggestion of the faculty, they formed a student council that consisted of officers elected from each division of each class. The council met once a month with the regent, Father Francis LeBuffe, and pro dean, Michael Dee, to discuss matters of concern to the students. Students also founded the Law School Forum, which sponsored monthly lunches at restaurants near the Law School where invited speakers discussed contemporary issues. More than a hundred students attended these luncheons. By the end of 1922 the forum had almost two hundred members and they declared, "Extra class activities are rapidly assuming a position of importance in the daily lives of Law Students."[71]

Because of the Law School's class schedule and the students' work schedules, the students usually could not play on Fordham University's athletic teams. Class officers encouraged their classmates to attend games to show their support for the Fordham Rams. On occasion, law students who had played varsity sports at college before coming to the Law School joined Fordham's teams. John F. Berrigan, for example, became a star shortstop and outfielder and was elected captain of the Fordham baseball team in 1915. In 1916 law students set up a committee to recruit players for the Fordham football team from classmates who had played football for their colleges before entering the Law School. These included quarterbacks from Yale and Cornell, a tackle from Holy Cross and another from Fordham College, and a fullback from Georgetown. The former captain of the Holy Cross track team joined Fordham's track team after entering the Law School. Some law student athletes were unable to balance law school and athletics, and they were dismissed from the Law School for missing too many classes. But the law students maintained an avid interest in athletics, and the class of 1925 organized a basketball team, "a hitherto unattempted innovation in the Law School."[72]

There was another kind of activity that brought students together, one that was far more painful. In a time before antibiotics and other life-saving medicines, the students sometimes lost their classmates to pneumonia, appendicitis, and other illnesses. When they did, class members attended the funerals and sent written condolences to surviving parents and family members. Activities of this sort contributed to the collegial, familial feeling at the Law School that became and continues to be a distinctive quality of Fordham.[73]

Most of Fordham Law School's graduates went into private practice. But some went into politics and took jobs in government, thus fulfilling Father Collins's hopes that the Law School would lead to a fuller representation of Catholics in the public life of New York City and in positions where professional training could make a difference. Clearly, Irish Catholic participation in New York politics was longstanding, but trained lawyers had something else to add to government positions.

Among the school's alumni was Ignatius M. Wilkinson. Wilkinson succeeded Francis P. Garvan when Garvan resigned the deanship in 1923. Wilkinson's appointment as dean began a pattern of decanal appointments from the ranks of Law School alumni that persisted to 2003. Wilkinson's tenure as dean extended almost to the Law School's fiftieth anniversary. It remains the longest in the school's history.

CHAPTER THREE

THE QUEST FOR

EXCELLENCE IN AN

ERA OF BIGOTRY

Ignatius M. Wilkinson served as Fordham Law School's fourth dean from 1923 to 1953, the period in which professional organizations pushed for ever-higher law school standards that eventually produced the modern law school. Dean Wilkinson played a leading role in national, state, and local bar associations in defining and adopting some of these standards and in persuading the New York Court of Appeals to apply them to the law schools in New York State. As dean, he implemented these and other higher standards at Fordham Law School. For example, he hired the first full-time Fordham Law faculty in 1930 and became the first full-time law dean at Fordham in 1936. He adopted a selective admissions policy in 1931, making Fordham Law School one of the first law schools to do so. He revived the Moot Court and he inaugurated instruction in law library research. He created the Law School Alumni Association and a placement office. All the while, Dean Wilkinson and the law faculty sought to make Fordham the best avenue into the legal profession for the New York City area's immigrants and their children, providing them with the opportunity to achieve respectability and upward socio-economic mobility in a life of professional public service.[1]

This chapter focuses on the history of Wilkinson's administration during the 1920s and explains the changes he initiated, the reasons for these changes, and their consequences. But these changes at Fordham Law School are best understood as a part of developments within legal education nationally.

Wilkinson assumed his responsibilities as dean in a period of exploding law school admissions. The dramatic escalation in Fordham Law School's student body began the year following the Allies' victory in World War I. Fordham enrollments had fallen to a six-year low of 320 students during the last year of the Great War, but they doubled to 667 in 1919 and peaked at 1,513 in 1927. Enrollments rose nationally, but not as much as the nearly fivefold increase in Fordham's law student population. Nevertheless, increases in the national law student population were significant, with a consequent rise in the number of the nation's lawyers. National enrollments prior to World War II peaked at 44,341 in 1927, the same year that enrollment at Fordham Law School reached its highest pre–World War II figure.[2]

The number of law schools continued to increase along with the number of law students, peaking at 195 in 1935, a 91 percent increase from the beginning of the twentieth century. Between 1920 and 1935, the number of law schools increased by 36 percent from 143 to 195. The national student population almost doubled from 20,992 in 1920 to 41,418 in 1935. During the first three decades of the twentieth century, the number of lawyers rose by 47 percent, from 109,140 in 1900 to 160,605 in 1930.[3]

By the 1920s and 1930s, law schools had become the gatekeepers at the point of entry to the practice of law, and bar associations garnered sufficient power to influence if not dictate the standards of legal education to which law schools eventually conformed. The exploding numbers of law students, law schools, and lawyers alarmed leaders in the legal profession, bar associations, and law schools. They were particularly concerned that unaccredited law schools, almost all of which were part-time programs, were outnumbering accredited, full-time law schools and the number of law students attending unaccredited part-time programs was substantially greater than full-time students enrolled in accredited institutions. The American Bar Association (ABA) responded to what its leaders viewed as an ominous growth in law schools and their graduates by redoubling their efforts to increase law school accreditation standards and to restrict entry into the profession by raising admission requirements. Fordham Law School was one of these unaccredited, part-time law schools.[4]

Bar admission standards continued to be lax into the 1920s. Thirty-two of the forty-nine jurisdictions in the United States had no educational requirement to take the bar examination. Only eleven states even required as little as a high school education or its equivalent to be admitted to practice. Not one jurisdiction required a law school education. The regulation of law schools was as haphazard as admission to the bar. In 1927 only sixty-five (about one-half) of the nation's law schools met the ABA's standards and were approved schools, and only one-third of the nation's law students attended Association of American Law Schools (AALS) member schools.[5]

Legal elites felt a particular urgency over standards of professionalism because those entering the profession through urban, part-time law schools were immigrants and the offspring of immigrants. Leaders of the bar believed these groups lacked the moral character, the understanding of the American legal and political system, and the appreciation of American values essential to the practice of law and to the leadership roles lawyers played. In 1928 law schools in four cities—Boston, New York, Newark and the District of Columbia—accounted for 56 percent of all part-time law students. Just under one-half of all part-time students (43 percent) attended eight law schools in Boston and New York City, and 31 percent attended five New York City law schools. Suffolk Law School in Boston became the largest law school in the world in 1928 when it enrolled 4,000 students, which represented about 13 percent of all part-time law students and almost 10 percent of the total number of law students that year. Brooklyn Law School was the second largest law school the following year with an enrollment of 3,312 students.[6]

The legal profession's elites openly declared their intention to raise barriers to entry in order to exclude immigrants and their children who were Catholics and Jews from eastern and southern Europe. They thereby intended to shape the social composition of the law profession in terms of ethnicity, class, gender, religion, and race. White Anglo-Saxon Protestants and other native-born children of native-born Americans dominated the legal profession early in the twentieth century. In 1910 they accounted for about 75 percent of lawyers nationwide. Some 20 percent were native-born sons of immigrant parents, and about 5 percent were themselves immigrants. However, lawyers who were immigrants or the children of immigrants constituted significantly higher proportions of practitioners in populous cities with large immigrant populations. In New York City, for example, these groups constituted a majority of lawyers, as 36 percent were the sons of immigrants and 16 percent were themselves immigrants; these groups represented just under one-half of the lawyers in Chicago (34 percent and 14 percent, respectively) and a little over one-third of the practicing bar in Philadelphia (26 percent and 7 percent, respectively). The efforts of elites to exclude newcomers failed. The number of lawyers with immigrant parents and the number of foreign-born lawyers increased in substantial proportions in these and other immigrant population centers, such as Boston and St. Louis.[7]

The motives of elite lawyers and legal academics to increase professional standards in the 1920s and 1930s were a mixture of professional idealism, concern for the public interest, racism, xenophobia, religious bigotry, fear of radicals, and economic competition. Fear of radicals produced the Red Scare after World War I and evolved into xenophobic, religious, and ethnic bigotry during the 1920s. The decade was tainted by waves of intolerance and prejudice directed at political radicals, Catholics, Jews, African Americans, Asian Americans, and other immigrant and minority groups. Profound social, economic, industrial, and demographic changes were transforming America and challenging established elites and traditional Protestant morality, causing fear and alarm in old-stock Americans. Old religious and ethnic antipathies resurfaced, taking their most virulent and violent expression in a resurrected Ku Klux Klan. The Klan recruited most of its members in small towns and rural communities whose citizens feared that their relatively homogeneous and dominant ethnic and Protestant religious structure and values and long-standing status arrangements were being threatened by the nation's increasingly dominant urban areas populated with heterogeneous ethnic groups who belonged to suspect religions and whose dynamism and high mobility generated a secular outlook and questionable standards of behavior.[8]

Small-town and rural Americans failed in their efforts to insulate their communities and their traditional Protestant values from the popular culture of the Jazz Age as new patterns of behavior penetrated their geographical isolation through radio, movies, romance magazines, and national service clubs. The automobile accelerated and expanded geographical mobility and personal contact among individuals who at an earlier time would have remained apart and relatively unknown to one another. In this era of upheaval, the Ku Klux Klan was the champion of Protestant Americans and Protestant establishments against those whom, because of irrational myths and stereotyping, they perceived to be responsible for undermining traditional America and American morality. In a most insightful analysis of the sources of religious and ethnic bigotry and Klan violence in the 1920s, historian Paul L. Murphy explained that "the ambitious immigrant, non–Anglo-Saxon, non-Protestant, whose frequent tendency to 'overachieve' led to actions to 'keep him in his place.' "[9]

Americans today seem to have forgotten that the main targets of religious bigotry and ethnic xenophobia in the 1920s were Roman Catholics and the ethnic groups most closely associated with Catholicism. The states with the largest Klan membership were in the North and Midwest, where a "quiet 'consensus of the 1920s' backed the Klan." Indiana, for example, had Klan membership estimated at between 250,000 and 500,000. The Klan penetrated the state's Protestant churches and local social organizations and permeated the political process. It dominated the state's Republican Party, which, in turn, controlled the state government. "In exploiting popular prejudices the Indiana Klan relied most heavily upon traditional fears of Roman Catholicism," wrote one of the state's most eminent historians. The theme it "harped on most consistently . . . was the alleged desire of the Church of Rome to dominate the government and schools of the United States, a theme in which existing prejudice against foreigners was fully exploited."[10]

Xenophobia and bigotry produced "the most important turning-point in American immigration policy" when Congress enacted an immigration law in 1921 that "imposed the first sharp and absolute numerical limits on European immigration" by establishing "a nationality quota system based on the pre-existing composition of the American population." This statute was amended by the National Origins Act of 1924, which manipulated the quotas and allowed six or seven times as many immigrants from northwestern Europe than for southern and eastern Europe, but which also established a limit on the total number of immigrants that could enter the United States each year.[11]

The pervasiveness as well as acceptability of anti-Catholic prejudice is illustrated by the fact that the highly respected American Legion replaced the Klan as the country's most energetic proponent of intolerance and repression. Though the most active group, the American Legion was not alone. It was one of a number of super-patriotic organizations and civic groups, such as the Daughters of the American Revolution and the National Civic Federation, that sought to protect America from the corrupting and revolutionary dangers posed by "radicals" and "foreigners."[12]

Although there was no single cause for his defeat, Al Smith's Roman Catholicism, Irish immigrant ancestry and New York City origins evidenced by his "New Yawkees" certainly prevented him from being elected to the presidency of the United States. Unlike Frederick René Coudert

Sr.—who rejected offers in the late nineteenth century to run for New York governor and President Grover Cleveland's two offers of appointment to the US Supreme Court because he understood that his Roman Catholicism was a "crippling political disability"—Smith refused to believe that such bigotry still existed in 1928. He did not take the Klan and what it stood for seriously, declaring that the Klan was "so abhorrent to intelligent thinking Americans of all denominations, that it must in time fall to the ground of its own weight." One biographer, Oscar Handlin, noted that Smith was simply not aware that "the dark secret prejudice against the urban foreigner was still nurtured by fear and desire." Smith was shocked to find that "anti-Catholicism was alive" as his enemies sought to make his candidacy "a worthless thing" by embarking on a "vicious campaign" in which they "attacked the Church and painted a horrendous picture of the downfall of free institutions at the hands of the priest whose tool Smith was. With the covert encouragement of local Republicans, numerous fundamentalist groups spread the tale of the Papist plot to conquer America at the ballot box." Smith refused "to pander to the mood of the times" or "to pretend that he was not what he was—a Catholic, a grandson of Irish immigrants, a poor boy from off the sidewalks of New York." He confronted the religious issue openly, forthrightly, and reasonably, but he failed to persuade his countrymen that "Catholics face no conflict of loyalties between their religious and political obligations" because "one's conscience was the ultimate guide to action," not church authority. He discovered that the bigotry his political opponents had injected into the presidential campaign pervaded large segments of the voting public. "The farmer and the small-town merchant, the fundamentalist and the prohibitionist, blinded by fear of the future, struck out in fury against the urban stranger who was the symbol of the new America." Some Protestant church leaders who disclaimed religious bigotry characterized Smith's home town of New York City as the location of "Satan's seat" and vehemently proclaimed that "no subject of the Pope" should be president.[13]

Failing to realize his dream of reaching the presidency was disappointing to Smith, but the manner in which he lost the election was devastating. Bigotry and prejudice caused even members of his own party to defect to the Republican Herbert Hoover, and Smith was unable to carry his own state of New York. Although the Klan regarded New York City to be the "enemy capital for the Invisible Empire" which it largely avoided, it was fairly active in nearby Long Island as well as upstate New York. In New York and around the nation, religious bigots did what they could to stoke the fires of prejudice against Smith. The success of bigotry and prejudice undermined Smith's understanding of what America stood for and the opportunities it offered to all Americans. He was left with the haunting question that asked, "If Americans were not really willing to accept an Irish Catholic as fully their equal, where then did he belong?" It was precisely to give the Al Smiths of the United States a place that Fordham University and its Law School were founded. It is not surprising that Al Smith Jr. attended both Fordham college and the Fordham Law School, although he graduated from neither.[14]

Genuine concerns about the quality of legal practice and practitioners also played an important role in raising the standards of professionalism in legal education and admission to the practice of law. This is evidenced by Dean Wilkinson's leadership in bringing about some of the important changes in academic standards during this period. Legal elites believed that standards of legal education and admission to the bar were insufficient to ensure that applicants for admission to the legal profession were qualified to practice law, and they did their best to prevent the unqualified from being admitted to the legal profession and to ensure that those who gained admission were well prepared to practice law.

The ABA and AALS redoubled their efforts to raise standards during the 1920s and 1930s. In addition to requiring two years of college before law school, they focused on raising law school academic standards and ensuring that lawyers received good legal educations. In 1924 the AALS and ABA increased faculty and library standards for member schools. They required member schools to have one full-time teacher for every one hundred students, and in 1928 the ABA followed the AALS in requiring member schools to employ at least three full-time professors. In 1927 the AALS raised its library requirements to a minimum of 7,500 volumes and a minimum annual maintenance expenditure of $1,000, and the ABA followed suit in 1928.[15]

The ABA and AALS understood their reforms as progress towards transforming the practice of law into an elitist profession. In addition to their desire to enhance the quality of the practicing bar, leaders of the bar believed that increasing educational standards, such as requiring some college education, would enable immigrants and their offspring to learn American values and ideals. These organizations and leaders of the bar also intended higher standards to exclude these groups from the practice of law.[16]

Motivated by a mixture of xenophobia and a desire to enhance professional standards, the ABA acted to reduce the number of unaccredited law schools and their graduates in the 1930s. It was assisted by a new organization which it sponsored and helped to create in 1930, the National Conference of Bar Examiners. This organization was led by Will Shafroth, who was also adviser to the ABA Section on Legal Education. The National Conference of Bar Examiners worked toward standardization and uniformity in legal education and bar admissions requirements. By 1932 seventeen states required at least two years of prelegal college education, and thirty-three states required at least three years of law study, either in a law school or by an apprenticeship, in order to take the bar exam and be admitted to practice.[17]

State bar associations began to think about ways to limit entry into the profession as they came to view it as overcrowded. Professional associations were also concerned about lawyers' incomes, which often were inadequate even where the number of lawyers was insufficient to meet the need for legal services. The number of state legislatures that adopted the ABA's college prerequisite for admission to law school increased each year during the 1930s. In addition, some state bar examiners raised the minimum passing grade on bar examinations and others used more stringent character requirements as means of limiting the number of lawyers. States increasingly required law school training in ABA-approved law schools in order to sit for the bar examination, and students consequently enrolled in ABA-approved law schools.[18]

The numbers shifted over the 1930s in a constant trend in favor of approved law schools. The decline in the number of unapproved law schools and their graduates was steady from 1931 on. In this year, enrollments in unapproved law schools outnumbered those in approved law schools 21,934 to 17,483, and the number of unapproved law schools exceeded that of approved law schools by 101 to 81. By 1936 the number of students in ABA-approved law schools, 22,029, exceeded those in unapproved law schools, 18,124, for the first time. The number of approved and unapproved law schools were almost equal, 94 and 96, respectively. In

1937 ABA-approved law schools finally outnumbered unapproved law schools 97 to 88. The following year, the number of ABA-approved law schools reached 101, enrolling almost 64 percent (23,827) of the nation's approximately 37,400 law students.[19]

The gap between approved and unapproved law schools continued to widen through the 1950s. By 1940 enrollment in ABA-approved law schools was twice that of unapproved law schools, and during World War II four times as many law students attended approved schools. Between 1930 and 1950, seventy law schools closed, sixty-nine of which were unapproved schools. By the middle of the 1950s the ratio of enrollments in approved law schools to those in unapproved schools reached 10 to 1, and more than 20 to 1 by the 1980s. Except in California, unapproved law schools became a thing of the past by the 1950s.[20]

ABA-approved schools became the gatekeepers to the legal profession in the interwar period. Not only did they succeed in eliminating unapproved law schools, they also succeeded in eliminating most part-time law programs and in reducing the number of part-time law students. By 1935 the number of full-time law students exceeded the number of part-time students in reporting schools, and they have remained a substantial majority ever since. By the 1950s part-time law programs became scarce. Dean Wilkinson recognized in 1929 that "the trend of official requirements in legal education undoubtedly is toward the standards recognized and approved by the American Bar Association and by the Association of American Law Schools." He pointed to the prelaw educational requirement adopted by the state of New York, which was "substantially the Association's standard," and to "the rules of a number of states, notably, Connecticut, Massachusetts, Maine, Minnesota and Ohio, which require in accordance with similar standards four years of law study where the same is evening or part-time work." The New York Education Department similarly incorporated into its rules for law schools the AALS standards relating to the minimum number of full-time professors and the size of law school libraries.[21]

Nationally, the efforts of the ABA and AALS, combined with the Great Depression and World War II, substantially diminished the rate of increase in the number of lawyers. Whereas the legal profession grew by 38,086 (31.1 percent) during the 1920s, it increased by 17,038 (10.6 percent) in the 1930s and by only 2,818 (1.6 percent) in the 1940s. The number of lawyers began to grow in more substantial numbers in the 1950s and 1960s, but it exploded in the 1970s. In the 1950s, the nation's lawyers increased by 29,223 (16.2 percent) and in the 1960s by 68,011 (32.4 percent). But in the 1970s, the number of lawyers increased by 247,111 (89 percent).[22]

The ABA adopted several other strategies to restrict entry into the legal profession. As early as 1909 it urged that United States citizenship be a prerequisite to admission to the bar, a rule that is said to have been directed against immigrants from southern and eastern Europe. By 1946 every state and the District of Columbia restricted admission to the bar to United States citizens, but the US Supreme Court ended this restriction in 1973 when it declared unconstitutional the exclusion of noncitizens. Residency requirements were another strategy state bars adopted to limit entry to the legal profession. The length of the residency varied among different jurisdictions, and some state supreme courts invalidated them, but forty-one jurisdictions still had some residency requirement when the US Supreme Court declared them unconstitutional in 1985. Many jurisdictions still maintain difficult residency requirements to limit entry of experienced lawyers from other jurisdictions. Lawyers in these states seek to protect themselves from out-of-state competition.[23]

Another strategy used to restrict entry to the bar was the character and fitness test. This was especially intended to exclude immigrants and their offspring. Two-thirds of American jurisdictions raised their standards and made their review procedures more stringent in checking for fitness and character. The number of applicants excluded by these tests was usually low, varying from virtually no exclusions to as many as 10 percent, depending upon the jurisdiction and the time period. Law schools adopted a fitness and character requirement for admission to law study, but they did not reject significant numbers of applicants based on it. They were primarily concerned about prior criminal records. By the 1980s Florida had the most vigilant screening processes for bar admission, but it excluded less than 1 percent of bar applicants in any given year. By then, fitness and character screening had come to focus on prior criminal records rather than ethnicity and religious backgrounds.[24]

The New York County Lawyers Association proposed a positive approach to remedy overcrowding in the legal profession: expanding lawyers' services. The association advocated "diverting some lawyers from general practice by giving them service in the courts and other govern-ment positions not now filled by lawyers." It recommended that lawyers be employed in the clerks' offices of surrogate courts to consult with members of the public seeking advice on minor matters that did not jus-tify the expense of retaining a lawyer in private practice. It suggested that lawyers be employed in the offices of registers and county clerks to main-tain records pertaining to and to register land titles. Various classes of court employees should be lawyers, from secretaries to judges, court clerks, and even court attendants. The rise of the bureaucratic state offered another inlet for lawyers' services. Lawyers could serve on legal advisory staffs of governmental commissions, boards, and other governmental agencies to counsel interested parties regarding the application and opera-tion of governing laws. Finally, the committee proposed that the govern-ment pay lawyers to offer free advice and representation to the poor. It proposed the creation of an "office of public defender, for the protection of the impecunious charged with crime." On civil matters, it recom-mended that clients of public relief and public works agencies be furnished at public expense with legal advice not only as to their rights in relation to such agencies but as well in their private affairs." It noted that "these people . . . [,] like other human beings," had domestic problems, issues relating to inheritance or personal injury claims, for which the advice of a social worker was not adequate. They should receive legal advice at gov-ernment expense, "as is the case with medical service."[25]

In addition to restricting entry to the legal profession and expanding legal services and government-supported legal counsel, the committee made several recommendations to eliminate "certain groups" from the list of lawyers entitled to practice law. It mentioned "a substantial number [of licensed lawyers] who . . . are not fitted to render proper legal services" because they had virtually abandoned the profession. A majority of the committee favored annual or other periodic registration. The report also recommended a "limitation of the number of times a candidate may take the written bar examination." Only two groups of lawyers were singled out as requiring special attention. The committee recommended that the association maintain constant vigilance "in the fight against 'ambulance-chasers,'" and it admonished that "the comparatively small number of lawyers who engage in unethical practices" should be "relentlessly driven out of the profession." The committee may have intended or expected that these reforms would operate disproportionately on lawyers belonging to certain immigrant groups, ethnicities, and religions, because it defensively asserted that "further restriction of admissions to the bar is not undemocratic."[26]

The ethno-religious composition of immigrant lawyers also changed. New York City lawyers who were from the British Isles and central Europe declined from 65 percent of first- or second-generation immigrants in 1900 to only 25 percent in 1960. Lawyers whose parents came from eastern and southeastern Europe rose from 3 percent in 1900 to 40 percent in 1960. New York City lawyers who were first- or second-generation immigrants represented 69 percent of the city bar by 1960. The number of Jewish lawyers increased significantly more than any other religious or ethnic group. In the first decade of the twentieth century, they accounted for a little over one quarter of new bar admissions in New York City, but they continually increased their proportion of New York City practitioners through the first half of the twentieth century. From 1911 to 1917, Jewish lawyers were 36 percent of new admittees; from 1918 to 1923, 40 percent; between 1924 and 1929, they were a solid majority of new bar admissions at 56 percent; but by 1930–34 they were an amazing 80 percent of the city's new lawyers. Their numbers declined to about one-half of new admissions by the end of the 1940s, but they leveled off at about 65 percent through the 1950s.[27]

The decline of the legal profession dominated by white, Anglo-Saxon Protestants came early in New York City. By 1920 they represented less than 25 percent of lawyers practicing in the city, and by the mid-twentieth century they made up only 10 percent. Jewish lawyers achieved majority status by 1938, according to a study conducted in that year. By 1960 Jewish lawyers represented 60 percent of the New York City bar, whereas Catholics and Protestants constituted only 18 percent each. Nationwide, Jewish law students continued to be over-represented in law schools, constituting about 20 percent of all law students in 1969 and 12 percent in 1979, although Jews were only 3 percent of the population.[28]

If part-time and evening law programs afforded working class men and women an opportunity to become lawyers, one would expect to see a difference in the class backgrounds of the legal profession as the number of part-time programs declined in the 1930s and 1940s. And, one does.

Through much of the first half of the twentieth century, substantial proportions of law students came from working class backgrounds and were either fully or partly self-supporting. As the number of part-time and evening law programs diminished, the class backgrounds of law students and lawyers narrowed. Earlier in the twentieth century, students whose fathers were relatively uneducated and worked in lower-paying occupations—such as clerical workers, unskilled laborers, craftsmen, and farmers—represented a substantial proportion of the law student population. The proportion of law students with these backgrounds steadily declined by the middle of the century in contrast to the steadily increasing proportion of students whose fathers worked in white collar occupations. Higher law school admissions standards and increasing competition to get into law school undoubtedly contributed to this narrowing of law students' class backgrounds. Because of these changes, in addition to the lowering of pass rates on bar examinations, lawyers increasingly came from relatively privileged backgrounds. And they continued to be white males for the most part as law schools, bar associations, and employers openly discriminated against blacks and women until well into the 1960s.[29]

New York Governor Malcolm Wilson reminisced about the working-class backgrounds of students who attended Fordham Law School's Bronx campus night division, which he entered in September 1933. Almost all of the students in the Bronx night school had day jobs. "We started out with sixty students in September of 1933," he recalled. "Without exception, all of us were working some place. Many of the men were married and all had jobs, but still made the sacrifice of going to law school at night." Attending law school during the Depression, students realized that they "were lucky to get a job to pay" tuition. Only nineteen years of age when he began law school, Wilson found the Bronx night school "very advantageous because everyone who was there was a serious student, and it was very helpful to have the influence of these older men who were out in the world." Wilson worked at the Lawyer's Mortgage Company in Rehabilitation, which was located at 342 Madison Avenue in Manhattan. He also tutored high school students between his job in Manhattan and the beginning of evening classes. "I took the Lexington Avenue subway to 183 Street and Jerome Avenue, walked to the home of Dr. Mark Healy on the Grand Concourse and tutored his high school student son for an hour—for which I was paid two dollars—and then walked across Fordham Road to the Biology Building where the Law School classes were conducted."[30]

Louis Lefkowitz attended the night school in lower Manhattan. A member of the graduating class of 1925 who later served as New York's attorney general from 1957 through 1978, Lefkowitz found law school "extremely difficult" in part because he needed to work to support himself and to pay his tuition. He worked as a clerk in a law office located at 15 Park Row, right across the street from Fordham Law School. He worked there from 9:00 A.M. until 5:45 P.M. during the work week and a half day on Saturdays and Sundays. From Monday through Friday, Lefkowitz would dash across the street to the school fifteen minutes before his classes began at 6:00 P.M., wolfing down a sandwich and gulping a cup of coffee as he went. Classes ended at 9:00 P.M. Four or five nights a week Lefkowitz served summons after class in the Bronx, Brooklyn, and Manhattan until 11:00 P.M. or 11:30 P.M., arriving home around midnight. "I sat down and worked till two, three o'clock in the morning. Got up at seven-thirty, eight o'clock to make nine o'clock at the office. Very tough," Lefkowitz reminisced. "I worked half a day Saturday and Sunday, the balance of the time I did my studying. . . . I did that for three years." Law School was also very difficult because "most of the students were graduates of college. Very few students were high school graduates," even though the Law School only required a high school diploma. Lefkowitz had only attended the High School of Commerce before entering Fordham Law School, and he had to wait a year and a half after graduating from high school at the age of sixteen because he was too young to attend the school.[31]

George A. Brooks was one of the college graduates. He enrolled in Fordham Law School upon graduating from Fordham College in 1924, and he graduated from the Law School cum laude as a member of the Manhattan night division class of 1927. Brooks enjoyed the advantage of not having to work when he attended law school. Although he and many of his classmates usually ate at home before class, he mentioned that "there was an interesting set up" at Childs Restaurant on Fulton Street. "The last table was, by custom, reserved for the Fordham Law School night attendants and if you couldn't eat at home, and you came down late, you'd take the end table and you'd get your meal then." Brooks was part of a four-man study group, all of whom had distinguished professional careers. "Bill Meagher became a founding partner of Skadden, Arps,

Slate, Meagher and Flom. He is the Meagher in the name of the firm," Brooks clarified. "Joe Noble became a partner in Bigham, Englar, Jones and Houston. . . . Al Power became General Counsel of the General Motors Corporation and I became Secretary of General Motors Corporation and Director of the New York Legal Staff of General Motors Corporation." Brooks also taught at the Law School from 1929 to 1935 and, after retiring from General Motors, from 1965 to 1985.[32]

Ignatius Wilkinson was dean of a part-time Catholic law school serving the very groups professional elites sought to exclude from the legal profession. His reaction to the proposed reforms and the prejudice that partially motivated them is therefore important in the history of legal education. Additionally, Wilkinson's response is important because he was in the vanguard of many of the reforms reformers sought to accomplish in the 1920s and 1930s.

With mixed motives, the ABA and AALS—as well as the Association of the Bar of the City of New York (ABCNY)—were pushing to increase the educational prerequisite for admission to law schools in the 1920s from a high school diploma to two years of college. Fordham required a high school education, or its equivalent, from its founding in 1905 until the 1924–25 academic year, when it raised its preadmission education requirement to one year of college. In anticipation of this higher education requirement, Fordham Law School began a one-year evening prelaw course in September 1923. One hundred and forty-one students enrolled in the first class. The school expanded the one-year course to two years in September 1926, the year before it increased the educational prerequisite for admission from one year of college to two years. The initial enrollment of the two-year course was three hundred eighty-four students. This prelaw department quickly expanded into Fordham University's Downtown College, or Fordham College Manhattan Division in 1928, and it graduated its first class in 1931.[33]

Wilkinson favored the higher educational prerequisite for several reasons. He believed that it was indisputable that the broader a student's prior education the better qualified he is to study law. This seems like common sense, but this view was inconsistent with the study Professor Wigmore conducted in 1909, which concluded that college work prior to law school had no effect on a student's performance in law school. A second reason was undeniable. Wilkinson thought that requiring more college prior to law school produced older and more mature students, because they entered law school at age nineteen or twenty instead of eighteen, "which in itself is a distinct advantage." He cited as "practical proof" the "high calibre of work done by the night school students," which he attributed principally to the high percentage of college graduates and older students in the night school. The only college degree and college courses the New York Department of Education accepted in satisfaction of the college education prerequisite were in the liberal arts and sciences. The BA or BS degree or courses that an accredited college accepted toward either of these degrees qualified applicants for admission to law schools. Professional or technical degrees, such as engineering, were not acceptable.[34]

Fordham Law School nevertheless deferred adopting the two-year college education prerequisite from 1926 to 1927 because of Wilkinson's concern over the effect it might have on "the calibre and number of our students." This was not an unreasonable concern. The few law schools that had raised educational prerequisites earlier experienced sharp declines in enrollment. However, when Fordham Law School raised the prerequisite from a high school diploma to one year of college in 1924, its effect on student enrollments was negligible, a drop of only ten students in the entering class from the preceding year, from 560 to 550. Wilkinson estimated a drop of about 40 percent in enrollments under the new rule, based on the prelaw school education of applicants for the 1925–26 academic year. He expected a gradual increase in qualified students over the ensuing years to the point they had been prior to the adoption of the two-year college requirement, but he projected a negative effect on the Law School's finances if enrollments did not increase. The lower enrollments necessitated increasing tuition from $180 to $200 per year, and the registration and university fees from $5 to $10 each. With these increases, the Law School would experience a substantial shortfall of $75,000 from the $250,000 in revenues for the 1925–26 academic year. The Law School was so profitable that, even with this one-third decline in revenue, Wilkinson estimated that the school would still operate at "a fair profit under the two year requirement," assuming "that the present rush to law study will continue."[35]

In New York, the educational prerequisite for law school admission in the 1920s was still only a high school diploma, but only New York Law

School and St. John's Law School had not adopted the two-year college requirement for admission. Columbia had adopted a college degree requirement in 1903, but it admitted Columbia University undergraduates with only three years of college, and in 1911 it relaxed its entrance requirement to three years of college for all applicants. The ABA favored the two-year college requirement, and the AALS required member schools to adopt this standard in 1925. The New York State Bar Association petitioned the New York Court of Appeals in 1924 to require two years of college for admission to the state's law schools. The Court of Appeals took no action. Wilkinson thought that "the factor that keeps them back, is the effect of such a rule on the country boy. Such a boy finds it difficult to secure a college education while usually it is relatively easy for him to attend a public high school, and meet the present requirement." Wilkinson's surmise is ironic inasmuch as the increased college requirement was apparently aimed at the "city boy" of immigrant stock.[36]

The ABCNY and the New York County Lawyers Association persuaded the New York Court of Appeals to hold a public hearing in March 1927 on the question of increasing the educational prerequisites for the state's law schools from a high school diploma to two years of college. Representatives of every law school attended. Wilkinson attended as Dean of the Fordham Law School and as a "specially designated representative" of the ABCNY. He spoke in favor of increasing the requirement to two years of college, the standard Fordham adopted in September 1927. The meeting persuaded the Court of Appeals to adopt the two-year college requirement, but it deferred implementation for "a reasonable time." Accordingly, those who entered a law school in New York State in September 1929 were required to have had one year of college in addition to a full high school education or its equivalent. The two-year college requirement began with the entering class of September 1930. Wilkinson was confident that Fordham Law School's enrollments would not be adversely affected by the statewide rule, because it did not suffer a decline in enrollments when applicants could have attended other area law schools that had lower entrance requirements.[37]

Enrollment figures demonstrate that implementing the two-year college requirement in 1927 did not materially reduce Fordham's enrollments. To the contrary, the Law School enjoyed its highest enrollment prior to World War II, 1,513 students, in that academic year. It also evidently had the beneficial effect on the Law School's reputation Wilkinson had hoped for, because it effected "a substantial improvement" in the "type of student" applying to and entering the Law School.[38]

Wilkinson was referring to the fact that the number of college graduates in each class increased. In 1927, the first year of the two-year college requirement, the law school enrolled 535 students, 60 percent of whom were graduates of approved colleges or universities. They graduated from 66 institutions, of which two-thirds were non-Catholic. Nevertheless, most Fordham Law students in this class had attended Catholic colleges or universities. Wilkinson was pleased that Fordham attracted applicants from a large number of non-Catholic colleges because he believed that this was evidence of the school's broad appeal and "a good augury for the future of the school." The class that entered in September 1928 was almost as strong. Of the 531 students admitted that year, approximately 55 percent were college graduates. Almost 40 percent of the morning and afternoon division students, 80 percent of the Manhattan evening division, and 50 percent of the Bronx division had college degrees. They received their degrees from 68 institutions, of which 44 or 65 percent were non-Catholic colleges or universities.[39]

Wilkinson boasted that Fordham's selective admission policy resulted in smaller declines in enrollment than all other New York City law schools except Columbia, which was the only other area law school with a selective admission policy. Wilkinson thought Columbia's modest increase in enrollments of just over 6 percent and Fordham's relatively small drop in enrollments of less than 15 percent were due, in part, to their "serious" policy of selective admissions. He implied that the college requirement at the Brooklyn, New York, and St. John's law schools was "nominal," and he stated that these schools and NYU Law School accepted any applicants who had a "law qualifying" certificate from the state, which verified that the holder satisfied the prelaw school education requirement. They did not demand "any further credential indicating the mental ability of the student." Fordham's "selective [admissions] process," Wilkinson concluded, produced "an increasingly desirable type of applicant" and enabled Fordham to maintain enrollments "substantially unimpaired" during "trying times."[40]

TABLE 3-1. COLLEGE GRADUATES IN ENTERING CLASSES

Year	Class size	No. and Percent of College Graduates	No. of Colleges	No. and Percent of Catholic Colleges	No. and Percent of Non-Catholic Colleges
1927	535	321 / 60%	66	44 / 67%	22 / 33%
1928	531	292 / 55%	68	24 / 35%	44 / 65%
1929	467	248 / 53%	54	31 / 57%	23 / 43%
1930	420	n.a.	n.a.	n.a.	n.a.
1931	466	312 / 67%	58	n.a.	n.a.
1932	478	n.a.	n.a.	n.a.	n.a.
1933	425	276 / 65%	69	n.a.	n.a.
1934	358	249 / 69.5%	65	n.a.	n.a.
1935	378	244 / 66.0%	69	n.a.	n.a.
1936	298	225 / 75.5%	70	n.a.	n.a.
1937	322	225 / 70.0%	75	n.a.	n.a.
1938	292	231 / 79.0%		n.a.	n.a.
1939	292	242 / 83.0%	65	n.a.	n.a.

Sources: Dean's Report for 1927–40; "September 1934," notebook of statistics, Fordham Law School archives; "Statistics Given to Dean 11/18/35," *ibid.*; "1937–1938 (West) About 10/10/37," *ibid.*

Wilkinson attributed declining enrollments to another factor that was affecting all of the city law schools and was one of the reasons bar associations sought to limit the number of new lawyers: the law of supply and demand. Wilkinson believed that the large number of lawyers admitted to practice in the 1920s created more lawyers than the New York metropolitan area could gainfully employ. Young lawyers had great difficulty finding positions, and, if they began their own practices, they could not find enough business to make a reasonable income. Recent investigations of negligence and "ambulance-chasing" lawyers in New York state courts and of bankruptcy lawyers in the federal courts revealed that the legal profession was overcrowded and that curtailment of unethical practices of negligence and bankruptcy lawyers had diminished "financial opportunities in the immediate future" and made law less "attractive to those whose sole purpose is to make the most money in the least time." Wilkinson therefore did not expect the decline in overall law student enrollments to recover, and he predicted further reductions in the future. He also believed that Fordham's proportionate reduction would continue to be smaller than other area law schools. However, enrollments declined precipitously through the following years as the nation slid more deeply into the Great Depression.[41]

Though dean of a law school most of whose students were targets of exclusion by legal elites, Wilkinson, in his appearance, his manner, and his stature, was himself one of the elites of the local bar. Dean Mulligan described Wilkinson as an "imposing" figure. Caesar Pitassy described him as "austere and pompous." Having "made some money," he lived on Park Avenue "and considered the Law School to be his own project. They used to say that when Wilkinson died he left the Law School to the Jesuits," Mulligan reminisced. Joseph McGovern characterized Wilkinson as "very autocratic." His favorite story about Wilkinson's intransigence involved McGovern personally. There was a school rule that one could never leave the classroom to go to the bathroom during an exam. At a faculty meeting, McGovern expressed his view that "it was completely out of line for a student's mark on a particular exam to be in direct relation to the condition of his kidneys." "Oh no, no, well, that's the rule," Wilkinson replied, "meaning that it would never be changed. Ipse dixit." So, McGovern made a motion to change the rule, and his motion was adopted by the faculty. During the next exam period, "the sign went up, 'Nobody leaves the classroom during examinations.' . . . That was typical under Wilkinson," McGovern reminisced.[42]

Wilkinson left a comprehensive record of his administration of the Law School, submitting biannual reports to the president of Fordham University beginning in December 1925. These reports provide much of the evidence of the Law School's history during his tenure as dean. Wilkinson was unable to begin resolving the problems that needed to be addressed until the 1924–25 academic year because he continued to teach his regular ten-hour load through the 1923–24 school year even though he became dean at the beginning of this academic year.[43]

Wilkinson surveyed the school and identified a number of problem areas that required immediate attention. He discovered that the administration and physical plant of a law school consisting of a few hundred students was inadequate for a school of 1,400 to 1,500 students. Although "the Woolworth Building was a very classy address," Judge William Hughes Mulligan later observed, "it was never intended to house a Law School." For example, "to get into the first year class, you had to walk through the second year class," even as late as 1939 when Mulligan entered the Law School as a first-year student.[44]

Most of the teachers' furniture and students' desks had been used since the Law School opened in 1905 and were "old and dilapidated." Moreover, the students' desks were moveable, which "caused difficulty and confusion to the monitors" who took student attendance "by means of seat numbers." Wilkinson installed new "lecture chairs," patterned on those he observed at Boston University Law School, which were affixed to the floor, at a cost of about $4,500 per class room. "In class you were assigned a seat and you kept it," recalled George Brooks some sixty years after his student days in the night division. "If you were in class, but [not] in that seat and the seat was vacant, you were marked absent. A proctor took class attendance by marking on a big sheet, the vacant places. There were penalties for excessive absences." Wilkinson also established "New Jersey and Connecticut Practice Rooms," an office for the Law School regent, and a "woman's lavatory and rest room." He also arranged to have the Woolworth Building paint the school's premises on the twentieth-eight floor, which, along with the other improvements, enhanced the utility and appearance of the Law School for both students and faculty.[45]

Wilkinson expanded the Fordham Law library in 1927, adding more book shelves and more seating to accommodate "a considerably greater number of students." He thought the changes he was making would be adequate "for some time in the future." Nevertheless, he would like to have had a new building custom built for the Law School. Wilkinson suggested this possibility when he informed Fordham University President William J. Duane in January 1929 that Brooklyn Law School had just built Richardson Hall on Pearl Street in Brooklyn for about $1 million and that St. John's College School of Law, which had begun operation just three years earlier, had announced plans to build a law school building in the business district of Brooklyn. Reminding Father Duane that the Law School's lease at the Woolworth Building expired in 1932, Wilkinson suggested that the president of Fordham University consider constructing a building for Fordham Law School in downtown Manhattan. He cautioned, however, that the building would have to be quite tall, because street noise was so loud that classrooms would have to be placed at least twelve stories above the street. Inadequate physical plant impeded the Law School throughout most of its history, even after the Law School built its own building and moved to Lincoln Center in 1961.[46]

Instead of constructing a new building in Manhattan, the Law School added a night division at Fordham University's Rose Hill campus in the Bronx. Classes were held in Larkin Hall, which was the Biology Building. The Bronx division opened in September 1925 to serve that borough's expanding population. The heavily Catholic population of the Bronx had doubled to 900,000 between 1910 and 1925. At that time it included "a heavy number of Irish and Italian families and also some Jewish families," Judge Mulligan recalled. "But, no matter what your ethnic background, you were identified by your parish. . . . The normal course in those days was for a boy to go to Fordham Prep or Regis, if he were bright, or some local Catholic high school and then automatically apply to Fordham College." Mulligan began his college education at Cathedral College in preparation for the priesthood, but he left and later attended Fordham College. "I would say that the vast majority of the students at the College then were locals. I could walk to school. There were some outlanders from Brooklyn, but the vast majority were in New York." With easier access to and from Manhattan via the subway system and Westchester by car or the Harlem and Hudson railroad lines, the Fordham campus was well situated for potential law students who worked in Manhattan and lived in the Bronx or nearby towns in southern Westchester. The Law School's Bronx division offered the same classes as the night program at the Manhattan campus, and courses were taught in three large classrooms in Larkin Hall.[47]

In addition to offering a legal education to a growing Bronx population, the Rose Hill night division also relieved some of the limitations presented by the Woolworth Building. Wilkinson immediately deemed the new division a success, pointing out that the night school in the Bronx had resolved some of the space problems at the Manhattan campus and enabled Fordham to educate more students at a higher level of instruction. It produced "a distinct scholastic improvement in the night school by limiting both sections to smaller teaching groups while at the same time accommodating a total night class materially larger than any heretofore registered in the school." By 1929 the Bronx night division was operating "as a complete unit," with enrollments ranging from 110 to 150 students in each academic class. It had its own administrator, Frank Delaney, who taught at Fordham Prep during the day and served as "Night Registrar." "He took attendance and answered any questions," recalled Joe McGovern, a student in the Bronx night school from 1930 to 1933. Acquiring competent faculty to teach in the Bronx was initially difficult, in part because of the commute from Manhattan where they practiced law. Wilkinson hired three new teachers in 1925 to teach in the Bronx, Arthur A. McGivney, William J. O'Shea, and Winthrop A. Wilson, but the latter two soon resigned. Wilkinson acknowledged that it was difficult to recruit and retain faculty who were willing to teach in the Bronx, and this had put "quite a strain on the school as a whole." Four years later he reported that the strain "seems now to be in large part solved," because he had appointed new teachers who were willing to commute from their Manhattan law offices. One such teacher was William Meagher, a Fordham Law School alumnus in the class of 1927 and, as mentioned, a founding partner of Skadden, Arps, Slate, Meagher and Flom, who began teaching in the Bronx in 1928. Many of Fordham Law School's most outstanding faculty also taught in the Bronx, such as John F. X. Finn, Eugene J. Keefe, Walter B. Kennedy, John T. Loughran, Joseph A. McGovern, and I. Maurice Wormser.[48]

Joe McGovern's recollections of his experience as an evening student suggest the appeal of the Bronx campus. McGovern enrolled in Fordham Law School after graduating from Fordham College in 1930. He taught at Regis High School in Manhattan during the day and went to classes at night at Rose Hill. "A number of our students, of course, worked at law firms," perhaps "as many as half." McGovern lived near the Bronx campus, and he enjoyed its bucolic setting. "There was a different atmosphere on campus, especially in the spring time—the trees were in bloom, very different from the atmosphere of the Woolworth Building." Nonetheless, McGovern's comment about his first year of law school will resonate with most first year law students: it was "the worst year that anyone could ever get out of college." Stress may have explained why students smoked in class, apparently with the teacher's permission, until March 1931 when

Dean Wilkinson apparently acceded to the demands of Father Charles J. Deane, Dean of Fordham College, that smoking in class be prohibited.[49]

The facilities available to law students in the Bronx division were meager. It had a "modest library," consisting of "all the New York State Court Reports, a number of textbooks, but it was limited," according the Joe McGovern. "If you wanted to go beyond that, you had to go down to the library in the Woolworth Building." The Bronx students also had to travel to the Manhattan campus to take their final examinations and to participate in Moot Court on Saturdays. Aside from the classrooms and the law book collection that was housed in the University Library, there were no other facilities in the Bronx, but that did not matter to McGovern, who looked back and saw "just damn good teachers and interested students." He remembered Professor Finn as "terrific" and "Dramatic! Dramatic! He had all these fictitious characters he would weave into his teaching." In short, "John Finn was a marvel," one of "the great ones." George Brooks described Finn as "a great teacher, very clear, very easy to understand. . . . very popular with the class." The teaching was "mostly Socratic, the old Harvard Law School system, the Ames System, I would call it," McGovern explained. When a teacher called on a student, the student stood and summarized the case and answered the teacher's questions, a teaching method that McGovern used when he taught at the Law School. But the teaching was pragmatic. "I always thought that Fordham was teaching you to practice the profession of law, and when I went to practice law," McGovern stated, "I had no trouble catching on immediately to the routine of a law firm, to writing memoranda to the boss or going to court. I had no problems. It just seemed to be a natural transition."[50]

McGovern graduated first in his class in 1933 and was hired by Vincent Leibell, a member of the first graduating class of Fordham Law School. Three years later, Wilkinson asked McGovern to teach at the school full-time for a salary of $3,000. It was during the Great Depression, a time when "you could get a steak dinner for a dollar" and a law school graduate was lucky to get a job that paid "maybe fifteen dollars a week." McGovern accepted, and he remained on the faculty full-time from 1936 to 1943 and, later, part-time from 1943 to 1966, when his responsibilities as chancellor of the State Board of Regents became too demanding. Two of McGovern's classmates from the Bronx evening division, Joseph Doran and William

White, eventually taught at the school, too. Yet another classmate was John O'Donnell, born in Ireland, with "just a nice touch of music in his brogue." He became counsel for a fellow Irishman, Michael Quill, head of the Transport Workers Union and served as his advisor during the major transit labor disputes of the 1940s, 1950s, and 1960s.[51]

A friendly, collegial spirit characterized the students at both the Bronx and Manhattan campuses. "I don't think there was ever a competitive spirit" in the Bronx, McGovern recalled. Student spirit at the Woolworth Building has been described in terms of the collegial environment for which Fordham Law School is known today. Recounting his student days at the Woolworth Building in the late 1930s, Caesar Pitassy recalled that "the students used to work with one another a lot. We were pretty friendly, and we studied together and discussed cases in the casebook during recess." Dennis McInerney confirmed this collegial spirit, noting that "there was a lot comradery [sic] in the group. We used to go out and have a few drinks together after classes." But not all night students had the time for after-class drinks or even to get to know their classmates. The variable was the kind of job one had, according to Richard Bennett. He explained that, "with mine, I know, I had no time for anything except going to Law School, and that is why you end up missing certain kinds of experiences like getting to have close associations with a lot of your fellow students. We were literally pouring into the Woolworth Building. We would go to class. Ten o'clock came and we would all took [sic] off for our homes." If you were one of these students, you did not "get to know intimately your fellow students." Ruefully, Bennett admitted, "I would have great difficulty in recalling the names of most of my class."[52]

Collegiality was characteristic of the Fordham culture even in an age of formality. Male students wore ties and jackets, and women were comparably dressed in business attire. Fordham Law students were indistinguishable from the business and professional tenants of the Woolworth Building. Interactions in the classroom manifested a similar formality and professionalism. When students were called on, noted Pitassy, they would stand up "and recite the case. You'd talk about the case, state the facts, and state what the holding was and then answer any questions that the Professor had." If a student did not know the material, he said so. For some professors, like John Blake, this was not sufficient. "He was less inclined to be lenient with you if your [sic] weren't prepared," Pitassy recalled. Blake "could be the most sarcastic man you ever ran into," and he was "the toughest Professor on a student reciting a case." Yet, Pitassy "got to be very fond of him. We got to be great friends," even though one was "a little afraid . . . of what he might say to you." Joe McGovern never had Blake as a teacher, but he got to know him very well as a faculty member. "He had a very clear, crisp mind and one thing I admired about him, he was teaching the cram course, and as a teacher in the Law School, he rarely gave the answers to questions. His whole purpose was to stimulate your thinking, make you reason things out for yourself." Some students complained that Blake did not answer their questions. Blake commented to McGovern one day, "Joe, you know, I suppose I'm a financially stupid guy because a lot of students don't want to take my bar review course because I haven't answered their questions in class. They don't realize that the cram course is going to be entirely different and I will lay it out for them as they wanted, but my idea of teaching is to make them think, and I don't care whether they take my course or not. I stick to my principles." Joe McGovern recalled that Finn would "give us a little pep talk: 'Now, you're going to have three hundred True/False questions. A good deal of those questions will be on subjects you never heard of in Law School but, remember, that's part of the test. Don't leave them blank. Take a good guess, that's part of the test because if you're not going to be a good guesser, you're not going to be a good lawyer.' "⁵³

Dean Wilkinson sometimes sent students to a professor's law office for help in preparing for the bar, and independent bar review courses had come onto the scene by 1924. Students studied together for the bar exam, and their professors also offered bar review courses. John Loughran and John Blake offered a bar preparation course at Fordham until Loughran was elected to the New York Court of Appeals in 1934. John F. X. Finn replaced Loughran.

Aspects of the Fordham Law School experience continued to rely on the earlier apprenticeship model of preparation for the bar examination. Aside from moot court, which was voluntary, and, after 1935, the *Fordham Law Review*, which was restricted to the top twenty students in a class, Fordham Law students from the 1930s through the 1960s had limited opportunities to do legal research and writing. Many students worked in law firms, "maybe as many as half," McGovern recalled from his student days, "so they had the opportunities to write briefs and do research in their law offices." He regarded this experience to be "a big help" in their learning how to become lawyers. Louis Lefkowitz was one of these students, and he found his work experience in a law office an important complement to his work as a Fordham Law student in the 1920s. Although working in the law office was "tough, it was invaluable to be a law clerk. I learned so much. It made my studying a lot easier." Lefkowitz was "a firm believer in getting a year or two of clerkship . . . something you don't get in law school." The fact that he could type and take shorthand helped in both his law office and at school, especially since he "was only a high school graduate."[54]

Wilkinson modernized somewhat the Law School's administrative procedures, many of which dated to the early years of the school. These changes were modest but important. Wilkinson designed a new application for admission, which elicited extensive information about the applicants' academic and personal backgrounds. He also reorganized the student files so that they could be used from the point of admission to postgraduate inquiries from bar examiners and character committees. Wilkinson's interest in complete files was more than a housekeeping matter. The New York State Education Department had tightened its rules for the filing of qualifying credentials of matriculated students prior to enrollment in law schools operating in the state. Wilkinson boasted that, with the changes they made, Fordham Law School was able to forward student credentials to the Education Department within two weeks of the opening of school.[55]

Nonetheless, the Law School's entire administrative staff during Wilkinson's era consisted of only three people: Dean Wilkinson, Registrar Charles Davis and Mary Long, Davis's assistant who succeeded him as Registrar. The admission process could be relatively informal, and Davis was apparently a compassionate Registrar. George Brooks related that when Davis died, "going through his desk they found a lot of 'IOUs' [for tuition] which had never been paid, because Mr. Davis, I guess, figured the students didn't have the money. So he just gently forgot it." Brooks believed that Davis was a friend of the philosopher George Santayana, who referred to Davis in one of his books.[56]

In addition to adopting more stringent admission standards, Dean Wilkinson raised the Law School's academic standards. One of his earliest reforms limited the number of times a student could retake a course or an examination he had already flunked. Though the Law School was stringent in administering examinations, certain weaknesses in the rules surfaced in the early 1920s. The faculty changed the rule regarding conditioned examinations, that is, failed examinations in June 1922. The faculty resolved that third-year students who were denied their degrees with their graduating class may have the opportunity to "clean their records in the condition [*sic*] examinations held in the following September," and, if successful, they may be awarded their degrees in October. However, this resolution did "not apply to Third Year students whose failures aggregate more than two major subjects, as they will be obliged to repeat their entire Third Year work." This rule nonetheless allowed a third-year student who had a failure in one minor subject to graduate with his or her class if the student's third-year average was at least 70 percent. Students who failed more than one minor subject or whose third-year average was less than 70 percent were allowed to remove these deficiencies by simply taking the conditioned examination in the following semester.[57]

The 1922 changes in academic standards "denied the degree to" forty graduating seniors that academic year. This rule prevented relatively large numbers of third-year students from graduating with their classes for the next few years. For example, twenty-four students in the graduating class of 1923 had more than two failures in major subjects and were denied their degrees. Thirty-nine such students in the graduating class of 1924 and thrity-one students in the class of 1925 were not permitted to graduate with their classes.[58]

Wilkinson thought the rules regarding failed courses were still defective in two respects. First, there was no limit on the number of times the student could repeat an exam. Wilkinson made the startling report that a few students had taken exams in a particular course as many as six or seven times "with the natural result that ultimately they found an examination" they were able to pass and so earn the law degree. Second, a student could continue taking courses and earn a degree even though "his work taken as a whole was of a poor grade." Wilkinson investigated other law schools' policies and found that at some, "notably Columbia and Harvard if a man failed a year completely he was not allowed to repeat the year and [at] Columbia if more than one D grade was obtained and not removed on subsequent re-examination the student could not continue as a degree candidate."[59]

Wilkinson thought the Harvard and Columbia law schools' rules were too "drastic and might operate too arbitrarily," so he worked out an alternative rule that would give a student one chance to make up a failed course or a failed year. Wilkinson thought that offering such students one chance, but only one chance, would "eliminate a lot of dead wood from the classes while it should not prevent any man who through some more or less excusable cause has failed a course or a year continuing in the school by removing his failure."[60]

The faculty adopted a modified version of the rule Wilkinson favored at its June 1925 meeting. The new rule required any third-year student who "has a condition in a minor or major subject in his previous years in the school" to repeat the course and pass the examination in the failed subject. If the student failed the repeated course, the "student is dropped definitely." And students had only one opportunity to pass the repeated course. First- and second-year students who failed a course and were permitted under the rules to take a reexamination in the failed subject were no longer given a conditioned examination at the beginning of the following semester. They were required after September 1928 to take the reexamination at the next regular examination period only. Wilkinson thought this change would impress upon students how serious Fordham Law School considered failing an exam.[61]

The 1925 rule resulted in comparable numbers of third-year students who failed and did not graduate with their class as the 1922 rule. Fourteen out of 428 who advanced to third year could not graduate with their class in 1926 because of failed exams; 31 out of 355 in 1927; 22 out of 410 in 1928; 14 out of approximately 465 in 1929; and 9 out of 392 in 1930.[62]

The second reason Wilkinson was unsatisfied with the rules regarding failed courses is that a student could continue taking courses and earn a degree even though "his work taken as a whole was of a poor grade." To obviate this problem, he devised an "elastic rule" which gave the dean the discretion to require any student to withdraw from school whose "work generally was of such low grade as to indicate that he could not pursue the study of law with profit." This rule was coupled with a requirement that all students must maintain a C average to be in good standing. It did not matter how many Ds a student had; his overall average must be at least 70 percent. Wilkinson put this rule into effect in the fall of 1925.[63]

On adopting the new policy, the dean sent a warning form letter to any student who was in academic jeopardy. It stated: "You are warned that, because of your low scholastic standing in your last year's work, you are required to improve your grades materially at the next examinations. Failure so to do will necessitate your withdrawal from the School." By December 1925 Wilkinson had sent warning notices to about 10 percent of the second- and third-year students. His goal was to ensure that students who reached third year "will be reasonably certain of completing the curriculum successfully." Students who were unable to maintain a C average were warned that they must achieve a C average in the next or midyear examinations or else withdraw from school. This resulted in some students having to withdraw during the academic year, but Wilkinson justified the policy on the grounds that the law school should eliminate "the unfit" as soon as their unfitness was demonstrated. He thought the warning letter announcing the new policy was having "a tonic effect on the student body" the first semester the policy was implemented.[64]

In the fall of 1928 Wilkinson was happy to report that he had to send warning notices to only twenty students, which led him to conclude that the rule was "improving the scholastic standards of the school." Nevertheless, the Law School modified this rule in 1931 to require students to maintain "a weighted average grade of at least 'C' in every scholastic year." The Law School also prohibited any student who had an outstanding failed course from beginning their third year. By 1932 Wilkinson was able to report that the Law School's policies had eliminated about one third of the students in the first two years, and a majority of these "unsatisfactory men" were gone by the end of the first year. It was unusual, therefore, for seniors to "run into serious scholastic difficulty." Wilkinson cited as an example the senior class of 1930–31. Of the 350 students in this class, only 9 failed to maintain the required C weighted average in their third year.[65]

The Law School's attendance policy sometimes barred students from taking final examinations and from graduating. The Court of Appeals rules required students to complete their courses "by good and regular attendance," and, since the Court of Appeals left it to law schools to administer this rule, Fordham would "have to certify to the regularity of his attendance" when the student applied to take the bar examination.[66]

Although attendance rules were stringent, they evidently did not operate with the severity with which they appeared on paper. In 1925 Wilkinson sought to correct a condition that had existed for several years, that
of "a man" cutting a subject he disliked. The Law School's attendance
regulations limited unexcused absences to five in a "half course" (a one
semester course) and eleven in a "full course" (a full year course). Apparently, one absence was equal to one class hour, because, with one class
session meeting for two class hours, "absence from three full lectures in
any half-term course and six full lectures in any full-term course would
bar a man from examination and require repetition in the succeeding year
of such subject." Though the regulation was not too liberal in any one
course, Wilkinson surmised, it was too liberal overall because it permitted
a student to miss approximately 17 percent of all of his classes without
penalty. Thus, if the student exceeded thirty hours of unexcused absences
during an academic year, he "will be deemed excessively absent and will
be barred from continuing in the course until the year has been repeated."
Wilkinson expected that this change would limit the total of unexcused
absences of any particular student to about 8 percent of his total class
hours.[67]

The only reasons that a student was excused from attending classes
were "death in the student's immediate family or the serious illness of the
student." However, even these reasons did not excuse a student's absences
if they exceeded the dean's understanding of "good and regular attendance." For example, an "excellent student" ran into attendance problems
in his third year. He was absent when his mother died during the fall
semester and when he was stricken with appendicitis in the spring term.
His appendix ruptured, and he contracted peritonitis. The student's
absence from class totaled 30 percent of his classes for the entire school
year and 50 percent for the spring semester. Wilkinson concluded that he
could not "in good faith say that the man is in regular attendance for the
year."[68]

Faculty did not take attendance. This job was performed in the early
years by proctors. By the late 1930s student workers in the Law School's
administration office took attendance. Caesar Pitassy recalled when he
attended Fordham Law School from 1938 to 1941 that "an afternoon student would take attendance for the morning, and a morning student

would take attendance for the afternoon." Presumably, a student also took attendance for the night school.[69]

Wilkinson proudly informed Fordham President Reverend Charles J. Deane, S.J., in October 1931 that the Law School's rigorous admission and academic standards had earned for it "an excellent standing as a strict school both among members of the profession and other law schools." The authorities at Cornell, Columbia, Harvard and Yale law schools frequently recommended students to Fordham Law School when they needed to transfer for reasons "other than poor scholarship." Wilkinson boasted that Fordham Law School graduates "are able to compete with those of other schools." The New York City bar had come to know the Law School and its alumni, and graduates "find no permanent difficulty in securing placement in satisfactory offices." Wilkinson observed that law offices that had previously restricted their hiring of office assistants to graduates of elite law schools, such as Columbia and Harvard, "have come to employ our graduates as well."[70]

On December 15, 1930, about a year following Black Tuesday and the Stock Market Crash of 1929, Wilkinson established a Placement Bureau to help Fordham Law graduates primarily, and current students secondarily, find employment "where necessary." The suggestion for the Placement Bureau actually came from Father John X. Pyne, S.J., the Law School regent and professor of jurisprudence, who saw the need "to centralize" the process of bringing together students looking for jobs and "members of the bar [looking] for clerks." Wilkinson was "not sanguine" about the success of this venture for two reasons. The first revealed how he understood the workings of job placement in legal offices. Wilkinson believed that the best employment opportunities for students and graduates were in the offices of alumni, and Fordham Law School was still too young in 1930 to have any sizeable number of alumni who had reached the status of employers of law clerks and assistant counsel. The second reason for Wilkinson's pessimism was one of the very reasons Father Pyne recommended the Placement Bureau's creation: business conditions since the Stock Market Crash had made placement difficult. Wilkinson set aside his skepticism and supported the creation of the Placement Bureau because of the goodwill he thought it would generate in students and graduates who witnessed the Law School's efforts to help them. He anticipated that this goodwill would more than compensate for the time and cost of the effort.[71]

Wilkinson appointed Professor George Brooks to run the Placement Bureau. Brooks estimated that he devoted about two hours per week to placement, for which he was paid. The bureau "was a very simple operation," as Brooks explained it. As requests to hire law students came in from employers, Brooks "would try to farm them out to the men who were looking for jobs." The initiative was completely on the student. "A fellow would say he's looking for a spot and I would say I think we have something here." After receiving the relevant information from Brooks, the student evidently arranged the job interview himself. Brooks also handled alumni placement: "Anybody that [sic] needed a job we tried to help them."[72]

The Placement Bureau sent out a mass mailing to 3,300 alumni in December 1930. The letter informed them that the Law School was beginning a placement service, and it asked them to return an enclosed card with certain information. Eight hundred and seventy-eight alumni complied by returning the completed cards. Wilkinson sent a second mailing in February 1931 to alumni who did not respond to the first mailing. This garnered another 192 replies. The 1,070 full responses yielded a return rate of about 32 percent, but the number of jobs it produced was disappointing. Seventy-three alumni reported that they were unemployed, and another 116 were employed but seeking to change jobs. The mailing only produced 20 possible job leads and, of these, only 2 jobs for Fordham graduates actually materialized.[73]

Inefficiencies in the placement process and anti-Catholic bias handicapped Fordham Law students in getting jobs while they were attending classes. The Law School received from three to five calls for law clerks each week from February to May 1931. Fordham was not as successful in filling these positions as it could have been. Students failed to register with the Placement Bureau, forcing the bureau to notify students of job opportunities by posting notices on the Law School's bulletin boards. This delayed the students' response time, and delay was the chief reason Fordham filled only thirteen of thirty-nine openings in the spring of 1931. The average salary for a student law clerk was eight dollars per week, but some employers offered the experience without compensation. Professor Brooks also reported that "racial and financial reasons" explained why Fordham

Law students were placed in only one-third of the jobs available. Not surprisingly, job placement for students and graduates became "exceedingly difficult" as the Great Depression deepened.[74]

Students may not have registered with the Placement Bureau because Brooks did not publicize it much. He decided not to give the bureau "extended publicity" because "the available positions [were] far less than the demand." The demand for jobs was twice as great as their supply, as Brooks had received 154 applications from students and graduates seeking employment and only 70 positions from employers. He feared that too much "encouragement or publicity would react unfavorably" under these conditions. Nevertheless, the bureau became increasingly popular among students as news of its increasing effectiveness in placing students spread by word of mouth. Though he had sought "chiefly to place students and graduates in law offices," the bureau's "real purpose," Brooks declared, was to place graduates. This purpose was best served, however, by securing positions for as many students as possible.[75]

The state of New York required law school graduates to clerk in a law office for one year in addition to passing the bar examination to be admitted to practice. The clerkship requirement had much to do with expanding the scope of the Placement Bureau to include students seeking employment during law school. Law firms were reluctant to hire law school graduates who accepted a position simply to fulfill their one-year clerkship requirement and then left at the end of the year. In addition, employers believed that college graduates who had also graduated from law school were too old and too educated to work for a law clerk's wages of $5 per week, and, in many cases, they were right. Many law school graduates refused to work for such a low salary, even though they were thereby meeting a condition for admission to the bar. Consequently, about 75 percent of the employment opportunities Fordham Law School received during the 1932–33 academic year were for students rather than graduates. Brooks reported that he placed Fordham students and graduates in fifty-one of the seventy positions the bureau received. Of these fifty-one placements, only twelve were filled by graduates of the Law School.[76]

Joe McGovern's employment experience on graduating from Fordham Law School in 1933 demonstrates the importance of the Law School's alumni. He did spectacularly well as one of the twelve graduates who were placed in law firms that year. McGovern recalled that the greatest problem confronting members of his graduating class was "getting a job after law school." The second- and third-greatest problems were: "Would you be paid anything if you had a job?" and "Could you get maybe fifteen dollars a week?" Fifteen dollars was three times the going rate for law clerks right out of law school. Graduating first in his class, McGovern "was happily surprised" when he got a job at Vincent Leibell's law firm starting at "twenty-five dollars a week." In recounting his experience in 1989, McGovern sought to explain the low salary by contemporary standards, noting that he actually did spectacularly well starting at a salary that was five times the going rate for law clerks.[77]

In 1935 the Placement Bureau changed its objectives. Instead of helping all of the students and graduates find jobs, the bureau concentrated on placing the best students in the best law offices. This shift in strategy appears to have been a consequence of two developments. One was the paucity of employment opportunities as New York City and the nation were in the throes of the Great Depression. The other was the resumption of the *Fordham Law Review* in 1935. Wilkinson regarded the law review as a job placement tool. Resumption of its publication enabled Professor Eugene J. Keefe, whom Wilkinson appointed to head the Placement Bureau when Professor Brooks left the faculty, "to begin a practice which is followed by many of our best law schools, that is to say to communicate with leading law offices in the city in the fall of the year and arrange interviews for our law review staff and other high ranking students in the school, for the purpose of securing them positions in satisfactory surroundings." A third explanation is Wilkinson's expectation that this new strategy would enhance the Law School's reputation in the city's "legal circles" and enable it to achieve greater success in placing "at least our good students in worthwhile offices upon graduation."[78]

The Placement Bureau's new orientation appeared to have the desired effect. In 1939, Fordham Law School alumnus Albert J. Clark, a partner in the law firm of Greene & Greene, reported to Fordham University President Father Robert I. Gannon, S.J., that he knew from personal experience that, "for many years, . . . the attitude taken by the large law firms [was] to disregard Fordham Law School graduates." He acknowledged that "the attitude is changing" and that this change was "due to the increased calibre of the students."[79]

Clark also reported that turning out better students was not sufficient to place the Law School's graduates in New York City's elite law firms. Graduates needed "organized help from the Alumni" to supplement the "splendid work" of the Law School in raising standards "so that it may further intrench [sic] its rightful rank with the Class 'A' law schools." Clark contrasted Fordham Law School's "nominal Alumni" association with the "potent and well organized" alumni associations of such first-rank law schools as Harvard and Columbia, which worked actively and hard to get their graduates placed in the top law firms. He urged that placing its graduates in good law firm positions could not be done by the Law School. Rather, it "can and should be cast upon the Alumni." Clark knew of "many men willing to undertake the task if only the ball gets rolling again."[80]

Shortly after becoming dean in 1923, Wilkinson tried to build the Law Alumni Association. He understood that, in addition to helping students and graduates get good jobs, there were various other ways in which the alumni were important to the Law School's success. Alumni could be very useful in recruiting prospective students. Wilkinson also viewed the alumni as an important lobbying group that could represent and protect the Law School's interests before the state and local governments and within bar associations. He thus informed Reverend William J. Duane, S.J., president of Fordham University in 1925 that an alumni association would be "extremely helpful . . . in sending prospective students to our doors," and it would give "us an organized group of professional men loyal to the school and its institutions" who, in times of need, would be "extremely helpful . . . in combating adverse legislation or arbitrary standards which in future might be sought to be imposed on us." For these reasons, Wilkinson advised, "it behooves us" to help the evolution of the alumni association "so far as lies in our power."[81]

Attempts had been made to form an alumni association before Wilkinson became dean, but they did not amount to very much. Wilkinson made the organization a priority soon after he assumed the deanship. Since Fordham Law School essentially served the New York City population, most of its 1,600 graduates lived in or near the greater city, which helped to "band them together." Marveling at the accuracy and thoroughness of the Law School's alumni information, Wilkinson called a meeting of representatives of every class to discuss the formation of a Law School alumni association in the spring of 1924. Those who attended were so enthusiastic about the project that they decided to call a general meeting to be held in the theater of the College of Saint Francis Xavier on West 16th Street. Over 100 alumni attended, and they adopted a constitution and elected officers. The Honorable Carroll Hayes, a justice of the Municipal Court, was elected as the Law Alumni Association's first president. Hayes later became president of the Catholic Lawyers Guild and at the request of Judge Samuel Seabury, he joined Judge Seabury's team of investigators, who conducted "the biggest investigation of municipal corruption in [the twentieth] century." The Law Alumni Association held two meetings during the 1924–25 academic year, a business meeting at the Catholic Club and a social meeting at the Hotel Pennsylvania. Both were attended well enough to indicate the possibility of establishing "a reasonably active and useful organization."[82]

In 1929 Wilkinson informed Father Gannon of the Alumni Association's critical importance to the success of the Law School's efforts to place its graduates. "On it practically hinges in large measure" the placement of the law school's graduates in top law firms, he acknowledged. In addition, the viability of a law review like those at "the more important law schools" was very much easier and more simplified by the support of the alumni, both in terms of financial support and in procuring articles on legal topics of interest. As he had earlier recognized, the alumni were "of the utmost importance in attracting desirable students" to the law school. Wilkinson recommended that the Law School hire a law alumni secretary for a reasonable salary who would devote almost all of his time to alumni relations. The alumni secretary could stimulate the growth of the association by preparing and keeping current a directory of law graduates. Emphasizing the close connection between a loyal alumni and job placement, Wilkinson suggested that the alumni secretary would also take charge of job placement of students before and after graduation. He noted that job placement was given great attention at the other law schools in the city. Placement and alumni relations were intertwined, but Fordham University appointed Edward P. Gilleran to the position of alumni secretary, and, administratively, the Law School's Alumni Association was incorporated into the general University Alumni Association.[83]

Through the end of the 1920s, the Law Alumni Association met once a year for an annual dinner. The number of alumni who attended these dinners, however, were relatively small, even though the attendees were enthusiastic. By 1934 the Alumni Association had become "absolutely quiescent." The president of the Law Alumni Association attributed this quiescence to the "general depressed business conditions." He thought it unwise to have any formal functions in this economic environment. However, the luncheon the Alumni Association held on May 12, 1934, to honor Professor I. Maurice Wormser was attended by almost 250 alumni. Wilkinson was encouraged by the luncheon's success, which he thought indicated that the Alumni Association was not "moribund." He was hopeful that it would restore normal activity when business conditions improved.[84]

With the nation still in the throes of the Great Depression at the end of the 1930s, the Law Alumni Association "lapsed into a state of complete inactivity." Depressed economic conditions, the poor job market for law school graduates, and the increasingly difficult struggle to make a living undermined interest in the Alumni Association. Wilkinson tried to revitalize the Alumni Association in the fall of 1938, but failed even to elect New York Court of Appeals Judge John T. Loughran as the association's president and a slate of new officers. The association continued in a state of desuetude through World War II. It was not until long after World War II, in the 1960s and 1970s, that the Alumni Association returned to life.[85]

Wilkinson also systematized and formalized a number of procedures relating to faculty hiring and employment. He replaced informal agreements with faculty with written employment contracts, and he introduced a standard salary scale based on faculty rank of lecturer, instructor, assistant professor, associate professor, and full professor. Wilkinson also increased teachers' salaries to reflect the extra work required to grade blue books as enrollment grew. Wilkinson rejected paying a flat fee to grade each book, as some suggested, because it was "characteristic of commercial or proprietary institutions." In 1925 the newly established salary rates were: $500–600 per course hour each year for full professors; $450–500 per hour for each associate professor in the day session and $400–450 for evening work; and $350–450 for day lectures and $300–400 for evening. Given the number of hours that the faculty taught and the fact that most were in practice or otherwise employed, these were reasonable payments at a time when a skilled laborer might make $3,000 to $4,000 a year.[86]

Hiring was fairly continuous during the 1920s and 1930s, with a stable core of professors and new part-time lecturers added as needed. The majority of the faculty were law graduates of Fordham, but there were a number with degrees from Harvard, Columbia, and Yale law schools. Faculty tended to stay for many years unless forced to leave for reasons of health. Francis X. Carmody, a well-known expert in New York Practice and seasoned instructor after many years at Brooklyn Law School, was hired in 1920 and remained until his death in 1928. In 1923 Walter B. Kennedy was appointed. He was a graduate of Holy Cross College and Harvard Law School (1909) who had practiced and taught at Catholic University's Law School in Washington, DC. He would remain at Fordham for the rest of his career. In 1924 Wilkinson hired John S. Roberts, class of 1922. Roberts had a PhD and taught part-time until poor health forced him to relinquish his work in the spring of 1937, at which time he was an assistant superintendent of schools in New York City. John F. X. Finn also joined the faculty in 1924 as a lecturer as did Arthur A. McGivney in 1925. The next year, Eugene J. Keefe, George W. Bacon, and Edward Q. Carr were appointed as lecturers. Along with Finn, McGivney, and Wormser, they held their positions until the 1950s and 1960s and were the core group of faculty who transmitted the culture of the school to new faculty and inspired generations of law students.[87]

There was always some turnover as faculty resigned for a variety of reasons. After teaching for eighteen years, John T. Loughran left in 1930, when he was elected to the State Supreme Court. For Wilkinson, his loss was "almost irreparable" because Loughran had taught a wide range of courses including Agency, Contracts, Criminal Law, Pleading, Torts, Evidence, Sales, Suretyship, and New York Civil Practice. A graduate later recalled of Loughran, "He was a natural teacher, was beloved by everyone, and had a tremendous memory." Teaching so many different courses was not unusual at schools like Fordham. Loughran also coedited and coauthored books with his Fordham Law School colleagues John S. Roberts and Francis Carmody. Laughran also taught bar review courses with colleagues John Blake and Walter Kennedy. Loughran, Wormser, and Kennedy were the most prolific authors on the faculty.[88]

Some lecturers resigned because the needs of their practice became too demanding. William Shea resigned in 1933 after several years of teaching because of health problems due to a heavy caseload. Joseph Force Crater lectured in the Law School until he resigned in 1927. He was appointed by Governor Franklin Roosevelt in April 1930 to fill an unexpired term on the New York Supreme Court. Crater became a household name when he disappeared four months later, apparently mired in political scandals. He had the reputation of "a 'playboy judge' who socialized with racketeers." On August 6, 1930, Crater "cashed two checks for large sums, bought a ticket to a Broadway show, hailed a taxi, and vanished forever." George Brooks, who knew Judge Crater as a student and as a faculty colleague, did not believe that Crater "voluntarily disappeared." Brooks explained, "The reason I say this is, to him the law was something very precious. I think it was the ambition of his life to attain the bench which he did and I don't think that he would have voluntarily done away with himself." Crater's case still fascinates New Yorkers and is evoked whenever a public figure disappears under questionable circumstances.[89]

During the 1920s, Dean Wilkinson played a leading role in achieving higher standards in legal education in New York State. He incorporated these achievements and built upon them by raising standards within Fordham Law School. Wilkinson continued his dual role as a reformer in legal education and as a reformer at Fordham Law School into the 1930s.

CHAPTER FOUR

THE GREAT DEPRESSION
AND EDUCATIONAL REFORM

Dean Wilkinson continued to be a leader in legal educational reform in New York State and at Fordham Law School well into the 1930s. With the urging of the president of Fordham University, he filed a motion in the New York Court of Appeals in 1934 and persuaded the court to adopt his motion to change its rules to permit a four-year night law school program. Wilkinson modified Fordham Law School's night curriculum in September 1934 to comply with the four-year night school program, bringing it into conformity with accreditation standards of the American Bar Association (ABA) and satisfying membership requirements of the Association of American Law Schools (AALS). Again at the urging of the president of Fordham University, Wilkinson continued to raise the Law School's academic standards and changed its faculty hiring practices in order to earn for the school the approval of the ABA as an accredited law school in 1936 and membership in the selective AALS in the same year. He also reestablished the *Fordham Law Review* in 1935. He was active in shaping the standards for admission to law practice in New York State.

One of the major reforms Wilkinson accomplished in the 1930s was persuading the New York Court of Appeals to change its rules to permit law schools to expand their night programs by spreading the three-year curriculum over four years. The need for this change first arose when the ABA and AALS adopted a resolution in the early 1920s that required part-time and night law programs to be the equivalent of full-time programs, but they were to be offered over four years instead of three years. The motivation behind this standard combined a concern to enhance professional standards and a desire to exclude poor urban immigrants from the profession.

Fordham Law School's part-time, evening curriculum was the same as the three-year day school curriculum. The need to adopt the four-year night school curriculum became acute in 1929 when the state of

Connecticut Board of Law Examiners decided to prohibit the graduates of Fordham Law School, New York University Law School, Brooklyn Law School, and Temple University Law School of Philadelphia from taking the Connecticut bar examination after January 1, 1930. Its stated reason was that "these schools are regarded as part-time institutions." The deans of these law schools expressed "strong disapproval" of Connecticut's action, characterizing it "as an arbitrary discrimination whose effect would be to place the youth of small means, whose only recourse is a part-time school, under a new handicap, and to tend to restrict entrance to the profession to young men of means." A member of the Connecticut Bar Examination Commission, James E. Wheeler, rejoined that it was merely adopting the standards recommended by the AALS, the ABA's Council on Legal Education, and the Carnegie Foundation.[1]

A spokesman for NYU Law School, Professor Henry B. Pogson, highlighted the arbitrary nature of Connecticut's action. In a statement that was equally applicable to Fordham and Brooklyn law schools, Professor Pogson asserted that Connecticut's exclusion of NYU Law School's *full-time graduates* "simply because they attend a university which also teaches part-time law students in separate divisions is neither intelligent nor intelligible." As for the part-time students, if they passed the same examinations as those students "who are able to devote all their time to study [law] there is no reason why they shouldn't be fitted to practice law." Perhaps anticipating Connecticut's action, NYU Law School adopted in April 1929 the ABA's and AALS's standards for part-time programs and extended its evening school to four years beginning with the entering class of September 1930.[2]

The *New York Times* defended Connecticut's decision on the bases of two distinct yet interrelated grounds. The editor cautioned that critics of the Connecticut Bar Examination Commission "should not overlook its commendable motive. The profession [of law] is crowded. It includes many incompetents. There ought to be stricter requirements for admission." According to the president of the New York State Board of Examiners, the editor reported, "most of the candidates who fail are lacking in intellectual ability." A former member of the New York Committee on Character and Fitness resigned because "the committee had no power to weed out 80 percent of the candidates [in]sufficiently educated to appear in court." He claimed that "their general knowledge was sometimes so limited that they had never heard of great figures at the bar." The deficit of "general knowledge" could be remedied with educational prerequisites for admission to law school. The *New York Times* consequently suggested that admission to the bar be restricted to college-educated candidates, a qualification that would exclude immigrants and their offspring. This effect notwithstanding, the *New York Times* editor maintained that bar examiners should "prevent the examination of young men who have not been trained to think and who are poorly informed about the history and government of their country. It is not enough for them to be able to repeat legal principles from memory."[3]

The *New York Times* identified an arbitrary feature of Connecticut's decision. Noting that "a student for three years in a law office is welcome in Connecticut," the *New York Times* editor opined that "it seems an inconsistency for Connecticut to exclude a graduate of the institutions named and allow an office student of three years to be examined. An industrious student at these colleges and schools should be able to learn as much law as a worker in an office for three years, whose hours of study are limited." To turn away an applicant "if he takes night or part-time courses of instruction must seem an injustice to many." Unjust or not, the *New York Times* supported Connecticut because "there are overcrowding and incompetency at the bar, and something must be done to reduce both."[4]

Part-time programs were under attack in New York State as well as Connecticut. A certain "local bar [association]" had petitioned the New York Court of Appeals to change its rules regarding part-time law schools, and Wilkinson believed that "the instigators of this movement" sought to eliminate part-time law programs entirely in New York State. He had persuaded some of the "instigators" that it was not possible to eliminate part-time law programs, and, even if it were possible, it would be undesirable to eliminate them "considering the public character of the profession of the law." Wilkinson undoubtedly was thinking of the undemocratic and elitist effect of eliminating part-time law school programs, namely, excluding the working classes—comprising largely Catholics, Jews, and southern and eastern Europeans—from attending law school and restricting the practice of law to those wealthy enough to attend law school without having to support themselves.[5]

Dean Wilkinson defended the three-year night program by explaining why a four-year curriculum "would be impracticable" under the current New York Court of Appeals rules. The four-year program would impose an unreasonable and unfair burden on part-time students. The Court of Appeals did not distinguish between full-time and part-time law programs, or, as Wilkinson put it, between "day and night work." It applied "the same minimum standard of weekly instruction" to both. All law students were required to take a minimum of ten class hours per week over thirty-two weeks per year for a minimum of three years. Wilkinson saw no benefit to night students to extend the night school to four years under these rules, because it would impose an additional year of a minimum of ten class hours per week over thirty-two weeks, requiring night students to attend one hundred and twenty more class hours than the "day men."[6]

There still was no generally accepted understanding of what constituted part-time and full-time law study. The New York "instigators" distinguished between them according to the time of day the courses were offered. Any law school operating principally before 4:00 P.M. was considered a full-time school, and any law school operating principally after 4:00 P.M. was a part-time school. If this distinction were adopted, Fordham's morning and afternoon sessions would be considered full-time programs and would operate under the three-year rule. The evening divisions in Manhattan and the Bronx would be considered part-time programs and would have to be extended to four years to satisfy ABA and AALS standards. Operating a three-year night program, Fordham Law School consequently was not an ABA-accredited law school or a member of the AALS.[7]

Wilkinson supported the extension of the part-time law school curriculum to four years if the Court of Appeals changed its rules to enable part-time students to take the same number of classroom hours over four years that full-time students took over three years. He thought the extra length of study could be of benefit to the night student. Wilkinson made his views known to William D. Guthrie—constitutional lawyer, Columbia Law School professor, and former president of the Association of the Bar of the City of New York (ABCNY)—who was to give an address on this subject to the New York State Bar Association at its annual meeting in January 1931. Wilkinson told Guthrie that "the night man did not require more classroom instruction than his day brother but required more free time for preparation of his case material outside of class so as to put him on an equality with the day student." Guthrie incorporated Wilkinson's views in his speech, and in the discussion that followed Wilkinson declared his support for the four-year night school and for a change in the Court of Appeals rules which clearly distinguished between full-time and part-time law study and that required fewer classroom hours per week for part-time students.[8]

Following the New York State Bar Association's meeting, Wilkinson emerged as a leader in shaping the rules regulating part-time legal education in New York State. As a member of the ABCNY and its Joint Conference on Legal Education and as dean of Fordham Law School, he influenced the course of legal education in New York State. In these capacities, Wilkinson drafted a resolution that petitioned the New York Court of Appeals to distinguish between full-time and part-time law schools, to define what constituted a full-time and a part-time law program, and to authorize part-time programs to be spread over four years with a reduced number of weekly class hours each year. The New York County Lawyers Association joined in the petition, and the ABA supported it by sending a representative to argue to the Court of Appeals on its behalf. According to Wilkinson, every law school in New York State supported the change, save St. John's Law School in Brooklyn. Wilkinson, among other lawyers, appeared before the Court of Appeals to argue on behalf of the ABCNY petition on June 5, 1931. He also submitted a written brief on behalf of Fordham Law School.[9]

On July 15, 1931, the New York Court of Appeals denied the petition to change its rules. In a per curiam opinion, the court explained that the proposed change "must be at least postponed until a more satisfactory definition can be worked out whereby to distinguish between full-time and part-time courses." The distinction between the two kinds of programs was based on the time of day the courses were offered. A "full-time law school" was one in which two-thirds of the courses were offered after 9:00 A.M. and before 4:00 P.M. A part-time school "is defined as any other." The court noted that the distinction, "roughly speaking," corresponded "to that between the day law schools on the one hand and the evening law schools on the other." It thought this definition inadequate and thus concluded that its consideration of the proposed rules change must await "a more satisfactory definition . . . to distinguish between full-time and part-time courses." The court thought that the proposed rule change would be "unjust to evening students" for two reasons. It found that many day students were "employed in gainful occupations during the night time and during free hours of the day," and that night students maintained "their standings in the law schools" and "their ratings" before the bar examiners. In light of these circumstances, extending legal studies to four years for all students would treat day and night students equally, the court opined, but this equal treatment would "operate harshly" on those students who had to work to support themselves while in law school. The court felt "constrained at this time to deny the applications," but it would reflect upon the "interesting data" the petitioners submitted, "and with the co-operation of the bar and of the faculties of the law schools may lead to action in the future." The ABCNY remained determined to persuade the Court of Appeals to adopt its proposal, gathering "comprehensive statistics and data" to refute the arguments of the petition's "opponent" and to support the arguments Wilkinson made.[10]

The ABCNY Joint Conference of Legal Education sent a survey to all ten law schools in New York State and four law schools outside of the state in the spring of 1932. It reported its findings in June 1935. All but three of the in-state law schools participated along with the four out-of-state law schools. The results are tabulated in Tables 4-1 to 4-3.

The vast majority of students in day schools were full-time students who devoted their entire time to their studies, and the vast majority of students in the night schools were part-time students who worked at jobs outside of law school for thirty to forty hours per week. The law schools with the best reputations offered only day courses, and, with the possible exception of Harvard Law School, they had the highest proportion of full-time students who devoted all of their time to their studies. Only Fordham and NYU law schools offered night programs, and they had the smallest proportion of full-time day students. Not only did these law schools have the most part-time day students, Fordham day students worked more hours at outside jobs than those of any other law school, and NYU day students worked almost as many. The overwhelming majority of night students at Fordham Law School and almost all of the NYU Law School night students were part-time students. One-half of the Fordham night students and two-thirds of the NYU night students worked at least forty

TABLE 4-1. DAY STUDENTS WHO WERE FULL-TIME AND PART-TIME AND HOURS OF WORK/WEEK, 1931–32

Law School	Total Students	F-T, No Work	P-T, Work 30+ Hrs.	P-T, Work 20–30 Hrs.	P-T, Work 1–19 Hrs.
U of Buffalo	206	125 (61%)	21 (10%)	28 (14%)	32 (16%)
Columbia	525	413 (79%)	4 (1%)	21 (4%)	87 (17%)
Cornell	139	100 (72%)	3 (3%)	9 (6%)	27 (19%)
Fordham	457	250 (55%)	95 (21%)	62 (14%)	50 (11%)
Harvard*	2807	917 (33%)	167 (6%)	204 (7%)	407 (15%)
NYU	561	316 (56%)	76 (14%)	66 (12%)	103 (18%)
Pennsylvania	196	137 (70%)	5 (3%)	11 (6%)	43 (22%)
Syracuse	102	69 (68%)	5 (5%)	7 (7%)	21 (21%)
U of Virginia	98	74 (76%)	5 (5%)	6 (6%)	13 (13%)
Yale**	235	214 (91%)	7 (3%)	10 (4%)	62 (26%)

Source: "Survey of Full-time and Part-time Law Students" conducted by the Joint Conference on Legal Education, Association of the Bar of the City of New York, June 15, 1935, included as Schedule C, Dean's Report, February 17, 1936.

*Harvard's enrollment was 1,517 students. But these figures are based on 2,807 replies, due to the questionnaire calling for replies for each of the three years. Dean Roscoe Pound asserted that the results, "while far from accurate, give a fair estimate of the work."

**Yale's enrollment was 318 students, but only 235 replied to the questionnaire.

TABLE 4-2. NIGHT STUDENTS WHO WERE FULL-TIME AND PART-TIME AND HOURS WORK/WEEK, 1931–32

Law School	Total Students	P-T Students (No Work)	F-T Students, 40 Hrs	F-T Students, 30–40 Hrs	F-T Students, 20–30 Hrs	F-T Students, 1–19 Hrs
Fordham	580	476 (82%)	289 (50%)	140 (24%)	24 (4%)	23 (4%)
NYU	254	242 (95%)	164 (65%)	56 (22%)	6 (2%)	16 (6%)

Source: "Survey of Full-time and Part-time Law Students" conducted by the Joint Conference on Legal Education, Association of the Bar of the City of New York, June 15, 1935, included as Schedule C, Dean's Report, February 17, 1936.

TABLE 4-3. DAY STUDENTS AND AVERAGE HOURS PER WEEK DEVOTED
TO LAW STUDIES, 1931–32

Law School	Full-Time (No Work)	40 Hrs	30–40 Hrs	20–30 Hrs	20-Oct Hrs	10-Jan Hrs
U of Buffalo	42	39.5	35.5	40	37	5
Columbia*	53	47	49	52	47	49
Cornell*	47	40	40	48	49	51
Fordham Day**	34.6	27.5	31	32.9	32.5	35
Fordham Night	33.1	29.6	30.8	32.2	32.5	34.3
Harvard	50	31	33	41	39	45
NYU Day**	36.1	30.6	31.1	32.6	34.4	34.5
NYU Night***	29.6	26.1	27.3	27.1	29.75	29.1
Pennsylvania*	48.55	27.5	37.5	42.95	38.95	45.95
Syracuse	48	41	42	46	46	45
U of Virginia	38.1	34.2	30	35.9	30	37
Yale*	47	40	47	42	47	46

Source: "Survey of Full-time and Part-time Law Students" conducted by the Joint
Conference on Legal Education, Association of the Bar of the City of New York, June
15, 1935, included as Schedule C, Dean's Report, February 17, 1936.
  *Require 14 hours of class per week, which increases the time devoted to law study.
  **Require 12 hours of class per week, which decreases the time devoted to law
study.
  ***Require 10 hours of class per week, which decreases the time devoted to law
study.

hours per week, and another quarter of the Fordham night students and
a little over one-fifth of the NYU law students worked more than thirty
but fewer than forty hours per week.[11]

The Joint Conference of Legal Education surveyed the number of
hours per week students devoted to their legal studies. These data show
that the time students devoted to law study varied substantially inversely
to the time devoted to work other than law study. Law students at Fordham and NYU who worked at outside jobs devoted the fewest hours
per week to their legal studies. Wilkinson calculated that Fordham Law
School's full-time students studied about two hours for every hour in

class, and part-time students studied only one and one quarter hours for every hour in class. He believed these results offered "a compelling argument" to extend the evening course to four years in order to reduce the number of classroom hours and allow more time for study to the "evening men." Wilkinson predicted that this step would afford the majority of evening students who worked a full business day the opportunity to study that was enjoyed by day students. He also thought it should enable evening students to do better in their classes, which would permit the Law School "to demand greater scholastic proficiency" of students without establishing different scholastic standards in the different divisions or "over-taxing" evening students.[12]

The Joint Conference of Legal Education reported that nineteen states distinguished between day law programs and night law programs. The New York State Education Department also wanted to distinguish day law programs from night law programs and to extend the latter to four years. Such distinctions in full-time and part-time programs had become "prevailing practice in university circles generally," that is, in other fields of study such as engineering. Brooklyn Law School, New York Law School, and St. Johns Law School, which failed to distinguish between full-time and part-time programs and conducted both full-time and part-time programs on a three-year basis, were contrary to general educational practice. The Joint Conference of Legal Education reported that the results of its survey supported its conclusion that extending evening programs from three to four years of substantially the same number of hours of class work was "sound in principle."[13]

Before the Joint Conference of Legal Education published its findings, Fordham University president, the Very Reverend Aloysius J. Hogan, S.J., directed Dean Wilkinson to place the Law School's night program on a four-year basis beginning with the entering class of September 1934 even though the New York Court of Appeals still required only three years. This was a gutsy move, because Wilkinson estimated that enrollments and revenues would decline significantly if Fordham adopted a four-year night school when the state only required three years and two other law schools in New York City were still offering three-year night school opportunities. Wilkinson predicted that if Fordham adopted the four-year night school plan in September 1934, the likely reduction in student enrollments would be 35 percent of its 1933–34 enrollment (a reduction from 1,094 to 711 students) and the loss of about 40 percent of its gross revenue for that year ($95,164 of $237,910) over the first four years of operation. Pointing out the importance of the Law School to the financial structure of the university, Wilkinson recommended against adopting the change, noting that it portended a "serious effect" on the finances not only of the Law School but of the "university generally," particularly with the continuing "bad business conditions" and "the hoped-for improvement" not materializing "as rapidly as had been expected."[14]

Wilkinson also advised Father Hogan to bear in mind that the rules regulating night schools may not change for some time. In his opinion, "the Court of Appeals [was] not likely in the near future, to change the rules regulating law study to require part-time work to be done over a longer period." Even if the Court of Appeals did approve of this change, "then the matter would have to be taken up, in all likelihood, with the State Education Department and with the representatives of the Section on Legal Education of the American Bar Association." All of this would take time. Wilkinson recognized the possibility that the Law School could "survive the change without showing an operating deficit." A 20 percent increase in tuition, from $200 per year to $240 per year beginning in the 1935–36 school year, would "remove the hazard of an operating deficit and possibly enable the School to return a modest operating profit."[15]

These data and the possibility of "greater scholastic proficiency" supported Father Hogan's decision to place the Law School's evening division on a four-year basis. He directed Wilkinson in November 1933 to make the night school a four-year program beginning in September 1934, provided that "the necessary State [Education Department] authorization can be secured." He also directed Wilkinson "to make the necessary application on behalf of the School" to the New York Court of Appeals "for such amendments to its rules as you deem requisite to the end in view," and to the New York State Education Department "to obtain approval of the re-arranged curriculum for the degree of LL.B." In addition to "greater scholastic proficiency," Father Hogan had a second reason for authorizing the four-year part-time program even without any changes in the Court of Appeal rules relating to minimum class hours: getting Fordham Law School on the list of ABA-approved law schools. After securing "favorable action" from "the above authorities," Father Hogan directed, Wilkinson was to "proceed to negotiate with the proper authorities of the American

Bar Association to the end that approval of the School by the Section on Legal Education of that body may be obtained as well."[16]

Dean Wilkinson filed Fordham Law School's petition to the New York Court of Appeals in late December 1933 asking the court to amend its rules to enable law schools to spread their part-time curricula from three years to four years without requiring more class time than that required of the three-year full-time programs. Wilkinson argued that this could be accomplished if the court were to reduce the minimum required hours of class per week from the current minimum of ten hours for all law students to eight hours for part-time law students. The petition asserted that Fordham Law School required all day and evening students to complete twelve class hours a week for three scholastic years, or thirty-six year hours in all, even though the Court of Appeals and the state of New York required only ten class hours a week over three years or thirty year hours. The rule change Fordham Law School requested would still result in the night students taking more total class hours of instruction than the minimum of thirty class hours the court presently required of all law students, "four (4) scholastic years of eight (8) hours weekly, or thirty-two (32) year hours of instruction."[17]

The petition Dean Wilkinson filed on behalf of Fordham Law School was almost identical to the one he and others submitted in 1931 on behalf of the ABCNY and the New York County Lawyers' Association. There was an important difference, however, which Wilkinson emphasized in his memorandum of law. The earlier petition would have *required* all of the law schools in New York State to change their part-time programs to four years, whereas Fordham's "requested amendment [to the Court of Appeals rules] is *entirely permissive* in character and would not require any law school to change its course in any way." Wilkinson pointed out that the opposition of St. John's School of Law to the 1931 petition was due to the mandatory nature of the requested rule change, and that St. John's would accept the requested change if it were permissive and left the decision whether to adopt a four-year night program "to the discretion of the institution."[18]

Wilkinson's substantive argument focused on the need to provide part-time evening law students with more time to prepare for class and to do collateral reading and research in order to put them on a par with full-time day students. Part-time students must devote substantial portions of their working day to their outside jobs, and they were in class five nights per week. Consequently, they had difficulty in mastering their courses in three academic years because they did not have sufficient free time to study. Spreading their courses over 4 years would afford them the necessary free time, but, under current court of appeals rules, they would be required to attend 1,440 class session hours over 4 years, whereas full-time students were required to attend only 1,152 class session hours over 3 years. The court of appeals could eliminate this disparity if it were to change its rules to permit part-time students to attend fewer than ten class hours per week over four years. The great need was not to require part-time students to take more class hours of instructions. Rather, it was to spread the same number of class hours over a longer period of time to afford them enough free time adequately to prepare for class.[19]

On January 16, 1934, the New York Court of Appeals granted Fordham's petition in full, permitting part-time law study of at least eight hours of class per week over four years. Upon receiving the court's order, Wilkinson applied to the New York State Education Department for approval of Fordham's proposed four-year night program. He explained in his letter to Assistant Commissioner Harlan H. Horner that the Law School required successful completion of "thirty-six (36) year hours of work for our degree," which it intended to continue, but it sought to divide these hours over four years for night school students, either nine year hours per week each year for four years or two years of eight hours per week and two years of ten hours per week, in accordance with the amended rules of the court of appeals. After submitting a detailed tentative four-year curriculum, Wilkinson satisfied Horner that the proposed change merely involved "a revision and adaptation of the law school's current program." The New York State Education Department quickly approved and registered Fordham's proposed four-year evening program. Wilkinson reorganized the night school curriculum to require students to take eight hours of classes per week for the first two years and ten hours of classes per week for the last two years, for "a total of thirty-six year hours in all, the exact equivalent of the work now required of . . . the day students in their three-year curriculum of twelve hours weekly."[20]

Extending the night school curriculum to four years in September 1934 produced a decline in Fordham Law School's part-time enrollments of 24 percent during the first year of the four-year program. The decline was significantly greater at the Bronx campus than at the Woolworth Building. Part-time enrollments during the 1934–35 academic year declined at the Bronx campus by 48 percent and in the Manhattan division by 11 percent. There was a drop of 3 percent in the day school enrollments as well, leading Wilkinson to surmise that there would have been a drop-off in the night school enrollments even without the change to the four-year curriculum. The declines in night school enrollments were partially recouped in the 1935–36 academic year, when night school enrollments at both campuses increased by 7 percent.[21]

Wilkinson was quite accepting of the reduced size of the student body, which he thought was the inevitable "net effect of the higher standards" and economic conditions. He also believed that the smaller student body was offset by gains in the scholarship of Fordham's students and the "capacity of our graduates, as well as in the reputation which the School has achieved and continues to enjoy in the community." The improvement in the Law School's standards would further enhance its reputation and attractiveness to "the right type" of law student in the future. The loss of revenue the Law School sustained would be made up "in large measure" by a tuition increase Father Hogan authorized for the 1936–37 academic year.[22]

Law School enrollments suggest that Wilkinson was correct in thinking that declining enrollments were due to economic and social conditions as well as the four-year evening program and its relatively high academic standards. The Law School's total enrollments had declined from 1,200 in 1930–31 to 1,077 the following year, and they remained between 1,000 and 1,100 through 1934–35, the year Fordham instituted the four-year night school program. In the following academic year enrollments dropped below 1,000 for the first time since 1920, to 897, and in 1936–37, the year Fordham raised tuition from $220 to $240, enrollments dropped again to 785. Wilkinson attributed the 1936 enrollment decline to the tuition increase and to "better business conditions generally which permitted prospective law students in some instances to pursue their law studies out of the city instead of in the city as had been necessary through the period of the depression." Enrollments rebounded somewhat to between 800 and 900 through the 1940–41 school year, but they did not return to pre-Depression levels until the late 1960s. The smaller student body was by design, which will be explained momentarily.[23]

The new president of Fordham University, Father Robert I. Gannon, S.J., praised Dean Wilkinson and the Law School faculty in 1936 for limiting the number of students "in the interest of maintaining higher standards," a policy which "represented his own ideas in the matter." Father Gannon endorsed the Law School's objective of achieving quality rather than quantity. This emphasis on educational excellence fit Father Gannon's character. Dean William Hughes Mulligan later described Father Gannon as "the Jesuit par excellence," a man of "great style, great poise," a "man of letters, a man of wit, a man of wisdom" and "an imposing appearance." Yet, he was also "genteel, very caring. He was also a Republican," Dean Mulligan commented. Interestingly, Mulligan also characterized Wilkinson as a man of Father Gannon's "caliber." "Wilkinson was equally imposing."[24]

Wilkinson predicted in 1936 that declining enrollments in law schools and other professional schools would continue over the next ten years. He based his prediction on demographic patterns that showed declining populations in New York City. Elementary school enrollments were falling off for a number of reasons. These included "a shift of population to other boroughs," immigration restriction, and "the general decline in the birthrate." Wilkinson anticipated lower enrollments in high schools, colleges, and "ultimately in the professional schools." If and when this time of lower enrollments arrived, Wilkinson surmised, "the wisdom of having been in the forefront of the movement for reasonably higher standards in legal education will become apparent." He predicted that "the law schools that will survive, without doubt, will be those schools which are recognized as the best schools," and these "must be the ones which through the imposition of proper standards of matriculation, study, and scholarship have graduated students who, being well trained men of character must achieve positions of influence and importance at the bar."[25]

The New York Court of Appeals mandated the four-year night school program for all law schools in the state in the summer of 1937, and Wilkinson again played a leading role in this decision. Because the Court of Appeals' four-year rule was permissive rather than mandatory, three of New York City's six law schools—Brooklyn, New York, and St. John's law schools—continued to operate their late afternoon and evening classes on a three-year basis. They adopted the four-year part-time curriculum in the spring of 1937 and put it into effect the following fall. Their decision to do so resulted from roundtable conferences of the Committee of Law School Deans of the Joint Conference on Legal Education of the State of New York. The Joint Conference was organized in 1932 and consisted of representatives of the state's ten law schools, bar associations, bar conferences, and members of character committees. Dean Wilkinson praised it for its contributions to improved standards in legal education. As a member of the Joint Conference's Committee of Law School Deans, Wilkinson succeeded in getting unanimous approval of the deans of the law schools in New York State of a resolution mandating the four-year night school. He then helped persuade the State of New York Education Department to require all law schools in the state to extend their part-time or evening curricula to four years effective September 1937. The Department made this decision after securing the agreement of the deans of Brooklyn, New York, and St. John's law schools to conform their evening programs to the four-year curriculum. This eliminated St. John's Law School's opposition to the four-year requirement. With St. Johns having withdrawn its earlier opposition, Dean Wilkinson saw "no reason why the Court should not take the action desired." He drafted an amendment to the New York Court of Appeals rules which mandated the four-year night school for all law schools operating in the state. He submitted the proposal to the court in the spring of 1937. The court, "with the consent of all of the law schools of the State," made the four-year curriculum mandatory for part-time students in the summer of 1937. As a result, "no sub-standard evening school" was permitted to open or operate in New York after 1937.[26]

The combined effect of the four-year night school requirement and higher academic standards tended to support Wilkinson's assessment that law schools with higher academic standards would lose fewer students than law schools with lower academic standards. He estimated that the increase in academic standards in New York State during the 1930s had "reduced [law student enrollments] in exact proportion to the increase in standards." In New York City, the law student population in 1928–29 was 10,800, and it declined by one-half in the 1937–38 academic year to 5,199. He noted that enrollments had declined by some 25 percent in the two years from 1936 to 1938, and, since the consensus of opinion was "that business conditions [had] been improving ever since 1932, this decline" could not be attributed to economic causes. Some 54 percent of the 10,800 New York City law students in the 1928–29 school year were enrolled in the two Brooklyn law schools. They sustained the most drastic losses in the 50 percent decline in the student population since that time, and Wilkinson suggested that their enrollments would decline further because of the higher academic standards they had adopted.[27]

And they did. In his dean's report for 1940, Wilkinson noted that "the three formerly sub-standard schools in this city" continued to experience "a marked drop" in enrollments "due to the continuing effect of the increase in the standards." Brooklyn, St. John's, and New York law schools became "standard" law schools when they adopted the four-year part-time curriculum in September 1937. They also raised their tuition to Fordham's level, which also contributed to a significant loss of students in these schools and a modest gain in enrollments at Columbia, Fordham, and New York University. Table 4-4 shows enrollments in New York City law schools. The figures demonstrate that Columbia and Fordham Law Schools experienced slight declines in enrollments in the last four years of the 1930s. The three "sub-standard" law schools lost more than half of their previous enrollments when they increased their standards in September 1937 to comply with the four-year night school curriculum mandated by the New York Court of Appeals. Wilkinson attributed almost all of their loss of students to the four-year night school and tuition increases. He estimated that only about 10 percent was attributable to "the economic

TABLE 4-4. NEW YORK CITY LAW SCHOOLS' ENTERING CLASS ENROLLMENTS, 1936–37 TO 1939–40

Law School	1936–37	1937–38	1938–39	1939–40	Change
Columbia	197	212	181	195	−01%
Fordham	300	320	292	292	−02%
NYU	334	354	298	251	−24.8%
Total	**831**	**886**	**771**	**738**	**−11.1%**
NY	113	133	53	61	−46%
Brooklyn	412	185	185	165	−60%
St. John's	676	377	344	300	−55.7%
Total	**1,201**	**695**	**582**	**526**	**−56.2%**

Source: Dean's Report, April 3, 1940, 3, folder 8, box 11, FLS, FU.

and other conditions of the times through which we are passing." The only law schools that experienced a steady and substantial decline in enrollments were the four law schools which, according to Wilkinson, continued to accept every applicant with minimum qualifications.[28]

Wilkinson believed the fact that Fordham was able to maintain enrollments during this period when the other city law schools, except for Columbia, were experiencing substantial declines was "a vindication of our policy of applying strict standards of admission to the School as well as strict internal scholastic standards to the students in the School." Columbia, of course, also had "a strict selective entrance system." Not only did Fordham maintain enrollment levels, it also experienced an increase in the number of applications. Wilkinson reported 456 applications for the entering class of 1938 and 474 for the class of 1939. He also reported in 1940 that Fordham applied its selective admission standards "a little more strictly in the last two years." It "accepted" only 64 percent and about 62 percent of the applications it received for the 1938–39 and 1939–40 school years, respectively. Fordham capped its enrollments in order to comply with ABA certification and AALS membership regulations. Nonetheless, the increased number of applications to Fordham evidently enabled the Law School to maintain its desired registration numbers and higher admissions standards.[29]

The more stringent admissions standards also helped Fordham to maintain enrollment levels after students were admitted. Wilkinson claimed that the school's selectiveness reduced first- and second-year failures. Table 4-5 supports his claim, showing that the failure rate of first-year students for most of the first half of the 1930s fluctuated between 13 percent and 17 percent. In the 1930–31 entering class, the last year college graduates were admitted without presenting a college transcript, the failure rate in the first year class was 22 percent. In 1931–32, the first year Wilkinson began applying the same selective admission process to college graduates as he had been applying to noncollege graduates, the first-year failure rate declined to about 17 percent, and it leveled off between 13 percent and 15 percent until Fordham adopted the four-year night school program in 1934. After "further tightening" of the admission process "over the intervening years," he boasted, the failure rate of the first-year class of 1938 dropped to about 10 percent or 11 percent.[30]

TABLE 4-5. FIRST YEAR DROP-OUT RATES

Year	Drop in Enrollment (%)	Dropped (%)*	Flunked (%)**	Total Left (%)***
1930–31	420, 141 (33.6%)	64 (15.2%)	77 (22%)	279 (66.4%)
1931–32	464, 120 (25.9%)	48 (10.3%)	72 (17.3%)	344 (74.1%)
1932–33	475, 99 (20.8%)	44 (9.3%)	55 (12.8%)	376 (79.2%)
1933–34	425, 107 (25.2%)	52 (12.2%)	55 (14.7%)	318 (74.8%)
1934–35	358, 93 (26.0%)	48 (13.4%)	45 (14.5%)	265 (74.0%)

Source: For 1930–32 entering classes, Dean's Report, May 15, 1934, 2–3, folder 5, box 11, FLS, FU; for 1933 and 1934 entering classes, Dean's Report, February 17, 1936, 2–3, folder 6, box 11, FLS, FU.

* Based on the original enrollment.

** Based on the original enrollment minus the number of "dropped" students.

*** Based on the original enrollment.

Drop-out rates of third-year students also continued to decline. The failure rate of third-year students in 1932–33 was 4 percent. It steadily dropped in 1933 to 2 percent; in 1934 and 1935 to 1 percent; and in 1936 it fell to 0 percent. Wilkinson concluded that, although the entering classes may have become smaller because of Fordham's "strict entrance standards," student retention was greater and that the overall number of students was not diminished as much as it appeared. Moreover, what the school lost in the smaller size of entering classes was "more than offset in the better scholastic results achieved with the selected student body."[31]

In April 1934 Wilkinson took up the issue of getting Fordham Law School placed on the ABA's list of approved law schools with John Kirkland Clark, president of the New York Board of Law Examiners and chairman of the ABA's Council on Legal Education. They had several conferences in which they discussed the matter with Mr. Will Shafroth, an advisor to the ABA on issues relating to legal education. Clark arranged for Shafroth to spend four days at the Law School in April 1934 to perform the required inspection for ABA approval.[32]

The Jesuits were an important catalyst in Fordham Law School becoming an ABA-accredited law school and a member in the AALS. In 1934, the Father General of the Jesuits established the National Jesuit Educational Association and created the office of Commissarius for Education which was held by the personal representative of the Father General. The Commissarius visited Fordham University and issued a report in February 1935 that stressed the importance of the Law School getting accredited by the ABA and becoming a member of the AALS. The three-year part-time curriculum was a big obstacle to ABA accreditation and membership in the AALS. Having achieved the four-year night curriculum, Wilkinson turned his attention to meeting the other standards required for ABA approval and AALS membership, and he had Fordham University's full support.[33]

Apart from the four-year night program, the ABA also had requirements relating to full-time teachers and the size and development of the law library, and it began to inquire about law school finances at the end of the 1920s. The Law School's finances posed a problem, but the ABA avoided it at this time. The "chief problem" standing in the way of Fordham's ABA accreditation became the full-time faculty requirement, although the law library at the Bronx campus also posed some difficulty, which the university resolved by closing the Bronx night school in 1938.[34]

Although most law professors in the early twentieth century taught on a part-time basis and pursued active law practices, the ABA and AALS began to require accredited and member law schools to employ full-time faculty shortly after World War I. In 1924 the AALS adopted a standard, against considerable opposition, that required at least one full-time instructor for every one hundred students. By 1930 the ABA brought its full-time faculty regulations for approved law schools into line with that of the AALS, requiring one full-time teacher for every one hundred law students. These professional standards undoubtedly contributed to the growing proportions of full-time faculties at law schools approved by the AALS and ABA. Even so, the Carnegie Foundation reported in 1928 that "it is now pretty generally conceded that the ideal faculty is one that includes both professional law teachers and practising lawyers. Each of these elements tends to be strong where the other is weak." With this perspective, it is not surprising to find that part-time teachers continued to represent significant portions of law school faculties to the late twentieth century. They constituted 33 percent of law faculties in 1930, and 39 percent over a half century later in 1984.[35]

What distinguished full-time from part-time faculty in the 1920s and 1930s was not the number of hours taught but whether the individual "devote[d] substantially all of his time to his teaching work." Neverthe-less, in the middle of the 1920s, the average teaching load of law teachers in most American law schools was less than eight hours per year, and in only fourteen law schools did teachers average ten or more hours per year. The "theory of requiring full-time teachers," Wilkinson informed Fordham's president, the Very Reverend Aloysius J. Hogan, S.J., in his Dean's Report of 1934, "is that the teacher devoting substantially all of his time to teaching duties will be better prepared than the practitioner, who has only a casual interest in his teaching work, while at the same time he will be available for consultation with the students and thus be able to exercise a direct and beneficent influence upon them." This principle had been written into the New York Regents' rules governing the registration of new law schools in New York State. The state's education department adopted a rule in 1929 that required registered law schools to employ at least three full-time professors, but the rule applied to new law schools and was not made retroactive to previously registered schools. If it were, Wilkinson thought Fordham could count as "full time men" the Fordham Law teachers who taught eight year hours.[36]

In 1929 Wilkinson assessed how complying with the ABA and AALS requirement of one full-time teacher for every one hundred students would affect Fordham Law School. He estimated that this rule would require Fordham to hire about ten full-time law professors with a maxi-mum teaching load of ten year hours at a salary of between $8,000 and $10,000 for the academic year. These salaries were considerably higher than the course hour rates at which Fordham faculty were paid. On these figures, the highest paid full professor would have received a maximum of $6,000 for ten year hours of teaching and the lowest paid lecturer only $3,000, amounts considerably below the estimated $8,000 to $10,000 full-time faculty would have commanded. Moreover, the typical Fordham Law teacher taught less than ten hours a year. Wilkinson correctly concluded that full-time faculty "would add considerably to the teaching expense" of the Law School. Nonetheless, he advised Fordham President Father Duane, S.J., in 1929 that good policy dictated "the establishment of some full time professorships."[37]

How many full-time positions Fordham should create was the ques-tion. Given Fordham's enrollment of 1,320 students in 1929–30, Wilkinson estimated that he would have had to create at least ten full-time positions and require the occupants to devote all of their time to the Law School in order to comply with the requirement of one full-time teacher for every one hundred students. He believed that Fordham could get away with only six full-time positions if he could convince the ABA that a full-time faculty member who taught in the morning and afternoon divisions could be counted as full-time in both. He thought he might be able to persuade some of the current faculty to consider "devoting themselves entirely to their law school work." This would entail establishing a separate office for each full-time faculty member, an ABA requirement, which Wilkinson thought could be done.[38]

Father Duane consented to building a full-time law faculty, but he proposed the full-time faculty as an alternative to beginning a Law School endowment which Dean Wilkinson had requested in 1929 and 1930. With Father Duane's consent, Wilkinson appointed two full-time teachers in the summer of 1930. Wilkinson persuaded two of the current part-time faculty to accept the full-time appointments, Professor Walter B. Kennedy and Associate Professor George W. Bacon. Wilkinson made these appointments not only to satisfy ABA and AALS standards, but also for pedagogical reasons. He agreed with the association's rationale for their full-time law professor standard, which was that teachers who spent all of their time at the Law School afforded greater accessibility to students who wished to consult with them. At Fordham, full-time faculty also made possible "a voluntary system of law clubs," which acquainted students with the art of law practice as distinguished from the "science of the law," and a "voluntary course" in the use of the law library and legal research. Professor Bacon was in charge of the law clubs, and Professor Kennedy taught the course in legal research. Wilkinson reported that Professor Kennedy had interested "a considerable portion" of the students in this work, the objective of which was to teach students the methods of finding answers to legal problems and the resources available for this purpose. The law school offered these activities to all students on an optional basis, but day students understandably took advantage of them more than evening students. Wilkinson did not require library work and research "because of the burden it would impose on men in the evening divisions."[39]

Wilkinson persuaded John Kirkland Clark and Will Shafroth that Fordham should not be required to employ one full-time law teacher for every one hundred students. For a school the size of Fordham, this rule would require ten full-time instructors, a number that Wilkinson asserted was "entirely unnecessary to achieve the purpose for which the standard and principle were intended." Nine of the Law School's part-time teachers who practiced "to a greater or less extent" taught "from seven to ten hours weekly." Undoubtedly, they were "genuinely interested in their teaching." They devoted so much of their workday to teaching that they had "to build" their activities as practitioners "around the work of the school." In addition, four members of Fordham's faculty were "full-time instructors in the strict sense of the word, all of whom are provided with adequate office facilities in the law school quarters." Needless to say, they were completely devoted to the Law School and its students. The four full-time faculty members were Walter B. Kennedy and George W. Bacon, appointed in the summer of 1930, and Eugene J. Keefe and Thomas L. J. Corcoran, appointed in September 1934. Moreover, it was not unusual for part-time faculty to use their law offices for student conferences. Indeed, Wilkinson "frequently" sent students to their law offices to discuss school matters. These part-time faculty exerted "a genuine influence on the entire student body," Wilkinson insisted, and he was confident that Mr. Shafroth, who had visited many of their classes, would agree that they were "capable teachers" and that Shafroth would so assure Clark. In addition, Wilkinson argued that it would be "anomalous" to require full-time teachers for night students. He pictured a scene in which the full-time teacher would be in his office all day waiting to consult with night students who would not arrive at the Law School until the evening hours because they were gainfully employed all day.[40]

It simply was not practical to secure a full-time faculty in a city like New York which offered so many opportunities to capable lawyers for remunerative law practices. To satisfy the standard of one full-time teacher for every one hundred students, the Law School would have to dismiss some of its "most experienced and dependable" faculty, because they "could not be induced" to accept full-time employment at the salary Fordham University could afford to pay. It was difficult to attract full-time law teachers at salaries that "would be proper or possible for a university to pay" who were willing "to forego absolutely the emoluments of private practice" and were also "equal in teaching skill" as the Fordham part-time faculty who had been teaching at Fordham "from eight to twenty-two years." If the primary purpose of a law school was "to train men for the practice of law," then practitioner-teachers strengthened the faculty and made a contribution "of great value" to the education of law students, one "which could not be had in the same way or to the same extent in a faculty composed exclusively of full-time men."[41]

Fordham expected to add a fifth full-time teacher in the 1934–35 academic year and one or two more in the 1935–36 academic year, Wilkinson informed Clark. That would raise the number of full-time faculty to six or seven by 1936, a number "entirely adequate for the needs of the school," in Wilkinson's opinion. To add any more would not serve any useful purpose. To the contrary, it would "necessarily . . . result in the disintegration of a teaching faculty of genuine skill and years of service in the school," Wilkinson concluded. Clark agreed with many of Wilkinson's arguments, and he asked the dean to put his views in a letter and to send it to him, which he did.[42]

At Clark and Shafroth's invitation, Wilkinson attended a meeting of the ABA's Council on Legal Education held on May 9, 1934, and presented his arguments to this body. Mr. Shafroth, spoke in support of Fordham, and "stated frankly" that he had not found a part-time faculty at any other law school that taught "the substantial number of hours per week" as did "most of [Fordham's] professors and associates." Wilkinson reported to Father Hogan that "a number" of the members of the council were "distinctly favorable" to Fordham's position and conceded that the Fordham Law School was "*sui generis.*"[43]

Nevertheless, the council decided not "to recede from the strict interpretation" of its standard and its application to Fordham Law School. Based on the Law School's enrollment of 850 to 950 students, Fordham would be required to have nine full-time teachers to satisfy the council's standard of one full-time teacher for every one hundred students. Moreover, to be considered full-time, law school teachers had to give "their entire time to the school." The council had "always interpreted this as excluding anyone who practiced on the outside in any degree or had an outside office connection." On this interpretation, Shafroth bluntly informed Wilkinson that he "would not be classed as a full-time teacher." Indeed, when he inspected the Law School in the spring of 1934, Shafroth found only two faculty "who could indisputably be classed as full-time," Professors Kennedy and Bacon. Fordham would have to hire another seven full-time faculty members to satisfy "a strict interpretation" of the ABA's standard on full-time faculty.[44]

However, interchanges with the ABA's representatives led Wilkinson to believe that the issue of full-time faculty was negotiable. Shafroth thought that, in view of Fordham's "situation and the attitude which the Council has displayed in the past toward your school," it was his "personal opinion" that the council would be willing to regard Wilkinson as a full-time teacher, and it might even include Father Pyne within this classification, though he could not give Wilkinson "any official assurance of this." Even so, Shafroth reported that the Law School did not provide enough offices for full-time faculty, finding only four offices, including Wilkinson's and Father Pyne's, were available to full-time faculty. The council would insist that each full-time teacher have a separate office. Shafroth was confident that Wilkinson could find the necessary office space, on an adjoining floor of the Woolworth Building if necessary.[45]

Wilkinson won a unique and remarkable concession from the ABA regarding full-time faculty. He persuaded the council to count Reverend John X. Pyne, S.J., as one of the Law School's full-time teachers. Father Pyne was the Law School's regent and professor of jurisprudence, and he devoted all of his time to the Law School, as the council required. Wilkinson insisted that Father Pyne was a full-time member of the faculty, explaining that Father Pyne taught Jurisprudence in all four sessions of the Law School, for which his long training in philosophy made him "particularly well qualified to present this course." He was also the spiritual adviser of the Catholic students, who constituted a majority of the student body, and in this capacity he unquestionably exerted "an influence on the students with the fair intent of the Association's rule." The problem with Father Pyne from the ABA's perspective is that he was not a lawyer, and he did not hold a law degree. At first the council resisted "under a strict interpretation of our rules." The ABA had "never in the past classed the Regent of a Jesuit school as a full-time teacher," Shafroth explained. If the council agreed to count Father Pyne as a full-time member of the faculty, Wilkinson bargained, Wilkinson would comply with the council's requirement of no substantial outside employment in order to secure his status as a full-time professor, "as the University will be willing to arrange that I sever my office association beginning with the year 1936–1937." The council relented and "finally determined" to count Father Pyne as a full-time member of the law school faculty at its December 29, 1935, meeting in New Orleans. Wilkinson proudly informed University President Father Gannon that "this is the first time that a Jesuit Regent has been accepted by the Council as a member of the [full-time] faculty . . . and represents a distinct victory as it seems to me for our position in this regard."[46]

Fordham's victory was much greater than satisfying the ABA's numerical standard for full-time faculty. The ABA's acceptance of Father Pyne, a Jesuit who was not a lawyer, and his course in Jurisprudence was tantamount to the ABA's legitimization of the Jurisprudence course and everything Catholic in the Law School. Father Pyne's predecessor in the Jurisprudence course, Father Francis P. LeBuffe, S.J., published a digest of his lectures which Father Pyne used. Father LeBuffe's jurisprudence derived from Scholasticism, which attempted to reconcile the classical philosophy of thinkers such as Plato and Aristotle with the theology of medieval Christian theologians such as St. Augustine and St. Thomas Aquinas. Scholasticism, especially Thomistic Schlasticism, was the predominant philosophy of the Roman Catholic Church and its universities in twentieth-century America. Reflecting Thomistic philosophy, Fordham Law School's course in Jurisprudence, as described by Father LeBuffe, was "rooted in the doctrine of Natural Law and natural rights and consequently in an objective, real standard of justice." Father LeBuffe argued that American political theory evolved from Roman Catholic thought, noting that the Declaration of Independence and the United States Constitution "have as their foundation the doctrine of the Natural Law." This "doctrine" identified God as the ultimate source of individual rights, of civil obligation as well as the government's power to govern and compel obedience. Father LeBuffe relied on Catholic and religious sources to support his jurisprudence. However, he also based his lectures on a wide variety of secular authorities that included political philosophers and ethicists, legal thinkers and treatise writers, decisions of the US Supreme Court and state appellate courts, and other authorities that were not associated with the Catholic Church and could be found in nonsectarian books on jurisprudence. Nevertheless, Father LeBuffe's course reflected a distinctively Roman Catholic natural law philosophy of law.[47]

The 1938 and 1947 editions of Father LeBuffe's book on jurisprudence reflect the philosophical debate that arose in the 1920s, raged in the 1930s, and peaked in the early 1940s between legal scholars who grounded their views of law on natural law philosophy and the legal realists, whose views of law were based on scientific naturalism, philosophical pragmatism, and positivism. Referring to the rise of totalitarian states in Germany, Italy, and the Soviet Union, Father LeBuffe declared that "man as man, with God-given, natural, pre-State rights, is, we are told, an exploded myth. . . . Against this totalitarian, absolutist philosophy of law this present book stands in flat contradiction." Father LeBuffe later made clear that his book was directed not only against totalitarian states, but also against "the total-itarian philosophy of Justice Holmes and his followers," that is, against the legal realists.[48]

Although there were many strands of legal realism, the realists shared the assumption of scientific naturalism that knowledge is discoverable only through "empirical, particular, and experimentally verifiable" scien-tific investigation. Believing "that truth was wholly dependent upon empirically established facts," many, but not all legal realist scholars rejected the possibility of proving the truth of ethical propositions and the validity of moral values through either deductive or inductive reasoning. These scholars consequently denied the fundamental assumptions of nat-ural law philosophy, "that human reason could discover certain immuta-ble metaphysical principles that explained the true nature of reality," and, as applied to law, that "human reason could discover certain universal principles of justice by philosophical analysis of the nature of reality." Consequently, these realists rejected the assumption of proponents of nat-ural law philosophy that immutable principles governed the universe.[49]

Rejecting the existence of immutable principles, legal realism stood as a direct contradiction to classical legal formalism, which assumed that judges decided cases through a process of impartial deductive reasoning from *a priori* principles. The realists argued to the contrary that judges decided cases according to their own personal values. In rejecting "ratio-nal justifications of ethical ideals, such as a 'higher law,'" critics claimed that the legal realists undermined the moral foundation of democratic theory. They also rejected "three cardinal principles of democratic govern-ment: the possibility of a government of laws rather than of men, the rationality of human behavior, and the practical possibility of popular government itself."[50]

By the late 1930s the critics of legal realism were alarmed at the moral relativism that flowed from the realists' rejection of objective, absolute principles of law and morality as the foundation of legal doctrine. Critics characterized scientific naturalism and legal realism as a form of skepticism, nihilism, and moral relativism that were undermining American democracy and were largely responsible for the spread of totalitarianism.[51]

Professor Edward Purcell reports that the "most severe and extreme attacks on legal realism and all forms of philosophical naturalism" in the 1930s were made by Catholic Thomists who thereby revivified neoscholastic philosophy and jurisprudence. Fordham Law School Professor Walter B. Kennedy, who was "perhaps the most widely respected Catholic legal scholar in the country," played a leading role in the Catholic opposition. Although he recognized that legal realism made some contributions to jurisprudence, beginning in the 1920s, Kennedy attempted to demonstrate the "imprecision and vagueness in both conception and analysis" of legal realism as well as the "naïve and uncritical acceptance to a number of dubious social science concepts" by legal realist scholars.[52]

In his *Fordham Law Review* article, "A Review of Legal Realism," Kennedy set out to show "four fundamental failures of Realism":

> Lack of consistent application of the scientific approach in its criticism of traditional law
>
> Overemphasis upon fact-finding and consequent submersion of principles and rules
>
> Absence of skepticism regarding the hypothetical theories of the social sciences
>
> The creation of a new form of word magic and verbal gymnastics

Kennedy claimed that legal realism was not really scientific. He contrasted the legal realists' skepticism of classical law with their "amazing faith in unscientific and experimental hypotheses." Although Kennedy acknowledged the value of extra-legal data in the legal process, he was critical of the unscientific *method* by which the legal realists acquired these data and their lack of skill and proficiency in using the data to improve legal rules and principles. He argued that they "conglomerate" "so-called scientific data, statistics and theories," often untested and unverified, from secondhand social science sources, and they welded them into loose generalizations which they called science. Kennedy concluded that "Realism, which worships at the altar of Scientism, has departed from the basic, essential practices of true scientific research."[53]

Dean Wilkinson also rejected legal realism and the New Deal which largely reflected the legal realists' assumptions about law. The dean's opposition to the New Deal likely predisposed him to oppose President Franklin Roosevelt's "court packing" scheme. Wilkinson achieved national recognition for his opposition to the President's plan to pack the Supreme Court. His outspoken opposition rallied law professors and legal practitioners to protest the plan, and his testimony before the US Senate Judiciary Committee evidently influenced its decision to reject the president's court packing plan. His opposition to the plan, and to the New Deal in general, was predicated, among other reasons, on his Thomistic philosophy and natural law jurisprudence. Wilkinson was one of eleven law school deans to testify before the US Senate Judiciary Committee on the president's plan. He argued, as did Chief Justice Charles Evans Hughes, that, as a practical matter, the court did not need more justices to keep up with its caseload as the president claimed. He also argued that the proposed plan would undermine the independence of the Court and was therefore an unconstitutional violation of the separation of powers. Wilkinson was the first person to place on the record the constitutionality of the court packing scheme.[54]

Most interestingly, Wilkinson warned that the court packing plan could set a precedent that "may be used some time in the future to subvert the rights of the individual and the protection of minorities." He noted that if the Supreme Court could be pressured to "respond always to the prevalent sentiment of the moment," it would eventually "become wholly subservient to the pressure of public opinion." Under the legal realist claim that whatever the law is is right, this could lead to the majority tyrannizing a minority. While the constitutional provisions at issue in the court packing episode included the commerce clause, the due process clause, and the general welfare clause as they related to social and economic issues, Wilkinson warned that other clauses of the Constitution that protected "the liberties of the citizen and the rights of minorities," such as the Bill of Rights and the Fourteenth Amendment, might be at issue. Presaging the jurisprudence of the Warren Court, he argued that the Supreme Court stands "as the sole guardian of persons, often poor and insignificant in themselves, whose natural rights enunciated in the Declaration of Independence and guaranteed them by the Constitution, were in danger of being destroyed because of an objective which was thought to be desirable by a majority." Wilkinson cited cases involving the First Amendment freedoms of speech, press, and assembly, the Fifth Amendment guarantees against self-incrimination and to representation of counsel to make his point. However, the first cases he referred to as examples of the court protecting the constitutionally secured natural rights of Americans were *Meyer v. Nebraska* and *Pierce v. Society of Sisters*. These two cases interpreted the Fourteenth Amendment's due process clause as a guarantee of liberty that protected the natural right and duty of parents "to give [their] children education suitable to their station in life," which included the natural right of Catholic parents to educate their children in Catholic schools. In attacking the Supreme Court, the president was attacking the bastion of fundamental rights. Wilkinson was a Republican and a political conservative, but his opposition to the president's interference with the independence of the court and to the New Deal was not simply an expression of political partisanship. It also stemmed from his Thomistic conception of law which encompassed absolute principles of natural rights, which he understood were secured by the Supreme Court under the doctrine of substantive due process of law. He opposed the New Deal legislation because it was based on legal realist views of law which were undermining the idea of absolute natural rights.[55]

Accused of being un-American by many Protestant Americans throughout the nation's history, Catholic scholars seized upon the intellectual crisis of the 1930s "to identify their beliefs with the basic and traditional ideas of American Democracy." Father LeBuffe claimed in the 1938 edition of his *Jurisprudence* book that "its philosophy . . . is thoroughly American." He went so far as to claim that this traditional Catholic philosophy was the philosophy of "our Founding Fathers." Father LeBuffe explained that he changed the title of his book in 1947 from *Jurisprudence with Cases to Illustrate Principles* to *The American Philosophy of Law with Cases to Illustrate Principles*, accenting the article *The*, "in the interest of sound Americanism and as a direct challenge to Americans at this peculiarly critical period of American legal thinking on national and international levels." Acknowledging the existence of other philosophies of law in the United States at the time, LeBuffe claimed "they are not *of America*." They are alien products: alien "in their origin" and "in their content." Referring specifically to the legal philosophy of Justice Holmes and his followers, Father LeBuffe declared that this alien legal philosophy conflicted with the philosophy of law on which the United States was built. He presented his book as a "flat contradiction" to the Holmesian positivist, totalitarian philosophy of law "of which Hitlerism and Stalinism are the logical outcome."[56]

In the end, the Catholic Thomists and philosophical proponents of absolute principles of natural law and natural rights lost the intellectual debate to the scientific naturalists and ethical relativists. They lost the debate in the 1940s and 1950s for several reasons. American scholars generally accepted the epistemological assumption that the scientific method was "the most reliable method of developing human knowledge," and, therefore, they assumed that a society that "most closely approximated the scientific method in its governing process was the most rational and desirable form of government." Most American intellectuals also assumed that all truths, even ethical truths, were "tentative, changing, and uncertain," and only social theories that acknowledged the tentativeness of truth "could support and justify democratic government." They therefore came to believe that "philosophical relativism implied . . . an open and democratic political structure," such as the United States, and that "theoretical absolutism logically implied political totalitarianism." Most American intellectuals consequently undertsood the cold war as a struggle between the relativist United States and the absolutist Soviet Union. Reinhold Niebuhr, the foremost American theologian of the twentieth century, provided a theological justification for the "firm conviction in the indeterminateness of the universe and in the relativity of all human knowledge" and the dangers of absolutist philosophies. Conceding that absolute truth existed because God existed, Niebuhr explained that "God's transcendence placed that truth beyond human reach, and man's inescapable finitude meant that God's absolute truth . . . could never completely become man's truth." Niebuhr claimed that "absolute philosophies necessarily led to political authoritarianism." American intellectuals accepted this relativist-absolutist dichotomy and believed that "a relativist culture was the empirical basis for democracy," and they were convinced "that the United States represented such a relativist culture." Political theory thus combined with intellectual criticism of philosophical absolutism and the advances of experimental science to render the philosophy of natural law and absolute principles untenable to most educated Americans.[57]

Members of the Jesuit Educational Association were divided in their views regarding the place of Catholic philosophy and theology in Catholic legal education after World War II. A small group wanted to include Catholic philosophy and theology in all courses taught in Catholic law schools. The other group shared Wilkinson's view: whereas "Catholic thought and Catholic principles naturally permeate all courses" taught by faculty who "are Catholic both in faith and in culture, by and large we have to teach the law as it is." Wilkinson feared that "the extremists" failed to understand that "a law school, whether part of a Catholic university or not, has to prepare its students to pass the bar examinations and to practice law." This is daunting enough, "and if too much energy is diverted into other fields," he cautioned, both Catholic and non-Catholic students "who normally would come to our schools will simply take themselves elsewhere." Nevertheless, Wilkinson thought that in all Catholic law schools "the law is taught against a Catholic background." Law is in "the realm of Caesar mostly" and is therefore "in the field of moral indifference." Law must be taught "as we find it." That said, Wilkinson noted that Fordham Law faculty "taught the law against our background of Catholic philosophy," and he, in his courses in Equity and Evidence, "frequently" developed "in connection with the case materials the scholastic, philosophic view and even at times where desireable the Catholic moral viewpoint."[58]

The appointment of Father Charles M. Whalen, S.J., to the faculty in 1962 marked a departure from the traditional approach to jurisprudence taught at Fordham Law School. Like his immediate predecessor, Father S. Oley Cutler, S.J., Father Whalen was a lawyer, having earned his LLB and LLM from Georgetown Law Center, but he also had earned credit toward the SJD in constitutional law at Harvard Law School. At the time of his appointment to Fordham, Father Whalen was teaching constitutional law at Georgetown Law Center, and he was serving as a consultant on constitutional law issues in the Office of General Counsel of the United States Catholic Conference and as an associate editor of *America Magazine*. The Provincial told Father Whalen that he would keep these latter two jobs, but that he was being reassigned to teach at Fordham Law School because his predecessor had flunked half the first-year class.[59]

Although Father Whalen brought the grading scale for the Jurisprudence course back to normal, he did flunk one student for which Dean Mulligan was very grateful. As Father Whalen recalled, one of his students had flunked first year twice, and he was repeating the first-year courses for the third time. It turns out that he was the son of a very well-known mafioso. When Mulligan learned that Whalen had flunked him, he went to the new Jesuit and expressed his deepest and most heartfelt appreciation, stating that the student's father "would never harm a Catholic priest."[60]

Father Whalen departed from his predecessors in the way he taught jurisprudence. He had been told by some of his Jesuit friends that the Catholic nature of Fordham Law School was manifested in its faculty, most of whom were Roman Catholic, and in the Jurisprudence course. Father Whalen changed the content of the Jurisprudence course because of his training as a Jesuit, which taught him that Jesuit education was "strongly non-proselytizing." Although Jesuit colleges offered students the opportunities to study theology and practice their faith, they also tried to educate "extremely well" in his view. But, he felt that students at the Law School had already been to college; so he tried to teach the most important issues and debates in jurisprudence, using a variety of approaches.[61]

Father Whalen did not use Father LeBuffe's jurisprudence casebook in recognition of the diverse student body. He assigned various readings, such as Walter Lippman's book *The Public Philosophy*; Book 1 on the meaning of justice and Book 6 on the role of women in Plato's *Republic*; and Harvard Law Professor Lon Fuller's study of the case of the Speluncean Explorers. He distributed notes on different versions of natural law, cautioning students not to think that natural law meant only one thing, the Scholastic version of natural law. He also assigned readings that introduced students to other approaches to the law, including legal positivism. Father Whalen tried to get students to think about and to chose the approaches to legal analysis and the answers to fundamental questions of justice that made the most sense to them. No one interfered with his approach to jurisprudence.[62]

Father Whalen wore a Roman collar during the first two or three years of his teaching at Fordham. But, he began to sense from students' reactions that his collar was an impediment to his teaching and their learning. So, he stopped wearing it at the Law School and began to dress as a layman. It was important to him and his philosophy of legal education that students understand that he was not trying to sell any Catholic line in his teaching. He was simply trying to make students aware of the big questions in jurisprudence and, when he began teaching the subject at the end of the 1960s, constitutional law.[63]

The third obstacle to ABA approval in the 1930s was the question of the Fordham Law library. Wilkinson acknowledged that there were gaps in the collection that needed filling and, beginning in 1925, he proposed strategies for bringing it into compliance with ABA and AALS standards. Deficiencies were attributable in part to the way in which the Law School updated the library's collection. In 1925 Wilkinson reported that graduating classes of the previous several years gave annual gifts which enabled the Law School to expand the library's collection with necessary acquisitions without having to use Law School funds. However, these voluntary gifts were not sufficient to develop and maintain the library to "its full usefulness." Consequently, sound policy dictated that "a definite sum be appropriated annually" for necessary additions and replacements. A good working law library at the university for the uptown section was a distinct problem. Though "a good start already [had] been made" to build a law library in the Bronx, more attention would have to be given to it "for the next several years."[64]

Wilkinson boasted in 1929 that the library in the Woolworth Building consisted of 12,500 volumes and was in compliance with any possible requirements the ABA and the AALS could impose. In that year, the AALS required at least 7,500 volumes "adequately housed and accessible to students" and the expenditure to expand the library's holdings of $7,500 over any five-year period, but a minimum expenditure of $1,000 each year. Unsurprisingly, Wilkinson recommended to Fordham President Father Duane that good policy dictated that the Law School set aside a definite sum in the neighborhood of $1,500 each year to expand the collection. However, the law library at the Bronx campus was "considerably below the 7,500 volume minimum" required by accrediting agencies. Wilkinson thought it could be brought up to meet the minimum standard "without such a great expenditure as to render it impossible of achievement."[65]

By 1936 it was not the law library in the Woolworth Building but deficiencies in the Bronx campus law library, along with too few full-time faculty, that remained the chief obstacles to Fordham Law School gaining the approval of the ABA's Council on Legal Education. Whereas the library in the Woolworth Building was in compliance with ABA and AALS standards, the Bronx Law library fell far short. The collection numbered only about 2,500 volumes. However, Governor Malcolm Wilson recalled that the uptown campus did not have a library "at all" when he was a student in the Bronx night division from 1933 to 1936. The library, "such as it was, was down in the Woolworth Building, and unless someone had access to a law office, where he or she could look up the law, you had to find time, going to law school at night and working daytime, to find your way down to Fordham, to the Law Library in the Woolworth Building." Despite the governor's recollections, Shaforth informed Wilkinson in 1935 that the ABA's Council on Legal Education would allow Fordham to operate the Bronx campus Law School provided they increased the Law library's collection by 5,000 volumes to the minimum 7,500 volumes. These were maximum conditions that the council required for its approval, but "less may be demanded finally."[66]

The faculty at the Bronx campus posed another problem since they were essentially part-time teachers. But, in an era of practice-oriented legal education, having practitioners as teachers was considered to be a good thing. Governor Wilson recalled that the faculty "were excellent." In the "world of the practical," he explained, "it was extremely useful to have men teach us who were out practicing law." They were doing what the students were planning to do, which made for a greater "rapport between us and these men who were out in the world which we hoped to enter." Nevertheless, the ABA and AALS demanded that Fordham "station" one full-time teacher for every one hundred students at the Bronx campus.[67]

Shafroth advised Wilkinson in October 1935 what Fordham would have to do to meet the requirements relating to the "uptown school." If Fordham were to provide "a minimum library of 7,500 volumes at that school" in addition to an office and one full-time teacher there for every one-hundred students or major fraction thereof to provide "sufficient contact between those students and their faculty," the Bronx campus "will not be an obstacle to your approval." Even here, Shafroth again suggested that the council might accept some lesser proposal, and he invited Wilkinson to offer any alternative suggestions, assuring him that they would "receive the careful consideration of the Council." He conceded that "it may be true that no useful purpose would be served by keeping any faculty members at the uptown school during the day," since the Bronx division was a night school, but he asked Wilkinson to demonstrate its futility, stating that the council did "not want to make a useless requirement." Indeed, he assured the dean that "we are anxious to meet you half way in this matter, and are very gratified that you are desirous of meeting our requirements."[68]

In a critical negotiation in the fall of 1935, Wilkinson held to some of his positions but bargained with Shafroth and the council in offering what he characterized as his "counter proposals." Increasing the Bronx campus law library to 7,500 volumes was acceptable to Wilkinson and Fordham's president, although it required Fordham to add about 5,500 volumes. And, since the student body in the Bronx night school was less than 150 students, only 1 full-time teacher was necessary to satisfy the ABA standard of 1 full-time teacher for every 100 students. If the council insisted on a strict reading of the standard, he agreed to appoint a full-time faculty person for the Bronx campus, but he "strongly urge[d]" that there was "no real need" to have him sit in an office in the Bronx all day when students did not arrive on campus until shortly before the evening classes began at 6:30. Applying the full-time faculty standard to the Bronx evening students was anomalous, Wilkinson insisted, because "a full-time teacher detailed exclusively to the uptown school would sit alone all day with substantially no students with whom to consult." In addition, he would have to do most if not all of the teaching in this division, requiring him to teach three to four evenings each week, which Wilkinson regarded as "distinctly undesirable." The Law School's general policy was not to require or even to permit any faculty member, whether full- or part-time, to teach more than two evenings. If the council was to demand a full-time teacher for the Bronx division, Wilkinson would provide an office for him there and make him available for student consultations beginning at 6:00 P.M., one-half hour before classes convened, but only on evenings on which he was scheduled to teach there. At other times he would be available in his office in the Woolworth Building.[69]

In another concession, Wilkinson expressed his willingness to add two more full-time teachers beginning with the 1936–37 academic year. He noted that he had appointed two new full-time professors in September 1934. If the council counted Wilkinson and Father Pyne as full-time faculty, these appointments brought the total number of full-time faculty to eight. It would be unwise to add many more, Wilkinson cautioned, because a few more full-time teachers would require either materially reducing the teaching load of or eliminating "some of the most depend-able teachers we have, who have been members of our faculty for many years and who could not be interested in affiliating themselves with the school on an absolutely full-time basis." This would damage the "scholastic and faculty standards of the school," Wilkinson warned. He proposed that, if two additional full-time faculty would satisfy the council, assuming the student body did not exceed 850, "we are willing to provide them." To ensure that the student body did not exceed this number, Wilkinson informed Shafroth that the Law School had decided to limit the entering class of September 1936 to approximately 320 to 330 students, and continuing thereafter. With the normal attrition of students, this strategy would keep the student body within the 850 student limit. Limiting the entering class to this size would also make the Law School's selective admissions practices even more selective and yield "still better material with which to work."[70]

Shaforth informed Wilkinson that the council would consider Fordham's position at its meeting in New Orleans on December 29, 1935. He added that the test that should be applied to the uptown school was whether the students there received "every advantage which they would in any approved school." Wilkinson quickly replied that the Bronx division was not operated as a separate law school, but was part of "the whole Law School." The Bronx students were not isolated from the Manhattan campus. The four full-time faculty all taught courses in the Bronx along with other part-time faculty who taught at the Manhattan campus as well. Bronx students took their final examinations at the Manhattan campus, and their exams were the very same exams taken by the Manhattan students. Moreover, many of the Bronx students worked in Manhattan during the day and could see their full-time teachers in their offices in the Woolworth Building more readily than they could if these teachers had offices in the Bronx. Bronx students had full access to the law library in the Woolworth Building, but if the Bronx library were expanded to include the required 7,500 volumes, "there could be no question then" that the students in the Bronx division would have the same advantages as students in the other divisions of the Law School.[71]

Wilkinson was happy to report that his negotiations with the ABA's Council on Legal Education to secure its approval "were successfully terminated" in May 1936 when the council extended its provisional approval of Fordham Law School, effective in the fall of that year. The council customarily granted provisional approval and then final approval after a reinspection of the Law School within two years. Mr. Shafroth reinspected Fordham Law School in May 1937, and the council granted final approval in the same month. Approval required Fordham to add two more full-time faculty, bringing the total to eight, and to keep the total student body to no more than 850 students. The two additional full-timers were Joseph W. McGovern and William R. White. Wilkinson evidently had persuaded the council that the presence of a full-time professor on the Bronx campus during the day was unnecessary, because he informed Shafroth that the three full-time professors assigned to teach classes in the Bronx division had scheduled office hours from 6:00–6:30 P.M. and from 8:30–9:00 P.M., one-half hour before classes and one-half hour after classes. Unfortunately, no students came to see these professors before class and only "a scattering number," perhaps not more than one or two students per professor, came to see them after class during the spring 1936 semester. The council made a concession on the Bronx campus law library, requiring an increase to only 5,000 volumes.[72]

Having won the ABA's approval for the law school, Father Hogan directed Wilkinson to "open negotiations" with the AALS to gain membership in the association. Wilkinson feared that the full-time faculty standard would present a greater problem with the AALS than with the ABA. The difficulty was that the AALS was "dominated by teachers employed on the full-time basis and which in consequence can see but one side of the question." Interestingly, Wilkinson did not feel the need to have the AALS's approval and did not think that the Law School would be hurt by not having its approval.[73]

Wilkinson submitted Fordham Law School's application for AALS membership in the fall of 1936, less than one month after the ABA placed the Law School on its list of approved law schools. Herschel W. Arant, dean of the Ohio State University College of Law and the secretary-treasurer of the AALS, visited the Law School in December to perform the required inspection for the AALS. Like the adviser to the ABA's Council on Legal Education, Will Shafroth, Dean Arant "found [the Law School's] internal standards excellent and was particularly impressed with [its] selective entrance requirements." The main issues Arant raised were some of the same issues that had delayed the Law School's approval by the

ABA. The AALS accepted the resolutions of these issues Wilkinson had negotiated with the ABA, including accepting Father Pyne as a full-time professor even though he did not have a law degree.[74]

As Wilkinson had predicted, the most troubling issue was that the executive committee of the AALS found the Law School "barely [complied] now with the full-time teacher requirement." Nevertheless, the committee decided not to question the number of full-time teachers so long as Fordham capped its enrollment at 850. Dean Arant asked Dean Wilkinson to add one or two more full-time teachers as soon as possible even though the executive committee would not require the Law School to do so. He had gone out on the limb for Fordham, assuring the executive committee that the Law School would more than meet the AALS standards. Adding a couple of full-time teachers "would be comforting to me," Arant explained, "since I recommended the school for admission" and assured the executive committee of "a willingness on your part to comply generously with our requirements rather than stop with the smallest measure of satisfaction or requirement that will get by." Adding more full-time faculty would not only be "comforting" to Arant, it would also prevent any future AALS inspector who might be less sympathetic toward Fordham's membership in the AALS from denying that Arant's faith in Fordham "had been abundantly justified."[75]

Wilkinson assured Arant that Fordham intended fully to comply with the AALS's standard for full-time faculty. The Law School's current enrollment was between 750 and 760 students, and Fordham's "definite policy" was to limit its enrollment to 850. Wilkinson understood that, should the school's enrollment exceed this number, it would be necessary to add another full-time teacher. As they had discussed during Arant's inspection to the Law School, the problem of adding more full-time faculty was finding a place for them. Moreover, the addition of full-time faculty would require Fordham "to dismiss competent men who while technically perhaps part-time teachers actually devote substantial time to the work of the school, as they teach not less than six hours weekly and who have been members of our faculty for from eleven to twenty-four years." Yet, a resignation due to illness and a request for a reduced teaching load of another part-time faculty member enabled Wilkinson to hire the seventh full-time teacher in the fall of 1937, bringing the total full-time faculty up to nine.[76]

Gaining AALS membership was quicker and easier than Wilkinson had anticipated. Wilkinson filed the Law School's application for membership in November 1936. Dean Arant inspected the school on December 14, and the AALS admitted Fordham Law School to its membership two weeks later at its annual meeting on December 29, 1936. The Law School joined some eighty-three other members of the association. Fordham became the third New York City law school to claim membership in the AALS, Columbia and New York University law schools being the other two.[77]

Though the AALS admitted Fordham to membership, the association's executive committee "reserved decision" on the size of the Bronx campus law library until Fordham University decided the future of this division. Wilkinson had informed them that it was "not entirely certain" that Fordham would continue this division indefinitely. In the end, Fordham University decided to discontinue the uptown campus at the end of the 1937–38 academic year and to "transfer the whole uptown evening school downtown beginning in September, 1938." This eliminated the need for further consideration of the Bronx law library.[78]

Closing the Bronx night school in 1938 did not materially affect night school enrollments. The number of applications increased from 1937 to 1940, and the Law School's rejection rate also increased. The entering classes of night students continued to be a majority of the total first-year class in each year from 1936 to 1940. Wilkinson boasted that, despite declining enrollments in other New York law schools, Fordham Law School's selective admission policy and high academic standards had enabled it to maintain qualitatively high enrollments and to attract as many students of "good scholastic caliber" as it wished to accept. Although the Law School could have accepted more applications, Wilkinson consciously kept total enrollments below 850 students to remain in compliance with ABA and AALS standards.[79]

The Law School's finances posed an additional potential obstacle to ABA accreditation and membership in the AALS, but these associations did not press the issue. Nevertheless, the ABA's Council on Legal Education announced in July 1928 that it had decided "the time has arrived when there should be a thorough investigation of the financial structure and practices of the law schools of the country." The council sent a questionnaire that year to all law schools requesting financial information and, if the law school was affiliated with a university, the financial relationship between the law school and the university. Through its "pertinent inquiries," the council sought to determine whether the law school was "dependent on fees for support," was "supported out of general funds" or was "specially endowed." It also asked for the law school's total income and expenditures for the preceding two years, the amount of any surplus or deficit for this period, and how any deficits were met and surplus funds disposed.[80]

Wilkinson inferred from the council's questionnaire that "financial independence or dependence of an institution" is "an important element in the rating of a law school." The Carnegie Foundation had expressed the same idea in its report of 1928, from which he freely quoted in informing Fordham President Father Duane of this development. Although money alone did not make a good law school, the Carnegie report opined, an institution that was not tuition dependent "obviously" had "a tremendous advantage." One of these advantages is that such law schools could determine the size of their student bodies, the amount of prelegal academic requirements and subsequent legal training to serve their conception of public service. The Carnegie Foundation was clearly calling for law schools to become financially independent.[81]

Wilkinson predicted in 1929 that the next requirement the AALS would impose on member law schools is that they have "some independent financial resources." He thought this demand would cause bar associations and state regulatory bodies also to adopt this requirement some time in the future. Although he did not think this action would occur in the short run, he advised Father Duane that they begin to prepare for it.[82]

Wilkinson recommended that Fordham University establish an endowment fund for the Law School out of the Law School's surplus revenues, which he estimated could make the Law School financially independent of tuition within a relatively short period of time. He thought an endowment would be easy to establish because "for some years past the school has been returning a substantial profit in its operations." Sound policy dictated that the university credit the Law School's profit to the Law School, and, "after deduction of the school's pro-rata share in general University overhead," to put the profit in a conservative investment and to use the interest thus generated to finance the Law School's operation. Wilkinson also suggested that, where the Law School's profits had been used by the university to finance other departments, those departments should be charged interest and amortization "as a running expense," and the university should credit these amounts to the Law School account as if these funds had been borrowed from a third party. Wilkinson estimated that, if the Law School's past profits were added to its future earnings, and if these funds were set aside and invested as a Law School reserve, at present levels of law student enrollments "a sufficient principal sum should be accumulated to make the school a financially independent unit for all time thereafter," and only "in a relatively few years."[83]

Recognizing the interconnection between a law school's financial resources and its quality as an academic institution, Wilkinson affirmed the importance of an endowment to the quality of the Fordham Law School. He predicted that, if his financial plan were adopted, "the future development of the school scholastically will follow logically and naturally therefrom." He elaborated the reasons he thought so, explaining that all of the signposts of an elite law school, such as a graduate school and "research work in the law," in addition to future requirements imposed by professional associations, would "require an adequate reserve of capital behind the school." He proposed the institution of an annual budget for the Law School which set out authorized expenditures for the forthcoming fiscal year. The financial plan Wilkinson outlined was dependent upon the action of the university's Board of Trustees.[84]

If the university were to agree to reorganize the Law School's finances along the lines Wilkinson proposed, "the next logical step" would be to institute a graduate program in law. He had proposed a graduate school shortly after he became dean, but this decision was wisely postponed because "it was impossible accurately to forecast" the effect on "the size and type of student body" stemming from the "changing entrance standards" of the period and the newly established night school on the Bronx campus. Barring the imposition of additional "onerous standards" by accrediting agencies, Wilkinson thought Fordham "should be in a position in the course of the next several years to institute graduate instruction, if your trustees deem such a course advisable."[85]

Wilkinson renewed his request to establish a Law School endowment in 1930, informing Father Duane that the ABA had begun to admonish universities not to use law schools as cash cows and to rate law schools, in part, on the basis of their finances. The ABA had recently elevated NYU Law School to a "Class A" law school, and NYU Law School Dean Henry

Sommer "intimated" to Wilkinson that NYU's elevation "was bound up with the question of devoting a substantial part of the law school revenues entirely to law school betterment." Furthermore, William Draper Lewis, retiring chairman of the ABA Section on Legal Education, in a speech delivered at the Section's 1929 Memphis meeting, admonished section members against using law schools as cash cows, either for themselves or for the universities with which they were associated. Acknowledging that the desire to make money was a natural human desire and not in itself immoral, Lewis nonetheless declared that "it is not practicable for schools designed to prepare for the important public profession of the law to be conducted for the pecuniary profit of the management, irrespective whether that management operates the school primarily for their personal benefit, or to gain funds to be expended on other departments of the institution of which the law school is nominally a part." Lewis warned that, "Once this condition exists, the controlling motive in every decision in respect to the school is not the best interests of the law student." Wilkinson advised Father Duane that the ABA and AALS were demanding that law schools secure independent financial resources or at least use all of their revenue to develop their programs and not to use any of their revenues for other departments of the university. Dean Sommer's experience suggested that the ABA was now insisting upon the latter requirement before confering a Class A rating on a law school. Wilkinson therefore renewed his request for an endowment fund for Fordham Law School, which he thought could be created by crediting the Law School for its past profits plus interest and by investing future earnings as a separate fund for the Law School.[86]

The Fordham University administration suggested using some of the Law School's surplus money to establish several full-time professorships as one way to begin moving toward a Law School endowment. It would also represent a start in acquiring and building a full-time faculty and reorganizing the Law School's financial structure in a way that would enable the Law School to get the Class A rating of the ABA, if and when it decided to seek it.[87]

By 1934 the ABA had made two unsuccessful attempts to get information relating to law schools' finances, and it was making its third try. In his 1934 Dean's Report, Wilkinson informed Father Aloysius J. Hogan, S.J., who had replaced Father Duane as Fordham University President in

1930, he had recently received an ABA questionnaire sent by the chairman of the Committee on Legal Education of the New York County Lawyers Association. Among other things this questionnaire asked for the income and expenditures of the Law School for the 1932–33 and 1933–34 academic years. It also asked what disposition was made of any surplus and how any deficit was met. It appeared that Father Hogan had decided in 1934 to credit the Law School's account for its surplus earnings which had been paid into the university's general funds over the years. But Fordham University did not return the Law School's surplus earnings; it continued to pay them into the university's general funds. Fordham University had decided to continue to use the Law School to subsidize its other divisions and general operations. Although the ABA did not press this issue in the 1930s, the question of how much of the Law School's revenue Fordham University used to finance other departments became a hotly contested issue with the ABA in the 1970s and 1980s.[88]

The bar examination became an effective obstacle to entering the practice of law. When they were introduced in the late nineteenth century, bar exams in most states consisted of a short, perfunctory oral interview with a local judge. States gradually changed the bar examination into an effective barrier to entry when they created central examining boards to replace judges and substituted lengthy written examinations for the *pro forma* oral interview. By World War I, thirty-seven of forty-nine jurisdictions had central boards of bar examiners, and, although evidence relating to the difficulty of bar exams is lacking, bar passage rates declined over the first three decades of the twentieth century, precipitously in some states. Bar passage rates varied directly with the local bar's interest in limiting the number of lawyers. The largest declines occurred in the urban, industrial states. For example, between 1904–6 and 1922–29, the bar passage rate in New York declined from 74 percent to 47 percent, and in Connecticut, it dropped from 73 percent to 45 percent. New Jersey's bar passage rate was low and remained so, hovering around 50 percent. By the 1920s, the lowest passage rates occurred in states that contained large cities, significant and growing immigrant communities, and many applicants for admission to the bar. The states with the highest pass rates were in the frontier states and states populated by small, homogeneous, rural communities that experienced little population growth, had small numbers of lawyers, and relatively few entrants to the legal profession. In these states, passage rates ranged from 100 percent in Delaware, 84 percent in Iowa, and 82 percent in Wyoming, to a low of 70 percent in Tennessee.[89]

Demographic trends and the downturn in economic conditions in the 1930s contributed to further declines in bar passage rates. Rapidly rising numbers of lawyers, particularly lawyers with immigrant backgrounds, and the contraction of the economy caused by the Great Depression led to lower pass rates. About three-quarters of the nation's jurisdictions failed a higher proportion of examinees, and the aggregate pass rate for all jurisdictions fell from 59 percent in 1927 to 45 percent in 1934. A comparison of law students bar pass rates to medical students medical board pass rates suggests a relationship between overcrowding and low examination pass rates. Whereas the number of medical students fell from 25,171 in 1900 to 21,597 in 1930, the number of law students nearly quadrupled from 12,408 to 46,751, and the number of law students in 1930 was more than double that of medical students. Between 1935 and 1939, the pass rate of the 35,890 examinees who took the medical board examinations was 88.5 percent, but the bar passage rate of the 82,650 examinees who took the bar examination was only 48 percent. Part of this disparity may have been attributable to more selective medical school admission policies, but not all of it. Yale Law School Dean Charles Clark acknowledged that low bar passage rates were "obviously" attributable to quotas that bar examiners applied, and he asserted that such quotas were not only appropriate, but necessary.[90]

A committee of the New York County Lawyers Association apparently agreed with Dean Clark, because it concluded in 1936 that the local bar was overcrowded, and it urged the imposition of quotas to limit the number of applicants admitted to the practice of law in New York. Dean Wilkinson opposed this finding and recommendation, and he presented evidence showing that the association's view was based on misinformation about the number of law school graduates. He demonstrated that student enrollments in the six New York City law schools had declined by almost 50 percent during the preceding eight years, from 10,814 in the 1928–29 academic year, just prior to the stock market crash in 1929, to 5,718 in the 1936–37 school year. Wilkinson argued that, to the extent that there were too many lawyers in New York City, the overcrowding was attributable to unusually high law school enrollments during the 1920s, which he maintained were largely corrected. Moreover, Wilkinson noted that 54 percent of the 5,718 students enrolled in the New York City law schools, more than one-half (3,085) attended the two law schools in Brooklyn, Brooklyn Law School and St. John's Law School. In his view, there may have been too many lawyers in Brooklyn, but not in Manhattan.[91]

The New York County Lawyers' Association was not convinced by Wilkinson's arguments, and it published a report in 1936 of a survey of New York City lawyers prepared by the Committee on Professional Economics, which was created in 1932 specifically to conduct the survey. The committee sent out the survey in September 1934 to all of the 15,000 lawyers practicing in New York City, and it received a total of 5,000 replies, 40 percent of which were from association members. Among other data, the report asserted that the median income of New York City lawyers in 1933 was $2,990. Some 42.5 percent of them earned an income "below the respectable minimum family subsistence level of $2,500 per year; one-third earned less than $2,000 a year; one sixth earned less than $1,000, and the income from practicing law for almost one tenth was at or less than $500 per year." The committee reported the startling fact that "a substantial number are on the verge of starvation, with almost ten per cent of the New York City Bar virtually confessed paupers, as indicated by applications for public relief." The committee reported "that in 1935 about 1,500 or 10 percent of our bar qualified for relief under a pauper's oath." It concluded that "overcrowding is largely responsible for this economic situation."[92]

Richard J. Bennett, class of 1942 and chairman of Schering-Plough at the time of his oral history, recounted the difficult economic times when he was a night student. He was lucky to get a job earning $15 per week when he graduated from Fordham University in 1938. While he was a law student, each evening he would meet his future wife, who worked near the Woolworth Building, and they would go to Chock 'Full O' Nuts. "I would permit her to have a cup of coffee for a nickel, always Chock'Ful [sic] O' Nuts, and I would allow myself the cream cheese and nut sandwich and the coffee and one donut. I think that cost was twenty cent [sic] a day." Mrs. Bennett "still to this day remembers that she was confined to a cup of coffee at Chock'Ful [sic] O' Nuts when she was also hungry. She would watch me eat the sandwich," Bennett concluded without any discernable expression of guilt.[93]

The Committee on Professional Economics recommended several ways to reduce the number of lawyers in New York City, including "determining [that is, limiting] the number of new lawyers to be admitted, year by year" through a "'quota system' whereby only so many new lawyers, chosen on a fair and impartial basis, are allowed admission as it is estimated the community will need." It also suggested better ways of testing for the character of applicants to New York's law schools. The committee thought that the state's educational standards were "commendably high as they stand," but, acknowledging the advancements in "the sciences of vocational and aptitude testing," it recommended that the association "study all such methods" relating to "guidance or testing" of law school applicants. It also recommended expanding the content of legal education within law schools, suggesting "the use of compulsory clerkships or apprenticeships [and] the extension of law school curricula."[94]

Leaders of the New York bar were very concerned about the "lack of education and culture of many of the men" who were entering the legal profession in New York City in 1934, which led them to believe that "the profession is over-crowded because of an over-stimulation of men to pursue the study of law and of an over-supply of law school graduates." Consequently, state and local bar associations gave legal education and entry to the profession their "continual attention." A New York State Bar Association report on legal education in 1934 recommended the elimination of the June bar examination and a limitation on the number of times an applicant would be permitted to take the examination "to three and no more." Law school deans generally approved eliminating the June bar examination, but Wilkinson thought that the second recommendation "was arbitrary in the extreme and vicious in the manner in which it was presented." Wilkinson was able to get the issue deferred until the New York State Joint Conference on Legal Education acted on the issue, which was referred to a subcommittee chaired by Dean Wilkinson.[95]

Wilkinson's subcommittee's findings are interesting. The New York Board of Law Examiners did not have a "fixed passing mark" for the bar examination. The method it used to determine a passing grade was "rather complicated," but the passing grade for the examinations given from 1931 to 1933 was slightly below 60 percent. The subcommittee concluded that the passing grade was "not excessively high." The examinations were comprehensive and "sufficiently difficult to furnish a real test of the applicant's knowledge of legal rules and principles and of his ability to apply the same to the practical problems confronting the practitioner." It determined the "severity" of the examinations and how they were graded by looking at the percentage of applicants' success or failure. Table 4-6 shows the results. The report noted that the pass rate for first-time exam takers in each of these examinations never reached 50 percent, and in most examinations it hovered around 40 percent.[96]

The study then inquired whether the low pass rates were due to the "poor caliber of the applicants" or to "the severity of the grading." It examined the results of the October 1933 examination and found that 1,405 applicants took this test, of whom 367 were first-timers. Of the entire class, only 1 percent or 14 earned a grade of 70 percent or better, and 6 percent or 84 test takers earned a grade as high as 63 percent. The passing grade was 58.8 percent and was separated by only 11 points from the highest grade of 70 percent. A mere 41 percent of the class earned a passing grade. The committee concluded that the examiners graded the examination "with considerable severity."[97]

Wilkinson believed that the bar examination standards in New York State were strict and that the bar examiners used a quota to restrict entry into the legal profession. "There is no absolute passing mark," he acknowledged. Rather, the passing grade "fluctuates depending on the results achieved by the particular group taking any examination." Consequently, one's examination was "marked not objectively on his own paper, but comparatively on the basis of the results achieved by the entire group

TABLE 4-6. FIRST TIMERS WHO PASSED BOTH GROUPS AFTER REVIEW

	March		June		October	
	No. Exam'd.	% Passing	No. Exam'd.	% Passing	No. Exam'd.	% Passing
1929	248	47	2,499	45	483	37
1930	273	45	2,221	39	528	40
1931	231	47	2,181	38	651	35
1932	237	40	1,757	43	565	35
1933	214	38	1,180	45	367	37
1934	175	42	1,454	49	418	42

taking the examination." Although "the Bar Examiners do not admit this to be the case," Wilkinson insisted, "it is obvious that in practice their methods result in their taking the top forty to fifty percent of a particular group and passing them." He thought this was "evident from the fact that although the standards in the law schools of the state have been improved vastly in ten years, the improvement is not reflected in any great increase in the percentage of success on the bar examination." The increased standards of all of the state's law schools, even those "formerly sub-standard schools in this city," improved "the quality considerably of any group taking a particular bar examination." He was certain that the bar examiners were holding these better applicants "to a higher standard of performance to achieve a passing grade" and thus capping the pass rate at 40 percent to 50 percent of the group taking the bar examination.[98]

Given the efforts of national and local bar associations to reduce the numbers of new lawyers by reducing the bar passage rate, which in New York State was below 50 percent, it was with understandable pride that Dean Wilkinson found that Fordham Law School graduates were remarkably successful in passing the New York bar examination and being admitted to practice. For example, Wilkinson estimated that all of the 300 to 325 members of the June 1930 graduating class who were eligible to take the bar exam did take it at one of the three times it was offered in the nine months following their graduation. He found that 255 (78 percent to 85 percent) of these graduates passed the bar exam and were eligible for admission to the bar on satisfying the requirements of the Committee on Character. Wilkinson believed that the 1930 results were "substantially representative of the results in other years."[99]

A detailed analysis of the Law School's graduating class of 1933 who took the bar examination revealed a direct correlation between law school grades and bar passage rates. Of the twenty-three members of the 1933 class who graduated with an average of B+ or better and indicated that they intended to take the bar examination in June 1933, twenty-two passed the bar. Wilkinson was unable to determine whether the twenty-third actually sat for the exam. If that person did not, then the bar passage rate for Fordham's best students was 100 percent. If that person took the exam and failed it, the passage rate was still 95 percent, an extraordinarily high rate in normal times, it was an extraordinary rate when the New York bar examiners were failing over 50 percent of exam takers. On the other hand, students who barely maintained the required C average and insisted on taking the June exam did not do well, though Wilkinson did not report how well or badly they fared. He explained that good students were usually able to review their law school courses "in the three weeks which elapse between graduation and the bar examination." Students who did not do so well in law school find "this time too short but usually cannot be dissuaded from taking a chance." If the poorer student waited until fall to take the October exam, Wilkinson mused, he would have "a very much better chance of passing the test," provided, of course, that he prepared adequately.[100]

Wilkinson surveyed the bar results of Fordham graduates in the classes of June 1934 and June 1935, and he again found a direct correlation between success in law school and success in passing the bar examination. He also found that at least 85 percent of the class of 1934 had passed the bar examination by the following March, and almost 75 percent of the class of 1935 had passed the bar examinations given in June and October of that year. Those who graduated with grades of B or better or who maintained a high C average had "little or no difficulty in passing" the bar. Students who barely passed their courses with a minimum C average continued to have difficulty.[101]

There was a sharp decline in the bar passage rates of Fordham graduates in 1936, the year the New York County Lawyers Association concluded that the local bar was overcrowded. The lower pass rates continued up to World War II. However, graduates who were B+ and B students continued to pass at relatively high rates. It was the C students who brought down the average. Counting those applicants who passed the entire or one-half of the June 1939 exam, 95.6 percent of the applicants who graduated with a B+ average passed the exam; 79.4 percent of the B group passed. Only 40 percent of graduates who maintained a C+ average passed, and 9 percent of the C students passed. The overall pass rate of the class of 1939 who took the June 1939 exam was only 68 percent.[102]

Despite their poor performance on the June 1939 bar exam, Wilkinson believed the C students had the capacity and the training to pass the exam. He attributed their high failure rate, especially that of the night school graduates, to insufficient time to prepare adequately for the June exam. The state administered this exam just three weeks after the students finished their law classes. Wilkinson thought that three weeks was not sufficient time for the C students to prepare for the bar examination, and he tried to persuade them to wait until the October exam. He was confident that if they waited much greater numbers would pass on the first try, because they would have had "an opportunity of a thorough review of their entire law school curriculum." Wilkinson tried to talk the C students out of taking the June exam, but he could not overcome the "tendency of a great many of them to gamble" on passing it, even "though they admit afterwards that they made no adequate review of their course." The majority of Fordham's C students eventually passed the bar exam by the second or third try. This was crucial to Wilkinson's claim regarding the competency of Fordham's C students, because about one-half of the law school's graduating class were C students.[103]

Several commercial courses were offered that prepared law school graduates for the bar exam. Most students in New York took the course offered by Harold Medina in the 1930s and 1940s. Most Fordham students took a course offered by Professors Blake and Finn, both of them Fordham Law faculty. These professors lectured over the course of about one month on subjects that were parts of old bar exams. Students took notes and studied the notes and outlines.[104]

The pass rate of the class of 1940 on the June bar exam was somewhat better than the class of 1939. Over 76 percent of the class passed the examination "in not over three and in most cases not over two tests." The exams were given in June and October 1940 and March 1941. The "average success rate of the first-timers as computed by the State Board of Law Examiners for the year 1940 was 66%." The class of June 1941 also did "particularly well in the June [1941] bar examinations," Wilkinson reported to the faculty. As far as he "could discover substantially 60% of the class had been completely successful in the tests." Information relating to bar passage rates disappears from the Law School records until several years after the end of World War II.[105]

In New York State in the 1920s, the Court of Appeals rules required law school graduates to serve a one-year law office clerkship, unless the graduate had also graduated from college, in addition to passing the bar examination before being admitted to practice. In 1929 the Court of Appeals decided to require law school graduates who were also college graduates to serve a six-month clerkship. A question arose in 1933 whether law school graduates who had also graduated from college should be exempt from the clerkship requirement. The Joint Conference on Legal Education, of which Dean Wilkinson was a member, conferred with the New York Court of Appeals on this issue, and Judge Frederick E. Crane of the Court of Appeals solicited Dean Wilkinson's views on the question.[106]

The question of law office clerkships in the 1930s offers insights into the interactions among contemporary views of legal education, the state of legal specialization and its effects upon the career paths of law school graduates, law firm hiring practices, and economic market forces. Dean Wilkinson thought the clerkship requirement should be eliminated in its entirety, not just for college graduates. The law office clerkship was "easy to defend in theory," Wilkinson conceded, since law schools did not purport to teach law students how to practice law. Law school graduates were expected to learn how to practice on the job. But, law firm clerkships did "not work out well in practice," Wilkinson maintained. Requiring all law school graduates to serve a clerkship greatly increased the number of law graduates seeking clerkships, which made it more difficult "to secure satisfactory positions in reputable offices," even in "ordinary times." In the depths of the Great Depression, the difficulty was even greater. Moreover, this requirement created a buyer's market. Prospective employers in many law offices, knowing that young graduates must serve a clerkship, were exploiting law clerks by reducing their salaries, if they paid them any salaries at all. Wilkinson suggested that restoring the rule on clerkships to that in place prior to July 1, 1929, which exempted college graduates from the clerkship requirement, would lessen the demand for clerkships, which should end the exploitation of law clerks and increase the feasibility of placing graduates in satisfactory law offices.[107]

Wilkinson agreed with an argument made by proponents of the current rule that "the law school graduate has little training in the art of practice, however well he may be versed in the science of law." But the answer to this argument, Wilkinson maintained, was that, although "theoretically . . . correct, . . . in practice it by no means works out that way." Few law graduates would "attempt to practice independently without some association with a law office . . . in order to gain such practical experience as may be necessary." Furthermore, serving a clerkship in a law office did not ensure that the clerk would gain the kind of practical experience necessary to open his own law office. Even in 1933, law firms had become large enough to departmentalize, and some small law offices had become

specialized in one particular field of the law. Placed in either kind of practice, the law clerk might spend all of his time doing specialized work
without gaining any experience in the general practice of law.[108]

Restoration of the older rule, under which college graduates were
exempt from the clerkship requirement, would have an indirect benefit
to the legal profession. Wilkinson argued that it would "stimulate men"
voluntarily to complete their college education before entering law school.
Whether Wilkinson's arguments influenced the decision of the Court of
Appeals is uncertain. However, the court amended its rules on March 25,
1933 and exempted college graduates from the law clerkship requirement.
Wilkinson was happy with the court's decision, not only because he
thought it was the right decision, but also because it reduced the time
required for a student to be admitted to the bar, an important consideration at the time because Fordham was preparing to lengthen the night
division from three to four years. Early in 1940, the New York Court of
Appeals made the decision Wilkinson had argued it should have made in
1933: it repealed the one-year clerkship requirement for applicants to the
bar who did not have a college degree.[109]

New York bar associations displayed "almost continuous activity" in
pushing for higher standards for law schools and admission to the bar in
1935 and 1936. Wilkinson attributed the causes to "the lack of education
and culture of many men who enter the practice of law, the generally
overcrowded condition of the profession, and a lack of sufficient legal
business for those at the bar as a consequence of the depressed times
through which the country has been passing now for six years." He also
noted that a small minority of lawyers lacked "those qualities of character"
that were important in every profession and particularly "one of the fidu-
ciary nature of that of the lawyer."[110]

The Joint Conference proposed limiting admission to the bar to law
school graduates who also graduated from college. This proposal was
predicated on the assumption that a college education was "the best
means of acquiring the general education and fitness needed as pre-legal
requisites" and "a full course of study at an approved law school" was the
"only method of obtaining adequate legal training" to practice law "under
present-day conditions." When Rollin W. Meeker, chairman of the Committee on Character and Fitness of the Third Judicial Department, was

appointed chair of the Joint Conference committee considering this proposal, he solicited Wilkinson for his views on the matter.[111]

Wilkinson replied with a lengthy discussion setting out his reasons for opposing the college degree prerequisite. Part of his argument was based on his experience as dean of Fordham Law School. Seventy percent of Fordham's students were college graduates, and Wilkinson found that a "college degree in itself [was] not a guarantee of the requisite intellectual or moral fitness" for the study of the law. Students who had only two years of college and achieved good undergraduate academic records made better students, in Wilkinson's experience, than college graduates with poor academic records. Instead of "an increase in quantitative requirements," Wilkinson recommended "a proper selective process" of admitting students to law school as an effective method of recruiting high caliber students.[112]

Perhaps a more important reason for retaining the two-year college prerequisite is that it was "supported by substance and reason," that is, by a philosophy of education and a theory of personal development that he derived from the views of Dean Huger Wilkinson Jervey of Columbia Law School. College administrators had concluded that a "boy" completed his secondary education and became a "man," at least "observably different from the boy that entered" college, by the beginning of his third year. Up to this point, the student was "being mentally disciplined and [was] absorbing information about the world." As part of his general education, he was acquiring logical, mathematical, and language tools, learning about the natural sciences and "the aspirations of literature and art. Colleges recognized this change" at a student's third year of college "by 'developing a conscious change of attack' to his education. The theory now is," by his junior year the student, "under skillful guidance," should begin "to find out things for himself, to specialize, to discover, to construct something with the tools and viewpoints he has gained." The achievement of these latter objectives was what law schools offered. The first two years of college work consisted of "general training and in the last two the student begins to specialize."[113]

Deans Wilkinson and Jervey agreed that requiring a college degree as an educational prerequisite to law study was "unjustified. The two-year requirement is not a mathematical compromise. It has substance and reality behind it." Wilkinson also cited as support for his position an earlier study conducted by the University of Chicago Law School which demonstrated that students who entered law school with three years of college work did better than those who entered with a college degree. Requiring a college degree exceeded ABA requirements and the academic prerequisites of most of the nation's law schools, even the best law schools. Wilkinson concluded that "there is no great basis in fact" supporting advocates of a college degree requirement "as the solvent of the conditions which they believe should be corrected."[114]

Consistent with Wilkinson's views regarding proper undergraduate preparation for law school studies, Fordham Law School had an arrangement with Fordham College in the 1920s and 1930s in which students who wished to go to law school and had successfully completed three years at the college were permitted to take their senior year at Fordham Law School. If they completed the first year of law school with "satisfactory marks," Governor Malcolm Wilson recalled, "they received their degree from the College. In other words, that was the substitute for the senior year at Fordham College." Apparently, this was a common practice in the 1920s and 1930s, because Governor Wilson claimed that many of his classmates entered Fordham Law School under this arrangement.[115]

Wilkinson's last argument against the college degree requirement emanated from his view of American higher education in the 1930s and its corrosive effect on moral development. He was "no believer in the value of a college education alone to guarantee character," because he believed "that much that is taught in many of our so-called best colleges today is destructive of good character." Wilkinson singled out departments of philosophy as the culprits, condemning the scientific naturalism, physical determinism, and moral relativism they espoused. In many of these departments, Wilkinson complained,

> students are taught that there is no essential difference between right and wrong; that there is no such thing as mind, or if there is we cannot know anything about it; that man is not possessed of a power within him of self-determination in view of a known end, or what the law recognizes as free-will, but that all of his actions are conditioned

reflexes determined by physical and chemical stimuli acting upon him from without, that there is no such thing absolutely as truth, not even mathematical truth; and similar philosophical rot. Many students hearing such stuff handed out by supposedly learned teachers do not fail to carry the lesson to its logical conclusion.

Rather than ensuring good moral character, America's colleges and universities were undermining it. "We have been sowing the wind for over a generation with many of these doctrines, and I am not surprised to find that now we are reaping the whirlwind," Wilkinson proclaimed. He favored the two-year rule and opposed compelling a student "to go on and be corrupted by theories" he had just described, because he was "certain that the moral character of many college graduates cannot help but be affected adversely by teachings of this kind." He believed that the "record of disbarments and disciplinary proceedings" in New York City, if examined closely, would probably "disclose that graduates of our best colleges and even of our best law schools are to be found among those who have violated the ethics of our profession as well as those who have not enjoyed these advantages."[116]

Wilkinson's opposition notwithstanding, the committee recommended that the college degree requirement proposal be adopted. The Joint Conference did not adopt the committee's recommendation, however, but referred it back to committee for reconsideration and further study. New York State did not adopt a college degree prerequisite until after World War II.[117]

On the eve of World War II, some of the law schools in New York State were either considering raising their admission standards, or they had already done so. Other law schools simply met the Court of Appeals mandated minimum two-year college prerequisite, at least nominally. The two-year standard had remained unchanged since the Court of Appeals put it into effect in 1927, and in 1940 all of the law schools in New York State conformed to or exceeded this standard, at least nominally. Wilkinson believed that Brooklyn, New York, NYU, and St. John's law schools accepted applicants who passed equivalency examinations in certain specified subjects instead of actually completing two years of college work, as was permitted by the New York Court of Appeals rules. NYU was thinking about increasing its requirement to three years, and Syracuse Law School did require three years of college. Columbia and Cornell Law Schools required the baccalaureate degree, except for students who were enrolled in a combined six-year college and law school program. Columbia, like Fordham, applied selective admission methods, and its entire student body consisted of college graduates.[118]

Fordham had "in fact increased our actual standards greatly by introducing and gradually applying with greater severity qualitative or selective standards of admission." In increasing its admission standards, the Law School was assisted by its obligation to keep its enrollments below 850 students in order to retain ABA accreditation and AALS membership. Employing higher admission standards, the proportion of Fordham Law students who entered the school with an undergraduate degree continued to increase "to a gratifying extent" through the 1930s. In the 1937–38 school year, 70 percent of Fordham Law students had a college degree. The following year that percentage increased to 79 percent, and it reached 83 percent in the 1939–40 academic year. The colleges represented in the 1939 entering class numbered 65, and the college graduates in the entire student body held their degrees from 108 colleges.[119]

Noting that four-fifths of Fordham's students entered the Law School with college degrees, Wilkinson raised a question whether Fordham should increase its prelaw education requirement from two years of college to either three years of college or a college degree. Wilkinson proposed that, if Fordham were to increase its prelaw education requirement, it "should go the whole way and demand a college degree either in liberal arts or general science or an equivalent degree, and not merely add completion of an additional year of college work as our entrance requirement." It is interesting that the New York Education Department listed these arts and sciences degrees as the only acceptable college degrees. Wilkinson suggested, however, that, if Fordham were to adopt a college degree prerequisite, it should follow the practice of law schools that had a degree prerequisite and accept graduates of schools of engineering who were "able to obtain a law student qualifying certificate because their courses have been found by the State Education Department to include at least two years of cultural work or its fair equivalent."[120]

Wilkinson conceded that there were some good reasons to adopt the college degree prerequisite for the entering class of 1941: It "would put us in the most select category of law schools in the country." He listed only eight law schools that had a college degree prerequisite: Columbia, Catholic University, Georgetown, George Washington, Harvard, Pennsylvania, Pittsburgh, and Yale. In 1940, Catholic University had only about fifty students and was "a negligible factor," in Wilkinson's opinion. Only two, Georgetown and George Washington, offered part-time programs. And, so far as he knew, only Columbia, Harvard, and Yale "employ in addition qualitative standards of admission," and "Harvard only within the last few years." Confessing that he had to check with Georgetown and George Washington to verify that they did not apply "qualitative standards," Wilkinson suggested that if Fordham were to adopt a college degree requirement, it could "boast . . . that we were the only law school conducting day and evening classes requiring a degree for admission and at the same time in addition selecting out students on the basis of their presumptive fitness for law study as indicated by their college records, and accordingly rejecting applicants with poor records."[121]

Joe McGovern taught at the Law School at this time, and he confirmed the high quality of Fordham's students, particularly the night students. He considered the classes he taught then to be the best he had ever seen. "I don't think in my overall thirty years of teaching, I ever saw a class superior to the night classes I had in say '39, '40 and '41. Boy, they were sharp, and they were in there to get everything they could get out of it," he boasted. "The students worked during the daytime. They weren't there for fun, they were there to learn. Gee, they were brilliant kids." McGovern believed the students' superior performance "had a lot to do with the hard times." With a law degree, they might earn "a little more on their job."[122]

This was a time of fewer applications and shrinking enrollments. Fordham was struggling to maintain its enrollments, which were declining to levels that made the school's mission of providing excellent legal education precarious. To maintain its student body at 850, Fordham had to enroll at least 300 new students each year. "For the last three years we have not found it possible to achieve this registration," Wilkinson informed Father Gannon in January 1941. The "principal cause" was the school's inability to receive "a sufficient number of qualified applications (under our selective entrance standards) for the day school." This inability was "undoubtedly . . . due principally to the times," a reference to the Great Depression. He reported that "diminution in law school registration" affected other law schools and was pervasive in the "Law School world generally in this city."[123]

Depressed economic conditions affected enrollments throughout Fordham University, forcing President Gannon to cut faculty salaries by five percent. In June 1941, Wilkinson explained the financial condition of the Law School to the faculty, which required him to ask them to take the five percent pay cut. Though the faculty regretted the salary reduction, they recognized its necessity, and they were "entirely cooperative." The dean passed on to President Gannon a few letters from faculty expressing their understanding of the "present necessity" and their willingness to accept the pay cuts. Professor Wormser was the most emphatic, writing that, "During twenty eight years of service to Fordham, I have been unswervingly loyal, and you may rest assured that my loyalty will always continue." However, the reduction in "our paltry salaries" persuaded Joe McGovern to return to practice and to teach part-time. The salary cuts were university-wide, and they were not restored until after World War II. The United States' entry into the war was almost six months to the day away.[124]

CHAPTER FIVE

WORLD WAR II AND ITS AFTERMATH

W orld War II profoundly affected law schools and legal education. After the United States formally entered the war in December 1941, hostilities greatly diminished the pool of male law students who were prime candidates for military service. Manpower shortages in the military and the risk of enrolled law students being drafted prompted law schools to adopt accelerated curricula which shortened the time to complete all of the requirements for the LLB degree. Accelerated curricula created a risk of lower standards.

The war cut deeply into student enrollments at Fordham Law School, as it did in law schools throughout the nation. The Selective Training and Service Act (the Burke-Wadsworth Bill) enacted in September 1940 required the registration of all eligible men between the ages of twenty-one and thirty-five. Between 1940 and 1943, enrollments in all American law schools dropped by 80 percent. Columbia Law School Dean Elliott Cheatham reported to the New York State Bar Association at its annual meeting in January 1943 that "the war has struck the law schools with greater severity than any other part of the universities." All law students were of military age, and the Selective Service Board did not exempt law students from induction.[1]

Fordham had been struggling to maintain enrollments in the last years of the Depression. The military draft sharply diminished the pool of potential law students even further as most qualified young men were called to military service. Men who were already enrolled in law school were drafted before they graduated. Many other men, both students and nonstudents, volunteered for military service. Although some draft boards deferred students until they finished law school, most did not. The military could not wait for student draftees to finish the school term in which their draft numbers came up. The armed services plucked them out of school during the academic semester.[2]

The New York Court of Appeals responded to the war emergency by adopting rules that attempted to accommodate departing law students and legal academic standards. Students who left school for military service during their last semester of law school were allowed credit for the full semester without taking final examinations, and they were allowed to receive their law degrees, provided they had completed at least half of the semester, were in good scholastic standing, and had met all of the scholastic requirements up to the semester prior to their being drafted. In no case were they given credit if they had attended fewer than eight weeks of classes in the semester in which they were drafted. The New York Education Department endorsed the court's rule, which the New York bar associations also supported. Dean Wilkinson drafted the New York rule and thus continued to be an important player in setting standards of legal education in New York State.

Dean Wilkinson also continued to play a formative role in shaping national standards of legal education in the United States. He was elected to the AALS's Executive Committee in the fall of 1941, and he served on the Association's Committee on Legal Education. The Executive Committee worked closely with the ABA's Council on Legal Education. Not surprisingly, the ABA's Council on Legal Education asked Dean Wilkinson to draft a regulation for this body that embodied the rule adopted by the New York Court of Appeals. He did, and the ABA adopted the regulation in June 1942. The ABA, AALS, the New York Court of Appeals, the New York Department of Education, and the New York bar associations were all in agreement on the matter. Law students across the nation who were drafted in the last semester of law school were granted their law degrees on the same bases that New York law students enjoyed. Wilkinson played a key role in establishing these rules.[3]

From June 1942 through February 1944, each third-year class at Fordham Law School had some inductees who received their degrees under the special rule. There were no other benefitted graduates of Fordham Law School until two members of the October 1945 class were granted their degrees under the accommodation rule even though the war had officially ended. The reason apparently is that students who were qualified for induction into the military were drafted before they reached their last semester of law school, and others who had intended to go to law school were drafted or enlisted before they had the opportunity to enroll in law school.[4]

At its regular meeting on June 4, 1942, the Fordham Law faculty extended the accommodation for graduating draftees to "students in the earlier years of the School" who were required to withdraw from school "by reason of their entry into the armed forces of the country." On furnishing proof of their entry into the armed services, either as inductees or as volunteers, they were awarded credit for the semester in which they withdrew, subject to the same conditions that applied to graduating seniors. The faculty decided "that this continue to be the policy of the School . . . until further Faculty action otherwise." How many Fordham law students left the Law School to serve in the military is uncertain.[5]

There was also the question of the bar examination. Students in their last year of law school who were subject to the draft were permitted to take the bar examination while they were still attending classes. This meant that, in addition to their regular classes, they took the bar cram course on Saturdays and Sundays. Richard J. Bennett, who graduated in June 1942, "was the happiest man in the world to go into the service, because [he] figured that nothing could be worse than that six months of 1942." He worked at an outside job full-time during the day, attended classes at Fordham Law School at night, and took the cram course on weekends. He found the whole experience of working and going to law school at night "absolutely horrendous in the sense of the scheduling." By the time he "got to the end of it, [he] was delighted to be going into Uncle Sam's service just to rest up."[6]

It was not until the end of the war that the New York Court of Appeals made an additional accommodation to veterans who were drafted out of law schools and thus prevented from taking the bar examination. Rule 3-A exempted these veterans from having to take the bar examination for admission to practice after they had received their law degrees. The theory behind this rule is that it would be rather difficult for one who had completed most or all of his legal education prior to his entry into military service to review for the bar examination when he returned some time later.[7]

Drastic reductions in students forced Fordham Law School to consider how it might recast its educational program in order "to weather the storm" of World War II. Wilkinson estimated annual deficits for the duration of the war in the neighborhood of $60,000 to $70,000, without taking into account "its pro rata share of general University expenses." To meet this crisis, he recommended combining the morning and afternoon sessions into one day session. This reduced the need for faculty, and the decline in revenue required the Law School either to lay off about one half of the full-time faculty or substantially the entire part-time faculty. Neither option was good. Eliminating the full-time faculty, most of whom were the most recently appointed, was unfair to those who had given up their law practices to devote all of their time to teaching. On the other hand, eliminating part-time faculty would sacrifice some of the school's most experienced and distinguished faculty.[8]

Another option was the accelerated curriculum that enabled students to complete three semesters within one calendar year by adding a summer session as a regular third term. Dean Young B. Smith of Columbia Law School informed Dean Wilkinson that Columbia wanted to run a summer school "as a means of keeping the Columbia Law School functioning." But, an accelerated curriculum that included a summer session of sixteen weeks was impracticable under the current New York Court of Appeals rules requiring an academic year to consist of thirty-two weeks and the entire course to total ninety-six weeks. Dean Smith asked Wilkinson to collaborate with him in drafting an amendment to the court's rules that would permit a law school term to consist of thirty weeks and the entire law course to extend over ninety weeks, but provided the total number of classroom hours not be decreased. Wilkinson drafted the amendment, which included a summer term consisting of the same number of classroom hours over fourteen weeks that comprised the fall and spring school terms of sixteen weeks and rolling enrollments in September, February, and June. The New York Court of Appeals adopted it on January 6, 1942. On the Court of Appeals' adoption of Wilkinson's amendment, four other New York City law schools—Columbia, New York University, Brooklyn, and St. John's—announced their intention of running a summer school term beginning in June 1942.[9]

Given diminished enrollments and anticipated financial deficits, Dean Willkinson and the Law School faculty believed that Fordham Law School "had little choice" but to offer a summer session and an accelerated curriculum regardless whether they believed it to be "scholastically desirable." Dean Wilkinson surveyed student interest in an accelerated curriculum should Fordham decide to offer it. More than half of the day students and slightly less than half of the night students expressed interest, which supported the faculty's belief that "a great many" of the law students would transfer to the other city law schools offering accelerated programs unless Fordham offered them the same opportunity to finish their legal educations on an accelerated basis.[10]

Wilkinson learned that Harvard Law School had decided to begin an accelerated curriculum in the summer of 1942, and entering students had the choice of beginning their classes in June, September, or February. Harvard also provided for graduation three times a year to correspond with the three entering classes. Harvard Law School's example may have had a determining effect on Fordham, because it was "quite clear" to President Gannon and his "Consultors," where decisions relating to the Law School's program resided, that the Law School should discontinue the afternoon division and to begin an accelerated curriculum of three school terms with rolling enrollments, beginning with the 1942 summer term.[11]

Wilkinson thought the accelerated curriculum promised to strengthen the Law School's financial condition significantly. He calculated that it would increase in the Law School's revenue in 1942 by 32.6 percent, from $67,500 to $89,850. Wilkinson estimated that the Law School could operate "at an actual expense" of $82,000, exclusive of "general University expenses ordinarily charged to us," if it reduced the part-time faculty's salaries by one half and the full-time faculty's salaries by one third "for the period of the emergency," provided he could persuade the Woolco Realty Company, manager of the Woolworth Building, to accept an annual rental of $20,000 with utilities or less, in addition to "reductions and economies" in other, smaller items. This reduction, combined with the "very considerable salary reductions for the Faculty" he had suggested, would lower the school's annual expenses to $87,000, leaving a small surplus of $2,850. If the Law School were to raise its tuition for day students from $270 to $300 and a *pro rata* tuition increase for night students, its revenues would increase by another $9,200, producing a commensurately higher surplus. Wilkinson provided Fordham University's president with all of this information in January 1942.[12]

Father Gannon disagreed with Dean Wilkinson's budget analysis, calling the estimated surplus of $2,850 "optimistic." The analysis failed to account for the ordinary charge from the university to the Law School, a charge of $74,312 in 1942 that could not be ignored—it included certain expenses that were "non-adjustables" and could not be eliminated, which brought the law school's total expense up to $161,312. Father Gannon was "doubtful how much assistance the other Schools can give" to the Law School in these financially difficult times. "The College boys are dropping out right and left," and the University might have to "very much increase the burdens of the full time men 'for the duration.'" Still, Father Gannon decided not to raise the Law School's tuition.[13]

The Law School adopted the accelerated program and opened a summer session in June 1942 with "approximately half" of the school's students having "filed notice of intention to pursue the accelerated course of studies." Frances M. Blake was one of the students who attended the Law School under the accelerated program. She completed Law School in two years, entering in 1943 and graduating in 1945. "Most everybody" accelerated their programs, Blake recalled. "Few people wanted to stay with the regular program. We dropped back and joined the incoming class that semester. Then the next semester we joined the class half a year ahead of us." Throughout World War II, the Law School's academic year was divided into three terms: summer, fall, and spring. Students could enroll at the beginning of each term—in June, September, and January—and they could graduate upon completing their studies at the end of each term. The three graduations were in June, October, and February. Students had the option of taking an accelerated course by attending all three terms until they satisfied the course requirements for the LLB degree. Day students could complete their three academic years in two calendar years, and night students could complete their four academic years in two and two-thirds calendar years.[14]

Students opted for the accelerated curriculum in substantial and accelerating numbers and proportions of the regular student body. Table 5-1 shows that 171 students were enrolled in the inaugural summer session in 1942, which was about 25 percent of the regular year enrollment. Thereafter, summer school enrollments grew substantially each year: 126 in 1943, 154 in 1944, and 270 in the last wartime summer session of 1945. Using the enrollments of the preceding academic years as a base, summer school enrollments steadily grew in relation to the regular term enrollments from 25 percent in 1942 to 90 percent in 1945.[15]

During the war, Fordham Law School's enrollments were a fraction of their prewar levels, and yet it was one of the nation's largest law schools.

TABLE 5-1. FORDHAM LAW STUDENT ENROLLMENTS DURING
WORLD WAR II

School Year	Regular Terms (Change from Preceding Year)	Summer School Enrollments	% of Summer to Regular Enrollment
1940–41	815	N/A	N/A
1941–42	681 (− 16%)	1942: 171	25%
1942–43	334 (− 51%)	1943: 126	38%
1943–44	220 (− 34%)	1944: 154	70%
1944–45	300 (+ 36%)	1945: 270	90%
1945–46	317 (+ 06%)	N/A	N/A
Total All Years	2,667		

Source: "Registration by Years Since the Foundation of the School," notebook memoranda, Fordham Law School Archives.

In the 1940–41 academic year, the last year of peacetime in the United States, the Law School's student enrollment was 811. In September 1941, even before the Japanese attacked Pearl Harbor on December 7, Dean Wilkinson predicted a total enrollment of only 700 for the 1941–42 academic year, explaining that he was allowing for "draft absentees" in his prediction. The actual figure was 681. It could have been much worse. New York Law School had to suspend operations and transfer its students to St. John's University School of Law in September 1941. And other law schools in New York City "were not as favorably situated with respect to enrollment as" Fordham Law School. The Law School's enrollment dropped by almost one half to 334 in September 1942. Surprisingly, even with this sharp decline, Fordham was the third-largest law school in the country. St. John's Law School in Brooklyn had the largest enrollment with 446 students, and George Washington Law School in the nation's capital had the second largest enrollment with 380 students. No other law school had an enrollment of 300 or more students.[16]

Wilkinson estimated that the Law School could continue to operate so long as the student body numbered no fewer than 200 students. The Law School's enrollments fell to within twenty students of "rock bottom" in the 1943–44 academic year. The 220 students enrolled during this school year represented a drop of 73 percent of Fordham's student population of 815 in the last year of peacetime. According to Frances M. Blake, who entered the Law School in 1943, there "were probably more women than men" among the students. Table 5-1 shows the sharp declines in student enrollments to 1944. But then enrollments sharply rose by 36 percent to 300 during 1944–45, and it rose a modest 6 percent in the academic year 1945–46 following the German and Japanese surrenders. According to an official report of the American Bar Association, the 300 students enrolled in the 1944–45 academic year made Fordham the "largest accredited under-graduate law school in America."[17]

The spike in student enrollments in the spring of 1944 was attributable to several causes. In contrast to the lawyers' lament of too many lawyers in the 1930s, there seemed to be too few lawyers in the 1940s because of the war. Wilkinson thought that "the dearth of lawyers had created an impetus to the study of law." In addition, law school student populations began to flourish with war veterans who had been drafted out of law school and were returning from the war wanting to finish their legal educations. A third cause was the affordability of legal education due to "muster-out pay and other Government aids to rehabilitation of soldiers."[18]

The 317 students enrolled in Fordham Law School during the 1945–46 academic year were still 61 percent below prewar enrollment figures. Table 5-2 suggests that the number of graduates in each graduating class paralleled the reduced enrollments. The Fordham student body jumped up to 739 students in the 1946–47 school year, but it would not reach the 800 level again for almost two decades following the end of World War II, when it reached 837 students in the 1963–64 school year.[19]

World War II deprived untold numbers of would-be Fordham Law students of their opportunity to study law and become lawyers. What is known is that the wartime student enrollments of Fordham Law School were a fraction of those before and after World War II. Table 5-3 shows the war's effect on the Law School's entering classes. Many of those who made it to Fordham were drafted out of law school before they could complete their studies to serve their county when it needed them. Again, the number is unknown. If one compares the number of students who entered Fordham Law School (Table 5-3) with the number who graduated

TABLE 5-2. NUMBER OF FORDHAM LAW SCHOOL WARTIME GRADUATES

Year	February	June	October	Total
1941		208		208
1942		141		141
1943	50	24	28	102
1944	15	32	21	68
1945	18	26	31	75
1946	14	47	73	134
1947	4	136		140
1948		201		201
Total All Years				1069

Source: "Number of Graduates of Fordham University School of Law During the Following Years, 1908–65," notebook memoranda, Fordham Law School Archives.

TABLE 5-3. FORDHAM LAW SCHOOL ENTERING CLASSES, 1939–45

Class	Morning	Afternoon	Evening	Total
1939–40	85	42	165	292
1940–41	78	39	169	286
1941–42	68	29	158	255
Summer 1942	22		16	38
September 1942	40		65	105
February 1943	27		56	83
Summer 1943	5		13	18
September 1943	17		46	63
February 1944	26		47	73
Summer 1944	18		36	54
September 1944	36		76	112
February 1945	37		107	144
Summer 1945				
				1523

Source: Figures stating enrollments in notebook memoranda, Fordham Law School Archives. I included the entering class of 1939 because this was the first class whose graduation was affected by the war.

during the war years (Table 5-2), it becomes clear that about one-third of enrolled students failed to graduate from the law school.

Events surrounding World War II led Fordham Law School to make student accommodations of another sort. After Adolph Hitler came to power in Germany in 1933, foreign-educated lawyers began to appear with some frequency among the Law School's student body. To practice law in the United States, they had to pass a state's bar examination, like any other lawyer. To sit for the bar exam, however, these foreign-educated lawyers were required to earn an LLB degree in an American law school. They enrolled in Fordham and other law schools to qualify for the New York bar. European émigrés who had studied law in European universities and matriculated through Fordham Law School were accommodated with special rules. Dean Wilkinson tailored each student's schedule to fill gaps in the student's prior education. Foreign-educated lawyers usually completed their American law degree in two academic years. The first foreign-educated lawyer enrolled in Fordham in 1931 and received his Fordham Law degree in 1933, and a steady though modest stream of such lawyers matriculated through the Law School through World War II. The Law School matriculated "a number of students from Belgium, Holland and Germany." It also began to receive students from Italy in 1937, and a law graduate of the University of Rome sought to establish an "exchange scholarship" between Fordham and the University of Rome, unsuccessfully it appears.[20]

One of these European émigrés, Jules Weinberg, hosted a dinner on June 18, 1945, at the Stockholm Restaurant to honor the law faculty and to pay tribute to Fordham Law School. Mr. Weinberg had received his Doctor of Laws degree from the University of Brussels and had attended the University of Louvain. He fled Belgium for the United States and took up residence in New York City during World War II. He attended Fordham Law School and graduated in June 1944. In hosting this dinner one year after his Fordham graduation, Mr. Weinberg expressed his gratitude to the Law School for receiving him as "a refugee." Fordham symbolized for him "the freedom of American educational opportunity." He announced that he was therefore establishing a "loan fund" for Fordham Law School students who needed financial aid.[21]

Toward the end of World War II, Fordham accommodated one of a number of Polish jurists who had fled Poland during the war and established a Polish Law Faculty at Oxford University in England. These jurists were unable to return to Poland because they had been "warned on good authority that there would be no guarantee of their personal safety." To the contrary, "the deportations [in Poland] still continue, and this means that any one whom the Russian police choose to regard as pernicious is packed off to heaven knows what destination, and is probably never heard of again." Dr. M. Z. Zedlicki was brought to the attention of Fordham University President Gannon by Oxford University Professor Francis de Zulueta, "Professor of Law and one of the leading Catholic figures in Oxford." Dr. Jedlicki had been on the faculties of law at the Universities of Cracow and Poznan before fleeing to England, and he was teaching the history of European law to law students at Oxford. Acting Dean Walter B. Kennedy arranged for Dr. Jedlicki to teach a course in European law, and Father Gannon thought he could offer him additional courses in one of the University's academic departments.[22]

Dean Wilkinson interrupted his deanship to assume the office of New York City Corporation Counsel in June 1943. The mayor who appointed him to this office was Fiorello La Guardia. La Guardia had earlier appointed Wilkinson as chair of a committee to study and recommend new ways for the city to set the wages of the city's 32,000 employees and handle their grievances. Wilkinson impressed La Guardia with the job he had done, and the mayor appointed Wilkinson as corporation counsel for the duration of World War II. His appointment made Wilkinson the head of the "largest law office in the world." William Hughes Mulligan identified the irony of the La Guardia/Wilkinson collaboration. "The two men were one of the oddest combinations of all time. La Guardia was small in stature, a man of the people, considered to be highly liberal. Wilkinson was tall, aristocratic and considered to be conservative." Nonetheless, it was a successful collaboration.[23]

Wilkinson appointed Professor Walter B. Kennedy as acting dean. Kennedy had been at Fordham Law School since 1923. He was respected by the students and faculty for his scholarship and student advisement, and he was also well regarded in the legal community for his expertise in labor relations. Kennedy consulted with Wilkinson frequently about Law School matters, and Wilkinson regularly attended faculty meetings. Thus, while he was corporation counsel, Wilkinson continued to maintain his close involvement in the direction of Fordham Law School. He also continued his activity in professional organizations. For example, he was elected president of the New York County Lawyers Association in 1945, where he had previously served as a vice president.[24]

In 1943 financial exigencies caused Father Gannon and his Consultors to decide to move from the Woolworth Building to 302 Broadway. Wilkinson may have succeeded in negotiating a reduction in the annual rent, because Father Gannon reported that "the annual drain" from the university to the Woolworth Building was $105,000, but the rent for the 1942–43 academic year was "less than $70,000." The Law School's portion of this "drain" was $33,000, which suggests that the Law School was paying close to one-half of the university's annual rent.[25]

Acting Dean Kennedy thought it was in the Law School's interest to remain at the Woolworth Building, but university priorities trumped Law School interests, and, in October 1943 the Law School moved to 302 Broadway, its sixth home since 1905. William Waldorf Astor had built the fifteen story office building in 1899 at a cost of $900,000, but its assessed value had fallen to $440,000 when Fordham University purchased the property for only $122,000 in the summer of 1943. Intending the building to serve as its downtown campus, the university installed a chapel, an auditorium, libraries, a moot court room, and a student lounge at a cost of $138,000, and it moved the Law School, the Graduate School of Education, and and the Graduate School of Business to this location. The move from the Woolworth Building to the 302 Broadway afforded the university twice the floor space and a savings of $50,000 a year. These savings paid for the $260,000 investment in about five years.[26]

Although the move from the Woolworth Building to 302 Broadway saved Fordham University money, it was not a good move for the Law School. The space allotted to the school was smaller than the space it had at the Woolworth Building. Space limitations stunted the Law School's growth and contributed significantly to its decline among local and national law schools. The Law School occupied the tenth through fifteenth floors of the building, taking over the six floors as existing tenant leases expired. The small floor plate of the building required that the law library occupy the fourteenth and fifteenth floors connected by an interior staircase. Because of the tight quarters and inadequate library, students did their research at the libraries of the local bar associations or the Practicing Law Institute.[27]

The combination of a wartime economy and the labor shortage created by the induction of men into the military created ample job opportunities during World War II. Fordham Law students and graduates who remained on the home front had little difficulty finding positions in law in the war-created prosperity. The "great majority of our students are satisfactorily placed today," Professor Keefe reported in February 1945. The Placement Bureau was able to interest only eleven Fordham Law students to apply for the fifty-four openings in the law officesand legal departments of insurance companies, banks, and commercial corporations about which Professor Keefe was notified. Indeed, most students obtained jobs without the assistance of the Placement Bureau. Moreover, Fordham could place a great number of night students at a minimum salary of $35 per week if they were available. Part-time jobs went unfilled even for day students. The problem facing the law school was not the underemployment of its students, but their overemployment. Acting Dean Kennedy complained in June 1945 that "a great many day school students were working a disproportionate number of hours" at outside jobs. He felt compelled to talk with these students about the maximum number of hours they were permitted to work outside the law school and still remain day students.[28]

In June 1944 Kennedy noted Fordham's success in breaking into the "sacrosanct precints" of the city's elite law firms. Kennedy gloated, "one peculiar feature of the Placement Bureau, of which we are all aware, is that offices which were formerly closed to Fordham men have opened their doors wide to them and reports indicate that once in these individuals are making good with the prophecy that after the war they will continue to be welcomed in the same sacrosanct precincts." In his June 1944 report on the Placement Bureau, Professor Keefe noted that it had placed Fordham students and graduates with firms such as Cadwalader, Wickersham & Taft and Lord, Day and Lord, among others. Other sources demonstrated that Fordham Law School graduates from the early 1920s through the 1940s had secured positions, including partnerships in firms such as Cahill, Gordon, Reindel and Ohl; Clearly Gottlieb; Steen and Hamilton; Coudert Brothers; Davis, Polk, Wardwell, Kelley; Donovan, Leisure; Newton and Irving; Drye, Newhall, Maginnes and Warren; Kenyon & Kenyon; Milbank, Tweed, Hadley and McCoy; Patterson, Belknap and Webb; Paul, Weiss, Rifkind, Wharton, and Garrison; Shearman & Sterling; Sunderland

and Keindl; White and Case; Wilkie, Farr, Gallagher, Walton and Fitzgibbon; Winthrop Stimson, Putnam and Roberts. A June 1944 report revealed placements in other law firms as well at salaries of $35 per week.[29]

Though "Fordham men" were very successful, Fordham women did not fare too well. "There still exists some difficulty in placing young women graduates," Professor Keefe reported in 1945. As middle-class women entered the work force in the 1940s, more women graduated from law schools, and they represented greater percentages of graduating classes during World War II even though they still constituted a minority of the law student population. The greater representation of women in law schools is attributable as much to the diversion of young men into military service as it is to women's interest in becoming lawyers. Table 8-4 shows the spike in the percentage of women graduates of Fordham Law School in the middle of the 1940s, but it also shows larger numbers of female graduates in earlier years in which women were a smaller percentage of the number of graduates. The most women graduates in a class graduated in the classes of 1923 through 1927, and the largest number of women in a single graduating class (thirty) before 1950 was in the graduating class of 1925. However, these women represented from 5.5 percent to 7.9 percent of their graduating classes. By contrast, fewer women graduated in the period of World War II, clustering between sixteen and eighteen graduates each year from 1943 through 1946. Yet, these women represented between 14.3 percent and 23.5 percent of the graduates of these classes. These were the only years in which women represented more than 10 percent of a Fordham Law School graduating class in the first half of the twentieth century. As was the case of women and jobs, women's presence in the law schools declined to pre–World War II levels when the GIs returned, and they did not represent a significant presence in law school student bodies until the 1970s. This postwar trend is also revealed in Table 8-4, which shows that women did not attend Fordham Law School in significant numbers and percentages after World War II until the mid-1970s.[30]

The New Deal's approach to government combined with some of the consequences of World War II to produce government assistance to returning veterans that greatly affected higher education generally and legal education specifically. In 1944 Fordham Law School entered into a contract with the Veterans Administration (VA) in which the VA provided financial aid to veterans who were "disabled to the extent of ten percent, or more" to enable them to complete their legal education. This contract preceded the enactment of "the broader program now passing through Congress known as the 'G.I. Bill of Rights.'" Congress enacted the GI Bill and President Roosevelt signed it into law in June 1944.[31]

The GI Bill had a significant impact on Fordham Law School, as it did on institutions of higher education generally. Financial assistance from the government enabled returning veterans to attend law school on a full-time basis, and the Fordham Law School's day school enrollment began to outnumber the night school enrollment shortly after World War II ended. Exactly two-thirds of the 180 veterans who entered the Law School in February 1946 were day students and one-third were night students. Significantly, nearly all of the day school students were war veterans attending the Law School "under the privileges of the G.I. Bill." Dean Wilkinson announced that the Law School was filled to capacity, making it "absolutely essential to maintain exceedingly high standards" and to eliminate "those not qualified" in order to make space available for entering students who "were qualified." Those admitted to the February 1946 class had an "exceedingly high college scholastic record," and 83 percent were college graduates. All applicants to the September 1946 entering class, except for returning veterans, were required to have a college degree. This entering class was "registered to capacity, mostly with returning veterans."[32]

But, enrollments were held below prewar levels for two reasons. The first was the limited space at 302 Broadway. Although the student body doubled from 317 in 1945–46 to 739 in 1946–47, total enrollments fell back into the six hundreds until the mid-1950s. The second reason the Law School kept these enrollments low was to ensure that it complied with the ABA's and AALS's student-to-faculty ratio.[33]

THE AFTERMATH OF WORLD WAR II

Student enrollments were not the primary concern of Fordham Law School during the last wartime school year. Rather, the faculty were looking ahead to the kind of law school Fordham might become with the return of peace. The AALS and ABA may have been a catalyst to Fordham's looking to the future, because these organizations were also busy exploring the administrative structure and intellectual content of legal education in 1944 and 1945. "Our main task," Acting Dean Kennedy informed Fordham University President Gannon, "is not to worry about students but to plan the type of law school that Fordham intends to build in the post-war period."[34]

The Fordham Law faculty engaged in its first substantive discussion of the nature and quality of the legal education they sought to offer in the postwar era at its September 1944 meeting. Fordham University President Robert Gannon, S.J., attended this meeting, and he urged the law faculty to adopt a college degree requirement for admission to the Law School beginning with the entering class of September 1946. However, Father Gannon recommended that the degree requirement should not be applied to returning veterans, because he did not think it "just" to change admission requirements affecting military personnel while they were "in the military service of their country." Father Gannon may have been influenced by AALS Emergency Resolution No. 8, which recommended a relaxation of entrance requirements for returning veterans. He also urged the faculty to eliminate the "unfit candidates" for Fordham Law degrees by "correct[ing] examination papers with a courteous and sympathetic ruthlessness."[35]

The faculty accepted Father Gannon's suggestions and increased the pre-Law School academic requirement for admission to a college degree beginning with the entering class of September 1946. They also applied the ABA/AALS two-year college requirement to war veterans. The faculty excepted one other group from the college degree requirement: Fordham University undergraduates who had enrolled in the prelaw course under the assumption that only two years of college were required for admission to the Law School and who "evidenced an intention of entering the School of Law at the conclusion of their pre-law course."[36]

Fordham Law School joined a select group of law schools when it adopted the college degree requirement for admission. Only eight law schools in the entire country required a college degree in 1946. Fordham was also one of the few law schools that also had a selective admission policy, which, combined with the college degree requirement, set it apart from almost all of the nation's law schools. Indeed, Wilkinson thought that Fordham Law School was the only law school with these high admissions standards that offered both day and night programs. He expressed his view of the Law School with the following auto analogy: "We prefer to build Cadillacs rather than Chevrolets. Both are good cars but they cater to different markets."[37]

Even law schools with a college degree requirement made exceptions for outstanding students. Dennis McInerney, for example, returned from military service after World War II and resumed his undergraduate education at Fordham University. "I'd been accepted at Columbia [Law School] in 1947 after my Sophomore year" of college, McInerney related. "In those days, that was not very unusual. Columbia gave me an LSAT-type test and said that my mark was sufficiently high that they would take me right away without finishing college. I had that option when I graduated from Fordham, but I thought it would be somewhat disloyal to go to any other law school when I was on the Fordham [College] faculty," a reference to his position of Philosophy instructor under Father Joseph Donceel, chairman of the Philosophy Department. McInerney did not appreciate "that Wall Street firms might prefer a Columbia law degree. I may not have even known what a Wall Street law firm was, and I felt very comfortable going to Fordham [Law School]." After graduating, McInerney eventually became a partner at the Wall Street law firm of Cahill, Gordon & Reindel, a position he still held when he gave this interview in 1989. He understandably concluded, "Of course, it worked out just fine. I'm glad I made that choice."[38]

In addition to raising the quantitative standard of pre-Law School college education to a college degree, the Fordham Law School also raised the qualitative standard. By the end of the 1940s, Fordham raised the minimum acceptable college average of C to B. The Law School also began to require marginal students whose undergraduate record averaged below B to take the Law School Aptitude Test (LSAT) administered by the College Entrance Board at Princeton, New Jersey. Fordham's selective admissions policy became more selective.[39]

At the end of World War II, Fordham was arguably still the second law school in New York City. With its selective admissions policy and academic standards, the "popular estimate" of the Law School, Acting Dean Kennedy reported to Father Gannon in November 1945, was that Fordham was "the most exclusive part-time law school in the metropolitan area and certainly in competition with Columbia." He did not think Fordham was "in serious competition with either Brooklyn Law School or St. John's." The only other law school "of greatest interest to us" was NYU School of Law. It was "very close to ours in many ways including the approximate scholastic standards." Nonetheless, Kennedy was confident that Fordham's academic standards and selective admissions policy placed it "in a position to compete favorable [*sic*] with any law school in the metropolitan district."[40]

But Fordham's fateful decision in the 1930s to continue using the Law School to subsidize the other divisions of Fordham University, which perpetuated the Law School's tuition-dependent financial structure, combined with the inadequate physical plant, forced the university's president and the Law School's dean to oppose ABA proposals for administrative and financial changes to improve legal education after the end of World War II. Dean Young B. Smith of Columbia Law School had recommended to the ABA that accredited law schools reduce their student-to-faculty ratio to one full-time teacher for every fifty students, one-half of the then current requirement of one full-time teacher for every one hundred students. Reflecting the growing importance of faculty scholarship within legal education, Dean Smith also recommended that law school libraries be developed, and he proposed that accredited law schools spend $15 per student each year on their law libraries to achieve this goal. Acting Dean Kennedy thought Dean Smith's proposals "doubtless represent the attitude of ivy law schools. The solutions in all his proposals, you will note, is obligatory disbursements of moneys, in order to reduce the 'profit motive' of proprietary or sub-normal law schools." After he had resumed his tenure as dean, Wilkinson attributed a different motive to Dean Smith's proposals to raise these standards, namely, to avoid the "rush into the law schools" after World War II that occurred after World War I. Smith sought "to prevent schools in the large cities from expanding too rapidly by making it expensive for them to do so."[41]

Father Gannon's objections to Dean Smith's recommendations highlighted the predicament of "unendowed" law schools attempting to maintain standards that were being determined increasingly by institutions that were relatively heavily endowed. His objections to Dean Smith's 50-to-1 student-to-faculty ratio recommendation were pragmatic and echoed Dean Wilkinson's opposition to the 100-to-1 ratio during the 1930s. For

Fordham Law School to adopt the fifty-to-one standard, Father Gannon asserted, "would necessarily eliminate the part-time teacher and thereby [cause] the law school to suffer the loss of experienced lawyers and very competent teachers." Also, Fordham simply could not afford Dean Smith's proposal for the library expenditures. It would require Fordham to spend "$12,000 a year for books alone." Father Gannon suggested that this financial burden could mean the extinction of law schools like Fordham, and he "urged that the unendowed school must be preserved as well as the endowed school." Wilkinson, in addition, denied "any necessary relation between the number of students and standards." He maintained that such an assumption was simply fallacious, which appears to have contradicted his earlier view that smaller classes would make teaching more effective.[42]

The Law School's financial condition brightened as returning veterans and the GI Bill rapidly increased Law School applications and enrollments. For some years after World War II, and again after the Korean Campaign in the 1950s, the numerous military veterans who made up large proportions of the student body were several years older than the students who had attended before the war. Judge Lawrence Pierce noticed that this greater "maturity level . . . was reflected in our class" when he was a student. He had enrolled in Fordham Law School in September 1948, after serving in Italy during World War II in a segregated unit where one of his friends was Benjamin Hooks, who later became president of the NAACP.[43]

The "rush into the law schools" that Columbia's Dean Smith feared in 1944 began with the rapid demobilization following the end of World War II. By the 1946–47 school year, Fordham Law School's enrollment jumped up to 739 students. Dean Wilkinson's estimated budget for that school year was based on an enrollment of 700 students, and it showed a huge surplus of almost $200,000. His estimated budget for the 1947–48 school year projected another substantial, though somewhat smaller, surplus of $145,000. With these huge surpluses derived from the Law School's tuition and fees, Fordham University could easily have afforded the proposals the ABA considered in 1946 to improve student-to-faculty ratios and to develop law school libraries. That is, it could have afforded them if the University had used the Law School's income to finance the Law School alone rather than divert the surpluses to subsidize the university's other divisions.[44]

Fordham Law School's opulent financial situation and Fordham University's diversion of Law School revenues to university funds were not unique. The ABA surveyed the nation's law schools in 1947 and discovered that exploding enrollments were producing "substantial financial surpluses." It also learned that "in several institutions" these surpluses were being applied "to other university purposes" than the law schools. Evidently, the council had learned that Fordham University was one of these institutions, because the council's chair urged Dean Wilkinson early in 1947 to apply to the Law School's operation each year "a sum at least equal to that derived from tuition and fees." To do otherwise was "undesirable" and contrary to the ABA's "general principle" that university administrations should devote surplus funds derived from law school tuition and fees exclusively to law school operations. This ABA communication was perhaps the earliest to inform Fordham Law School that the ABA considered Fordham University's diversion of the Law School's income to general university funds to be undesirable and in conflict with the ABA's general principles.[45]

Two years later, the ABA's Council on Legal Education sent out another questionnaire to the nation's law schools touching on a variety of subjects, including law school and university finances. Fordham University President Gannon was "somewhat amazed" at the questionnaire's inquiries, some of which he believed "are not the business at all of the American Bar Association." Nevertheless, he informed Dean Wilkinson that he would provide answers if the dean felt they must be answered. Wilkinson did, and again reminded Father Gannon that the ABA was "somewhat insistent that in approved schools any surplus be devoted to the school rather than to general University purposes."[46]

Dean Wilkinson opposed the ABA and AALS proposals to lower student-to-faculty ratios and to increase library expenditures for practical reasons and, in his view, for their flawed theoretical soundness. Both proposals presented the Law School with space problems because of the cramped quarters at 302 Broadway. The library proposal would have required Fordham to spend approximately $13,750 per year, which, while "not prohibitive," would have required the purchase of many new books which were "not needed in our library" and would have presented "problems of library space."[47]

It is revealing that Wilkinson did not think the Law School's library needed to expand its holdings, because the Law library did not have "the range of books that [Dennis McInerney] saw when [he] started in a Wall Street law firm." Moreover, students did not use the school's library to study as they do today. *Law Review* editors would often go to other local libraries, such as those at the Practicing Law Institute, the Association of the Bar of the City of New York, and the New York County Lawyers Association, all of which had better libraries, compared with Fordham Law library's limited collection, limited work space, and limited hours of operation. Wilkinson's opposition to expanding the library's holdings and facilities suggest a view of legal education and academia that did not place much importance on student research and faculty scholarship.[48]

Wilkinson led the opposition to the proposal to reduce the student-to-faculty ratio to 50-to-1 at consecutive AALS meetings. He made two arguments. Wilkinson argued from "the principle involved," which was central to his theory of legal education. A "well-balanced faculty required a sufficient number of full-time men" as well as "a fair number of active practitioners" in order "to bridge the gap between the theoretical instruction in the law school and the actualities of practice." As he "would not dream of urging" an AALS rule requiring part-time teachers, because each law school should be permitted to develop its own program, so would he oppose a rule requiring law schools "to maintain substantially only a full-time staff." The proposal would have required "a very considerable cut in the part-time faculty," who Wilkinson regarded as "an important part of the School."[49]

Wilkinson also opposed the student/faculty proposal on practical grounds. He focused on the impact this standard would have on law school faculties across the country. Harvard's law faculty, for example, which numbered thirty-three full-time teachers would have to add ten more. "What in the name of Heaven would Harvard or any other school do with such a number," Wilkinson wondered. Looking at the enrollments and full-time faculties of AALS member law schools, Wilkinson calculated that the proposed rule would require these schools to add a total of sixty-seven full-time teachers in one year, and he questioned whether law schools would be able to find the sixty-seven new full-time teachers to comply with the proposed standard. Some of the Catholic law schools, most notably Loyola of Chicago, voted in favor of the proposal, but "Harvard and a number of the best schools in the Association stood with me in the matter," Wilkinson reported to Fordham University's president, Father Gannon. In 1950 Wilkinson succeeded in getting the AALS to adopt a compromise student/faculty proposal of 75-to-1. He believed this ratio preserved the central role part-time law faculty played in legal education, especially at Fordham, and it required Fordham Law School to hire only one additional full-time teacher at current enrollments.[50]

Practical realities severely affected Wilkinson's views and partially explain his opposition to proposals that presaged the future of legal education. His opposition to enhancing professional standards was out of character for him, but the space limitations at 302 Broadway prevented the Law School from developing in the ways that he surely knew were occurring among first-rank law schools. Unable to provide offices for full-time faculty, the Law School could not expand its full-time faculty and was forced to rely primarily on its part-time faculty for instruction. Its inability to add more classrooms also restricted the Law School in several ways. Pedagogically, the most serious problem is that it rendered impossible adding more courses and providing different methods of instruction. For example, the seminar was emerging as an important method of legal instruction which, when done correctly, offered law students an opportunity to engage in scholarly research. Seminars were correctly taught in classes of limited enrollments, which required more classrooms than the Law School had at its current location. The scarcity of classrooms also limited the size of the student body. Too few classrooms and forced limitations on student enrollments restricted the school's ability to expand its faculty and enrich its curriculum. Dennis McInerney recognized decades after his student days at 302 Broadway that conditions there were inadequate by today's standards. At the time, however, "it didn't occur to us that this was, in comparison to what the students now have, some kind of deprivation because we had no basis for comparison." Nevertheless, he stated that "we were in a building that probably should have been condemned years before—and I believe it was torn down not long after Fordham moved."[51]

Dean William Hughes Mulligan agreed. The building at 302 Broadway "was an old office building which did not readily become adapted to school requirements," Mulligan remembered. The city's fire code required the installation of a second staircase, which took up about one quarter of the space the Law School had planned to use. "It was really a miserable place," Mulligan complained. "The elevators were archaic. The [sic] bounced up and down." However, the Woolworth Building had also been unsuitable for a law school. "Neither building was suited for our operation—thank God for Lincoln Center."[52]

Financial considerations also pushed Wilkinson to oppose proposed reforms. It is not that the Law School's revenues were insufficient to finance the changes the AALS reforms would have required. Wilkinson acknowledged that this was not the case. Rather, the Law School was unable to absorb these costs because the university diverted the enormous surpluses the Law School produced to finance its general operations. For example, in the 1947–48 academic year, the Law School's revenues totaled $257,506 and its expenditures were $186,684.36, leaving a 27.5 percent surplus of $70,821.64. It reported to the ABA's Council, Section of Legal Education and Admission to the Bar that this surplus was "allocated to Plant expansion—and return [sic] to general University funds for deficits during war years." Fordham University declined to give any further details of how it allocated the Law School's surplus because the ABA's "report itself does not call for details," and the central administration asserted that these "details are for our own information." In addition to the surplus, the Law School's expenditures included "Indirect Expenses" of $63,481.71 paid to Fordham University. The Law School generated a surplus of about $54,000 in the 1951–52 school year, and the university diverted it into its general funds.[53]

The Law School's profitability was a mixed blessing. The costs of its operations were low for a variety of reasons that were undermining the stature Fordham Law School had achieved in its first half century. The law school was housed in a low-cost but inadequate building that impeded its development. Faculty salaries were low in large part because most members of the faculty were part-time. Even full-time faculty salaries were relatively low. The most serious obstacle to the Law School's financial well-being and future development was the lack of an endowment that might have made the school independent of tuition and fees to finance its operations. Fordham Law School was one of the few leading law schools in the nation that was entirely dependent on student tuition.

World War II stimulated discussions among legal educators of administrative and intellectual aspects of legal education. The AALS saw the wartime disruption to legal education as an opportunity to assess law school curricula. In 1942, the Executive Committee of the AALS, of which Dean Wilkinson was a member, circulated a letter to law school deans asking them to undertake with their faculties a "comprehensive reexamination and appraisal of law school programs," which the committee considered long overdue. Dean Wilkinson, with the faculty's approval, appointed a faculty committee in early 1943 known as the Post-War Committee to survey the Law School's curriculum and consider possible changes for the postwar period, particularly the possibility of expanding course offerings in the field of public law.[54]

The Post-War Committee reported that the Law School's curriculum was "greatly in need of revision." The faculty had made very few changes in the curriculum since its founding. The most recent change was the addition of three important electives in the 1938–39 school year: Administrative Law, Labor Law, and Taxation. The faculty adopted these public law courses because of their "increasing importance in consequence of developments in government during recent years," a clear reference to the New Deal and the expansion of the administrative state. Incorporating these electives was the most significant change in the Law School curriculum since the opening of classes in 1905. Earlier changes included moving Agency from second to first year; moving Bankruptcy from third to second year; dropping Carriers from second year and New York Code of Civil Procedure from third year; and adding Damages and Wills to second year and a second course in Equity and New Jersey Practice to third year. Notwithstanding these changes, students took the same courses for most of the law school's first half century. Despite the committee's conclusion that the Law School's curriculum needed to be revised, the faculty took no action to revise it.[55]

The Fordham University central administration also made substantive suggestions regarding teaching methods and formats and course content in 1945 that anticipated some of the most important developments in the intellectual content of legal education in the closing decades of the twentieth century. But their suggestions were incompatible with the university's reliance on the Law School to subsidize its general operations. The university administration recommended that the case method be used only in the first two years of courses, a recommendation the faculty ignored. Fordham's president wanted to broaden the Law School's curriculum beyond technical law subjects. He "was particularly interested" in developing "more than pure professionalism in our students." Speaking on behalf of Father Gannon from his personal experience with medical schools, Father William J. Mulcahy, S.J., who had recently been appointed director of the university's City Hall Division, noted that the medical schools he knew "created excellent doctors who were ignoramuses" because of the narrowness of medical education. Father Mulcahy asserted that this was also true of law schools, but "to a lesser degree . . . because of the nature of the subject matter taught in the law schools." Nonetheless, he cautioned that lawyers who were educated "only along legal lines might well be dangerous to the community at large if they were totally ignorant of economic, political [*sic*] and sociological fundamental principles."[56]

Father Gannon also urged the law faculty to incorporate some of the social sciences into substantive law courses. Father Mulcahy on behalf of Father Gannon advanced a view earlier expressed by Roscoe Pound, that "much more work could be done" in teaching law students the "fundamental sociological, economical and political sciences." Especially at this time, Father Mulcahy admonished, "the lawyer . . . should have at least some basic knowledge of these very important subject matters." The Jesuits did not advocate adding courses in these subjects to the law school curriculum. Rather, they thought these principles and subject matters should be taught within established law subjects. This was a surprising recommendation when one considers the opposition of Dean Wilkinson and Fordham's law faculty to legal realism. Perhaps the Jesuits' goal was to teach social science principles and subject matter as an antidote to legal realism as Father Shealy taught a Catholic perspective on social work and sociology as an antidote to socialism. The Law School faculty chose not to infuse their courses with the social sciences, which was sound legal educational pedagogy at this time. Even the legal realists in their heyday before World War II and their intellectual descendants in the 1950s, 1960s, and 1970s stuck to traditional content in their law courses.[57]

Father Laurence J. McGinley, S.J., who succeeded Father Gannon as Fordham University's president in 1949, repeated his predecessor's request to broaden the intellectual content of the Law School's curriculum. He "urged the faculty" in September 1951, "to direct their efforts not merely to training competent lawyers but wherever possible to developing graduates who would be leaders in legal thought." McGinley believed law students were too smug, lacked a sense of "social responsibility," and needed to develop "a greater sense of public obligation." He suggested that "we ought to reexamine our methods," presumably to produce leaders who would shape legal rules and the public policies they advanced. He recommended that some of the school's top students "should be actively promoted so that 20 years from now they could have some impact on the legal thought to counteract some trends" in the law.[58]

Beginning in 1947, the Carnegie Corporation and the ABA subsidized a massive seven year survey of the legal profession, including legal education. The first director of the survey was Arthur T. Vanderbilt, the dean of NYU School of Law at the time of his appointment. Some of the survey's salient observations and conclusions are summarized below and serve as a measure of where Fordham Law School was situated within the contours of legal education.[59]

The survey found that the aspirational vision of legal education was much different from that of earlier in the century, and it was similar to the vision expressed by Father Gannon and Father McGinley. The report stated that the objectives of legal education had evolved beyond merely training "men" for the legal profession, and that law schools should now provide "a center where scholars may contribute to an understanding of law and government and may participate creatively in their growth and improvement." The expanded roles of lawyers in public life required an expanded view of legal education beyond training to solve the problems of individual clients. The survey reported that, reflecting these goals, "historical, sociological, and even psychological data are now considered in the law-school classrooms as part of the training for the bar." Some law schools, such as Columbia and Yale, appointed to their law school faculties scholars in the social sciences, particularly economics and political science, and other fields such as philosophy and history with a consequent reorientation of legal research along more academic scholarly lines. However, these experiments in integrating the social sciences and philosophy with traditional law courses were quite limited and "decidedly irregular." The survey found that law school curricula consisted of traditional, practice-oriented courses designed to help law students pass the bar examination. Even the major schools suffered "from a kind of intellectual ennui." Consequently, by far the greatest number of law schools around 1950 performed "the routine work of basic legal instruction well enough," and they were "completely orthodox and conventional in their outlook."

Fordham Law School was in the mainstream of American law schools as these sources described them.[60]

ABA inspectors reported that law schools were inadequately financed and lacked the funds required to study and develop curricula. Insufficient funding also contributed to pressures to mass-produce lawyers and contributed to large classes and overcrowded conditions. As before World War II, metropolitan law schools offering part-time instruction were seen as the "problem children" of legal education. Investigators found that "the bulk of evening training" consisted of spoon feeding information to students to pass the bar examination, and the survey concluded that part-time evening programs were not adequate substitutes for full-time day programs. Even so, the legal profession generally agreed that part-time programs should be available, but their standards should be raised to full-time standards.[61]

Another important development was a growing emphasis on higher qualitative as well as quantitative standards to measure the quality of legal education. Historically, professional associations emphasized quantifiable standards to assess the quality of law schools and legal education. They focused on such factors as years of pre–law school education, years of law study, the number of books in law libraries, and the number of full-time faculty. Bar leaders were now placing greater emphasis on qualitative standards, such as the quality of the content of law courses and of the "mind and character" of law school graduates admitted to the practice of law. However, they did not make recommendations as to how to assess these factors or how to improve the substantive quality of legal education.[62]

The survey of the legal profession did make recommendations concerning the nature and quality of pre–law school education, which shed light on leading lawyers' and judges' conceptions of the ideal lawyer as a well-rounded, socially conscious public servant with a strong commitment to professional ethics and moral values. Though they recognized the need for lawyers to be educated to meet the new conditions of American life, both judges and lawyers steadfastly refused to recommend prescribed courses in prelegal education. Still, their universal view was that law students were "woefully unprepared" in subjects needed to study law, naming economics, government, and history as examples. The survey was critical of law students for failing to learn these subjects and of colleges for failing adequately to educate them in cultural norms and the liberal arts. It acerbically asserted that no law teacher in any class of any law school can refer "to Plato or Aristotle, to the Bible or Shakespeare, to the Federalist or even the Constitution itself with any assurance that he will be understood." The survey was also critical of law students' inability "to think straight or to write and speak in clear, forceful, attractive English." It found that colleges did not "arouse in their students abiding interests in the physical, social, and ethical aspects of the world in which they live and in the best that art and letters have to offer." They failed to stimulate "in their students any personal sense of responsibility for the destiny of the body politic."[63]

Fordham Law School's curriculum and character at the time of the survey was dominated by Dean Wilkinson's imprint. Achieving his vision of the Law School in the 1920s and the 1930s placed Fordham among the nation's leading law schools. In the final years of his tenure, he worked to maintain this vision at a time when forces were pushing for educational change that would transform the profiles of the leading law schools. In the opinions of Dean Mulligan and Fordham University's president and academic vice-president, Father Edwin A. Quain, S.J., Fordham Law School was no longer among them by the 1950s.

NYU School of Law overtook Fordham as the second most prestigious law school in New York City by the 1950s. Under Dean Arthur Vanderbilt, NYU Law School acquired "various business enterprises which produced tax exempt income that financed the school's operations," setting it apart from the inadequately financed law schools. The best known of these businesses was the Mueller Macaroni Company, which provided NYU Law School with substantial revenue until it was sold in the 1970s. These business enterprises enabled NYU to build its new five million dollar law school building on Washington Square South, which it completed in 1951. This new facility opened many doors for NYU Law School, including Dean Russell Niles's plan "to attract superior students from the better colleges throughout the United States," Dean Wilkinson informed Father McGinley. Wilkinson was skeptical that Dean Niles would be able to attract such students, notwithstanding his "fine Law School building." He anticipated NYU's current student body to "be one of his real problems," not only because it was "largely drawn from the City of New York and its environs," but because it was "a very different student body from the type which we have here at Fordham." With some hubris, Wilkinson suggested that if Dean Niles "could induce some good Fordham material to matriculate with him it might serve as a leaven," but Wilkinson was "inclined to think that the lump with which he has to deal would be hard to make any impression on."[64]

Fordham Law School also had the opportunity to acquire a business enterprise that could have financed its operations. Wilkinson had discussed this opportunity with Father McGinley in 1950. As with NYU's Dean Vanderbilt, "a former client of my [law] office," Wilkinson recounted, "came to me with the suggestion that Fordham purchase his flourishing manufacturing business from which he wanted to retire." The name of the business is unknown, because Father McGinley and Dean Wilkinson "determined not to go into [the project] for various reasons." Wilkinson also considered a "tax arrangement" with a business in which the Law School would benefit from business income that would be tax exempt to the Law School. Wilkinson and Father McGinley deemed this tax arrangement "most undesirable from a public relations standpoint," so Fordham Law School did not acquire any businesses that might have provided it with independent sources of income as did NYU Law School. Also unlike NYU, Wilkinson and his immediate successors did not express any interest in recruiting students from the better colleges around the nation. By spring of 1951, Wilkinson acknowledged that NYU had joined Columbia as Fordham's competitor.[65]

Faculty governance was very limited under Dean Wilkinson. In the last years of the Wilkinson era, the faculty met at least twice per year, with part-time faculty joining full-time faculty as equal participants. All faculty members had full voting rights. The principal function and responsibilities of faculty meetings was to decide matters relating to admission standards, the nature of examinations, and curriculum issues. The limited scope of faculty governance is reflected in the fact that only one of the three faculty committees at that time related to governance, namely, the Committee on Curriculum. The other two committees were the Committee on Law Review and the Committee on Moot Court. The curriculum was prescribed for the first two years, and students had very limited choice of electives in the third year for day students and the fourth year for evening students. The school offered no continuing education courses for practicing attorneys, but none of the other New York City law schools did either. Continuing education courses were only offered by the Practicing Law Institute.[66]

Under Dean Wilkinson, the faculty played a limited, consultative role in matters affecting faculty interests. Procedures to determine questions of tenure, promotion, and salary went largely unaddressed, because the faculty was small and no problems arose around these issues. The faculty had an informal rather than an institutional role in matters relating to hiring, promotions, and tenure. The dean solicited applications for teaching positions, and he and senior faculty interviewed interested candidates. The dean also consulted Law School alumni. If they reacted favorably to a candidate, he was invited to lunch with the entire faculty. If the faculty were also favorable, the dean recommended the appointment to the academic vice president, who then made the official recommendation to the university president. The dean consulted faculty members individually, but he possessed the sole power to decide whether to recommend the appointment. Not one of the Law School dean's recommendations for faculty appointments was denied by the university for the period from 1947–48 to 1957–58.[67]

The bases upon which the decision to hire a new faculty candidate was made and the decisions relating to promotion and salary were the usual considerations reflecting Fordham's vocational perspective on legal education, with certain exceptions that reflected the Law School's religious affiliation. The faculty candidate's education, law practice, interest in teaching, potential to become a good teacher, and recommendations all played a role. Because Fordham Law School was a Catholic institution, other factors were also considered. For example, "an attitude of irreligion or anti-religion would be a factor" in the hiring process. However, the Law School's Jesuit affiliation would "not prevent us from retaining non-Catholics on our faculty," nor would a candidate's political affiliation or political activity, so long as it did not prevent him from devoting full-time to the Law School. But, the school "would not employ a member of the Communist Party" or anyone who would not swear allegiance to the United States. The "nature of candidate's domestic life" was also considered, but race was not a consideration. These factors were also considered in decisions concerning faculty promotion along with considerations of "work and length of service" and "ability to work cooperatively with fellow faculty members."[68]

Dean Wilkinson recommended faculty salary increases after meeting with the individual faculty members. He recommended increases for the "lowest grades at least every second year and under present conditions [in 1949] every year," a reference to the school's attempt to make up for the decreases in faculty salaries during World War II. The only criteria for salary increases were an "ability to work cooperatively with fellow faculty members" and "continued interest in faculty commitments and duties."[69]

Faculty salaries were determined by the central administration. The dean sent his recommendations to the academic vice president who consulted with the vice president for business and finance who, in turn, made the official recommendation to the university president. There was no known refusal of a salary increase in the period from 1947–48 to 1957–58. Consistent with Dean Wilkinson's practice-oriented vision of legal education, the Law School did not provide faculty sabbaticals for scholarly research and writing, but it encouraged younger faculty in particular to gain practical experience in private practice.[70]

Fordham's faculty at mid-century consisted of twice as many part-timers as full-timers, and it was inbred as most of them were Fordham Law School alumni. Of the seven full-time faculty, four were Fordham Law School graduates. Of the fifteen part-time teachers, thirteen were graduates of the Law School. The full-time faculty's maximum teaching load was eight hours per week, only two hours per week more than that of the part-timers. However, the part-timers' average weekly teaching load was only three hours. In 1949, the full-time faculty's average salary was $7,464 and the median salary was $8,550. These figures declined to $6,620 and $7,050, respectively, in 1953. By 1953 all full-time faculty members received a pension contribution of 5 percent in addition to their salaries. Law faculty salaries were higher than those in the other divisions of Fordham University. Maximum salaries of full-time instructors were "about 1/3 to 1/2 higher" and minimum salaries were "about 1/2 to 100% higher" than those of full-time faculty in other divisions. In addition, salary increases of the Law School faculty were "generally more liberal."[71]

The Law School and, presumably, the university subscribed to the tenure principles adopted by the American Association of University Professors in 1940. The Law School recognized tenure as a protected faculty status after four to five years of service, on average, and promotion to the rank of associate professor. Seventy percent of the full-time faculty were tenured in the fall of 1957. Consistent with the AAUP Statement of Principles Number 32, which permitted termination only for adequate cause, retirement, or financial exigency, a law teacher would be dismissed only for "grave cause" and after notice of the charges and a hearing before a faculty hearing committee at which the faculty member was entitled to legal representation. He had a right of appeal to the ultimate deciding authority, who was the president of Fordham University. The Law School did not have any procedure for terminating a term appointment prematurely or for reviewing the dean's decision not to renew a term appointment.[72]

Dean Wilkinson encouraged the Fordham Law faculty to write articles for the *Fordham Law Review*, but the Law School did not provide support for faculty scholarship. It did not have a publication fund to support faculty research and writing, and it did not give grants-in-aid or defray the expenses associated with faculty publications. Although Dean Wilkinson reported that secretarial assistance was available to the faculty, faculty "stenographic assistance" was not separately budgeted. The dean encouraged faculty to attend meetings of professional organizations and to participate in the educational activities of professional associations such as the ABA and AALS, but amounts expended for these purposes were paltry, ranging from $65.41 in the 1945–46 academic year to $271.73 in 1947–48.[73]

Fordham Law School continued to maintain distinctively high admissions and academic standards in Wilkinson's last years as dean. It was one of eight law schools that required a college degree as the academic prerequisite for admission. Although Fordham Law School did not require course work in any particular pre-law subjects, it did "recommend that students pursue as far as possible the old classical education embracing the study of the 'humanities' so called." Wilkinson did not consider non-theory courses in assessing whether the applicant satisfied the Law School's degree requirement and its required minimum college scholastic average, and the Law School did not accept degrees in technical subjects, such as engineering or business administration. The bachelor's degree itself was not sufficient. The Law School's selective admission policy required that the applicant's college academic record demonstrate that he or she was capable of law study. However, from the 1946–47 school year to the 1952–53 school year, Wilkinson's last year as dean, the number of applications to the Law School declined, but more applicants were accepted and enrolled. Of the applicants who enrolled in 1952, 5 percent had an undergraduate GPA of A; 30 percent had a B average; and the great majority, some 64 percent, graduated college with a C+ average. Wilkinson, who made all admissions decisions, admitted three students with averages below C+. He preferred Fordham graduates over other "equally qualified students," and about one quarter of the students accepted to the Law School came from departments within Fordham University. The other students enrolled in the 1949–50 school year graduated from approximately 125 colleges and universities, most of which were located outside of New York State. Nevertheless, most of the Law School's students came from the New York metropolitan area and lived at home.[74]

Drop-out rates continued to be significant after World War II. In the academic year immediately following the conclusion of the war, 1945–46, 34 percent of the day students and 43 percent of the night students dropped out. The greatest proportion of students who left were in the first year: 17 percent of the day students and 21 percent of the night students dropped out. Fewer students dropped out the next academic year: 24 percent of the day students and 36 percent of the night students. Fewer students still dropped out during the 1947–48 academic year: 16 percent of the day students and 30 percent of the night students. Students who reached their senior year generally graduated, although a few either dropped out of school voluntarily or were failed out of school. Significant numbers of voluntary and involuntary withdrawals continued into the 1950s.[75]

Wilkinson's view of legal education continued to be practice-oriented at a time when the Vanderbilt study revealed that bar leaders urged law schools to prepare lawyers not only to represent clients but also to become public leaders. His vision also conflicted with that of Fordham University's central administration, which shared the Vanderbilt study's view and urged the Fordham Law faculty to become more interdisciplinary and academically oriented. Leaders in legal education also urged these changes, and the better law schools eventually adopted them. Wilkinson, on the other hand, expressed his "firm conviction that the first and principal business of any good law school is to train men for the practise [sic] of their profession and not as it is contended to be in some places to equip men to staff Government agencies and become criminologists and the

like." Indeed, he thought that "training a man to be a competent practising [*sic*] lawyer" would "equip him to engage in the other—governmental
and otherwise—activities" in which lawyers had taken a leading role
"throughout the history of our country." The law school's curriculum
"necessarily takes into account the content of the New York bar examinations," Wilkinson reported to the ABA in 1949. He was satisfied with the
relationship of the "curriculum and methods of the School to the bar
examinations" and did not think any improvement was needed or desirable. He noted that there was "a high degree of conformity between bar
examination results and school grades." Wilkinson also clung to his vision
of legal educators as experienced practitioners who served as part-time
teachers and brought "into the classroom something of the actualities of
practice and thus [bridged] the gap between the theory or science of the
law and its art and practice."[76]

Dean Wilkinson's vision of legal education explains his unyielding
opposition to trends that were occurring in the better law schools in the
mid-twentieth century. William Hughes Mulligan entered Fordham Law
School as a student in 1939 and joined the faculty in 1946. He later recalled
his years as a student and as a faculty member when Wilkinson was dean.
As much as he respected Wilkinson for his remarkable accomplishments,
Mulligan had to admit that Wilkinson "ran the school like a despot on a
shoe string," and he adamantly clung to "a curriculum which he would
never change." Wilkinson "considered the Law School to be his own project," Mulligan opined. "They used to say that when Wilkinson died he
left the Law School to the Jesuits and I think that probably was the reason
why [Fordham University President Robert] Gannon did not fully accept
the excellence of the Law School."[77]

Wilkinson's ideal law school professor was the practitioner who taught
part-time. Faculty scholarship, to the extent that faculty published,
reflected this pragmatic orientation, with important exceptions. The publications of the Fordham Law faculty consisted of law review articles and
treatises intended for the practicing bar. Casebooks manifested a similar
pragmatic quality. Through the 1950s and into the 1960s, the Fordham
Law faculty did not engage in significant academic scholarly research, and
the Law School deans did not encourage it. The full-time faculty devoted
their time to teaching and to supervising and conducting extra-curricular

activities, such as the *Fordham Law Review* and the Moot Court, and lawyering skills, such as legal drafting.

Fordham Law School experienced a decline in status following World War II. A number of factors disadvantaged the institution and contributed to its slippage from being the number two law school in New York City and among the top twenty law schools in the nation. These factors included the following: the university's diversion of Law School surplus revenues away from the Law School to subsidize other divisions of the university; the Law School's financial structure, which rendered it dependent on tuition and fees; the Law School's inadequate building which prevented its development and growth; Dean Wilkinson's vision of legal education, which served the Law School well before World War II but was quickly becoming obsolete in the postwar era; and the failure of the Law School's faculty to produce the kind of academic legal scholarship that was becoming the hallmark of the nation's best law schools. The Law School's decline became evident in the last years of Dean Wilkinson's tenure.

Paul Fuller
Dean, 1905–13

H. Gerald Chapin
Professor, 1905–19

Ignatius M. Wilkinson
Professor, 1911–53; Dean, 1923–53

I. Maurice Wormser
Professor, 1913–55

Francis J. Mcintyre
Professor, 1913–65

John Whalen
Dean, 1914–19

Frederick L. Kane
Professor, 1914–47

Francis P. Garvan
Dean, 1919–23

John A. Blake
Professor, 1919–47

Lloyd M. Howell
Professor, 1922–50

Edmond Butler
Professor, 1923–54

Leo T. Kissam
Devoted Alumnus and Benefactor,
Class of 1923

Raymond D. O'Connel
Professor, 1924–46

Ruth Whitehead Whaley
First black woman admitted to the
bars of New York and North Carolina,
Class of 1924, *cum laude*

John F. X. Finn
Professor, 1924–56
Dean, 1954–56

Arthor A. McGivney
Professor, 1925–58

Gorge W. Bacon
Professor, 1926–65

Edward Q. Carr
Professor, 1926–84

Eugene J. Keefe
Professor, 1926–68

Lois Stein
Devoted Alumnus and Benefactor,
Class of 1926

William R. Meagher
Professor, 1928–45, 1974–78

George A. Brooks
Professor, 1929–35, 1965–88

Victor S. Kilkenny
Professor, 1930–59

Ned Doyel
Devoted Alumnus and Benefactor,
Class of 1931

Hon. David N. Edelstein
Devoted Alumnus–U.S.D.C.,
Class of 1934

Joseph W. McGovern
Professor, 1936–66

William R. White
Professor, 1936–79

Francis X. Conway
Professor, 1938–71

Bernard J. O'Connell
Professor, 1946–67

Joseph A. Doran
Professor, 1946–68

William Hughes Mulligan
Professor, 1946–1971
Dean, 1956–71

Edward Freeman
Professor, 1946–81

John E. McAniff
Professor, 1946–82

Leonard F. Manning
Professor, 1948–83

John D. Calamari
Professor, 1952–91

Hon. John F. Keenan
Devoted Alumnus–U.S.D.C.,
Class of 1954

Raymond P. O'Keefe
Professor, 1955–63

Martin Fogelman
Professor, 1956–2004

Joseph R. Crowley
Professor, 1957–85
Associate Dean, 1982–85

Robert A. Kessler
Professor, 1957–88

Hon. Kevin Thomas Duffy
Devoted Alumnus–U.S.D.C.,
Class of 1958

Ludwick A. Teclaff
Professor, 1959–2003
Law Librarian, 1959–86

Ernest Earl Phillips
Professor, 1960–2003

Manuel R. Garcia-Mord
Professor, 1961–65

Hon. Joseph M. McLaughlin
Professor, 1961–81
Dean, 1971–81

Charles Whelan, S.J.
Professor, 1962–2006

Robert M. Byrn
Professor, 1963–94
Associate Dean, 1986–88

Joseph M. Perillo
Professor, 1963–2003
Acting Dean, 1981–82

Thomas M. Quinn
Professor, 1965–2003

Edward F. McGonagle
Professor, 1964–2007

Michael R. Lanzarone
Professor, 1969–2007
Associate Dean, 2003–4

Peter O'Connor
Professor, 1973–88

Edward J. Yario
Professor, 1973–78, 1983–92

Abraham Abramovsky
Professor, 1979–2007

Rev. Donald L. Magnetti
Professor, 1981–2008

Georgene M. Vairo
Professor, 1982–96
Associate Dean, 1985–95

Mary C. Daly
Professor, 1983–2004
Director, Stein Institute, 1989–2004

Dehorah A. Batts
Professor, 1984–94

Janet R. Tracy
Professor, Law Librarian,
1986–2005

Ann Moynihan
Clinical Professor, 1994–2006
Associate Dean, 2005–7

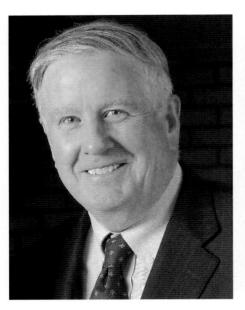

John D. Ferrick
Dean, 1982–2002; Leonard F. Manning
Distinguished Professor, 2002–2003;
Sidney C. Norris Chair of Law,
2003–present

William M. Treanor
Professor, 1991–2002
Dean, 2002–10
Paul Fuller Chair of Law, 2006–10

CHAPTER SIX

MODERNIZING FORDHAM LAW SCHOOL

Dean Wilkinson died unexpectedly on June 22, 1953. The selection and appointment of Wilkinson's successor demonstrated that the Law School's governance was completely in the hands of Fordham University's administration. Fordham University President Reverend Laurence J. McGinley, S.J., appointed Professor George W. Bacon acting dean until a new dean could be selected. Professor Bacon was in his early sixties in 1953 and considered too old to be appointed the regular dean. In addition, Bacon was a Protestant, and he did not "believe that a Protestant should become Dean of a Catholic Law School." Bacon served as acting dean until June 30, 1954, when Father McGinley announced to the Law School faculty the appointment of Professor John F. X. Finn as the new dean at a special meeting he convened after saying a memorial Mass in the chapel at 302 Broadway on the first anniversary of Wilkinson's death. Father McGinley oversaw the search for the new dean, which was conducted by the university's central administration. Father McGinley also announced the appointment of Professor William Hughes Mulligan as assistant dean. Professor Mulligan succeeded Finn as dean two years later, and he served as dean until June 1971.[1]

Dean Finn symbolized the old order in legal education that mixed an active law practice with legal academia. But, Finn carried it to an extreme. "John established that he was more interested in practicing law than Deaning," Mulligan explained. Fordham University's academic vice president, Reverend Edwin A. Quain, S.J., informed the president in July 1956 that Finn had not "decreased his active practice of the law to any notable degree since taking the Office of Dean" two years earlier. It was "common knowledge among downtown lawyers and faculty that the Dean [was] actively engaged in the practice of Law," and he was "certainly absent from the Dean's Office a great deal of the time." This upset some of the Law School's faculty and alumni, and Father McGinley thought that the dean should be full-time. Nor was Finn "in any sense an administrator," in Father Quain's view, who believed he lacked "both the temperament and the judgment for the position." Mulligan carried the whole burden of running the Law School. Father McGinley more or less fired Finn as dean. Fordham University issued a press release on August 19, 1956, stating that Father McGinley had appointed Finn "co-ordinator for Fordham University Law School Development," that Finn would continue as professor of law, but that he would "also resume private practice" at Lorenz, Finn and Giardino, the law firm with which he had been associated since 1923.[2]

Evidently, Father McGinley simply appointed Mulligan as Finn's successor. "Father McGinley called me in during the summer and told me that I was to be the Dean," Mulligan later recalled. There was no dean's search and no search committee. Mulligan, who had graduated *cum laude* from both Fordham College in 1939 and Fordham Law School in 1942, was a successful lawyer, having become a partner in the law firm of Manning, Hollinger and Shea before joining the Fordham Law faculty in 1946. Mulligan's ties to Fordham were deep. He was a collateral descendant of Archbishop John Hughes, who founded Fordham in 1841. Mulligan's father told the priest at William's baptism that he named the boy Hughes after "Archbishop John Hughes who was the first Archbishop of New York, the builder of St. Patrick's Cathedral and the founder of Fordham University."[3]

In the half century of its existence, Fordham Law School declined from an elite institution of legal education to a trade school. Mulligan acknowledged this unfortunate fact on the occasion of the Law School's fiftieth anniversary in 1955. As associate dean, Mulligan informed Academic Vice President Edwin A. Quain, S.J., that he was "convinced that we are a 'trade school.'" Mulligan attributed a large part of the blame for the Law School's decline to Dean Wilkinson, because he had "intended to run a 'bread and butter Law School.'" Both men agreed that it was not "desirable that this point of view be maintained for the future."[4]

Mulligan was dedicated to modernizing Fordham Law School and propelling it into the mainstream of American legal education. He succeeded in transforming it from a part-time to a full-time law school early in his tenure as dean. Mulligan succeeded also in getting a new building suited to the kind of legal education he sought to deliver: it provided more classrooms for various kinds of courses, such as seminars; more library space; more space for student-edited journals and student scholarship; and more space to accommodate a larger faculty and faculty scholarship. He began the process that eventually eliminated the faculty's inbreeding by hiring faculty from diverse backgrounds. He made greater efforts to engage the faculty in scholarly research and publication, which the new building made possible, by requiring publication for tenure and promotion and supporting faculty scholarship with financial support. He wanted to recruit students beyond the New York metropolitan area and across the nation, and, recognizing the need for a student dormitory and student scholarships to accomplish this goal, he struggled to persuade the Fordham University administration to devote the necessary financial resources.

Unfortunately, Father McGinley and the Fordham University administration considered the Law School a bread-and-butter institution, though with a different meaning than Wilkinson's. Father Quain's view notwithstanding, Fordham University continued to use the Law School as a cash cow, diverting the Law School's surplus revenue to subsidize Fordham University's other schools and divisions through the rest of the twentieth century. The university continued to house the Law School in an inadequate building, and this deficiency was not corrected until 1961, and then only temporarily. University budget priorities and space limitations precluded the Law School's development and rendered the Law School incapable of regaining and improving upon its earlier stature among the nation's best law schools.

The Law School undoubtedly generated enough revenue to fund a first-rate operation, but empirical data demonstrates that it was underfunded. Like most law schools of the time, Fordham Law School was tuition-dependent. However, in its fiftieth anniversary year of 1955, its enrollment was the tenth largest of 125 reporting law schools, and its tuition for full-time students was the fifteenth highest in the nation. Yet, the school's library ranked "77th out of 127 [reporting law] schools" in the size of its collection and "110th out of 127 schools" in the amount of its annual library expenditures to increase its collection. The law library's expenditure per student was "about the lowest of any of the [ABA] approved schools," according to John G. Hervey, adviser to the ABA's Section of Legal Education and Admissions to the Bar.[5]

Because the Law School's tuition and student enrollment were among the highest in the country and the number of full-time faculty employed was relatively small, Fordham had the financial resources to recruit the highest-quality faculty by offering premium salaries. But it could not.

Mulligan lamented that the Law School's "salary scale is not as yet high enough to attract successful lawyers away from the lucrative practice of law," and Father Quain agreed. Although it was located in a city with one of the nation's highest costs of living, Fordham Law School's median faculty salary for the 1953–54 school year placed it eighty-fourth out of 119 reporting law schools and eighteenth out of 34 reporting church-related schools. Its faculty salaries were "the lowest in the New York area," and its full-time faculty-to-student ratio was "the highest in the New York area," according to ABA adviser Hervey.[6]

Hervey informed Dean Finn in March 1955 that his section "expressed deep concern at the salary scale which prevails" at Fordham Law. They were of the view "that there is a close relationship between salaries paid, the competency and stability of the staff, and the adequacy of the instruction offered." The Law School was a "professional one," Hervey opined, and "the earnings of competent law teachers should approximate the earnings of practitioners of equal ability." Nevertheless, Fordham law faculty salaries were significantly below those of New York City practitioners.[7]

Fordham University's underfunding of the Law School and diverting of the Law School's profits to subsidize its general operations sparked a conflict in 1955 between the ABA and Fordham University. Hervey concluded that the Law School did not have "any problems that money will not cure," and he believed that the Law School was generating the money to cure them. He warned Dean Finn that the ABA Council on Legal Education "will be most critical" of the university's siphoning off these surplus revenues, and that he would "have some harsh words to say about" Fordham University's financial arrangements with the Law School in his talk "before the administrative round-table on 'Things Monetary in Legal Education'" at the annual ABA meeting in December 1955. This marked the beginning of a decades-long dispute between the ABA and Fordham University over the university's appropriation of the Law School's surplus revenues. The dispute became increasingly acrimonious in the 1970s. The members of the ABA's council believed the university's financial priorities contributed to the decline of Fordham from the first-rate law school it had been and prevented it from becoming again.[8]

The building that housed the Law School and its location in the legal district encouraged the Law School community to regard the Law School as a part-time institution. The school's physical plant was too small to educate all full-time students in one day division, forcing the Law School to split the day school into two separate divisions—a morning and an afternoon—in order to accommodate the large number of students it was required to enroll because of its total tuition dependency and its role as the university's financial subsidizer. Of course, the third division was the night school, which enabled "a great many excellent young men" to get their legal education who would otherwise be deprived of this opportunity. The inadequate law library and the absence of additional room for study forced day students to leave the Law School when they were not in class. Requiring day students to attend classes only in the morning or only in the afternoon was "almost an invitation to those students to work for the other half of the day."[9]

The school's proximity to law offices was another "encouragement to students to become part-time students." Thus, locating the Law School in lower Manhattan, the center of Manhattan's law practice, which was an advantage when most law students worked in these offices and attended the Law School on a part-time basis, was now an impediment to quality legal education when the best law schools, indeed, most law schools offered only full-time programs to full-time students. The "three-session system" combined with "enticing employment opportunities" in nearby New York law offices and courts tended to "aggravate the problem" according to the ABA inspection report. Full-time students were required to sign a certificate stating that they would not work more than twelve hours at outside employment, but enforcement of this rule was "something of a problem," and this pledge was not kept by many students. The teachers were not very demanding of the students, which caused Mulligan to complain that day students were "not taxed enough in their work at school, they have no place to study and lounge at the school, and gradually they become more and more involved in work in Law offices downtown."[10]

Mulligan made scheduling changes to cut down on outside employment by full-time day students and to end Fordham's image as a part-time law school. He persuaded the full-time faculty to change the current "block" schedule of classes to a "checkerboard" schedule. Thus, the day classes were divided into two sections instead of morning and afternoon divisions. The students in the two sections attended classes on alternative mornings and afternoons. The dean intended this change as a "method of forcing full time study." Mulligan eased these changes into the course schedule during the 1958–59 academic year.[11]

The Law School's location also had "a deleterious effect on the full-time faculty." Again, at the Law School's inception and through most of its first half century, the faculties of the nation's law schools consisted mostly of practicing lawyers who taught part-time. This began to change prior to World War II and by the middle of the twentieth century the trend was toward full-time faculties who devoted all of their time to teaching and publishing legal scholarship. Fordham Law School's full-time faculty were "in theory, permitted 'an occasional brief or consultation' in a downtown law firm" during the academic year, but they used summers to engage in legal practice rather than scholarly research and publication. However, Mulligan and Father Quain were "in complete agreement" that it had become "increasingly clear . . . that rule is not carefully observed because the men inevitably become more and more involved in legal practice." One of the reasons is that it was "very difficult, if not impossible, to secure employment in the summer unless some association is permitted with the employing firm during the course of the academic year," with the understanding that full-time employment with the firm was permitted only during the summer months. The Fordham Law faculty felt compelled to supplement their low salaries with fees they could earn practicing law. The faculty's involvement in the practice of law accounted for their "failure . . . to write for legal journals and to produce books such as would bring prestige to the school."[12]

The faculty's failure to engage in legal scholarship was also attributable to the nonscholarly academic environment at Fordham. Fordham University's criteria for promotion and tenure clearly did not require scholarly publications. Promotion and tenure determinations were made on the "candidate's genuine service to the University." In evaluating this service, the qualities considered included "years of service in rank, degrees held, previous teaching experience and the recommendation of departmental chairmen and deans." Other factors considered included the candidate's "influence on students and colleagues; mastery of the classroom and academic presentation; participation in learned societies; research; professional excellence in circles outside the University, etc." The university's merit system of salary increments adopted in the spring of 1958 also focused on teaching and personality. In 1967 Fordham University adopted the 1940 Statement of Principles of the American Associations of University Professors (AAUP), which included the AAUP's tenure policies and procedures, although the university still did not place much emphasis on scholarly publications. Law faculty were subject to Fordham University's criteria and principles in tenure and promotion decisions. Mulligan formalized the Law School's tenure and promotion process by creating an advisory faculty tenure and promotion committee, and he placed greater emphasis on scholarship, but this factor remained relatively unimportant in these decisions.[13]

Deploring the lack of faculty publications in the past, Mulligan conceded that the solution to the problem of inadequate faculty research and writing was not simple, and he acknowledged that at least some of the difficulty was attributable to the absence of support given by the university to faculty scholarship, even though Father McGinley placed a great deal of "importance [on] having a full-time faculty who would write." The inadequate physical accommodations at 302 Broadway, "both librarywise and officewise," had "a stultifying effect upon any academic efforts," Mulligan confessed. So did the lack of research funds for teaching fellows and secretarial help that Mulligan tried unsuccessfully to get from the university. He admonished the university administration that hiring faculty "who are capable and inspired to become leaders in molding legal thought will further depend upon the facilities provided in large measure." However, he also continued to stress to the faculty the importance of legal writing and complained to them "that the great majority of the faculty have not in recent years cooperated in this respect."[14]

Mulligan acted against his interest in getting more faculty members to publish in scholarly journals, as did the university administration. The first faculty fellowship awarded to a law school faculty member appears to have gone to Professor Eugene J. Keefe in June 1960, even though Mulligan thought that "Keefe was definitely not a scholar. He was a fun-loving bachelor who loved to hit spots like the Oak Room of the Plaza and the Stork Club. He was extremely well dressed, always wore gold cuff links which he would flash in class with a very distinctive gesture and proceed to conduct his classes." No one had "ever accused him of being a Blackstone." On the other hand, Keefe was "a great companion," and he had a "wonderful sense of humor and he was loved by everybody." Awarding faculty fellowships on the basis of good fellowship rather than commitment to scholarship was sure to undermine Mulligan's goal of getting faculty publications.[15]

Mulligan further impeded his goal of securing a publishing faculty by awarding the Law School's only endowed chair on the basis of seniority rather than scholarly production. Professor Bacon was awarded the Alpin W. Cameron Chair "in recognition of his able and faithful service during the course of his more than thirty years on the faculty." Bacon had not published anything for more than a decade, and Mulligan later acknowledged that Bacon was awarded the Cameron Chair "on the basis of his being the senior professor on the full-time faculty." When Professor Bacon resigned his Cameron Chair, Mulligan recommended that it go to Professor Thomas J. Snee, who had genuine scholarly credentials by the standards of the 1950s, including a PhD, which set him apart from most of the nation's law professors. Nevertheless, it appears that the Cameron Chair went to Professor Snee "as the next senior man." Seniority was also the determining factor in the award of the Law School's second endowed chair in 1961, the Agnes and Ignatius Wilkinson Professorship of Law. "In point of service," Mulligan was "the next senior full-time professor, followed by Professor Manning." Apparently it was not considered appropriate for the dean to receive this chair, and Mulligan recommended Professor Manning.[16]

Despite the institutional obstacles to faculty scholarship, Mulligan continued to admonish the faculty to engage in scholarly research and writing. In 1958 Mulligan informed the faculty that "in the future rank, promotion and salary will depend to a great deal upon scholarly achievements." Mulligan's statement was more aspirational than real, and he did not follow through. Father Charles Whalen served for many years in the 1960s and 1970s as chair of the faculty committee on appointments, promotions, rank, and tenure. He recalled that the most important consideration in hiring new faculty members and in promotions and tenure was the candidate's teaching skills. "Writing was applauded, but it didn't play the important role it would in the future, in particular under Dean John Feerick." Father Whalen's statement did not mean that faculty scholarship was unnecessary. Deans Mulligan and McLaughlin stressed the importance of writing and required faculty publication for tenure and promotion. However, according to Father Whalen, "the emphasis was on teaching in and out of classroom," and faculty scholarship was not reviewed as vigorously as it was under Dean Feerick. Not only were full-time faculty expected to spend a substantial amount of their time with students, faculty teaching schedules sometimes precluded scholarly research and writing. For example, Professor Thomas Quinn recalled that he was overloaded with courses that left no time for writing. Nevertheless, he was still expected to publish, and he met the publication requirement by writing the UCC Newsletter for the practicing bar instead of scholarly articles to be published in law reviews.[17]

The 1958 ABA inspection report confirmed that the law faculty was "distinctly a teaching faculty" which gave "very little emphasis [to] research and scholarly production." The faculty's orientation was "almost necessarily so," the inspectors reported, because of the "small full-time faculty, [the large] size of the student body, and the arrangement of the School in three divisions." The report further concluded that "the full-time staff is too small to meet the needs of a multiple-division school of this size. Little can thus be expected beyond basic instruction in large classes." Mulligan hoped that the new building at Lincoln Center that was in the planning stages would enable the Law School "to raise the sights a little more beyond the classroom in the direction of seminar and small group instruction and scholarly research."[18]

It must be stated, however, that the Fordham Law faculty were not unusual in their low scholarship productivity and in the nature of the faculty's publications during the Mulligan years. Law professors in the period from the 1940s into the 1970s, legal historian Laura Kalman recently observed, "published little beyond casebooks, treatises, or the occasional doctrinal article, if that much." These were the kinds of publications Fordham faculty produced and Mulligan appreciated. Despite the disincentives to engage in legal scholarship, the faculty responded to Mulligan's entreaties to publish by publishing. In September 1958 Mulligan proudly informed Father McGinley of faculty publications in the *Fordham Law Review*. But the nature of the publications did not distinguish the faculty as important legal scholars.[19]

Another factor contributing to the Law School's decline was its continued reliance on part-time faculty to keep teaching salaries low. Fordham's law faculty was primarily a part-time faculty at a time when law school faculties in the best law schools were expected to be full-time teachers and scholars who eschewed the practice of law. The practice experience and practical perspective part-time faculty brought to legal education that Wilkinson and the legal academy valued so highly earlier in the century were increasingly devalued within the legal academy in the second half of the twentieth century. Moreover, the demands of their law practices gave part-time law teachers only rare opportunities to engage in academic scholarly pursuits. Unfortunately, Father Quain commented, the Law School's "location downtown has encouraged us to take on part-time men whose busy lives in practice do not make them ideal teachers in a *serious law school* even with full credit given to the eminence of some of them in their particular fields." The Law School's full-time faculty favored moving the Law School to Fordham University's Bronx campus in 1955. However, the current dean, John F. X. Finn, and the alumni opposed the move, and the Law School remained at 302 Broadway.[20]

In 1955 the Law School's ratios of full-time to part-time faculty and full-time faculty to students were both very poor. Father Quain reported to Father McGinley that Assistant Dean Mulligan "tells me that our ratio of 9 full-time to 15 part-time is exactly that of St. Louis University which has a total of 259 students," fewer than one-half of Fordham's student body. The Law School "has, at the present time, about 675 students. There is no school of comparable size with so unfavorable a faculty ratio," Father Quain lamented. The following year Fordham was "a bad last" among New York State's AALS-approved law schools in terms of full-time faculty. The ratio of students to full-time teachers was 76-to-1, placing Fordham Law School as the "second lowest of the entire 127 schools listed" among the law schools reporting to the ABA during the 1954–55 academic year. The Law School and university administrations recognized the need to hire more teachers and were "anxious to strengthen" the Law School's full-time faculty. Although many faculty at the Law School and Fordham University President McGinley continued to believe that a "balance between" full-time and part-time teachers was "essential" and "extremely advantageous," Fathers McGinley and Quain recommended that "steps be taken to replace" part-time men, who were "rather old," with "full-time men." The full-time faculty did not outnumber the part-time faculty until the 1959–60 academic year. The "primary difficulty" in hiring more full-time faculty was that "they have no office space to give a full-time man if they took one on the faculty." There was also an acute shortage of space for books in the law library as well. Fordham was "third from the last" among New York law schools in the number of books in the library. These conditions "cannot be ameliorated until we get larger quarters," Mulligan maintained. Convinced this was true, Father Quain concluded that "both of these items point once again, to the urgency of new and larger quarters for the Law School."[21]

In 1958 the ABA inspectors identified another problem with the faculty that detracted from the Law School's stature. It noted a "considerable remnant of inbreeding" on the law faculty that had "characterized the earlier school still exists." Inbreeding was not unusual among law faculties at this time. "Our faculties tend to reproduce themselves; and in the process may by the continual inbreeding be producing even narrower law students than they were themselves," Harvard Law School Dean Erwin Griswold complained. Only one of the six Fordham Law School alumni on the twelve member full-time faculty did graduate work in another law school, and he earned an LLM from New York University. The six non-Fordham alumni received their degrees from Yale, New York University, Harvard, Columbia, St. John's, and St. Louis Law Schools (supplemented by an LLM degree). Of the seventeen part-time faculty, two were Jesuit priests who taught the course in Jurisprudence, and eleven were Fordham Law alumni. The four other part-timers earned their law degrees from Columbia, Syracuse, Yale, and Cornell Law Schools. Mulligan sought to get away from the inbreeding by diversifying the faculty in terms of educational and religious backgrounds. Approximately two-thirds of the faculty Mulligan appointed during his deanship were graduates of law schools other than Fordham Law School.[22]

The Law School experienced a tremendous turnover in the faculty during Mulligan's deanship. It lost many of the faculty it regarded as its most "eminent and experienced" faculty through death and resignation during the 1950s and 1960s. In the 1950s, it lost Dean Wilkinson and Professors I. Maurice Wormser, Edmund B. Butler, and John J. X. Finn, all of whom died, and Arthur A. McGivney, Edward Q. Carr, Victor S. Kilkenny, and Godfrey P. Schmidt, all of whom resigned. The "severe attrition" of the 1950s continued into the 1960s with the loss of Professors Julian A. Ronan, George W. Bacon, Eugene J. Keefe, Thomas J. Snee, Joseph McGovern, Raymond O'Connell, and Joseph A. Doran. "Old-timers" who remained on the full-time faculty included John E. McAniff, Leonard Manning (appointed in 1948), and Raymond P. O'Keefe. John Calamari, appointed in 1952, became an "old-timer" during this period.[23]

Mulligan "had great aspirations for the Law School," Judge McLaughlin recalled. He decided that a new building "was the place to launch, to catapult, the School into national prominence." Mulligan believed that the new Law School building in Lincoln Square would afford Fordham Law School the opportunity to match the Jesuit standard of preeminence in education, to become "without doubt the best Catholic law school in the United States," and to "compete successfully with the so-called Ivy League schools." Mulligan understood that national prominence was not possible without a faculty that produced scholarship. "In those days, very few of them wrote anything, and to do that, they had to be in the building. So Mulligan required the faculty to sign in and to sign out."[24]

Under Mulligan's leadership, the faculty decided in the late 1950s to rebuild and expand the faculty by bringing in "young lawyers of proven ability and scholarship who would continue the tradition of excellence for many years to come." They "rejected the idea of recruiting glamour 'big names.'" This decision was based on the belief that "quality law faculty must be built from within" by "established law teachers" retaining "qualified young lawyers" and helping them build their reputations on the "basis of effective teaching, research, publication and public service." This policy bore fruit by the mid-1960s, when an AALS researcher who studied Fordham Law School as part of a research project on legal education commented about the "quality explosion" at Fordham due to the finding that faculty "research, publication and involvement in public service were all on the rise."[25]

To achieve national prominence, the Law School needed greater funding from Fordham University. Mulligan believed the Fordham University administration supported the Law School's ambitions. In 1955 the university's academic vice president, Father Edwin A. Quain, S.J., acknowledged that the Law School was underfunded, and he advised President Father Laurence J. McGinley that the university was going to have to provide it with more money. Quain observed that the Law School's library acquisitions were low, and the law library compared unfavorably in this and other respects with the law libraries of St. John's and Georgetown. Father Quain also recognized the growing importance of scholarships to attract the best students. "Judging from the statistics on scholarships available in

Law Schools, it would seem that we will have to do something on this matter very soon," he advised Father McGinley. In light of all of this information, he informed Father Rector that "it seems certain that the Law School is for the next few years going to cost us considerably more money than it has in the past if we wish to bring it up to the level that our Law School ought to reach."[26]

Father McGinley seemed to indicate in 1959 that he agreed with his academic vice president's assessment of the Law School's need for greater financial support. He acknowledged that the school's physical facilities were one of the primary reasons it was unable to achieve its vision of excellence in legal education. Consequently, the university decided that the Law School and library would be the first buildings constructed at Lincoln Square. Father McGinley conceded that the Law School had had to function from the start with an inadequate physical plant, and he assured Mulligan that "your Law School for the first time in its history will be given the physical facilities to permit it to produce great lawyers in the 'grand manner.'"[27]

The Law School building at Lincoln Center was dedicated in 1961 at a ceremony in which Attorney General Robert F. Kennedy gave the keynote address and was followed with speeches by U.N. Ambassador Adlai E. Stevenson and Professor Arthur E. Sutherland of Havard Law School. Chief Justice Earl Warren of the United States Supreme Court laid the cornerstone of the building.[28]

The Lincoln Center facility encouraged Mulligan to believe that Fordham University supported his ambition to transform Fordham Law School into a first-rate law school, but his belief was misplaced. The university refused to provide the necessary funding to achieve this goal. It manifested its lack of support in the 1960s.

Mulligan recognized in 1965 what Dean Vanderbilt of New York University Law School saw almost two decades earlier—that a law school "must emerge as a national rather than a local law school" if it was to continue to improve its academic status. To become a national law school, Mulligan believed that Fordham Law School had to recruit students "beyond the normal geographic limits which have confined our interest for the past sixty years." Mulligan understood that none of the law schools that ranked with Fordham in academic stature were "purely 'local.'" Rather, they recruited "students on a national basis with a consequent broadening of influence on bench, bar and public service." He realized that achieving this objective required "substantially increased student scholarship funds as well as convenient dormitory facilities" that took advantage of the "singularly attractive situs of the law school in Lincoln Square which is the cultural center of the nation." Mulligan noted that the "rate of progress" would depend to a great extent on "the continuing generosity of the alumni and friends of the law school." But, he also believed that the university "encouraged these ambitions" to achieve national prominence and would support the Law School's efforts by increasing the faculty salary scale and by supporting "eventual" dormitory construction and increased student scholarship assistance.[29]

Mulligan's optimism over the university's support was misplaced. The university failed to provide the needed funding. The Law School had to wait about thirty years before the student dormitory was completed and available to house students. Rather than provide the needed scholarships to attract the best students, the university established a low ceiling on law school student scholarship funds: "No doubt, Dean Mulligan and his legal beagles will in time find ways to pierce Father Rector's suggested 'ceiling' figure, but this kind of statement should keep them busy with their law books for a while," Dr. Joseph Cammarosano snidely remarked.[30]

The modest scholarship funds the Law School received it did not use to attract excellent incoming students. Rather, it used these scholarships to reward editors of the *Fordham Law Review*, "which has been of great value in increasing the caliber of the *Law Review*," Mulligan rationalized. Still, he complained, "We are competing with Columbia and New York University insofar as scholarships are concerned, and they for the most part are for the full scholarships, whereas many of our scholarships are only one-quarter and one-half scholarships." The Law School's inadequate student aid explained "the serious limitation" Fordham faced "in attracting the top-flight scholar by reason of our limited scholarship funds." Mulligan informed Father McGinley in 1959 that he knew of "five Jesuit college graduates who are the sons of Law School alumni who were given Root-Tilden scholarships at New York University, which is indicative of the fact that we are losing the best boys who would normally be attracted to this school."[31]

Clearly, the caliber of applicants to Fordham Law School was adversely affected by the school's limited scholarship fund. An ABA report issued in February 1962 indicated that "the calibre of the students applying [to Fordham]—at least on the basis of LSAT scores—was under such schools as Boston College and Georgetown." Mulligan informed the faculty that "we are being rejected by some of the best applicants who are probably listing us as a second or third choice. We are losing to schools which are making much greater scholarship allowances." Mulligan proclaimed that "we need scholarship funds desperately." He asked the university for "additional scholarship help . . . which in the past has been neglected due to the pressing need for funds for the new law school." Fordham could not compete for the best students with law schools, especially Catholic law schools, that offered larger and more scholarships and that actively recruited applicants nationally. One of these law schools was Notre Dame. Its dean, Joseph O'Meara, wrote to the presidents of colleges and universities around the country asking them to encourage their "*exceptionally talented* students" to apply for available tuition scholarships at Notre Dame. Mulligan was not in a position to make similar solicitations. Moreover, Fordham was not trying to recruit students nationally. Its applicants were primarily residents of the New York City metropolitan area, and most of them had graduated from Catholic colleges and universities. Fordham University graduates supplied the largest number, followed by Holy Cross, St. John's, Columbia, Manhattan, New York University, Iona, Notre Dame, St. Peter's, Villanova, and Georgetown. One or more students were graduates of about seventy other schools, including Yale, Harvard, Princeton, Brown, Dartmouth, Vassar, Hamilton, Colgate, and Marymount.[32]

Relations between the Law School and the Fordham University administration began to sour in the summer of 1967. In July 1967 Mulligan expressed his desire "to project Fordham into the mainstream of American legal education." The dean and the Law School faculty believed that the first steps to make Fordham a "truly great law school" were to increase the size and the salaries of the faculty, "and most importantly, . . . to provide additional grants to students who will be pressed by any increase in tuition." Mulligan also required a fully qualified administrative staff.[33]

Reverend Leo McLaughlin, S.J., succeeded Father McGinley as Fordham University's president in 1965. He and his executive vice president, John J. Meng, were not about to provide the financial support required to make the Law School truly great when they believed that Mulligan and the law faculty were not capable of making Fordham Law a truly first-rate law school. Reviewing the proposed law faculty salary increases and Mulligan's proposal to increase the law faculty in March 1967, Father McLaughlin wondered "how we justify increments which are so far above the average increments in the entire University," inasmuch as "we are agreed, I think, that the [Law School] faculty is not truly outstanding." He was even "more concerned about the fact that Mulligan needs more than encouragement in getting some 'stars' on his faculty." He feared that giving Mulligan authority to hire associate professors at "the salaries authorized will merely encourage the continuation of the mediocrity." McLaughlin confided to Dr. Meng that "I sometimes have the fear that neither the Dean of the Law School nor the Faculty of the Law School have any real concept of what is meant by a truly great Law School." He asked Dr. Meng whether it was "too late to tell the Dean that he may have additional faculty only if the additional faculty are truly outstanding?"[34]

Approving three or four additional faculty positions, Dr. Meng did urge Mulligan to hire stars. "In these appointments, top-flight quality and major faculty rank should be primary considerations," Meng advised. "Perhaps we can utilize the goodwill of some of the friendly 'legal lights' of New York to assist in such recruiting." Mulligan and the law faculty disagreed with this approach to building an outstanding faculty. They preferred to hire young faculty with great potential as law teachers and legal scholars. This is the course they pursued.[35]

The Law School probably would not have been able to hire established "stars" even if it had wanted to. The faculty salary structure was too low to pay what would have been required to attract a star to Fordham. In addition, the university did not provide research support for faculty scholarship, which would have dissuaded serious scholars from accepting a Fordham offer. Moreover, the Law School's student-to-faculty ratio was so high that the faculty could only cover the basic courses. The top law schools were hiring scholars to do research in areas of their own interests, and they structured their academic programs to enable the faculty to engage in scholarship. Professors were required to teach one basic course that the law school needed to be taught and any other course or courses that grew out of their scholarly interests. Fordham Law School could not offer this kind of teaching package in the 1960s. To the contrary, the Fordham Law faculty were frequently overloaded with courses. Professor

Thomas Quinn was so burdened with courses that he had no time to write, although he did make time to write for the practicing bar. Given the lack of strong fund-raising and the terrible student-to-faculty ratio, the Law School only had room in the curriculum and money in the budget to hire faculty to teach the traditional courses. The Law School's challenge in its second half century was to overcome these and other disabilities to regain its stature as one of the top law schools in the United States. One of these disabilities was the disparaging view of the Law School held not only by Fordham President McLaughlin but by other Jesuits as well. "They used to say," recalled Mulligan, "that when Wilkinson died he left the Law School to the Jesuits and I think that probably was the reason why Gannon did not fully accept the excellence of the Law School."[36]

Thus, the university administration posed insurmountable obstacles to the Law School's ambitions by refusing to increase the Law School's salary structure required to recruit entry-level "stars" to the faculty and by refusing to authorize a substantial increase in the size of the full-time faculty to comply with ABA/AALS standards by reducing the high student-to-faculty ratio. Mulligan informed Dr. Meng that the Law School's starting salary was below the "opening salary for law school graduates from $10,000 to $15,000 per annum" paid by Wall Street law firms. Consequently, the Law School's salary structure was utterly inadequate to "cajole" lawyers to teach students who will command a higher starting salary without experience than the beginning teacher with "experience and top-flight scholastic qualifications." The Law School would have to have "a substantial boost for all salaries if we are to continue to strive for excellence," Mulligan admonished.[37]

Given the Fordham University administration's dismal view of the Law School, Mulligan was unsuccessful in persuading the administration that law faculty salaries were inadequate. Rejecting comparisons between the Law School's salaries and those of local law schools and the practicing bar in New York City, as the ABA standards directed, the administration compared them primarily to Fordham University–wide faculty salaries and AAUP university averages and secondarily to national law school averages, which were not very relevant to the New York City area with its high cost of living. Yet, insofar as faculty salaries were concerned, Dr. Meng expressed the perspective of the central administration when he told Mulligan: "I must frankly state my conviction that [the Law School's] salaries are not out of line with those paid in other good institutions and that the increments provided to the Law School are among the highest in the University."[38]

By spring of 1968, a breach opened between the Law School and the university administration over the place of the Law School within the university, the mission of the Law School, and the question of who should determine the Law School's policies and priorities. On May 9 the Law faculty unanimously adopted resolutions which proclaimed that the "Law School has entered a period of institutional and educational crisis" and that this crisis stemmed in significant part from the fact that non–Law School personnel within other divisions of Fordham University were making decisions that "vitally affect the institutional and educational policies of the Law School," decisions and policies that were within the Law School's exclusive discretion. These decisions were interfering with the consistent progress of the Law School, and they may have put in jeopardy the Law School's accreditation. The faculty further resolved that they were "charged with the primary responsibility for determining" the Law School's educational policies, and they sought to meet with Father McLaughlin to discuss "these several pressing crises" and to reach "an understanding concerning the future status of the Law School within the University." There is no record that this meeting took place.[39]

Mulligan warned the administration that its "attitude of hostility" toward the Law School "can only lead to a rapid deterioration of faculty morale." He reminded University Vice President for Academic Affairs Arthur W. Brown that Law School Assistant Deans Robert McGrath and Robert Hanlon had resigned in 1969. Hanlon had accepted a comparable position at the new Hofstra Law School, which, "without alumni or students," was offering Hanlon "more money than Fordham where he has served in outstanding fashion." The central administration's disregard of Mulligan's recommended salary increases for Hanlon of the preceding two years "constitute the major reason for his departure." Mulligan informed the administration that Professor Rice also "indicated his intention to leave the law school because of his inability to support a growing family on his present salary."[40]

Not only was the university underpaying the law faculty and administrators, the dean discovered that it was also charging the Law School for faculty salaries for which the university was compensated from other funds or was not incurring. The university was charging the Law School for Professor Leonard Manning's full salary even though the income generated by Professor Manning's endowed chair was "devoted entirely to supporting his salary." Mulligan argued that the amount should be credited to the Law School. The salaries of the two Jesuits on the law faculty were retained by the university. Mulligan believed it was not "equitable" to charge these against the lay faculty because they were "really a paper transaction" and represented "an expense which is not incurred." Perhaps even more inequitable was the university's charging Father Charles Whalen's entire salary to the Law School when one half of his salary was paid by *America* magazine, where he was an editor.[41]

Unmoved by Mulligan's pleadings, the university reduced recommended increases in Law faculty salaries in early 1969 as an economy measure to offset deficits of the preceding three years. The administration defended its action by noting that the Law faculty's salaries were "the highest group of salaries within the University." Mulligan replied that Law faculty salaries were the highest salaries in every university, except for those universities that had medical schools. "The reason for this is obvious," Mulligan maintained; "law teachers are professional attorneys and their worth has to be gauged on the basis of the competing salaries in the profession and in other law schools." He noted that the three full-time faculty members he had hired the preceding year took "a considerable decrease in salary." Mulligan conceded that an English teacher should be paid at the same salary as a law teacher, in an ideal world, and he even understood the resentment the English teacher might feel "because he is not, in fact, as well compensated." But, the Law School "must compete in the real world in which we live," and, in this world, the faculty's salaries were not high, "but, at best, modest."[42]

Mulligan further argued that average faculty salaries were not the "sole criterion" on which to compare law schools. Other factors, such as the student-to-teacher ratio and tuition were "essential elements in making this determination." The real question was how many faculty at a law school received the average salary and how many students did they have to teach. When one analyzed the student-to-faculty ratio, tuition, and average salary at other law schools, Fordham Law School was "in a very poor competitive position," Mulligan complained, and it was "lagging far behind" its competitors.[43]

ABA data on law school student populations, student-to-faculty ratios, full-time tuition, and student aid supported Mulligan's position. Table 6-1 shows that Fordham Law School lagged far behind other law schools in these regards. St. John's University Law School, for example, had slightly fewer students than Fordham, a comparable number of faculty and student-to-faculty ratio, and it charged $100 less in full-time tuition, but its student aid fund was six times larger than Fordham's. Boston College Law School had almost a third fewer students, but its faculty was larger than Fordham's and its student-to-faculty ratio was substantially lower. Boston College charged $100 more in full-time tuition, but it had three

TABLE 6-1. LAW SCHOOLS, STUDENTS, FACULTY, TUITION, AND STUDENT AID 1968

School	Students	Faculty	Student-to-Faculty Ratio	Tuition	Scholarship, Loan, Grant Funds
Boston College	546	21	21	$1,700	$ 217,000
Catholic U.	429	16	26	$1,600	$ 81,000
Columbia	902	41	21	$1,900	$ 710,000
Cornell	407	24	17	$1,900	$ 343,000
Georgetown	1146	34	34	$1,750	$ 303,000
George Washington	1158	43	27	$1,620	$ 329,000
Harvard	1581	65	25	$1,850	$1,500,000
New York University	1003	59	17	$2,000	$ 600,000
Pennsylvania	549	28	20	$2,150	$ 404,000
St. John's	741	18	41	$1,500	$ 400,000
St. Louis	342	17	20	$1,600	$ 135,000
Santa Clara	213	12	18	$1,600	$ 98,000
Stanford	433	24	18	$1,920	$ 381,000
Yale	542	39	14	$2,150	$ 825,000
Fordham	768	19	41	$1,600	$ 66,000

Source: ABA Section on Legal Education and Admission to the Bar, Law Schools Charging Tuitions of $1,600.00 or More, Table of Law Schools of Comparable Size, Table of Law Schools in New York State.

and one-quarter times more in student aid. Georgetown Law Center's student body was one and one-half times larger than Fordham's and its faculty one and four-fifths larger, and Georgetown had a substantially better student-to-faculty ratio. It charged $150 more per year in tuition than Fordham, and its student aid was three and one-half times greater. Fordham Law School was not even close to the New York City law schools it regarded as its competitors. Columbia and New York University Law Schools were simply in another league from Fordham's. New York University's student aid was almost ten times greater and Columbia's was almost eleven times greater than Fordham's. Both schools had student-to-faculty ratios that were about half of Fordham Law School's student-to-faculty ratio.[44]

The Law School's student-to-faculty ratio was problematical, as were other aspects of its teaching program. The ratio reported to the ABA counted as full-time faculty Dean Mulligan and Professor Ludwik Teclaff, the Law librarian, neither of whom carried a full teaching load. It also included the semi-retired Professor Keefe and Father Whalen, who had "never taught a full program." The ABA required that in each law school "at least three-fourths of the hours of instruction . . . should be offered by full-time teachers." The Law School was in violation of this rule. Forty percent of the fall semester courses in the second and third years in the night division were taught by part-time faculty. Part-time teachers taught 60 percent of the night courses in the spring semesters of these years.[45]

As soon as he received the ABA's report of median and average law faculty salaries for 1969–70, Mulligan forwarded it to Father Michael P. Walsh, S.J., who had replaced Father McLaughlin as university president in 1969. Mulligan highlighted fifteen law schools with which Fordham Law School "considered ourselves in competition," and they are represented in Table 6-2. He included the size of their faculties as well. Mulligan noted that Fordham's salaries were the "lowest of all except Villanova which ties us for median salary and has a lower average." Fordham's salaries lagged behind those of Georgetown and Boston College, and the Law School was "particularly low in our number of full-time teachers." Mulligan maintained that, in light of the Law School's high tuition, "it seems quite obvious that we are not receiving an appropriate allocation for faculty salaries."[46]

TABLE 6-2. COMPETITOR LAW SCHOOLS' SALARIES AND FACULTY SIZE
1969–70

Law School	Median Salary	Average Salary	Faculty Members
Columbia	$28,000	$25,850	37
Cornell	$26,000	$25,023	21
Michigan	$25,750	$24,992	36
Yale	$25,000	$24,679	46
New York University	$25,000	$24,625	48
Pennsylvania	$24,500	$24,780	27
Rutgers Newark	$24,495	$23,230	26
Virginia	$21,000	$20,254	36
NY State-Buffalo	$20,258	$19,963	26
Boston College	$20,000	$19,550	19
Boston University	$19,500	$20,380	30
Georgetown	$18,500	$19,251	33
Fordham	$18,000	$18,655	17
Villanova	$18,000	$16,894	15
Harvard	—	—	—
Notre Dame	—	—	—

Source: ABA Section on Legal Education, summarized in table prepared by Dean Mulligan.

Despite the ABA data on salaries, Fordham Academic Vice President Paul J. Reiss rejected Mulligan's claim that the law faculty were underpaid, and his position reflected the administration's perspective that law faculty salaries should be commensurate to those of other Fordham University faculty. He informed Father Walsh that Fordham Law faculty salaries were "entirely consistent with the salaries which [Fordham University] is providing for the rest of its faculty." The Law School's ambition of getting its faculty salaries up to "the mid-point or higher" among its competitor law schools was unrealistic, Reiss argued. Fordham University "as a whole does not provide salaries at this level." Reiss asserted that "we have to be realistic about our situation here. We are not in a good competitive position on salaries with respect to the universities with which the Law School's competitor law schools were associated. "It is unreasonable, therefore, for us to expect that the salaries for the Law School will be competitive." He did not explain why Fordham was unable to pay competitive salaries to the law faculty when other Catholic law schools were better able to and especially when the Law School was generating large surpluses. Sadly, the university's administration positioned itself in direct opposition to the Law School's goal of enhancing its standing within legal education.[47]

Fordham University was in a period of desparate financial crisis in the second half of the 1960s. University President Father Leo McLaughlin, S.J., announced in September 1967 that "Fordham was faced with the greatest crisis in its long history of crises." The university had suffered a $500,000 deficit in 1966, which doubled to $1 million in 1967 and was estimated to grow to $3,719,264 for the 1968–69 academic year. The financial crisis was attributable to several causes. Father McLaughlin's "greatness" program, an innovative educational program that brought onto the university faculty eminent professors and scholars, such as Margaret Mead and Marshall McLuhan, required greater financial resources than the university possessed. In addition, the university had embarked upon a $62 million building program that included the Lincoln Center campus, a program it could not afford. Fordham University was tuition dependent, and student enrollments were declining as many of the best and brightest Catholic high school students were now welcomed at the nation's most prestigious colleges and universities that had previously excluded them, such as Columbia, Harvard, and Yale. The *Gellhorn Report*, which is described below, concluded that "impecunious Catholic students" increasingly enrolled in tax-supported institutions or secular institutions that offered them financial aid. In 1965, 820,000 Catholics were enrolled in secular colleges and universities, but only 320,000 were enrolled in Catholic institutions of higher learning. The Vatican Council's decree on religious liberty was interpreted by many priests and nuns as a "license to become . . . an autonomous agent," which permitted them to leave their religious orders and to marry. Jesuits on the Fordham faculty, who were paid virtually nothing and left the order, had to be replaced with lay faculty at full salary. Consequently, as student enrollments and corresponding tuition revenues were declining, a major university expense, the faculty payroll, was increasing dramatically.[48]

According to Father McLaughlin, Fordham University's fund-raising was "totally inept." The university would spend its meager endowment of $14 million dollars in order to continue functioning through this crisis. Father Timothy Healy, S.J., was the university's executive vice president at that time. He later recalled that the university had exhausted its reserves at the end of the 1960s. Law Professor Joseph Sweeney recalled that the university was facing the prospect of closing, a recollection that is confirmed by Robert Kidera, vice president for university relations and development, who concluded in 1967 that, without state aid, Fordham University faced three choices: to close its doors, to give itself to the state, or to become nonsectarian.[49]

Fordham University opted to qualify for state aid. It commissioned Columbia Law professors Walter Gellhorn and Kent Greenawalt to identify what measures Fordham University would have to adopt "to shed identification as a religious institution in the conventional sense and, instead, gain acceptance as a completely independent institution of higher learning." Father Schroth recounts that when Gellhorn and Greenawalt issued their findings on October 17, 1968, in what has become known as the "Gellhorn Report," they "created a sensation" that was covered by the *New York Times* and dominated the university community's discourse for months thereafter. The "Gellhorn Report" listed sixteen steps the university should take to become nonsectarian. Father Schroth asserts that "for the most part the [Gellhorn] plan was not implemented." Nevertheless, many believed then and now that Fordham did implement it, and, in doing so, "sold its soul." Enough of the Gellhorn Report was implemented, such as transforming the exclusively Jesuit Board of Trustees into a lay-dominated board and recognizing that Fordham University is an autonomous corporation owned by its board of trustees and not the Jesuits or the Catholic Church, increasing the number and diversity of lay persons in the university administration and faculty, to establish the university's independence from the Jesuits and qualify it as a nonsectarian institution. Moreover, it changed enough to establish its nonsectarian status and qualify for state and federal aid, which caused many Fordham alumni to greet with skepticism Father McLaughlin's claim that the Gell-horn Report required Fordham "to change 'some characteristics,' not to 'change our character.'"[50]

In October 1968 Father McLaughlin acknowledged that Fordham University could look forward to increased state and federal aid. However, he also announced another deficit year due to insufficient tuition income. Father McLaughlin proposed a reduction in spending, an increase in tuition, a faculty hiring freeze, and "increased income from Lincoln center." Given its desparate financial condition, it is understandable that the Fordham University administration would look to the profitable Law School to extricate it from insolvency.[51]

The law faculty considered the Law School to be independent of Fordham University. They began to explore the possibility of establishing the school's autonomy from the university, "in view of the grave concern that the financial strictures now being imposed could and undoubtedly will jeopardize the professional standing of the law school." Mulligan found it "increasingly difficult to justify cut-backs [in proposed salaries] in the face of what seems to be a clear profit after all costs of some $200,000 per annum to the law school." A $200,000 surplus was about one-third of the Law School's $638,000 budget. With the Law School increasing its tuition in the fall, "the students and faculty are understandably concerned about our professional accreditation," the dean informed Vice President for Academic Affairs Dr. Brown.[52]

The law faculty and students met with Father Walsh in October 1969 and proposed that "the Law School should be autonomous in every way." Father Walsh's reaction to the Law School's demand for "fiscal autonomy" was to agree to "set them up as a separate school but they no longer will be called or be able to use the name Fordham University. If they were to separately incorporate, we would insist upon another name." The meeting ended in a stalemate.[53]

The university's unresponsiveness to the needs of the Law School, and the "growing University bureaucratization" prompted the dean to appoint a self-study committee chaired by Professor Robert M. Byrn. The committee consisted of Professors Leonard F. Manning, John D. Calamari, E. Earl Phillips, and Joseph C. Sweeney. Professor Barry Hawk served as the committee's reporter. The self-study committee and the administration's reaction to it reflected the deepening chasm between the Law School and the administration regarding the Law School and its place within Fordham University.[54]

Professor Byrn asked for complete detailed financial information relating to the Law School, including the portion of general university overhead expenses allocated to the Law School along with an explanation of the university's accounting procedures and the basis of the overhead allocation. He also asked for an accounting of total contributions made by Fordham Law alumni and others.[55]

Father Walsh and his executive vice president, Dr. Joseph Cammarosano, were utterly uncooperative. Cammarosano distrusted and disliked the members of the law school community. He was "opposed to placing this kind of [financial] information in the Law School's hands, for they would use it simply to exploit a political advantage." He believed that the Law School did not understand "that it is an integral part of the University and does not exist apart from it." It existed only so long as the university willed that it exist—it had "no sovereign power." This power was "reserved to the University." Moreover, the Law School could not have fiscal autonomy and still enjoy the benefits of its affiliation with Fordham University. Not only was it improper for an educational institution to "seek to maximize its return in every academic area," Cammarosano opined, some activities and some schools "may have to pay for others," because a university "must have balance." He deplored the Law School's "atomistic" conception of units within a university, because it would force the university to close unprofitable units, such as the Physics and Classics departments. He asserted that the Law School's thinking was "completely anathema to the idea of the University." Disclaiming any wish "to vulgarize the discussion further," he nonetheless maintained that "even the academic world needs a few 'loss leaders,'" because a university must offer a "balanced program, even if it means that some areas cannot pull their own freight and must be subsidized by other areas." There the business analogy ended from the Law School's perspective, as Cammarosano understood it. "A University cannot be likened to General Motors or some commercial firm which is quick to jettison its unprofitable operations." His understanding of the Law School's perspective led him to conclude that "the principle of fiscal maximization which is implied in the Law School argument would require just that."[56]

Fordham University unfortunately relied too heavily on revenue derived from tuition and fees and too little on revenue derived from fund-raising and endowment income. This predisposed Father Walsh and Cammarosano to use the profitable Law School to subsidize Fordham University's unprofitable programs. They were unwilling to return to the Law School the financing it required to achieve its goal of becoming a first-rate law school in the changing world of legal education at the beginning of the 1970s. With his understanding of a university and of university finances, Cammarosano smugly advised Father Walsh that the "people at the Law School are not terribly well versed in . . . [nor] understand the concept of a University."[57]

Cammarosano carried his argument to a point of absurdity by posing a hypothetical and then arguing as if it were factual. He asserted that it was conceivable that at some point in the past other units in the university had "carried" the Law School. Assuming they did, Cammarosano suggested that they "paid for the new building and fine campus the Law School now enjoys." Why "could not these other units, principally the College, insist on some kind of indemnity payment?"[58]

Cammarosano conceded that the Law School "may be bringing in more than it is paying out." But, he suggested that its profitability may have been due less to its "standing" than to "that of the entire University." Fordham University was "a joint product," he reasoned, and the Law School benefited from the "first rate undergraduate division" and other units of the university, which rendered it difficult "to know precisely each unit's true share of University income." Cammarosano asked rhetorically, "Are not the people at the Law School willing to concede that their success may, in part, stem from other sectors of the University and that, therefore, they do not have full claim to what they bring in?" It seemed to him that "the Law School has gotten away with this kind of nonsense for too long a time." Menacingly, he warned that "it had better start to pay some attention to the fact that it is not a merchant prince residing in some autonomous City State, but rather that it is a citizen of a larger entity and ought to start to behave accordingly."[59]

Father Walsh waited one month before communicating his refusal to comply with Professor Byrn's request for the Law School's financial information. He informed Byrn that he was unable to supply some of the requested information to the self-study committee because "we have not yet done a sufficiently good study of the cost per unit of the University." Although the Law School already had the requested "detailed breakdown of Law School income and total Law School budget," Father Walsh maintained, the university had not yet determined the "breakdown and detailed expenses allocated to the Law School." He was similarly dismissive of Professor Byrn's request for information regarding Law School alumni contributions, stating that "it would be almost impossible for us to determine the total contributions by Law School alumni."[60]

The "restiveness" of the Law School's constituent members "intensified" as they witnessed the "mushrooming University administrative bureaucracy" actively impinge on the Law School's "internal self-governance." The University conferred on "committees of faculty and students from other schools in the University" the authority to make decisions relating to matters as central to the Law School's operations as its budget, which gave them the capability "of undermining" the Law School's educational policies. For example, the University Budget Committee, consisting of faculty and students from other schools within Fordham University, had the power to review and veto items budgeted by the Law School, which took control over institutional and educational policies away from the Law School. Moreover, in reducing the Law School's budget, faculty and students on the budget committee controlled the size of the law faculty and the holdings in the Law library, both of which could "significantly affect the curriculum." The law faculty and students believed that the university budget committee's reductions in budgeted items "intrude[d] upon [the Law School's] faculty control of institutional policies" and constituted a clear violation of ABA and AALS standards.[61]

In December 1969 the law faculty issued a bold declaration of exclusive self-governing authority. They affirmed AALS rules requiring ultimate responsibility for the internal governance of the Law School be in the hands of the law faculty, "a responsibility that the faculty must not surrender, under any circumstances" to the central administration or to any other group, such as a university faculty/student committee or the University Faculty Senate. For any of these to "arrogate to themselves" any of the law faculty's responsibility "would literally endanger the continued existence of the Law School."[62]

The faculty approved the self-study report, which expressed open hostility between the Law School and the university. It reported "a sharp deceleration of the Law School's progress" in the second half of the 1960s, and attributed the principal cause to "dramatic reversals of University policy." The report asserted that the university refused to provide the Law School with needed "financial support for expansion in a number of vital areas," and it maintained that the university lacked "a basic understanding . . . of the requisites for excellence in legal education." Ironically, university administrators held the same view of the Law School's dean and faculty. The Law School's faculty, students, and alumni were "increasingly concerned" over the university's "apparently negative attitude" toward the Law School.[63]

The Fordham Law community was particularly troubled by Fordham University's policy "of diverting Law School income to other programs in the University." Even though the university refused to honor the Law School's requests for detailed financial statements, the self-study committee determined from the data available to it that over the five fiscal years from July 1, 1965, to June 30, 1970, the university had "derived in excess of three-quarters of a million dollars in *profit* from law school tuition and fees alone." These figures did not include donations and gifts by law alumni to the Law School, "all of which are presently diverted by the University to programs outside the Law School."[64]

In calculating its "profits," the Law School took into account the university's charge for overhead. The administration's method of allocating overhead was to charge each school within the university 14.2 percent of total salaries. The effect of the administration's allocation was to charge divisions with relatively highly paid faculty, such as the Law School, more than those with lower salaried faculty, regardless of the amount of university resources they consumed. Obviously, this bore "no relationship either to actual total overhead or to actual utilization of administrative services by individual schools within the University." In addition, the Law School had its own registrar and admissions and placement offices, which should have reduced the charge to the Law School for these services, but the administration's method of allocation did not provide for such reductions. Interestingly, an AALS study of legal education at that time revealed that between 60 and 70 percent of the nation's law schools were not charged overhead. The AALS found that most universities saw no need to "indulge the attribution of overhead," and it recommended "the majority practice" as a better method for law schools to assess their financial position.[65]

Almost all of the law schools that responded to the self-study survey (thirty-one of thirty-six) reported that they received from their universities funding that exceeded their revenues from tuition and fees. This was true of all of the state law schools (sixteen of sixteen), 73 percent (eight of eleven) of the private law schools and 78 percent (seven of nine) of the Catholic-affiliated law schools. These results approximated similar findings by the AALS, which concluded that, among the nation's law schools, there was "very little current concern with the possibility of a university drain on law student generated income for the benefit of other university operation." This was not the case at Fordham, where the committee found that the university "consistently derived a profit from Law School tuition and fees and where the reasonable requirements of the Law School are not being met." The failure to meet the school's budgetary needs was a violation of ABA and AALS rules.[66]

The self-study report accused Fordham University "of operating the Law School to produce a profit" for the university. Consequently, although the Law School generated the funds it required "to achieve a margin of excellence," it did not receive them. Moreover, other law schools surveyed by the self-study committee acquired these funds through "separate law school fund raising." Fordham Law School did not have this source of funding, even though Fordham Law's alumni were the "most generous and loyal of all of Fordham's alumni."[67]

Deprived of adequate financial support and hampered by the interference of the university administrative structure, Fordham Law School compared unfavorably to other law schools in a number of critical areas reported to the ABA and AALS. One of Fordham's most serious deficiencies related to the sizes of the faculty and the student body. Fordham Law School was the fifteenth largest law school in the United States based on the number of students. Of thirty-two schools of comparable size, twenty-three had much lower student-to-faculty ratios. Of the nine schools with which Fordham compared favorably, several were unaccredited, and none had as good a reputation as Fordham's. The Law School ranked eighteenth in tuition, based on a tuition of $1,600 in 1969, which was raised to $1,900 for the 1970–71 academic year. Yet, its student-to-faculty ratio was the worst among the "top-charging 25 law schools." Most law schools had student-to-faculty ratios of 1-to-30 or lower. Fordham Law School's ratio of 1-to-41 placed it in the bottom 16 percent of all law schools. The ABA "encouraged" law schools to keep their student-to-faculty ratios between 20 to 30 students per full-time teacher. The Law School's shortage of full-time faculty prevented the faculty from devoting "sufficient time" to research, publication, and public service. It also prevented the Law School from providing faculty sabbaticals and rendered the Law School "extremely hard pressed" if a teacher became ill.[68]

Inadequate numbers of full-time faculty had other adverse consequences for the quality of legal instruction. Each member of the full-time faculty taught an average of 184 students, an excessive number. Furthermore, the Law School made "excessive use of part-time faculty." Indeed, the night division did not comply with an ABA Standard for Legal Education (Factor B:3:2), which required that at least three-fourths of the hours of instruction in each division be taught by full-time faculty. The Law School's accreditation was "in jeopardy" because of the night division's failure to meet this standard. The self-study deplored the "University policy, recommended to us in the past, of using part-time teachers as substitutes for badly needed full-time faculty members."[69]

Inadequate numbers of faculty prevented the Law School from fully implementing its new curriculum, particularly its plan to offer more seminars and electives. The faculty's "desired goal" was to follow the example of the best law schools by allowing every faculty member to offer an elective or seminar in "his special area of competence." Unable to effectuate its revised curriculum, Fordham Law School was impeded from attracting serious young scholars to its faculty. The self-study report concluded that "the most dramatic result of the University's failure to provide the Law School with a numerically adequate faculty" was the sacrifice of "a highly desirable tutorial writing program." The current number of faculty was simply too small to provide the "required close faculty supervision" the writing program demanded.[70]

The lack of adequate numbers of faculty forced the dean to employ a "judicious rearrangement of schedules" just to cover the required courses in the new curriculum. He succeeded in covering core courses "only by the most liberal interpretation of accepted academic practice" relating to the number of unrelated courses taught by individual full-time faculty and "the excessive use of part-time teachers." Although the best law schools recognized that a law professor could not be "considered an expert in more than two fields," one-half of Fordham Law's faculty taught more than two unrelated course areas, and two of these taught five unrelated areas. The faculty expanded the number of electives only by violating AALS and ABA standards relating to teaching loads, and it still failed to offer as many electives as many other law schools.[71]

In addition to unreasonably onerous teaching loads, inadequate university financial support for research assistance and faculty secretaries also contributed to the law faculty's deficiencies in research, publication, and public service. Whereas the self-study committee's survey revealed that thirty-four of thirty-nine law schools provided research assistance at an average cost of $12,350 per year, Fordham Law School had "no budget at all for student research assistance." Many other law schools also provided, on average, one secretary for every professor. Fordham Law School's secretary-to-faculty ratio was 1-to-7 when fully staffed, but this ratio was 1-to-10 at the time of the self-study report.[72]

Quoting the ABA Standards for Legal Education, the 1969 self-study committee declared that "competitive compensation" was "the *sine qua non* for attracting and retaining a quality faculty." Yet, the Law School's faculty salaries were "markedly less" than those offered "at those law schools with which Fordham Law School most closely competes for students" and those its graduates reasonably could expect to earn in a Wall Street law firm after two years of practice. In *all* of the law schools with which Fordham competed for students, average law school faculty salaries were substantially higher than faculty salaries in their affiliated universities as a whole. In ten of thirteen of these schools that reported faculty salary information, law faculty salaries were "from 50% to 100% higher than university [faculty] salaries as a whole (including the law school itself in the latter average) for the year 1968–1969." Fordham University refused to give the Law School information regarding faculty salaries in other schools and divisions of the university, so the self-study committee could not accurately specify the relationship of law faculty salaries and those paid to faculty in the other schools and divisions of Fordham University. However, the university's policy was to keep the law faculty salaries as close to those other salaries as possible. It is highly unlikely that the Law School's faculty salaries were 50 percent to 100 percent greater than the salaries of Fordham University's faculty. Compared to the other reporting law schools, Fordham Law salaries ranked "last as to median salary, twelfth (of thirteen) as to average salary, twelfth as to maximum salary and eighth as to minimum salary for the year 1968–1969." Median and average Fordham Law School salaries were lower than the salary of a second-year associate at a Wall Street law firm. The effect of the Law School's inability to pay competitive faculty salaries was unstated, but this must have been a substantial impediment to recruiting outstanding young scholarly professors, an impediment made more substantial by the onerous teaching loads the faculty had to carry and the absence of research support.[73]

The lack of student aid and a dormitory continued to disadvantage the Law School in competing for bright students. The school's scholarship fund was $70,000 when its full-time tuition was $1,600 per year during the 1968–69 academic year. Fifty-eight of 138 law schools in the United States had larger scholarship funds, and, of the 25 law schools with the highest tuition, Fordham's scholarship loan funds placed it second from the bottom. Of the 32 law schools whose student bodies were comparable to Fordham's, 23 had greater scholarship loan funds, and only marginal schools had smaller funds than Fordham's. The self-study committee compared the Law School's tuition and student aid with the ten law schools in New York State and 13 church-related law schools and found that Fordham ranked in the top percentile in tuition and the bottom percentile in student aid. The difficulties in student recruitment were compounded when the university reduced the Law School's travel budget, which precluded Fordham Law representatives from recruiting students from out-of-town colleges. The consequence of this inadequate funding was that Fordham was "losing students to more competitive law schools."[74]

The law library was also starved for funds. The size of its collection placed it thirty-third among accredited law schools. It ranked "much lower" in the ratio of the number of students using the library to the number of volumes available. Nevertheless, Fordham University reduced the law library's book acquisition budget for the 1969–70 school year from $60,500 to $41,000. Other law schools were upgrading their libraries. The allocation of only $41,000 was just $1,000 higher than the minimum required by the AALS for member law schools, and it was $30,000 less than the estimated average for leading law schools according to the American Library Association. Interestingly, law students negotiated with the university and succeeded in getting a good portion of this cut, $14,200, restored to the library's acquisition budget. However, reductions in the library staff forced the library to reject many gifts of books because it lacked the personnel to process them. The self-study committee anticipated "a rapid drop" in both the library's ranking and its usefulness.[75]

Placement services and continuing legal education were suffering because of inadequate funding. The self-study report claimed that Fordham Law students "have never been more sought after" by law firms, but they were "stinted" in placement services because the Law School was operating without a placement director, essentially "because the salary offered is inadequate." In addition to serving as the placement director, Assistant Dean Robert McGrath also supervised the Law School's continuing legal education program. Unfortunately, "that program too has been in abeyance," the committee reported. However, in 1970 the Law School hired Helen P. Solleder to the new position of Law School director of placement to replace McGrath. Mrs. Solleder was hired at a salary that was one-third greater than her predecessor's, although Brother Kenny "questioned this rather significant increase." However, Fordham Law School's placement service was still controlled by the University Placement Office. The Student Bar Association informed the self-study committee that "Fordham ranks poorly in financial support of extra-curricular student activities." The self-study report thus concluded that "in all areas in which a quality law school must have strength—library, faculty, curriculum and students—Fordham Law School is losing ground," and it just could not "afford to lose any more ground."[76]

The self-study committee thus proposed a plan to eliminate the deficiencies it identified, and each of its recommendations required substantially greater financial support. For example, the committee proposed increasing the library's holdings to 200,000 volumes within the next five years, increasing its annual book acquisitions budget to $80,000 and its staff to five professional librarians, six clerks and "sufficient student help." Two hundred thousand volumes was the average for leading law libraries, according to the Association of Research Libraries, but an adequate staff for a library of this size was six professional librarians and nine clerks. The staffing recommendation would have left the Law Library inadequately staffed.[77]

The self-study report recommended an increase in faculty size to between twenty-five and twenty-eight full-time professors in addition to the dean and the law librarian, two teaching-research associates and "an adequate part-time faculty." The recommendation on the size of the faculty was the minimum required to enable the Law School to implement curricular reforms. The curricular goal was to have every faculty member teach a seminar or an elective in "his special area of expertise," and to reinstate the second-year tutorial writing program under the administrative guidance of teaching-research associates, who would also be responsible for the first-year research and writing course and coordination of all writing and Moot Court programs. It recommended an increase in secretarial support to a minimum of six secretaries, which would have reduced the ratio of secretaries to full-time faculty to 1-to-4 or -5. The report recommended a student research budget of between $10,000 and $15,000, and "an adequate convention-travel budget." The report was unable to recommend specific goals for student aid without more study of necessary aid to the disadvantaged. Nevertheless, the committee declared that doubling of scholarship loan funds would be a "starting point." And it urged funding for student recruitment.[78]

The self-study report also made recommendations "to insure the internal self-governance of the Law School, to regularize" its position within Fordham University and "to provide procedures for closing the gap between our deficiencies and our goals." The most important of these recommendations was to give the Law School dean the authority to prepare and administer the Law School's budget "according to his estimate of the" Law School's "reasonable requirements." This was the practice in forty-one of forty-two law schools that responded to the self-study committee's survey. This was also an ABA requirement for accreditation.[79]

The dean should submit the Law School's proposed budget directly to the university administrator who had ultimate authority to determine the budget prior to its submission to the board of trustees. The law school budget should not be reviewed by any dean, faculty member, student, or other person from any other school or division in Fordham University. Although a university budget committee such as Fordham University's was used to review law school budgets in seven of the ten responding Catholic-affiliated law schools and one-third of the state-supported law schools, the AALS frowned on and criticized such review. The self-study committee urged that the responsible university administrator should not reduce any budget item without first consulting with Fordham Law School's dean. In such a consultation, the "reasonable requirements" of the Law School, and not those of Fordham University, should be given "primary consideration." Prior to this consultation, the university should provide the dean with a "complete financial statement of the Law School's operations for the most recent fiscal year." The report concluded that the Law School's budget was "grossly inadequate to meet the reasonable requirements of the Law School," and that the Law School was "losing ground in every area" in which it needed to be strong if it was to offer a "quality legal education." The Law School refused to allow its "quest for excellence" to be "thwarted," even if it meant that the Law School would "no longer be available as a financial reservoir for other schools and programs in the University."[80]

The Law School's quest for excellence required greater financial autonomy from the university. To attain greater financial autonomy, the report recommended that the Law School conduct its own annual fund-raising appeal, "separate from any other University fund raising venture." Separate law school fund-raising was becoming the trend in the 1960s. Only 50 percent of law schools "engaged in active separate fund raising" in the 1950s, but 76 percent (thirty-one of forty-one responding schools) in the Law School's study engaged in this practice. Of the ten schools that did not have separate fund-raising appeals, six were affiliated with Catholic universities. The report acknowledged that problems associated with appeals to law school alumni were "particularly acute at Fordham," because Law School alumni were aware that the school operated at a profit and that their contributions would "immediately be diverted" to a university program having no connection with the Law School that they had no wish to support. The Committee asserted that the Law School and the university had to work out the "mechanics" of the alumni appeal. It urged that gifts designated by the donor for the Law School's use be delivered to the Law School and not be diverted to any other university use. If the donor specified a gift to the Law School for a "particular purpose," the gift should be used for this purpose and no other.[81]

The university got around restricted gifts to the Law School by reducing funds the Law School would have received by the amount of the gifts. For example, alumni gifts to the Law School Scholarship Fund resulted in the university reducing the amount of scholarships it provided to the Law School. In light of this, Mulligan complained that "it is extremely difficult to honestly say to an alumnus that the law school will benefit from any gift since normally the University merely retains the check as part of the unrestricted funds."[82]

The self-study committee insisted that all "moneys and other things of value" the Law School received as gifts should be "a supplement to the budget and in no event shall be offset ('washed out') against any item in the budget," with the exception of income from an endowed chair. This supplemental income would provide the Law School with a "margin of excellence," the committee maintained, identifying such uses as student recruitment and student scholarships and loans over and above scholarships to disadvantaged students, financing distinguished visiting professors, and special library collections. Ending the university's practice of offsetting gifts and donations to the Law School would bring it into conformity with the practice of the overwhelming majority of responding law schools and universities. Thirty-three of thirty-seven responding schools (89 percent) "reported no wash out; 2 reported wash outs on endowment income only, and one school reported a complete wash out." All of these law schools received more than they contributed to their universities from their fees and tuition, and they all engaged in separate fund raising. Some of the deans at these schools reacted with "Surprise, condemnation, and outrage" at the idea of washouts.[83]

The Law School's ambitions and the ABA and AALS standards required the Law School to maintain control over the tuition and fees it charged its students. Such control placed the Law School in direct opposition to the university's policy of using it to subsidize the university. The report recommended that the university "shall not" increase the Law School's tuition and fees "without first consulting with the Dean." This was the practice in the majority of reporting private law schools. Tuition at these schools was established either by the university after consultation with the law school dean or by the law school with the formal approval of the university. The report also boldly declared that Fordham University may not increase the Law School's tuition and fees "for the purpose of using Law School income as a financial reservoir for other schools or programs in the University." The AALS was clearly opposed to this practice because "draining off law school income," particularly after raising tuition, "would 'constitute an unfairness to law students in causing them to bear more than their fair share of educational costs.' "[84]

The self-study committee also tried to gain greater Law School control over faculty salaries by severing the connection the university maintained between Law School faculty salaries and salaries of faculty in other schools and divisions within the university and by adhering to ABA/AALS principles to determine competitive law faculty salary levels. In determining law faculty salaries, "primary (if not exclusive) consideration" should be given to salaries at those law schools with which Fordham Law School must compete for students and at law firms with which the Law School must compete to recruit and retain faculty. Faculty salaries in other schools and units of Fordham University were of little relevance in making these determinations. Furthermore, the high cost of living in New York City must be given due consideration. "An inadequately compensated full-time faculty rapidly becomes a part-time faculty," the report knowingly declared. "This is recognized by all law schools," it added.[85]

The Law School requested greater autonomy over decisions relating to the salaries, rank, and tenure of individual law professors. The report recommended that the university's authority to change faculty salaries should be restricted only to salaries "as a whole." This was the practice in the "great majority of responding schools." Similarly, the "large majority . . . of private and Catholic-affiliated law schools" established their own criteria for faculty promotion. Sixteen of twenty-one (or 76 percent) of these law schools reported that they "autonomously establish the criteria for promotion." An even higher proportion of these law schools, sixteen of eighteen (or 89 percent), reported that their criteria for promotion differed from those of other divisions of their universities. "The most reported differences in criteria were acceleration of law school promotion, lessening of publication requirement and a greater emphasis on public services."[86]

In another recommendation, the self-study committee attempted to take away from the university all control over promotions. It proposed that the university "shall formally approve all faculty promotions recommended by the Law School." The "overwhelming majority" of law schools, thirty-two of thirty-nine (or 82 percent), reported that their university administrations did not reject "a single faculty promotion" they recommended during the preceding three years. The committee reported that these figures were consistent with the results of an AALS study, which found that 838 of 913 (or 92 percent) of law school recommendations for promotions were accepted by the university over a ten-year period. However, this was not the case at Fordham Law School. During the preceding three years, the University rejected several recommendations for promotion submitted by the dean.[87]

"Fordham Law School stands at a crossroads," the self-study report concluded. "Either we re-accelerate our progress in the quest for excellence or we go into a decline." Decline meant "at best mediocrity and at worst . . . loss of accreditation." Mindful of the Law School's traditions and the preferences expressed by the faculty, students, and alumni, the self-study committee "opted for excellence." The question, however, was whether Fordham University would support the Law School's quest for excellence.[88]

Professor Byrn transmitted the self-study report to Fordham University President Father Walsh with a cover letter that asserted and defended the need for the Law School's financial independence from the university. The Law School's recent experience demonstrated that it "must have internal control over its own quest for excellence if it is to survive," it began. The school must retain "sufficient funds" from the tuition and fees paid by its students to meet its "reasonable needs." Because of past budgetary "deficiencies," Byrn declared, "it will be necessary to retain substantially all of this income for the foreseeable future." The Law School will also have to engage in separate fund-raising to achieve "the margin of excellence," which will require an amount over and above the revenue produced by tuition and fees. Consequently, "there must be no wash-out of regularly budgeted items by this fund raising," Byrn admonished. Conceding that the university derived no real benefit from a mediocre law school, he proclaimed that the Law School derived no real benefit from its association with Fordham University "which inhibits the school's quest for excellence. Mediocrity is unacceptable," he declared. He asserted that implementation of the report's recommendations was a matter of "particular urgency," and he asked that Father Walsh meet "at [his] earliest convenience" with a committee composed of Dean Mulligan and representatives of the faculty, students, and alumni.[89]

Father Walsh's initial response to the self-study report was quite negative. Father Walsh informed Byrn "how terribly disappointed" he was over "the narrowly limited scope" of the self-study report, "especially the almost total concern for such self-interested problems as faculty compensation and other peculiarly temporary problems instead of long range, academic projections." He had expected "a clearer statement" of the Law School's "priorities," a "more precise definition of [its] objectives, and an explanation of the various alternatives for achieving those objectives." He was "disappointed in not finding them."[90]

Father Walsh believed that the self-study's real objective was to achieve the Law School's "academic and fiscal autonomy." He informed Byrn that the university could not grant this autonomy to the Law School without extending it to all units of the university. If it did so, the university would soon become "little more than a loose federation of autonomous, self-sustaining trade schools," which "hardly accords with the concept of a university." In Father Walsh's view, the self-study report's demands were "unrealistic and to the rest of the University most unfair." But, he accepted Professor Byrn's invitation to discuss the self-study report and arranged to meet with Law School representatives on March 20, 1970.[91]

Prior to the meeting, Father Walsh discussed the administration's strategy with Executive Vice President Commarosano and Vice President for Academic Affairs Reiss. He wanted "to take a positive approach" at the meeting, and he acknowledged to his team that he had "no doubt whatsoever" that the Law School "do need more faculty. Their student-faculty ratio is so much out of line with other law schools." He hoped to "lift them up to the number 25" over time, emphasizing that perhaps they could satisfy their faculty needs "by joint appointments of personnel in the behavioral sciences or other areas of the university." He also was not opposed to independent Law School fund-raising within certain guidelines they would have to work out to avoid conflicts with the "overall development plans of the University." He favored more scholarship money, but he was concerned that it would be given to editors of the *Fordham Law Review* rather than to recruit bright students. He also acknowledged that the Law School needed more travel money for "recruiting purposes" and for more faculty members to attend annual conventions. As for the meeting with the Fordham Law representatives, he cautioned Cammarosano and Reiss that "it is important for us to go there, keep our cool, and try to make it a more positive experience" than his initial response to the self-study report. Father Walsh made a surprising admission, given the low regard the administration had for the Law School. "Our Law School has an extraordinary reputation and, I notice, not from the faculty or Dean but from associates in other schools around this area and the general public."[92]

The March 20, 1970, meeting proved to be very productive. Representatives of the administration and the Law School reached agreement on most of the self-study report's recommendations and left some issues to be worked out in the future. The administration agreed that the dean shall be the Law School's "budget administrator" and prepare the school's annual budget according to "his estimate of the reasonable requirements of the Law School." The administration also agreed that the dean shall submit the budget to the "university Administrator(s)" with the "ultimate authority" over budgets prior to its submission to the board of trustees. However, the administration refused to exempt the Law School's budget from review by the university's budget committee. This exemption would have to be extended to the budgets of all of the university's departments, schools, and units, which would have required the dissolution of the university's budget committee. Father Walsh "doubt[ed] very much that the faculty and students" in those other areas of the university "would consent to a dissolution of this Committee." The administration suggested a compromise under which it would attempt to persuade the committee to review "only major categories and not examine individual items in each School and Department Budget." Until then, "some items" in the Law School budget would have to be reviewed by them.[93]

The university's position on the budget is puzzling. It refused to give detailed budgetary information to the dean of the Law School at the very time it gave detailed budget information to a university committee consisting of deans, faculty, and students from other divisions in the university. The university also seems to have given the budget committee significant authority to review and adjust the budgets of the various schools, departments, and units of Fordham University. It is difficult to explain this administrative process.

The administration accepted all but one of the remaining recommendations on the budget process. It agreed not to reduce any item in the Law School budget without prior direct consultation with the dean and to give primary consideration to the reasonable requirements of the Law

School in such consultations. Cammarosano considered this concession "a significant compromise on the part of the Administration," and he "remained unalterably opposed to" disclosing to the Law School dean financial information regarding the Law School's operations. Consequently, the Law School withdrew its request that the university give to the dean prior to the consultation "a complete financial statement of the Law School's operations for the most recent fiscal year." This represented a significant concession on the part of the Law School. The administration "agreed in principle" to the interpretation of "reasonable requirements of the law school" that enabled it "to attain and maintain a high and competitive position" in relation to other accredited law schools in virtually all areas of the Law School's operations, namely, full-time student-to-faculty ratio, student aid, student and faculty recruitment, curriculum, research assistance and secretarial support, faculty salaries and benefits, teaching loads, faculty promotions and leaves of absence, participation in professional organizations and conventions, library facilities and personnel, and student extra-curricular activities.[94]

The Law School and the university administration reached substantial agreement on issues related to the Law School's independent fund-raising activities. The administration agreed to this in principle, with the understanding that the Law School's separate fund-raising process would have to be worked out with the administration, the university development office, and the Fordham Law Alumni Association. The university also agreed in principle to the Law School's recommendation that unsolicited gifts designated by the donor for the use of the Law School would be delivered to the Law School and not diverted to other university uses.

In 1970 the university attempted to clarify the rules regarding fund-raising for the Law School. It entered into a five-year contract with the Law Alumni Association which provided that the association would participate in the university's annual giving program. In return for annual financial support from the university of $5,000 per year, the association agreed to comply with the university's current fund-raising practices when it solicited funds for the Law School. There could be trouble if the Law School solicited its alumni who had also graduated from one of the other schools of Fordham University. Executive Vice President Cammarosano also wanted to avoid situations in which Fordham Law alumni who might be administrators of trusts and estates "get the arm placed on them by Bill [Mulligan] and his people" and siphon off funds to the Law School that might otherwise come to the university. This was "where we and the Development Office have to stay on our toes," he informed Father Walsh.[95]

The university struggled with rules to determine the uses of unassigned gifts to the Law School and to avoid competition in fund-raising between the university and the Law School. These rules provided that all gifts "specifically assigned by the donor to the Law School" would be "considered as a supplement to the budget and in no event shall be offset ('wash out') against any item in the budget," except for income from an endowed chair, which could be credited to the salary of the chair's holder. For donations restricted to the Law School but not "earmarked as to their use," the university administration and the Law School dean would determine the use to which they would be put. To avoid conflict between the university and the Law School in soliciting funds from law firms, the Law School's "solicitation must first be cleared with the University Development Office." The Law School was permitted to solicit its alumni "on a personal basis," but the university's development office was also free to solicit Fordham Law alumni who had also attended some other school of the university.[96]

The university thus controlled how unrestricted gifts to the Law School would be used as well as whom the Law School may solicit, which proved to be complicated and difficult. The administration proposed that "the Law School would be restricted to soliciting those persons who attended *only* the Law School and no other unit of the University." However, where the Law School approached an alumnus for a gift from his or her firm, the solicitation must "first be cleared" with the university development office to avoid any conflict between the Law School and the university in fund-raising activities. The Law School agreed not to solicit funds outside its own alumni unless the source was "uniquely concerned with the Law School or a Law School program" or "otherwise expressed a unique interest therein."[97]

Although the administration agreed that the Law School dean would give primary consideration to the "reasonable requirements" of the Law School in drawing up the school's budget, it telegraphed that the university would not necessarily allow the use of law school revenue exclusively for this purpose. This became apparent in the discussions regarding tuition and fee increases. The administration rejected the Law School's proposal that its tuition and fees would not be increased to provide "a financial reservoir for other schools or programs in the University." The administration's proposal, to which the Law School agreed, stated that tuition and fees would not be raised "unless the Law School derives a significant benefit from the increase." This would permit tuition increases to provide "a financial reservoir" for the university, so long as the Law School received "a significant benefit" from the increase.[98]

The administration and the Law School made major concessions regarding faculty salaries and promotions. The administration conceded that, in determining faculty salaries, primary, if not exclusive, consideration would be given to salaries in law schools with which Fordham competed for students and salaries in law firms from which the Law School recruited its faculty. The Law School and the administration agreed that the administration be permitted to change the salaries of individual law faculty, but not "without prior consultation with the dean." The administration agreed to allow the Law School to establish the criteria for faculty promotions, so long as they were not inconsistent with procedures and criteria established by the University Promotions Committee. The administration rejected the recommendation that would have required the university to approve all faculty promotions recommended by the Law School. It retained the right to review promotions to ascertain whether the persons recommended met the criteria.[99]

The test of the agreement was how well it was implemented. On that score, the future did not look very promising. The university's agreement to peg law school faculty salaries to competitor law schools and law firms did not improve the salary structure before Mulligan resigned as dean. In his last year, 1970–71, law faculty salaries "dipped to the lowest point in comparison with other schools than at anytime in the last ten years," he informed Father Walsh. Tables 6-3 and 6-4 show that Fordham's median salaries were lower than all of its competitor law schools in 1969, and they fell even lower the following year. Fordham's median salary of $18,500 was $250 above the national median and placed it, along with 7 other law schools, sixty-third among the 140 reporting law schools. The other seven were state law schools, four of which were in the South, and three of which were in the Midwest. Fordham also compared poorly to law schools

TABLE 6-3. MEDIAN SALARIES FOR 1970 AND 1969 FOR SELECTED
LAW SCHOOLS

Law School	Median Salary 1970	Fringe Benefits 1970	Median 1969	Difference
2. Rutgers (Newark)	$29,624	—	$24,495	$5,129
3. Harvard*	$29,000	$4,886.5	—	—
4. Columbia*	$28,000	$5,600	$28,000	no change
5. Cornell*	$27,500	$4,125	$26,000	$1,500
6. NYU*	$27,000	$3,510	$25,000	$2,000
7. Yale*	$26,500	$4,213	$25,000	$1,500
8. Boston University*	$25,500	$3,060	$19,500	$6,000
10. Michigan*	$25,200	$3,780	$25,750	$ − 550
15. St. John's	$24,000	$2,640	—	—
18. Penn*	$23,500	$2,509	$24,500	$ − 1,000
21. Virginia*	$23,000	$4,200	$21,000	$2,000
33. Georgetown*	$21,750	$1,784	$18,500	$3,250
34. SUNY Buffalo*	$21,728	$3,558	$20,258	$1,470
38. Notre Dame*	$21,000	$2,100	—	—
41. Boston College*	$20,600	$ 625.2	$20,000	$600
46. Brooklyn	$20,000	$2,520	—	—
58. Villanova*	$19,000	$1,900	$18,000	$1,000
63. Fordham	$18,500	$1,850	$18,000	$500
63. Georgia	$18,500	$1,850	—	—
78. New York	$18,000	$1,620	—	—

*Law schools Mulligan identified as Fordham Law School's competitors.

For 1970, see Median Faculty Salaries for Academic Year 1970–71, attached to
Millard H. Ruud, to Deans of the Approved Law Schools, November 20, 1970, box 6,
folder Law School Dean—1970, Walsh Papers, FU; for 1969, see ABA Section on Legal
Education, summarized in table prepared by Dean Mulligan, enclosed in Mulligan to
Father Walsh, February 12, 1970, box 26, folder Law School, Finlay Papers, FU.

in New York State. Mulligan complained "that all of the New York State
schools, with the exception of New York Law School, are ahead of us."
New York Law School's median income of $18,000 placed it 78th and was
just $500 per year less than Fordham.[100]

TABLE 6-4. MEDIAN FACULTY SALARIES AT ABA-APPROVED
LAW SCHOOLS 1970–71

Law School	Median Faculty Salary	Fringe Benefits
1. U of California (Hastings)	$29,624	—
2. Rutgers (Newark)*	$29,624	—
3. Harvard*	$29,000	$4,886.5
4. Columbia*	$28,000	$5,600
5. Cornell*	$27,500	$4,125
6. New York University*	$27,000	$3,510
7. Yale University*	$26,500	$4,213
8. Boston University*	$25,500	$3,060
10. Michigan*	$25,200	$3,780
15. St. John's University	$24,000	$2,640
18. Pennsylvania*	$23,500	$2,509
21. Virginia*	$23,000	$4,200
33. Georgetown*	$21,750	$1,784
34. U of NY Buffalo*	$21,728	$3,558
38. Notre Dame*	$21,000	$2,100
41. Boston College*	$20,600	$ 625.2
46. Brooklyn	$20,000	$2,520
58. Villanova*	$19,000	$1,900
63. Fordham	$18,500	$1,850
63. Georgia	$18,500	$1,850
78. New York	$18,000	$1,620

*Law schools Mulligan identified as Fordham Law School's competitors.

Median Faculty Salaries for Academic Year 1970–71, attached to Millard H. Ruud, to Deans of the Approved Law Schools, November 20, 1970, box 6, folder Law School Dean—1970, Michael P. Walsh Papers, FU.

Even Father Walsh was "disturbed" that other Catholic law schools were "significantly ahead of us" in faculty salaries. He specifically mentioned Notre Dame, Georgetown, Santa Clara, and Boston College. Father Walsh asked Mulligan how "our median faculty salary could be raised." He would appreciate any suggestion apart from the "obvious one of raising every member of the faculty to a significant degree." However, Table 6-5 shows that Fordham lagged behind Boston College and Georgetown in every salary category based on the number of years since obtaining the first law degree, a measure used by the ABA. It seemed early in the history of law school rankings to suspect that they manipulated figures to make themselves look better than they were, but Father Walsh was certain "many institutions have fooled around with their median faculty salary and know exactly where to concentrate in order to get a better picture."[101]

Not only was Fordham University keeping law faculty salaries low, it continued to use the Law School as a cash cow and increased the funds it diverted from the Law School to help it balance its deficit-ridden income and expense statements in 1970. Cammarosano employed two strategies to get more money from the Law School. One was to deduct from Law School revenues the amount of money the university "made available" to the Law School for student aid rather than the amount of funds it actually expended for student aid, which amounted to $21,187 in 1970.[102]

Cammarosano's second strategy to divert Law School income to general university operations was more significant and controversial. It was to charge the Law School rent for its building at Lincoln Center in addition to the $192,000 the university charged the Law School for physical plant expense. Interestingly, although Cammarosano insisted that the Law School should pay rent, Brother Kenny, university treasurer and no friend of the Law School whom some law faculty called "the Black Knight," objected because the Law School had paid off the cost of the building. "I am aware of your argument that the building is free and clear of debt and was more than paid for by the 'profits' earned by the Law School prior to its move to Lincoln Center," Cammarosano acknowledged in his discussion with Brother Kenny. Cammarosano countered, "But were these alleged 'profits' deposited in some kind of a building fund for the Law School or did the University use general funds received from all sources, including some of its other schools, to pay for this building?" The executive vice president revealed that his objective in taking these positions was to avoid returning the Law School's current surplus revenues to the Law School. He candidly stated that "the point I want to make is that if we add another $21,187 to the Law School's Financial Aid program and make provision for an appropriate rental charge, the alleged Law School 'profit' would quickly evanesce." And as the profit evanesced, so too would the

TABLE 6-5. 1970 SALARIES BY NUMBER OF YEARS SINCE FIRST
LAW DEGREE

0–5 Years Since First Law Degree

School	High	Median	Low	Faculty Members
Boston College	$17,760	$14,985	$14,430	3
Cornell	$27,025	$23,575	$19,550	4
Georgetown	$21,640	$18,394	$17,312	4
Fordham	$16,800	$16,700	$16,000	3

6–15 Years Since First Law Degree

School	High	Median	Low	Faculty Members
Boston College	$30,525	$22,200	$15,260	7
Cornell	$37,950	$32,200	$27,025	9
Georgetown	$27,591	$23,533	$18,935	18
Fordham	$28,300	$18,500	$17,000	8

Over 15 Years Since First Law Degree

School	High	Median	Low	Faculty Members
Boston College	$23,587	$23,000	$22,366	2
Cornell	$37,950	$33,925	$28,175	8
Georgetown	$33,542	$26,509	$18,394	13
Fordham	$27,500	$20,500	$17,000	8

Information is derived from ABA Section of Legal Education and Admissions to the Bar, Take-Off Compensation of Full-time Teachers for Academic Year 1970 by Number of Years Since Obtaining First Degree in Law, box 6, folder Law School Dean—1971–72 Walsh Papers, FU.

university's obligation under its agreement with the Law School to return the revenue to the Law School.[103]

Fordham University's stated policies and practices prior to the move to Lincoln Center support Brother Kenny's contention that Law School surpluses were used to pay for the Law School's building. When the ABA inspected the Law School in 1958, it required the university to explain why it was using the Law School's "substantial profit" for university funds and not for the Law School. The university answered that it was taking the Law School's profits on the "theory" that it would "shortly expend several millions in the erection of a new building for the School of Law." The university's justification, combined with the ABA inspectors' finding that the Law School "more than pay[s] its own way and that this has been the picture over a great many years," explain why the inspectors thought it was "not surprising" that Fordham Law School was "primarily a 'gate-receipt' operation." They questioned "whether the [Law] School gets its fair share of institutional resources or whether the current rate of profit turn-over indicates a kind of exploitation." Fordham University did not make available the detailed financial information that would have enabled the ABA to answer this question in 1958. According to Brother Kenny in 1970, the Law School had paid off the Law School building, but the Law School did not have the financial records to show this. In what may have been an extraordinary presaging of Cammarosano's position in 1970, Mulligan mused in 1958 that the university's refusal to make available financial information "does point up the problem of our establishing eventually that the excess of tuition income over operating costs has in some way been allocated for the construction of the new Law School."[104]

An event occurred during the 1969–70 academic year that reflected the growing division between the Law School faculty and the Fordham University administration. The law faculty organized a faculty union. Admittedly, they would not have taken this action had the faculty of the other divisions of Fordham University not announced their intention to organize the entire university faculty into a union under the auspices of the American Association of University Professors (AAUP). Professor Joe Crowley, a specialist in labor law, advised the law faculty to organize themselves into a separate union to maintain their independence from any collective bargaining agreement Fordham University might reach with the AAUP. Fordham University fought both faculties "tooth and nail" to defeat their efforts to unionize. Under the expert guidance of Professor

Crowley, the law faculty were certified as a separate union by the National Labor Relations Board whereas the other Fordham University faculty failed to unionize. It is ironic that the law faculty would not have unionized had it not been for the impending unionization of the other Fordham faculty, and it became one of two law school faculties that unionized. Nevertheless, many law school faculty regarded the union as an expression of the distrust and "deep animosity" that existed between themselves and the Fordham University administration. They also credit the union with their subsequent success in raising salaries to levels that were competitive with their peer law schools.[105]

William Hughes Mulligan tendered his resignation as dean on June 15, 1970, effective at the end of the 1970–71 academic year. Father Walsh accepted his resignation "with a great deal of reluctance." Mulligan had served as dean for fifteen years, and he had been on the faculty for twenty-five years.[106]

Contrary to popular belief, Mulligan did not resign to join the federal bench. He resigned the deanship to become a full-time faculty member. "There was no talk of the bench at the time," according to Judge McLaughlin. Mulligan "had just had it with the student revolutions in the late '60s, and after the really big one in '70 he resigned." McLaughlin explained that Kent State happened within two weeks of the bombing of Laos and Cambodia, and students "all over the country went into an uproar over that." Students in the Northeast decided to march on Washington in protest. They agitated to be exempt from final exams, "demanding that we simply graduate them or pass them without exams." Fordham was the only law school in the New York City "neighborhood" that refused. "NYU, Columbia, etc., capitulated," McLaughlin related. Students from those other law schools picketed Fordham, and the faculty met with student leaders from 4:00 in the afternoon until 2:00 in the morning for "easliy [sic] ten days." The court of appeals convened in special session and declared that no one would be permitted to take the July bar exam who had not taken meaningful examinations to graduate law school. "We felt fully vindicated," McLaughlin gloated, "but when that was all over Mulligan had had it, and he decided to return to the full time faculty as a professor." Though Mulligan had intended to continue as a member of the faculty and to hold the Wilkinson Chair of Law, he was appointed to the Second Circuit Court of Appeals shortly after his resignation as dean became effective in the summer of 1971.[107]

CHAPTER SEVEN

STRUGGLE FOR AUTONOMY

J oseph M. McLaughlin succeeded William Hughes Mulligan as the Law School's dean in July 1971. During his tenure, McLaughlin accelerated changes that Mulligan had initiated which transformed the Law School from the Wilkinson model to that of mainstream American law schools. His most important contributions to the evolution of the Law School included changes in the nature of the faculty the Law School recruited, an increased emphasis on the importance of legal scholarship, and a more academic vision of legal education. McLaughlin also contributed to the modern Fordham Law School by establishing a Career Planning Center (or Placement Office) and significantly improving the placement of the Law School's students and alumni, reviving the Fordham Law School Alumni Association, and creating a Law School Development Program with increased emphasis on fund raising and separating the Law School's fund raising from that of Fordham University. Nevertheless, Fordham University's central administration inhibited the Law School's development by persisting in its long-standing policy of appropriating Law School revenue to subsidize the university's other divisions.

In his letter of resignation of June 15, 1970, Mulligan informed Fordham University President Father Michael P. Walsh, S.J., that he intended to resign as dean of the Law School effective July 1, 1971. "I do believe that fifteen years is about the maximum lifespan for a law school dean in these critical times," he explained, adding, with some irony given his tender age on becoming dean, "I firmly believe that someone younger than I should take over." He also had been teaching at the Law School for twenty-five years. Mulligan intended to continue as a member of the faculty, but stepping down as dean was best for the Law School and for him, he commented, "particularly since I am still at such a tender age."[1]

Announcing his resignation one year before it was to take effect, Mulligan gave the Law School and the university plenty of time to find his replacement. In contrast to Mulligan's appointment as dean, Father Walsh appointed a seven-person search committee comprising four law faculty members, Fordham University's academic vice president, Paul J. Reiss, one law student representative, and one representative of the Law Alumni Association. Although the search committee solicited recommendations from the deans of the nation's leading law schools and contacted forty-two of the sixty-seven candidates who were nominated, the faculty's near unanimous support of one candidate rendered this nation-wide search a mere formality. This candidate, of course, was one of their own, Professor Joseph McLaughlin. The committee sent his name along with those of two other candidates to Father Walsh. "Walsh, of course, saw right through this, and was a little bit angry, and rejected" the committee's first recommendations, McLaughlin recalled.[2]

The second search produced only two nominations, Professor Cornelius Scanlon of the University of Connecticut Law School and Joseph McLaughlin. The search committee strongly preferred Professor McLaughlin for a number of reasons that related as much to the nominees' respective visions of the role of dean as to their personal qualifications. Scanlon viewed the role of dean "as a catalyst," whereas McLaughlin saw the dean "as a leader," and the committee believed that the Law School "badly" needed leadership. McLaughlin would "move the faculty to follow his lead," Professor Robert M. Byrn opined, and he thought McLaughlin would "get more out of the faculty. We need someone to shake us up. So do the students," he remarked. Father Charles Whalen agreed. "There has been little wind in the sails of the Law School this year," he informed Father Walsh. "We need a strong dean to get us moving again," and he thought McLaughlin "would definitely [be such] a 'leader.'" While Scanlon was "simply qualified" to be dean, Professor Martin Fogelman summarized, he did not compare with the "outstanding demonstrated qualities of McLaughlin," who was "far, far superior." Fogelman also emphasized that Scanlon was seriously deficient in the area of scholarship, not having published. McLaughlin, on the other hand, had "written extensively," and his scholarship was erudite, in Professor Fogelman's estimation.[3]

McLaughlin also enjoyed the strong support of the Fordham Law alumni. Dennis McInerney informed Father Walsh that almost one-half of the alumni who made recommendations "strongly endorsed" McLaughlin. McInerney was one of them, and he knew McLaughlin especially well, having worked closely with him when he was an associate in McInerney's law firm. McInerney and his partners believed that McLaughlin had "such exceptional ability as a practicing lawyer" that he would have been offered a partnership had he not left the firm. McInerney was convinced that, although Scanlon was qualified, McLaughlin "would be infinitely superior as our new Dean."[4]

Reiss supported the search committee's preference for McLaughlin. Indeed, he concurred in all of the committee's decisions, assured Father Walsh that the committee genuinely tried to get more candidates in the second round, and he was "particularly disappointed" that they could not get more. He agreed with other members of the committee that Scanlon's "one major deficiency" was his "failure to have published anything at all." The Law School needed a dean "who has and will continue to publish in the field of Law," Reiss opined. The dean must understand the role of the law professor "in research and publication and who will encourage this in his faculty." Among Reiss's reasons for preferring McLaughlin was "virtually the unanimous support of the faculty" that he enjoyed, a "very great asset." He also had a "very distinguished record as both a teacher and as a scholar."[5]

However, Reiss did not think McLaughlin was the perfect candidate. Among McLaughlin's negatives were his background. He had no experience "with legal education at other institutions," although he had lectured at other law schools, such as Harvard and NYU Law Schools. Reiss also questioned McLaughlin's understanding of the "full range and complexity of problems and issues facing the [Law] School." He was "not particularly satisfied" with McLaughlin's answer to the question of what the Law School needed most—"money." Acknowledging that money was "a critical problem" requiring "our full attention," Reiss nonetheless thought it a "gross oversimplification" to think that money would solve all of the school's problems and that no improvement was possible "within the present financial limitations." The third "mild negative" was the possibility McLaughlin might have trouble dealing with students "due to the impression he gives of being overconfident of his positions or point of view, of being a bit smug and self-satisfied or of 'talking down' to others." Nonetheless, McLaughlin's "strong points" outweighted the mild negatives, and he was Reiss's choice for dean. Father Walsh appointed McLaughlin dean of Fordham Law School on May 19, 1971, effective July 1, 1971.[6]

McLaughlin had two major priorities on becoming dean. His "first priority was to expand the curriculum" and to make it more accessible to students by reducing the number of required courses and expanding the number of electives. His second priority was "to broaden the faculty." There were only fifteen or sixteen full-time faculty in 1971, "and I'll bet 90% of them were Fordham Law graduates," McLaughlin reminisced almost twenty years later. "While I bow to no one in my admiration for the Fordham-trained lawyer, I felt we ought to expand a little bit to get some variety on the faculty." He hired eight new faculty "right away" in one of the largest, if not the largest hiring years in the Law School's history. The new dean characterized the new hires as the "famous McLaughlin eight," and he proudly announced, incorrectly, that "not one of them was from Fordham."[7]

McLaughlin diversified the faculty by hiring lawyers who had attended law schools other than Fordham and by hiring women faculty. To broaden the faculty, McLaughlin changed the process of faculty recruitment and adopted the process used by major law schools. He went to the AALS "slave market." Job applicants approached Fordham as "the word got out . . . that Fordham was doing some hiring." The faculty hiring committee received "lots of resumes and invited people to come and be interviewed." McLaughlin chaired the faculty hiring committee because he believed that, "at least at that point in the Law School development, you had to have a guiding hand to lend coherence in the faculty selections." He "stayed pretty much on top of" faculty hiring during his entire tenure as dean.[8]

To expand the full-time faculty by eight in his first year was quite an accomplishment, McLaughlin reminisced, because Fordham University was in the midst of a financial crisis at the time. However, "we had Father Walsh, and he was extremely well-disposed toward the Law School," McLaughlin explained. The president of Fordham University recognized the Law School's need to expand and to diversify its faculty, and he was pleased with the new appointments. The part-time faculty also "bloomed" under McLaughlin. The Law School continued to hire part-timers as "a good way to get a lot of people, a lot of faculty people, without having to pay a lot of money," McLaughlin strategized.[9]

Fordham University's financial crisis may have been more perceived than real. Father James C. Finlay, S.J., who replaced Father Walsh as president of Fordham University in 1972, recalled years later that there was much concern that Fordham was in financial difficulty when he assumed the presidency. However, Executive Vice President Joseph R. Cammaro-sano persuaded Father Finlay that the university's financial situation "was not nearly as perilous as most people believed. It wasn't good, but we were not about to collapse." Clearly, the university "had to continue tightening our belts," and Cammarosano taught Father Finlay "a great deal about fiscal stringency and about budget control." After his first year as president, Fordham University "began to do fairly well." Despite a better financial situation than generally believed, Finlay perpetuated the illusion of financial exigency to keep the Law School budget down.[10]

It was in this time of financial difficulties that the Law School finally won the freedom to establish its own fund raising. For the first time in its history, the Law School embarked upon its own fund-raising campaign during the 1971–72 academic year. The creation of the Law School's annual fund as a separate fund-raising effort from Fordham University arose from the adversarial nature of the Law School's and university's relationship. "We were not getting a fair, or any share, of our alumni's contributions," McLaughlin complained. The Law School community believed that the law alumni "were probably the most generous benefactors out there, and there was a large number of alumni who had no particular devotion to the University and probably weren't giving." They finally persuaded Father Walsh to approve separate fund-raising by the Law School. This development produced a great deal of resentment among university administrators, however, and the university development office hassled the Law School over when solicitation letters should be sent out and whose letters should be sent first. "We had some fights over that," McLaughlin recalled.[11]

In December 1971 Fordham Law Alumni Association President Denis McInenery happily announced to law alumni the First Annual Law School Fund, stating that, "*for the first time*, the Law School itself is appealing to you directly for funds to fulfill its own special needs." He urged Fordham Law alumni to take full advantage of this "new opportunity to contribute directly to the future of Fordham Law School." The separate Law School fund-raising presented a question of how the donations would be handled. McInerney suggested that the Law School follow the example of many other law schools and establish a charitable corporation to operate its fund-raising, and a law school committee decided to establish the foundation for the 1972 fund-raising mailing. It also considered a separate law school bank account as an alternative to the corporation.[12]

Father Walsh was guarded in his reaction to the information about the Law School's separate fund-raising and plans for the money. He did not see the need to set up a separate corporation or a separate bank account. Fordham University's development director could keep a record of contributions. He also maintained that McLaughlin would have to get the approval of the university's executive vice president on the disposition of the funds. "It would be somewhat demoralizing to other Deans to know that one Dean had a special kitty with no supervision with regard to its use," he explained.[13]

Fordham University administrators rejected the idea of a Law School Foundation, and so the Law School agreed to "a separate bank account" for the fund administered in the Treasurer's Office. The university would not charge the Law School for this service. The Law School and university administrators compromised on the method of allocating these funds, though the Fordham president had final authority. The dean of the Law School would submit to the president of Fordham University by September 1 for his approval the categories within which funds were to be spent. The allocation of funds among these categories was to be decided "internally in the Law School," by a an advisory committee consisting of representatives of the alumni, faculty, and students. These allocations did not need the president's approval, but the dean was required to make an annual report on how these funds were used. The use of these funds outside the approved categories did require the president's approval.[14]

It was clear that the university was unwilling to relinquish control over the Law School's funds and how they were used. McInerney later related that the university was opposed to the Law School's separate fund-raising because this move "would simply be moving money from the University coffers into the Law School coffers where the Law School would have some say in how the money would be spent." This was precisely what the board of directors of the Fordham Law Alumni Association sought to achieve, and they asked McInerney, as president of the Alumni Association, to negotiate with the university. The Alumni Association's position was "that separate fundraising would result in substantially greater contributions to the University as a whole, and should at least be given a chance." The alumni leaders also realized that the Law School was not getting the contributions it could be getting from alumni who had attended other undergraduate schools "and who had told us time and again that they didn't care to support Fordham University unless they could be assured the money was going to Fordham Law School." Of course, the Law School succeeded in getting its own fund-raising program, and it had grown "tremendously since those days," under "the excellent leadership of people like Jim Gill," McInerney recounted. The Law School and the university were raising "multiples of—what the University was raising in its combined annual drives." McInerney's law firm—Cahill, Gordon and Reindel—had a matching grant program, and he asserted that Fordham Law alumni gave "approximately twice per person as much as graduates of the Ivy League law schools or other schools" employed by his firm.[15]

There was cause for concern about Fordham University's diversion of Law School funds to university uses. A Helbig family devise to the Law School offers a blatant example. McLaughlin was very close to Father Frederick J. Helbig, S.J., whose parents had a substantial estate. Frederick and Clara Helbig executed a will leaving a sizeable portion of their estate to the Law School for student scholarships. Professor Joe McGovern drafted the will and served as executor. Two years after Father Helbig's parents died and their will had been probated, he informed McLaughlin that he was thumbing through the Law School catalogue and did not see his parents' scholarship. Checking with McGovern, McLaughlin learned that McGovern had sent the money and relevant papers to Brother Kenny, the Fordham University treasurer. McLaughlin telephoned Father Walsh and asked him to "check out what's going on." After checking, Father Walsh called back and said, "to quote him verbatim, 'Brother Kenny pulled a fast one.'" Brother Kenny had deposited the money, but he was using it for other purposes.[16]

McLaughlin was aware of the need for financial support beyond the revenue derived from student tuition and fees to operate a first-rate law school, and he intensified his pleas to alumni to contribute this support with substantially increased contributions. Alumni contributions reached $105,000 during the 1974–75 school year and $150,000 the following year. Forty-one percent of this money was devoted to scholarships for qualified students who would otherwise be financially unable to attend law school. "This, we feel, is in the best tradition of Fordham Law School," the dean informed the alumni. "We have always prided ourselves on our reputation as a provider of a quality legal education to striving, qualified students from low income families, whatever their race or religion might be."[17]

Louis Stein endowed the Fordham-Stein Prize in 1976 to restore the reputation of the Law School in the wake of the Watergate scandal. Mr. Stein explained how he decided to establish the Fordham-Stein Prize on the occasion of the fifteenth Stein award on October 25, 1990. "In 1976 I celebrated my fiftieth class reunion," he related. Two events had happened that held great significance for him. His granddaughter graduated from Fordham Law School, and "the Watergate fiasco had broken at that time, and two of Fordham's outstanding alumni were involved." He was referring to John Mitchell and G. Gordon Liddy. Feeling "depressed and hurt," he arranged a dinner with Bill Mulligan, Joe McLaughlin, John Feerick, Joe Crowley and several others at the 21 Club where Stein proposed to endow a program that would give an honorarium "to the outstanding member of the legal profession who did most to preserve our democratic way of life." He intended this program to "offset any idea that the morals and ideals of Fordham Law School were anything but the highest. Two alumni had taken a path that certainly did not meet with the approval of the School, and that had to be clarified in the eyes of the legal profession. . . . This program was expanded in 1986 to include a chair in legal ethics that is now in full force," Stein proudly declared. He believed that "Fordham has set the pace of what they expect the legal profession to give to the community as a whole." Reflecting his humility, Stein declared: "I can tell you, I'm proud and thrilled and overjoyed at the success which our wok [sic] has been received at Fordham. That far outweighs any accolades that my peers may feel are due to me."[18]

In 1976, the Law School received several major bequests that provided a "substantial foundation" for the Bacon-Kilkenny Distinguished Visiting Professor's Chair. The Law School's goal was to complete the Bacon-Kilkenny Chair's endowment by 1978. The sixty-five-member Alumni Fund Raising Committee, chaired by William Meagher, raised $124,000 in 1975–76. However, almost all of these funds had to be used for operating expenditures. This meant that the Law School was able to allocate to the Bacon-Kilkenny Chair only 4.5 percent of the funds thus raised, which was less than $6,000. McLaughlin proudly announced at the beginning of the 1976–77 school year that the Law School had received a total of $600,000 for the Bacon-Kilkenny Chair. However, the university required a $1,000,000 endowment for a chaired professorship. As of August 1979, the Law School was able to raise only $700,000 to fund the Bacon-Kilkenny Chair. The faculty consequently decided to fill the chair in alternate years. Professor Maria Marcus chaired the first search committee for an appointment in the 1980–81 academic year, which resulted in Professor Douglas A. Kahn of the University of Michigan becoming the first occupant. The Bacon-Kilkenny Chair was never fully funded, and it continues to be a biannual appointment to this day.[19]

McLaughlin increased the annual fund contributions tenfold, from $31,000 in 1971–72 to $300,000 in 1981–82. He urged alumni to increase their contributions with a quotation from Peter Finlay Dunn's Mr. Dooley: "your gift reduces your riches, thereby making it that much easier for you to enther th' Kindgom iv Hiven." Nevertheless, the Law School's fund-raising remained inadequate through the 1970s and early 1980s. McLaughlin informed the alumni in his annual report for the 1977–78 school year that "other law schools, who share leadership with Fordham, raise three to five times as much as we do in their fund drives." He cautioned that, "unless we can begin to close the gap," Fordham Law School will lose its place among the nation's excellent law schools.[20]

Although the Law School succeeded in establishing an independent fund-raising campaign, albeit under the close control of the university, few of the other goals set forth in the 1969 self-study had been realized when McLaughlin became dean in July 1971. Lack of progress in achieving these goals prompted the law students and faculty to propose during the 1971–72 academic year the Law School's first five-year plan to restore it to its former position of excellence. Because these plans elaborated the problems and recommendations contained in the 1969 self-study report, this summary will mention only those parts of the plan that add to our understanding of how the Law School and its relationship to Fordham University were seen by the various actors in this history. It should be noted, however, that the faculty adopted the student's proposal and based its own five-year plan on that of the students'. This project was a coordinated effort of the entire law school community.

The Student Five Year Plan Report concluded that there had been "no substantial broad-based follow through" in dealing with the serious problems at the Law School that had been identified in the 1969 self-study report, and in the intervening two years "the problems have worsened, and on balance the Law School has deteriorated." It explained that Fordham Law students had "witnessed and experienced" in recent years "a distressing stagnation" in the legal education offered at Fordham. Although the basic law courses were adequately covered, the curriculum reflected "a lack of concern for advanced study and individual development." Related programs were in "disarray or non-existent," and essential services, such as placement and financial aid, were "undersupported or very limited." The student report asserted that "An all-pervading spirit of apathy, and one might even say Law School inferiority, grips the students," and recent graduates feared they were entering the profession "underprepared for their responsibilities." The student commission "squarely placed [the blame] on the University Administration for a gross undercommitment of resources and concern to our Law School."[21]

The students' harsh assessments are strikingly contradicted by the cordial and collegial relationships they had with their teachers, by the success they enjoyed in finding jobs, and by the extraordinary support the Law School received from the alumni when McLaughlin revived the Fordham Law Alumni Association. One of the distinguishing qualities of Fordham Law School today is the collegial spirit that permeates the relationships among the administration, faculty, students, and staff. Alumni who attended the Law School in the Mulligan and McLaughlin eras attest to the presence of this spirit when they were students. Bob Reilly, for example, remembered that faculty and students "respected and enjoyed each other's company, and the relations of the students and faculty were close." The teachers "were wonderful, . . . interesting and creative and fun." The "delightful, and humorous Deans Reports of McLaughlin are unique in American legal education and express the fun and cultured approach and impish side of the Fordham experience." The Fordham Law Alumni Association "embodied the great spirit of the school and each year held the largest annual alumni gathering of any law school in America—the Annual Luncheon at the Waldorf." Students and faculty believed that Fordham Law School was providing a high-quality legal education.[22]

Professor Robert M. Byrn has offered an explanation of the apparent disconnect between the negative assessments of the student and faculty self-studies and the high regard in which students and faculty held the Law School and in which major law firms and corporations held its graduates. As chair of the Byrn Self-Study Committee that produced the faculty self-study report, his statement of the self-study's purpose is authoritative. It "was not meant to disparage the quality of legal education at Fordham. It was a Brandeis Brief for funding." Professor Gail Hollister, who was a student at this time, independently expressed a similar view of the student self-study's purpose: to persuade the Fordham University administration to increase funding for the Law School.[23]

The self-studies may have presented an unduly negative picture of the Law School for their intended effect, but they did identify deficiencies. Students had "two major grievances" with the Law School's curriculum. Simply stated, there were too many required courses and too few elective courses, and there were too many examinations worth "an excessive number of credits" given at the end of the school year. The first grievance created a condition in which students were "forced to 'choose,' by default, courses which they [had] no desire to study." Students were "not only bored," but their "own lack of interest" encouraged them to do only "the minimum work required to pass the course." To remedy these grievances, the students proposed a basic curriculum that reduced the number of required courses to fourteen worth forty-two credits in the first and second years of the day school and the first three years of the night school. They also recommended that upper-class students be allowed to take a total of up to three courses on a pass/fail basis.[24]

Students identified three major problems with the elective courses the Law School offered: students were permitted to take too few electives; the Law School offered too few electives; and the electives it offered were too concentrated in the area of commercial law. Fordham offered thirty-five electives. "No other law school of national importance offers so few," the report maintained. Among the nation's major law schools, Duke University Law School offered the lowest number of electives, fifty-four. Columbia and New York University law schools offered 113 and 146 electives, respectively. Fordham Law students were permitted to take only eighteen credits of electives. The lowest number of elective credits students were permitted to take at major law schools was fifty, at the University of California at Berkeley. Most major law schools allowed their students to take between fifty and sixty-six credits of electives, but the University of Chicago Law School set the cap at eighty-nine elective credits. Fordham had seven electives in commercial law, beyond the five required courses in this area, only one elective each in criminal law, trial practice, and real property and only two each in constitutional law and tax law. The report concluded that the limited number and variety of electives the Law School offered resulted in students' "legal unpreparedness" for law practice. It recommended increasing the range and the number of electives to "an amount equaling at least one-half the student's entire course load."[25]

The students' most significant recommendations were in the areas of legal writing and research and clinical education. Legal writing was being taught in large lecture courses which precluded individual appraisal and guided development. Of the schools the students sampled, Fordham Law School, which required only one semester of legal research, "stood next to last in number of semesters of required legal writing and research." Several schools required one full year of legal research and writing in addition to a legal thesis researched and written under a faculty advisor. The student commission proposed a writing program that is similar to the Law School's current writing program.[26]

The students were critical of the Law School for failing to offer enough clinical courses, opportunities for independent student research and writing under faculty supervision, and interdisciplinary study. Asserting that legal research and writing are "critical to the proper development of the student" and that the "practical application of legal theories to actual situations cannot be left to unsupervised" practice after graduation from law school, it concluded that "clinical education should also be an essential part of the students' education." Of the eighteen law schools sampled for the students' five-year plan, Fordham Law School was the only one "without a clinical education program in operation." Eleven of these schools gave "semester credits" to their clinical courses, and a twelfth required at least one semester of clinical work. Similarly, Fordham Law School was distinguished from the sampled law schools in that independent student research under faculty supervision was "completely ignored." Twelve of the eighteen sampled law schools gave semester credit for independent research, and several allowed ten to sixteen credit hours for "an approved independent project." Acknowledging that law was generally recognized as requiring "a broad based knowledge of other fields of concentration, especially the social sciences," the report noted that interdisciplinary study and joint degree programs were "becoming necessary adjuncts to legal education." The majority of the seventeen university-affiliated law schools the students sampled offered joint degree programs or permitted students to take up to six credit hours per semester in courses offered by other graduate programs. Of these law schools, however, only Fordham and St. John's Law Schools did not offer interdisciplinary study or a joint degree. The report concluded that Fordham Law School's curriculum and activities neither challenged nor motivated students to use their legal skills. These deficiencies produced "a general and pervasive apathy among the student body whose only desire is to get out."[27]

Although much of the old Fordham Law School remained, McLaughlin accelerated the process of creating the new Fordham Law School. The Fordham Law faculty's conception of legal education differed from trends in the American law schools the students identified. The faculty defined the Law School's mission in a traditional, vocationally oriented manner. The mission statement proclaimed that the Law School's mission remained "unchanged: the preparation of men and women for the practice of law." Nevertheless, the school denied that it was simply producing "legal technicians." Its basic mission was to educate "future leaders of the bar" to become engaged in creating, interpreting, and administering laws governing "the world community, the nation, state and municipality." The faculty proclaimed that the Law School was "necessarily committed to the advancement of research and scholarship," but to do so *within the parameters of its own discipline.* A "corollary" to its "primary role of educating lawyers" was its responsibility to provide continuing legal education for the practicing bar. The faculty acknowledged the need for greater variety in course offerings and for developing courses that were more relevant to students' interests.[28]

In contrast to Mulligan's view that the Law School's purpose was to prepare students to pass the bar examination, McLaughlin undoubtedly played an influential role in the faculty's adoption of a new conception of legal education as an intellectual discipline in addition to a course of professional studies that conformed more to developments in the best law schools. The faculty recognized that the "all-required curriculum" designed to pass the bar examination was "no longer responsive to the dynamics of society" and actually "stifles student interest and ignores the need for interdisciplinary training as a necessary complement to strictly law-oriented courses." The report acknowledged that some of the Law

School's students sought a legal education "as an intellectual experience rather than preparation for a professional career." The school's curriculum must "be flexible enough to accomodate [sic] these students" as well as those who were career-oriented. The curriculum must be broadened also to "allow students flexibility" in choosing their career paths among the options of a "traditional law practice," "the law teacher's podium," or "serving the disadvantaged." The curriculum must reflect "the heterogeneity and varied aspirations of our student body." This was a much different understanding of legal education than that asserted in the self-study report just two years earlier.[29]

The faculty's recommendations for curriculum reform encompassed traditional educational values, an awareness of new areas of the law and different understandings of the instrumental nature of law. The curriculum should provide students with "a firm grounding in basic legal rights and responsibilities" that were "indispensable for any lawyer," and "the maximum latitude in choice of a curriculum" that was both "relevant to society and meaningful to [their] own career aspirations." The curriculum should include new law courses ranging from ecology to international business, and the curriculum should be supported by "a broad range of clinical and internship courses, a strong faculty, an integrated writing and moot court program, interdisciplinary study, influential student publications, continuing legal education, faculty research, and a fully developed library." Many of the faculty's comments and recommendations regarding specific components of the Law School echoed those of the student commission. For example, they acknowledged that the number of electives were "grossly inadequate" and small writing tutorials highly desirable, but the school had neither the classrooms nor the faculty to greatly expand the number of electives or to offer tutorial writing sections.[30]

The faculty thought the Law School did better in its clinical offerings than did the students. Clinical education, consisting of field work and classroom instruction, was relatively new in American law schools, but the report announced that, in the 1972–73 academic year, the Law School would have "limited clinical programs in Legal Aid, Securities Regulation, Environmental Law, Federal Criminal, and Labor Law." The faculty were considering other clinical programs in poverty law, urban problems, and civil rights. A special faculty/student committee was considering the appointment of a clinical and research professor at the rank of associate professor for the 1973–74 school year. He would supervise all clinical and internship programs and do some limited amount of teaching. He would also serve as director of research, in which capacity he would solicit and coordinate research grants to the Law School.[31]

McLaughlin was a strong advocate of interdisciplinary legal studies, and the faculty report made a number of recommendations to encourage interdisciplinary study. It endorsed joint degrees and urged the exploration of combined programs with other schools in Fordham University. The faculty also recommended interdisciplinary courses be taught in the Law School, such as Law and Economics, Law and Medicine, Law and Psychiatry, and Professor Katsoris's course in Accounting for Lawyers. They also suggested that the Law School invite professors in other schools in Fordham University to teach courses that would be open to both law students and nonlaw students, a move the university administration had desired.[32]

Continuing legal education was completely lacking in the student five-year plan, but it was an important component in the faculty's. The faculty declared that the Law School's "tradition of professionalism" induced it to "become deeply enmeshed in continuing legal education," enlightening practitioners of recent legal developments. The Law School had entered into an agreement with the New York State Bar Association to cosponsor all of the association's continuing legal education programs offered in New York City. The Law School offered its own programs independently of the State Bar Association. During the 1971–72 academic year, it sponsored a program on Law and the Performing Arts, a natural topic given the school's location in Lincoln Center. The report recommended that the responsibilities of a director of continuing legal education be assigned to "one of the deans."[33]

Students reported that many of the problems with the educational program were related to the faculty. There were too few full-time professors to expand the curriculum. Faculty compensation was "unconscionably low," and it was "unrealistic" to expect the Law School to compete for "quality faculty" or to prevent its being "pirated of its best young faculty" by law schools that offered higher salaries and better working conditions. The conditions of the Fordham Law faculty were poor. They were each "spread into too many specialized areas of law," and the secretarial support was at such an "atrocious level" that faculty were "stymie[d]" in attempting to meet their professional responsibilities in research and public service. A "more serious shortcoming" from the students' perspective was "the total absence of funds for student research assistance" to support faculty scholarship. "The University stands alone in its total failure to provide funds for a Law School of our size," the students reported. Students also recommended the expansion of student publications and the establishment of independent student research programs and credit for study in some of the graduate school programs of Fordham University. In addition to increasing the number of issues published by the *Fordham Law Review* and the *Journal of Urban Law* to six, students recommended the creation of a third journal, entitled the *International Journal of Law and World Order*, "devoted to the development of a better understanding of world problems and the needs and uses of international law."[34]

The faculty agreed and endorsed the students' proposed solutions to the problems associated with the faculty, even though they were expensive. They recommended increasing the number of full-time faculty "to 30 plus the Dean, Librarian, a proposed Legal Writing Associate Professor and Associate Clinical Professor . . . as soon as possible to assure implementation of the new curriculum." This number would reduce the student to full-time faculty ratio from fifty-two to one to thirty-four to one, thus bringing the student to full-time faculty ratio closer to the ABA-recommended ratio of between twenty and thirty to one. According to the ABA, the majority of law schools had a thirty to one ratio. They also recommended increasing the part-time faculty by four, from twelve to sixteen. To retain high-quality faculty, students recommended substantial increases in full-time and part-time faculty salaries. To assist the faculty in meeting their scholarly and public service obligations, they recommended hiring enough secretaries to provide one secretary for every four faculty members, the average ratio at other law schools.[35]

Students and faculty made other recommendations to improve the teaching effectiveness and scholarly production of the faculty. A faculty research fund of $24,000 should be established to compensate student research assistants at the rate of $4 per hour. Each faculty member should be allotted 400 hours of student research assistance each year. Proclaiming that sabbaticals or paid leaves of absence were "necessary to serious legal scholarship" and that most law schools provided these opportunities, the faculty report urged the initiation of a sabbatical program within two years. Moreover, the increase in faculty was also compelled to keep the full-time faculty's teaching load from exceeding twelve hours per year and to allow the faculty time to engage in "in-depth specialization necessary for scholarly and professional development." The faculty report endorsed the practice at most law schools of limiting each faculty member to two areas of specialization, stating that "two areas is the maximum" number in which a professor could "hope to develop that expertise necessary to excellence in the classroom and to meaningful publication and public service." Without going into detail, the faculty report concluded its section on the faculty by declaring that the present salary scale was "inadequate," and, if it was not increased, the five-year plan "will have to be scrapped."[36]

The lack of student recruitment and the small amount and distribution of student aid were major problems. Students complained that the Law School's failure to attract students "from far afield" contributed to its reputation as a "regional" law school and to the rarity of its graduates who practiced beyond the metropolitan area. Not surprisingly, they urged greater efforts to recruit students and "a sorely needed residence facility" to house students from "far afield," and they also suggested that student aid be used more effectively to "shape the character of [the] student body and, therefore the Law School."[37]

The lack of student scholarships inhibited the Law School's efforts to recruit minority students and thereby diversify the student body. For example, Professor Joe Crowley and a black Fordham Law alumnus, Simon Gourdine, worked hard to recruit black students. Gourdine was a high-profile executive with the National Basketball Association (NBA). In 1970 the NBA hired Gourdine as assistant to the commissioner, the first time a black man (or woman) was appointed to such a high position in the history of professional sports. When he became NBA commissioner in 1974, Larry O'Brien appointed Gourdine deputy commissioner, and this appointment made Gourdine the highest-ranking black executive in sports. Gourdine and Professor Crowley found black applicants, but the applicants would not come to Fordham Law School because the school could not give them the scholarship money they were offered at other law schools. The Law School succeeded in recruiting minority students in significant numbers in the late 1980s when it became competitive in offering minority and other applicants financial aid.[38]

The student report recommended that the Law School's administration be expanded. Students proposed the creation of an Office of Student Affairs, staffed by an assistant dean and a secretary, to focus on the student body and its problems, such as academic advisement, course selection, and student aid. The report made the controversial recommendation of involving students in the admissions and readmissions processes, and the practical suggestion that student aid be used more effectively to "shape the character of [the] student body and, therefore the Law School" by granting some aid "solely on academic achievement" to attract "excellent undergraduates," some aid to needy students and to minority students, and a portion of student aid to students who "enhance the reputation of, and contribute to the improvement of, the Law School," such as the editor-in-chief or managing editor of the *Fordham Law Review*, members of the National Moot Court team, and the president of the Student Bar Association. Students considered the amount of student aid in 1972, $110,000, as "atrociously low" and "almost criminal in light of the number of students competing for assistance." The "almost total lack of loan money" was almost as serious a problem. Students recommended the creation of an Office of Student Affairs staffed by an Assistant Dean and a secretary and the expansion of the "understaffed" Placement Office, whose services were "inadequate at best," which should be headed by a placement professional and staffed with an executive secretary and two clerk typists.[39]

McLaughlin recalled that "we had [no] real placement office . . . until the early 70s, when it was crystal clear we needed one." Fordham was "about the only school around that had nothing in place." John Feerick also could not remember the Law School "having any formal placement process," and he was quite certain it had none in the 1950s and 1960s. Feerick recalled that one circulated one's resume to law firms and then went to the firms themselves seeking an interview. The firms usually granted the interview. The school "had a long history of editors of the *Law Review* finding employment in the larger firms."[40]

McLaughlin hired Leslie Goldman to be the first director of placement. Elizabeth Walters succeeded Goldman, and Maureen Provost succeeded Walters. According to McLaughlin, it was during the 1970s and 1980s that Wall Street discovered Fordham Law School.[41]

Bob Reilly, a member of the class of 1975, was a student when the Law School originated the Career Planning and Placement Center, commonly referred to as the Placement Office. "Leslie Goldman operated out of one room, she and her secretary," he recalled. "It was barely a closet. . . . All the job leads consisted of sort of looking on her rolodex, and she would hand out one sheet of paper with the names of the firms that were coming on campus to interview. You had no idea who these firms were," he commented. Students like Reilly, who had no lawyers in the family or did not graduate from elite colleges and universities, appear to have been in a predicament that most students who are disadvantaged by class, race, or sex are in today. They "had no prior recognition of any of the names of any of the firms or what they did or what the culture of these firms was like." This was typical of Fordham Law students in the 1970s. Reilly graduated when starting salaries "were just about ready to explode, but they had not exploded yet." The going rate at Wall Street law firms in New York City was about $21,000 a year. "Immediately thereafter, the salaries began to gallop forward to $25,000 to $30,000 to $35,000. They were making leaps every single year that were just enormous."[42]

Reilly's recollections of his student days confirm McLaughlin's comment about Wall Street discovering Fordham Law School. This comment should be understood in context. Members of the *Fordham Law Review* had been hired by Wall Street firms since prior to World War II. In the 1970s these firms began recruiting graduates who had not served on the *Fordham Law Review*. Reilly relates a conversation with McLaughlin when Reilly was a student in which the dean explained to Reilly that the Lincoln Center Law School building did not have any interview rooms because "no Wall Street firm would come here to interview" in 1961. By the time Reilly was a third-year student, many Wall Street firms were coming to interview on campus, and by 1991, some 300 firms from around the nation were conducting on-campus interviews. "It is just astonishing how the acceptance of Fordham Law School had changed in this short period of time," Reilly commented. He acknowledged that "Dean McLaughlin was very much a factor in that, and of course, Dean John Feerick has been spectacular in helping to build that reputation."[43]

McLaughlin reported that in November and December 1973 seventy-five law firms, government agencies, corporations, banks, and accounting firms interviewed Fordham Law students at the Law School. He estimated that approximately one-half of the senior class were placed in jobs by the end of the first semester, a tribute to the efforts of Leslie Goldman. Goldman resigned in June 1977 to take a position with Dewey Ballantine. She was replaced by Elizabeth P. Walters, and Frances Blake, a graduate in the Fordham Law School class of 1945 and daughter of Professor John A. Blake, was hired as executive director of placement and alumni affairs.[44]

The Fordham Law Alumni Association became more actively involved in placement through its placement committee, which instituted a career counseling program in the 1974–75 school year. Each first-year day and second-year evening student was assigned an alumni advisor to assist with job placement. Even without this program, the *ABA Journal* in January 1975 listed Fordham Law School among the sixteen law schools with the largest alumni representation among partners in the nation's law firms with fifty or more lawyers. In August, the *Journal* ranked Fordham Law School seventh among law schools in the United States in the number of alumni who were the chief legal officers in the 500 largest publicly held corporations in the United States. In February 1976 the *New York Law Journal* reported that Fordham was one of six law schools that supplied 88 percent of new partners whose appointments were announced in the *Journal* within a three-month period. In a survey of American law school graduates conducted by *Juris Doctor* in summer 1978, "Fordham law alumni rank[ed] fifth in median income among those in private practice and eighth among those not in private practice." In announcing these achievements to the alumni, McLaughlin paraphrased Shakespeare and commented that "we have need neither to gild [refined gold] nor to paint [the lily], but merely to flaunt, our auric assets."[45]

Fordham graduates were fairly successful in securing judicial clerkships in the 1970s. In 1976, eleven students obtained judicial clerkships, ten federal and one in a New Jersey state court. Fourteen graduates in the class of 1977 received clerkships with federal judges on the Second Circuit Court of Appeals and the Eastern and Southern District Courts. This achievement was exceeded by only two other law schools. However, Professor Fogelman reported in 1978 a declining interest in judicial clerkships among the "better qualified students." He reported that seven students obtained federal judicial clerkships and three students would be clerking for state judges.[46]

McLaughlin boasted that, owing to the "extraordinary talents and plain hard work of Elizabeth Walters," her staff, and the Law Alumni Placement Committee, headed by Bob McTamaney, a survey of the class of 1978 revealed that 90 percent had been placed in jobs *"prior to graduation."* This exceeded the preceding year's achievement of placing 70 percent of the class shortly after graduation. On-campus interviews increased by 40 percent during the 1977–78 school year as more than 500 students participated in over 2,000 on-campus interviews. The Placement Office broadened its contacts with various segments of the legal profession to afford more employment opportunities for students and alumni. The Placement Office processed more than 500 alumni positions in 1977–78.[47]

In May 1979 Walters reported that over 150 organizations interviewed on campus, which generated over 2,800 interviews. Only 5 students obtained judicial clerkships, Professor Fogelman reported. During the 1979–80 academic year, approximately 160 law firms, government agencies, corporations, and banks conducted more than 3,000 on-campus interviews. Almost 80 percent of the graduating class that participated in these interviews received job offers by May. McLaughlin lauded the Law School's alumni because they had been invaluable in the placement of graduates in 1978–79. The Connecticut, New Jersey, Westchester, Long Island, and Washington, DC, chapters conducted placement seminars for the students, and over 500 students were assigned alumni advisors under the Alumni/Student Counseling Program, which was in its fifth year.[48]

The following year McLaughlin was more explicit in identifying the critical role the alumni were playing in the success of the Law School. He contrasted the Law Alumni Association in 1979 with that of forty years earlier, when Dean Wilkinson deplored "the state of innocuous desuetude" into which the association had fallen. Comparing the activity of the association in 1979 with that of "the inert organism of the thirties and forties," McLaughlin commented that "the Law Alumni Association pervades and enriches the life of the Law School," from student orientation to alumni placement to Continuing Legal Education." Moreover, John D. Feerick, "more than anyone else, [was] responsible for the revivification of the Law Alumni Association" and for establishing the precedent of alumni involvement in every phase of the Law School's operation. In recognition of Feerick's service, the Law School conferred on him the Alumni Achievement Award in 1980.[49]

Placement services were working for the day school graduates, but not so well for the night students, according to the 1979 ABA Accreditation Committee. Acknowledging the Placement Office's "notable success," the committee also "pointed out that the evening students feel that they are not getting sufficient assistance either from the Placement Office or from any of the other administrative support offices." According to the 1979 self-study report of the faculty, Fordham Law graduates ranked sixth in median income of lawyers in private practice nationally and sixth in terms of graduates who were partners in large New York City law firms. The *Harvard Business Review* (September/October 1980) reported that the Fordham Law School ranked sixth among the 170 accredited law schools in the number of alumni serving as vice president or president of a major American corporation during the 1970s.[50]

Walters resigned as of May 1, 1981. Maureen Provost was named the new placement director. In her first year, Ms. Provost reported that over 130 organizations conducted over 2,700 on-campus interviews.[51]

The faculty report noted an expanded role played by the library in the Law School's teaching and research missions. Though it had doubled its holdings since moving to Lincoln Center, the library "still ranks about 33rd in the nation," and it still had "gaps in older materials" due to "a very restricted acquisitions policy" prior to moving to its current location. The library's goal under Dr. Ludwik A. Teclaff was to shift from a collection that merely supported teaching to a "collection capable of supporting serious research." To achieve this goal, the report recommended a budget for the 1972–73 academic year of $93,000 and annual increases of 10 percent to 15 percent each year thereafter. The faculty and students agreed that increases in library funding were required as were increasing the library staff, expanding the physical space, particularly the stack areas, and reducing the noise level by placing carpet on the floor of the main reading room. The faculty report acknowledged that the implementation of its recommendations would "almost certainly require some expansion of the Law School building."[52]

The five-year plan called for "on-going review of its implementation." The faculty committee appointed in September 1975 to make this review reported that its proposals were partially achieved. The committee concluded that the Law School had fully implemented the "most significant change" the 1972 self-study report proposed, namely, moving from "a largely 'required' curriculum" to one offering students the freedom to select their courses after first year. This conclusion is questionable even though the number of elective courses rose from thirty-five to seventy-five. The reduction in the number of required course hours from sixty-six to forty-two was offset by the increase in the number of recommended course hours, which brought the total number of course hours in the core curriculum back to sixty-five, which was only one course hour lower than the previously required sixty-six. The 170 elective course hours available at Fordham Law School were fewer than the 182 available at law schools with comparable resource rankings. Most students took this core curriculum, although the expanded number of elective courses afforded them substantial flexibility in course selection, which enabled students to follow their interests and prepare for the wide variety of career paths that were open to lawyers in the mid-1970s. Interestingly, Fordham Law School required its students to take a course in Professional Responsibility when only about half of the nation's law schools had such a requirement and two-thirds of the state bar examinations examined this area.[53]

The review committee identified some problems with the revised curriculum. One serious problem was the lack of "rough equivalence" between the day and night schools. Although no equivalence was required, the report urged that it be "self-imposed." Night students had fewer opportunities to take courses with writing requirements, fewer clinical courses, and fewer courses taught by full-time faculty. Although progress was made in reducing class sizes in first-year courses, the recommended goals were not met. Nor did the Law School implement the recommended Legal Writing Program, though it did restructure legal writing classes. The 60 to 140 students assigned to each legal writing instructor precluded individualized attention. Little was done to expand student independent study, to increase interdisciplinary courses and interdisciplinary teaching, and to permit cross-registration with other graduate schools at Fordham University.[54]

The clinical program expanded with new courses, but clinical opportunities were not as numerous or as varied as students would have liked. The Law School added clinical courses in Consumer Problems and Environmental Law to established clinical courses associated with the Criminal Defender Program, the district attorneys' offices in New York County and the Bronx, and the United States attorneys' offices in the southern and eastern districts. These courses were comparable to externships today, with ten hours per week of fieldwork combined with individual or group instruction and assessment by a Fordham Law School professor. There were no live-client clinics.[55]

The Law School fell short of its goals relating to faculty size and faculty secretarial support. The twenty-six full-time faculty were six shy of the recommended thirty-two, if one included the positions of legal writing associate professor and clinical associate professor that were not created. Faculty size became a more acute problem in 1975 as the size of the student body increased beyond that anticipated in the five-year plan. The five faculty secretaries were one and one-half short of that required to provide one secretary for every four professors. But, the Law School met its goal of providing faculty research support, allotting each full-time faculty member 150 hours of student research assistance and allowing the faculty to participate in the university's program of sabbaticals.[56]

The review committee recognized the Law School's need to replicate its "very good" reputation within the metropolitan professional circles in the academic world, where "Fordham is an unknown quantity." Recognizing that reputations are built upon public relations as well as on substantive achievement, the committee made several suggestions to improve Fordham Law School's reputation within the legal academy. One form of public relations was faculty "attendance and active participation at conventions of international, national and regional associations, as well as in the committees of such associations." The Law School should encourage faculty participation with "ample funding." The review committee also recommended publication of legal works aimed at a national audience, which should be encouraged with temporarily reduced teaching loads and adequate research and secretarial support. Another way of enhancing the Law School's reputation was by exchanging faculty with other law schools. The report noted that the Law School hosted only one visiting professor in the preceding twelve years. It urged Fordham to solicit professors from leading law schools to visit at Fordham, and to encourage Fordham faculty members to visit at other leading law schools. The report endorsed the Admissions Office's policy of recruiting qualified students from outside of the Northeast as contributing to the Law School's national reputation.[57]

Some progress was made in meeting the 1972 recommendations for the law library, but progress was "at an extremely slow rate." The library's book acquisition budget was increased from $65,000 in 1971 to $100,000 in 1975. The Law School supplemented these amounts each year by $5,000 to $7,000 from its fund-raising efforts. The library's collection had reached 162,000 volumes by 1975, but this placed the library fifth among the eleven law schools in New York State, behind Columbia, Cornell, NYU, and SUNY Buffalo. The collection was growing, but at a slower pace than other comparable law school libraries. Approximately two-thirds of Fordham's collection was composed of series, and three-quarters of its budget was allocated to continuing these series. In funds spent per student, the law library ranked eighth out of the eleven law schools in New York State.[58]

The Law School's annual expenditure "to round out the collection" was less than one-half of the $22,000 the 1972 plan estimated, and its annual spending to acquire new materials was far less than the plan's estimated $15,000. The failure to meet these spending goals resulted in "a paucity of material" to support a number of existing courses taught at the Law School and to support "serious research." Dr. Teclaff estimated that about $600,000 was needed to acquire the necessary books and materials to enable the Fordham Law library to become a fully equipped research library. The review committee concluded that "very little can be done within the present budget." In addition, only one of the two additional professional librarians were added to the library staff. At least one more was needed to enable the library to provide a professional librarian for the entire time that the night school was in session and to provide better library service during the day. The ABA, in a recent inspection, recommended that the library add two nonprofessional positions to assist in cataloguing and acquisitions. The Law School requested these positions in the 1974–75 budget, but the university rejected the request. On the positive side, the 1972 recommendation to reduce the noise level in the library's main reading room was largely achieved.[59]

The issue of faculty salaries remained contentious in the spring and summer of 1971. Pursuant to an agreement with Father Walsh, Fordham Law School appointed a Law School Bargaining Committee in April 1971 consisting of Joe Perillo, Joseph Crowley, and Earl Phillips to negotiate with the Fordham University president on faculty salaries and fringe benefits. The negotiations were complicated because Mulligan was ending his tenure as dean, and McLaughlin was beginning his tenure. They were further complicated because Father Walsh resigned as Fordham's president, and Father James C. Finlay replaced him. Negotiations extended over the following year. The administration acknowledged that the faculty salaries had fallen below those paid at competing law schools, and it agreed to adjust these salaries to bring them up to the level at these other law schools. But, the administration's position seemed to be self-defeating, if not disingenuous, because it insisted on tying annual salary increments and fringe benefits paid to the law faculty to those paid to faculty in other schools in the university.[60]

The administration did not provide sufficient funds to meet the curricular and staffing goals of the Law School for the 1972–73 academic year. In order to increase the number of electives the Law School offered, it would have to add six new faculty positions. It also had to replace three full-time faculty who resigned at the end of the 1971–72 school year, Professors Kelly, Sprizzo, and Sheridan. The nine hires would bring the number of full-time faculty to twenty-seven, giving the Law School a student to faculty ratio of one to thirty-nine and moving toward McLaughlin's goal of reducing the ratio to one to thirty, "as in the better law schools." He requested authorization to make lateral hires of "experienced personnel" at salaries of about $21,000. The additional faculty necessitated additional faculty secretarial support and office space. These required additional financial outlays. On top of these increased expenditures, McLaughlin requested another assistant dean.[61]

The administration authorized a Law School budget increase of $57,000, aside from salary increases and new faculty positions, for the 1972–73 school year. Reiss informed McLaughlin that he could allocate the $57,000 according to his own priorities, but he suggested that this amount would enable McLaughlin to hire the new assistant dean he had requested, add one professional librarian, modestly increase the annual increment for the purchase of new books for the library, purchase chairs for library carrels and add two secretaries. Funds for the *Law Review* would have to come from the Law School's fund-raising efforts, as would funds for the *Urban Law Journal* which began publication in 1971. Reiss also informed McLaughlin that the Law School's budget increase was "a unique exception" because all of the other schools and departments within Fordham University had been instructed to maintain a zero budget increase, aside from faculty salaries.[62]

Deficiencies reported in the student and faculty self-studies in 1969 and the 1970s presaged difficulties in the Law School's reaccreditation by the ABA. It was up for the ABA's periodic reinspection in the fall of 1973. The contentious relationship that had emerged between the university and the Law School over the latter's autonomy and financial support spilled over to the ABA reinspection team. The newly appointed president, Father James Finlay and the ABA visitation team got off to a bad start, and their relationship spiraled downward through the reinspection and its aftermath. The relationship between Fordham University and the ABA was poor throughout Father Finlay's tenure as Fordham's president.

The ABA had changed its process of accreditation in 1973. It created an accreditation committee that focused on the quality of the law school. The ABA expected accredited law schools to exceed the ABA's minimum standards and to meet the standards of excellence they held out to students. If a law school, like Fordham, held itself out to be a premier law school, but its students were average and its publication standards were average, then it was not a premier law school and should not claim that it was.[63]

The ABA assessed the quality of law schools by certain indexes. For example, it measured the adequacy of the faculty by such factors as the ratio of students to full-time faculty; the number of core and required courses taught by full-time faculty; the adequacy of the physical plant to provide sufficient space for small classes and elective courses and to meet other educational needs; the adequacy of the library measured by its book collection, research resources and services, and library personnel. If a law school was lacking in these criteria, the accreditation committee then looked into the law school's finances to determine whether it was receiving sufficient financial support to accomplish its educational mission. At this time, the ABA thought a university with which a law school was affiliated could reasonably divert about 20 percent of the law school's revenue for general university expenses. If it diverted more than that, the ABA required the university to explain and justify the larger diversion. This was a time, however, when many universities used law schools to subsidize their other schools and programs, and many of these universities did not change this practice until the late 1970s and 1980s.[64]

Fordham University was one of these universities, as were many other Catholic and nonsectarian universities. Fordham University's resistance to the ABA's new reaccreditation process is indicative of the resistance the ABA received from many university administrations to its new process. Dean James P. White, who was the ABA consultant involved with Fordham Law School's reaccreditation from 1974 to 2001, recalled that Dean McLaughlin wanted the ABA to help the Law School get the funding from Fordham University that it deserved. The dean understandably asked the ABA visitation team to give special attention to the Law School's newly inaugurated separate program of fund-raising. Father Finlay objected to "the idea of independent agencies telling us how we should go about our fund raising." Cammarosano shared Father Finlay's resistance, who commented that "it is ironic that the University should pay for a visitation which will explore ways and means for reducing the University's income." Reiss signaled the administration's concern to McLaughlin, saying that the inspection team should instead "take a hard look" at the new curriculum and its implementation, an area where they "could, perhaps, be of some assistance to us."[65]

The reinspection report focused on the Law School's finances, which outraged university administrators. It also contained contradictory conclusions that further alienated the Fordham administration. The report declared that the Law School "meets, and, in many cases, exceeds the standards and requirements of both [ABA and AALS] associations, and that its accreditation should remain intact." It also identified a number of problems. "One of the critical problems," the report recounted, was what appeared to the visitation team to be the improper "financial balance" between the income the Law School generated and the support the university gave back to the Law School. The "imprecise nature of the budget data" in the university's financial statements rendered the visitation team unable to assess the proper balance with certainty. Nevertheless, the report concluded that insufficient financial resources had created deficiencies in a number of areas that were correctable by providing sufficient funds.[66]

The visitation team concluded that various aspects of the Law School suffered from being underfunded. For example, the twenty-five full-time faculty was large enough to cover required courses in both the day and evening divisions, but the Law School had to rely on the twenty-two part-time faculty to cover the elective courses. The full-time faculty's median salary of $23,600 was "below regional standards and [was] well below the median salary paid by the neighboring law schools with which Fordham should be competing." The five faculty secretaries were inadequate, and their pay structure, which was tied to university staff guidelines, "impose[d] a low ceiling on these salaries and prevent qualitative improvement." Although the Law librarian, Professor Ludwik A. Teclaff, brought "distinction to the Law School" as a librarian and a legal scholar, the report recommended that the other four librarians develop "greater professionalism" by attending professional conferences and workshops, acquiring the proper degrees, teaching courses in legal writing and research, and producing scholarly publications. Law librarians did not stay long at Fordham, and the visitation team believed the "chief cause of the short tenure" was likely due to "the disparity between salaries paid to professional librarians at Fordham and those paid at other comparable law schools." The library's 152,000 volumes was "a fine collection" of publications, but its current book budget of $94,000 would have to be increased by "upwards of $25,000 annually" to develop in "fields of expanding law," such as energy, the environment and civil rights and in "fields peripheral to law" if it hoped to achieve its goal of becoming "a top rank law library." The report found that its book appropriation for the 1972–73 academic year placed it eighth out of nine comparable law schools. It concluded that, "if Fordham aspires to greatness, it must have the funds to continue its development intensively for several more years and gradually thereafter."[67]

The report was critical of the Law School's fund-raising program and suggested that Father Finlay reneged on an agreement regarding the Law School's separate fund-raising his predecessor had entered with the Law School, which Father Finlay and the university administrators found highly offensive. The Law School and Fordham University reached this agreement in the fall of 1971. A Law School committee consisting of two Fordham Law alumni, Dennis McInerney and Matt Mone, two faculty members, Robert M. Byrn and Barry Hawk, and one student representative, SBA President Tony Siano, worked out the logistics with the development office. The separate Law School fund raising presented a question of how the contributions would be handled. At McInerney's suggestion, the committee decided that Fordham Law School should follow the example of many leading law schools and establish a charitable corporation to operate its fund-raising, and it sought to establish the foundation for the 1972 fund-raising mailing. The committee also considered a separate Law

School bank account as an alternative to the charitable corporation. The Law School's separate fund-raising raised a question of who would control the funds thus raised.[68]

Fordham University and Fordham Law School reached an agreement establishing a separate law school fund-raising program in 1971, but the university retained control over it and the funds it generated. The university agreed that all contributions sent directly to the Law School in response to its annual fund solicitations "must be assumed to be for Law School use," but it insisted that all contributions sent directly to the university "must be assumed to be for University use." If, however, the recipient had "reasonable grounds to believe that the donor's intention" was otherwise, an inquiry into the donor's intent was required. The donor's intent on the use of the contribution "must be followed." Law alumni who were also alumni of other schools within Fordham University would receive a solicitation only from the university's development office, but the "letter of solicitation" would include "*inter alia*, a solicitation for the Law School Fund." The purpose was to allow such alumni the opportunity to direct his or her contribution to the Law School or to the university. The Law School agreed not to solicit any "persons outside the Law Alumni." However, the university allowed the Law School to keep contributions made by a nonalumnus who was solicited by a Fordham Law alumnus, on his or her own initiative, and to allow the Law School subsequently to place such donors on its "list for an annual solicitation." The university would remove such donors from its list of potential donors.[69]

The ABA disapproved of the university's substantial control of the Law School's fund-raising. Not only did the development office mail the Law School's solicitations, more importantly, Father Finlay "screened out the 300 most affluent law alumni, and . . . ordered the Dean not to solicit them for law school gifts until after they [had] been solicited by the President on behalf of the University." The visitation team reported that the law faculty considered this restriction a violation of the Law School's agreement with the university, and the university president's "failure to live up to the terms of his 1971 agreement with the Law School" was a "major concern" of the faculty. Moreover, the Fordham president's policy regarding the solicitation of the most affluent Fordham Law alumni, the report opined, was "contrary to the current of sophisticated fund raising in the better law schools," such as Columbia, Chicago, Harvard, NYU, Pennsylvania, and Virginia, and, in the visitation team's opinion, would "diminish the effect of both fund raising efforts." The team had urged on Father Finlay "the necessity of his restoring parity to the Law School's solicitation effort," but the president "clearly indicated his unwillingness to do so." The visitors considered his refusal "extremely detrimental to both the University and the Law School."[70]

The ABA report reached certain conclusions regarding the Law School's financial circumstances despite its complaints that the university failed to provide adequate financial information. It stated that the visitation team was convinced that the Law School was "generating more than sufficient income to meet its present deficiencies and to bring the School to the level of excellence of which it is capable." The Law School's revenue was also "more than sufficient" to provide "very substantial" contributions to the university's other departments, even after the Law School absorbed "appropriate overhead costs properly chargeable to the Law Program." The team met with Father Finlay and McLaughlin to discuss these problems, and members felt that they had conveyed to the Fordham administrators a better understanding of their need for more precise financial information and a better balance between Law School income and university support. The report recommended that the team revisit the Law School in a year to determine the extent to which needed changes had been implemented.[71]

Father Finlay reacted quickly and angrily to the ABA report. He informed the visitation chairman, Dean John B. Neibel, that the report's comment that the university president failed to live up to the terms of the 1971 agreement with the Law School concerning its fund raising "comes close to being a personal affront to myself." He noted that this agreement was made not by him but by his predecessor, Father Walsh, and that he consulted Father Walsh to confirm that his understanding of the agreement was the same as Father Walsh's. Finlay asserted that he had "made every effort, according to my lights, to live up to that agreement," and he found it "quite inappropriate . . . that my honesty should be impugned in this way," especially in a document "that will have wide distribution."[72]

Father Finlay also found the 1973 ABA report lacking in proportion and disappointing in what he did not find in it. He expressed "a little wonderment" that it devoted more than one-third to the law library, "particularly when there are no major reasons for complaint." The report also focused heavily on financial questions, but the "faculty gets only a page and a half of treatment and the course of study scarcely two pages." Finlay complained that "it is the lack of proportion that disappoints me." He reassured Dean Neibel that he had "every intention of working to see that our Law School" achieved greater progress, and explained that his "negative comments on the Report were dictated by a desire to set a record straight."[73]

Academic Vice President Reiss alerted Father Finlay of a more dangerous and unacceptable feature of the visitation report. Reiss saw that the ABA was trying to help the Law School achieve a better allocation of its revenue from the university. It was asserting itself into the university's financial affairs and institutional policies and pressuring the university to conform them to the ABA's priorities for Fordham Law School. Reiss thought it "outrageous" that the visitation committee presumed to be "a watchdog on the University's operations over the next year to assure itself that its recommendations are followed." He also believed it was "totally improper" that the committee "assume the right to enter into agreements with the President" and then announce them to the faculty through its report, "following which it takes unto itself the responsibility for policing the 'agreements.'" Reiss concluded that the visitation committee's actions represented "an unwarranted interference by the ABA with the operations of Fordham University."[74]

Reiss's major objection was directed not only at the ABA's interference with the university's financial affairs but also at what he perceived to be the ABA's imposition of higher accreditation standards on Fordham Law School than it applied to other law schools. The visitation committee, having concluded that the Law School satisfied and "in many cases, exceeds the standards and requirements of [the ABA and the AALS], and that its accreditation should remain intact," by "what right," Reiss demanded, did "this Committee establish additional standards such as an acceptable allocation to the Law School of University resources . . . and then hold the University accountable to this Committee for meeting these standards?" Reiss adamantly maintained that it was "for Fordham University to decide how it should operate its law school and allocate its resources." What the law faculty salaries should be in relation to any selection of other law schools was "our decision to make, not that of the ABA."

Reiss insisted it was "improper and indeed dangerous to accept the principle that the ABA and its visiting committee are to set these objectives for
us." Ignoring the aspirations of the Law School's dean and faculty to make
the law school as good as it could become, Reiss insisted that, if the ABA
accredited third-rate law schools and Fordham University wanted to run
one "(which, of course, it does not)," Reiss noted, then "by what right
does the ABA tell us that New York Law or Brooklyn Law can do that
but Fordham can't—that it has set higher standards for Fordham." The
visitation committee had also "overstepped its role in suggesting that it
should review progress on its recommendations over the next year, especially in financial matters and that the ABA would itself be overstepping
its authority if it were to accept the Committee's recommendation in this
regard."[75]

In a second letter to Neibel, Father Finlay incorporated the points Reiss
had made to him and informed Neibel that Fordham University rejected
the ABA's "unacceptable" and "insulting" presumption of authority to
investigate the Law School's and the university's financial condition. Finlay made additional points. He bluntly stated that it was the "prerogative
of the University and its Trustees" to decide how the university "should
operate its law school and allocate its resources," including the level of
faculty salaries, "and not that of external agencies." Finlay reminded
Neibel that he agreed with the visitation committee's objectives for the
Law School, but it was "both improper and dangerous for us to accept
the principle that the ABA and its visiting Committee are to set these
objectives for us." Reasserting Fordham's determination to develop the
Law School "to the highest level its resources will allow," Finlay refused
"to place ourselves under the tutelage of such committees now, no matter
how well intentioned." He sent a copy of this letter to Millard H. Ruud,
the executive director of the AALS. Ruud assured Father Finlay that his
comments would be "placed in the hands of the appropriate officials of
this Association."[76]

The ABA and AALS agreed that it would be improper for the visitation
committee "to act in any continuing capacity," and they informed Father
Finlay "that will not be done." However, these organizations insisted on
addressing the principle issue, the allocation of financial resources.[77]

The ABA's Council of the Section of Legal Education and Admissions
to the Bar and its Accreditation Committee considered its conflict with

Fordham University at its July 1974 meeting. The council concluded that the Law School was "in substantial compliance with the Standards" of the ABA, but it requested that the president of Fordham University and the dean of the Law School submit by January 1, 1975, "a detailed response to concerns expressed" in the visitation committee's report regarding various matters: the law school budget; the Law School's alumni relations and its solicitation to alumni; continuing education; reduction of the noise level in the law library; development of greater professionalism among the library staff; and enrichment of the library's book collection.[78]

The ABA Council and its Accreditation Committee were particularly concerned about the Law School budget. They reiterated the visitation committee's discomfort over its inability to determine the proper balance between the Law School's revenue and the support the university returned to the law program because of "the imprecise nature" of the budget data. The council cited a number of ABA Standards for Approval of Law Schools in this regard: Standard 105, which declared that "an approved school should seek to exceed the minimum requirements of the Standards"; Standard 209, which required that "financial resources of the law school shall be adequate to sustain a sound educational program"; and Standard 405, which required an approved law school to "establish and maintain conditions adequate to attract and retain a competent faculty."[79]

The ABA Council and Accreditation Committee suggested that Fordham Law School may be in violation of Standard 405 relating to the faculty. This standard included several subsections which specified the kinds of conditions necessary to attract and retain competent faculty. Salaries should be sufficient to attract and retain "persons of high ability." Standard 405 defined "sufficient" to mean "prevailing compensation of comparably qualified private practitioners and government attorneys and of the judiciary," and as "comparable with that paid faculty members at similar approved law schools in the same general geographical area." This standard also required that faculty members be afforded "reasonable opportunity for leaves of absences and for scholarly research," "reasonable secretarial and clerical assistance," and an established and announced policy regarding academic freedom and tenure. The ABA Council and Accreditation Committee suggested that Fordham Law School's faculty salaries failed to meet this standard when it noted that they were "among the lowest quartile among metropolitan law schools." Indeed, Fordham

Law School's median faculty salary placed it behind every law school in New York State except New York Law School, which supported the visitation team's contention that faculty salaries violated ABA Standard 405. These bodies manifested "considerable concern" that Fordham Law School did not have "the financial resources available for its use as necessary to provide the type of legal education to enable it to accomplish the objectives of an educational mission." The ABA asked Fordham University to submit more detailed financial information to make this determination.[80]

Father Finlay asked the ABA to justify its request for a "further report" of financial information and to clarify the ABA's role in establishing standards for law schools. He also wanted to know whether the ABA had established uniform standards, which it applied equally to all law schools, or whether it had established different standards which it applied to different law schools depending upon its judgment of what standards specific law schools were capable of attaining. He insisted that Fordham continued to meet the ABA's standards, as he understood them, and that it sought "the highest possible levels of attainment for its School of Law."[81]

Despite his protestations of unfair and discriminatory treatment by the ABA, Father Finlay submitted additional financial information to the ABA, but his report was incomplete. It included "only the direct expenditures of the [Law] School, exclusive of financial aid, fringe benefits, physical plant expenses, and allocable proportion of general University expenses." His report also did not include "funds expended by the [Law] School from revenues received in its own fund raising efforts." Fordham administrators contended that the Law School was sufficiently funded to accomplish "an education mission."[82]

To support its contention that the Law School was adequately funded, Fordham's report included a table of individual and total faculty salaries for each year from the 1970–71 to the 1974–75 academic years. The number of faculty increased from twenty-one in 1971 to twenty-seven in 1974. Total faculty salaries increased from $403,270 in the 1970–71 academic year to $729,800 in 1974–75, an increase of $326,530, or 81 percent. The median salary rose $7,600 from $18,400 in 1970–71 to $26,000 in 1974–75, which represented a 41 percent increase during the period. The report also indicated changes in the Law School's fund-raising program that gave it

greater control; identified a number of continuing legal education programs and institutes the Law School conducted; and specified a number
of actions the Law School took to meet the deficiencies in the law library.
For example, it reduced the noise level in the main reading room by car-
peting and partitioning it from the copy machine and the circulation desk.
It created a separate travel fund to encourage the attendance of librarians
at professional conventions and workshops as ways to develop their professionalism. The law library succeeded in hiring an evening reference
librarian and was searching for a day reference librarian. The Law School
raised the librarian salaries, but Father Finlay conceded that the assistant
librarian's salary had to be increased more to assure the continued service
of a fully qualified and competent person. The university increased the
budget for new book acquisitions by $7,000, which was less than the
$16,000 Law School had requested and the $25,000 the 1973 ABA report
stated was necessary to get the collection up to where it should be. Father
Finlay explained that the Law School's administration had decided to
reach the $25,000 goal in "two or three states."[83]

The ABA Council and its Accreditation Committee did not retreat
from their demand for complete financial information and stated that the
Law School was not in compliance with certain of its standards. The council accepted as satisfactory those parts of Fordham's report dealing with
the noise level in the law library, alumni relations, and the development
of the librarians' professionalism. However, they found the information
Father Finlay submitted regarding the Law School's budget and enrichment of the library's book collection was inadequate to satisfy the ABA
that Fordham Law School was in compliance with ABA Standards 105,
201, 209, and 405, despite the recent increases in faculty salaries and funds
for library acquisitions.[84]

To make its determination whether Fordham Law School was in compliance with its standards, the ABA Council requested specific information
concerning the Law School's income from tuition and fees, gifts and
endowments restricted to the Law School, overhead recovery on Law
School contracts and grants, other direct income, and its shared allocation
from unrestricted university endowments and gifts. The council also asked
for detailed information concerning certain Law School expenses: administrative expenses other than library acquisition costs and salaries, faculty
salaries, fringe benefits on salaries, scholarship assistance, physical plant

expenses, and indirect expenses, that is, allowable proportion of general university expenses. Father Finlay was asked to state "with precision" the criteria the university used to determine the proportion of general university expenses allocable to the Law School. The council wanted to know the amount of the surpluses, if any, resulting from the Law School's operation during 1972–73, 1973–74, and 1974–75, and the purposes for which the surpluses, if any, were used.[85]

On April 25, 1975, James P. White, the ABA's consultant on legal education, met with Father Finlay, Cammarosano, Reiss, and McLaughlin in the president's office to discuss the council's concerns and to enable the university to make "an adequate response to their questions." At this meeting, Dean White informed them that the ABA and AALS "had made a significant change in the application of their standards for evaluation of law schools between 1973 and 1975. They were now stressing essentially qualitative norms rather than the quantitative norms that had been used previously." During this period, thirty-seven law schools were inspected, and of these only three "received approval without any comment." Five law schools had been given orders "to show cause why they should not be de-certified." Six other schools were "close to show cause." Fordham Law School was in a category with twenty-three other law schools. These schools met the qualifications for accreditation, but they had "some problems relating to the quality of their program [sic]."[86]

The ABA now looked upon reinspection visitations "as devices to stimulate growth in legal education both as to quality and diversity." White assured the Fordham administrators that there was "obviously no question of removing Fordham's accreditation." The ABA considered Fordham Law School to be "a very good Law School." However, members of the visitation committee believed that it could be "substantially better with a minimal increase in resources." They had questions about "the uses to which tuition was being put, also gifts and the charges made against the Law School for supporting services." When pressed for details, Mr. White "had difficulty in responding to specifics." He conceded that there were "no hard and fast standards for costs in legal education," although the ABA and AALS were trying to develop them.[87]

Cammarosano expressed alarm over the information that the ABA was demanding Fordham University give to its council. He regarded the request as an intrusion into the "purely internal affairs of the University," which would set a "very dangerous precedent and could, quite conceivably, be violative of our own academic freedom." Cammarosano believed that Fordham's administrators should not give the council the requested information.[88]

One can understand Fordham's resistance to what appeared to be the ABA's inappropriate interference into the governance of the university to meet ambiguous standards that seemingly kept changing. Father Finlay contacted Lloyd H. Elliott, president of George Washington University and chairman of the Council on Post-Secondary Accreditation, to complain about the ABA's behavior. He informed Elliott that the 1973 ABA visitation committee inspected the Law School and concluded that it did "meet and in many cases exceed the standards and requirements" of both the ABA and AALS. Despite this favorable finding, the ABA asked Father Finlay for a further report of Fordham University's finances, including revenue and expenditures allocable to the Law School. He suggested that the ABA's request was "designed to pressure the University to consider the Law School as an autonomous fiscal entity within the University." Finlay asserted that the ABA attempted to justify its request for information by citing standards that had "little relevance" to the issue and "in no way justify the position the Accreditation Committee is taking."[89]

Father Finlay maintained that the ABA's approach to reviewing Fordham Law School's reaccreditation "raises serious questions as to the proper role and function of accreditation for professional schools." First, should a law school, which met all of the relevant accreditation standards, be denied accreditation because "the accrediting group decides that the university might have more resources which it should allocate in some fashion to the school?" Second, should a university have the "freedom to allocate its total resources as its Trustees see fit as long as it meets the relevant standards in each of its schools." Father Finlay believed the ABA had committed "serious abuses of authority," and he turned to the Council on Post-Secondary Accreditation for help because a university, on its own, "is obviously not in a very strong position to deal with these threats to institutional freedom and prerogatives." He asked for Dr. Elliott's advice and for information on "any actions in which COPSA might be involved in connection with these issues."[90]

Dr. Elliott brought the matter before the Council on Post-Secondary Accreditation at its meeting in April, 1975. Evidently, he telephoned Father

Finlay on May 22 to discuss the council's action. Father Finlay noted that there seemed to be "widespread hostility to the ABA's attitude and agreement with us that allocation of resources within the University properly belongs to Trustees." Dr. Elliott asked Father Finlay to keep him informed of his dealings with the ABA. He was especially interested in the "shift in application of norms." Father Finlay complied, and the Council on Post-Secondary Education monitored the ABA's accreditation process.[91]

In May 1975 the ABA warned Father Finlay that Fordham University was jeopardizing the Law School's accreditation by "your adamant resistance to furnishing of financial information requested of you by the Council." R. W. Nahstoll, chairman of the ABA's Section of Legal Education and Admission to the Bar, insisted that the requested information was needed to evaluate Fordham Law School as an ABA accredited institution. He warned that, if the council did not receive the information by July 1, 1975, it would consider at its July meeting "taking steps appropriate to the withdrawal of approval from your law school."[92]

Fordham was not the only Jesuit law school that was having problems with the ABA and AALS in the mid-1970s. Father Finlay learned this in a letter Father John A. Fitterer, S.J., president of the Association of Jesuit Colleges and Universities, sent to him with helpful information and advice on how to deal with these accrediting organizations. An unidentified member of the ABA who was "active in the law school accreditation process" and "quite a good friend of the Jesuits" offered "some unsolicited advice concerning our Jesuit Law Schools in general and your own School of Law specifically." The general problem was "the use of law school revenue for university purposes," Father Fitterer reported. If this revenue was "inequitably apportioned" to other divisions of the university, "then both law school students and faculty can initiate a grievance."[93]

The ABA was interested in preventing "a drain of too much revenue," Father Fitterer informed Father Finley, because it could diminish the "quality of legal education at the school." It had been in contact with seven or eight Jesuit law schools concerning this and related issues. As the "major accrediting agency," the ABA was "anxious" to maintain "a high level of quality" in the legal education law schools offered, and it was "now trying to serve as a buffer between law schools and the new accreditation-consciousness of the [US] Office of Education." The ABA was feeling pressure from the federal government to maintain professional excellence in the nation's law schools. "The new Guaranteed Student Loan regulations," Father Fitterer remarked, "will prompt more federal action on both career readiness of law school graduates and refund policies." The ABA was also working jointly with the state agency responsible for law school accreditation.[94]

Father Fitterer offered suggestions on how Fordham University could satisfy the ABA and continue to divert revenue from the law school into other parts of the university. It was important to establish "a reasonable basis for apportioning indirect costs," because this was, after all, the "device which permits siphoning law school revenue to broad university support." The computation of overhead costs "should be *consonent* [sic] throughout the university," he cautioned. "Keep median salaries high," Fitterer suggested, because the "ABA uses the median as its measure." Maintaining "high [median salaries] may be the least expensive way of satisfying ABA requirements." He suggested that "some Jesuit law schools" were having trouble with the ABA because "experience has indicated" that salaries are "near or below media [sic] levels; . . . library support is near median or lower; . . . tuition is very high." Fitterer unequivocally declared that "salaries and library support must be made more competitive by more fairly apportioning law school revenue to legal education." This strategy "would be better assurance" that the university could "still utilize a part of law school revenue for university support." The issue was "*equitable apportionment*," Father Fitterer opined. "Otherwise, students can sue on the basis that not a sufficient part of their tuition is directed at insuring a high quality of legal education." Not only could law students sue, "law school faculty can charge discriminatory salary practices." He concluded by informing Father Finlay that the Jesuits's "old friend" suggested that "Fordham tone down its reaction to ABA policies and processes."[95]

Dean White recalled that Fordham was more aggressive than most law schools at this time. His recollection appears to be accurate. Father Finlay failed to tone down his rhetoric as Father Fitterer advised. Following a meeting with then Professor White, Father Finlay wrote to Nashtoff and as much as accused the ABA of being arbitrary and of violating fundamental principles of due process in its dealings with Fordham. Father Finlay's account of Fordham's meeting with White to clarify the ABA's position supported Father Finlay's characterization. White could not explain why the ABA's Accreditation Committee was unable to determine whether the Law School met the standards for accreditation when the 1973 ABA inspection report concluded that it not only met but in many cases exceeded the standards for accreditation and that its accreditation should continue. White informed the Fordham administrators that the Accreditation Committee sought the information to determine whether the university possessed additional resources that "could be made available to the School of Law." White was unable to identify any standard that specified the proportion of available resources that must be allocated to the Law School. Nor could he name a standard that specified "what would be considered available resources." It appeared to Fordham administrators, and White admitted, that the ABA simply wanted to learn whether there were additional resources that might be allocated to the Law School and to decide according to "some unstated norm" whether these resources should be allocated to the Law School. They believed that the ABA would make this decision "with no reference to specific deficiencies" in the Law School and without "reference to any assessment that the educational program was any less than excellent." Fordham University administrators expected the ABA to supply them with "clear and consistent norms which are applied universally to all Law Schools." An explanation of these norms "should make obvious the need for the data in order to judge whether or not a School of Law, any School of Law, meets the standards for accreditation." Father Finlay explained, "Our problem was one of principle." But, "Mr. White was singularly unable to explain the relevant norms. In fact, he as much as admitted that such norms do not exist."[96]

Nahstoll did not budge at all in his reply to Father Finlay's letter. "I sense some foot-dragging on the part of your office with regard to supplying the financial information which has been requested several times," he cautioned. Quoting ABA Standard 210, which requires that the relationship with the university with which a law school is affiliated "shall serve to enhance the program of the law school," he informed Father Finlay that it was with respect to this standard that the ABA needed "to know to what purposes are being applied the revenues of your law school." Disclaiming any "wish to appear arrogant about the matter," Nahstoff reminded Father Finlay that "the deadline by which it is imperative for you to supply the requested information is coming fast upon us." He reiterated the ABA's intention of considering the withdrawal of Fordham

Law School's accreditation if it did not receive the requested information by July 1, 1975. In a telephone conversation, Father Finlay assured Nahstoff that he would submit the requested information by the July 1 deadline.[97]

Father Finlay missed the deadline by one day, but the information was not complete because the 1975 fiscal year had just ended, and the auditors had not had the opportunity to audit the university's financial records. However, Father Finlay submitted the Law School's income and expense statements for 1973 and 1974. These statements revealed that the Law School generated surpluses of $155,672 out of total revenues of $2,310,103 or 6.7 percent for the 1972–73 academic year and $176,983 out of total revenues of $2,504,246 or 7 percent for the 1973–74 academic year. The university applied these surpluses to its Plant Funds and Funds Functioning as Endowment accounts "to replenish the University's badly depleted reserves. Because the University's budget has been balanced since 1970," Father Finlay maintained, "no funds have been transferred from the Law School to any other school or department of the University."[98]

As the ABA requested, Father Finlay explained two expense items the ABA had indicated were troublesome. The first, "Physical Plant Expenses," represented "the Law School's share of the total cost" of operating and maintaining the Lincoln Center Campus, "which is comprised of two structures." The Law School's cost was "determined by applying the ratio of the total square feet of space in the Law School to the total square feet of space at Lincoln Center to the total cost of maintaining and operating the Lincoln Center campus." The physical plant expenses allocated to the Law School for 1972–73 and 1973–74 were $362,271 and $404,868 respectively.[99]

The other expense that needed clarification was "Indirect Expense." This entry represented "the Law School's share of General Administration and General Institutional Expenditures." Included in this account were outlays for "audit, consultants, legal, insurance, Alumni, University Relations, Computer, Personnel, Development, etc." The Law School's proportion of these expenses was determined "by taking the ratio between the FTE (full-time equivalent) student population at the Law School and the FTE student population for the entire University and then applying the ratio to the total General Administration and General Institutional expenditures." For fiscal years 1973 and 1974, the university assigned to the

Law School indirect expenses of $253,016 ($1,220,000 in present-day dollars) and $280,099 ($1,220,000 in present-day dollars) respectively. For 1973, the Law School's share of physical plant expenses and indirect expenses totaled $615,287 and represented 28.6 percent of the Law School's total expenses of $2,154,431. For 1974, these two charges amounted to $654,967 and represented 29.4 percent of the Law School's total expenses of $2,327,263. In addition to these items, the university charged the Law School $200,000 per year for plant replacement. Fordham failed to explain how it determined the amount for plant replacement. If one added plant replacement costs to the other two university allocations, the total paid to the university in 1973 was $815,287, or 37.8 percent of the Law School's total expenditures. For 1974, the total paid to the university was $884,967, or 38 percent of the Law School's total expenditures. But then, one would have to add the surpluses the Law School earned and which the university absorbed to get the total amounts paid by the Law School to the university. For 1973 the surplus of $155,672 raised the total paid to Fordham University to $970,959, or 42 percent of the Law School's total revenue of $2,310,103. For 1974 the surplus of $176,983 raised the total amount paid to the university to $1,061,950, or 42.6 percent of the Law School's total revenue for that year. These diversions of the Law School's revenue were more than twice as large as the ABA's recommended standard of 20 percent.[100]

The conflict between the ABA Council and Fordham University revealed that the two antagonists had conflicting understandings of the nature of the Law School's affiliation with Fordham University. The ABA and Fordham Law School's administration and faculty viewed the Law School's relationship to the university as analogous to the relationship of the commonwealths of the British Empire to Great Britain: affiliated but self-governing and autonomous for the most part. Father Finlay and the university administration, on the other hand, rejected this view and insisted "that Fordham University operates as one unified and integrated institution." It did not consider any of its various schools "as a separate unit for the purpose of financial accounting."[101]

The university's failure to consider any of its various schools "as a separate unit for the purpose of financial accounting" gave rise to accounting practices and funds distribution policies to which the ABA objected. For example, Fordham University considered the money it received from the state of New York for the degrees its various schools conferred, that is, Bundy Aid, as "an unrestricted institutional grant," and it did not "credit the funds to its several schools." The university received $2,631,000 in Bundy money for the 1974–75 academic year. Of this amount, it received $600 for each of the 333 law degrees the Law School conferred for a total of $199,800. This amount, along with the other Bundy grants, went into the University's general funds. On the expense side of the ledger, the plant replacement cost of $200,000 the university charged to the Law School was part of an allowance for all of the university's schools and divisions, not only the replacement cost of the law school's building. Father Finlay did not explain how the dollar amount charged to the Law School was determined, nor did he explain whether the university used "the same criterion in budgeting plant replacement expenditures in other divisions of the university," even though the ABA expressly asked for this information. But he did say that these funds were "transferred to general University plant funds," and they were "utilized as determined by the University Board of Trustees for particular [University] needs." Funds that were transferred out of this account and into current funds "would not be allocated to specific Schools but to the University operating budget." Father Finlay claimed that the current law school building had been built with funds from this general university account.[102]

After considering the information Father Finlay submitted, the Accreditation Committee of the ABA Council concluded at its December 1975 meeting that Fordham University "continue[d] to refuse to provide information upon which the Council can determine compliance, by Fordham University," with ABA standards for accreditation. Stating that "the Council has reason to believe that the School of Law, Fordham University, is in violation of the Standards," White's letter asserted that the council "hereby notifies" the president of Fordham University and the dean of the Law School "of the apparent violation of the Standards . . . and asks for an explanation of this violation." The bases for this judgment were the university's failure to make available for the Law School's use the Bundy money it received from New York State, the university's failure to limit the $200,000 of Law School revenue it transferred to the plant replacement fund to the Law School's use, and the university's diversion of the Law School's surplus to the university's endowment fund "with no apparent intention to use these funds for the educational program of the law school." Once the Accreditation Committee received the requested financial information, the council would then determine whether Fordham University and its Law School were in compliance with ABA standards. If the council were to determine that the Law School was not in compliance, "it will take appropriate action for removal of the Fordham University School of Law from the list of Law Schools approved by the American Bar Association." If Fordham Law School were removed from the list, Dean White explained, the Law School's "graduates would not be eligible to take the bar examination in almost every admitting jurisdiction."[103]

The ABA Council reaffirmed its concern that the funds Fordham University made available to the Law School for its "educational program," particularly for "financial aid and library were marginal for a school of its size and professed educational objectives." It could not determine whether that Law School had "as strong an educational program as it might have if it were not a part of Fordham University" and was able to retain for the sole use "of its educational program all of the tuition paid by its students and the state aid appropriated on the basis of the degrees awarded by it." However, the council found that the existing ABA standards did not address the "diversion of law school generated income" to general university purposes. It consequently rescinded its "December resolution" and specifically asked the Accreditation Committee to draft new standards that "specifically address themselves to the problem of a University that utilizes substantial amounts of revenue generated by a law school for non-law school purposes when the educational program of the law school needs additional resources to surpass minimum compliance with other States and to provide the kind of educational program which it professes to provide in its catalog and other public pronouncements."[104]

At their August 1976 meeting, the ABA Council and the Accreditation Committee again acted inconsistently and withdrew their resolution stating that the ABA standards for reaccreditation did not address the diversion of law school–generated funds to general university purposes. They resolved that Standards 201 and 210 required that law students' tuition and New York State institutional Bundy money "be devoted to the educational program of the School of Law." These bodies found serious deficiencies in Fordham Law School's program of legal education because of inadequate funding. They found deficiencies in the law library's "collection, study facilities, and professional administration," in the "number of and compensation paid to full-time members of the law faculty," and in "the absence of a program of continuing legal education." They concluded that financial resources "committed" to the Law School were "not adequate to sustain a sound educational program," even though adequate "financial resources are available." They asked the president of Fordham University and the dean of the Law School to appear before the Accreditation Committee at its November 1976 meeting to discuss these and other matters related to their concern over Fordham's failure to comply with standards for reaccreditation.[105]

The university sought help from outside counsel in preparing for the impending meeting. Fordham alumnus Leo A. Larkin prepared a memorandum that addressed the ABA's complaints, mustering the actions Fordham University had taken since the 1973 reinspection to meet the specific deficiencies the 1973 report identified and presenting arguments to rebut the ABA's continuing concerns over the adequacy of the university's financial support of the Law School. Larkin identified several options available to Fordham University in dealing with the ABA. They all had serious drawbacks.[106]

One option was to negotiate a settlement with the ABA. The university could agree to some increases in the salaries and number of faculty, additional annual funds for library book acquisitions, improvements in the administration of the library and the professionalization of the library's staff, and changes in the Law School's program of education. An obvious disadvantage of this option was the increase in the cost of operating the Law School. A more important disadvantage was the implicit recognition of the ABA's expertise in and authority to order such "improvements" in legal education. In any dispute over these matters, the "ABA would probably prevail" because of its "presumed expertise" and the "well-established law that the courts will not substitute their judgment for that of qualified administrators."[107]

A second option presented even greater difficulties. Fordham could agree to allocate a percentage or all of the Law School's surplus and Bundy money to correct the alleged financial deficiencies the ABA identified. However, this option would entail the university's surrendering some of its control over the allocation of its funds, and it would establish a precedent that the ABA would exploit in the future, in Larkin's view. If the

Fordham Law's first location, Collins Hall, was named in memory of Fordham president John Collins, S.J.

Construction of the Morse Building, 140 Nassau Street, cost $178,000.

The Woolworth Building was the tallest building in the world when Fordham Law first moved into the 28th floor.

Larkin Hall. The Law School maintained a Rose Hill presence for the Evening Division until 1935.

The Law School occupied the top four floors of the Vincent Building, 302 Broadway.

SPRING/SUMMER 1994

VOL. 27 NO. 2

75 Years *of*
Women
at Fordham Law

The Ethics of Cloning
Building a 21st Century Library
Jesuits in Training

Cover of Fordham Magazine, celebrating 75 years of women at Fordham Law.

Current building in the year that it opened, 1961. Above: under construction.

university were to allocate all of the Law School's surplus and all of the Bundy money attributable to Fordham Law graduates, it risked sacrificing "the University's sovereignty" and encouraging the ABA "to challenge in the future the propriety of the University's charges to the Law school."[108]

Alternatively, Fordham University could resist the ABA's threatened withdrawal of accreditation. It could continue the Law School without accreditation. This was undesirable because it would diminish the Law School's and the University's reputations, and Fordham Law graduates might not be qualified to practice in any jurisdiction outside of New York State. The University could terminate its affiliation with the Law School. This would require the Law School to move from the Lincoln Center campus and adopt a new name. Larkin cautioned that the ABA might suggest this. However, he thought this alternative "probably would be a disservice to the law school." These alternatives entailed a determination of university policy and were therefore "beyond the purview of legal judgement."[109]

Finally, Fordham could "contest in court the proposed withdrawal of accreditation." In such litigation, Fordham University would charge the ABA "with espousing a selective enforcement program against Fordham for arbitrary reasons, causing, among other consequences, interference with administration of the University, unjustified damage to the reputation of the University and law school, possible termination of law school affiliation with the University, prejudice to the out-of-state students (whose recruiting the JVT recommended in its December 1973 report), excessive and uncontrollable costs of legal education, and possible violation of antitrust laws." The ABA could thus be liable for damages "for impairment of the reputation of the University and Law School, irreparable injury to the students and, in particular, the out-of-state residents." A lawsuit would also subject the ABA "to the risk that its standards and their application will be declared arbitrary and invalid." For these reasons, Larkin did not think the ABA would risk litigation in New York courts.[110]

Father Finlay, along with Reiss and McLaughlin, represented Fordham University and Fordham Law School in a tension-filled, contentious seventy-five minute meeting with the ABA Accreditation Committee at the Rockefeller Plaza law offices of Webster and Sheffield on November 20, 1976. Mr. Nahstoll opened the meeting by confronting Father Finlay with the ABA's "real basic hangup" regarding the "relationship between the Law School and financing." Nahstoll claimed that the university was taking 40 percent of the Law School's tuition income for general university expenses. When one added the Bundy money attributable to the Law School, the university was appropriating "one half of the tuition revenue of [the Law] School, and this [was] far in excess of what other schools are directing from the Law School to the University." A member of the Accreditation Committee added that "the average in private Law Schools is from 20% to 30%." A possible consequence of this divergence of Law School funds was the Law School's unacceptably high student-to-faculty ratio, which was somewhere between forty to one and fourty-four to one. The ABA Committee thought Fordham University's allocation of law school income to general university purposes was "sufficiently excessive" under ABA standards "for you people to justify it." The problem, however, was that it did not have sufficient financial information to determine whether the university was "ripping off the Law School."[111]

The Law School also complained that it did not have adequate financial information to make the kind of long-range planning it would have preferred. Its 1979 self-study concluded that the "necessary data is not available to the Law School." It acknowledged the bad blood financial issues had created between members of the Law School community and university administrators. "Prior attempts to obtain sufficient financial data for detailed planning have led to needless acrimonious exchanges between University administrators and the Law School." University administrators rejected the Law School's complaint, stating, "it is simply not true." They insisted that they had given the "revenue and expenditure analysis" to the law faculty. University administrators acknowledged that the self-study discussed the university and the Law School "almost as though they are separate entities, often more or less in opposition to each other," and they believed that some members of the Law School undoubtedly "view university administration as essentially 'the enemy.'" Nevertheless, the self-study report "limited" its recommendations for the Law School's development so that they would fall "well within the capabilities of the income generated by the Law School."[112]

Father Finlay was the principal spokesman for the university in its dealings with the ABA, and he assumed an aggressive and adversarial posture right at the start. He informed the Accreditation Committee that he was "acting under clear instructions from our Trustees," and he was instructed to say that it appeared to them that the ABA was attempting to tell the university and its board of trustees how to allocate university funds, which they insisted was unacceptable. Although he said he "did not want to mention this at the outset" of the meeting, Finlay warned the ABA representatives that, "if it comes to a question of challenging the right of Trustees to make appropriate allocations of funds, I am instructed to let this group know that the University and the Trustees are willing to go to court on this issue."[113]

In the end, the Accreditation Committee persisted in demanding more financial information in order to determine whether too much of the Law School's revenue was being diverted to general university support. They wanted a clear explanation of how the university allocated income and expenses to the Law School and to the other divisions in the university so they could be sure "that the Law School gets its fair share from within the University." The meeting ended with Father Finlay acceding to the committee's demand for more detailed financial information and the opportunity for an ABA representative to go over the figures with Fordham University's financial officers and auditors.[114]

Father Finlay provided the requested financial information under protest. He reminded ABA consultant White that Fordham University's system of accounting consisted of "central budgets," and the university did not have a separate accounting of the Law School's income and expenses "in a complete and accurate manner." He reiterated the university's position that the Law School was "not an independent fiscal or academic entity within the University," but "an integral unit of the University." He reasserted the university's "disagreement with the approach of the [Accreditation] Committee which is utilizing the internal fiscal arrangements within the University as an indicator of whether a sound educational program is being conducted at the Law School." University administrators insisted that the best way to determine whether the Law School was offering a sound legal education and was eligible for accreditation was to evaluate "the educational program itself." Father Finlay asked the ABA to explain "the objective standards" it was using to evaluate student-to-faculty ratios. He also insisted that the Law School's part-time faculty be included in any evaluation of the faculty resources of the Law School. Noting that the Law School was located "in the midst of an unsurpassed center of legal resources," Finlay claimed that its part-time faculty included "experts, even prominent authorities, in particular fields" who provided "impressive strength and diversity to the faculty." This was true, but the Law School's reliance on part-time faculty appears to have been motivated primarily to expand its curriculum and electives with as little expense as possible. Father Finlay nevertheless concluded that the Law School not only merited reaccreditation, but that it offered a "superior educational program as measured by its reputation and by the results it has been achieving."[115]

After reviewing the information in May 1977, the ABA Accreditation Committee concluded that "a considerable proportion of funds attributed to the [Law] School are not available for law school instructional, library, administrative, and financial aid purposes." It remained concerned that the Law School still was not receiving "the resources which are appropriate for a school of its reputation and kind," and it urged Fordham University's president and central administration "to insure" that the "necessary resources" were made available to the Law School "to maintain and enhance the quality of its faculty, its instructional program, its financial aid program, and its general academic character." The committee admonished the university "to make every effort to improve the quality" of the Law School's academic program. It therefore ordered a reinspection of the Law School during the 1977–78 academic year. Owing to a variety of factors, the reinspection was postponed until September 1979. Six years after the 1973 inspection, the ABA's Accreditation Committee still had not formally resolved to reaccredit Fordham Law School. Nevertheless, the accreditation of a member law school remained in effect until the ABA formally rescinded the accreditation. Consequently, Fordham Law School did not lose its accreditation at any point during this long, drawn-out process.[116]

Following the September 1979 reinspection, the ABA Accreditation Committee found that the Law School was not in compliance with ABA Standards with regard to faculty size, the number of support staff in the library, its clinical offerings, and its physical plant. The 26 member full-time faculty was too small for the 972 full-time equivalent student body, and the resulting student-to-faculty ratio of 37 to 1 was too high. The insufficient number of faculty constituted a "serious deficiency that violated [ABA] Standards 201 and 402." The "unreasonably low" number of library support staff violated Standard 605. Although the reinspection report found that the Law School offered a good basic program of legal research and writing, the ABA Accreditation Committee concluded that it failed to provide "adequate training in professional skills," which violated Standard 302(a)(ii). It also concluded that the Law School's physical plant was no longer adequate for its programs, which violated Standards 701 and 705. The building was adequate in 1961 for the student body of 700, but it was too small for the enrollment that had increased by one-third to 1,098 in 1979. Not only were classrooms overcrowded, many were poorly designed and students were unable to hear the instructor because of window air-conditioners. The building lacked sufficient space for student organizations and lockers for students, and ventilation in the library was a problem. The Accreditation Committee also found "a severe communication problem between the Law School, its Dean and its Faculty and the central administration." On the positive side, the law library's collection was vastly improved by 1979. The librarian member of the Accreditation Committee "thought the library collection was really very solid and he would have been thrilled to have found it in his own university when he took over the library there."[117]

The most serious deficiency was related to Fordham University's handling of the Law School's finances. The Accreditation Committee found that "a very large portion" of the Law School's revenue was not available to meet the needs of the Law School's programs. The reinspection report had calculated that the university was taking over thirty percent of the Law School's revenue for general university expenses, which was simply too high. Given the "serious deficiencies" in these programs and the resources needed to eliminate them, the committee concluded that there was a "serious question" whether Fordham University was providing adequate financial resources to the Law School as required by Standards 201 and 209, and whether the Law School's affiliation with Fordham University was "enhancing the School's programs" as required by Standard 210.[118]

The Law School's 1979 self-study report summarized a 1975 study of the nation's law schools by Professor Charles Kelso that supported the ABA's skepticism over the adequacy of Fordham University's financial support of the Law School. Professor Kelso found that Fordham ranked forty-fifth among the nation's law schools on a "resource index" he developed. Kelso based his index on the student-to-faculty ratio and ratios of the number of volumes in the library to the number of students and the number of faculty.[119]

The 1979 self-study report nevertheless concluded that Fordham's "position in the spectrum of legal education . . . stands very high." It quoted and cited a variety of professional journal articles to support this conclusion. The report quoted the *National Law Journal*'s 1978 finding that, although Fordham Law School was "not usually rated as one of the top ten" law schools in the nation, it "was statistically the fifth hardest to get into." Only Yale, Harvard, Columbia, and Stanford were more selective. In the same year, *Juris Doctor* found that the Law School's graduates "rank[ed] sixth in median income" among private practitioners, being "surpassed by graduates of the same four schools plus Georgetown." The *New York Law Journal* reported in 1976 that, "among new partners admitted to large New York law firms, Fordham graduates ranked within the first six." The self-study report cited a 1975 *ABA Journal* article and concluded that "Fordham shared seventh place with Minnesota, Pennsylvania and Virginia in the number of graduates occupying the position of chief legal officer of the five hundred largest publicly held corporations in the United States." By these measures, the Law School was doing just fine.[120]

It is not surprising that Father Finlay and the chairman of the university's board of trustees appointed an ad hoc committee of three members of the board to review the findings of the ABA's Accreditation Committee and the 1979 reinspection report and to report to the full board. They appointed John D. Feerick, Walter Wriston, and Professor Theodore J. St. Antoine of the University of Michigan Law School. They agreed with Father Finlay that the Accreditation Committee's report was not "particularly threatening." Noting that the ABA's "major complaint" against Fordham was diverting too much of the Law School's income from the Law School, the ad hoc committee (hereafter cited as Feerick Committee) defended the university's accounting methods and allocations and concluded that, depending upon whether one used the ABA's or the university's calculations, the university returned to the Law School at worst 87 percent and at best 98.6 percent of the Law School's revenue. Although the ABA did not provide Fordham with comparable allocation figures from other law schools, the Feerick Committee concluded that the university's "good faith" allocations "should certainly be within acceptable limits."[121]

The Feerick Committee affirmed the objections to the ABA's financial analysis that Fordham University officials had raised years before. It viewed the ABA's actions as unjustifiable interference with university autonomy, and it denied that an outside accrediting organization had the authority to allocate the university's revenue among its various "expense centers." The committee unequivocally asserted that this discretion resided in the university's board of trustees, and it opposed "the ABA's attempt to re-allocate University revenues [as] an impingement on the Board's authority." It declared its support for the university administration's and Law School's efforts to maintain and improve the quality of legal education at Fordham.[122]

Father Finlay decided to comply with the ABA's demands for further information. The Accreditation Committee asked Father Finlay and Dean McLaughlin to give it a written report by October 1, 1980 of the actions taken to remedy the deficiencies regarding the faculty and the library support staff and their plans to provide an adequate physical plant. It also asked for the Law School's current financial data. The Law School reported that it increased the number of faculty to 29, but the FTE enrollment increased to 1,010. Not surprisingly, the ABA Accreditation Committee found that the resulting ratio of students to full-time faculty of 35 to 1 was still "a serious deficiency that violated Standards 201 and 402." It also found that the current physical plant, "when used by a total student body of 1,140," was still deficient and continued to violate Standards 701 and 705, and it would do so until the addition was built in 1983–84 at a cost of $8 million. In light of these "serious deficiencies," the "serious question" remained whether the university was providing adequate financial support for the Law School's program as required by Standards 201 and 209 and whether the Law School's affiliation with Fordham University enhanced the Law School's programs as required by Standard 210. The committee advised Father Finlay and Dean McLaughlin that unless it received their assurances by April 1, 1981 that the deficiencies were being satisfactorily resolved, it would issue a notice for a hearing pursuant to Rule IV. In the meantime, the executive committee of the AALS resolved "that the membership in good standing of the School of Law of Fordham University in the Association be continued."[123]

Father Finlay informed the ABA Accreditation Committee of the actions Fordham was taking to cure the deficiencies. He authorized the

Law School to appoint thirty-three full-time faculty, and the board of trustees approved an addition to the Law School building. At its April/ May 1981 meeting, the committee concluded that these actions did not assure that the deficiencies in faculty size and space were being satisfactorily resolved, and it postponed further action until it received fuller information. It deferred consideration of whether it should issue a notice for a hearing until its October/November 1981 meeting. Father Finlay informed the committee in September 1981 that the Law School had reduced its student-to-faculty ratio to 31.3 to 1, but the committee found that this ratio "remains unfavorable and in non-compliance with Standards 201 and 401–405." The committee further found that the student body had increased to 1,034 students, thus "placing a strain on the School's already deficient physical plant" and increasing the violation of Standards 701 and 705. These deficiencies indicated that "the substantial portion of the [Law] School's tuition revenue" was not made available to the Law School, which "raises serious questions whether" the affiliation of the Law School with the university enhanced the school's programs as required by Standard 210. The committee again deferred whether to issue a notice for a hearing until its fall 1982 meeting, and it asked for a "further report" as to "further improvements in the student/faculty ratio and the physical facilities" of the Law School.[124]

Reacting to the ABA's criticism of the student-to-faculty ratio, the university authorized three new full-time positions and one visitor for the 1981–82 academic year. With faculty who were leaving, the net affect was only one new full-time faculty addition. However, the Law School only appointed three new faculty. They were Donald L. Magnetti, S.J., a 1979 graduate of Fordham Law School who held a PhD in Middle Eastern Linguistics from Johns Hopkins University and was a member of the Coudert Brothers law firm; Daniel J. Capra, a graduate of the University of California at Berkeley, Boalt Hall Law School, who was currently teaching at Tulane Law School; and David Schmudde, who earned his JD at the University of Florida Law School and an MS in Economics at North Carolina State University and was a member of the Brauner & Baron law firm at the time of his appointment to the Fordham Law faculty. This left two vacancies, which partially explains why the student-to-faculty ratio remained unacceptably high at about 31 to 1. An important datum supported the ABA's claim that the university was not returning substantial law school revenue to the Law School during the 1981–82 school year: law school expenditures per FTE JD student. Fordham Law School's expenditure of $3,277 per FTE student placed it 157th among the 166 reporting law schools. The only other law school in New York State that finished lower was St. Johns, which expended $3,138. Only three other Catholic law schools finished lower than Fordham: Loyola-Chicago (158th at $3,267), Duquesne (160th at $3,183), and Gonzaga (165th at $2,839).[125]

The issue of Fordham Law School's reaccreditation remained unresolved through the end of McLaughlin's tenure as dean and Father Finlay's tenure as president of Fordham University. Neither the ABA nor Fordham University backed down from their positions. The ABA persisted in its refusal to accept Fordham University's accounting methods and funds allocation policies. Fordham University persisted in pursuing them as it also expanded the faculty and planned to build an addition to the Law School building that would satisfy the space requirements of the increased student body.

McLaughlin resigned as dean when he was appointed to the US District Court for the Eastern District of New York in 1981. When asked what were his proudest decanal accomplishments, Judge McLaughlin identified the curriculum and faculty changes he oversaw. What made him proudest, "was the changing around of the curriculum to a more modern-type curriculum; the expansion of the base of the faculty. Those two achievements were, I think, the top of my priority list," and they were both achieved very quickly.[126]

CHAPTER EIGHT

RESURGENCE OF

FORDHAM LAW SCHOOL

John Feerick succeeded Joseph McLaughlin as dean on July 1, 1982. McLaughlin resigned as dean almost a year earlier when he was appointed to the United States District Court for the Eastern District of New York. He assumed the bench in October 1981. Professor Joseph Perillo was named acting dean and served for almost one year. In his first Annual Report to the Alumni, Dean Feerick acknowledged Professor Perillo's contribution to the Law School as acting dean. Normally, Dean Feerick noted, an acting dean is a mere caretaker, but "Joe Perillo did not behave like an acting dean. Things got done," he declared. The curriculum was expanded with the addition of an "innovative Legal Process course," plans for the renovation and expansion of the Law School building "proceeded apace," the full-time faculty expanded with "significant additions," and Feerick did not find any "leftover problems" when he became dean "except the ubiquitous (but, one hopes, not eternal) financial challenges."[1]

The extraordinarily positive impact Feerick had on the Law School as its appointed dean was presaged when Father Finlay, the president who appointed Feerick stated, "half jokingly," that "one of the best things I ever did for Fordham was to persuade John Feerick to accept the Deanship of the Law School. I'm very proud of him." Finlay had had his eye on Feerick since he had appointed Feerick to the Fordham University Board of Trustees in 1978, and Feerick functioned effectively as a "trustee liaison with the Law School and Dean McLaughlin." In 1977, Dean McLaughlin recognized John Feerick as "the guiding genius of the Law Alumni Association" and "the shadow Dean of the Law School."[2]

Nevertheless, the law faculty overwhelmingly preferred Professor Joseph Crowley to be their new dean, even after a thorough dean's search had been completed. The faculty's great esteem for Crowley was one of the reasons for their preference. Additionally, the faculty were suspicious of Feerick because they saw him as a favorite of Father Finlay's. After considering at least forty candidates, including a University of Chicago Law School professor by the name of Antonin Scalia, the search committee recommended two candidates for the position of dean, Joseph Crowley and John Feerick. Almost every member of the faculty who did not serve on the search committee signed a letter stating their choice of Crowley to be the new dean of Fordham Law School. Father Finlay ignored the letter and appointed Feerick.[3]

John Feerick was a senior partner in the Skadden Arps law firm and knew little about law school administration when he was appointed dean. Before assuming the deanship, Feerick visited a number of the nation's leading law schools, such as Stanford and Yale, and he studied their administration processes and structures. Wisely, Feerick's first act as dean was to appoint Joe Crowley his associate dean, and Crowley helped Feerick transition into academia. Feerick quickly earned the faculty's trust and respect.[4]

Feerick became dean because of his deep commitment to public service and his deep love for Fordham Law School. He made the "tough" decision to leave law practice and become dean of the Law School because "there was something strong within me saying it was time to give something back to the world." Feerick had performed plenty of public service while in private practice, but he never had the opportunity to do it on a full-time basis. The Law School had become "so much a part of [his] life," and it was now offering him the opportunity of performing public service full time. He seized the opportunity.[5]

And it was a good thing for the Law School, because John Feerick turned it around and guided it toward achieving the goals he had set out for his deanship. Dean Feerick's primary objectives were substantially to improve the quality of the legal education offered by Fordham Law School and to catapult the Law School into national prominence. The key to the changes he brought about was money. Feerick recounted that, when he became dean he had to "deal with a lot of economic challenges" that required his full attention. The most pressing challenge stemmed from the Law School's capital campaign for a major renovation and expansion of its physical plant. "I spent well over half of my time my first two years engaged in fundraising and the activities that are associated with planning an expansion of a Physical Plant," he recalled.[6]

The Law School's inadequate building was recognized by the school's community as one of the primary reasons for many of the Law School's deficiencies during the 1970s and early 1980s. The school's building was one of the best in the nation when it opened in 1961, but it had become inadequate by the 1973 reaccreditation visit, a mere dozen years later. In April 1983, the total net square footage per FTE Student at Fordham Law School was 39.2, lower than every other law school in the nation but one, which was 38.1. The Law School's 1984 addition remedied this deficiency, albeit only temporarily. It doubled the Law School's physical plant, adding "21 new faculty offices; a new student cafeteria and student lounge; a tiered amphitheater seating 256 and two tiered classrooms seating 140 each; a new faculty library and an additional moot court room; a number of seminar rooms and student activities rooms; and an expansion of the library to provide a new reading room, additional carrels, preparation for developing technology and stack areas for new acquisitions." The new addition actually created two new floors in the library.[7]

Even with the 1984 building expansion, insufficient physical space continued to hamper the Law School for the next two decades. The Law School building required repeated renovations to meet the increasing space needs of the developing faculty, administration, curriculum, and student organizations and activities. Building renovations were completed in 1984, 1987, 1989, 1990, 1993, and 1994. The 1994 renovations to the physical plant created additional student activity rooms, five seminar rooms, and one classroom in addition to making the building accessible to disabled persons.[8]

Even with these renovations, the 1994 ABA visitation report identified the Law School's physical plant as the school's most serious problem: "too many people . . . for the limited amount of space." The ABA visitors concluded that "without additional space and faculty," the Law School would "not be able to continue [its] high student enrollments and maintain the quality of its program."[9]

The problem of inadequate physical facilities persisted through Feerick's deanship and well into that of Dean William Treanor. The 2001 ABA Visitation Report found that the Law School building facilities were "minimally adequate to support the School's operation." The history of inadequate physical facilities and their debilitating impact on the Law School's education mission persisted into the twenty-first century, but a new build-ing is scheduled to be built and operational by the year 2014.[10]

The inadequate allocation of Law School revenue to support Law School programs also confronted Feerick when he became dean. In April 1982 the ABA issued a report of Total Law School Expenditure Per FTE Student. Fordham Law School's $3,277 per FTE student was almost at the bottom of the nation's law schools in this category, and it was well below every law school in New York State except St. John's Law School, which spent $3,138 per FTE student. The other law schools in New York State and their expenditures per FTE student were: New York University ($13,311); Columbia ($10,052); Cornell ($8,080); Brooklyn ($5,760); Syracuse ($5,634); New York Law School ($4,787); Yeshiva ($4,308); Hofstra ($4,026); SUNY Buffalo ($3,896). Fordham's per-student expenditure also placed it well behind competitor Catholic law schools, such as Georgetown ($7,331); Notre Dame ($6,416); Boston College ($4,630); Villanova ($4,510); and Seton Hall ($3,696).[11]

Legal education was rapidly becoming more expensive in the 1970s and 1980s because of larger student enrollments, expanding academic services, and curricular changes. These developments required larger faculties and larger administrative structures. The number and variety of elective courses greatly expanded, and interdisciplinary courses such as Law and Economics, Legal History, Legal Philosophy, and Law and Social Science were offered at the leading law schools. Clinical education came into being in the late 1960s and expanded over the next few decades. Formal legal writing programs also began in this period. These developments required low student-to-faculty ratios; the ABA set the standard for student-to-faculty ratios at twenty to one. The changing nature of legal education also required more library resources and personnel to assist students and faculty with research projects. Computer technology arrived in the early 1980s and became pervasive in the 1990s, further driving up the cost of legal education. ABA standards required law schools to have the necessary resources to implement and support these sweeping changes.[12]

Concerned that Fordham University continued to underfund the Law School, the ABA's Accreditation Committee kept Fordham under its supervision from 1980 through its next reinspection in September 1987. It was unrelenting in its demand for complete and accurate financial infor-mation and transparency in Fordham University's accounting for the Law

School's revenue and the university's allocation of those revenues. Fordham University had to file financial reports with the ABA each spring and fall from 1980 to the ABA reaccreditation visit in September 1987.[13]

The Fordham University administration under Father Finlay was equally unrelenting in refusing ABA demands for greater financial transparency and a greater allocation of the Law School's revenue to the Law School's educational mission. A change in the university's posture came only after John Feerick became dean of the Law School and Father Joseph O'Hare replaced Father Finlay as Fordham University's president in 1984. ABA reaccreditation consultant, Dean James P. White, recalled that Father Finlay did not like criticism and was fairly aggressive in his disagreement with the ABA's assessment over funding. Father O'Hare "had a different attitude." Dean Feerick was "such a wonderful human being" and did not want conflict between the university and the ABA. He tried to ameliorate their differences, and he was largely successful. Feerick was "very respected in the ABA and in the legal profession." He "participated actively" in the ABA section on legal education, whereas his immediate predecessors did not. Feerick was on the Fordham University Board of Trustees when he was appointed dean of the Law School, and "this made a great difference." The trustees had confidence in him and trusted him, and he influenced their thinking. Dean Feerick found Father O'Hare and Fordham University administrators "instantaneously responsive and helpful" and their dealings were characterized by "civility [and] understanding" leading to "fair" outcomes on fiscal matters. Dean White, who represented the ABA, found a "cordial, mutually supportive relationship" between the Law School and senior university officials. He stated that Feerick was able to get more financial support from Father O'Hare.[14]

Fordham Law School "was regarded as a good law school" Dean White recalled. After Columbia and NYU, it was probably the best law school in New York City. White thought Fordham Law School "had tremendous potential" and a "well-regarded dean," but it "was not living up to its potential." He believed Fordham "could be a much better law school if it used the revenue it took in. Ultimately, it did," White concluded.[15]

Although the relationship between the ABA and Fordham University administrators improved during Father O'Hare's presidency, greater transparency and greater financial support for the Law School remained imperfect. In dealing with the first ABA site inspection after Father O'Hare became president, Executive Vice President Joseph R. Cammarosano urged Father O'Hare to maintain the university's confrontational posture toward the ABA. He objected to the ABA's demand "that the Law School retain all of the tuition and other revenue generated by it for its own purposes." Cammarosano conceded that the university's accounting methods had enabled the university to charge the Law School a greater amount for overhead expenses and direct costs than it could document, explaining that, "in prior years," the university's "accounting arrangement," which simply assumed "a 65:35 split of the Law School's tuition and fee income with the University," had enabled the university to resist the ABA's demand that the Law School retain all of its revenue, whether generated by tuition and fees or by fund raising. The administration had "traditionally assumed" the 35 percent coefficient for overhead expenses. This percentage evidently was added to the university's allocation of the Law School's operating surpluses for the five fiscal years from 1985 to 1990 to repay the Law School's debt to the university for the building expansion in 1984. Cammarosano urged Father O'Hare to resist the ABA's demand that the Law School retain all of its revenue, which would have required the university to provide the ABA with accurate financial information, advising Father O'Hare that the university was not obligated to comply with the ABA's demand.[16]

Cammarosano may have been understating the percentage of the Law School's revenues the university diverted to general university operations. Professor Joseph Perillo recalled "many conversations with [Executive Vice President] Paul [Reiss] (when I was acting dean)," during the 1981–82 academic year, in which "Paul told me again and again that the formula was 55% for the law school, and 45% for the University whether it involved a chair endowment or an application fee." Professor Joseph Sweeney adamantly insisted that the university took "at least" 55 percent of the Law School's revenue. Judge Joseph McLaughlin affirmed that Perillo's and Sweeney's recollections are close to the mark, and Dean Feerick believed that the university was taking 60 percent and the Law School 40 percent of the Law School's revenues when he became dean in 1982. Judge McLaughlin understandably cautioned "that the only person who would really know the truth was . . . Brother Kenny, who took this knowledge to his grave."[17]

Father O'Hare evidently decided not to follow Cammarosano's advice completely. He provided the ABA with "an analysis that reflect[ed] more closely the costs of the School of Law." The ABA's 1987 reinspection report acknowledged Fordham's more accurate analysis of the university's allocation of the Law School's income and expenses, but it commented that there were "no fixed, exact rules" that governed the "university's determination of the proper allocation of costs," although such determinations should be "rational." The report implied that the reinspection team disagreed with "some of the premises" on which the university based its allocations. The report explicitly questioned the sixty-five to thirty-five allocation of Law School revenues between the Law School and the university. Allocating 35 percent for the university was "a substantial overhead, higher than would be standard for most law schools," the report observed, and it again concluded that this "allocation of costs to the university needs to be examined carefully."[18]

Father O'Hare changed Fordham University's allocation policy. He decided to allow the Law School to "receive a dollar for dollar return of any tuition increase that might go into effect" during the 1988–89 academic year, and the Law School "would, in turn, pay the University for documented overhead expenses and other allocable costs incurred on its behalf out of this tuition and fee revenue." The full-time tuition rose from $10,360 in 1987 to $17,900 in 1993. The average annual tuition increase during this period was 9.5 percent, and the total increase of $7,540 represented a 72.8 percent rise in tuition from 1987 to 1993.[19]

The university changed its allocation because "the ABA [was now] demanding a more precise and explicit accounting of overhead charges." This policy change had a substantial financial impact. Restricting the financial allocation of Law School revenue to documented university overhead and other allocable costs reduced the university's take to about 28 percent of Law School revenue for fiscal 1987. Cammarosano explained that, "if the coefficient for overhead expenses were 35 percent, as had been traditionally assumed, the dollar cost to the Law School would have worked out to $4,017,318 ($11,478,053 x 0.35 = $4,017,318) or $838,588" more than the university actually allocated to it for overhead. Cammarosano acknowledged that "the reason for the lower figure of 28 percent" was that a 35 percent coefficient was "more than can be presently documented."[20]

The university and the Law School agreed on a new approach to calculating the actual costs the university allocated for overhead expense. The new approach was consistent with the advice Father John A. Fitterer had given to Father Finlay in May 1975 in that it employed "various allocation formalae [*sic*] which, to the extent possible, use[d] objective criteria and [applied] these criteria equally to all 10 units" of the university. This new approach would have "substantially" reduced the Law School's share of university overhead expenses to about 22 percent.[21]

Despite these policy and accounting changes, the Law School's contributions to Fordham University's general expenses continued to exceed ABA maximum standards. Because the Law School and Fordham University were "largely tuition driven" and had "a small endowment," enrollment levels played a determinative role in their financial conditions. Declining enrollments in the various divisions of the university produced serious financial difficulties that caused the university to "look to the graduate schools for additional revenues." The university administration believed that the Law School was obliged to help the university through the financial exigencies it experienced in the late 1980s and early 1990s. In addition, the university assessed the Law School $750,000 each year for the "next several years to help defray the costs" of the Lincoln Center Student Dormitory until it became self-supporting. Although unexpectedly high enrollments in the Law School's first year class for the 1993–94 school year produced a $1 million surplus in tuition revenue, the Law School had to borrow just over $4 million for renovations because it was "overcrowded and need[ed] more space" for student organizations, clinical programs, and faculty offices. "Simply put," the 1994 ABA reinspection report asserted, "finances lie at the heart of this institution's future hopes and aspirations and must be addressed quickly and directly."[22]

Although Fordham University agreed to let the Law School keep the revenue from its tuition increase in the 1988–89 academic year, it quickly retreated to its traditional policy of relying on Law School revenue to subsidize general university operations. From 1989 to 1995, Fordham University diverted Law School surpluses to offset the university's operating losses. It was not until the fall of 1995 that Fordham University decided to comply with ABA guidelines and charge the Law School "a total of 20% for all overhead." The university also eliminated the $750,000 assessment the Law School had been paying to the university to cover operating losses of the new dormitory because the dormitory had reached a financial break-even point. The Law School did not expect surpluses in the future because it planned to limit the size of the student body to 1,400 JD students and 50 LLM students and to keep tuition increases small. Nonetheless, the Law School and the university discussed an agreement to split any future law school surpluses at the 80 percent/20 percent split it applied to indirect (overhead) expenses.[23]

Although Fordham University agreed in 1995 to limit the Law School's "total overhead rate" to 20 percent, the university continued to overcharge the Law School for overhead and indirect expenditures into the twenty-first century. The 2001 ABA visitation report found that overhead and indirect expenditures charged to the Law School between fiscal year 1994 and fiscal year 2000, as a percentage of the Law School's total revenue as reported by the university, varied from a high of 24.9 percent in fiscal year 1994 to lows of 21.4 percent and 19.01 percent in fiscal years 1999 and 2000, respectively. However, if one considers the overhead and indirect expenses *actually charged* by the university, the lowest percentages of Law School revenue allocated for these expenses increased to 27.7 percent and 24.9 percent for 1999 and 2000, respectively. The Law School's 2001 self-study, relying on the same financial data the university supplied to the ABA, found that the university allocated certain indirect charges to direct expenses which, if included in indirect expenditures, increased indirect expenditures for fiscal 1994 to 33.77 percent, for fiscal year 1999 to 33.03 percent, and for fiscal year 2000 to 29.79 percent. Consequently, negotiations between the Law School and the Fordham University administration to limit the university's total overhead charges to 20 percent continued into the twenty-first century.[24]

The ABA inspection team concluded, moreover, that the Law School shifted $1 million of its revenue "in addition to the normal overhead amounts in each of the fiscal years of 1998, 1999, 2000 and 2001 . . . to the University to help it balance its budget." This was money that "would have financed the Law School's operations" had it not been diverted to subsidize Fordham University. These subsidies limited the Law School's "ability to fund desirable programs and build endowment." Obviously, these subsidies also inhibited the Law School from moving into the top tier of American law schools.[25]

These Law School subsidies to the university highlight Dean Feerick's great success in fund-raising, which supplemented increasing percentages of the Law School's budget. Whereas revenue from tuition and fees funded virtually all of the Law School's expenses before he became dean, between 1994 and 2001 approximately 2 percent of the budget was financed by endowment income, and the Annual Fund and other fund raising efforts supplied between 8 percent and 9.5 percent of the budget. The Law School's dependence on tuition for its revenue was "its single biggest financial challenge" as it entered the twenty-first century. But, these gifts made a difference in the quality of the Law School and were "crucial to the Law School's ability to innovate."[26]

Building its endowment was one of the Law School's "needs and aspirations." In 2001 the Law School completed a $10,000,000 endowment campaign and sought to raise additional funds for a national scholarship program to attract "high quality students to the Law School." It began the "quiet phase of a major capital campaign" on July 1, 2001. The Law School also had to find new sources of revenue to finance the escalating costs of its operations in the last years of the twentieth century. The school's expenditures increased 68 percent between fiscal 1995 and 2000, largely because of increases in the size of and compensation paid to the tenure-track and clinical faculty. Dean Feerick understood that realizing his goal of achieving national prominence was not possible without "a major endowment to support students in meeting the costs of their education" and to build "the academic programs that promote[d] academic excellence." Consequently, he devoted most of his efforts as dean to raising the funds that were indispensable to Fordham becoming recognized as one of the "preeminent law schools in the country." The school's alumni played a critical role in satisfying the Law School's needs and achieving its aspirations.[27]

The years Feerick served as president of the Law Alumni Association taught him the critical importance of the alumni to improving the quality of the Law School. He spent a lot of time "trying to reach out to the graduates of the Law School to impress on them, as much as [he] could, how important they were to the future of Fordham Law School." He was "very proud of the response of our alumni during my tenure," Feerick proclaimed. For example, it was the alumni's financial support that made possible the 1984 expansion of the Law School's building. Leo Kissam, class of 1923 and senior partner of Kissam, Halpin & Genovese, bequeathed $2,600,000 to the Law School, which it received shortly after Feerick became dean. Kissam's bequest was the largest gift in the Law School's history up to 1983, and it was used to add two new floors atop the library and a faculty office wing. The Law School's library bears Kissam's name to honor his generosity. Ned Doyle, class of 1930, made an "equally extraordinary gift" during the building and expansion program, which made possible the new building that houses classrooms, a cafeteria, an amphitheater, and atrium. The Law School honored him by naming the new structure the Ned Doyle Building. The atrium was named the "Edith Guldi Platt Atrium" in recognition of a generous gift given by her husband, Bill, and her three sons, Harold (1971), Jonathan (1976), and Bill (1977). Lou Stein's remarkable generosity was used to create "a major institute of law and ethics, to complement the majestic Fordham-Stein Prize program," and it is called the Louis Stein Center for Law and Ethics. The Norman and Rosita Winston Foundation made possible the Sidney C. Norris Chair of Law by donating $1 million in 1984, two years after Feerick became the Dean. Mr. Norris was a graduate in the class of 1927, and he served as legal counsel to the N. K. Winston & Co. development company.[28]

The alumni readily responded to the role model Feerick presented to them as an alumnus and as dean. "We've been blessed with very good Deans," Dennis McInerney opined, "and certainly Dean Feerick is a gem, no question. He is really an inspiration to alumni who, if they reflect on it and realize how much he's given to Fordham Law School, would be embarrassed not to try to do something remotely comparable."[29]

Feerick tremendously increased contributions from alumni and foundations to the Law School during his tenure as Law School Dean. Each year produced a higher total than the year before. For example, contributions to the Annual Fund between 1984 and 1986 more than doubled from $288,000 to $653,000. Under the leadership of Fordham's "million dollar man," Jim Gill (1956), the Annual Fund for 1988 reached $1 million for the first time in the Law School's history. In just four years, the Fordham Law Alumni Association increased the Annual Fund giving from $288,000 to $1 million. The total giving and the number of donors to the Annual Fund continued to increase through the 1990s under the leadership of alumni leaders such as Gill, Dennis McInerney (1951), Michael Stanton

(1959), Donald Zoeller (1958), and Maureen Scannell Bateman (1968). The 1993 Annual Fund yielded $2,248,000, and the Law School raised another $13.2 million in gifts and pledges in the Fordham University Capital Campaign. The 1995 Annual Fund, chaired by Ms. Bateman, yielded an unprecedented $4 million, and Louis Stein contributed another $1.1 million to the Law School. The dean reported the most successful fund-raising year in the Law School's history to that time with a total of $7.3 million in gifts and pledges raised during the 1998–99 year. The alumni helped the Law School conclude the campaign successfully in 1998 as their contributions of $33 million exceeded the Law School's goal by $8 million. This campaign resulted in the creation of five new academic chairs, more than sixty new student scholarships, and the establishment of the Joseph R. Crowley Program in International Human Rights. During his tenure, Feerick built the Law School's endowment to about $50 million. Although many alumni contributed to the remarkable increase in funds raised, the 2001 self-study concluded that it was "ultimately the product of the Dean's leadership and in large part of his incredible personal efforts." Feerick's last year as dean was the most successful fundraising year to date with over $11 million in gifts and pledges in 2001–2.[30]

Alumni giving financed the ever-increasing need for student financial aid to meet the escalating costs of tuition, books, room, and board. Alumni generosity helped to finance increasing numbers of student-edited journals, ever-expanding career planning programs, student publications, student services, and student research assistance for full-time faculty, which, in addition to faculty summer research grants made possible by the alumni, enabled the faculty to produce higher quality and more scholarly publications. The alumni also made it possible for the Law School to acquire and integrate information technology, computers, and technical equipment in the library and throughout the Law School and to make it available to faculty, students, and administrators. The development and expansion of the live-client and simulated clinical skills programs in addition to the graduate LLM program were largely funded by alumni contributions and other outside financial support. The Law School expanded its curriculum and educational programs and improved the quality of the legal education it offered to students because of the generosity of its alumni and friends.[31]

The Law School Development Program is the only school-based fundraising project at Fordham University. After 1997, the university's development office assigned four full-time professionals to assist the Law School, but this staff did not provide sufficient support in a timely manner. The size of the staff constituted one-third the number of professional development personnel devoted to law school and alumni development work at law schools of comparable size. In January 1998 the director of law school development was given an office in the Law School, which has integrated fundraisers into the Law School and contributed to an increased awareness among the faculty and administration of the importance of fundraising. It also helped the dean to begin an "outreach program at law firms in New York City where [the Law School has] a critical mass of alumni." More than 250 alumni work on fundraising projects. Although the Law School's development office was understaffed, it assisted Dean Feerick and alumni to raise a total of more than $27 million between 1994 and 2000.[32]

Feerick devoted most of his time as dean to raising the funds required to enable the Law School to regain national recognition as a premier law school. He relied on his associate deans and faculty for the internal governance of the Law School. Susan Santangelo was hired to assist Dean Crowley when he was appointed the first associate dean in 1982. Ms. Santangelo has performed outstanding service as the associate dean's administrative assistant and later as director of faculty administration. Bob Byrn succeeded Joe Crowley, who died in December 1985. But, the Law School's direction noticeably changed after Georgene Vairo assumed the associate dean's position in 1987.

The 1986 ABA inspectors characterized Fordham Law School as "a quality institution, providing a generally high level of legal education in both its day and evening divisions." The student body was "well qualified for the study of law," and the faculty were, "in general, good to excellent teachers," actively involved in the service of the school, and "active researchers and writers." The administration was "excellent," alumni support was "strong" and was "increasingly shown in tangible form." Faculty and student morale was "very high."[33]

Feerick had his work cut out for him nevertheless. The Law School suffered from deficiencies in virtually all aspects of its operation. A fundamental problem was the absence of a well-conceived vision of the legal education the faculty sought to offer their students and the best ways of providing it. It was therefore "essential" that the Law School "define its mission, derive its objectives and goals from that mission, and then determine the policies and actions necessary to carry out the mission, objectives and goals." The first ABA inspection report after Feerick became dean observed that the Law School had not articulated its mission.[34]

At the ABA site evaluation of Fordham Law School in November 1986, the full-time faculty understandably still wore the stamp of Dean Feerick's predecessors. The size of the full-time faculty (thirty-seven) was about the same size as in 1982. Although Dean McLaughlin had added many full-time faculty who had attended other law schools, the ABA Evaluation team still found it too inbred, observing that the ten full-time faculty and Dean Feerick who were Fordham Law alumni were "giving the school a definite home-grown flavor." Six full-time faculty were women and two were minorities. The number of full-time faculty was still too small for the 811 full-time and 411 part-time students, which equated to a full-time equivalent of 1,085 students. The resulting student-to-faculty ratio of over 29 to 1 was just below the 30-to-1 ratio that would have violated the ABA student-faculty ratio standard. This problem was "mitigated by the extensive use of adjunct professors drawn from the bench and bar in compliance with [ABA] standard 403(b)."[35]

The ABA inspectors evaluated the nature and quality of the faculty's scholarship as poor, and their criticism identifies an important reason why Fordham Law School had declined from its earlier stature. Although most of the faculty engaged in ongoing legal research and produced "a steady stream of books, articles, law letters, CLE materials, and other legal writing," the inspectors described the faculty's scholarship as essentially descriptive. They concluded that, as a group, the faculty "appears to do a fine job of disseminating legal knowledge," but they "*do not advance legal knowledge* through scholarly inquiry." One reason is that much of the faculty's legal writing "seems to address the questions of 'What?' and 'How?' more than it does the question of 'Why?'" Another reason is that, all too often "faculty publication has been in the school's review, and other material seems to focus substantially on New York law or law of direct importance to the New York bar." Still another reason is that "several" faculty wrote columns in the *New York Law Journal*, and others "contribute heavily to law letters and CLE materials," which "activity is healthy in itself," but, "when done to the exclusion of more scholarly inquiry it may detract from a school's image both external and internal."[36]

Particularly problematic was the faculty's tendency "to favor publication in its own journals." Senior faculty apparently regarded publication in the *Fordham Law Review* as a requirement of school loyalty. Profesor Hugh Hansen "was told in no uncertain terms by the senior faculty that I should only publish in the *Fordham Law Review*. It was a matter of loyalty and a show of support for the journal. It was to show our students that we cared about their efforts and to help them compete against other schools' journals." The ABA inspectors noted that "the best indication of a law faculty's scholarly vigor is its publication of articles in outside journals." Such publications could "enhance a law school's national and regional reputation" and help recruit faculty and students. The ABA report reached the damning conclusion that, "to the extent that change and advancement comes to the law through scholarly articles" published in outside law reviews, the Fordham Law faculty "appears to have consigned itself to the sidelines of scholarly debate and commentary on the law."[37]

John D. Calamari and Joseph M. Perillo were notable exceptions to the ABA's characterization of the faculty's scholarship. These scholars had achieved a national reputation as leading authorities on contract law with their 1970 publication, *The Law of Contracts*. Their national reputation brought distinction to the Fordham Law School in the 1970s and beyond, and their treatise went through six editions, the last two of which acknowledged their stature by being retitled, *Calamari and Perillo on Contracts*. They also published an innovative casebook on contract law that went through multiple editions. The innovation was the use of the problem method in a more thoroughgoing manner than had been employed previously. Professor Helen H. Bender became a third author of this casebook in the second edition published in 1989. Professor Perillo was designated to update and revise the most authoritative multivolume treatise on contract law, *Corbin on Contracts*. Professor Ludwik A. Teclaff was a third exception. The ABA had earlier noted that Teclaff, law librarian, professor of law, and legal scholar specializing in national and international water law and the environment, had brought "distinction to the Law School" as a librarian and as a legal scholar.[38]

The level of institutional support for faculty research and writing in 1986 apparently adversely affected their quantity and quality. In the summer of 1985, the Law School began a program of faculty summer research grants of $4,600 for each faculty member engaged in summer research and writing projects. The ABA visitors noted that this amount was "not strong compared to the summer support at many other schools." The amount allocated to each professor for research assistants ($750) was "a low level of support within the experience of the inspection team," and it appeared that many faculty "did not use up their allocation." The level of secretarial support also appeared low, though the dean was raising the standards and salaries for secretaries to improve their efficiency and competence. Even so, the number of faculty secretaries (eight) was too small for the size of the thirty-seven member full-time faculty, but the secretaries' office was too small for additional personnel and required renovation to accommodate a larger number of secretaries.[39]

One consequence of the "failure of the school to review its mission" was its "continued use over a period of years of the same basic program" of instruction. The 1986 report characterized the required and elective courses as "typical" and "traditional." As with many law schools, the growth of elective offerings was "*ad hoc,*" reflecting the "time-to-time interests of full time faculty, prospective adjunct instructors, and students." In short, the Law School "tended to allow its curriculum to grow rather haphazardly." Furthermore, the inspectors were "uncertain whether [the faculty] will improve coordination between course offerings."[40]

The inspectors found other problems with the curriculum. The legal writing program "may not be sufficiently rigorous," and the training in professional skills appeared to be "inadequate." The school's clinical education in 1986 took the forms of externships and simulation courses. The externships were not well supervised by faculty, and were "little more than a way for judges, agencies and corporations to get free legal researchers." The externship program was one of two "major problems" with the clinical offerings. The other was the total absence of "school-sponsored live clinical experience for students." The Law School recognized some of these problems and hired a director of legal writing and a full-time director of clinical programs to correct them. They were largely responsible for transforming these areas of the curriculum.[41]

Fordham Law School achieved extraordinary changes between 1986 and 1994. The 1994 ABA report concluded that Fordham Law School had "experienced significant growth and development" since its last inspection. This must be the case, they reported, for any law school "whose Dean's sobriquet is 'John the Good' must have a number of things going for it, and this is true of Fordham." The faculty had "lost its 'home grown' flavor and had become more scholastically diverse and productive." They noted that "colloquia, symposia, lectures and seminars featuring prominent contributors to the law frequent Fordham's halls." The graduate program had grown beyond "the toddler stage" and had found "its stride." New student-edited journals "seem to flare up with only a little kindling," and the number had grown to five. The inspectors accurately identified an important reason for this growth when they reported that it took place "under the benevolent gaze of the dean, who takes the view that 'if it's a good idea, we'll find a way to make it work.' "[42]

In contrast to 1986, the 1994 self-study included a carefully thought-out mission statement that expressed the Law School's commitment to "excellence in legal education through teaching, scholarship, and public service" and identified interrelated goals to fulfill its commitments. In its teaching mission, the Law School sought to "provide its students with a comprehensive understanding of legal doctrine and a solid foundation of analytical reasoning, lawyering skills, and professional values." It also offered students "opportunities for developing interdisciplinary, jurisprudential, and comparative perspectives on law and legal institutions," in addition to practical lawyering skills through clinical training programs.[43]

The faculty's legal scholarship was central to the Law School's mission, enriching legal instruction and contributing to the development of law and legal education. Representing "a wide range of scholarly perspectives," the faculty were "committed to extensive academic and professional research and publication about the law, legal institutions, and the role of law in society." The Law School aimed to foster in students an appreciation for lawyers' unique responsibility to the community for "the quality of justice" and for public service both as lawyers and as private citizens through its clinical offerings and public service programs, which provided legal and other services to the indigent. Faculty and administrators were also encouraged to contribute their time and experience to advance the profession and to serve the public. The Law School promoted diversity in the legal profession by actively recruiting members of ethnic and racial minorities to its student body, its faculty, and its administrative staff.[44]

Fordham Law School's commitment to excellence in all of these regards reflected the Jesuit "educational ideals of rigorous thought, justice, and service to others," preparing its graduates to be "dedicated to the highest standards of ethics, excellence, and professionalism." The Law School's "distinctive characteristic is a shared commitment to being a community" with students, faculty, administrators, and alumni having "diverse perspectives and diverse individual goals," yet "acting with civility, courtesy, and mutual respect" and offering mutual support "in pursuing the community commitment to excellence."[45]

This new vision of the Law School's mission and of legal education is attributable to a small group of forward-looking older faculty and to the faculty appointed after 1985. Nearly 40 percent of the forty-nine full-time faculty in 1994 were appointed during this period. ABA inspectors concluded that the nature of the law faculty and of their legal scholarship changed "significantly" between 1986 and 1994. Whereas the faculty in 1986 had "a definite home-grown flavor," the Fordham faculty in 1994 were "increasingly diverse" in terms of educational backgrounds. They had received their initial law degrees from seventeen different law schools; sixteen held LLM degrees and seven had earned PhDs. The faculty appointed during Feerick's deanship up until 1994 had graduated from the following law schools: Harvard (9), Yale (6), NYU (6), Columbia (5), Pennsylvania (2), Stanford (1), Michigan (1), Howard (1), Florida (1), Suffolk (1), and Syracuse (1). Four had earned an LLM degree, and sixteen had advanced degrees in other fields: eight MAs, one MPhil, and six PhDs. Three had been Fulbright Fellows at universities in three different countries across the Atlantic; and one subsequently had earned the DEA, *droit international économique*: Univ. de Paris I–Sorbonne. Twenty had served as law clerks to federal judges: four to US district court judges; twelve to US Court of Appeals judges, and four to US Supreme Court Justices. Counting the federal judicial clerkships, they all had significant legal experience prior to joining the faculty. Whereas in 1986 only two faculty members were from minority groups, in 1994 the faculty included six minorities: one Asian, four African-Americans, two of whom had been appointed in 1993, and one Latino, who was appointed effective in the

1994–95 academic year. Women made up 16 percent of the faculty in 1986, but 26 percent in 1994.[46]

As the ABA inspectors found the profile of Fordham faculty appointed after the mid-1980s had changed "significantly," they also found that the scholarship they produced had "changed dramatically." Whereas the 1986 ABA inspection report criticized the Fordham faculty for consigning itself "to the sidelines of scholarly debate and commentary on the law," the 1994 report praised the faculty for changing "its primary focus from its own law journals to outside law reviews" and for demonstrating "an impressive growth in overall scholarly productivity over the past seven years." Between 1986 and 1994, the faculty published over fifty articles in "traditional law reviews," many of which "were placed in some of the nation's most prestigious journals." They also published over thirty books and treatises, 70 percent of which were published since 1990. Yet, many faculty continued to support Fordham's own journals by publishing almost twenty articles in them. "It is clear," the 1994 ABA inspection report concluded, "that the faculty has made immense progress in [legal scholarship] in recent years."[47]

The 1994 self-study identified three factors that were "instrumental in our flourishing scholarship." First, Dean Feerick and Associate Dean Georgene Vairo provided increased financial incentives in the form of summer research grants and merit salary increases based in part on scholarly publication. Second, the faculty recruitment process focused on hiring new faculty with demonstrated research and writing interests. Third, the reappointment, tenure, and promotion process emphasized publication.[48]

These factors reflected the fundamental reason for the law "faculty's impressive record of publication": an institutional commitment to high-quality legal scholarship. In addition to Feerick and Vairo, this commitment is attributable to a coterie of the Fordham Law faculty, some of whom had joined the faculty before 1985, many of whom were appointed after 1985, who shared a vision of legal education and legal scholarship that had become the prevailing vision of the faculties of the nation's leading law schools and the nation's leading legal scholars. These faculty members not only produced excellent legal scholarship that focused on the "why" in addition to the "what" and the "how," they worked to acquire new faculty members committed to the highest quality of legal scholarship and to develop the scholarship of these young, entry-level professors.

The ABA inspectors interviewed individual faculty members who confirmed "that [these] other, perhaps more subtle, influences [played] a major part in Fordham's scholarly surge." These interviews identified "a supportive 'atmosphere' or an intellectual 'excitement' that was not previously evident." Faculty credited "the Dean's personal interest in their work," the administration's support, and "the inspiration provided by their colleagues" for creating the faculties' new scholarly orientation. The Law School community had "made a conscious and collective commitment to developing a culture of scholarship," and the ABA report concluded that "the effect has been striking." Striking indeed. The quality of the Law School's legal history faculty was ranked sixteenth in terms of scholarly impact in the highly regarded Brian Leiter Law School Rankings in 2003–4. The Constitutional Law faculty was runner-up for the top twenty that year.[49]

The faculty continued to be "productive in scholarly terms" into the twenty-first century. Between 1994 and 2001 it published 190 scholarly articles in leading law reviews, including *Harvard Law Review, Yale Law Journal, Stanford Law Review, New York University Law Review, Columbia Law Review, University of Chicago Law Review, Cornell Law Review, University of Pennsylvania Law Review, Michigan Law Review, Virginia Law Review, Texas Law Review, Duke Law Journal, Georgetown Law Journal, Northwestern University Law Review, UCLA Law Review,* and *Vanderbilt Law Review.* Faculty published over 100 articles in specialized journals and periodicals in addition to writing, editing, and contributing to many books. Indeed, a "study of the academic distinction of American law faculties" published in the *Journal of Legal Studies* in 2000 ranked the Fordham Law School faculty twentieth in publications in leading law reviews.[50]

Feerick was justifiably proud of the faculty's "widespread scholarship. I regard our faculty as among the best in the United States," he declared. The dean mentioned two other sources of pride. One was the "tremendous surge of public service activities at the School, started by the students." The other was the dedication of the Law School administrators.[51]

The ABA inspectors were "convinced that teaching at Fordham generally is at the level of teaching at good law schools in this country." All of the students the inspectors spoke to "were at pains to express their general satisfaction with and respect for the faculty as a group," even when they were critical of specific faculty members. The faculty's primary focus in the classroom was on "rigorous analysis," but they gave "due attention" to methodology and policy. This faculty assessment is strikingly different from earlier ones.[52]

The size of the full-time faculty continued to be too small for the size of the student body through the mid-1990s. The JD program enrollment had grown since 1986 by more than one-third to 1,451 full-time equivalent students (1,155 full-time and 395 part-time), and the student-to-faculty ratio was 29.6 to 1, slightly higher than in 1986. When one added the forty students enrolled in the LLM program, as one should since they took classes with the JD students, the effective ratio rose to about 30.4 to 1. The ABA regarded the student-to-faculty ratio to be a "continuing concern." As in 1986, "the extensive use of adjunct faculty" who were "drawn from a rich pool of practicing New York lawyers who are eminent practitioners in their respective fields" offset the relatively unfavorable student-to-faculty ratio to "some extent." Some eighty-six adjunct faculty taught "traditional classroom courses." Whereas in earlier years the Law School offered too few electives, through these adjuncts it was able to offer "a virtual cornucopia of small-enrollment, specialized courses."[53]

By the first year of the twenty-first century, the full-time tenured, tenure-track, and long-term contract clinical faculty had grown to sixty-four members. The Law School hired twelve tenure-track faculty between 1994 and 2001, three of whom were minorities and four were women. Two minority women faculty were hired in the clinic on renewable contract lines. The profile of the total full-time faculty was as diverse as it was in 1994 in terms of its legal educational diversity—the Law School did not consider hiring Fordham Law School alumni between 1994 and 2001—advanced degrees in law, advanced degrees in fields other than law, judicial clerkships, and significant prior legal experience. One new hire had clerked for the Supreme Court of Israel. Fifty-four members of the full-time faculty were tenured or tenure-track, including four members of the clinical faculty who were offered tenure-track positions in the mid-1990s.[54]

The Law School was committed to faculty diversity. Dean Feerick charged the faculty recruitment committee each year to increase the diversity of the faculty, and the faculty intensified its efforts to achieve this goal. Nevertheless, the Law School's efforts to recruit minority faculty were not as successful as the dean and the faculty would have liked. Between 1994 and 2001, the Law School hired two tenure-track minority faculty and nine nonminority tenure-track faculty. The ABA inspectors reported that it had "made impressive additions to enrich its faculty." These included one black woman and one Asian American man the Law School hired who deferred their appointments for one year in order to clerk for justices of the United States Supreme Court; another black woman who accepted a lateral appointment and a black man who accepted a lateral non-look-see visit. The Law School also hired two minority women to the long-term contract clinical faculty. In 2001 the full-time tenured and tenure-track faculty included two tenured black men, one untenured black woman, one tenured Hispanic man, and one tenured Asian American man. One tenured black woman left the faculty when she was appointed to the US District Court for the Southern District of New York. The four black faculty members it had hired in the 2000–1 academic year reflected the Law School's intensified efforts to diversify its faculty.[55]

By the beginning of the twenty-first century, Feerick finally succeeded in bringing the student-to-faculty ratio into compliance with the ABA standard of 20 to 1. In the fall semester of 2000, the enrollment in the JD program was 1,344 full-time equivalent students (1,125 full-time and 328 part-time students). In the spring 2001 semester, 1,290 full-time equivalent students (1,093 full-time and 296 part-time students) were enrolled. Applying the ABA formula, the student-to-faculty ratio for the fall semester was 18.36 to 1, and for the spring semester it was 18.23 to 1.[56]

The director of clinical programs oversaw "significant development" in the professional skills curriculum in the last years of the twentieth century. Despite the faculty's ambivalence about live-client clinics, the director established two by 1994, one a litigation clinic and the other a mediation clinic. A third live-client clinic, a prosecution clinic, was established under the supervision of adjunct faculty. By the beginning of the twenty-first century, the three live-client clinics had expanded to eleven, and clinical faculty increased from four to twelve full-time and four part-time teachers. Student enrollment quadrupled (from thirty to one hundred and twenty) as did the space dedicated to the professional skills program. Support staff increased to meet the needs of the expanded clinical program. The clinical program also increased the number of simulation courses to eleven, two of which were interdisciplinary in approach and were cotaught by law, social work, and psychology faculty. The program correspondingly diminished its reliance on externships "as a professional skills instructional vehicle" as it improved the management of the externship curriculum.[57]

The Law School developed interdisciplinary relationships with other professional schools at Fordham University and offered interdisciplinary approaches to clinical casework in four of the live-client clinics: Family and Child Protection, Children's Disability and Special Education, Battered Women's Rights, and Criminal Defense. Faculty from the Law School, the Graduate School of Social Services, and the Graduate Program in Psychology supervise the clinical work of students from these three programs enrolled in these clinics, and clinical law faculty and social services faculty teach the seminars associated with these clinics.[58]

The educational purpose of the live-client clinics was to offer students opportunities to develop professional skills and judgment through actual practice in different areas of the law and different communities. In addition to the interdisciplinary clinics, the Law School offered the following live-client clinics: Civil Rights, Community Economic Development, Housing Rights, Mediation, Securities Arbitration, Low-Income Taxpayer, and Justice and Welfare Rights. The Securities Arbitration Clinic was established in 1998 through the leadership of Professor Constantine Katsoris and the support of Securities Exchange Commissioner Arthur Levitt. Fordham was one of just two law school in the nation to offer this clinic. These clinics, and the interdisciplinary clinics, furthered the Law School's commitments to interdisciplinary legal education and to public service. The 2001 ABA site inspection report concluded that the Law School had made "tremendous progress in [its] clinics," and that the clinics "enhance the image of the School in the community." Indeed, the *US News & World Report* survey for 2000–01 ranked the Law School Clinical Program seventeenth in the nation.[59]

The growth of the Professional Responsibility curriculum and faculty was one of the most striking changes in the Law School's curriculum during the Feerick years. In 1986 the Law School offered only one one-credit course in Professional Responsibility, which was taught by one professor, and all students were required to take it. The 2001 ABA reinspection report stated that the Law School's Professional Responsibility program "is nationally recognized." Students were now required to take one three-credit course and were able to select it from the six courses and seminars in Professional Responsibility the Law School offered. In addition, the curriculum included other courses in which Professional Responsibility was taught in the context of substantive law. The ABA inspectors characterized these courses as "unique" and acknowledged the intricate "skill set required of the instructors" who taught them, because they "have a command of both the substantive area taught and the principles of professional responsibility." The Law School also offered an innovative Advanced Seminar in Ethics and Public Interest Law, which was required for second-year students accepted into the Stein Scholars Program, a three-year program for "selected students who work in public interest settings and who undertake specialized academic work in legal ethics." The Stein program offers students specialized academic experiences in legal ethics, including roundtable discussions, public interest internships, and advanced seminars in public interest law and legal ethics. The Stein Scholars Program also sponsors conferences, programs, and symposia for the "entire law school community" on ethical issues arising in the context of public interest law and private practice.[60] ABA inspectors concluded that the "Law School thus gives its students the clear message that professional responsibility is an integral and important part of the profession."

The inspectors observed in 2001 that Fordham Law School has played a "major role in establishing the 'contextualization approach' to the teaching of legal ethics." This contribution is attributable to another unique quality of the Professional Responsibility program: the courses and seminars are "almost exclusively taught by tenured faculty members whose scholarship is in the area of legal ethics and professionalism and who have assumed leadership roles in both the academy and the bar."[61]

The Legal Writing Program, which had been a deficiency in earlier years, improved and expanded enormously through the end of the twentieth century. By 2001, it consisted of sixty-one courses and enrolled over nine hundred students. The director of legal writing was a tenured member of the full-time faculty. She supervised fifty-three adjunct professors and thirty-four teaching assistants, and she is assisted by a legal writing coordinator. The ABA inspectors reported in 2001 that "the quality of the adjunct Legal Writing Faculty is high, capitalizing on the School's location." Upper-division students were required to complete a "supervised analytic writing" course. This requirement could be satisfied by taking one of the fifty-five seminars or one of the thirty-five to forty advanced writing and drafting courses the Law School offered in 2001 or by taking an independent study with a professor. ABA inspectors evaluated the curriculum available to satisfy the upper-class legal writing requirement as "impressive in its scale and reach."[62]

The law faculty resolved an important curriculum deficiency of the past in eliminating almost all of the required courses and enormously expanding the elective courses. The upper-division legal writing requirement was one of only three upper-division course requirements remaining in the Law School's curriculum at the turn of the twenty-first century. The other two were one course in Professional Responsibility and one course in Corporations. The Corporations requirement was a vestige of the past when the Law School had a greater array of required upper-division courses.[63]

The Law School established study-abroad programs in addition to student and graduate exchange programs at foreign law schools that continue to the present. It has an exchange agreement with the Amsterdam Law School, the College of Management Law School in Israel, and a reciprocal preferential admissions arrangement with the Université de Paris I–Sorbonne. The Law School established its first summer program abroad, participating in "a unique cross-border partnership" with the law schools of University College of Dublin in the Republic of Ireland and Queens University Belfast in Northern Ireland. One half of the summer program is held at Queens and the other half at University College Dublin. The courses, which focus on human rights, dispute resolution, international business transactions, and comparative contract law, are taught by faculty from Fordham and Irish Law Schools.[64]

In recognition of the globalization of law and law practice, the Law School has developed a "significant international presence." It established the Mulligan Chair in International Legal Studies in 1999–2000 to bring leaders in the field to teach at Fordham Law School. Senator George Mitchell was the inaugural chair-holder, but his involvement in the Irish peace negotiations prevented him from assuming the chair until fall 2000. He was joined by the second holder, Professor Dominique Carreau, director of Graduate Studies in International Economic Law at the Université de Paris I–Sorbonne. In addition, the Law School has tried to include one foreign law professor among its visiting teaching faculty each semester. Two have visited a number of times: Professors Valentine Korah of the University of London, and Baruch Bracha of Tel Aviv University. The US Information Agency has given the Law School grants to conduct conflict resolution training programs in Northern Ireland and New York City which brings together Irish Catholic and Protestant community leaders.[65]

The Law School established a Graduate Program which has grown substantially. The program enrolled eighty students in the 2000–1 academic year, divided almost equally between the LLM program in Banking, Corporate, and Finance Law and the LLM program in International Business and Trade. About 90 percent of the students hailed from thirty-seven different countries, and they included Fulbright Fellows, a University of Rome La Sapienza Scholar, several UN Diplomats, foreign PhD candidates, and experienced lawyers and honors graduates from the world's leading universities. Different Fordham Law faculty have served as director of the Graduate Program, and the constant in its administration is assistant dean for Graduate Program Administration, Estelle Fabian, who, with her staff provides the essential administrative services for the program. In spring 2000 the US Department of State and the Open Society Institute designated the Graduate Program as a host institution to receive Muskie Fellows from Eastern European Countries who would like to study in the United States.[66]

The Law School broadened opportunities for law students to study in other schools within Fordham University. It established two arrangements with the Graduate School of Business Administration. The first permits a law student to take two preapproved courses in GSBA for credit toward the JD degree. The other is a joint JD/MBA degree in which a student is able to earn both degrees within three-and-one-half calendar years. It also established a joint JD/MSW program with the Fordham University Graduate School of Social Service. The Law School established a third joint degree program with the Graduate School of Arts and Sciences, a joint JD/MA in International Political Economy and Development.[67]

The number and variety of institutes, conferences, lectures, colloquia, and other programs proliferated in the last decades of the twentieth century and enriched the intellectual life of the Law School and community and, according to the ABA inspectors in 2001, they enhanced the reputation and recognition of the Law School. The oldest and most prestigious institute is the Fordham Corporate Law Institute, and its primary activity, the Annual International Antitrust Law and Policy Conference, brings to the Law School leading scholars, government officials, academics, and lawyers from the United States and Europe to discuss trends in competition law. The proceedings are published each year in book form with the editorial assistance of the *Fordham International Law Journal*, and the papers presented are published as a separate issue of the *Journal*. The 2001 self-study characterized it as "the foremost international competition law conference," and it has gained this reputation among foreign and domestic academic, government, and business circles. The Center on European Union Community Law and International Antitrust sponsors lectures at the Law School by high-level officials from the European Union, such as members of the European Court of Justice and staff and directors-general from the directorates of the Commission and the Council of Ministers' legal service. The Annual Conference on International Intellectual Property Law and Policy provides a forum for academics, judges, practicing attorneys, and government officials to discuss in depth key issues in international intellectual property. In 2001–2, the *US News & World Report* survey ranked the Law School's US and International Intellectual Property Programs in the top twenty.[68]

The number of institutes, conferences, and symposia relating to domestic law issues also expanded. The Institute on Law and Financial Services focuses on three areas: banking, securities, and insurance. The institute offers a series of lectures on the bank regulatory system for practicing lawyers, regulators, representatives of trade groups, interested faculty, and selected students. The Louis Stein Center for Law and Ethics sponsors national conferences, an annual symposium with the *Fordham Urban Law Journal*, and continuing legal education programs on a variety of public interest subjects. Papers and other materials produced by the Stein Center are published in the *Fordham Law Review* and *Fordham Urban Law Journal*. The Philip D. Reed Professorship in Civil Justice and Dispute Resolution was established by the family of Philip D. Reed and the Philip D. Reed Foundation. The Reed Professorship sponsors programs that discuss contemporary issues in civil litigation by noted scholars and leading members of the bar. The William and Burton Cooper Chair in Urban Legal Issues was endowed by the family of William and Burton Cooper to sponsor conferences, lectures, and course work relating to urban legal issues.

The coordinator works closely with the *Fordham Urban Law Journal* in accomplishing its mission. The Law School sponsors other conferences and programs that bring over 5,000 legal academics and professionals to the school each year.[69]

The Law School has had "a long history of dedication to public service that is deeply rooted in the Jesuit tradition of commitment to service and education," and this dedication is expressed in its mission statement. In 1995 the faculty adopted guidelines that called for faculty members to commit a minimum of fifty hours per year to pro bono work. In the closing years of the twentieth century the school's public service programs experienced "tremendous growth," and by the beginning of the twenty-first century was ranked nationally among the top ten law schools in public service. Undoubtedly, Dean Feerick was the "primary motivator for this growth, creating the environment" shared by the entire Law School community in which public service is "highly valued" and "seriously supported with financial and staff resources." Professor Thomas Quinn "complemented" Feerick's leadership as the occupant of the Sidney C. Norris Chair of Law to Public Service, "the first fully-endowed professorship in the nation devoted to law in the public interest." The Law School has built "a significant core group of faculty members" whose prior legal experience was in public service and who are actively engaged in the Law School's public service programs. Many of the public interest activities and programs are administered by Assistant Dean Thomas Schoenherr, "a pioneer law school public interest administrator" and "an acknowledged leader in the field," and two full-time professionals in the Public Interest Resource Center. These administrators and faculty members have made the Public Service Program "one of the School's signature programs."[70]

The Stein Scholars Program has become "the primary source of public interest student leadership at the Law School." This program is administered by the Louis Stein Center for Law and Ethics. Stein Scholars engage in academic course work, summer internships, and community service designed to give them training and practical experience in public service law. Course work includes an advanced seminar in which students work in small groups in conjunction with public interest law offices on projects that result in analytical papers. Summer internships are supported with a stipend intended to help students engage in public interest activities at a time when they could be working in private law firms earning lucrative salaries. Students interested in international human rights issues may engage in externships abroad in countries such as South Africa, Israel, and Northern Ireland. The service component of the Stein Scholars Program has become part of the Public Interest Resource Center and is therefore available to all Fordham Law students.[71]

The Law School also established the Joseph R. Crowley Program in International Human Rights in 1997 to promote teaching, scholarship, and advocacy in international human rights law. The Crowley Program affords students with the opportunity to research human rights issues around the world and to advocate solutions to international human rights problems. In addition to holding many events that bring human rights academics and practitioners to the Law School, the Crowley Program makes arrangements each summer for students to work with human rights organizations in New York, London, Israel, Guatemala, the West Bank, Rome, Haiti, and other countries. It also established six new courses in the field.[72]

Feerick achieved extraordinary improvements in two areas of the Law School that the ABA had identified as problem areas before he became dean. One was the Law School library. The new addition to physical plant doubled the space allocated to the library. Its collection met "the curricular and research needs of the Law School," and continued "to improve relative to the collections of other law schools of similar size." Its membership in a consortium with Columbia, NYU, the University of Pennsylvania, and Yale "rationalize development of the international collection." The law library also became a depository of the federal government. Through his fund-raising efforts, Feerick made the Fordham Law library "one of the best funded law libraries in the United States." The ABA site inspectors acknowledged that "the financial resources available to the library have increased significantly from 1995–2001." This was a particularly remarkable achievement inasmuch as the Law School lacked a significant endowment. Its market value in fiscal year 2002 was $57,800,143.[73]

Many of the earlier problems in the law library were spatial. Thus, 1984 building renovations greatly expanded the library's physical space. It now occupied "nearly half the total area of the expanded law school building," and it had two "attractive reading rooms" and a faculty library. The seating area exceeded the minimum standards set by the ABA and AALS. The new basement stack area was expected to give the library enough space to grow for the next fifteen years, until 2001. As predicted, by 2001 the "library facility [was] at maximum capacity."[74]

The book collection had been "identified as one of the great strengths of the library" by ABA inspectors in 1980, and it was "built carefully" by Dr. Ludwik Teclaff when he was law librarian. The total "title count" in 1985 was approximately 130,000 volumes. By comparison, Columbia's Law Library numbered about 260,000 titles, Cornell's was 148,000 titles, and NYU's numbered 137,000 titles. Fordham Law library's extensive special collection of international materials on the European Economic Community distinguished it from all other law libraries in the area. It was built by a gift of $330,000 from the Norman K. Winston Foundation beginning in 1981.[75]

Dr. Teclaff, a member of the full-time teaching faculty and internationally renowned legal scholar, resigned as law librarian and joined the full-time faculty at the end of 1985. He was replaced by Janet R. Tracy. Ms. Tracy devoted "full time to law library administration, [did] not teach, and [had] no administrative responsibilities outside the library." Her position as law librarian was unusual in that Ms. Tracy was an assistant dean as well as a voting member of the law faculty, but she was "not on the law faculty tenure track and [did] not have any other form of job security." The ABA inspection report asserted that it was "inconsistent with ABA Standard 205 for a law school to deny to a law librarian who is a member of the faculty the rights and procedures respecting reappointment or termination which are accorded to faculty members generally." Apparently, this standard applied even to law librarians whose responsibilities and activities were purely administrative and included none of those required of a law school tenure-track faculty member. Responding to the ABA report, Deans Feerick and Byrn stated that they would present Fordham University with a proposal "under which she may receive tenure," and Ms. Tracy was appointed to the tenured faculty with the title of professor of research and library services.[76]

Other problems with the Law Library remained unresolved in 1994. None of the other four professional librarians had tenure or any other form of job security. Moreover, the ABA inspectors concluded that it was "apparent that the Fordham law librarians [were] underpaid," that they "still [earned] salaries below that of most academic law librarians in the New York City area," and that the Law School "should be considering steps to bring its librarian salaries into line with other librarian salaries in the area." The Law School's policies regarding librarians' salary levels and job security "tend[ed] to cause rapid turnover and some loss of stability in the functioning of the library," and the Inspectors recommended that the Law School reconsider these policies. Their report noted that three professional librarians had left Fordham within the past year. Critical in 1980 of the dearth of opportunities for the law librarians' professional growth, the 1986 inspection revealed that there was still "little opportunity for real improvement in this regard until 1986" because of two factors: limited funds and limited staff. With the recent increase in staff, the ABA expected that the level of staff participation in professional activities would "rise considerably." These problems were essentially resolved by 2001, as the financial resources made available to the library "increased significantly from 1995 to 2001."[77]

With Dean Feerick's leadership, the Law School succeeded in improving the quality of its students even as it was maintaining high enrollments and increasingly diversifying the student body. The 1994 ABA inspection report concluded that the students were among the strengths of the Law School. "By all objective measures," the report asserted "the quality of those students has improved" between 1986 and 1994. Moveover, "the number of minority students has increased." The Law School enrolled only 11 percent of the applicants to the entering class of 1993. The 555 students represented 172 colleges and universities, and 63 had earned a graduate or professional degree, including nineteen MBA's, twelve PhDs, and two MDs. Forty-two percent were women, which was close to the national average, and a remarkable 26 percent were minorities. The extraordinary increase in the proportion of minority students from 7.9 percent in 1986 was the result of the affirmative steps the Law School took to diversify the student body. The median LSAT score of 163 placed the entering class at the ninety-first percentile in 1993. In 2000, the median LSAT rose one point to 164.[78]

The students were very active in the life of the Law School, and they reflected the Law School's strong orientation toward public service. The Fordham Student Sponsored Fellowships, begun in 1989, awards summer grants to first- and second-year students who work in public interest law programs. The "first-of-its-kind auction to raise money for a student-run, volunteer public service organization" was held at Fordham Law School in March 1992, and it catapulted Fordham's Public Interest Resource Center to national prominence. Some 700 students, more than half the enrollment, were engaged in some form of public service through the Public

Interest Resource Center during the 1994–95 school year. In two consecutive years, 1993 and 1994, the Law School's Student Sponsored Fellowship program, under the leadership of Thomas Schoenherr, received an award from the National Association of Public Interest Law "for its outstanding growth." The Fordham Student Sponsored Fellowship raised $175,000 in 1996, the largest sum ever generated by a student group in an American law school. The Law School "significantly increased its efforts to encourage" students to engage in pro bono activities and broadened opportunities for them to do so. The Stein Scholars Program affords students training and practical experience in public interest law, preparing them "to serve as leaders in promoting ethical conduct and service to the community." The Law School's programs in legal ethics and professional responsibility are arguably the most extensive in the country.[79]

The Law School supported a wide variety of student activities and organizations. These included five student-edited law reviews: the *Fordham Law Review, Fordham Urban Law Journal, Fordham International Law Journal, Fordham Intellectual Property, Media and Entertainment Law Journal*, and the *Fordham Environmental Law Journal*. The Moot Court Board, under the direction of Professor Maria Marcus, runs the Irving R. Kaufman Moot Court Competition—an annual national competition in which thirty teams participate—and prepares teams to compete in seven interschool moot court competitions each year. The other twenty-two student organizations the Law School supported in 1994 grew to thirty-eight by 2000 with wide-ranging foci and memberships that reflected the increasing ethnic, racial, religious, gender, sexual-orientation, and political diversity of the student body.[80]

When students were asked to characterize the atmosphere at Fordham Law School, "the first word used by virtually every student interviewed was 'friendly.'" They noted that Fordham had a reputation for maintaining a friendly environment and that the administration stressed the value of such an attitude "from the very first day." That this feeling is genuine was confirmed by a student, "a self-confessed skeptic who acknowledged having had such misgivings prior to arriving at the law school," but "insisted 'No, it really is a friendly place!'" *The Princeton Review* gave the Law School laudatory mention because its "students appear quite satisfied with their choice of schools, finding little to criticize." The 1994 ABA inspection report recounted that students viewed the administration as "accessible, available and generally quite responsive to student complaints." It concluded that "Fordham is obviously a 'user friendly' law school where student needs are given high priority."[81]

Before John Feerick became dean, the Law School was unsuccessful in recruiting minority students. Shortly after he became dean, Feerick implemented policies and programs that substantially improved the Law School's record in this regard. The ABA inspectors concluded in 1994 that the Law School "can be proud of its progress" in recruiting "an ethnically diverse student body." Recruitment procedures produced "dramatic results, especially in enrollment of African Americans, which more than doubled from 25 in 1992 to 55 in 1993." The percent of minority students in each entering class from 1988 to 1993 more than doubled (see Table 8-1). Increasing numbers of minority students received increasing amounts of aid in the forms of loans and grants. From 1989 to 1993 the number of minority students receiving such aid rose from 81 to 182, and they received about three times the amount of grants (from $255,800 to $777,925) and loans (from $134,650 to $446,520) for total amounts of aid from $390,450 to $1,224,445.[82]

The Law School did not have an affirmative action plan for student admissions, but it considered race as one of many factors in the admission process. However, the school employed strategies specifically designed to recruit students from racial and ethnic minorities. The effectiveness of these strategies resulted in the Law School's increased minority enrollments for 1998 and 1999, which compared favorably to national averages,

TABLE 8-1. PERCENT OF MINORITY STUDENTS IN ENTERING CLASS, 1988–93

Year	% of Class Minority
1988	11
1989	14.5
1990	17
1991	17
1992	22
1993	26

Source: Report on Fordham University School of Law, February 28 to March 3, 2001, May 22, 2002 (follow-up visit).

and these enrollments were evenly balanced among racial groups (see Table 8-2). The Law School provides academic and financial assistance to retain students in need. A national ranking of institutions that granted the largest number of graduate and professional degrees to minority students in the United States during the 1995–96 school year was published in the July 23, 1998 issue of *Black Issues in Higher Education*. Among ABA approved law schools, Fordham ranked eighth for African Americans, nineteenth for Hispanic Americans, and twenty-fifth for Asian Americans. A survey published in the September 1998 issue of the *Hispanic Business* magazine ranked Fordham Law School fifth among the nation's law schools that are "doing the best job of attracting Hispanic enrollment." Another survey published in the magazine's September 2000 issue ranked Fordham Law School in the top ten law schools, and Fordham was the only law school in the northeast to rank that high. ABA inspectors randomly interviewed minority students in 2001, and the students reported "satisfaction with the environment of the Law School."

The recruitment, retention, and graduation of minority students sharply increased after 1989 as seen in Table 8-3. From 1990 to 2005, the proportion of minorities in the graduation class was in double digits, ranging between 15 percent and 25 percent and in most years averaging around 20 percent.[83]

The Law School virtually eliminated any disparity in the enrollments of male and female students by the end of the twentieth century. As Table 8-4 shows, through most of the twentieth century, the percentage of women in each graduating class was in the single digits. In the first seventy

TABLE 8-2. MINORITY ENROLLMENT, FORDHAM VS. NATIONAL, 1998–99

	1998		1999	
	Fordham	*Nationally*	*Fordham*	*Nationally*
African American	8.80%	7.4%	7.93%	7.4%
Hispanic American	7.58%	5.7%	7.51%	5.71%
Asian American	7.99%	6.3%	8.76%	6.3%

Source: Report on Fordham University School of Law, February 28 to March 3, 2001, May 22, 2002 (follow-up visit).

TABLE 8-3. NUMBER AND PERCENT OF MINORITY GRADUATES, 1977–2005

Year	Total Number of Graduates	Number and % of Minority Graduates	Black, not of Hispanic Origin	Mexican American	Puerto Rican	Other Hispanic American	Asian or Pacific Islander	American Indian
1977	315	14 / -4.40%	8 / -2.50%	0 / 0%	1 / -0.32%	0 / 0%	5 / -1.60%	0 / 0%
1978	326	19 / -5.80%	5 / -1.50%	0 / 0%	6 / -1.80%	2 / -0.61%	6 / -1.80%	0 / 0%
1979	322	14 / -4.30%	8 / -2.50%60%	0 / -0.93%	3 / -0.31%	1 / -0.62%	2 / 0%	0
1980	309	11 / -3.60%	2 / -0.65%	0 / 0%	3 / -0.97%	0 / 0%	6 / -1.90%	0 / 0%
1981	337	19 / -5.60%	11 / -3.30%	0 / 0%	5 / -1.50%	0 / 0%	3 / -0.89%	0 / 0%
1982	306	13 / -4.20%	2 / -0.65%60%0%	0 / -0.98%	3 / 0%	0 / -2.60%	8 / 0%	0
1983	330	16 / -4.80%	2 / -0.61%	0 / 0%	6 / -1.80%	1 / -0.30%	7 / -2.10%	0 / 0%
1984	399	20 / -5%	5 / -1.30%	0 / 0%	3 / -0.75%	3 / -0.75%	9 / -2.30%	0 / 0%
1985	379	14 / -3.70%	4 / -1.10%	0 / 0%	4 / -1.10%	2 / -0.53%	4 / -1.10%	0 / 0%

Year														
1986	332	20	−6%	6	−1.80%	0	0%	4	−1.20%	4	−1.20%	6	−1.80%	0	0%
1987	361	17	−4.70%	7	−1.90%	0	0%	1	−0.28%	3	−0.83%	6	−1.70%	0	0%
1988	392	17 (4.3%)		4	−1%	0	0%	3	−0.77%	2	−0.51%	8	−2%	0	0%
1989	397	33	−8.30%	12	−3%0%	0	0%	0	−1.80%	7	−3.50%	14	0%	0	
1990	393	72	−18.30%	17	−4.40%	13	−3.30%	0	0%	31	−7.90%	11	−2.80%	0	0%
1991	393	72	−18.30%	17	−4.40%	13	−3.30%	0	0%	31	−7.90%	11	−2.80%	0	0%
1992	396	41	−10.40%	15	−3.80%	1	−0.25%	3	−0.76%	11	−2.80%	11	−2.80%	0	0%
1993	429	88	−20.50%	29	−6.60%	1	−0.23%	8	−1.90%	20	−4.70%	30	−7%	0	0%
1994	412	64	−15.50%	16	−3.90%	0	0%	2	−0.49%	15	−3.60%	31	−7.50%	0	0%
1995	430	80	−18.60%	20	−4.70%	1	−0.23%	8	−1.90%	18	−4.20%	32	−7.40%	1	−0.23%
1996	519	119	−22.90%	48	−9.20%	3	−0.58%	17	−3.30%	25	−4.80%	24	−4.60%	2	−0.39%
1997	413	96	−23.20%	31	−7.50%	0	0%	14	−3.40%	15	−3.60%	34	−8.20%	2	−0.48%

TABLE 8-3. (CONTINUED)

Year	Total Number of Graduates	Number and % of Minority Graduates	Black, not of Hispanic Origin	Mexican American	Puerto Rican	Other Hispanic American	Asian or Pacific Islander	American Indian
1998	430	100	40	3	15	10	31	1
		−23.30%	−9.30%	−0.70%	−3.50%	−2.30%	−7.20%	−0.23%
1999	449	95	36	2	15	12	30	0
		−21.20%	−8%	−0.45%	−3.30%	−2.70%	−6.70%	0%
2000	448	108	41	2	18	18	29	0
		−24.10%	−9.20%	−0.45%	−4%	−4%	−6.50%	0%
2001	466	72	24	0	9	12	27	0
		−15.50%	−5.20%60%	−1.90%	−2.60%	−5.80%	0%	
2002	459	91	29	0	20	11	31	0
		19.80%	−6.30%	0%	−4.40%	−2.40%	−6.80%	0%
2003	414	104	38	0	19	13	33	1
		−25.10%	−9.20%	0%	−4.60%	−3.10%	−8%	−0.24%
2004	492	125	44	2	15	28	36	0
		−25.40%	−9%	−0.40%	−3%	−5.70%	−7.30%	0%
2005	429	112	31	1	10	24	45	1
		−26.10%	−7.20%	−0.23%	−2.30%	−5.60%	−10.50%	−0.23%

Source: Fordham Law School Registrar's records.

TABLE 8-4. NUMBER AND PERCENT OF WOMEN GRADUATES, 1921–2005

Year	Total Number of Graduates	Number of Female Graduates	Percentage of Female Graduates
1921	119	4	3%
1922	222	9	4%
1923	252	15	5.9%
1924	357	21	5.8%
1925	382	30	7.8%
1926	399	22	5.5%
1927	328	26	7.9%
1928	389	13	3.3%
1929	451	14	3.1%
1930	371	7	1.8%
1931	347	16	4.6%
1932	282	13	4.6%
1933	245	9	3.7%
1934	292	6	2.1%
1935	308	5	1.6%
1936	258	22	8.5%
1937	106	8	7.5%
1938	188	12	6.4%
1939	210	14	6.7%
1940	187	9	4.3%
1941	208	11	5.3%
1942	141	7	5%
1943	102	17	16.7%
1944	68	16	23.5%
1945	75	17	22.7%
1946	134	18	13.4%
1947	140	9	6.4%
1948	201	11	5.5%
1949	217	10	4.6%
1950	156	17	10.9%
1951	158	11	7%
1952	155	3	1.9%
1953	155	10	6.5%

TABLE 8-4. (CONTINUED)

Year	Total Number of Graduates	Number of Female Graduates	Percentage of Female Graduates
1954	161	7	4.3%
1955	152	9	5.9%
1956	178	12	6.7%
1957	180	8	4.4%
1958	167	3	1.8%
1959	203	10	4.9%
1960	180	3	1.7%
1961	190	6	3.2%
1962	163	4	2.5%
1963	158	7	4.4%
1964	196	5	2.6%
1965	201	5	2.5%
1966	199	10	5%
1967	216	12	5.6%
1968	221	14	6.3%
1969	209	10	4.8%
1970	136	11	8.1%
1971	190	19	10%
1972	236	17	7.2%
1973	268	18	6.7%
1974	331	25	7.6%
1975	300	40	13.3%
1976	291	56	19.2%
1977	315	65	20.6%
1978	326	92	28.2%
1979	322	98	30.4%
1980	309	101	32.7%
1981	337	119	35.3%
1982	306	93	30.4%
1983	330	131	39.7%
1984	399	173	43.4%
1985	379	158	41.7%
1986	332	126	38%

1987	361	149	41.3%
1988	392	158	40.3%
1989	397	176	45%
1990	393	158	40.2%
1991	393	158	40.2%
1992	396	177	44.7%
1993	429	190	38.6%
1994	412	172	41.8%
1995	430	185	43%
1996	519	203	39.1%
1997	413	166	40.2%
1998	430	197	45.8%
1999	449	191	42.5%
2000	448	198	44.2%
2001	466	211	45.3%
2002	459	222	48.4%
2003	414	211	51%
2004	492	262	53.3%
2005	429	213	49.7%

Source: Fordham Law School Registrar's records.

years of the Law School's existence, in only six did women constitute 10 percent or more of the graduating class, and four of these years were war years. The percentage of women graduates spiked to 23.5 percent during World War II, but this was due to the sharp decline in male law students who went into military service. The proportion of women in each graduating class did not return to World War II levels until the mid-1970s, averaging in the single digits for all but two of the years between 1947 and 1974. A significant increase in women law students began in 1975 and continued into the twenty-first century, and women averaged between 38 percent and 45 percent of each graduating class between 1983 and 2001. The gap between men and women gradually narrowed each year, and in 1999 the ratio was fifty-one to forty-nine. Females slightly outnumbered males in some of the entering classes at the beginning of the twenty-first century. The number of females exceeded that of males in the graduating classes of 2003 and 2004, and it was just shy of half in 2005. The increased representation of women in the student body was the result of active recruitment efforts that produced a larger pool of women applicants and a higher rate of conversion of accepted students to enrolled students.[84]

A student residence was a prerequisite to Fordham's becoming a national law school. The Law School had been requesting one since the 1960s. Although Feerick expected the Law School "to remain committed to the greater metropolitan area," he understood the importance of a geographically diverse student body. A student residence at the Lincoln Center campus finally opened in the fall of 1992, and, as predicted, it enabled the Law School to compete more effectively and more broadly for students because it opened to the Law School additional student markets around the nation that were previously inaccessible due to the absence of residence facilities. In 1994 the proportion of out-of-state students rose sharply to 32.7 percent of the student body. In 2000 this portion of the student body increased to 38.7 percent overall and 45.3 percent of the full-time day students. These results were achieved through specific strategies devised to recruit out-of-state students.[85]

Career planning and placement was the Law School's first area of service that "received a great deal of development." At the conclusion of his first decade as dean, Feerick was confident that Fordham's program in career planning and placement was "the equal of any law school in the country," and it provided a range of services to students and alumni "that's unparalleled in the history of Fordham Law School." He was "eternally grateful" to the directors who developed the program—Maureen Provost, Carol Vecchio, and Kathleen Brady—as well as to every one who worked in that office. Another office Feerick singled out is the Office of Student Affairs, and he acknowledged the assistant deans of student affairs, Professor Gail Hollister, who was succeeded by Linda Young who, in turn, was succeeded by Bob Reilly. Feerick praised them for their "tremendous contributions" "to the *esprit de corps* of the Law School." Feerick also expressed his gratitude to Bob Reilly for his "extraordinary work" in alumni relations, and for "really being always there for me, no matter the problem, no matter what the subject, no matter what the hour."[86]

The Placement Bureau evolved into the modern Career Planning and Placement Center from 1979 to 1986. In 1979, the office was staffed by one full-time placement director, and in 1986 it was staffed by six full-time individuals: one director, one associate director, one assistant director, and three secretaries. Career counseling and advisement and support services, such as workshops discussing resume writing, interviewing skills and managing a job search, videotaped mock interviews program, career panels, student observer program, alumni advisor program, minority programs, and the Employer Information Directory had become important components of the job search process. "Fordham was a leader in initiating these changes" after Maureen Provost became director. She expanded the services available to students and alumni.[87]

The number of on-campus interviews tripled from over 2,000 in 1978, mainly large law firms based in New York City, to close to 6,000 in 1985, including small, medium, and large firms in New York City and corporations, government agencies, and public interest agencies in nineteen states and Puerto Rico. One-third of the on-campus interviews occurred in early interview week in August, but on-campus interviews were spread over eleven weeks from September to November in addition to a spring semester season of interviews.[88]

The Law School's Career Planning and Placement Office "received the greatest acclaim from students, faculty and alumni alike," the ABA inspectors reported in 1986. These services had been "substantially upgraded" in the preceding several years. In addition to the three full-time professionals and part-time consultants, the alumni were "actively involved in placement." Fifty to sixty percent of graduating students acquired their jobs through the on-campus interview process in 1986, and 9 percent received judicial clerkships with federal and state judges. Seventy-eight percent of graduates had jobs by graduation, and just over 90 percent had jobs within six months of graduating. Because most students who attended the Law School in the 1980s lived in the metropolitan area, the vast majority of law school graduates worked there. Of the class of 1985, 80 percent worked in New York City, 6 percent in other parts of New York state, 5 percent worked in New Jersey, and 2 percent in Connecticut. Fordham law graduates were more successful in passing the New York exam than average. For both repeaters and first-time exam takers, the bar passage rates were 90 percent in 1982, 82 percent in 1983, and 88 percent in 1985, "substantially better than the overall pass rate in New York."[89]

Table 8-5 shows that the overwhelming proportion of law school graduates still practiced in New York City (79.9 percent in 1985) and New York

TABLE 8-5. GEOGRAPHIC DISTRIBUTION OF FORDHAM LAW SCHOOL
CLASSES OF 1984 AND 1985

	1984		1985	
Location	Number	Percentage	Number	Percentage
New York City	272	79.5%	262	79.9%
New York State	27	7.9%	20	6.1%
New Jersey	15	4.4%	18	5.5%
Washington, DC	8	2.3%	3	0.9%
Connecticut	6	1.7%	6	1.8%
California	2	0.6%	2	0.6%
Florida	2	0.6%	1	0.3%
Illinois	2	0.6%	1	0.3%

Source: "Long-Range Plan of the Fordham University School of Law, 1986," 63.

State (6.1 percent), with another 5.5 percent in New Jersey and about 1 percent each in Connecticut, Massachusetts, and Washington, DC. Graduates worked in fourteen other states in 1985.[90]

Table 8-6 compares known Fordham Law job placements with national placements for the graduating class of 1984. It shows that Fordham Law graduates entered private practice at approximately the same rate as law school graduates nationally, just under 60 percent. However, significantly higher percentages of Fordham graduates worked at large (58 percent greater) and very large firms (104 percent greater) than the national averages. About one-third of Fordham's graduates practiced in these firms. They also went into government jobs and business at significantly higher rates—56 percent higher and 72 percent higher, respectively—but they entered academics slightly under the national rate. Fordham Law graduates settled in the same geographical region as the Law School at a rate that was about 12 percent higher than the national average. These statistics show that in 1984 Fordham Law School was primarily a local law school which nevertheless placed a significantly higher percentage of its graduates in the nation's largest and most prestigious law firms than law schools generally. The two biggest challenges confronting career planning in 1986 were computerization of the system and expansion of the interviewing

TABLE 8-6. CLASS OF 1984: NATIONAL PLACEMENT AND FORDHAM LAW
SCHOOL PLACEMENT

Class of 1984	National Placement	Fordham Placement
Total Employed	92.3%	96.0%
Private Practice:	57.4%	59.3%
Very Small Firms (2–10)	22.0%	19.3%
Small Firms (11–25)	8.4%	9.2%
Medium Firms (26–50)	6.4%	3.7%
Large Firms (51–100)	6.0%	9.5%
Very Large Firms (100 +)	9.1%	18.6%
Government	10.9%	17.0%
Business	10.8%	18.6%
Academic	1.8%	1.4%
Placed in same geographical region as Law School	71.1%	79.5%

Source: "Long-Range Plan of the Fordham University School of Law, 1986," p. 60.

space. The self-study committee recommended that the Career Planning
Center extend its contacts to geographic areas outside of New York,
including the establishment of alumni chapters in other cities.[91]

As Table 8-7 shows, Fordham students and alumni experienced increasing success in securing judicial clerkships in the federal and state courts
from 1979 to 1987. The number of federal court of appeals clerkships tripled from two to six; federal district court clerkships tripled from five to
sixteen; the number of clerkships in the highest appellate court of the state
quadrupled from one to four; and the total number of clerkships more
than tripled from eight to twenty-six. In 1986, Fordham ranked second
among the nation's law schools in the number of clerkships secured in the
Second Circuit Court of Appeals.[92]

There were not more judicial clerkships because many of the top-
ranked students were reluctant or unwilling to relocate in another part of
the country or because of the expense of traveling for an interview. Many
top night students did not pursue clerkships because of "family responsibilities, financial constraints and other personal circumstances." Many

TABLE 8-7. JUDICIAL CLERKSHIPS, 1979–80 TO 1986–87

Year	Federal Court of Appeals	Federal District Court	Highest State Court	Total
1986–87	6	16	4	26
1985–86	5	17	1	23
1984–85	2	11	3	16
1983–84	2	9	3	14
1982–83	1	13	1	15
1981–82	0	13	0	13
1980–81	2	7	0	9
1979–80	2	5	1	8

Source: "Long-Range Plan of the Fordham University School of Law, 1986," p. 67.

top-ranked students bypassed a judicial clerkship to pursue "markedly higher salaries offered by major law firms." In 1986 the disparity in salaries for major law firms and federal clerks was great, $52,000 as compared to $27,000. The disparity was increasing. Cravath announced that its starting salary in 1987 would be $65,000. Many Fordham law students finished school with large debts incurred from college and law school tuition and living expenses, rendering it difficult if not impossible for them to postpone high salaries in major law firms.[93]

The career paths of Fordham Law graduates in the last years of the twentieth century were not too different than those of the mid-1980s. Compared with Table 8-6, Table 8-8 shows that somewhat greater proportions of graduates were going into private practice and smaller percentages were going into private industry, but the proportion of graduates going into government service and public interest work was about the same. Larger numbers of graduates went into private practice than in earlier years, and those numbers increased through the end of the twentieth century. The number of graduates who went into business and industry declined at the end of the century. But the other employment categories were fairly consistent.[94]

The Law School's goal of achieving a more geographically diversified student body was succeeding, judging by the geographical dispersion of

TABLE 8-8. TYPES OF EMPLOYMENT 1994–1999

	1994	1995	1996	1997	1998	1999
Private Practice	64%	65%	65%	66%	68%	70%
Business and Industry	12%	18%	17%	15%	13%	11%
Government*	16%	16%	19%	16%	17%	15%
Public Interest	01%	01%	01%	02%	02%	01%

*including judicial clerkships
Source: Self-Study 2001 Fordham University School of Law, January 10, 2001, 71.

graduates in their first jobs after graduation. Table 8-9 shows that the overwhelming majority of law school graduates remained in the New York area. However, a comparison with Table 8-5 demonstrates that graduates were entering new job markets, and they were finding employment in greater numbers in markets graduates had earlier penetrated. For the first time in the Law School's history, JD graduates were securing their first jobs in foreign countries.[95]

Not surprisingly, the vast majority of Fordham Law graduates took the New York State Bar Examination. Table 8-10 shows that their bar passage rates in the last years of the century continued to be better than average, often by significant margins. As one of the measures the ABA used to determine the quality of a law school, the bar passage rates signified that Fordham Law School was providing a high-quality legal education to its students.[96]

The last ABA inspection report of John Feerick's tenure as dean did conclude that the Law School was "providing high quality legal education." In his last report to the alumni, Feerick identified some of the Law School's achievements during his penultimate year as dean, 2000–1, that added to his other accomplishments over his twenty-year tenure as dean and led to the ABA's affirmative evaluation. The ABA conferred its E. Smythe Gambrell Award on the Louis Stein Center for Law and Ethics for excellence in promoting professional values. The Stein Center inaugurated the Institute in Religion, Law & Lawyer's Work with lectures, programs, and workshops on the intersection of law and religious values. The Law School expanded its programs in corporations and securities law with the

TABLE 8-9. GEOGRAPHICAL DISTRIBUTION OF FIRST EMPLOYMENT, 1994–99

Graduation yr.	1994	1995	1996	1997	1998	1999
New England (CT, ME, MA, NH, RI, VT)	3.0%	1.5%	2.2%	2.1%	2.8%	2.7%
Mid-Atlantic (NY, NJ, PA)	89.8%	95.0%	93.3%	92.3%	94.6%	90.4%
East No. Central (IL, IN, MI, OH, WI)	1.3%	.6%	.2%	.6%	.5%	.4%
West No. Central (IA, KS, MN, MO, NE, ND, SD)	.3%	0	0	0	0	.2%
South Atlantic (DE, DC, FL, GA, MD, NC, SC, VA, WV)	2.3%	1.2%	1.7%	1.5%	.8%	2.1%
East So. Central (AL, KY, MS, TN)	1.3%	.6%	.2%	.6%	0	.2%
West So. Central (AR, LA, OK, TX)	0	0	.2%	.6%	0	0.2%
Mountain (CO, ID, MT, NV, UT, WY)	.3%	0	0	0	.5%	.2%
Pacific (AK, CA, HI, OR, WA)	1.3%	0	1.5%	.6%	.5%	.8%
International	.7%	.3%	.5%	1.8%	.3%	2.8%

Source: Self-Study 2001 Fordham University School of Law, January 10, 2001, 72.

TABLE 8-10. NEW YORK STATE BAR EXAMINATION PASS RATES, 1993–2000

Exam Date	Fordham Overall	Fordham 1st timers	All applicants Overall	All applicants 1st timers	ABA Law Schools 1st timers
July 1993	86.0%	87.7%	75.0%	82.0%	
February 1994	59.4%	83.3%	82.0%	53.0%	
July 1994	92.0%	95.5%	79.0%	86.0%	
February 1995	73.2%	87.1%	52.0%	71.0%	
July 1995	87.9%	90.1%	72.0%	78.0%	
February 1996	67.6%	82.1%	54.0%	69.4%	
July 1996	84.0%	86.0%	71.0%	78.0%	81.0%
February 1997	56.1%	85.7%	51.0%	67.0%	74.0%
July 1997	78.0%	86.0%	71.0%	78.0%	81.0%
February 1998	65.0%	59.0%	48.0%	65.0%	71.0%
July 1998	84.9%	88.7%	70.1%	77.9%	82.0%
February 1999	49.0%	65.0%	51.0%	64.0%	69.0%
July 1999	81.5%	85.9%	68.4%	75.0%	79.4%
February 2000	54.8%	82.6%	45.0%	60.0%	68.0%
July 2000	80.2%	84.7%	68.0%	75.0%	79.0%

Source: Self-Study 2001 Fordham University School of Law, January 10, 2001, 66.

creation of the Center for Corporate Securities and Financial Law and the inauguration of the Eugene P. and Delia S. Murphy Conference on Corporate Law, the A. A. Sommer Jr. Corporate Securities & Financial Law Lecture, the Albert A. DeStefano Lecture on Corporate Securities and Financial Law, and the *Fordham Journal of Corporate and Financial Law*. US Supreme Court Justice Anthony Kennedy was the first Jurist in Residence.[97]

The Public Broadcasting System selected the Joseph R. Crowley Program on International Human Rights for a documentary on the faculty's and students' human rights activities in Ghana in June 2001. Only in its fifth year, the Crowley Program had achieved a stature comparable to more established programs at Columbia, Harvard, and Yale.[98]

The faculty continues to be recognized for its outstanding scholarly achievements. In a study of the academic distinction of law school faculties, Fordham's was ranked in the top twenty for its publications in the nation's leading law reviews. Indeed, the faculty publishes "in all of the top reviews and in many of the leading peer-reviewed journals." They were advancing the scholarly discussions of the leading legal questions of the day through these publications in addition to filing amicus briefs in the US Supreme Court, writing books, publishing articles in leading legal treatises, and participating in conferences and symposia at Fordham and other law schools.[99]

At the end of Dean Feerick's tenure, Fordham Law School was among the top 5 percent of the nation's law schools with the most diverse student bodies as it achieved the highest GPA and LSAT medians among entering students in its history. The median GPA was above 3.5 and the LSAT median was in the ninety-two percentile. The Francis J. Mulderig National Merit Scholars Program, which funds merit-based full-tuition scholarships for students of outstanding intellect and character, contributed to this success. At the same time, the Law School maintained its commitment to creating opportunities for students to obtain a legal education who might not be able to afford one by providing 1,100 students with need-based scholarships and loans. It also created new services and enhanced existing ones to assist students to acclimate to the demands of law school and to successfully complete their legal studies, including programs providing tutors and student advisors for students performing below average. Law students demonstrated their extraordinary commitment to public service. For example, the graduating class of 2001 had given 57,504 hours to public service and community service projects, averaging 404.95 hours per student over the course of their law school careers. This is almost three times the fifty hours of pro bono service per year the ABA suggests for practicing attorneys. The Career Planning Center reported that nine months after graduation nearly 98 percent of the class of 2000 were employed with an average salary of $94,000.[100]

In his first report to the Alumni, Dean William M. Treanor expressed his appreciation to Feerick for his leadership over his twenty-year tenure as dean. He declared that:

> No single individual in the history of the School has done more than John Feerick to advance our educational mission, to secure our future as a center of academic learning, and to create a place that is special for its scholarship, its ethical values, and its commitment to the public interest. He truly defines the phrase, "in the service of others."

The record of John Feerick's deanship abundantly supports Dean Treanor's eloquent testimonial. The Law School improved and expanded virtually every aspect of its operations.[101]

Two challenges that had long plagued the Law School remained to greet Dean Feerick's successor. The "single biggest administrative challenge is space," according to the 2001 ABA site inspection report. It noted that "nearly every aspect of the School's operation is confined in cramped quarters," and the current facility "is minimally adequate to meet the School's needs and poses a potential problem." The ABA accreditation committee concluded that the Law School and Fordham University should "consider carefully . . . the need for adequate physical facilities in which to carry out the School's program of legal education." The other problem related to the Law School's relationship with Fordham University. "Still to be ironed out is the exact extent of University charges to the School," a dismaying finding made by ABA inspectors in 2001. Although Dean Feerick turned the Law School around and sent it on an upward trajectory, demanding challenges confronted Dean William Treanor as the Law School approached its centenary.[102]

NOTES

CHAPTER ONE: THE FOUNDING OF FORDHAM LAW SCHOOL

1. Different sources report different numbers of students in Fordham Law School's first entering class. At the beginning of classes, the *Fordham Monthly* stated that nine students were enrolled, and more students were expected. *Fordham Monthly* 24 (October 1905): 25. Robert I. Gannon, S.J., agreed. Gannon, *Up to the Present: The Story of Fordham* (Garden City, NY: Doubleday, 1967), 126. A member of the first class, Judge Vincent L. Leibell, however, set the number at ten in an interview he gave fifty years later. *Fordham Life* 1 (October, 1955): 7. He was probably the source for Dean Joseph McLaughlin's unequivocal assertion that ten students were enrolled in the Law School's opening class. *Dean's Report to Alumni for the Academic Year 1972–73*, 4, box 24, folder Dean's Reports 1971–1989, Fordham Law School Papers, Walsh Library, Fordham University (hereafter cited as FLS, FU). In reporting a tribute to Dean Fuller on his retirement, the *Fordham Monthly* praised him in 1914 for increasing enrollment "from eight at the end of its first year to over three hundred at the present time." *Fordham Monthly* 32 (March 1914): 248. The *Fordham University Bulletin of Information*, which included the Law School, listed the students in each law class by name. Understandably, the *Bulletin* for the 1905–6 school year did not include such a listing. In the first listing after the opening of the Law School, the *Bulletin* included eight students in the second-year class for the academic year 1906–7. *Fordham Bulletin of Information* (1906–7): 98. The following year's *Bulletin* listed seven students in the third-year class. *Fordham Bulletin of Information* (1907–8): 129. The *Bulletin* for 1908–9 at page 140 listed six students in the first graduating class in June 1908. Ibid (1908–9): 140. Beginning in 1910, the *Bulletin* stated that the number of students in the first class of 1905–6 was thirteen. For tuition and class schedules, see *Catalogue of St. John's College* (1905–6): 124, and *Fordham University Bulletin of Information* (1906–7): 95, 97.

2. Virginia Kays Veenswijk, *Coudert Brothers, A Legacy in Law: The History of America's First International Law Firm, 1853–1993* (New York: Truman Talley Books/ Dutton, 1994), 33–34; William Hughes Mulligan, "The Fiftieth Anniversary of Fordham University School of Law," *Catholic Lawyer* 2 (1956): 209; Mulligan, "Fifty Years of Fordham Law School," *Fordham Law Review* 24 (1955): xi.

3. On Fuller's social prominence, see "What Is Doing in Society," *New York Times*, April 29, 1902; "What Is Doing in Society," *New York Times*, May 2, 1903; "Paul Fuller Dies; Adviser on Mexico," *New York Times*, November 30, 1915; "**its earliest and greatest**," *New York Times*, December 2, 1915. The quotations in the text can be found in Veenswijk, *Coudert Brothers*, 70 and 81, which cites the original sources; on President

Cleveland's offers see ibid., 90–93. Coudert Sr. had previously turned down appointments to the New York Supreme Court and the New York Court of Appeals, ibid., 79; "Death of F. R. Coudert," *New York Times*, December 21, 1903.

4. "**achieved a reputation**," *New York Evening Post*, August 14, 1915; "**bibliophile**," Veenswijk, *Coudert Brothers*, 119, quoting an unidentified source; "**prodigious**," "**diversified**," "**all manner**," "**the learning of**," Frederic R. Coudert, "Memorial of Paul Fuller," Association of the Bar of the City of New York Reports, 18 (1916): 162; **knowledge of French and Spanish**, John Jay Chapman, "Memories of Paul Fuller" (Butler Library Microform Collection, Columbia University, 1916), 6; **foreign governments,** Coudert, "Memorial of Paul Fuller," 162; **Graceful and incisive**, ibid., 123, 63.

5. "**original multinational law firm**," "Coudert Brothers Votes to Disband Storied Law Firm," *Wall Street Journal*, August 19, 2005, quoting legal consultant Ward Bower of Altman Well Inc.; Coudert, "Memorial of Paul Fuller," 162; **on the opening of the Paris office**, see Veenswijk, *Coudert Brothers*, 44. The Insular Cases include DeLima v. Bidwell, 182 U.S. 1 (1901); Downes v. Bidwell, 182 U.S. 244 (1901); Hawaii v. Mankichi, 190 U.S. 197 (1903); U.S. v. Dorr, 195 U.S. 138 (1904); Rasmussen v. U.S., 538 U.S. 981 (1903); Dowdell v. U.S., 221 U.S. 325 (1911).

6. "**the man who**," *New York Evening Post*, August 14, 1915.

7. Veenswijk, *Coudert Brothers*, 67–70.

8. Chapman, "Memories of Paul Fuller," 9; "The Hundred Born at Stormy Meeting," *New York Times*, June 17, 1909, 2; "Hundred Become Just Ninety-Six," *New York Times*, June 22, 1909, and "Schwab is Not Downcast," *New York Times*, June 23, 1909; "Democrats Gather for Harmony Talk," *New York Times*, September 9, 1909; **New York State Bar Association**, "Bar Votes Down Praise of Roosevelt," *New York Times*, January 26, 1908; **New York Law Institute**, "Law Institute Election," *New York Times*, May 24, 1913; **character committee**, "Bar Committee," *New York Times*, February 18, 1914. **New York State Bar Association**, "Bar Votes Down Praise of Roosevelt," *New York Times*, January 26, 1908; **New York Law Institute**, "Law Institute Election," *New York Times*, May 24, 1913; **The court system was rank**, Herbert Mitgang, *The Man Who Rode the Tiger: The Life of Judge Samuel Seabury and the Story of the greatest Investigation of City Corruption in This Century* (New York: The Viking Press, 1963); **William Jerome candidacy**, "'If He Didn't Get It,'" *New York Times*, October 25, 1905; **committee to nominate New York justices**, "Bar Nominating committee," *New York Times*, June 5, 1906; **code of ethics**, "Untermyer Wants Corporate Reformers," *New York Times*, January 6, 1911.

9. The quotations are in Veenswijk, *Coudert Brothers*, 127, 66–67; see also, Chapman, "Memories of Paul Fuller," 8. The *New York Times* reported the dissolution of the Coudert Brothers law firm in August 2005, explaining that the firm failed because its members maintained this professional orientation into the twenty-first century and

prided themselves on being different from other law firms that came to resemble the business corporations they represented, focusing on marketing, profits, and corporate-style organizational structures and operations. Resisting these trends to transform a professional practice into a business enterprise, the *Times* reported, Coudert Brothers lawyers practiced pure law and were, "in a sense, above such concerns." Fuller shared the Coudert brothers' values of scrupulous personal integrity, the importance of honor and strict adherence to the highest professional ethics, and the ideal of the lawyer as public servant. These values and professional attitudes suffused the legal education Fordham Law School offered its students. As a leader of the bar, a partner in a preeminent law firm, a civic leader, and a scholar, Fuller was a role model of the kind of lawyer Fordham Law School sought to produce. See "Law Firm That Opened Borders Is Closing Up Shop," *New York Times*, August 30, 2005.

10. Woodstock Letters 36 (1907), 386.

11. **"a happy selection,"** Gannon, *Up to the Present*, 126; **"was indeed fortunate,"** Hughes Mulligan, "Fiftieth Anniversary," 207, 209. These statements are also quoted in Veenswijk, *Coudert Brothers*, 156.

12. **Fuller elaborated his constitutional theories in,** Paul Fuller, "Some Constitutional Questions Suggested by Recent Acquisitions," *Columbia Law Review* 1 (1901): 108; and Fuller, "Expansion of Constitutional Powers by Interpretation," *Columbia Law Review* 5 (1905): 193. **Fuller's discussion of** *McCulloch v. Maryland,* 17 U.S. (4 Wheat.) 316 (1819) is in Fuller, "Expansion of Constitutional Powers by Interpretation," 201. The **modern Supreme Court precedent** referred to is *Reid v. Covert,* 354 U.S. 1 (1957). The Supreme Court's jurisprudence of individual autonomy at the turn of the twenty-first century privileges certain constitutionally secured personal rights from unduly burdensome governmental regulation. See, for example, Planned Parenthood of Southeastern Pennsylvania v. Casey, 505 U.S. 833 (1992); Lawrence v. Texas, 539 U.S. 558 (2003). The best authority on the theory of popular constitutionalism is Larry D. Kramer, *The People Themselves: Popular Constitutionalism and Judicial Review* (New York: Oxford University Press, 2004).

13. **"paramount purpose,"** **"protection of all,"** **"greatest enabling act,"** and **"should be put,"** Paul Fuller, "Some Constitutional Questions," 118; Fuller, "Expansion of Constitutional Powers by Interpretation," 214; see also Fuller, "Are Franchises Affected by Change of Sovereignty?" *Columbia Law Review* 3 (1903): 241. Justice Story's opinion is Prigg v. Pennsylvania, 41 U.S. (16 Pet.) 539, 612–20 (1842). See Robert J. Kaczorowski, "The Supreme Court and Congress's Power to Enforce Constitutional Rights: An Overlooked Moral Anomaly," *Fordham Law Review* 73 (2004): 173–85.

14. "In Memoriam Paul Fuller," *Fordham Law Review* 2 (January 1916): 17, 18, quoting letter from Paul Fuller to Professor Thorpe of the University of Pittsburgh, n.d.

15. Veenswijk, *Coudert Brothers*, 156. There are almost no official law school records prior to the 1920s. A book of Fordham Law faculty minutes, 1907–33, Fordham Law School Archives (hereafter cited as FLSA), provides some, but not much, information of faculty meetings. The best sources for the Law School's first twenty years are the annual *Catalogue of St. John's College*, renamed in 1906 to the *Fordham University Bulletin of Information*, and the *Fordham Monthly*, a student publication of information regarding the college and professional schools, student activities, the faculty and alumni. The *New York Times* supplemented these sources with a fair amount of information on the activities and personnel of the Law School.

16. *Fordham Law Week* 24 (January 1906): 173; **on editors' positions and editorials,** see *Fordham Monthly* 24 (November 1905): 70–71; **on involvement with legal periodicals and legal expertise,** see *Fordham Monthly* 24 (January 1906): 173; "**started a tradition,**" and "**an excess of modesty,**" Dean's Report to Alumni for the Academic Year 1972–73, 2, folder Dean's Reports 1971–89, box 24, Fordham Law School Papers, Walsh Library, Fordham University (hereinafter cited as FLS, FU).

17. **All quotations** are in Saul Gordon, *Fordham Law Review* 3 (March 1917): 95–97 and "March Book Reviews," *Fordham Law Review* 3 (March 1917): 120; *Fordham Monthly* 24 (January 1906): 173; *Fordham Monthly*, 24 (November 1905): 70–71; H. Gerald Chapin, *Code Practice in New York* (New York: Baker, Voorhis, 1918); Chapin, *Cases on Torts* (St. Paul: West Publishing Co., 1917); Chapin, *Handbook of the Law of Torts* (St. Paul: West Publishing Co., 1917). Review of torts volumes, Saul Gordon, *Fordham Law Review* 3 (March 1917): 95–97; "March Book Reviews," ibid., 120. *McPherson v. Buick Motor Co.*, 217 N.Y. 382 (1916).

18. "**protected Jim's interest,**" Gene Fowler, *Beau James: The Life and Times of Jimmy Walker* (New York: Viking, 1946), 126; "**prevailed upon his old friend**" and "**a man of excellent character,**" ibid., 223; "**a sick man,**" "**Jim's old friend,**" ibid., 222; **Warren's death,** ibid., 234; "**an incorruptible,**" Kenneth T. Jackson, ed., *The Encyclopedia of New York City* (New Haven: Yale University Press, 1995), 1233. For Warren's views on legal ethics, see infra note 34 and accompanying text. There is a mistaken belief that Walker was a partner in the McIntyre & Downey law firm. Herbert Mitgang mistakenly identifies Walker's police commissioner as Charles B. Warren, and writes that Walker was Warren's law partner, which would have made him a partner in the McIntyre & Downey law firm. Herbert Mitgang, *The Man Who Rode the Tiger: The Life of Judge Samuel Seabury and the Story of the Greatest Investigation of City Corruption in This Century* (Philadelphia: J. B. Lippincott, 1963), 166. In its obituary of Francis McIntyre, the *New York Times* perpetuated this impression when it reported that Walker "had his law office in the McIntyre & Downey suite from 1917 until he took office as Mayor at the beginning of 1926." "Francis M'Intyre, Democratic Aide," *New York Times*, May 13, 1965. The obituary also mentioned that "Various other well-known

persons were associated with the firm, among them the late Joseph A. Warren, who became Police Commissioner under Mayor Walker." However, Walker's biographer states unequivocally that "Jim had no law partners, as is commonly supposed, but occupied one small room in a suite maintained by intimate friends. "He identified the McIntyre law firm. Fowler, *Beau James*, 126. The New York City Police Department website, http://www.nyc.gov/html/nypd/html/pchistory.html, lists Joseph A. Warren as Police Commissioner from April 12, 1927 to December 18, 1928. Fowler thus correctly identifies Police Commissioner Warren as Joseph A. Warren, and he also notes that, contrary to common belief, Walker had no law partners. Fowler, *Beau James*, 126.

19. *Fordham Law Week* 25 (June 1907): 381–82; *Fordham University Bulletin of Information* (1906–7): 92–95; *Fordham Monthly* 25 (November 1906): 88; "Judge J. E. Corrigan Dies Unexpectedly," *New York Times*, January 9, 1935; "Death of Corrigan Shock to Jurists," *New York Times*, January 10, 1935; *Fordham Monthly* 25 (November 1906): 88; Julius Goebel Jr., *A History of the School of Law, Columbia University* (New York: Columbia University Press, 1955), 244–46.

20. *Fordham Monthly* 25 (November 1906): 88; *Fordham Monthly* 27 (April 1909): 481; *Fordham Monthly* 30 (May 1912): 348; Goebel Jr., *History of the Law School*, 244–47. **The quotations regarding Professor Clifford** are at 246–47. In discussing Gifford as a legendary professor, Goebel was explaining Gifford's legendary reputation at Columbia Law School as well as Gifford's anecdotes being a part of Columbia's traditions. The equally high regard with which Fordham Law students held Gifford suggests that they recognized his distinctive qualities as their law professor. See, *Fordham Monthly* 32 (June 1914): 393; "Slap at Columbia by Retiring Dean," *New York Times*, November 21, 1909; "Fordham School Prospers," *New York Times*, September 26, 1913. Dean Harlan Fiske Stone also lauded Gifford. See Goebel Jr., *History of the Law School*, 245–46, quoting Harlan Fiske Stone, "Memorial of Ralph W. Gifford," Association of the Bar of the City of New York Year Book (1926): 451–54.

21. **Keener at Harvard Law School,** Goebel Jr., *History of the Law School*, 135–37; Arthur E. Sutherland, *The Law at Harvard: A History of Ideas and Men, 1817–1967* (Cambridge, Mass.: Harvard University Press, 1967), 186–87, 201; **Columbia recruits Keener**, William P. LaPiana, *Logic and Experience: The Origin of Modern American Legal Education* (New York: Oxford University Press, 1994), 94; Goebel Jr., *History of the Law School*, 147–48; **resigned from Columbia**, Goebel Jr., *History of the Law School*, 197; **practiced law and returned to teaching at Fordham Law School**, *Fordham Monthly* 31 (June 1913): 412; *Fordham Monthly* 32 (May 1914): 345.

22. **"the student must,"** William A. Keener, *A Selection of Cases on the Law of Quasi-Contracts*, I (Cambridge, Mass.: C. W. Sever, 1888–89): vi, also quoted in Robert Stevens, *Law School: Legal Education in America from the 1850s to the 1980s* (Chapel Hill: University of North Carolina Press, 1983), 56, 57; **"knowledge of,"** LaPiana, *Logic*

and Experience, 57, quoting, Keener, "The Inductive Method in Legal Education," *17 Reports of the American Bar Association* (1894): 482; **"the student is practically doing,"** LaPiana, *Logic and Experience*, 109, quoting, Keener, "The Inductive Method," 482; **on Keener's method of teaching law**, see LaPiana, *Logic and Experience*, 135; Goebel Jr., *History of the Law School*, 140, 154; Stevens, *History of Legal Education*, 60.

23. Committee on Honors, November 1965, folder Law School Dean, 1966, box 6, Leo P. McLaughlin Papers, Walsh Library, Fordham University.

24. "In Memoriam, Dean Ignatius M. Wilkinson, 1887–1953," *Fordham Law Review* 22 (1953): 232–34.

25. Ibid.

26. "John T. Loughran, 1889–1953," *Fordham Law Review* 22 (1953): xii; "Chief Judge Loughran," *New York Times*, April 1, 1953; "Judge Loughran Dies At Age of 64," *New York Times*, April 1, 1953.

27. "Francis M'Intyre, Democratic Aide," *New York Times*, May 13, 1965.

28. "I. M. Wormser, 68, of Fordham Dead," *New York Times*, October 23, 1955. Casebook and case method innovator William Keener selected Wormser and John Loughran to bring out the second and subsequent editions of his contracts casebook, *Keener's A Selection of Cases on the Law of Contracts*, which they published after Keener's death in 1914, 1915, and 1920. In 1933, Wormser brought out another edition of this casebook with John F. X. Finn, who had joined the Fordham Law faculty in 1924. Wormser's earliest joint venture was with George F. Canfield, Dwight Professor of Law at Columbia University, who taught there for thirty-six years. They produced four editions of *Cases on Private Corporations*, in 1913, 1925, 1932, and 1948. Goebel Jr., *History of the Law School*, 172–75, 277. **"Without a doubt,"** William Hughes Mulligan, interview by Michael Sheahan, September 30, 1988, Transcript No. 22, Book 3, 5, Oral History Project, Fordham Law School Archives (hereinafter cited as OHP, FLSA). Wormser coedited casebooks on corporation law with other scholars as well. He coedited with Charles B Elliott, *Illustrative Cases on Private Corporations* in 1914; he published *Illustrative Cases on Corporations* with William L. Clark Jr. in 1916, and, in 1936, he and Robert S. Stevens published *Illustrative Cases on Corporations*. Wormser and Clark Jr. collaborated in writing a hornbook entitled *Handbook of the Law of Private Corporations*, which they published in 1916. With Columbia Law School scholar and former Dean, George W. Kirchwey, who was characterized as "a profound or productive scholar," Wormser produced two editions of Kirchwey's Cases on the Law of Mortgage in 1917 and 1924. Goebel Jr., *History of the Law School*, 166. He also published two editions of his own casebook on mortgage law, *A Selection of Cases and Other Authorities on the Law of Mortgages*, in 1925 and 1935. With a former student, Saul Gordon, Wormser published *Gordon's Annotated Forms of Agreement* in 1923. Wormser also wrote five books on corporation law and thirty-five articles, which he published

in legal journals, on a wide variety of law topics. Additionally, Wormser served as editor of the *New York Law Journal* from 1919 to 1931.

29. Frederic R. Coudert Jr., *Certainty and Justice: Studies of the Conflict Between Precedent and Progress in the Development of the Law* (New York: D. Appleton and Company, 1913). Veenswijk details Coudert's life and character in *Coudert Brothers*. On Professor Burgess, see Goebel Jr., *History of the Law School*, 210.

30. *Fordham University Bulletin of Information* (1906–7): 89.

31. *Fordham University Bulletin of Information* (1908–9): 131.

32. **"with the fundamental," "some of the problems,"** *Fordham University Bulletin of Information* (1912–13): 10; **Jurisprudence,** Alfred Z. Reed, *Training for the Public Profession of the Law: Historical Development and Principal Contemporary Problems of Legal Education in the United States with Some Account of Conditions in England and Canada* (New York: Charles Scribner's Sons, 1921, reprinted by William S. Hein Company, Buffalo, N.Y. 1986), 300; **on Columbia Law School**, see Goebel Jr., *History of the Law School*, 339–40; **Legal Ethics,** Alfred Z. Reed, *Present-Day Law Schools in the United States and Canada* (New York: The Carnegie Foundation for the Advancement of Teaching, 1928), 254–55; **"some of the problems,"** *Fordham University Bulletin of Information* (1906–7): 92.

33. *Fordham Monthly* 24 (May 1906): 355, 356.

34. **Warren's comments** are in *Fordham Monthly* 28 (November 1909): 2–3. The article he referred to is John C. Meyer, "Boards of Legal Discipline," *Law Notes* 13 (1909): 84–87.

35. **"hoped that,"** *Fordham Monthly,* 27 (April 1909): 483; *Woodstock Letters,* 36 (1907): 387; William A. Keener, *Selections on the Elements of Jurisprudence* (St. Paul: West Publishing Co., 1896): 1–15; Stevens, *History of Legal Education,* 39; Schroth, S.J., *Fordham: A History and Memoir,* 129, 275; *Fordham Law Week* 25 (April 1907): 275; see also *Woodstock Letters* 38 (1909): 305–6.

36. **"Fordham was,"** William Hughes Mulligan to Dean John C. Fizgerald, December 6, 1954, folder 3, box 1, FLS, FU; **"a chair,"** and **"Father Shealy,"** *Woodstock Letters* 36 (1907): 387; Keener, *Selections on Jurisprudence,* 1–15; Stevens, *History of Legal Education,* 39; Schroth, S.J., *Fordham: A History and Memoir,* 129; *Fordham Law Week* 25 (April 1907): 275; **"creating, perhaps,"** *Fordham Monthly* 27 (April 1909): 483; see also *Woodstock Letters* 38 (1909): 305–6.

37. This summary of Father Shealy's philosophical framework is based on the following: Gerald C. Treacy, S.J., *Father Shealy—A Tribute* (Fort Wadsworth, N.Y.: Mount Manresa, 1927), 1–3, 11–12, 15, 26–28; "Opening Address—School of Social Studies by Father Shealy," reprinted in ibid., 95, 100–1; *Woodstock Letters* 24 (1923): 92; Schroth, S.J., *Fordham: A History and Memoir,* 129–30. The best work on the thought of legal scholars and social scientists relating to the rational, ethical basis of democratic

government is Edward A. Purcell Jr., *The Crisis of Democratic Theory: Scientific Naturalism and the Problem of Value* (Lexington, Ky.: University Press of Kentucky, 1973). As his definition of "science" suggests, Father Shealy was very traditional in his thinking. He feared that the Catholic faith was threatened by modern thought, such as philosophical and scientific naturalism, socialism, evolution and women's equal rights. Although he taught the Church's views on "the rights of the workingman to develop his full mental and moral growth," he feared "the tyranny of the lower classes . . . [and] the autocracy of the gutter more than he feared the tyranny of the ruling class." Shealy believed that "'the revolt against authority' was the greatest evil that plagued the modern world" Schroth, S.J., *Fordham: A History and Memoir*, 130.

38. *Fordham Monthly* 26 (April 1908): 318–19; *Fordham Monthly* 26 (May 1908): 355, 357, quoting, "No True Education Without Moral Training," a lecture Father Shealy presented at the Albany Cathedral and reported in the Albany, N.Y., *Times-Union*, March 13, 1908.

39. Joseph Warren, "Fordham's Innovation in the Teaching of Law," *Fordham Monthly* 28 (November 1909): 2, 3–4.

40. *Fordham Monthly* 26 (October 1907): 37–38; "Revised Remarks of Gov. Malcolm Wilson prepared for Delivery at the Opening of Fordham's Sesquicentennial Celebration at the Rose Hill Campus, September 30, 1990," 7, following the interview with Honorable Malcolm Wilson by Robert Cooper Jr. on March 14, 1989, Transcript No. 45, Book 3, OHP, FLSA.

41. **"was probably the first,"** William Hughes Mulligan, "Fifty Years of Fordham Law School," *Fordham Law Review* 24 (1955): xi, xii; **Attitudes toward jurisprudence and "borderland" subjects, "relatively narrow," Reed,** *Training for the Public Profession of the Law*, 299–303, 410; **"new subjects,"** Reed, *Present-Day Law Schools*, 255 (emphasis added); **"it is a fallacy,"** Reed, *Present-Day Law Schools*, 255n3; Stevens, *History of Legal Education*, 39.

42. **Governor Hughes's speech**, *Fordham Monthly* 26 (June 1908): 408–14; *New York Times*, June 11, 1908; **Justice Hendrick**, *Fordham Monthly* 27 (June 1909): 608, 611; **McAdoo's speech**, *Fordham Monthly* 28 (July 1910): 548–53; "Gov. Glynn at Fordham," *New York Times*, June 10, 1914. Legal ethics and resistance to commercialism were also emphasized in other speeches to law students. See, for example, *Fordham Monthly* 26 (April 1908): 415; *New York Times*, January 27, 1909; **Conference of Bar Association Delegates**, Stevens, *History of Legal Education*, 172.

43. Fordham Monthly 29 (July 1911): 522–23.

44. **For tuition and class schedules,** see *Catalogue of St. John's College* (1905–6): 124; *Fordham University Bulletin of Information* (1906–7): 95, 97. Tuition of $100 in 1905 is approximately $2,520 in present-day dollars. The monetary conversion is approximated according to the Consumer Price Index and was calculated at http://www.measuringworth.com/uscompare (hereafter cited as CPI).

45. **"as the transit,"** *Woodstock Letters* 34 (1905): 437; **On the move to 42 Broad-way**, see *Woodstock Letters* 34 (1905): 437; *Woodstock Letters* 36 (1907): 387; *Fordham Monthly* 24 (January 1906): 172; *Fordham Monthly* 24 (March 1906): 263; *Fordham Monthly* 25 (May 1907): 325.

46. **"is peculiarly adapted,"** *Fordham Monthly* 24 (January 1906): 172; **enrollments** are discussed in Schroth, S.J., *Fordham: A History and Memoir,* 112; "Fordham's Fine Record," *New York Times,* September 29, 1912, 18; "Fordham School Prospers," *New York Times,* September 26, 1913.

47. **On the move to the New York** *Evening Post* **Building**, see *Fordham Monthly* 26 (May 1908): 370. **On the move to the Morse Building**, see *Fordham Monthly* 29 (February 1911): 249; *Fordham Monthly* 29 (May 1911): 433, 434; *Fordham Monthly* 30 (July 1911): 533; "Fordham Law School Moves," *New York Times,* May 24, 1911. **On the move to the Woolworth Building**, see Anonymous, "Prologue" (unpublished manuscript in FLSA, n.d.): 16; Schroth, S.J. *Fordham: A History and Memoir,* 111. **On New York buildings**," see Sarah B. Landau and Carl W. Condit, *Rise of the New York Skyscraper 1865–1913* (New Haven, Conn.: Yale University Press, 1996); David W. Dunlap, *On Broadway: A Journey Uptown Over Time* (New York: Rizzoli, 1990). **For information on the Woolworth Building**, see Jackson, *Encyclopedia of New York City,* 1273; Gail Fenske, *Woolworth Building: An American Cathedral* (New York: Princeton Architectural Press, 1992).

48. *Fordham University Bulletin of Information* (1907–8): 126; *Fordham University Bulletin of Information* (1908–9): 136, 138. In addition to Jurisprudence, which met two hours per week for the full year, the first-year courses were: Common Law and Code Pleading (two hours per week, first semester); Contracts (three hours per week, full year); Criminal Law and Procedure (two hours per week, second semester); Domestic Relations (one hour per week, full year); Property, Personal and Real (two hours per week, full year); and Torts (two hours per week, full year). One would substitute Civil Procedure for Common Law and Code Pleading, Constitutional Law for domestic relations, and add legal writing to complete the first-year curriculum today. In the second year students took the following courses: Agency (two hours per week, first half year); Bills and Notes (two hours per week, second half year); Carriers (one hour per week, second half year); Corporations (two hours per week, full year); Equity (three hours per week, full year); Evidence (two hours per week, full year); Real Property (two hours per week, full year); and Sales (one hour per week, first half year). The third year courses were all half-year courses. Students took Bankruptcy (two hours per week, first half year); Conflict of Laws (two hours per week, first half year); Constitutional Law (two hours per week, second half year); Damages (two hours per week, first half year); Insurance (two hours per week, second half year); Mortgages (two hours per week, second half year); New York Code of Civil Procedure (two hours per week,

first half year); Partnership (two hours per week, second half year); Practice in the New York Courts (two hours per week, second half year); Quasi-Contracts (two hours per week, first half year); Suretyship (two hours per week, first half year); and Trusts (two hours per week, second half year). *Fordham University Bulletin of Information* (1907–8): 126–27, *Fordham University Bulletin of Information* (1908–9): 136–38.

49. **Fordham adopted Langellian method,** *Fordham University Bulletin of Information* (1912–13): 10; unless otherwise cited, quotations are in Mulligan, "Fiftieth Anniversary," *Catholic Lawyer* 2 (1956): 209; **"debarred from using,"** Reed, *Training for the Public Profession of the Law,* 382.

50. *Fordham University Bulletin of Information* (1912–13), 7–8.

51. Ibid., 9.

52. Ibid., 10. The casebooks faculty used were included in the list of courses required in each year. See, for example, *Fordham University Bulletin of Information* (1906–7), 92–94. **The characterization of Professor Ames as "the first in a new breed of academic lawyer"** is by Stevens, *History of Legal Education,* 38; **Ames as making the case method work** is in Goebel Jr., *History of the Law School,* 137. However, Stevens and LaPiana give equal credit to William A. Keener. Stevens, *History of Legal Education,* 55–57; LaPiana, *Logic and Experience,* 3.

53. **Seven of seventy-six law schools,** Richard L. Abel, *American Lawyers* (New York: Oxford University Press, 1989), 48–49; **major reform,** Stevens, *History of Legal Education,* 37; Reed, *Training for the Public Profession of the Law,* 393, 411, 448.

54. **First entering class,** *Fordham Monthly* 24 (October 1905): 25. Students' names, degrees, and colleges from which they graduated are listed in the *Fordham University Bulletin of Information* from 1906 through the 1940s.

55. **Class recitations,** Book of Fordham Law School Faculty Meeting Minutes, 1907–33, Faculty Meeting of June n.d., 1908, 6, FLSA, [hereafter cited as Faculty Meeting of (date, page), FLSA]; **the student's work in the classroom,** *Fordham University Bulletin of Information* (1911–1912): 12; **"get up and recite,"** Caesar L. Pitassy interview by Robert Cooper Jr., May 19, 1989, 10, Transcript No. 56, 1989 Interviews, Book 3, OHP, FLSA; **"state the facts,"** ibid., 10–11; **"not prepared"** and **"make a note of it,"** ibid., 11; **"could read your lips,"** ibid., 12; **"he looked at your"** and **"And he was,"** ibid., 13.

56. **For decisions regarding examination rules and grading,** see, Faculty Meeting of September 1907, 5, FLSA; Faculty Meeting of June n.d., 1908, 6, FLSA; Faculty Meeting of September 21, 1908, 7, FLSA; Faculty Meeting of January 23, 1909, 8, FLSA; Faculty Meeting of June 6, 1912, 18–19, FLSA; Faculty Meeting of June 11, 1920, 40, FLSA; **"given the opportunity,"** *Fordham University Bulletin of Information* (1908–9): 133; **"no member of the faculty,"** Faculty Meeting of Mar. 29, 1910, 10, FLSA; **conditioned examinations,** ibid.; Faculty Meeting of Sept. 1907, 5, FLSA; Faculty Meeting

of Sept. 21, 1908, 7, FLSA; Faculty Meeting of June 8, 1922, 44, FLSA; **students denied degrees and subsequently allowed to graduate on passing a conditioned examination,** Faculty Meeting of June 4, 1910, 12, FLSA; Faculty Meeting of June 6, 1912, 18, FLSA; Faculty Meeting of June 3, 1913, 22, FLSA; Faculty Meeting of June 3, 1914, 23, FLSA; Faculty Meeting of June 1, 1915, 28, ibid.; Faculty Meeting of June 7, 1916, 30, FLSA; Faculty Meeting of June 6, 1917, 33, FLSA; Faculty Meeting of June 5, 1919, 37, FLSA; Faculty Meeting of June 11, 1920, 39, FLSA; Faculty Meeting of June 9, 1921, 41, FLSA.

57. **"the attendance,"** Faculty Meeting of September 1907, 5, FLSA; Faculty Meeting of, Mar. 29, 1910, 10, FLSA; Faculty Meeting of June 4, 1910, 12, FLSA; Faculty Meeting of June 3, 1913, 22, FLSA; Faculty Meeting of June 3, 1914, 23–25, FLSA; Faculty Meeting of June 5, 1924, 48–49, FLSA.

58. The data are taken from the class lists and list of graduates reported in the *Fordham University Bulletin of Information* for 1906–7 to 1914–15. See Excel Spreadsheet entitled "Drop Out Rates 1906–27 Class by Class," on file with author.

59. **"full-fledged bona fide,"** *Fordham Monthly* 26 (November 1907): 92; **"full-fledged,"** *Fordham Monthly* 27 (May 1909): 555; see also, *Fordham Monthly* 28 (November 1909): 72; *Fordham Monthly* 28 (April 1910): 394; *Fordham Monthly* 40 (May 1922): 569; Faculty Meeting of Sept. 21, 1908, 7, FLSA.

60. **On the 1911 pass rate**, see *Fordham Monthly* 30 (December 1911): 45; **on the 1912 pass rate**, see *Fordham Monthly* 30 (July 1912): 397, 399; **on the 1913 mid-term exam pass rate**, see *Woodstock Letters* 42 (1913): 125; **on the June 1913 pass rate**, see *Fordham Monthly* 31 (July 1913): 461, 462; **on the 1922 pass rate**, see *Fordham Monthly* 41 (November 1922): 120–21; see also Schroth, S.J., *Fordham: A History and Memoir,* 123.

61. **The bar requirements** are presented in the *Fordham University Bulletin of Information* (1906–7): 96; (1910–11): 112; (1912–13): 12; (1913–14): 10; (1920–21): 11; **New Jersey continued,** *Fordham Monthly* 40 (May 1922): 569.

62. Veenswijk, *Coudert Brothers,* 180–85; "B.B. Odell Approves New Constitution," *New York Times*, October 28, 1915.

63. **"Fuller's death was reported in** "Paul Fuller Dies, Adviser on Mexico," November 30, 1915, 6; **"lost its earliest,"** Faculty notice, "Died," *New York Times*, December 2, 1915. **"really sincere desire,"** "In memoriam Paul Fuller," *Fordham Law Review* 2 (1916): 18.

CHAPTER TWO: WORLD WAR I AND ITS AFTERMATH

1. **"on the lowest imaginable,"** "John Whalen Dead: Lawyer and Banker," *New York Times,* January 1, 1927; **"Mr. O'Conor was the greatest jurist,"** John Bigelow, ed., *Letters and Literary Memorials of Samuel J. Tilden,* 2 (New York: Harper, 1908), 643.

2. **Quotations are in** "John Whalen Dead; Lawyer and Banker," *New York Times,* January 1, 1927.

3. **Whalen's estate and bequests,** "Whalen Eulogized in Cathedral Rites," *New York Times,* January 4, 1927; "John Whalen Estate Gets Accounting," *New York Times,* September 20, 1930; Whalen left half his estate (valued at about $3 million) to the Archdiocese of New York (actually to the Archbishop to disburse) and also $250,000 to purchase a new organ for St. Patrick's Cathedral, "Bequest to Cardinal Protested by Heirs," *New York Times,* December 6, 1938; "5,000 at St. Patrick's As Organ is Dedicated," *New York Times,* February 12, 1930. *Woodstock Letters* 42 (1913): 127 (Chapel). *Fordham Monthly* 32 (March 1914): 248. One newspaper account reported that Whalen's estate was valued at $4,000,000. "Prayer Book a Clue to an Irish Heiress," *New York Times,* June 18, 1930. "**the Grand Gallery Organ,**" is at http://www.nycago .org/Organs/html/StPatCath.html; **still in use,** telephone conversation between Chelsea Walsh and Robert Evers, Administrator of Music, St. Patrick's Cathedral, September 20, 2005. $100,000, $250,000, $3,000,000, and $4,000,000 in 1930 are approximately $1,280,00, $3,210,000, $38,500,000, and $51,400,000 in present-day dollars, respectively. The monetary conversion is approximated according to the Consumer Price Index (hereinafter cited as CPI) and was calculated at http://www.measuringworth.com/ uscompare.

4. **On the move to the Woolworth Building,** see Anonymous, "Prologue" (unpublished manuscript in Fordham Law School Archives [hereafter cited as FLSA], n.d.): 16; Raymond A. Schroth, S.J., *Fordham: A History and Memoir* (Chicago: Loyola Press, 2002), 111; **for information on the Woolworth Building,** see Kenneth T. Jackson, ed., *The Encyclopedia of New York City* (New Haven: Yale University Press, 1995), 1273; Gail Fenske, *Woolworth Building: An American Cathedral* (New York: Princeton Architectural Press, 1992).

5. **On the 1917 graduation,** *Fordham Monthly* 36 (October, 1917–18): 1, 56. **Mulry,** *Fordham Monthly* 40 (October 1921–22): 1, 4; **for the Fordham Law students' subscription and the Liberty Loan Campaign,** see "$140,000,000 Added to Loan Sale Here," *New York Times,* October 26, 1917.

6. Alfred Z. Reed, *The Study of Legal Education* (New York: Carnegie Foundation, 1917), 1.

7. Book of Fordham Law School Faculty Meeting Minutes, 1907–33, Minutes of the Faculty Meeting of Wednesday, May 22, 1918, 35, FLSA, (hereafter cited as Faculty Meeting of (date, page), FLSA); Faculty Meeting of Thursday, June 5, 1919, 37, FLSA.

8. Alfred Z. Reed, *Legal Education and the War* (New York: Carnegie Foundation, 1918), 1.

9. **For Fordham Law School enrollments,** see worksheet entitled, "Dropout Rates 1906–27 Class by Class," on file with the author. **On enrollment data for Georgetown**

and Columbia Law Schools, see *The First 125 Years, 1870–1995: An Illustrated History of The Georgetown University Law Center* (Washington, DC: Georgetown University Law Center, 1995), 59 and Julius Goebel Jr., *A History of the School of Law Columbia University* (New York: Columbia University Press, 1955), 259, 483n2.

10. *Woodstock Letters* 42 (1913): 125–26.

11. **Enrollment data** are taken from *Fordham University Bulletin of Information* for the respective academic years; **"owing to war conditions,"** Faculty Meeting of Thursday, June 5, 1919, 37, FLSA.

12. **On the military take-over and rumors of Fordham's closing,** "Fordham Law School to Continue," *New York Times*, September 10, 1918; Herbert L. Parker and Thomas Ehrlich, *New Directions in Legal Education* (New York: McGraw-Hill, 1972), 64; Albert J. Harno, *Legal Education in the United States* (San Francisco: Bancroft-Whitney Company, 1953), 134–35.

13. **Regarding the five largest law schools in 1920,** see Alfred Z. Reed, *Training for the Public Profession of the Law: Historical Development and Principal Contemporary Problems of Legal Education in the United States with Some Account of Conditions in England and Canada* (New York: Charles Scribner's Sons, 1921, reprinted by William S. Hein Company, Buffalo, N.Y., 1986), 452. **Reports of student enrollments for each academic year and of students turned away** are in the *Fordham Monthly* 39 (October 1920): 46; *Fordham Monthly* 40 (October 1921): 56; *Fordham Monthly* 41 (October 1922): 59; **"a complete morning division,"** Faculty Meeting of June 9, 1921, 42, FLSA.

14. *Fordham University Bulletin of Information* (1921–22): 11. **On prohibited transfers and staggered classes,** see *Fordham University Bulletin of Information* (1922–23): 12.

15. **"to that graduate,"** *Fordham Bulletin of Information* (1928–29): 9. **On the first Chapin Prize,** see Faculty Meeting of June 7, 1928, 58, FLSA. **On the $100 Chapin Prize,** see Faculty Meeting of June 5, 1930, 65, FLSA; *Fordham Bulletin of Information* (1929–30): 9. $100 in 1914 was approximately $2,210 in present-day dollars. $110 in 1915 was approximately $2,420; $125 in 1917 was about $2,090; and $150 in 1920 was about $1,610 in present-day dollars. On workers' wages see Susan B. Carter et al., eds., *Historical Statistics of the United States: Earliest Times to the Present*, Millenial ed., 5 vols. (New York: Cambridge University Press, 2006), 2:265–83. **On Columbia scholarships,** see Goebel Jr., *History of the Law School,* 449n101. The Fordham scholarship is described as such in the *Fordham Bulletin of Information* for each year until the 1912–13 academic year. Thereafter, the award was described as **"a prize of fifty dollars ($50) in gold."** *Fordham Bulletin of Information* (1913–14): 10. Average annual wage income of $550 in 1905 is about $13,800 in present-day dollars; $700 in 1915 is about $15,400 in present-day dollars; $1,426 in 1920 is about $15,300 in present-day dollars. The New

York male clerical wage of $1500 in 1923 is about $18,900 in present-day dollars. The monetary conversion is approximated according to the CPI and was calculated at http://www.measuringworth.com/uscompare.

16. Data based on lists of enrolled students in the law school catalogues, 1906–21.

17. **"ladies were to be admitted,"** Faculty Meeting of September 21, 1918, 7, FLSA. **On the shift in policy,** ibid. The minutes of this date stated: "In a letter from the Rev. Rector of the University under date of July 6, 1918, he writes 'it has been decided that, owing to objections raised against it, women will not be admitted to the classes of the Law School this Fall.'" See also *The Women of Fordham Law School, 1918–19—1993–34* (Fordham Law School, 1993). **"The University recognizes,"** *Fordham Bulletin of Information (1919–20)*: 10. Fordham University opened the all-female Thomas More College in 1964; this was merged with Fordham College in 1974, Schroth, *Fordham: A History and Memoir*, passim. **On the Yale data,** see "Milestones in the Education of Women at Yale" in *Historical Statistics of the College and University, A Yale Book of Numbers*, ed. Beverly Waters (2001), www.yale.edu/oir/pierson_update.htm. One woman received a law degree from Yale Law School in 1886 after she was "mistakenly" admitted when she applied using her initials. Women were then excluded until 1919.

18. Robert Stevens, *Law School: Legal Education in America From the 1850s to the 1980s* (Chapel Hill: The University of North Carolina Press, 1983), 82; Joan Hoff, *Law, Gender, and Injustice: A Legal History of U.S. Women* (New York: New York University Press, 1991), 162–63. **On Margaret Brent and Luce Terry,** see http://tinyurl.com/women-laywers-bar; Karen Berger Morello, *The Visible Bar: The Woman Lawyer in American 1638 to the Present* (New York: Random House, 1986), 3. The Library of Congress cites as authority on Luce Terry: J. Clay Smith, ed., *Rebels in Law: Voices in History of Black Women Lawyers* (Ann Arbor: University of Michigan Press, 1998), 2.

19. Bradwell v. Illinois, 83 U.S. (16 Wall.) 130 (1873). Justice Bradley's concurring opinion is in ibid., 141–42 (Bradley, J., concurring).

20. See infra chapter 4, notes 47–63 and accompanying text, for a discussion of the Law School's course in Jurisprudence and the faculty's natural law philosophy.

21. Bradwell v. Illinois, 83 U.S. (13 Wall.) 130, 141–42 (1873) (Bradley, J., concurring) (emphasis added). **On the "cult of true womanhood,"** see William H. Chafe, *The American Woman: Her Changing Social, Economic, and Political Role, 1920–1970* (New York: Oxford University Press, 1972); William H. Chafe, *Women and Equality: Changing Patterns in American Culture* (New York: Oxford University Press, 1978); Mary P. Ryan, *Womanhood in America: From Colonial Times to the Present* (New York: New Viewpoints, 1983). **On the law of coverture,** see Marylynn Salmon, *Women and the Law of Property in Early America* (Chapel Hill: University of North Carolina Press, 1986); Richard H. Chused, "Married Women's Property Law: 1800–1850," *Georgetown Law Journal* 71 (1983): 1397; Richard H. Chused, "Late Nineteenth-Century Married

Women's Property Law: Reception of the Early Married Women's Property Acts by Courts and Legislatures," *American Journal of Legal History* 29 (January 1985): 24. **On the law of marriage**, see Hendrik Hartog, *Man and Wife in America: A History* (Cambridge: Harvard University Press, 2000); Michael Grossberg, *Governing the Hearth: Law and the Family in Nineteenth-Century America* (Chapel Hill: University of North Carolina Press, 1985).

22. **Information on Bradwell** is in Edward T. James, Janet Wilson James, and Paul Boyer, eds., *Notable American Women 1607–1950: A Biographical Dictionary,* 1 (Cambridge, Mass.: Harvard University Press, 1971), 223–25; **Lockwood** is in ibid., 2, 413–16; **Masfield** is in ibid., 492–93; for **Kate Stoneman**, see Katheryn D. Katz, "Kate Stoneman: A Pioneer for Equality," in *Pioneering Women Lawyers*, ed. Patricia E. Salkin (Chicago: Commission on Women in the Profession, American Bar Association, 2008), 1–13. See also, Hoff, *Law Gender & Injustice*, 169; Stevens, *History of Legal Education*, 82; Virginia G. Drachman, *Sisters in Law: Women Lawyers in Modern American History* (Cambridge: Harvard University Press, 1997). Bradwell was also admitted to the US Supreme Court bar in 1892. Hoff, *Law Gender & Injustice*, 169; **ABA and ABCNY membership**, Abel, *American Lawyers*, 90.

23. **Census data** from US Department of the Interior, Bureau of the Census, *Women in Gainful Occupations, 1870–1970* (Washington, D.C.: 1979), 42; Stevens, *History of Legal Education*, 83; **on law school enrollments**, see Alfred Z. Reed, *Legal Education and the War,* 3n2; **on 1920 enrollment of women**, see Abel, Richard L. Abel, *American Lawyers* (New York: Oxford University Press, 1989), 90.

24. **"owing to war conditions,"** Faculty Meeting of Thursday, June 5, 1919, 37, FLSA; **on enrollments of women**, Reed, *Legal Education and the War*, 3n2; **on women enrollments at NYU Law School**, see ibid., 10; **on women enrollments at Brooklyn Law School**, see Jeffrey B. Morris, *Brooklyn Law School: The First Hundred Years* (Brooklyn: Brooklyn Law School, 2001), 36. **Women enrolled nationally in law schools**, estimated from data in Reed, *Legal Education and the War*, 3n2.

25. Abel, *American Lawyers*, 90–91; **the proportion of women lawyers** is in Reed, *Training for the Public Profession*, 442–43 and Cynthia Fuchs Epstein, *Women in Law* (Garden City, N.Y.: Anchor Books, 1983), 4. **On Columbia and Harvard Law Schools**, see ibid., 50. **On Georgetown**, see "Georgetown Law Center to Celebrate 50 Years of Women," Georgetown Law Center Press Release, February 23, 2002 (available online at http://tinyurl.com/georgetown-50-years); **on Notre Dame**, Victoria L. Vreeland and Karen K. Koehler, "Proud to Be a Lawyer . . . a Female Lawyer," Washington State Bar Association, October 2001 (available online at: http://www.wsba.org/media/publications/barnews/archives/2001/oct-01-proud.htm).

26. **Quantitative data** are in "Number of Graduates of Fordham University School of Law During the Following Years: 1908–1960," FLSA; **"single-issue fight for suffrage,"** Hoff, *Law, Gender & Injustice*, 182, 202–3. **Regarding ethnic cultures**, Irish

women in New York City who were college educated tended to become school teachers and nurses. In 1900, the daughters of Irish immigrants who taught in the public schools exceeded the combined total of female teachers who were descendants of English and German parents; one-fifth of New York City's public school teachers were the daughters of Irishmen who had been born in Ireland. This does not include the women who entered religious orders. Lawrence J. McCaffrey, "Overview: Forging Forward and Looking Back," in *The New York Irish,* ed. Ronald H. Bayor and Timothy J. Meagher (Baltimore: The Johns Hopkins University Press, 1996), 213, 230–31.

27. *Fordham Monthly* 40 (October 1921): 56; *Fordham Monthly* 40 (November 1921): 129; *Fordham Monthly* 40 (June 1922): 650.

28. **The source of the data on graduation rates** is the *Fordham University Bulletin of Information,* which lists students in each class by year and those who graduate each year. Graduation rates were derived by counting the number of students in an academic year's entering class and comparing that number to the number of students who graduated three years later. However, see *The Women of Fordham Law, 1918–19 to 1993–94,* 5, which claims that "three-quarters of the women entrants did not survive through graduation was not especially remarkable; two-thirds of men didn't make it either." The data clearly contradicts this statement.

29. "Georgetown University: A Mostly White Enclave in a Black City," *The Journal of Blacks in Higher Education,* No. 35 (Spring 2002): 54–57; Jervis Anderson, *This Was Harlem: A Cultural Portrait, 1900–1950* (New York: Farrar Straus Giroux, 1981), 108; Martin Duberman, *Paul Robeson: A Biography* (New York: The New Press, 1989), 20–22, 32, 53–54.

30. J. Clay Smith Jr., *Emancipation: The Making of the Black Lawyer, 1844–1944* (Philadelphia: University of Pennsylvania Press, 1993), 402, 405.

31. **On Ruth Whitehead Whaley,** see *New York Times,* December 25, 1977; *New York Times,* August 11, 1948; *The Women of Fordham Law,* 6; **on Oliver D. Williams,** see "Negro Wins Fordham Scholarship," *New York Times,* April 8, 1924; "The Judicial Candidates: II," *New York Times,* November 1, 1963; "Democrats Gain Judicial Sweep," *New York Times,* November 6, 1963. See also "Nominees' Color Discounted Here," *New York Times,* November 8, 1963. Williams was the third African-American to be elected to the State Supreme Court.

32. "Garvan Heads Law School," *New York Times,* April 7, 1919.

33. There is no biography of Francis Garvan. Information about his life, family, and career was assembled from several sources. See, for example, "New Dean for Law School," *Fordham Monthly* 37 (April 1919): 172; "Garvan Heads Law School," *New York Times,* April 7, 1919; "Francis P. Garvan, Lawyer, Dies Here," *New York Times,* November 8, 1937; "Frances P. Garvan," *New York Times,* November 9, 1937. **Quotations relating to Jerome** are in "Jerome Dies at 74; Long Tammany Foe," *New York Times,* February 14, 1934.

34. **"one of Hartford's,"** "Patrick Garvan Dead," *New York Times*, September 23, 1912; **on Garvan's family**, see "Garvan Dies After Blood Transfusion," *New York Times*, March 5, 1910; "F. P. Garvan to Wed," *New York Times*, March 28, 1910; "Francis P. Garvan, Lawyer, Dies Here," *New York Times*, November 8, 1937; "John S. Garvan, 73, Dies," *New York Times*, March 20, 1954. **Brady's investments and financial affairs** are discussed with some detail in "Brady's Fortune May Be $1,000,000,000," *New York Times*, August 6, 1913; see also, "A. N. Brady's Death Was Kept Secret," *New York Times*, July 24, 1913; "Told of Big Losses Suffered by Brady," *New York Times*, November 22, 1914. The monetary conversions are approximated according to the CPI, http://www.measuringworth.com/uscompare.

35. **On Brady**, see "A. N. Brady as a Financier," *New York Times*, July 24, 1913; **on Garvan inheritance**, see "Told of Big Losses Suffered by Brady," *New York Times*, November 22, 1914; "Fordham Gets $260,369," *New York Times*, January 30, 1921; "Buys Old Colonial House," *New York Times*, February 12, 1919.

36. Robert I. Gannon, *Up to the Present: The Story of Fordham* (New York: Doubleday, 1967), 160. The monetary conversion is approximated according to the CPI, http://www.measuringworth.com/uscompare.

37. **On A. Mitchell Palmer's activities as alien property custodian**, see "Nation Gets Ehret Property," *New York Times*, May 4, 1918; "German Chemical Plant is Seized," *New York Times*, July 30, 1918; "Tribute From Cummings," *New York Times*, May 12, 1936; "4,500 German Dye Patents Available," *New York Times*, March 12, 1919.

38. "Garvan Succeeds Palmer," *New York Times*, March 4, 1919; "Palmer is Sworn in," *New York Times*, March 6, 1919.

39. U.S. v. Chemical Foundation, Inc., 272 U.S. 1, 14 (1926); "Dye Sales Stand; Government Loses," *New York Times*, October 12, 1926. **The lower court decisions** are reported in U.S. v. Chemical Foundation, Inc., 5 F.2d 191 (3rd Cir. 1925); United States v. Chemical Foundation, Inc., 294 F. 300 (D. Del. 1924). See also "Dye Patents Hearing Set," *New York Times*, October 7, 1924; "Dismiss Dyes Suit, Clearing Garvan," *New York Times*, March 27, 1925. See also, "Seeks to Question Custodian Garvan," *New York Times*, July 12, 1919; "Washington, June 21," *New York Times*, June 22, 1919; "Assails Garvan, Attacks Palmer," *New York Times*, June 22, 1919; "Must Give Up Alien Funds," *New York Times*, August 1, 1919; "Palmer Vindicated in Alien Seizure," *New York Times*, April 22, 1920.

40. **On Garvan appointment as director of investigations**, "Garvan Succeeds Palmer," *New York Times*, March 4, 1919; **appointment as assistant attorney general**, "Francis P. Garvan Promoted to Assistant Attorney General," *New York Times*, June 3, 1919; **on the "Red Scare,"** see Robert K. Murray, *Red Scare: A Study in National Hysteria, 1919–1920* (New York: McGraw-Hill, 1964); **on Murray's discussion of the Seattle strike**, see ibid., 64–68. **The Wilson administration's repression of civil liberties**

during World War I is vividly recounted in Paul L. Murphy, *World War I and the Origin of Civil Liberties in the United States* (New York: W. W. Norton & Company, 1979); Harry N. Scheiber, *The Wilson Administration and Civil Liberties* (Ithaca, N.Y.: Cornell University Press, 1960); Zechariah Chafee Jr., *Free Speech in the United States* (Cambridge: Harvard University Press, 1941). See also Geoffrey R. Stone, *Perilous Times: Free Speech in Wartime* (New York: W. W. Norton, 2004), 135–234; David M. Rabban, *Free Speech in Its Forgotten Years* (New York: Cambridge University Press, 1997), 248–341.

41. Murray, *Red Scare*, 68–72.

42. Murray, *Red Scare*, 71–72, quoting the *New York Times*, May 1, 1919; the *Atlanta Constitution*, May 1, 1919; the *San Francisco Examiner*, May 1, 1919; the *Chicago Tribune*, May 1, 1919; and the *Salt Lake Tribune*, May 2, 1919.

43. Murray, *Red Scare*, 73–77, quoting the *Salt Lake Tribune*, May 3, 1919; and the *Washington Post*, May 3, 1919.

44. Murray, *Red Scare*, 77–80, quoting the *Salt Lake Tribune*, June 3, 1919; the *San Francisco Examiner*, June 3, 1919; and the *Atlanta Constitution*, June 3, 1919.

45. Murray, *Red Scare*, 82–104.

46. **On Garvin appointment as assistant attorney general**, "Francis P. Garvan Promoted to Assistant Attorney General," *New York Times*, June 3, 1919; **on federal, state, and local cooperation**, see "Unite For Action on Bomb Plotters," *id.*, June 7, 1919; Murray, *Red Scare*, 73; **on Lusk Committee**, see Todd J. Pfannestiel, *Rethinking the Red Scare: The Lusk Committee and New York's Crusade Against Radicalism, 1919–1923* (London and New York: Routledge, 2003).

47. **"Convinced that the nation," "took steps which,"** "Flynn to Direct Search for Reds," *New York Times*, June 4, 1919; **"general supervision,"** and **the reorganization of the Bureau of Investigation**, see "Palmer Recasts Force of Helpers," *New York Times*, July 17, 1919; "Flynn to Direct Search for Reds," *New York Times*, June 4, 1919; **on enlisting aid of local police**, see "Unite For Action on Bomb Plotters," June 9, 1919; "Urges Police to Co-Operate," ibid.; **on joint effort**, see "Plan Bolshevist Inquiry," *New York Times*, June 10, 1919; "Bomb Views of Radicals," *New York Times*, October 3, 1920. **On Emma Goldman**, see her autobiography, *Living My Life* (New York: Alfred A. Knopf, 1931). There are many biographies of Goldman. See, for example, John Chalberg, *Emma Goldman: American Individualist* (New York: Harper Collins Publishers, 1991); Richard Drinnon, *Rebel in Paradise: A Biography of Emma Goldman* (Chicago: University of Chicago Press, 1961). **On the Red Scare in New York**, see Pfannestiel, *Rethinking the Red Scare*.

48. "Eliot and Carnegie Scored at Dinner . . . No Doctrinal Training." *New York Times*, February 4, 1914.

49. Thomas McAvoy, *Roman Catholocism and the American Way of Life* (Notre Dame: University of Notre Dame Press, 1960), 74; John T. McGreevy, *Catholicism and American Freedom* (New York: W. W. Norton & Company, 2003), 142–45.

50. **All quotations** are in "Want Law Schools to Bar Socialists, Movement is Begun in New York State Association of Legal Instructors," *New York Times*, April 4, 1920. The *New York Call* was a daily socialist newspaper founded in 1908. It lost its mailing privileges under the Espionage Act of 1917, and after additional attention from government agents, it finally closed down in 1923. *Encyclopedia of New York City*, "Newspapers," 813.

51. *Fordham Monthly* 35 (October 1916): 51.

52. *The First 125 Years: An Illustrated History of Georgetown University Law Center*, 88–89.

53. The Red Mass dates to the middle of the thirteenth century and is celebrated annually in the Catholic Church for judges, prosecutors, attorneys, government officials, law professors, and law students. It requests guidance for all who seek justice and provides a time to reflect on the divinely ordained power and responsibility of the legal profession.

54. **On organization of the St. Thomas Acquinas Law School Sodality**, see *Fordham Monthly* 40 (January 1922): 270; **on Glennon's speech**, *Fordham Monthly* 40 (February 1922): 342.

55. **Third Communion Breakfast, first annual retreat**, and **quotations**, *Fordham Monthly* 40 (June 1922): 650; *Fordham Monthly* 40 (May 1922): 569; *Fordham Monthly*, 40 (June 1922): 650; **quotations** are in *Fordham Monthly* 41 (March 1923): 385; *Fordham Monthly* 41 (April 1923): 454; *Fordham Monthly* 42 (January 1924): 287; *Fordham Monthly* 42 (December 1923): 210.

56. The Honorable Malcolm Wilson, interview by Robert Cooper Jr., March 14, 1989, Transcript No. 45, Book 3, 10, Oral History Project, FLSA (hereafter cited as OHP, FLSA).

57. *Woodstock Letters* 36 (1907): 387.

58. **For discriminatory practices among elite universities and law schools**, *see* Marcia Graham Synnott, *The Half-Opened Door: Discrimination and Admissions at Harvard, Yale, and Princeton, 1900–1970* (Westport: Greenwood Press, 1979); Jerold S. Auerbach, *Unequal Justice: Lawyers and Social Change in Modern America* (New York: Oxford University Press, 1976).

59. The Honorable Louis J. Lefkowitz, interview by Robert H. Cooper Jr., March 3, 1989, Transcript No. 42, Book 2, 13–15, OHP, FLSA.

60. Louis Stein, interview by Robert Cooper Jr., October 25, 1990, Transcript No. 139, Book 3, 1–2, OHP, FLSA. Mary C. Daly, interview by Deborah S. Gardner, November 14, 2001, 11, Fordham University Law School Oral History Project, 2003, FLSA.

61. See *Fordham University Bulletin of Information*, 1906–23 for St. John's College, the School of Social Service and the School of Law.

62. *Fordham University Bulletin of Information*, 1914–23.

63. Forty-eight applications were randomly selected from each entering class. This number yielded a margin of error of plus or minus 9 percent, on average, but this margin fluctuated according to fluctuations in the number of students in each entering class. The margin of error ranged from a low of 7.68 percent to a high of 14.52 percent. After collecting and analyzing the results on a year-to-year basis, we aggregated the data in five-year clusters to make more vivid any trends they revealed. The five-year aggregates are: 1925–29, 1930–34, 1935–39, 1940–44, and 1945–47. We again sampled forty-eight applications from each entering class from 1948 to 1968. The margin of error fluctuated from year to year between 10.25 percent and 11.89 percent, according to the size of the entering class. We also aggregated these yearly data into five-year clusters: 1948–52, 1953–57, 1958–62, and 1963–68.

64. Data are in an Excel spreadsheet file titled "Ethnicity and Religion by Countries of Origin Totals: Period Totals," on file with the author.

65. Data are based on worksheet titled "Ethnicity and Religion by Countries of Origin Totals: Foreign Born Totals."

66. Ibid.

67. As is, the margins of error for each division are much higher than those for the entire entering classes. For example, the margins of error for the morning division ranged between 13.91 percent (1945) to a high of 21.93 percent (1946); for the afternoon division, it ranged between 16.30 percent and 27.25 percent; and for the evening division it ranged between 11.17 percent and 21.16 percent.

68. The margin of error for these data relating to the entire student body is approximately 11 percent. The margin of error for each division is higher. For the morning division A, the margin of error ranged from a low of 18.97 percent (1965) to a high of 22.27 percent (1952). For figures collected in the afternoon division B, the margin of error ranged from a low of 16.81 percent (1964) to a high of 22.26 percent (1957). For figures collected in the evening division, the margin of error ranged from a low of 18.34 percent (1959) to a high of 24.46 percent (1966).

69. Stevens, *History of Legal Education*, 127–28n34.

70. Students attempted to revive the law review in 1922. They went so far as to elect officers, but the effort failed when the students recognized the need for subscriptions before publication could begin. *Fordham Monthly* 41 (January 1923): 247–48.

71. *Fordham Monthly* 40 (March 1922): 414; *Fordham Monthly* 41 (December 1923): 188.

72. *Fordham Monthly* 24 (March 1906): 264; *Fordham Monthly* 27 (December 1908): 207; *Fordham Monthly* 28 (December 1909): 207; *Fordham Monthly* 28 (May 1909): 555; *Fordham Monthly* 29 (January 1910): 213, 215; **on Berrigan**, see "Berrigan Fordham Baseball Captain," *New York Times*, June 7, 1915; **on students in sports**, see "Fordham on the Gridiron," *New York Times*, September 17, 1913; "After Law School Men," *New*

York Times, March 15, 1916; "Committee to Aid Fordham Team," *New York Times*, October 17, 1915; "Joseph Higgins to Enter Fordham," *New York Times*, September 20, 1916; **on students dropped**, see *New York Times*, January 10, 1915; "Fordham Dismisses Three Athletes," *New York Times*, March 14, 1915; Class of 1925, **a hitherto unattempted innovation**, *Fordham Monthly* 41 (February 1923): 320.

73. *Fordham Monthly* 28 (January 1910): 3, 214–15; *Fordham Monthly* 41 (January 1923): 250.

CHAPTER THREE: THE QUEST FOR EXCELLENCE
IN AN ERA OF BIGOTRY

1. **Biographical information on Ignatius M. Wilkinson** compiled from Fordham Law publications: "In Memoriam: Ignatius M. Wilkinson, 1887–1953," *Fordham Law Review* 22 (1953): 232; Dean's Report to the Alumni, 1985–1986, 14, folder Dean's Reports 1971–1989, box 24, Fordham Law School Papers (hereinafter cited as FLS), Walsh Library, Fordham University (hereinafter cited as FU); and *Fordham University School of Law: 90th Anniversary Celebration* (1995), 4–6. See also "Dean Wilkinson of Fordham Dies," *New York Times*, June 23, 1953, and numerous other articles in the *Times*. Dean Wilkinson ended his work in the law firm in 1931.

2. "Registration by Years Since the Foundation of the School," notebook, Fordham Law School Archives (hereafter cited as FLSA). **On national trends in law school enrollments**, see Alfred Z. Reed, *Present-Day Law Schools in the United States and Canada* (New York: The Carnegie Foundation for the Advancement of Teaching, 1928), Appendix I, 530; Richard L. Abel, *American Lawyers* (New York: Oxford University Press, 1989), 277–78, Table 21.

3. Abel, *American Lawyers*, 277–78, Table 21 and 280, Table 22.

4. Ibid., 254, Table 5 and 54; Robert Stevens, *Law School: Legal Education in America from the 1850s to the 1980s* (Chapel Hill: The University of North Carolina Press, 1983), 79.

5. Stevens, *History of Legal Education*, 173–74.

6. Abel, *American Lawyers*, 254 and 54; Stevens, *History of Legal Education,* 79.

7. Abel, *American Lawyers*, 85–86, 109; Stevens, *History of Legal Education,* 176; Jerome E. Carlin, *Lawyers on Their Own* (New Brunswick, N.J.: Rutgers University Press, 1962), 22n27; Jerome E. Carlin, *Lawyers' Ethics* (New York: Russell Sage Foundation, 1966), 21.

8. This discussion of the sources and nature of bigotry and the Ku Klux Klan in the 1920s relies most heavily on Paul L. Murphy, "Sources and Nature of Intolerance in the 1920's," *The Journal of American History* LI (June 1964): 60–76. For a detailed history of the Ku Klux Klan in this period, see David M. Chalmers, *Hooded Americanism: The History of the Ku Klux Klan*, 2nd ed. (New York: New Viewpoints, 1981).

9. Murphy, "Sources and Nature of Intolerance in the 1920s," 69.

10. **"Quiet 'consensus of the 1920s,'"** ibid., 69; **"In exploiting"** and **"harped on,"** Emma Lou Thornbrough, "Segregation in Indiana during the Klan Era of the 1920's," *The Mississippi Valley Historical Review* 48 (March 1961): 610; John Higham, *Strangers in the Land: Patterns of American Nativism 1860–1925* (New York: Atheneum, 1968), 290–99.

11. Higham, *Strangers in the Land*, 310–12, 320–24.

12. Murphy, "Sources and Nature of Intolerance in the 1920's," 60–76; Thornbrough, "Segregation in Indiana during the Klan Era of the 1920's," 594–618; Higham, *Strangers in the Land*, 290–99.

13. **"crippling political disability,"** Virginia Kays Veenswijk, *Coudert Brothers, A Legacy in Law: The History of America's First International Law Firm, 1853–1993* (New York: Truman Talley Books/Dutton, 1994), 79, 81, 90–93; **"so abhorrent,"** Oscar Handlin, *Al Smith and His America* (Boston: Little, Brown and Company, 1958), 125; **"the dark secret prejudice,"** and **"anti-Catholicism,"** ibid., 131; **"to pander to the mood,"** ibid., 129; **"to pretend that he was not,"** ibid., 130; **"Catholics face no conflict,"** ibid., 131; **"The farmer and the small-town merchant,"** ibid., 132.

14. **"enemy capital,"** Chalmers, *Hooded Americanism*, 254; **"If Americans,"** Handlin, *Al Smith's America*, 135; *Fordham Monthly* 41 (October 1922): 60. **For the Klan in New York and national presidential campaign**, see Handlin, *Al Smith's America*, 118–36; Chalmers, *Hooded Americanism*, 254–65, 300–3; and Robert A. Caro, *The Powerbroker: Robert Moses and the Fall of New York* (New York: Vintage Books, 1975), 148, 199, 201.

15. Stevens, *History of Legal Education*, 172–73.

16. Ibid., 174–77.

17. Ibid., 177.

18. Abel, *American Lawyers*, 176, 178.

19. Ibid., 180, 190n77; see also 55, 72, 254, Table 5 and 278, Table 21.

20. Ibid., 55, 72, 254, Table 5 and 278, Table 21.

21. Ibid., 72, 254, Table 5; **quotations** are in Dean's Report, January 1, 1929, 10, folder 2, box 11, FLS, FU.

22. Abel, *American Lawyers*, 281, Table 23.

23. **On limiting bar admission to citizens**, see Abel, *American Lawyers*, 68, 72; see also Jerold J. Auerbach, "Enmity and Amity: Law Teachers and Practitioners, 1900–1922," in *Law in American History*, ed. Donald Fleming and Bernard Bailyn, (5 Perspectives in American History, Boston: Little Brown, 1971), 585. The Supreme Court struck down this practice in In re Griffiths, 413 U.S. 717 (1973). **On state residency requirements**, see Abel, *American Lawyers*, 68–9; Allan Ashman, "Residency Requirements for Admission to the Bar: Gordon and its Progeny," *American Bar Association Journal* 71 (March 1985): 64–7. The case voiding residency requirements is Supreme Court of New Hampshire v. Piper, 470 U.S. 274 (1985).

24. **On test for fitness and character**, see Abel, *American Lawyer*, 69–70; see also Deborah L. Rhode, "Moral Character as a Professional Credential," *Yale Law Journal* 94 (January 1985): 491, 499, 501, 515, 520–22, 530–36; Deborah L. Rhode, "Ethical Perspectives on Legal Practice," *Stanford Law Review* 37 (January 1985): 589.

25. **"diverting some lawyers,"** New York County Lawyers' Association Committee on Professional Economics, *Survey of the Legal Profession in New York County* (New York: New York County Lawyers' Association, 1936), 60; **Offices of registers and county clerks,** and **"office of public defender,"** ibid., 64; **" 'clients' . . . be furnished,"** ibid., 65.

26. **All quotations** are in ibid., 60–61.

27. Abel, *American Lawyers*, 85–86.

28. Ibid.

29. Ibid., 88–111.

30. The Honorable Malcolm Wilson, interview by Robert Cooper Jr., March 14, 1989, Transcript No. 45, Book 3, 4, Oral History Project, Fordham Law School Archives (hereafter cited as OHP, FLSA).

31. The Honorable Louis J. Lefkowitz, interview by Robert H. Cooper Jr., March 3, 1989, Transcript No. 42, Book 2, 1–5, OHP, FLSA.

32. George A. Brooks, interview by Robert Reilly, December 5, 1988, Transcript No. 34, Book 1, 18, OHP, FLSA.

33. Gannon, *Up to the Present*, 161, 177.

34. **Quotations from Wilkinson's report** are in Gannon, *Up to the Present*, 18–19. Fordham Law School's educational requirements for admission are stated in the *Fordham University Bulletin of Information* (1922–23): 9; ibid. (1923–24): 9; ibid. (1924–25): 9; ibid. (1925–26): 7; ibid. (1926–27): 6; ibid. (1927–28): 6. See also Dean's Report, January 11, 1929, 1, folder 3, box 11, Fordham Law School Papers, Walsh Library, Fordham University (hereafter cited as FLS, FU). **For Professor Wigmore's study**, see Abel, *American Lawyers*, 47. **For the nature of acceptable college credit and bachelor degrees**, see Charles J. Deane, S.J., to Ignatius M. Wilkinson, July 27, 1932; Dean to Father Deane, July 29, 1932; Deane to Wilkinson, July 30, 1932, folder 1, box 10, FLS, FU.

35. **Wilkinson's data and estimated effects of the two-year college rule** are in Dean's Report, December 10, 1925, 20–25, folder 1, box 11, FLS, FU; **"a fair profit,"** ibid., 24; **"that the present rush,"** ibid., 25. The law school increased tuition from $150 to $180 per year in September, 1923. *Fordham University Bulletin of Information* (1923–24): 11. Following Wilkinson's cautionary hypothetical, the Law School raised tuition from $180 to $200 in September 1926. It also raised the matriculation fee and university fee from $5 to $10 each. Ibid. (1926–27): 10.

36. Dean's Report, December 10, 1925, 18–19, folder 1, box 11, FLS, FU; Alfred Z. Reed, *Present-Day Law Schools in the United States and Canada* (New York: The Carnegie Foundation for the Advancement of Teaching, 1928), 135. The AALS followed the

ABA's lead and resolved that member law schools require one year of college beginning in 1923 and two years of college beginning in 1925. Ibid. **On Columbia Law School**, see Julius Goebel Jr., *A History of the School of Law Columbia University* (New York: Columbia University Press, 1955), 187, 233–34.

37. Dean's Report, January 11, 1929, 2–3, folder 2, box 11, FLS, FU.

38. Ibid., 1.

39. **"a good augury,"** ibid., 2. See Table 3-1 for details.

40. As Wilkinson predicted, Brooklyn, St. John's, and New York University law schools suffered the greatest enrollment declines between 1929 and 1931: over 50 percent (Brooklyn), about 44 percent (St. John's), and just under 65 percent (New York University). The effect of the college requirement on NYU's enrollments is unclear. It did experience a drop in enrollments of almost 17 percent in these years, but the decline was probably attributable more to discontinuing its afternoon division and its Bronx evening division and to extending its night school from three years to four years for students admitted after 1929. Dean's Report, January 11, 1929, 5–6, folder 2, box 11, FLS, FU; Dean's Report, February 20, 1930, 2–3, 4–5, folder 3, box 11, FLS, FU; Dean's Report, January 28, 1932, 4–5, folder 3, box 11, FLS, FU. **On Columbia Law School's selective admission policy**, Goebel Jr., *History of the Law School*, 234–35.

41. Dean's Report, February 20, 1930, 3–4, folder 3, box 11, FLS, FU.

42. William Hughes Mulligan, interview by Michael Sheahan, September 20, 1988, Transcript No. 22, Book 3, 5, OHP, FLSA; Caesar L. Pitassy, interview by Robert Cooper Jr., May 18, 1989, Transcript No. 56, Book 3, 10, OHP, FLSA; Joseph W. McGovern, Esq., interview by Robert Cooper Jr., April 3, 1989, Transcript No. 49, Book 2, 32, OHP, FLSA.

43. Dean's Report, December 10, 1925, 1, folder 1, box 11, FLS, FU.

44. William Hughes Mulligan, interview, 14.

45. **"old and dilapidated,"** and **"caused difficulty,"** Dean's Report, December 10, 1925, 2–5, folder 1, box 11, FLS, FU; **structural changes** are reported in ibid.; **"In class you,"** and **"if you were,"** George A. Brooks, interview by Robert Reilly, December 5, 1988, Transcript No. 34, Book 1, 19, OHP, FLSA.

46. Dean's Report, January 11, 1929, 7–9, folder 2, box 11, FLS, FU.

47. The biology building was named after Reverend John Larkin, S.J., president of Fordham University from 1851 to 1854; see Schroth, *Fordham: A History and Memoir*, 28; **"a heavy number," "But, no matter," "I would say,"** William Hughes Mulligan, interview, 3.

48. "A distinct scholastic improvement," Dean's Report, December 10, 1925, 17, folder 1, box 11, FLS, FU; **on hiring of McGivney, et al.**, see ibid. **Enrollments and additional faculty hires**, Dean's Report, December 11, 1929, 9, folder 3, box 11, FLS, FU; **"quite a strain"** and **"seems now,"** ibid.; **"He took attendance,"** Joseph W.

McGovern, Esq., interview, 4; **Meagher and other faculty,** ibid., 12–13, 19; Donald M. Dunn, Esq., interview by Robert Cooper, Jr., May 9, 1989, Transcript No. 54, Book 1, 5–6, OHP, FLSA.

49. Joseph W. McGovern, Esq., interview, 4; **on smoking in class,** Dean to Reverend Charles J. Deane, S.J., November 10, 1926; Father Deane to Wilkinson, March 11, 1931; Dean to Father Deane, March 12, 1931; Dean to Father Deane, March 16, 1931; Dean to Father Deane, March 25, 1931, folder 1, box 10, FLS, FU.

50. **"modest library,"** Joseph W. McGovern, Esq., interview, 5; **"terrific," "dramatic, dramatic,"** ibid., 12; **"Mostly Socratic,"** ibid., 13; **"I always thought,"** ibid., 24; **"a geat teacher,"** George A. Brooks, interview, 22.

51. **"you could get"** and **"maybe fifteen,"** Joseph W. McGovern, Esq., interview, 9; **"just a nice touch,"** ibid., 11; see also ibid., 7, 34–35.

52. Caesar L. Pitassy, interview by Robert Cooper Jr., May 18, 1989, Transcript No. 56, Book 3, 6, 9 OHP, FLSA; Dennis McInerney, Esq., interview by Robert Cooper Jr., May 1, 1989, Transcript No. 51, Book 2, 11, OHP, FLSA; **"I don't think,"** Joseph W. McGovern, Esq., interview, 6; Richard J. Bennett, interview, by Robert Cooper Jr., May 11, 1989, Transcript No. 55, Book 1, 20–21, OHP, FLSA.

53. **On collegiality and law students' attire,** see Dean's Report, 1936, 15–16, folder 6, box 11, FLS, FU; Dean's Report, 1938, 15, folder 7, box 11, FLS, FU; **on Blake, "and recite the case," "He was less inclined,"** Caesar L. Pitassy, interview, 10–11, 26; **McGovern quotations** are in Joseph W. McGovern, Esq., interview, 22–23, 32–33; **on faculty law office,** see Thomas L. J. Corcoran to Ignatius M. Wilkinson, January 13, 1934, folder 2, box 12, FLS, FU; **independent bar review** courses are in Francis X. Carmody to Ignatius M. Wilkinson, November 28, 1924, folder 1, box 12, FLS, FU. See also "Judge Loughran Dies at Age of 64; Chief of State' Appeals Court Named to Bench by Lehman in 1934—Head Since 1945," *New York Times,* April 1, 1953, 29.

54. Joseph W. McGovern, Esq., interview, 14–15; The Honorable Louis J. Lefkowitz, interview by Robert Cooper Jr., March 3, 1989, Transcript No. 42, Book 2, 3–5, OHP, FLSA.

55. Dean's Report, December 10, 1925, 11, 13–17, folder 1, box 11, FLS, FU.

56. George A. Brooks, interview, 57.

57. **"clean their records,"** Faculty Meeting of June 8, 1922, 44, FLSA; **"not apply to Third Year,"** ibid.

58. Faculty Meeting of June 7, 1923, 46–47, FLSA; Faculty Meeting of June 5, 1924, 48–49, FLSA; Faculty Meeting of June 5, 1925, 50–51, FLSA.

59. **Quotations** are in Dean's Report, December 10, 1925, 6, folder 1 Box 11, 6, FLS, FU.

60. **"drastic and might operate,"** and **"eliminate a lot of dead wood,"** ibid.; **policy on failed examinations** is Exhibit A, attached to ibid.

61. Faculty Meeting of June 5, 1925, 51, FLSA.

62. **Numbers of failed students**: fourteen in 1926, Faculty Meeting of June 16, 1926, 52–53; thirty-one in 1927, Faculty Meeting of June 9, 1927, 55–56; twenty-two in 1928, Faculty Meeting of June 7, 1928, 58–60; fourteen in 1929, Faculty Meeting of June 6, 1929, 62–63; nine in 1930, Faculty Meeting of June 5, 1930, 66; **for the September 1928 rule change**, Dean's Report, January 11, 1929, 5, folder 2, box 11, FLS, FU.

63. Dean's Report, December 10, 1925, 6, folder 1, box 11, FLS, FU

64. **"you are warned,"** Exhibit B attached to Dean's Report, December 10, 1925, folder 1, box 11, FLS, FU; **"will be reasonably certain,"** and **"a tonic effect,"** Dean's Report, December 10, 1925, 7.

65. **"improving the scholastic standards,"** Dean's Report, January 11, 1929, 5, folder 2, box 11, FLS, FU; **"a weighted average,"** Dean's Report, January 28, 1932, 6–7 folder 4, box 11, FLS, FU; **"run into serious scholastic difficulty,"** Exhibit C: Ignatius M. Wilkinson to the Reverend Charles J. Deane, S.J., October 7, 1931, attached in ibid.

66. Wilkinson to Reverend Laurence J. McGinley, April 22, 1949, folder 6, box 10, FLS, FU.

67. **"absence from three,"** Dean's Report, December 10, 1925, 8, folder 1, box 11, FLS, FU; **"will be deemed,"** Exhibit C: Rules Regulating Students' Attendance, attached to ibid.

68. **"death in the student's immediate family,"** Dean's Report, December 10, 1925, 8, folder 1, box 11, FLS, FU; Exhibit C: Rules Regulating Students' Attendance, attached to ibid.; **"in good faith,"** Wilkinson to Reverend Laurence J. McGinley, April 22, 1949, folder 6, box 10, FLS, FU.

69. Caesar L. Pitassy, interview, 11.

70. Exhibit C: Ignatius M. Wilkinson to the Reverend Charles J. Deane, S.J., Fordham University, October 7, 1931 attached in Dean's Report, January 28, 1932, 6–7, folder 4, box 11, FLS, FU. Dean Wilkinson made no exceptions to the rule that prohibited students who failed to maintain "the required average for promotion" at another law school to transfer to Fordham. Ignatius M. Wilkinson to the Reverend Robert I. Gannon, September 9, 1940, folder 2, box 10, FLS, FU.

71. Dean's Report, January 28, 1932, 12, folder 4, box 11, FLS, FU. The precise starting date is in the first Placement Bureau Report, July 31, 1931, folder 1, box 12, FLS, FU.

72. **"was very simple, "would try to farm them out," "A fellow would,"** George A. Brooks, interview, 30; **"Anybody that needed,"** ibid., 33.

73. George A. Brooks to Ignatius W. Wilkinson, July 31, 1931, folder 1, box 12, FLS, FU; Dean's Report, January 28, 1932, 13, folder 4, box 11, FLS, FU.

74. **"racial and financial reasons,"** George A. Brooks to Ignatius W. Wilkinson, July 31, 1931, folder 1, box 12, FLS, FU; **"exceedingly difficult,"** Dean's Report, May 15, 1934, 19, folder 5, box 11, FLS, FU.

75. Report on the Placement Bureau for the Year 1932–33, folder 11, box 11, FLS, FU.

76. Ibid.

77. Joseph W. McGovern, Esq., interview, 9. Fifteen dollars in 1933 is approximately $248 in present-day dollars; $25 in 1933 is approximately $414 today. The monetary conversion is approximated according to the Consumer Price Index (hereinafter cited as CPI) and was calculated at http://www.measuringworth.com/uscompare.

78. Dean's Report, February 17, 1936, 18, folder, 6, box 11, FLS, FU.

79. Albert J. Clark to Reverend Robert J. Gannon, January 31, 1939, folder 9, box 10, FLS, FU.

80. Ibid.

81. Dean's Report, December 10, 1925, 13, folder 1, box 11, FLS, FU.

82. **"a reasonably active,"** and **"band them together,"** ibid., 12–13; Herbert Mitgang, *The Man Who Rode the Tiger: The Life of Judge Samuel Seabury and the Story of the Greatest Investigation of City Corruption in This Century* (New York: The Viking Press, 1970), 175; **"the biggest investigation,"** ibid., vii.

83. **"On it practically hinges,"** Dean's Report, January 11, 1929, 6, folder 2, box 11, FLS, FU; **"the more important law schools,"** and **"of the utmost importance,"** ibid., 7.

84. Dean's Report, May 15, 1934, 17–18, folder 5, box 11, FLS, FU.

85. **"lapsed into,"** Dean Wilkinson to Gannon, May 14, 1948, folder 5, box 10 FLS, FU. Wilkinson referred to the "moribund Law Alumni Association" in this letter. Dean's Report, February 20, 1930, 5–6, folder 3, box 11, FLS, FU; January 28, 1932, 8–9, folder 4, box 11; May 15, 1934, 17–18, folder 5, box 11; February 17, 1936, 17, folder 6, box 11; February 28, 1938, 16, folder 7, box 11; April 3, 1940, 20–21, folder 8, box 11; Walter B. Kennedy to Rev. Robert I. Gannon, December 6, 1944, folder 3, box 10, FLS, FU.

86. Dean Wilkinson did not explain what determined who received the maximum and minimum salaries, but it was probably based on years of service. The figures are in Dean's Report, December 19, 1925, 10. The ranges of salaries in 1925 converted to present-day values are as follows: $300–350 = $3,670–4,280; $400–450 = $4,900–5,510; $500–600 = $6,120–7,340. Skilled labor wages of $3,000–4,000 in 1925 are equivalent to $36,700–49,900 in 2009 (see CPI, http://www.measuringworth.com/uscompare).

87. Dean's Report, Feb. 28, 1938, 17, folder 7, box 11, FLS, FU; Wilkinson to Edward Gilleran, February 7, 1938, folder 9, Box 10, FLS, FU; "A Dean at Fordham," *New York Times*, December 31, 1945; *Fordham University Bulletin of Information: School of Law* (1923–24): 17; Dean's Report, February 20, 1930, 6, folder 3, box 11, FLS. FU; Dean's Report, January 11, 1929, folder 2, box 11, ibid.

88. William Hughes Mulligan, interview, 13. **Loughren resignation** is in Dean's Report January 28, 1932, 9, folder 4, box 11, FLS, FU.

89. Dean's Report, December 10, 1925, 17, folder 1, box 11, FLS, FU; Wilkinson to President Charles J. Deane, March 25, 1931, folder 1, box 10, FLS, FU; Wilkinson to Reverend Dean, January 27, 1927, folder 1, box 10, ibid. Wilkinson to Reverend Deane, July 12, 1927, folder 1, box 10, ibid.; **On Crater's resignation**, see Dean's Report, January 11, 1929, folder 2, box 11, ibid.; Dean's Report, May 15, 1934, 18, folder 5, box 11, ibid. **"a playboy judge,"** and **"cashed two checks,"** William Safire, "Where is Judge Crater?" *New York Times*, Thursday, July 12, 2001; **"voluntarily disappeared,"** George A. Brooks, interview, 30; see also "Aide Denies Crater Destroyed Papers; Hunt is Pressed," *New York Times*, September 5, 1930.

CHAPTER FOUR: THE GREAT DEPRESSION
AND EDUCATIONAL REFORM

1. **"these schools,"** "Connecticut Bans 3 Law Schools Here," *New York Times*, June 5, 1929; **"as an arbitrary,"** ibid.

2. **Professor Pogson's statements** are in ibid.; on **NYU adopts four-year night program,** see "Says N.Y.U. Changed Law Requirements," *New York Times*, June 6, 1929.

3. "Admission to the Bar," *New York Times*, June 6, 1929.

4. Ibid.

5. Dean's Report, February 20, 1930, 7–8, folder 3, box 11, Fordham Law School Papers, Walsh Library, Fordham University (hereinafter cited as "FLS, FU").

6. **"it would be impracticable,"** "Connecticut Bans 3 Law Schools Here," *New York Times*, June 5, 1929; **"day and night work"** and **"same minimum standards,"** Ignatius M. Wilkinson to the Reverand Charles J. Deane, S.J., October 7, 1931 attached in Dean's Report, January 28, 1932 as Exhibit C; **"day men,"** Dean's Report, January 28, 1932, 18, folder 4, box 11, FLS, FU; **on the New York Court of Appeals minimum requirements,** see Dean's Report, January 28, 1932, 15. Wilkinson did not think the Connecticut decision would affect Fordham Law School's curriculum, "Says N.Y.U. Changed Law Requirement," *New York Times*, June 6, 1929. The Connecticut Bar Examination Committee had approved Fordham's morning and afternoon divisions three years earlier. Wilkinson remarked that its approval "undoubtedly rests on the fact that the hours at which they are conducted stamp them as full time schools." Unfortunately, Fordham offered its two-credit-hour course in Connecticut Practice at 6 P.M. Wilkinson asked the Connecticut Bar Examination Committee whether taking this two-hour course in the evening division "would in any way militate against" a day student who took "thirty-four thirty-sixths of his three year course" in the day school and render him ineligible to sit for the Connecticut Bar Examination. Dean Wilkinson to Joseph L. Melvin, May 20, 1926, folder 1, box 12, FLS, FU. The Committee's reply could not be found. Dean's Report, January 28, 1932, 18.

7. Dean's Report, February 20, 1930, 7–8, folder 3, box 11, FLS, FU.

8. Dean's Report, January 28, 1932, 15–17, folder 4, box 11, FLS, FU.

9. Ibid., 15–19. Wilkinson appended his brief as Exhibit D, *In the Matter of the Rules Relating to Admission to the Bar*, Memorandum on Behalf of Fordham University, School of Law. Wilkinson acknowledged that "the spokesman" for New York University made an argument, and the *New York Times* reported that Cornelius W. Wickersham and George A. Spiegelberg, chairs of the Committees on Legal Education of the Association of the Bar of the City of New York and New York County Lawyers Association were to argue on behalf of the petition along with representatives of the ABA and other law schools in New York State. See "Hears Plea June 5 on Bar Standards," *New York Times*, June 1, 1931.

10. **Quotations** are in *In the Matter of the Petition of the Association of the Bar of the City of New York et al.*, for Amendment of the Rules of the Court of Appeals Relative to the Study of Law, 257 N.Y. 211, 177 N.E. 423 (1931); see also "comprehensive statistics," Dean's Report, January 28, 1932, 19, folder 4, box 11, FLS, FU.

11. Dean's Report, May 15, 1934, 23–24, folder 5, box 11, FLS, FU. See Tables 4-1 and 4-2. Wilkinson thought the 82 percent of evening students who worked at outside jobs was unusually low. In "normal times," 95 percent of "evening men" worked at some occupation during business hours. Conversely, Wilkinson thought the 17.9 percent of evening students who devoted all of their time to their studies was abnormally high, and he attributed this abnormality to the paucity of available jobs due to prevailing "business conditions."

12. Dean's Report, May 15, 1934, 25, folder 5, box 11, FLS, FU. See Table 4-3.

13. **"prevailing practice,"** Survey of Full-time and Part-time Law Students conducted by the Joint Conference on Legal Education, Association of the Bar of the City of New York, June 15, 1935, 11, included in Schedule C in Dean's Report, February 17, 1936, folder 6, box 11, FLS, FU; **"sound in principle,"** ibid., 13.

14. Dean's Report, May 15, 1934, 2–3, folder 5, box 11, FLS, FU; Dean Wilkinson to Very Rev. Aloysius J. Hogan, S.J., October 17, 1933, attached as Exhibit D in Dean's Report, May 15, 1934. The 1934 figures of $95,164 and $237,910 are approximately $1,520,000 and $3,810,000 in present-day dollars, respectively (see CPI, http://www.measuringworth.com/uscompare).

15. **Quotations** are in Dean's Report, May 15, 1934, 2–3, folder 5, box 11, FLS, FU; see also Dean Wilkinson to Very Rev. Aloysius J. Hogan, S.J., October 17, 1933, attached as Exhibit D in Dean's Report, May 15, 1934. The 1935 sums of $200 and $240 are approximately $3,130 and $3750 in present-day dollars (see CPI, http://www.measuringworth.com/uscompare).

16. **Father Hogan's statements** are in Aloysius J. Hogan, S.J., to Ignatius M. Wilkinson, November 17, 1933, attached as Exhibit D in Dean's Report, May 15, 1934, folder 5, box 11, FLS, FU. See note 33 and accompanying text.

17. *In the Matter of the Rules for the Admission of Attorneys and Counselors at Law*, Petition of Fordham University, attached as Exhibit D in Dean's Report, May 15, 1934, folder 5, box 11, FLS, FU. A copy of the Petition is in folder 8, box 14, Fordham Law School Archives (hereafter cited as FLSA).

18. **"requested amendment,"** and **"to the discretion,"** ibid. (emphasis added). See also In the Matter of the Petition of the Association of The Bar of The City of New York et al., for Amendment of the Rules of the Court of Appeals Relative to the Study of Law, 257 N.Y. 211, 177 N.E. 423 (1931); Reply Brief on behalf of St. John's College School of Law, 21.

19. *In the Matter of the Rules for the Admission of Attorneys and Counselors at Law*, Memorandum in Support of Petition of Fordham University for an Amendment to the Rules, n.p., quoting, Memorandum of Law in Support of Petition of the Association of the Bar of the City of New York and the New York County Lawyers' Association, 12–13, attached as Exhibit D in Dean's Report, May 15, 1934, folder 5, box 11, FLS, FU. A copy of the Memorandum of Law is in folder 8, box 14, FLSA.

20. A copy of Judge Cuthbert W. Pound's judgment order is in folder 8, box 14, FLSA. Ignatius M. Wilkinson to Honorable Harlan B. Horner, January 19, 1934, included in Exhibit D in Dean's Report, May 15, 1934, folder 5, box 11, FLS, FU. The amended rule is reprinted in Wilkinson to Horner, January 23, 1934, included in Dean's Report, May 15, 1934. The Education Department's approval was sent in Horner to Wilkinson, Feb. 27, 1934, included in Dean's Report, May 15, 1934. See also the following correspondence included in Dean's Report, May 15, 1934; Horner to Wilkinson, January 20, 1934; Wilkinson to Horner, February 7, 1934; Horner to Wilkinson, February 9, 1934; Wilkinson to Horner, February 15, 1934; Wilkinson to Horner, February 26, 1934; Wilkinson to Horner, February 28, 1934; **"a total of thirty-six,"** Dean's Report, May 15, 1934, 12.

21. Dean's Report, February 17, 1936, 4, folder 6, box 11, FLS, FU.

22. **Quotations** are in ibid., 28–29. Interestingly, Wilkinson reported that NYU Law School's entering classes "for the last two years has been only as large as our own entering class this year," even though NYU had been on a four year night standard since 1930 "and does not, I believe, attempt any selection of its students." Ibid., 6.

23. Faculty Meeting of June 6, 1935, Faculty Meetings, 1933–44, folder 9, box 11, FLS, FU; Faculty Meeting of September 19, 1935, ibid.; **"better business conditions,"** Faculty Meeting of September 17, 1936, ibid. The tuition of $220 and $240 in 1936 dollars are approximately $3,140 and $3,710 in present-day dollars (see CPI, http://www.measuringworth.com/uscompare). Total enrollments are listed in "Registration by Years Since the Foundation of the School," in Notebook of Memoranda, FLSA.

24. **"in the interest of maintaining,"** Faculty Meeting of September 17, 1936, folder 9, box 11, FLS, FU. **For the descriptions of Father Gannon and Dean Wilkinson see**

William Hughes Mulligan, interview by Michael Sheahan, September 20, 1988, Transcript No. 22, Book 3, 4–5, OHP, FLSA.

25. Dean's Report, February 17, 1936, 29–30, folder 6, box 11, FLS, FU.

26. **"no reason why,"** Ignatius M. Wilkinson to Dean Herschel W. Arant, April 26, 1937, appended as Exhibit B in Dean's Report, February 28, 1938, folder 7, box 11, FLS, FU; Dean's Report, February 28, 1938, 18–20; **"no sub-standard evening school,"** Dean's Report, February 28, 1938, 20; Faculty Meeting of June 10, 1937, folder 9, box 11, FLS, FU; Wilkinson to Will Shafroth, October 30, 1936, folder 2, box 13, FLS, FU; **"with the consent,"** Ignatius M. Wilkinson, "A Decade of Progress in Standards of Legal Education in New York," *Proceedings of the . . . Annual Meeting of the New York State Bar Association* (1940): 90, 92–93.

37. **"reduced [law student enrollments],"** Dean's Report, February 28, 1938, 20, folder 7, box 11, FLS, FU; **"that business conditions,"** ibid., 9.

28. **"the three formerly,"** Dean's Report, April 3, 1940, 3–4, folder 8, box 11, FLS, FU; **"the economic and other conditions,"** ibid., 4; **adopted the four-year night school** is in ibid., 2.

29. **On enrollments,** Dean's Report, April 3, 1940, 3, folder 8, box 11, FLS, FU; **"a vindication of our policy,"** ibid., 4; **application figures,** ibid., 2; **"a strict selective system,"** ibid.; **"a little more strictly,"** ibid.

30. Wilkinson's Dean's Report for 1940 made statements that were incorrect or, at least, inconsistent with earlier dean's reports. For example, he erroneously stated that 1939–40 was the last year in which college graduates were admitted to the Law School without having to produce and, therefore, without a review of their transcript of their college record. Dean's Report, April 3, 1940, 12, folder 8, box 11, FLS, FU. However, he had earlier reported that the last year the academic records of college graduates were not reviewed 1930–31. He had also reported that the entering class of September 1931 was the first "completely selected" class in which the academic credentials of every applicant were evaluated, whether or not the applicant held a college degree. Dean's Report, May 15, 1934, 2, folder 5, box 11, FLS, FU. Similarly, Wilkinson said the first year failure rate of the entering classes of 1930 and 1931 were 23 percent and 14 percent, respectively. However, in his 1934 report he placed these figures at 22 percent and 17.3 percent. Another 15 percent of the original class of 1930 left voluntarily during the first year, and about 10 percent of the 1931 class dropped out voluntarily in the first year. The attrition rates of the first year classes for these years, combining voluntary withdrawals and academic dismissals, declined from about one-third (33.6 percent) to one-fourth (25.9 percent). Ibid., 2.

31. **Statistics** are in Herschel W. Arant to Dean Ignatius M. Wilkinson, January 26, 1937, appended in Exhibit B, Dean's Report, February 28, 1938, folder 7, box 11, FLS, FU; **"strict entrance standards,"** and **"more than offset,"** Dean's Report, April 3, 1940, 12, folder 8, box 11, FLS, FU.

32. Dean's Report, May 15, 1934, 13–14, folder 5, box 11, FLS, FU; Ignatius M. Wilkinson to John Kirkland Clark, April 19, 1934, copy appended as Exhibit C in ibid.

33. Gannon, *Up to the Present*, 196–201; Dean's Report, February 20, 1930, 8, folder 3, box 11, FLS, FU. See note 16 and accompanying text.

34. Gannon, *Up to the Present*, 196–201; Dean's Report, February 20, 1930, 8, folder 3, box 11, FLS, FU; Ignatius M. Wilkinson to John Kirkland Clark, April 19, 1934, copy appended as Exhibit C in Dean's Report, May 15, 1934, folder 5, box 11, FLS, FU.

35. **"It is now pretty generally conceded,"** Alfred Z. Reed, *Present-Day Law Schools in the United States and Canada* (New York: The Carnegie Foundation for the Advancement of Teaching, 1928), 261. As early as 1892, the ABA recommended that every law school have at least one teacher who devoted "his life to the study and teaching of law as a science." Ibid. The AALS adopted a standard in 1916 that took effect in 1919 that required member law schools to employ at least three teachers who devoted substantially all of their time to the school. In 1921, the ABA adopted the ambiguous standard that required accredited law schools to employ a sufficient number of teachers who devoted all of their time to the law school "to ensure actual personal acquaintance and influence with the whole student body." ibid., quoting Resolution (1) (d) of the 1921 American Bar Association Resolutions. **Statistics on full-time and part-time faculty** are in Richard L. Abel, *American Lawyers* (New York: Oxford University Press, 1989), 173; Dean's Report, January 11, 1929, 12, folder 2, box 11, FLS, FU.

36. **"devote[d] substantially all,"** Dean's Report, February 20, 1930, 9, folder 3, box 11, FLS, FU; **on average teaching loads,** see Abel, *American Lawyers*, 173, 263–66, 265n2–5, 266n1–5, 540–41; **"theory of requiring,"** Dean's Report, May 15, 1934, 13–14, folder 3, box 11, FLS, FU; **for the New York State Regents** see Dean's Report, January 11, 1929, 12, folder 2, box 11, FLS, FU; Dean's Report, January 28, 1932, 10, folder 4, box 11, FLS, FU.

37. **"would add considerably,"** and **"the establishment,"** Dean's Report, January 11, 1929, 12, folder 2, box 11, FLS, FU. Full professors received between $500 and $600 per year hour; associate professors who taught in the day division were paid between $450 and $500 per year hour and those who taught in the night school were paid between $400 and $450; lecturers in the day division earned between $350 and $450 per year hour, and lecturers in the evening school received between $300 and $400. The salaries of $8,000 and $10,000 in 1929 are approximately $100,000 and $125,000 in present-day dollars. The salaries of $6,000 and $3,000 in 1929 are approximately $75,100 and $37,600 in present-day dollars (see CPI, http://www.measuringworth.com/uscompare). Wilkinson did not explain what determined who received the maximum and minimum salaries, but it was probably geared to years of service. Dean's Report, December 10, 1925, 10, folder 1, box 11, FLS, FU.

38. **"devoting themselves,"** Dean's Report, February 20, 1930, 10, folder 3, box 11, FLS, FU.

39. **Full-time faculty as an alternative to a Law School endowment,** ibid., 11–12. For a discussion of the endowment issue, see infra notes 81–88 and accompanying text; **"a voluntary system,"** Dean's Report, January 28, 1932, 10–11, folder 4, box 11, FLS, FU; **"because of the burden,"** ibid., 11–12.

40. **Quotations** are in Ignatius M. Wilkinson to John Kirkland Clark, April 19, 1934, copy appended as Exhibit C in Dean's Report, May 15, 1934, folder 5, box 11, FLS, FU. **Full-time faculty were named** in Ignatius M. Wilkinson to Will Shafroth, October 16, 1935 and Wilkinson to Shafroth, November 29, 1935, appended as Exhibit A in Dean's Report, February 17, 1936, folder 6, box 11, FLS, FU.

41. **"most experienced and dependable,"** Dean's Report, May 15, 1934, 14, folder 5, box 11, FLS, FU. **All other quotations** are in Ignatius M. Wilkinson to John Kirkland Clark, April 19, 1934, copy appended as Exhibit C in Dean's Report, May 15, 1934.

42. **"entirely adequate,"** and **"necessarily . . . result,"** Ignatius M. Wilkinson to John Kirkland Clark, April 19, 1934, copy appended as Exhibit C in Dean's Report, May 15, 1934, folder 5, box 11, FLS, FU.

43. Dean's Report, May 15, 1934, 14–15, folder 5, box 11, FLS, FU; **quotations** are in ibid., 15.

44. **"to recede from,"** Dean's Report, February 17, 1936, 10, folder 6, box 11, FLS, FU; **other quotations** are in Will Shafroth to Ignatius Wilkinson, October 11, 1935, appended as Exhibit A in Dean's Report, February 17, 1936, folder 6, box 11, FLS, FU.

45. **Full-time faculty negotiable** reported in Dean's Report, May 15, 1934, 15, folder 5, box 11, FLS, FU. **Quotations** are in Will Shafroth to Ignatius Wilkinson, October 11, 1935, appended as Exhibit A in Dean's Report, February 17, 1936, folder 6, box 11, FLS, FU.

46. **"particularly well qualified,"** **"an influence,"** and **"as the University,"** Ignatius Wilkinson to Will Shafroth, November 29, 1935, appended as Exhibit A in Dean's Report, February 17, 1936, folder 6, box 11, FLS, FU; **"under a strict,"** **"never in the past,"** and **"this is the first time,"** Dean's Report, February 17, 1936, 11; Shafroth informed Wilkinson of the council's decision regarding Father Pyne in Will Shafroth to Ignatius Wilkinson, December 31, 1935, appended as Exhibit A in Dean's Report, February 17, 1936.

47. **"rooted in,"** and **"have as their,"** Francis P. LeBuffe, S.J., *Outlines of Pure Jurisprudence* (New York: Fordham University Press, 1924), i. **Religious sources** included the Old and New Testament, St. Augustine, St. Thomas Acquinas, *Summa Theologica*; Bellarmine, *De Laicis*; Suarez, *De Legibus*; Pope Leo XIII's encyclical, *The Condition of the Working Classes*. **The secular authorities LeBuffe quoted and cited** include Blackstone, *Commentaries on the Law of England*; Edmund Burke, *The French*

Revolution; Wigmore, *The Law of Torts*; Lorimer, *Institutes of Law*; Kent's *Commentaries on the Constitution*; Sir. Paul Vinogradoff, *Historical Jurisprudence*, Kinkead, *Jurisprudence, Law and Ethics*; Austin, *Jurisprudence*; Dillon, *The Laws and Jurisprudence of England and America*; Lord Shaw of Dunfermline, *The Law of the Kinsmen*; Roscoe Pound, *The Spirit of the Common Law*; Pollock, *First Book of Jurisprudence* and *Essays in the Law*; Holland, *Jurisprudence*; Burlamaqui, *The Principles of Natural and Political Law*; James Wilson, *Works*; Aristotle, *Politics*; Ryan and Millar, *The State and the Church*; Bouvier, *Law Dictionary*; Lorimer, *Institutes of Law*; Taylor, *The Science of Jurisprudence*; Bryce, *Studies*; Cicero, *De Republica*; The Declaration of Independence; President George Washington's "Farewell Address"; President Warren G. Harding, "Inaugural Address"; Joseph Story, *Equity Jurisprudence*; Holland, *Natural Law and Legal Practice*; Robinson, *Elements of American Jurisprudence*; Ritter, *Moral and Civil Law*; Rickaby, *Aquinas Ethicus, Political and Moral Essays* and *Moral Philosophy*; Salmond, *First Principles of Jurisprudence*; Markby, *Elements of Law*; Spalding, *Introduction to Social Service*. Compare LeBuffe's book with William A. Keener, *Selections on The Elements of Jurisprudence* (St. Paul, Minn.: West Publishing Co., 1896).

48. **"man as man,"** Francis P. LeBuffe, S.J., and James V. Hayes, *Jurisprudence with Cases to Illustrate Principles* (New York: Fordham University Press, 1938), v; **"the totalitarian philosophy,"** LeBuffe and Hayes, *The American Philosophy of Law with Cases to Illustrate Principles* (New York: Crusader Press, Inc., 1947), v. **Catholic legal scholars associated Justice Holmes's legal doctrine with totalitarianism in the 1940s.** Edward A. Purcell Jr., *The Crisis of Democratic Theory: Scientific Naturalism & the Problem of Value* (Lexington: The University of Kentucky Press, 1973), 168.

49. This discussion is based on the superb study of Edward A. Purcell Jr., *The Crisis of Democratic Theory: Scientific Naturalism & the Problem of Value* (Lexington, Ky.: The University of Kentucky Press, 1973). **"empirical, particular," "that human reason,"** ibid. 3; **"that truth was," "human reason could,"** ibid., 176.

50. **"rational justifications," "three cardinal principles,"** ibid., 11. See also 87, 96–100, 159–60. Impressed with the mechanical stimulus-response theories of behavioral psychology and the theories of Freudian psychologists who emphasized the unconscious and the irrational in human behavior, many legal scholars rejected the idea of the rational human imbued with free will. These scholars accepted the idea that humans lacked free will and an independent reason.

51. Purcell Jr., *The Crisis of Democratic Theory*, 5.

52. **"most severe and extreme,"** and **"perhaps the most,"** Purcell Jr., *The Crisis of Democratic Theory*, 163–64. **Professor Walter B. Kennedy's articles** include: "Pragmatism as a Philosophy of Law," *Marquette Law Review* 9 (1925): 63; "Utility of Legal Philosophy," *New York Law Review* 3 (1925): 353; "Men or Laws," *Brooklyn Law Review* 2 (1932–33): 11; "The New Deal in the Law," *United States Law Review* 68 (1934): 533;

"Principles or Facts?" *Fordham Law Review* 4 (1935): 53; "The Scientific Approach in the Law," *United States Law Review* 70 (1936): 75; "Functional Nonsense and the Transcendental Approach," *Fordham Law Review* 5 (1936): 272; "More Functional Nonsense—A Reply to Felix S. Cohen," *Fordham Law Review* 6 (1937): 75; "Realism, What Next?" *Fordham Law Review* 7 (1938): 203; "Realism, What Next? II," *Fordham Law Review* 8 (1939): 45; "A Review of Legal Realism," *Fordham Law Review* 9 (1940): 362; "Psychologism in the Law," *Georgetown Law Review* 29 (1940–41): 139.

53. **"four fundamental failures,"** "Kennedy, "A Review of Legal Realism," 364; **"amazing faith,"** ibid., 365; **"so-called scientific data," "Realism, which worships,"** ibid., 366.

54. "Fordham Dean Dissents," *New York Times*, February 17, 1937; "The Menace to the Individual," *New York Herald Tribune*, March 4, 1937; Ignatius M. Wilkinson, "The President's Plan Respecting the Supreme Court," *Fordham Law Review* 6 (1937): 179 (Wilkinson's statement before the Judiciary Committee of the United States Senate, April 7, 1937, with some additional footnote material). Edward Gluck, a member of the ABA Committee on Legal Education informed Wilkinson that, although some thought had been given to the question of the constitutionality of the court packing plan, "it had not been raised on the record" until Wilkinson "had made the point" in his testimony before the US Senate Judiciary Committee. Ignatius M. Wilkinson to Will Shafroth, April 16, 1937, folder 2, box 13, FLS, FU. The Dean's testimony before the US Senate Judiciary Committee is published in US Senate Committee on the Judiciary, 75th Congress, 1st Session, *Reorganization of the Federal Judiciary Hearings on S. 1392* (Washington, D.C.: Government Printing Office, 1937): 1131–58.

55. **"may be used,"** Wilkinson, "The President's Plan Respecting the Supreme Court," 179; **"respond always"** and **"become wholly,"** ibid., 183; **"the liberties,"** and **"as the sole guardian,"** ibid., 185; **whatever the law is is right**, Purcell Jr., *The Crisis of Democratic Theory*, 161; **"to give [their] children,"** *Meyer v. Nebraska*, 262 U.S. 390, 400 (1923); *Pierce v. Society of Sisters*, 268 U.S. 510 (1925). See also Wilkinson's articles: "The Lawyer and the Defense of Constitutional Democracy in America," *Fordham Law Review* 7 (1938): 301; "Editorials: Law, Liberty, and Tradition," *Thought, Fordham University Quarterly* 16 (1941): 213; "Some Aspects of the Constitutional Guarantees of Civil Liberty," *Fordham Law Review* 11 (1942): 50.

56. **"to identify their beliefs"** Purcell Jr., *The Crisis of Democratic Theory*, 170; **"its philosophy," traditional Catholic philosophy, "our Founding Fathers,"** LeBuffe and Hayes, *Jurisprudence With Cases to Illustrate Principles*, v; **"in the interest of,"** LeBuffe and Hayes, *The American Philosophy of Law*, v; **"they are not of *America*," "in their origin," "in their content," flat contradiction," "of which Hitlerism and Stalinism,"** ibid., vi; in his Preface to *The American Philosophy of Law*, LeBuffe expressed his intention to summarize the American "natural law philosophy, the principles of

which are woven into the very fabric of our American law." American jurisprudence was "rooted in natural law and natural right and consequently in an objective standard of justice" which he traced back to the Middle Ages. The Founding Fathers' "philosophy of law and of state" "was natural law philosophy, deeply rooted in theistic principles." Ibid., v–vii. Quoting Chief Justice Robert G. Simmons of the Nebraska Supreme Court, Father LeBuffe asserted that "Our whole governmental structure recognizes the hand of God in the affairs of man. Our basic religious beliefs and our democracy are inseparable." ibid., vii, quoting Chief Justice Robert G. Simmons, 33 *American Bar Association Journal*, 3 (1947): 220. Acting Dean Walter B. Kennedy explicitly asserted "that America is founded upon the Catholic philosophy of law." Walter B. Kennedy to Rev. Robert I. Gannon, S.J., February 14, 1944, folder 3, box 10, FSL, FU.

57. **"the most reliable method,"** and **"most closely approximated,"** Purcell Jr., *The Crisis of Democratic Theory*, 206; **only social theories, "tentative, changing,"** and **"could support,"** ibid., 205; **"philosophical relativism,"** and **"theoretical absolutism,"** ibid., 236; **"firm conviction,"** and **"God's transcendence,"** ibid., 243; **"absolute philosophies,"** ibid., 247; **"a relativist culture,"** and **"that the United States,"** ibid., 157. See also, ibid., 177, 204, 209, 238–39.

58. **Quotations** are in Ignatius M. Wilkinson to Rev. Robert I. Gannon, S.J., January 5, 1949, folder 5, box 10, FLS, FU. Dean William Hughes Mulligan continued to oppose efforts within the Jesuit Law School Association to require Catholic law schools to teach law "in the light of principles of natural law and of Catholic faith and morals." Dean William Hughes Mulligan to Rev. Edward F.Clark, S.J., January 6, 1958, folder 6, box 5, FLS, FU.

59. Interview with Father Charles M. Whalen, Wednesday, September 20, 2006. Father Whalen received an AB, a PhL, and an STL from Woodstock, and he held an LLB and LLM from Georgetown University, where he was editor-in-chief of the *Georgetown Law Journal*. During his tenure as a Fordham Law professor, he was associate editor of *America Magazine*, covering legislative and judicial developments on church/state issues. Dean's Annual Report to the Alumni 1995–96, 13, Kissam Law Library.

60. Interview with Father Charles M. Whalen, Wednesday, September 20, 2006.

61. Ibid.

62. Ibid.

63. Ibid.

64. Dean's Report, December 10, 1925, 12, folder 1, box 11, FLS, FU.

65. **"adequately housed,"** Dean's Report, January 11, 1929, 11, folder 2, box 11, FLS, FU; **"considerably below,"** and **"without such,"** ibid., 12. The amounts of $7,500, $1,000, and $1,500 in 1929 are equivalent to $93,900, $12,500, and $18,800 in present-day dollars, respectively (see CPI, http://www.measuringworth.com/uscompare).

66. Honorable Malcolm Wilson, interview by Robert Cooper Jr., March 14, 1989, Transcript No. 45, Book 3, 8, Oral History Project, Fordham Law School Archives (hereinafter cited as OHP, FLSA). Will Shafroth to Ignatius Wilkinson, October 11, 1935, appended as Exhibit A in Dean's Report, February 17, 1936, folder 6, box 11, FLS, FU.

67. Honorable Malcolm Wilson, interview, 16.

68. Will Shafroth to Ignatius Wilkinson, October 11, 1935, appended as Exhibit A in Dean's Report, February 17, 1936, folder 6, box 11, FLS, FU.

69. Ignatius M. Wilkinson to Will Shafroth, November 29, 1935, appended as Exhibit A in ibid.

70. Ibid.

71. "**every advantage**," Will Shafroth to Dean Ignatius M .Wilkinson, December 5, 1935, appended in Exhibit A in ibid.; "**the whole Law School**," and "**there could be**," Ignatius M. Wilkinson to Mr. Shafroth, December 9, 1935, appended as Exhibit A in ibid.

72. "**were successfully terminated**," Dean's Report, February 28, 1938, 11, folder 7, box 11, FLS, FU; Will Shafroth to Dean Ignatius Wilkinson, May 7, 1936, copy of telegram, appended in Exhibit A in ibid.; **full-timers**, Ignatius M. Wilkinson to Mr. Shafroth, April 28, 1936, appended in Exhibit A in ibid. Ignatius M. Wilkinson to Mr. Shafroth, February 21, 1936, ibid. **Conditions of the ABA's provisional approval** are set out in Will Shafroth to Dean I. M. Wilkinson, May 11, 1936, appended in Exhibit A, ibid. At the June 1936 faculty meeting, Wilkinson reported to the faculty that the ABA "had approved this school, the approval to become effective on the re-opening of the school in September, 1936." Faculty Meeting of June 4, 1936, folder 9, box 11, FLS, FU; Faculty Meeting of June 10, 1937, ibid.

73. "**dominated by teachers**," Dean's Report, May 15, 1934, 14–15, folder 5, box 11, FLS, FU.

74. "**found [the Law School's] internal**," Dean's Report, February 28, 1938, 12–13, folder 7, box 11, FLS, FU. To trace the details of Dean Wilkinson and Dean Arant's interactions, see, Ignatius M. Wilkinson to Dean Herschel W. Arant, July 22, 1936, appended in Exhibit B in Dean's Report, February 28, 1938; H. W. Arant to Dean Ignatius M. Wilkinson, July 23, 1936, ibid.; Ignatius M. Wilkinson to Professor George Gleason Bogert, June 24, 1936, ibid.; George G. Bogert to Dean I.M. Wilkinson, July 1, 1936, ibid.; H.W. Arant to Dean I.M. Wilkinson, July 14, 1936, ibid.; Ignatius M. Wilkinson to Dean Herschel W. Arant, July 31, 1936, ibid. Regarding Fordham's application, Dean Arant's inspection and the AALS's admission of Fordham Law School to membership, see, H.W. Arant to Dean Ignatius M. Wilkinson, November 10, 1936, ibid.; Ignatius M. Wilkinson to Dean Herschel W. Arant, November 12, 1936, ibid.; H.W. Arant to Dean Ignatius M. Wilkinson, December 4, 1936, ibid.; H.W. Arant to Dean Ignatius M. Wilkinson, January 26, 1937, ibid.

75. H.W. Arant to Dean Ignatius M. Wilkinson, January 26, 1937, appended in Exhibit B in Dean's Report, February 28, 1938, folder 7, box 11, FLS, FU.

76. Ignatius M. Wilkinson to Dean W. Arant, February 2, 1937, appended in Exhibit B in Dean's Report, February 28, 1938, folder 7, box 11, FLS, FU; Ignatius M. Wilkinson to Dean Herschel W. Arant, October 4, 1937, ibid.; H.W. Arant to Dean Ignatius M. Wilkinson, October 7, 1937, ibid.

77. Regarding Fordham's application, Dean Arant's inspection and the AALS's admission of Fordham Law School to membership, see H. W. Arant to Dean Ignatius M. Wilkinson, November 10, 1936, appended in Exhibit B in Dean's Report, February 28, 1938, folder 7, box 11, FLS, FU; Ignatius M. Wilkinson to Dean Herschel W. Arant, November 12, 1936, ibid.; H.W. Arant to Dean Ignatius M. Wilkinson, December 4, 1936, ibid.; H.W. Arant to Dean Ignatius M. Wilkinson, January 26, 1937, ibid. The correspondence includes the following: Ignatius M. Wilkinson to Dean Herschel W. Arant, July 22, 1936, ibid.; H. W. Arant to Dean Ignatius M. Wilkinson, July 23, 1936, ibid.; Ignatius M. Wilkinson to Professor George Gleason Bogert, June 24, 1936, ibid.; George G. Bogert to Dean I.M. Wilkinson, July 1, 1936, ibid.; H.W. Arant to Dean I.M. Wilkinson, July 14, 1936, ibid.; Ignatius M. Wilkinson to Dean Herschel W. Arant, July 31, 1936, ibid. Announcement to be inserted in *The Fordham Alumni Magazine* (February 1937), folder 9, box 10, FLS, FU.

78. **"reserved decision,"** and **"not entirely certain,"** Dean's Report, February 28, 1938, 12–13, folder 7, box 11 FLS, FU; **"transfer the whole,"** Ignatius M. Wilkinson to Dean Herschel W. Arant, April 26, 1937, appended in Exhibit B in Dean's Report, February 28, 1938, ibid; H. W. Arant to Dean Ignatius M. Wilkinson, April 28, 1937, ibid.

79. Dean's Report, April 3, 1940, 5, folder 8, box 11, FLS, FU. Minutes of the Faculty Meeting of September 16, 1937, folder 9, box 11, FLS, FU; Dean's Report, February 28, 1938, 9–10, folder 7, box 11, FLS, FU. The breakdown in the entering classes for the period are reported in Table 4-5.

80. Dean's Report, January 11, 1929, 14, folder 2, box 11, FLS, FU.

81. Ibid., quoting Alfred Z. Reed, *Present-Day Law Schools in the United States and Canada* (New York: The Carnegie Foundation for the Advancement of Teaching, 1928), 101.

82. Dean's Report, January 11, 1929, 15, folder 2, box 11, FLS, FU.

83. Ibid., 15–16.

84. Ibid., 16.

85. Ibid., 16–17.

86. Dean's Report, February 20, 1930, 11–12, folder 3, box 11, FLS, FU.

87. Dean's Report, February 20, 1930, 12, ibid.

88. **Quotations** are in Dean's Report, May 15, 1934, 25–27, folder 5, box 11, FLS, FU; **continued diversion of surplus revenues into the university's general funds,** see

Ignatius M. Wilkinson to The Reverend Robert I. Gannon, May 15, 1941, folder 2, box 10, FLS, FU; Wilkinson to Father Gannon, May 26, 1941, ibid.

89. Abel, *American Lawyers*, 64–65, 72; Tables 15 and 16, 266–68.

90. Ibid. 64–65.

91. Faculty Meeting of June 10, 1937, Faculty Meetings, 1933–44, folder 9, box 11, FLS, FU. Wilkinson reported enrollments for the six New York City law schools, as shown in Table 4N-1.

TABLE 4N-1. TOTAL ENROLLMENT OF NEW YORK CITY LAW SCHOOLS

1928–29	10,814
1929–30	9,248
1930–31	8,481
1931–32	6,215
1932–33	5,835
1933–34	6,610
1934–35	6,452
1935–36	5,905
1936–37	5,718

92. New York County Lawyers' Association Committee on Professional Economics, *Survey of the Legal Profession in New York County* (New York: New York County Lawyers' Association, 1936) (hereafter *Survey of the Legal Profession in New York County*); questionnaires sent and replies received, ibid., 6; **median income**, ibid., 16; **"below the respectable minimum,"** ibid., 57; **"that in 1935,"** ibid., 16n*; **"a substantial number,"** and **"overcrowding,"** ibid., 57. The median income of lawyers in 1933 of $2,990 is approximately $49,500 in present-day dollars. The respectable minimum family subsistence level of $2,500 is approximately $41,400 in present-day dollars; $2,000 is approximately $33,100 in present-day dollars; $1,000 is approximately $16,600 in present-day dollars; and $500 is approximately $8,280 in present-day dollars (see CPI, http://www.measuringworth.com/uscompare).

93. **Quotations** are in Richard J. Bennett, interview by Robert Cooper Jr., May 11, 1989, Transcript No. 55, Book 1, 9, 22, OHP, FLSA; see also Dennis McInerney, Esq., interview by Robert Cooper Jr., May 1, 1989, Transcript No. 51, Book 2, 12, OHP, FLSA. The weekly income of $15 in 1936 is approximately $228 in present-day dollars (see CPI, http://www.measuringworth.com/uscompare).

94. **Quotations** are in *Survey of the Legal Profession in New York County*, 59–60.

95. **Quotations** are in Dean's Report, May 15, 1934, 19–22, folder 5, box 11, FLS, FU.

96. **Quotations** are in Report of the Committee on Whether to Limit Applicants in the Number of Bar Examinations Permitted of the Joint Conference on Legal Education of the State of New York, 4–5; pass rate table is in ibid., 6.

97. Ibid., 7.

98. Dean's Report, April 3, 1940, 15, folder 8, box 11, FLS, FU.

99. Ignatius M. Wilkinson to The Rev. Charles J. Deane, S.J., October 7, 1931, attached in Exhibit C in Dean's Report, January 28, 1932, folder 3, box 11, FLS, FU.

100. Dean's Report, May 15, 1934, 16–17, folder 5, box 11, FLS, FU.

101. Dean's Report, February 17, 1936, 12–15, folder 6, box 11, FLS, FU; Dean's Report, April 3, 1940, 15–17, folder 8, box 11, FLS, FU.

102. Dean Wilkinson reported the June 1939 bar exam results in Dean's Report, April 3, 1940, 15–17, folder 8, box 11 FLS, FU.

103. Ibid.

104. Caesar L. Pitassy, interview by Robert Cooper Jr., May 18, 1989, Transcript No. 56, Book 3, 14–15, OHP, FLSA.

105. Minutes of Faculty Meeting of June 5, 1941, folder 9, box 11, FLS, FU; Minutes of Faculty Meeting of June 4, 1942, folder 9, box 11, FLS, FU.

106. Bar requirements in the 1920s and the issue of 1933 are explained in Dean's Report, May 15, 1934, 22–23, folder 5, box 11, FLS, FU; for Dean Wilkinson's consultation with the court of appeals and Judge Crane see ibid. and Ignatius M. Wilkinson to Hon. Frederick E. Crane, February 24, 1933, appended as Exhibit F in Dean's Report, May 15, 1934. See also Dean's Report, April 3, 1940, 10, folder 8, box 11, FLS, FU.

107. **Quotations** are in Ignatius M. Wilkinson to Hon. Frederick E. Crane, February 24, 1933, appended as Exhibit F in Dean's Report, May 15, 1934, folder 5, box 11, FLS, FU; see also Dean's Report, May 15, 1934, 22–23; Dean's Report, April 3, 1940, 10.

108. **Quotations** are in Ignatius M. Wilkinson to Hon. Frederick E. Crane, February 24, 1933, appended as Exhibit F in Dean's Report, May 15, 1934, folder 5, box 11, FLS, FU; Dean Wilkinson repeated these views in Dean's Report, May 15, 1934, 22–23; Dean's Report, April 3, 1940, 10.

109. **Benefit to the bar** is in Ignatius M. Wilkinson to Hon. Frederick E. Crane, February 24, 1933, appended as Exhibit F in Dean's Report, May 15, 1934, folder 5, box 11, FLS, FU; **the court of appeals actions** are reported in Dean's Report, May 15, 1934, 22–23 and Dean's Report, April 3, 1940, 10.

110. **Quotations** are in Dean's Report, February 17, 1936, 21–22, folder 6, box 11, FLS, FU.

111. Rollin W. Meeker to Ignatius M. Wilkinson, October 9, 1934, appended as Exhibit B in Dean's Report, February 17, 1936.

112. Ignatius M. Wilkinson to Rollin W. Meeker, October 11, 1934, appended as Exhibit B in Dean's Report, February 17, 1936.

113. Ibid.

114. Ibid.

115. Honorable Malcolm Wilson, interview by Robert Cooper Jr., March 14, 1989, Transcript No. 45, Book 3, 1, OHP, FLSA.

116. **Quotations** are in Ignatius M. Wilkinson to Rollin W. Meeker, October 11, 1934, appended as Exhibit B in Dean's Report, February 17, 1936.

117. Rollin W. Meeker to Ignatius M. Wilkinson, October 12, 1934, appended as Exhibit B in Dean's Report, February 17, 1936, 25.

118. Dean's Report, April 3, 1940, 7–8, folder 8, box 11, FLS, FU.

119. **"in fact increased,"** ibid., 7; **"to a gratifying extent,"** ibid., 6.

120. **"should go the whole way,"** and **"able to obtain,"** ibid., 8.

121. Ibid., 11–12.

122. Joseph W. McGovern, Esq., interview by Robert Cooper Jr., April 3, 1989, Transcript No. 49, Book 2, 38–39, OHP, FLSA.

123. Ignatius M. Wilkinson to the Reverend Robert I. Gannon, January 7, 1941, folder 2, box 10, FLS, FU.

124. Minutes of Faculty Meeting of June 5, 1941, folder 9, box 11, FLS, FU; **"entirely cooperative,"** Ignatius M. Wilkinson to The Rev. Robert I. Gannon, June 12, 1941, folder 2, box 10, ibid.; **Professor Wormser's statements** are in Maurice Wormser to Dean Wilkinson, June 4, 1941, ibid.; see also Francis J. MacIntyre to Ignatius M. Wilkinson, June 6, 1941, ibid.; Thomas E. Kerwin to Ignatius M. Wilkinson, June 10, 1941, ibid.; **"our paltry salaries,"** Joseph W. McGovern, Esq., interview 38, OHP, FLSA; **for restoration of salaries after World War II,** see Robert I. Gannon, Memorandum to All Deans, January 25, 1946, folder 3, box 10, FLS, FU.

CHAPTER FIVE: WORLD WAR II AND ITS AFTERMATH

1. **"the war has struck,"** "State Bar Fearful of 'Bootleg' Law," *New York Times,* January 24, 1943. Ignatius M. Wilkinson to Edward P. Gilleran, August 6, 1942, folder 9, box 10, Law School Papers, Walsh Library, Fordham University (hereafter cited as FLS, FU).

2. Minutes of Faculty Meeting of June 4, 1942, folder 9, box 11, FLS, FU; **some board deferments,** Ignatius M. Wilkinson to Rev. Robert I. Gannon, July 21, 1941, folder 2, box 10, FLS, FU.

3. Minutes of Faculty Meeting of June 4, 1942, folder 9, box 11, FLS, FU; Albert J. Arno to Deans of Approved Law Schools, April 29, 1943, folder 2, box 13, FLS, FU; Ignatius M. Wilkinson to Reverend Robert I. Gannon, April 17, 1946, folder 4, box 10, FLS, FU; Wilkinson to Very Reverend Laurence J. McGinley, December 18, 1950, folder 6, box 10, FLS, FU; Wilkinson to Dean Edwin R. Keedy, August 5, 1942, folder 7, box 8, FLS, FU; Elliott Cheatham to Wilkinson, June 8, 1942, folder 9, box 10, FLS, FU.

4. The June 1942 class of one hundred and forty-one included eight members who had to withdraw during their last semester but were allowed to graduate with their class, and the February 1943 class of fifty had seven such members. The number of drafted graduating students declined to three, two, and two in the next three graduating classes. Minutes of Faculty Meeting of June 4, 1942, folder 9, box 11, FLS, FU; Minutes of Faculty Meeting of January 28, 1943, folder 10, box 11, FLS, FU. The June 1943 class had three accommodated graduates; the October 1943 class had two, and the February 1944 class had two. Minutes of Faculty Meeting of June 4, 1943, folder 10, box 11, FLS, FU; Minutes of Faculty Meeting of September 29, 1943, folder 10, box 11, FLS, FU; Minutes of Faculty Meeting of February 10, 1944, folder 10, box 11, FLS, FU; Minutes of Faculty Meeting of September 27, 1945, folder 10, box 11, FLS, FU.

5. Minutes of Faculty Meeting of June 4, 1942, folder 9, box 11, FLS, FU.

6. Richard J. Bennett, interview by Robert Cooper Jr., May 11, 1989, Transcript No. 55, Book 1, 18–19, 21–22, Oral History Project (hereinafter cited as OHP), Fordham Law School Archives (hereinafter cited as FLSA).

7. To qualify for the Rule 3-A exemption, applicants must have been drafted out of law school; they must have been honorably discharged after active military service for at least one year; they must have completed at least two-thirds of their legal education or have received a law degree from an accredited law school; and they must have filed an affidavit stating that they intended to practice law in New York State. "Veterans Spared on Tests for the Bar," New York Times, August 2, 1945; Walter B. Kennedy to Edward P. Gilleran, October 2, 1945, folder 9, box 10, FLS, FU; Ignatius M Wilkinson to Reverend Robert I. Gannon, May 3, 1946, folder 4, box 10, FLS, FU.

8. Ignatius M. Wilkinson to the Reverend Robert I. Gannon, January 13, 1942, folder 3, box 10, FLS, FU. The estimated deficits of $60,0000 to $70,000 in 1941 are approximately $874,000 to $1,020,000 in present-day dollars (see CPI, http://www .measuringworth.com/uscompare).

9. Ibid.; Ignatius M. Wilkinson to Very Reverend Laurence J. McGinley, December 18, 1950, folder 6, box 10, FLS, FU. Wilkinson initially opposed establishing a summer school, thinking that it was "unwise" from a "scholastic standpoint." In the days before air conditioning, he did not believe "any worthwhile study can be accomplished during July and August, particularly in the case of evening students." The longer classroom periods over the two week foreshortened summer term compounded the problem. Wilkinson set aside his opposition, however, because of "practical considerations." If Fordham did not offer the same program that the other city law schools offered, it ran the "risk of losing a considerable number of our reduced quota of students to the other institutions." A summer term had one advantage, an important advantage, in that it would enable Wilkinson to "find places for all of the faculty" and thus avoid the difficulty created by the temporary closing of the Law School's afternoon division. Ignatius M. Wilkinson to The Rev. Robert I. Gannon, January 13, 1942, folder 3, box 10, FLS, FU.

10. Ignatius M. Wilkinson to the Reverend Robert I. Gannon, January 29, 1942, folder 3, box 10, FLS, FU.

11. Ignatius M. Wilkinson to Robert I. Gannon, February 5, 1942, folder 3, box 10, FLS, FU; Robert I. Gannon to Ignatius M. Wilkinson, February 20, 1942, folder 3, box 10, FLS, FU.

12. **Quotations** are in Ignatius M. Wilkinson to The Rev. Robert I. Gannon, January 13, 1942, folder 3, box 10 FLS, FU; Ignatius M. Wilkinson to The Rev. Robert I. Gannon, January 29, 1942, folder 3, box 10, FLS, FU. The estimated increase in revenue of $67,500 to $89,850 in 1942 is approximately $888,000 to $1,180,000 in present-day dollars; the actual expense of $82,000 in 1942 is approximately $1,080,000 in present-day dollars; the annual rental of $20,000 in 1942 dollars is approximately $263,000 in present-day dollars; annual expenses of $87,000 in 1942 is approximately $1,150,000 in present-day dollars; the surplus of $2,850 in 1942 is approximately $37,500 in present-day dollars; the tuition increase from $270 to $300 in 1942 is approximately $3,550 to $3,950 in present-day dollars; the increased revenue of $9,200 in 1942 is approximately $121,000 in present-day dollars (see CPI, http://www.measuringworth.com/uscompare).

13. **Quotations** are in Robert I. Gannon to Ignatius M. Wilkinson, February 20, 1942, folder 3, box 10, FLS, FU; see also Gannon to Wilkinson, February 26, 1942 and Wilkinson to Gannon, March 3, 1942, folder 3, box 10 and box 11, FLS, FU. The university's charge of $74,312 in 1942 is approximately $978,000 in present-day dollars; the Law School's total expense of $161,312 in 1942 is approximately $2,120,000 in present-day dollars (see CPI, http://www.measuringworth.com/uscompare).

14. Minutes of Faculty Meeting of June 4, 1942, folder 9, box 11, FLS, FU; Walter B. Kennedy to William W. Gager, July 8, 1943, folder 2, box 13, FLS, FU; Frances M. Blake, interview by Robert Reilly, October 18, 1988, Transcript No. 23, Book 1, 1, OHP, FLSA.

15. "Registration by Years Since the Foundation of the School," notebook memoranda, FLSA.

16. Minutes of Faculty Meeting of September 18, 1941, folder 9, box 11, FLS, FU; Ignatius M. Wilkinson to The Rev. Robert I. Gannon, November 19, 1941, folder 2, box 10, FLS, FU; Minutes of Faculty Meeting of January 28, 1943, folder 10, box 11, FLS, FU; Ignatius M. Wilkinson to The Rev. Robert I. Gannon, January 4, 1942, folder 3, box 10, FLS, FU.

17. Minutes of Faculty Meeting of January 28, 1943, folder 10, box 11, FLS, FU; Ignatius M. Wilkinson to Reverend Robert I. Gannon, January 4, 1942, folder 3, box 10, FLS, FU; **"were probably more,"** Frances M. Blake, interview, 2; **"largest accredited,"** Walter B. Kennedy to Reverend Robert I. Gannon, January 13, 1945, folder 3, box 10, FLS, FU. George Washington University Law School had a larger enrollment, but it had a graduate school and its enrollment figure included its "post-graduate class and

an extraordinary number of special students." Its undergraduate enrollment was not as large as Fordham's.

18. Minutes of Faculty Meeting of February 10, 1944, folder 10, box 11, FLS, FU; Walter B. Kennedy to Reverend Robert I. Gannon, September 19, 1944, folder 3 and folder 2, box 10, FLS, FU.

19. **Enrollments** are in "Registration by Years Since the Foundation of the School," notebook memoranda, FLSA.

20. **"a number of students,"** Dean Wilkinson to Edward P. Gilleran, Alumni Secretary, February 3, 1937, folder 9, box 10, FLS, FU. The first foreign educated lawyer who was named in the faculty meeting minutes and recommended for a law degree from Fordham Law School was a Dr. Milde, a Doctor of Law awarded by the University of Breslau, Germany. He entered Fordham Law School in September 1931 and received his LLB in June 1933. Minutes of Faculty Meeting of June 8, 1933, folder 9, box 11, FLS, FU. See also Minutes of Faculty Meeting of June 4, 1936, folder 9, box 11, FLS, FU; Minutes of Faculty Meeting of June 9, 1938, folder 9, box 11, FLS, FU; Minutes of Faculty Meeting of June 8, 1939, folder 9, box 11, FLS, FU; Minutes of Faculty Meeting of June 5, 1941, folder 9, box 11, FLS, FU; Minutes of Faculty Meeting of June 4, 1942, folder 9, box 11, FLS, FU; Minutes of Faculty Meeting of January 28, 1943, folder 10, box 11, FLS, FU; Minutes of Faculty Meeting of September 29, 1943, folder 10, box 11, FLS, FU; Minutes of Faculty Meeting of June 1, 1944, folder 10, box 11, FLS, FU; Minutes of Faculty Meeting of February 8, 1945, folder 10, box 11, FLS, FU; Minutes of Faculty Meeting of March 15, 1945, folder 10, box 11, FLS, FU; Minutes of Faculty Meeting of September 27, 1945, folder 10, box 11, FLS, FU; Minutes of Faculty Meeting of June 6, 1946, folder 10, box 11, FLS, FU.

21. "Law School Notes," n.d., folder 9, box 10, FLS, FU.

22. **"warned on good authority"** and **"the deportations,"** Professor Zulueta to Father Gannon, December 7, 1945, folder 3, box 10, FLS, FU; **"Professor of Law,"** Father Gannon to Walter B. Kennedy, August 3, 1945, folder 3, box 10, FLS, FU; Kennedy to Father Gannon, August 7, 1945, folder 3, box 10, FLS, FU; Father Gannon to Dean Kennedy, August 31, 1945, folder 3, box 10, FLS, FU; Dr. M. Z. Jedlicki's resume, enclosed with Professor Zulueta's letter to Father Gannon, December 7, 1945, folder 3, box 10, FLS, FU; Kennedy to Father Gannon, September 4, 1945, folder 3, box 10, FLS, FU.

23. Wilkinson was appointed to the committee in March 1943. His report proposed a major revision in the way wages were fixed for the system's 32,000 workers and the way grievances should be handled. These included an impartial arbitration committee (which the Board of Transportation did not want) and the appointment of a deputy commissioner to the Board to handle labor relationships with the city's transit system workers. La Guardia selected Edward C. McGuire to hold this position. McGuire was

43 years old, a 1923 graduate of Fordham Law School, and experienced with labor matters. "Transit Report to Mayor Today," *New York Times*, April 28, 1943; "Mcguire to Rule on Transit Labor," *New York Times*, July 18, 1943; Wilkinson to Gilleran, March 29, 1943, folder 9, box 10, FLS, FU. **"largest law office,"** "Wilkinson Quits City Job," *New York Times*, November 26, 1945." **"The two men were,"** "Interview of William Hughes Mulligan by Michael Sheahan," September 20, 1988, Transcript No. 22, Book 3, 12, OHP, FLSA; "Thacher to Serve City for War Term," *New York Times*, January 10, 1943; "Wilkinson Named as City's Counsel," *New York Times*, June 7, 1943; "Wilkinson in City Post," *New York Times*, July 16, 1943; William E. Nelson, *Fighting For the City: A History of the New York City Corporation Counsel* (New York: New York Law Journal, 2008), 163. Wilkinson's salary of $17,500 per year is stated in "Wilkinson Named as City's Counsel," *New York Times*, June 7, 1943. For a history of the LaGuardia mayoralty, see Thomas Kessner, *Fiorello H. La Guardia and the Making of Modern New York* (New York: McGraw-Hill, 1989). A small coincidence: LaGuardia and Wilkinson were both admitted to the New York Bar at the same term of court in 1910, http://www.courts.state.ny.us/history/bios/thacher_thomas.htm.

24. "Appointed as Acting Dean of Fordham Law School," *New York Times*, June 14, 1943; "Edison Dispute Arbiter Named," *New York Times*, October 17, 1945; Minutes of Faculty Meeting of June 1, 1944, folder 10, box 11, FLS, FU; Kennedy to Gilleran, June 26, 1944, folder 9, box 10, FLS, FU; "Edison Dispute Arbiter Named," *New York Times*, October 17, 1945; **New York County Lawyers Association,** Faculty Minutes, June 1, 1944, box 10, folder 9, FLS, FU.

25. Robert I. Gannon, *Up To the Present: The Story of Fordham* (Garden City, N.Y.: Doubleday, 1967), 239–40. The University's "drain" of $105,000 in 1942 is approximately $1,380,000 in present-day dollars; the rent of $70,000 in 1942 is approximately $921,000 in present-day dollars; the Law School's portion of the drain, $33,000 in 1942, is approximately $434,000 in present-day dollars (see CPI, http://www.measuringworth.com/uscompare).

26. Walter B. Kennedy to Father Robert I. Gannon, July 29, 1943, folder 3, box 10, FLS, FU; "Broadway Parcel Sold by Astor," *New York Times*, October 24, 1942; "Building Acquired for Fordham Units," *New York Times*, September 12, 1943; Gannon, *Up To The Present*, 240. The cost of $900,000 in 1899 is approximately $11,200,000 in present-day dollars; the assessed value of $440,000 in 1943 is approximately $5,460,000 in present-day dollars; the purchase price $122,000 in 1943 is approximately $1,510,000 in present-day dollars; the renovations of $138,000 in 1943 are approximately $1,710,000 in present-day dollars; the savings of $50,000 in 1943 are approximately $620,000 in present-day dollars; the investment of $260,000 in 1943 is approximately $3,220,000 in present-day dollars (see CPI, http://www.measuringworth.com/uscompare).

27. Edward B. Schulkind, "The President's Corner," *The Advocate* 4 (October 1954): 2.

28. **great majority of our students**, "A Brief Report on Placement Bureau From September, 1944 to Date," February 6, 1945, folder 10, box 11, FLS, FU; law offices, legal departments, ibid.; **"a great many day school students,"** Minutes of Faculty Meeting of June 4, 1945, folder 10, box 11, FLS, FU. The weekly wage of $35 in 1945 is approximately $417 in present-day dollars (see CPI, http://www.measuringworth.com/uscompare).

29. **"sacrosanct precincts"** and **"one peculiar feature,"** Minutes of Faculty Meeting of June 1, 1944, folder 10, box 11, FLS, FU; "A Brief Report on Placement Bureau from September, 1944 to Date," February 6, 1945, folder 10, box 11, FLS, FU; Placement Bureau Report, June 22, 1944, folder 11, box 11, FLS, FU; Minutes of Faculty Meeting of June 1, 1944, folder 10, box 11, FLS, FU. **The list of law firms** is taken from a database of Fordham alumni who graduated prior to 1960. The weekly wage of $35 in 1944 is approximately $427 in present-day dollars (see CPI, http://www.measuringworth.com/uscompare).

30. **"There still exists,"** "A Brief Report on Placement Bureau from September, 1944 to Date," February 6, 1945, folder 10, box 11, FLS, FU. **On the history of women and work and women and law in the first half of the twentieth century,** see William Henry Chafe, *The American Woman: Her Changing Social, Economic, and Political Roles, 1920–1970* (New York, N.Y.: Oxford University Press, 1972); Virginia C. Drachman, "The New Woman Lawyer and the Challenge of Sexual Equality in Early Twentieth Century America," *Indiana Law Review* 28 (1995): 227; Lydia Yu-Yeh Wang, "American Women in Legal Education: A Historical Perspective," *EurAmerica* 29, (1999): 197. For the period of World War II, see Karen Anderson, *Wartime Women: Sex Roles, Family Relations, and the Status of Women During World War II* (Westport, Conn.: Greenwood Press, 1981); D'Ann Campbell, *Women at War in America: Private Lives in a Patriotic Era* (Cambridge: Harvard University Press, 1984).

31. Minutes of Faculty Meeting of June 1, 1944, folder 10, box 11, FLS, FU. **On the GI Bill of Rights,** see Keith Olson, *The G.I. Bill, the Veterans, and the Colleges* (Lexington: University of Kentucky Press, 1974).

32. Minutes of Faculty Meeting of February 8, 1945, folder 10, box 11, FLS, FU. The proportion of day and night students enrolled in the preceding fall was just the reverse. Of the 370 students enrolled in September 1945, 107 were in the day school and 263 were in the night school. Minutes of Faculty Meeting of September 27, 1945, folder 10, box 11, FLS, FU. **The quotations and February 1946 enrollments** are in Minutes of Faculty Meeting of January 31, 1946, folder 10, box 11, FLS, FU. **On the proportion of day school and evening school enrollments,** see Table 5-3. On the September 1946 entering class, see Ignatius M. Wilkinson to Edward P. Gilleran, July 29, 1946, folder 9, box 10, FLS, FU.

33. Minutes of Faculty Meeting of February 8, 1945, folder 10, box 11, FLS, FU; Ignatius M. Wilkinson to Rev. Robert I. Gannon, January 7, 1947, folder 4, box 10, FLS, FU. **Enrollments** are in "Registration by Years Since the Foundation of the School," notebook memoranda, FLSA.

34. Walter B. Kennedy to Rev. Robert I. Gannon, September 19, 1944, folder 3, box 10, FLS, FU.

35. See Walter B. Kennedy to Edward P. Gilleran, October 2, 1945, folder 9, box 10, FLS, FU. **Quotations** are in Minutes of Faculty Meeting of September 28, 1944, folder 10, box 11, FLS, FU. The faculty discussed the AALS's Emergency Resolution No. 8 at its February 1945 meeting. Minutes of Faculty Meeting of February 8, 1945, folder 10, box 11, FLS, FU.

36. Minutes of Faculty Meeting of February 8, 1945, folder 10, box 11, FLS, FU; **"evidenced an intention,"** announcement of admissions requirements, n.d., folder 9, box 10, FLS, FU; Robert I. Gannon to Father Mulcahy and Dean Wilkinson, January 3, 1946, folder 4, box 10, FLS, FU.

37. Wilkinson to Dean John G. Hervey, August 8, 1949, folder 4, box 13, FLS, FU.

38. Dennis McInerney, Esq., interview by Robert Cooper Jr., May 1, 1989, Transcript No. 51, Book 2, 10–11, OHP, FLSA.

39. Ignatius M. Wilkinson to Rev. Henry O'Carroll, January 17, 1949, folder 5, box 10, FLS, FU; Wilkinson to Reverend Gannon, June 2, 1953, folder 2, box 5, FLS, FU.

40. Walter B. Kennedy to Rev. Robert I. Gannon, November 21, 1945, folder 3, box 10, FLS, FU.

41. Minutes of Faculty Meeting of September 28, 1944, folder 10, box 11, FLS, FU; **"doubtless represent,"** Walter B. Kennedy to Rev. Robert I. Gannon, September 19, 1944, folder 3, box 10, FLS, FU; **"rush into"** and **"to prevent schools,"** Ignatius M. Wilkinson to Rev. Robert I. Gannon, January 7, 1947, folder 4, box 10, FLS, FU. The $15 proposal in 1944 is approximately $183 in present-day dollars (see CPI, http://www.measuringworth.com/uscompare).

42. Minutes of Faculty Meeting of September 28, 1944, folder 10, box 11, FLS, FU. The library cost of $12,000 in 1944 is approximately $146,000 in present-day dollars (see CPI, http://www.measuringworth.com/uscompare).

43. Judge Lawrence W. Pierce, interview by Robert Cooper Jr., July 26, 1990, Transcript No. 76, Book 3, 2, OHP, FLSA.

44. Dean Wilkinson's estimated revenues for the 1946 summer session and 1946–47 academic year totaled $298,878.75; estimated expenses totaled only $108,036. The estimated surplus was $190,842.50. "Estimated Budget," folder 4, box 10, FLS, FU. The projected surpluses of $200,000 in 1947 and $145,000 in 1948 are approximately $1,920,000 and $1,290,000 in present-day dollars respectively. His estimated budget for projected expenses of $112,462 and receipts of $257,506.50 to arrive at a surplus of

$145,044.50. "Requested Budget for School of Law," included in Ignatius M. Wilkinson to Rev. Robert I. Gannon, July 24, 1947, FLS, FU. Projected expenses of $112,462, receipts of $257,506.50, and surplus of $145,044.50 in 1948 are approximately $1,000,000, $2,290,000, and $1,290,000 in present-day dollars, respectively (see CPI, http://www.measuringworth.com/uscompare).

45. Laurence W. DeMuth for Joseph A. McClain Jr. to Dean Ignatius M. Wilkinson, March 13, 1947, folder 4, box 10, FLS, FU.

46. **"somewhat amazed"** and **"are not the business,"** Rev. Laurence J. McGinley to I. M. Wilkinson, July 8, 1949, folder 6, box 10, FLS, FU; **"somewhat insistent,"** Wilkinson to Very Reverend Laurence J. McGinley, July 7, 1949, FLS, FU. See also Wilkinson to Rev. Robert I. Gannon, March 25, 1947, folder 4, box 10, FLS, FU.

47. Ignatius M. Wilkinson to Rev. Robert I. Gannon, November 4, 1946, folder 4, box 10, FLS, FU. The library expense of $13,750 in 1946 is approximately $151,000 in present-day dollars (see CPI, http://www.measuringworth.com/uscompare).

48. **"the range of books"** and **student use of the law library**, Dennis McInerney, Esq., interview, 13.

49. **"the principle involved," "well-balanced faculty," "a fair number," "to bridge the gap," "would not dream," "to maintain substantially,"** Ignatius M. Wilkinson to Rev. Robert I. Gannon, S.J., Jan 7, 1947, folder 4, box 10, FLS, FU; **"a very considerable cut," "an important part,"** Ignatius M. Wilkinson to Rev. Robert I. Gannon, November 4, 1946, folder 4, box 10, FLS, FU.

50. **Quotations** are in Ignatius M. Wilkinson to Reverend Robert I. Gannon, January 5, 1949, folder 5, box 10, FLS, FU; Ignatius M. Wilkinson to Very Reverend Laurence J. McGinley, January 4, 1951, folder 6, box 10, FLS, FU.

51. **"It didn't occur to us,"** Dennis McInerney, Esq., interview, 11; **"we were in,"** ibid., 12.

52. **All quotations** are in William Hughes Mulligan, interview, 15.

53. **"allocated to Plant expansion," "report itself,"** and **"details are,"** "Work Sheet Data for Figures Entered on Report For Law School To American Bar Association," April 7, 1948, folder 4, box 13, FLS, FU; Wilkinson to John G. Hervey, April 9, 1948, folder 4, box 13, FLS, FU. Revenues of $257,506, expenditures of $186,684.36, and surplus of $70,821.64 in 1948 are approximately $2,290,000, $1,660,000, and $631,000 in present-day dollars respectively; "Indirect Expenses" of $63,481.71 in 1948 are approximately $566,000 in present-day dollars. In the 1951–52 school year, the Law School received $246,101 in revenue and expended $192,148.21 in expenses for a surplus of $53,952.79. Report to Council, March 23, 1953, 6, folder 5, box 13, FLS, FU; see also, ibid., 7. Receipts of $246,101, expenditures of $192,148.21, and surplus of $53,952.79 in 1952 are approximately $1,990,000, $1,550,000, and $436,000 in present-day dollars, respectively (see CPI, http://www.measuringworth.com/uscompare).

54. **"comprehensive reexamination,"** Executive Committee to Law School Deans, November 30, 1942, folder 8, box 8, FLS, FU; Minutes of Faculty Meeting of January 28, 1943, folder 10, box 11, FLS, FU. The **Post-War Committee** consisted of Professors Walter B Kennedy, Raymond D. O'Connell, and George W. Bacon. Ibid.

55. **"greatly in need of revision,"** Minutes of the Faculty Meeting of February 10, 1944, folder 10, box 11, FLS, FU; **"increasing importance,"** Dean's Report, April 3, 1940, folder 8, box 11, FLS, FU. There may also have been some pressure to teach the new courses stemming from non-lawyers and corporations that were engaging in the unauthorized practice of the the law. See Wilkinson to Leon Sarpy, February 25, 1947, folder 4, box 13, FLS, FU; Leon Sarpy to Wilkinson, February 19, 1947, folder 4, box 13, FLS, FU; ABA Committee on Unauthorized Practice of the Law School Questionnaire, February 1947, folder 8, box 13, FLS, FU. Minutes of Faculty Meeting of February 10, 1944, folder 10, box 11, FLS, FU; Minutes of Faculty Meeting of June 1, 1944, folder 10, box 11, FLS, FU. See also correspondence relating to the faculty's recommendations in folder 3, box 10, FLSA. The curriculum was listed in the Law School catalogue. In the 1950s, the faculty made modest curricular adjustments. In the first year, they dropped Criminal Law and Procedure and added Criminal Law; they divided Real and Personal Property into two separate courses, and they added a new course entitled Introduction to Law. In the second year, the faculty dropped two courses, Bills and Notes and Bankruptcy, and added two courses, Negotiable Instruments and Creditors' Rights. Equity was dropped from the third year, and two electives were added: Trade Regulation and Connecticut Practice. These conclusions are based on courses listed in *Fordham University School of Law Announcements*, 1909–10, 1929–30, 1940–41, 1946–47, 1955–56.

56. **On the prevailing method,** see ABA Questionnaire, December 6, 1949, 47, folder 3, box 13, FLS, FU; **the university administration's recommendations and Father Mulcahy's quotations** are in Minutes of Faculty Meeting of September 27, 1945, folder 10, box 11, FLS, FU; see also Minutes of Faculty Meeting of September 21, 1950, folder 10, box 11, FLS, FU. **For developments in legal education,** see Laura Kalman, *Yale Law School and the Sixties: Revolt and Reverberations* (Chapel Hill: The University of North Carolina Press, 2005), 18–28.

57. Father Mulcahy's comments are in Minutes of Faculty Meeting of September 27, 1945, folder 10, box 11, FLS, FU. Dean Pound had urged that "the modern teacher of law should be a student of sociology, economics, and politics." N. E. H. Hull, *Roscoe Pound and Karl Llewellyn: Searching for an American Jurisprudence* (1997): 67; Kalman, *Yale Law School and the Sixties*, 18–28.

58. **Quotations** are in Minutes of Faculty Meeting of September 20, 1951, folder 10, box 11, FLS, FU.

59. Albert P. Blaustein and Charles O. Porter, with Charles T. Duncan, *The American Lawyer: A Summary of the Survey of the Legal Profession* (Chicago: The University of Chicago Press, 1954), v; see also, ibid., vi, 2.

60. "a center where scholars," Blaustein and Porter, with Duncan, *The American Lawyer*, 162, quoting a special committee of Harvard Law School; "historical, sociological," ibid., 170; "decidedly irregular," ibid., 172. For law school curricula consisted of traditional, practice-oriented courses, see Robert Stevens, *Law School: Legal Education in America from the 1850s to the 1980s* (Chapel Hill: The University of North Carolina Press, 1983), 210, quoting Lowell S. Nicholson, *The Law Schools of the United States* (Baltimore: Lord Baltimore Press, 1958), 21; "from a kind," ibid.; "the routine work," "completely orthodox," Blaustein and Porter, with Duncan, *The American Lawyer*, 173, quoting Albert J. Harno, *Legal Education in the United States* (San Francisco: Bancroft-Whitney Co., 1953), 163.

61. Blaustein and Porter, with Duncan, *The American Lawyer*, 177, quoting Elliot E. Cheatham; ibid., 177–78.

62. "mind and character," Blaustein and Porter, with Duncan, *The American Lawyer*, 181.

63. "woefully unprepared," ibid., 188; "to Plato or Aristotle," "to think straight," and "arouse in their students," ibid., 189. The survey also collected information from American law schools. Fordham Law School is not listed among those that participated. Chief Justice Vanderbilt's committee did send the questionnaire to Fordham, but Dean Wilkinson was unable to submit the information in a timely manner. Laurence J. McGinley to Dean Wilkinson, January 6, 1951, folder 6, box 10, FLS, FU; Wilkinson to McGinley, January 8, 1951, folder 6, box 10, FLS, FU; McGinley to Wilkinson, January 15, 1951, folder 6, box 10, FLS, FU. "Report of Committee on Pre-Legal Education," folder 9, box 11, FLS, FU. Respondents declared that prelegal education should emphasize "intellectual discipline" rather than information about "particular subjects;" colleges should educate would-be lawyers "to meet new conditions in life," and develop the "capacity for independent thought and action." The ideal prelaw college education was a liberal arts curriculum. The survey yielded the following course recommendations, listed in order of highest score with the number of recommenders in parentheses: courses in English language and literature (72); government (71); economics (70); American history (70); mathematics (65); English history (63); Latin (60); logic (56); philosophy (50); accounting (47); American literature (45); physics (44); modern history (43); sociology (42); psychology (39); ancient history (38); chemistry (38); medieval history (37); ethics (34); biology (30); scientific method (25); physiology (21); French (20); Spanish (20).

64. Quotations are in Wilkinson to McGinley, January 2, 1951, folder 6, box 10, FLS, FU. The $5,000,000 NYU Law building in 1951 is approximately $41,300,000 in present-day dollars (see CPI, http://www.measuringworth.com/uscompare).

65. "a former client," "came to me," "determined not to," "tax arrangement," "most undesirable," Wilkinson to McGinley, January 2, 1951, folder 6, box 10, FLS,

FU; see also Wilkinson to McGinley, March 5, 1951, ibid.; Wilkinson to McGinley, March 15, 1951, ibid.; Wilkinson to McGinley, March 9, 1951, ibid.; McGinley to Wilkinson, March 26, 1951, ibid.; Wilkinson to McGinley, March 27, 1951, ibid.; McGinley to Wilkinson, April 4, 1951, ibid.

66. ABA Questionnaire, December 6, 1949, 23–24, 46–49, folder 3, box 13, FLS, FU.

67. **The hiring process** is described in I. An Inquiry Into American Law Schools, October 31, 1957, 88–94, folder 7, box 4, FLS, FU. See also ibid., 146a. Fordham University's President, in consultation with the vice presidents for academic affairs and finance set the starting salaries of law faculty. See, for example, Edwin A. Quain, S.J., to Professor George W. Bacon, December 22, 1953, folder 2, box 5, FLS, FU; George W. Bacon to Reverend Edwin A. Quain, January 5, 1954, folder 2, box 5, FLS, FU.

68. **"an attitude of irreligion," "not prevent us," "would not employ," "Nature of candidate's," "ability to work,"** I. An Inquiry Into American Law Schools, October 31, 1957, 92, folder 7, box 4, FLS, FU; Ignatius M.Wilkinson to William Hildebrand Jr., August 9, 1950, folder 8, box 5, FLS, FU; see also Hildebrand Jr. to Wilkinson, August 11, 1950, ibid.; Wilkinson to Hildebrand Jr., August 14, 1950, ibid.; ABA Questionnaire, December 6, 1949, 49, folder 3, box 13, FLS, FU; Edwin A. Quain, S.J., to Professor Bacon, September 11, 1953, folder 2, box 5, FLS, FU; George W. Bacon to Reverend Edwin A. Quain, August 6, 1953, ibid.; Minutes of Faculty Meeting of September 24, 1953, folder faculty minutes, 1954–1960 FLSA.

69. **"lowest grades,"** ABA Questionnaire, December 6, 1949, 49, folder 3, box 13, FLS, FU. See also, ibid., 23–28, 51; **"ability to work,"** and **"continued interest,"** I. An Inquiry Into American Law Schools, October 31, 1957, 112, folder 7, box 4, FLS, FU.

70. **The process for determining salary increases** is described in ibid., 107–113; see also ibid., 98–106; II. An Inquiry Into American Law Schools, 12–18, folder 8, box 4, FLS, FU.

71. ABA Questionnaire, December 6, 1949, 51, folder 3, box 13, FLS, FU; see also 23–24, 46–49. For the 1953 faculty salary, see Report to Council, Section of Legal Education and Admission to the Bar, American Bar Association (hereafter cited as Report to Council) March 23, 1953, 10, folder 5, box 13, FLS, FU. Average and median faculty salaries of $7,464 and $8,550 in 1949 are approximately $67,100 and $76,900 in present-day dollars, respectively; average and median salaries of $6,620 and $7,050 in 1953 are approximately $53,100 and $56,500 in present-day dollars (see CPI, http://www.measuringworth.com/uscompare).

72. **"grave cause,"** I. An Inquiry Into American Law Schools, October 31, 1957, 113, folder 7, box 4, FLS, FU. **The tenure principles and procedures** are in ibid., 113–19.

73. I. An Inquiry Into American Law Schools, October 31, 1957, 113, statement attached to page 113, folder 7, box 4, FLS, FU; ABA Questionnaire, December 6, 1949, 49–50, folder 3, box 13, FLS, FU. Expenditures for professional meetings of $65.41 in

1946 and $271.73 in 1948 are approximately $714 and $2,420 in present-day dollars (see CPI, http://www.measuringworth.com/uscompare).

74. The Law School received 1,152 applications for the 1946–47 academic year. It accepted about 26 percent (296) of the applicants, and 226 or about 19.6 percent of the applicants enrolled in the school. In the following academic year Fordham accepted 44 percent (335 out of 758) of the applicants and 30 percent (228) enrolled. In 1948–49, it accepted 50 percent (345) of the 693 applicants, and 37 percent (257) of all applicants entered the Law School. For the 1952–53 academic year, the Law School accepted 58 percent of applicants, and 32 percent (245) of all applicants matriculated. ABA Questionnaire, December 6, 1949, 54, 63, folder 3, box 13, FLS, FU; Report to Council, March 23, 1953, 3, folder 5, box 13, FLS, FU. Not surprisingly, day students tended to be younger than evening students. With a college degree prerequisite for admission, virtually all Fordham law students were at least twenty-one years of age. The overwhelming majority of the day students, 87 percent, were between 21 and 30 years of age. About one-third (32 percent) were between the ages of 21 and 25 and 50 percent were between 25 and 30. Only 10 percent were between 30 and 35, and 3 percent were over 35 years of age. Only 11 percent of the night students were between 21 and 25 years of age. The overwhelming majority, 77 percent, were between the ages of 25 and 35, 43 percent were between 25 and 30, and 34 percent were between 30 and 35. About 12 percent of night students were over the age of 35. ABA Questionnaire, December 6, 1949, 64, folder 3, box 13, FLS, FU. Some 75 percent of day students and 81 percent of night students were residents of New York state and lived at home. Report to Council, March 23, 1953, pp. 63–65. **"recommend that students,"** ABA Questionnaire, December 6, 1949, 57, folder 3, box 13, FLS, FU; **"equally qualified students,"** ibid., 54; see also, ibid., 53–57.

75. ABA Questionnaire, December 6, 1949, 60–61, folder 3, box 13, FLS, FU. Report to Council, Section of Legal Education and Admission to the Bar, ABA, March 23, 1953, 1, 4, folder 5, box 13, FLS, FU.

76. **"firm conviction"** and **"training a man,"** Wilkinson to John G. Hervey, December 7, 1948, folder 4, box 13, FLS, FU; **"necessarily takes into account," "curriculum and methods,"** and **"a high degree of conformity,"** Report to Council, March 23, 1953, 45, folder 5, box 13, FLS, FU; **"into the classroom,"** Wilkinson to McGinley, January 4, 1951, folder 6, box 10, FLS, FU.

77. William Hughes Mulligan, interview, 5.

CHAPTER SIX: MODERNIZING FORDHAM LAW SCHOOL

1. "History," folder faculty minutes, 1954–1960, Fordham Law School Archives (hereinafter cited as FLSA); **"believe that a Protestant,"** William Hughes Mulligan, interview by Robert Cooper, Jr., September 20, 1988, Transcript No. 22, Book 3, 14

Oral History Project (hereinafter cited as OHP), Fordham Law School Archives (hereinafter cited as FLSA). **Correspondence regarding the dean's search** is in box 26, folder Correspondence: Candidates for Dean of Law School—October 1953–July 1954, Laurence J. McGinley, S.J., Papers, Walsh Library, Fordham University (hereinafter cited as FU). Fordham University Vice President for Academic Affairs Reverend Edwin A. Quain, S.J., told Assistant Dean Mulligan years later that Mulligan was the search committee's first choice, but they considered him too young. He was only thirty-six years old at that time. Even after Mulligan was appointed dean two years later, Mary Long called him "Billy," and she still considered him "a child." Mulligan interview, 18.

2. **"John established,"** Mulligan interview, 20; **Father Quain's quotations** are in Memorandum from Rev. Edwin A. Quain, S.J., to Father Rector, July 5, 1956, box 26, folder School of Law 1956, McGinley Papers, FU; Fordham News Service, "For Release Sunday, August 19, 1956," folder Faculty Minutes 1954–60, FLSA.

3. **"Father McGinley called me,"** William Hughes Mulligan, interview, 20; **"Archbishop John Hughes,"** Fordham News Service, "For Release Sunday, August 19, 1956," folder Faculty Minutes 1954–60, FLSA.

4. **All quotations** are in Reverend Edwin A. Quain, S.J., to Father Rector, March 1, 1955, box 26, folder School of Law 1955, McGinley Papers, FU.

5. **All quotations but Hervey's** are in Reverend Edwin A. Quain, S.J., to Father Rector, March 1, 1955, box 26, folder School of Law 1955, McGinley Papers, FU; **"about the lowest of any,"** John G. Hervey to Dean John F. X. Finn, March 21, 1955, box 26, folder School of Law 1955, McGinley Papers, FU.

6. **All quotations** but Hervey's are in Reverend Edwin A. Quain, S.J., to Father Rector, March 1, 1955, box 26, folder School of Law 1955, McGinley Papers, FU; **"the lowest in,"** and **"the highest in,"** John G. Hervey to Dean John F. X. Finn, March 21, 1955, box 26, folder School of Law 1955, McGinley Papers, FU.

7. **Quotations** are in John G. Hervey to Dean John F. X. Finn, March 21, 1955, box 26, folder School of Law 1955, McGinley Papers, FU.

8. **Quotations** are in John G. Hervey to Dean John F. X. Finn, September 13, 1954, box 26, folder School of Law 1954, McGinley Papers, FU

9. **Quotations** are in Reverend Edwin A. Quain, S.J., to Father Rector, March 1, 1955, box 26, folder School of Law 1955, McGinley Papers, FU.

10. **Except as otherwise noted all quotes** are in Reverend Edwin A. Quain, S.J., to Father Rector, March 1, 1955, box 26, folder School of Law 1955, McGinley Papers, FU; **"aggravate the problem,"** and **"something of a problem,"** ABA Inspection Report, April 28–29, 1958, 7, attached to John G. Hervey to Dean William Mulligan, June 28, 1958, box 26, folder 1958, McGinley Papers, FU.

11. Minutes of Faculty Meeting of November 15, 1957, folder Faculty Minutes 1954–60, FLSA; Minutes of Faculty Meeting of June 4, 1959, folder Faculty Minutes 1954–60, FLSA.

12. **Quotations** are in Reverend Edwin A. Quain, S.J., to Father Rector, March 1, 1955, box 26, folder School of Law 1955, McGinley Papers, FU. For example, Professor John D. Calamari formally requested permission to prepare a memorandum of law for a New York City law firm—Delson, Levin and Gordon—during the academic year "because of the manifest impossibility of securing employment in the summer if contact is completely broken with a firm during the academic year." Calamari justified his law services pedagogically, asserting his conviction "that this contact with the more practical aspects of the law will materially enhance my competency as a law teacher," a justification Acting Dean Bacon endorsed. John D. Calamari to George W. Bacon, February 8, 1954, box 5, folder 2, Fordham Law School Papers, Walsh Library, Fordham University (hereinafter cited as FLS, FU). George W. Bacon to Reverend Edwin A. Quain, February 8, 1954, box 5, folder 2, FLS, FU.

13. **"candidate's genuine service," "years of service,"** and **"influence on students,"** are in "Recruitment, Retention and Recompense of Faculty," memorandum in box 11, folder Faculty, Tenure and Salary, 1949–61, McGinley Papers, FU; for tenure and promotion policies, see "Memorandum from Edward F. Clark, S.J., to Rev. Arthur A. North, S.J., Dean W. H. Mulligan, et al., March 21, 1958, box 5, folder 6, FLS, FU; Memorandum on Rank and Tenure, n.d., Minutes of Faculty Meeting of February 27, 1958, FLSA; Paul J. Reiss to Professor Leonard Manning, October 13, 1970, box 6, folder Law School Dean—1970, Michael P. Walsh Papers, Walsh Library, Fordham University (hereinafter cited as Walsh Papers, FU); Mulligan to Father Clark, January 28, 1957, box 5, folder 6, FLS, FU; Father Clark to All Deans, July 25, 1957, ibid. On Dean Mulligan's efforts, see I. An Inquiry Into American Law Schools, October 31, 1957, 102 104–06, 110, and 98–112, box 4, folder 7, FLS, FU; ABA Questionnaire, December 6, 1949, 23–28, 49, 51, box 13, folder 3, FLS, FU; AALS Committee on Law School Administration and University Relations, "II. An Inquiry Into The Adequacy and Mobilization of Certain Resources in American Law Schools to Educate for the Legal Profession," n.d. (hereinafter cited "II. An Inquiry Into American Law Schools"), 12–18, box 4, folder 8, FLS, FU.

14. **"importance [on] having," "deplored the lack,"** Minutes of Faculty Meeting of September 5, 1956, FLSA; Minutes of Faculty Meeting of February 25, 1957; **"stultifying effect," "in the planning of,"** secretarial help, **"who are capable,"** Mulligan to Father Clark, December 17, 1957, box 5, folder 6, FLS, FU; **teaching fellows,** Minutes of Faculty Meeting of December 20, 1957; **"that the great majority,"** Minutes of Faculty Meeting of September 12, 1957, FLSA.

15. **Quotations** are in Mulligan interview, 16.

16. **"in recognition,"** Mulligan to Father Clark, January 6, 1958, box 5, folder 6, FLS, FU; concerning Professor Snee's chair, see Mulligan to Rev. McGinley, September 17, 1958, box 5, folder 5, FLS, FU; **"on the basis of,"** and **"In point of service,"** Mulligan to Father McGinley, November 6, 1961, box 25, folder School of Law 1961, McGinley Papers, FU; see also Minutes of Faculty Meeting of June 5, 1957, FLSA; Thomas C.

Cronin to Henry J. Kennedy, October 18, 1961, box 25, folder School of Law 1961, McGinley Papers; Kennedy to Father Cronin, October 16, 1961, "box 25, folder School of Law 1961, McGinley Papers, FU; "Estate of Ignatius M. Wilkinson, Article Sixth," enclosed in ibid. Professor Snee published two textbooks and law review articles in addition to writing a doctoral thesis for his PhD in psychology and a couple of short articles published in the *Journal of Psychology.* See Thomas Snee and Lawrence X. Cusack, *Documents and Data for Estate Planning* (Englewood Cliffs, N.J.: Prentice-Hall, 1963); Snee and Cusack, *Principles and Practice of Estate Planning* (Englewood Cliffs, N.J.: Prentice-Hall, 1959); Snee, "A Statutory Approach to the Tax Problems of the Mortgagor Consequent Upon Reduction of the Mortgage Debt," *Fordham Law Review* 21 (1952): 42; Snee, "Acceptance of Rent as a Waiver of Notice," *Fordham Law Review* 17 (1948): 88; Snee, "The Superiority of the Performance of Fourth Grade Children: An Analysis of the Witmer Clinical Standards" (PhD Dissertation, University of Pennsylvania, 1933); Snee, C. F. Terrence, and M. E. Crowley, "Drug Facilitation of the Audiogenic Seizure," *Journal of Psychology* 13 (1942): 223; Snee and D. E. Lush, "Interaction of the Narrative and Interrogatory Methods of Obtaining Testimony," *Journal of Psychology* 11 (1941): 229. For publication standards in law schools at this time, see infra, note 19 and accompanying text.

17. **"in the future rank,"** Minutes of Faculty Meeting of February 27, 1958, folder Faculty Minutes, 1954–60, FLSA; **"Writing was applauded,"** and **"the emphasis was,"** Interview with Father Charles M. Whalen, Wednesday, September 20, 2006; **Deans Mulligan and McLaughlin's emphasis on writing,** letter from Professor Robert M. Byrn to Robert Kaczorowski, Sept. 3, 2010; interview of Professor Joseph Sweeney by the author, September 14, 2010, FLSA; interview of Professor Thomas Quinn by the author, September 10, 2010.

18. **All quotations** are in ABA Inspection Report, April 28–29, 1958, 9, attached to John G. Hervey to Dean Willliam Mulligan, June 28, 1958, box 26, folder 1958, McGinley Papers, FU.

19. **"published little beyond,"** Laura Kalman, *Yale Law School and the Sixties: Revolt and Reverberations* (Chapel Hill: The University of North Carolina Press, 2005), 23. When Professor Thomas J. Snee published a text book on Estate Planning, Mulligan held him up as an example to their colleagues. In the same vein, when Professor George W. Bacon reached the university mandatory retirement age of 65 in 1958, Mulligan recommended that he be retained for several reasons, among which was his desire to publish a casebook in Contract Law. Mulligan wanted to afford Bacon this opportunity because he thought the casebook would add to Bacon's reputation "in the Law School world as an expert in contract and sales law." Minutes of Faculty Meeting of February 25, 1957, FLSA; Mulligan to Father Clark, January 6, 1958, box 5, folder 6, FLS, FU; Father Clark to Reverend Father Rector, January 31, 1958, box 26,

folder School of Law 1958, McGinley Papers, FU. Mulligan reported that Professor Leonard F. Manning published "a leading article" in the current issue of the *Fordham Law Review*, which also published a book review by Assistant Professor Robert A. Kessler. The journal's next issue included "a leading article" by Associate Professor John D. Calamari, and Professor Kessler's article on "clerkship" would soon appear in the *New Jersey Law Journal*. Professors Calamari and Raymond P. O'Keefe were planning to use research they completed in their capacities as research consultants to the New York State Law Revision Commission as the bases of future law review articles. "The long struggle for faculty publication is beginning to pay dividends," Mulligan asserted with a sense of satisfaction. **All quotations** are in Mulligan to Father McGinley, September 16, 1958, folder School of Law 1958, box 26, McGinley Papers, FU.

20. **Quotations** are in Reverend Edwin A. Quain, S.J., to Father Rector, March 1, 1955, box 26, folder School of Law 1955, McGinley Papers, FU. **On the move to the Bronx** see Minutes of Faculty Meeting of September 5, 1956, FLSA.

21. **"tells me," "has, at the present time,"** Edwin A. Quain, S.J., to Father Rector, February 17, 1955, box 26, folder School of Law 1955, Laurence J. McGinley Papers, FU; **"a bad last," "they no office," "third from the last," "cannot be ameliorated," "both of these items,"** Mulligan to Father Rector, February 18, 1957, box 26, folder School of Law 1957, McGinley Papers, FU; **"second lowest,"** Mulligan to Father Clark, January 4, 1957, box 5, folder 6, FLS, FU; **"anxious to strengthen," "steps be taken,"** Edwin A. Quain, S.J., to Professor George A. Bacon, December 22, 1953, box 5, folder 2, FLS, FU. The discrepancy in the numbers of listed full-time and part-time faculty with the numbers Father Quain reported to Father McGinley may be resolved if Dean Finn were added to the fourteen regular part-time faculty and Assistant Dean Mulligan were added to the eight full-time faculty. Reverand Edwin A. Quain, S.J., to Father Rector, March 1, 1955, box 26, folder School of Law 1955, McGinley Papers, FU; Minutes of Faculty Meeting of September 5, 1956, FLSA. Father McGinley's views echoed those given to him in a hand written letter from Professor I. Maurice Wormser. See, I. Maurice Wormser to Reverend Laurence J. McGinley, S.J., August 9, 1955, box 26, folder School of Law 1955, McGinley Papers, FU; Mulligan to Reverend Laurence J. McGinley, October 29, 1959, box 5, folder 5, FLS, FU. **On space limitations**, see Mulligan to Father Clark, January 4, 1957, box 5, folder 6, FLS, FU.

22. **"considerable remnant of,"** ABA Inspection Report, April 28–29, 1958, 8, supra note 18; see also, ibid., 2; **"Our faculties tend,"** Kalman, *Yale Law School and the Sixties*, 27, quoting Joel Seligman, *The High Citadel: The Influence of Harvard Law School* (Boston: Houghton Mifflin, 1978), 122. **The law school changed the part-time faculty designation to "adjunct" in 1958**, Memorandum on Rank and Tenure, n.d., Minutes of Faculty Meeting of February 27, 1958, FLSA; Minutes of Faculty Meeting of June 5, 1958, ibid. Although Mulligan continued his predecessors' practice of

appointing alumni, he did so with less frequency. A growing majority of the professors Mulligan hired received their legal education at some of the nation's foremost law schools and their undergraduate educations at some of the nation's most highly regarded colleges and universities. He was most strongly impressed by those candidates who had graduate degrees in law and other areas, because he believed their graduate degrees indicated their interest in academics. Mulligan sought to diversify the faculty in terms of religious affiliations. For example, he made one appointment to the faculty in 1959, Martin Fogelman, a Jewish lawyer who had been teaching as an adjunct at the Law School for the preceding three years. In the 1960s, Mulligan tried to interest another Jewish lawyer, Carl Felsenfeld, to join the full-time faculty. Felsenfeld had impressed Mulligan with a paper he delivered at a Fordham Law School sponsored conference, and Mulligan wanted to hire him because of his professional qualifications and because he was "unlike most of the current faculty." Mulligan to Father McGinley, January 3, 1957, box 26, folder School of Law 1957, McGinley Papers, FU. Carl Felsenfeld declined Mulligan's offer at that time, but he started teaching part-time and later joined the full-time faculty when he retired as general counsel for City Bank of New York. Conversation by the author with Professor Carl Felsenfeld, September 27, 2006. Among the professors Mulligan brought onto the Fordham faculty were Joseph Crowley, Martin Fogelman, Robert Kessler, Manuel Garcia-Mora, Joseph McLaughlin, Malachy Mahon, the first Fordham Law School graduate to clerk for a Justice of the United States Supreme Court, Justice Tom Clark, Reverend Charles M. Whalen, S.J., Reverend Thomas Quinn, S.J., Robert Byrn, Joseph Perillo, Constantine N. Katsoris, Edward F. C. McGonagle, Earl Phillps, Charles Rice, Joseph Sweeney, Barry Hawk, John Sprizzo, Ludwik Teclaff, and Michael R. Lanzarone. Mulligan also appointed Robert Hanlon as assistant dean for admissions in 1963 and William Moore assistant dean for admissions in July 1970 to replace George McKenna. For Dean Mulligan's policies and appointments, see Mulligan to Father McGinley, November 17, 1959, box 25, folder School of Law 1960, McGinley Papers, FU; Library Report, Faculty Meetings June 1965, FLSA. Minutes of Faculty Meeting June 9, 1961, FLSA; Minutes of Faculty Meeting June 7, 1962, ibid.; Minutes of Faculty Meeting June 6, 1963, ibid.; Minutes of Faculty Meeting June 4, 1964, ibid.; Minutes of Faculty Meeting June 1966, ibid.; Minutes of Faculty Meeting June 6, 1968, ibid.; Dean's Report to Alumni 1970, enclosed with Mulligan to Father Walsh, December 4, 1970, box 6, folder Law School Dean 1970, Walsh Papers, FU; Fordham University School of Law 75 Years: 1905–80, 14–16, folder Histories, FLSA.

23. **Quotations** are in Report of the Self-Study Committee of the Fordham University School of Law on the Status of the Law School in the University, December 1, 1969, 1, box 30, folder 1, FLS, FU (hereafter cited as 1969 Report of the Self-Study Committee).

24. **"had great aspirations," "was the place," "In those days,"** The Honorable Joseph McLaughlin, interview by Robert Reilly on April 9, 1990, Transcript No. 107, Book No. 3, 18, OHP, FLSA; **"without doubt," "compete successfully,"** William Hughes Mulligan to Edward F. Clark, S.J., March 26, 1957, box 5, folder 6, FLS, FU.

25. **Quotations** are in 1969 Report of the Self-Study Committee. Mulligan hired many of the faculty who became notable "old-timers" in the late twentieth century. His dear friend Joseph R. Crowley was one of them. They had been seminarians together at Cathedral College, but they both left before ordination and finished college at Fordham. Mulligan was the best man at Crowley's wedding during World War II. Mulligan said that Crowley was "probably the most popular professor at the Law School. . . . He was self-effacing, had a tremendous sense of humor and was in many scrapes with me in college and law school." Cancer took Crowley's life suddenly and without warning in early December 1985. Mulligan always thought that Crowley was "a great man," and he "missed him." Robert Kessler was another full-time appointment. He was a graduate of Yale College and Columbia Law School, and Kessler was teaching at Rutgers Law School when Mulligan hired him in 1957. William Hughes Mulligan, interview, 19. See also infra notes 35 and 36 and accompanying text.

26. **Quotations** are in Reverend Edwin A. Quain, S.J., to Father Rector, March 1, 1955, box 26, folder School of Law 1955, McGinley Papers, FU. Whereas Fordham's law library for the 1953–54 academic year had 26,484 volumes and spent $4,300 for new books, St. John's law library had 32,000 volumes and spent $24,000 for new books. Georgetown's law library had 46,640 volumes and spent $10,500 for new acquisitions.

27. **"Your Law School,"** Laurence J. McGinley, S.J., Greetings From the University To our Fordham Law Alumni, Faculty, Friends delivered at an informal luncheon on January 20, 1959, enclosed in L. J. McGinley to William H. Mulligan, January 8, 1959, box 5, folder 5, FLS, FU. Father McGinley's reference to the "grand manner" was from Oliver Wendell Holmes. Quoting Justice Holmes, McGinley declared "that the function of the law school was the training of lawyers and that the function of the great law school was the training of 'great lawyers in the grand manner.'"

28. Dean's Annual Report to the Alumni 1989–90, inside front cover, box 24, folder Dean's Reports 1971–89, FLS, FU.

29. **All quotations** are in Dean's Report to Alumni—1965, attached to Mulligan to Father McLaughlin, January 10, 1966, box 6, folder Law School Dean—1966, Leo P. McLaughlin Papers, FU.

30. J. R. Cammarosano to Reverend Timothy S. Healy, January 14, 1966, box 6, folder Law School Dean—1966, Leo P. McLaughlin Papers, FU.

31. **"which has been,"** Memorandum for Faculty Meeting of June 4, 1959, folder Faculty Meeting 1959, FLSA; **"We are competing,"** Minutes of Faculty Meeting of June 5, 1958, FLSA; **"the serious limitation," "in attracting," "five Jesuit college,"**

Mulligan to Father McGinley, March 9, 1959, box 26, folder School of Law 1958, McGinley Papers, FU; Dean Mulligan's early attempts to get more scholarship funds and the university's response are in Reverend William J. Mulcahy, S.J., to Reverend Laurence McGinley, S.J., March 29, 1957, box 26, folder School of Law 1957, McGinley Papers, FU; Father McGinley to Father Mulcahy, April 11, 1957, ibid. Mulligan to Father McGinley, March 21, 1958, box 26, folder School of Law 1958, McGinley Papers, FU; Rev. McGinley to Mulligan, April 1, 1958, ibid.; note attached to ibid.; Mulligan to Edward B. Schulkind, May 11, 1959, box 5, folder Alumni Law 1954–59, McGinley Papers, FU. Fordham Law School's scholarship fund in 1959–60 compared unfavorably with most of the other law schools in New York City and New York State, as shown in Table 6N-1.

TABLE 6N-1. NEW YORK STATE LAW SCHOOL SCHOLARSHIP FUNDS 1959–60

Law School	Scholarship Money	Number of Scholarships
New York University	$280,000	287
Columbia	$106,380	152
St. John's	$ 42,000	44
Syracuse	$ 29,242	41
Albany	$ 22,810	60
Fordham	$ 16,000	42
Brooklyn	$ 15,822	56
New York	$ 4,000	6

Source: Memorandum from John G. Hervey, Adviser to the ABA Section of Legal Education and Admissions to the Bar, January 11, 1961, folder Faculty Meetings 1961, FLSA. Note that Cornell University Law School did not report its scholarship information.

Many competitor Catholic law schools had significantly larger scholarship funds than Fordham Law School in 1959 (see Tables 6N-2 and 6N-3).

When Catholic law schools are compared to the law schools with the largest student aid, only Georgetown of the Catholic law schools is in the same league.

32. **"the caliber,"** **"additional scholarship help,"** Minutes of Faculty Meeting of February 15, 1962, folder Faculty Meetings 1961, FLSA; **"we are being rejected,"** Memorandum in folder Faculty Meetings 1961, FLSA; **"we need scholarship,"** Untitled memorandum, ibid.; *"exceptionally talented students,"* Joseph O'Meara to Rev. Laurence J. McGinley, S.J., November 17, 1955, box 26, folder School of Law 1955, McGinley

TABLE 6N-2. LARGEST CATHOLIC LAW SCHOOL SCHOLARSHIP FUNDS 1959–60

Law School	Scholarship Money	Number of Scholarships
Georgetown	$120,804	104
Notre Dame	$ 45,000	33
St. John's	$ 42,000	44
Villanova	$ 39,600	35
Boston College	$ 21,600	22
Fordham	$ 16,000	42

Source: Memorandum from John G. Hervey, Adviser to the ABA Section of Legal Education and Admissions to the Bar, January 11, 1961, folder Faculty Meetings 1961, FLSA.

TABLE 6N-3. LARGEST LAW SCHOOL SCHOLARSHIP FUNDS NATIONWIDE 1959–60

Law School	Scholarship Money	Number of Scholarships
Harvard	$385,768	428
Tulane	$134,375	89
U. of Pennsylvania	$121,800	165
Georgetown	$120,804	104
U. of Michigan	$106,794	162

Source: Memorandum from John G. Hervey, Adviser to the ABA Section of Legal Education and Admissions to the Bar, January 11, 1961, folder Faculty Meetings 1961, FLSA.

Papers, FU. **On feeder colleges** see Mulligan to John J. O'Connor, October 1, 1958, box 26, folder School of Law 1958, McGinley Papers, FU.

33. **"to project Fordham,"** Mulligan to Dr. John J. Meng, July 20, 1967, box 5, folder Law School Dean—1967, McLaughlin Papers, FU; **"truly great law school," "most importantly,"** John G. Hervey, Inspection Report Fordham University School of Law May 4–5, 1967, box 5, folder Law School Dean—1967, McLaughlin Papers, FU; see also John J. Meng to Dean Mulligan, March 1, 1967, ibid.; John J. Meng to Dean Mulligan, July 26, 1967, ibid.

34. Leo McLaughlin, S.J., to Dr. John J. Meng, March 7, 1967, ibid.

35. John J. Meng to Dean Mulligan, March 1, 1967, box 5, folder Law School Dean—1967, McLaughlin Papers, FU. For the law faculty's attitude, see supra note 25 and accompanying discussion.

36. **"they used to say,"** Mulligan interview, 5; interview of Professor Thomas Quinn by author, September 10, 2010, FLSA.

37. **All quotations** are in Mulligan to Dr. John J. Meng, February 8, 1968, box 5, folder Law School Dean—1968, McLaughlin Papers, FU. Opening salaries of $10,000 to $15,000 in 1968 are approximately $61,600 and $92,500 in present-day dollars (see CPI, http://www.measuringworth.com/uscompare).

38. John J. Meng to Dean Mulligan, July 26, 1967, box 5, folder Law School Dean— 1968, McLaughlin Papers, FU. Meng informed Mulligan that the *Chronicle of Higher Education* in February 1968 had reported the national median salary for law school full professors at $17,300 ($107,000 in present-day dollars) and associate professors at $13,800 ($85,100 in present-day dollars). Fordham law faculty's median salaries were $18,250 ($113,000 in present-day dollars) for full professors and $14,500 ($89,400 in present-day dollars) for associate professors. Meng argued that these figures supported the university's refusal to increase law faculty salaries significantly. John J. Meng to Dean Mulligan, February 19, 1968, box 5, folder Law School Dean—1968, McLaughlin Papers, FU. Meng further informed Mulligan that the "overall average compensation" of Fordham University's full professors was "calculated to be $19,114" for the 1968–69 school year ($118,000 in present-day dollars). The proposed average total compensation for the Law School's full professors was above that average and "well above the 'A' rating of the AAUP for average compensation" of $21,500 ($133,000 in present-day dollars), Meng insisted. Associate professors in the Law School received an average total compensation of $16,500 ($102,000 in present-day dollars), which exceeded the AAUP "AA" average compensation of $15,500 ($95,600 in present-day dollars) by $1,000 ($6,160 in present-day dollars) and that of Fordham University–wide associate professors' average of $13,500 ($83,200 in present-day dollars) by $3,000 ($18,500 in present-day dollars). Meng did not understand why Mulligan believed the proposed salary figures he gave to the Dean were inadequate. Meng to Mulligan, March 7, 1968, box 5, folder Law School Dean—1968, McLaughlin Papers, FU.

39. **All quotations** are in Faculty Resolution, attached to Mulligan to Reverend McLaughlin, May 10, 1968, box 5, folder Law School Dean—1968, McLaughlin Papers, FU.

40. **All quotations** are in Mulligan to Brown, February 3, 1969, box 6, folder Law School Dean—1969, Walsh Papers, FU.

41. **All quotations** are in Mulligan to Brown, February 3, 1969, box 6, folder Law School Dean—1969, Walsh Papers, FU; V.P. A.A., memorandum entitled Faculty Salary Increments by Percent, 1969–70, March 11, 1969, ibid.

42. **All quotations** are in Mulligan to Brown, February 3, 1969, box 6, folder Law School Dean—1969, Walsh Papers, FU.

43. **All quotations** are in Mulligan to Reverend Walsh, March 21, 1969, box 6, folder Law School Dean—1969, Walsh Papers, FU.

44. ABA Section on Legal Education and Admission to the Bar, Law Schools Charging Tuitions of $1,600.00 or More, Table of Law Schools of Comparable Size, Table of Law Schools in New York State, attached to Mulligan to Reverend Walsh, March 20, 1969, box 6, folder Law School Dean—1969, Walsh Papers, FU. $100 in 1968 dollars is approximately $616 in present-day dollars; $150 in 1968 dollars is approximately $925 in present-day dollars (see CPI, http://www.measuringworth.com/uscompare).

45. **All quotations** are in Report on Compliance with Standards of ABA at Fordham Law School, March, 1968, box 6, folder Law School Dean—1969, Walsh Papers, FU.

46. ABA Section on Legal Education, summarized in Table 6-2 prepared by Dean Mulligan, enclosed in Mulligan to Father Michael P. Walsh, February 12, 1970, box 26, folder Law School, James C. Finlay Papers, FU. $1,000 in 1969 is approximately $5,850 in present-day dollars. Thus, Fordham Law School's median salary of $18,000 is approximately $105,300 in present-day dollars, whereas Boston College's median salary of $20,000 is approximately $117,000 in present-day dollars, and New York University's median salary of $25,000 is approximately $146,250 in present-day dollars (see CPI, http://www.measuringworth.com/uscompare).

47. **Quotations** are in Paul J. Reiss to Father Walsh, February 18, 1970, box 26, folder Law School, Finlay Papers, FU.

48. **"Fordham was faced,"** Raymond A. Schroth, S.J., *Fordham: A History and Memoir* (New York: Fordham University Press, rev. ed., 2008), 275, quoting Father McLaughlin; **"impecunious Catholic students,"** Walter Gellhorn and R. Kent Greenawalt, "An Independent Fordham? A Choice for Catholic Higher Education" (unpublished report, October 1968): 2, FLSA; **"license to become,"** Schroth, *Fordham: A History and Memoir*, 267; see also, ibid., 264–90. Robert Reilly reports that Fordham College and the College of Business Administration "had for decades enrolled the best and the brightest Catholic high school students were severely hurt" by this exodus of Catholics to secular institutions. Email from Robert Reilly to Robert Kaczorowski, Sept. 16, 2010, FLSA. **For comment on the Gellhorn Report**, see infra note 50 and accompanying text.

49. **"totally inept,"** Schroth, *Fordham: A History and Memoir*, 275; on Kidera's conclusion, see ibid.; Father Healy's recollection was reported in the email from Robert Reilly to Robert Kaczorowski, September, 16, 2010, FLSA.

50. **"to shed identification,"** Gellhorn and Greenawalt, "An Independent Fordham?" 1, FLSA; **"created a sensation,"** Schroth, *Fordham: A History and Memoir*, 284;

"for the most part," ibid., 286; "to change," ibid., 287. Father Schroth explains why he believes Fordham did not implement the Gellhorn Report in ibid., 286–87.

51. "increased income from Lincoln center," Schroth, *Fordham: A History and Memoir*, 287; Professor Joseph Sweeney confirmed the university's dire financial condition in interview by Robert Kaczorowski, September 14, 2010, FLSA.

52. All quotations are in Mulligan to Dr. Arthur W. Brown, June 9, 1969, box 6, folder Law School Dean—1969, McLaughlin Papers, FU; see also Brian P. Crosby to Reverend Michael Walsh, May 6, 1969, box 6, folder Law School Dean—1969, Walsh Papers, FU. The budget figure is for fiscal 1968–69. See Meng to Mulligan, June 24, 1968, box 5, folder Law School Dean—1968, Walsh Papers, FU; $200,000 in 1968 dollars is approximately $1,230,000 in present-day dollars; $638,000 in 1968 dollars is approximately $3,930,000 in present-day dollars (see CPI, http://www.measuringworth.com/uscompare).

53. Meng to Mulligan, June 24, 1968, box 5, folder Law School Dean—1968, Walsh Papers, FU.

54. Robert M. Bryn to Rev. Michael P. Walsh, January 9, 1970, folder 1, box 30, FLS, FU.

55. Robert M. Byrn to Reverend Michael P. Walsh, October 16, 1969, box 6, folder Law School Self-Study, Walsh Papers, FU.

56. Quotations are in Joseph Cammarosano to Father Walsh, October 23, 1969, box 6, folder Law School Self-Study, Walsh Papers, FU.

57. Ibid.

58. Cammarosano to Father Walsh, October 23, 1969, box 6, folder Law School Self-Study, Walsh Papers, FU. Cammarosano's musing ignored the fact that Fordham University's Treasurer, Brother James Kenny, claimed that the Law School had paid for its own building. See infra notes 103–4 and accompanying text. Cammarosano compounded the absurdity by making a bogus economic efficiency argument. If the Law School received all of the money to which it laid claim, it was entirely within the realm of possibility that it eventually "would have more money than it needed and started to spend it uneconomically simply because it had it," thus leaving "unattended" other "and more worthwhile needs," presumably in other divisions of the university. He argued that this would "make for a gross misallocation of resources in the educational community."

59. Cammarosano to Father Walsh, October 23, 1969, box 6, folder Law School Self-Study, Walsh Papers, FU.

60. Father Walsh to Professor Byrn, November 14, 1969, box 6, folder Law School Self-Study, Walsh Papers, FU.

61. Report of the Self-Study Committee of the Fordham University School of Law on the Status of the Law School in the University, December 1, 1969, 1–2, 4, box 30,

folder 1, FLS, FU (hereinafter cited as Report of the Self-Study Committee, December 1, 1969).

62. Ibid.

63. Report of the Self-Study Committee, December 1, 1969, 1. Professor Byrn transmitted the report to Father Walsh with Robert M. Bryn to Rev. Michael P. Walsh, January 9, 1970, box 30, folder 1, FLS, FU. There is a copy of this letter in box 6, folder Law School Self-Study, Walsh Papers, FU.

64. Report of the Self-Study Committee, December 1, 1969, 5.

65. Ibid.

66. Report of the Self-Study Committee, December 1, 1969, 13–14; see also Appendix A, Survey of Accredited Law Schools in the United States, 28–29, 31–32; **"very little current concern,"** Appendix A, 33.

67. Report of the Self-Study Committee, December 1, 1969, 6. The self-study committee approached its mandate "principally, but not exclusively, by comparing Fordham Law School to other university-affiliated law schools," particularly the fifteen or so law schools with which Fordham Law School competed for students, Robert M. Bryn to Reverend Michael P. Walsh, January 9, 1970, box 30, folder 1, FLS, FU. It sent out questionnaires to over one hundred accredited law schools and received replies from forty-nine. These included eighteen private law schools, eleven law schools affiliated with Roman Catholic universities, and twenty state-supported law schools. Report of the Self-Study Committee, December 1, 1969, 2–3; Appendix A, Survey of Accredited Law Schools in the United States, 23. The law schools are listed in Appendix A.

68. Report of the Self-Study Committee, December 1, 1969, 7; Appendix C, Faculty Size and Curriculum, 54.

69. **"excessive use,"** Report of the Self-Study Committee, December 1, 1969, 7; **"University policy,"** ibid., 15.

70. **All quotations** are in ibid., 8. A committee of faculty and students had studied the curricula of twenty law schools from 1966 to 1967 and issued reports concluding that "an effective curriculum demanded fewer required courses and more elective courses relevant to the changing nature of the profession." Report of the Self-Study Committee, December 1, 1969, Appendix C, Faculty and Curriculum, 55. Headed by Professor Calamari, the committee proposed in April 1967 "sweeping changes in the entire law school curriculum." Minutes of Faculty Meeting June 6, 1967, FLSA. The faculty adopted most of the committee's proposed curriculum revisions in May, 1967 and planned to implement them that September. Appendix C, Faculty and Curriculum, 55.

71. **Quotations** are in Report of the Self-Study Committee, December 1, 1969, Appendix C, Faculty Size and Curriculum, 55. The Law School offered the following

electives in 1969–70: Accounting, Administrative Law, Admiralty, Advocacy, Bankruptcy, Close Corporations, Domestic Relations, International Law, International Business Transactions, Trade Regulation, SEC, Mortgages, Jurisprudence, Comparative Law, Insurance, Federal Courts, Suretyship, Estate Planning, Labor Law, Advanced Labor Law, Legislation, Law of the Urban Poor–Urban Education, and Protection of the Environment. Electives offered at many other law schools which Fordham was unable to offer were: Patents, Corporate Reorganization, Business Planning, Municipal Law, Trademark and Copyright, International Organizations, Performing Arts, Oil and Gas, Business Taxation, Law and Medicine, Surrogates' Practice, and Land Use Planning.

72. Ibid. Functioning under these adverse conditions, some faculty members nonetheless contributed to legal scholarship and performed important public service. Their publications were directed to law practitioners. For example, Professors John Calamari and Joseph Perillo published their new Hornbook on the Law of Contracts; Professor Martin Fogelman authored the Annual Review of New York Insurance Law and Professor Joseph McLaughlin authored the Annual Survey of New York Practice, both of which were published in the *Syracuse Law Review*. Professor Robert Byrn published articles on New York Tort Law and on abortion. Several professors served as editors to legal newsletters and periodicals. Thus, Professor Thomas Quinn was the editor of the *Uniform Commercial Code Law Letter*; Professor Joseph Sweeney was the case notes editor of the *Journal of Maritime Law & Commerce*; and Professor Ludwik Teclaff was an associate editor of the *Journal of Maritime Law & Commerce*. Professor Byrn testified before a joint committee of the New York Legislature and submitted a statement to a legislative committee in the New Jersey Assembly investigating the legalization of abortion. He was also very active in "numerous debates, panels, TV and radio programs" on the subject, and, for these public services Byrn was awarded a Papal Medal—*Pro Ecclesia et Pontifice*—which Cardinal Cooke presented to him. Professor Quinn served as chairman of the Community Services Committee of the AALS and director of the Fordham Law School Urban Law Center. Professor Teclaff was elected president of the New York Law Library Association and served on a wide range of professional library positions, including the Committee for Liaison with the Library of Congress for the Association of American Law Libraries, the Law and Political Science subsection of the Association of College and Research Libraries of the American Library Association, and secretary of the Committee on International Water Resources Law of the International Law Association. Teclaff also served as codirector of the Marine Environment Legal Research Project of the New York University Law Center. Dean's Report to Alumni, 1970, attached to Mulligan to Father Walsh, December 4, 1970, box 6, folder Law School Dean—1970, Walsh Papers, FU; Mulligan to Rev. Walsh, February 12, 1970, ibid.; Reverend Walsh to Mulligan, February 16, 1970, ibid.

Research assistance of $12,350 in 1969 is approximately $72,300 in present-day dollars (see CPI, http://www.measuringworth.com/uscompare).

73. **"the *sine qua non*,"** Report of the Self-Study Committee, December 1, 1969, 8; **"at those law schools,"** ibid., Appendix A, 40. **All remaining quotes** in this paragraph are in ibid. **Wall Street second-year associate salaries,** Report of the Self-Study Committee, December 1, 1969, 19–20.

74. Report of the Self-Study Committee, December 1, 1969, 9. The scholarship fund of $70,000 and tuition of $1,600 in 1969 are approximately $410,000 and $9,360 in present-day dollars, respectively (see CPI, http://www.measuringworth.com/uscompare).

75. **On the law library's rank,** see Report of the Self-Study Committee, December 1, 1969, 6; **law library's finances,** ibid., Appendix B, Library Report, 50. The reduction in the book budget from $60,500 to $41,000 in 1970 is a reduction of approximately $334,000 to $226,000 in present-day dollars; $1,000 in 1970 is approximately $5,520 in present-day dollars; $30,000 in 1970 is approximately $166,000 in present-day dollars; $14,200 in 1970 is approximately $78,400 in present-day dollars (see CPI, http://www.measuringworth.com/uscompare).

76. **Quotations except Brother Kenny's** are in Report of the Self-Study Committee, December 1, 1969, 9; **"questioned this,"** Brother James Kenny to Father Walsh, February 11, 1970, box 26, folder Law School, Finlay Papers, FU.

77. **"sufficient student help,"** Report of the Self-Study Committee, December 1, 1969, 9; see also ibid., Appendix B, Library Report, 50–51. The book budget of $80,000 in 1969 is approximately $468,000 in present-day dollars (see CPI, http://www.measuringworth.com/uscompare).

78. **"an adequate part-time,"** **"his special area,"** **"an adequate convention-travel,"** **"starting point,"** Report of the Self-Study Committee, December 1, 1969, 10, and Appendix B, Library Report, 50–5. The recommended research budget of $10,000 to $15,000 in 1969 is approximately $58,500 to $87,800 in present-day dollars (see CPI, http://www.measuringworth.com/uscompare).

79. **Quotations** are in Report of the Self-Study Committee, December 1, 1969, 12–13.

80. **"reasonable requirements,"** **"primary consideration,"** **"complete financial statement,"** **"grossly inadequate,"** **"losing ground,"** **"quality legal education,"** Report of the Self-Study Committee, December 1, 1969, 13–14; **"quest for excellence,"** and **"no longer be,"** ibid., 15; Appendix A, Survey of Accredited Law Schools in the United States, 28–29, 31–32.

81. **Quotations** are in Report of the Self-Study Committee, December 1, 1969, 15–16. Many Law School alumni sent checks made out to Fordham University, but they restricted their donations to the use of the Law School. See, for example, Caesar L.

Pitassy to Dean Mulligan, December 29, 1965, box 1, folder Alumni Association (Law), McLaughlin Papers, FU; Leo McLaughlin, S.J., to Caesar L. Pitassy, January 3, 1966, ibid.; Leo T. Kissam to Dean Mulligan, December 19, 1965, ibid.; Mulligan to Father McLaughlin, December 13, 1965, box 4, folder Law Alumni Scholarship Fund, McLaughlin Papers, FU; McLaughlin to Kissam, December 29, 1965, ibid.

82. Mulligan to Father McLaughlin, December 20, 1968, box 5, folder Law School Dean—1968, McLaughlin Papers, FU.

83. Report of the Self-Study Committee, December 1, 1969, 16–17.

84. Ibid., 18.

85. Ibid., 19.

86. Ibid., 19–20. In thirty of thirty-nine (or 77 percent) of these law schools, the recommended salaries of individual faculty members were not reduced by the university during the preceding three years. In only two of nine reporting Catholic-affiliated law schools did the university reduce individual salaries.

87. Ibid.

88. Ibid., 21.

89. Robert M. Byrn to Father Michael P. Walsh, January 9, 1970, box 30, folder 1, FLS, FU. There is a copy of this letter in box 6, folder Law School Self-Study, Walsh Papers, FU.

90. Father Walsh to Professor Byrn, February 9, 1970, box 6, folder Law School Self-Study, Walsh Papers, FU.

91. **All quotations** are in Father Walsh to Professor Byrn, February 9, 1970, box 6, folder Law School Self-Study, Walsh Papers, FU; see also, Father Walsh to Professor Byrn, February 25, 1970, ibid.

92. **Quotations** are in Father Walsh to Cammarosano, March 10, 1970, box 6, folder Law School Self-Study, Walsh Papers, FU. See also Cammarosano to Father Walsh, March 11, 1970, ibid.; Father Walsh to Members of the Law School Self-Study Committee, February 25, 1970, ibid.; Father Walsh to Cammarosano, February 25, 1970, ibid.; Cammarosano to Father Walsh, February 23, 1970, ibid.

93. **"his estimate of,"** Joseph R. Crowley to Father Walsh, April 10, 1970, box 6, folder Law School Self-Study, Walsh Papers, FU; **"doubt[ed] very much," "only major categories,"** Father Walsh to Professor Crowley, April 30, 1970, ibid. The self-study committee's recommendations and the disposition of each item in the March 20, 1970 meeting were set forth, according to Cammarosano, "in a very forthright and statesmanlike fashion," in a memorandum prepared by Professor Joseph R. Crowley and sent to Father Walsh. See Joseph R. Crowley to Father Walsh, April 10, 1970, box 6, folder Law School Self-Study, Walsh Papers, FU. The administration's view is set forth in the memorandum sent by Father Walsh to Professor Crowley, April 30, 1970, ibid. The administrators' internal discussion of these issues and Professor Crowley's

memorandum are expressed in Cammarosano to Father Walsh, April 22, 1970, ibid.; Reiss to Father Walsh, April 27, 1970, ibid.

94. **"a significant compromise," remained unalterably,"** Cammarosano to Father Walsh, April 22, 1970, box 6, folder Law School Self-Study, Walsh Papers, FU; **"a complete financial statement,"** Professor Crowley to Father Walsh, April 10, 1970, ibid.; **"agreed in principle," "reasonable requirements," "to attain and maintain,"** Father Walsh to Professor Crowley, April 30, 1970, ibid.

95. Agreement, Denis G. McInerney and Reverend Michael P. Walsh, July 1, 1970, box 6, folder Law School Dean—1969, Walsh Papers, FU; **"get the arm placed," "where we,"** Cammarosano to Rev. Walsh, March 23, 1970, box 6, folder Law School Dean—1970, ibid.; Rev. Walsh to Cammarosano, March 24, 1970, ibid. The annual support of $5,000 in 1970 is approximately $27,600 in present-day dollars (see CPI, http://www.measuringworth.com/uscompare).

96. Agreement, Denis G. McInerney and Reverend Michael P. Walsh, July 1, 1970, box 6, folder Law School Dean—1969, Walsh Papers, FU; **"specifically assigned," "earmarked as to," "solicitation must," "on a personal basis,"** Dr. Joseph R. Cammarosano to Rev. Michael P. Walsh, March 31, 1970, ibid.; Walsh to Cammarosano, April 6, 1970, ibid.; Rev. Walsh to Cammarosano, March 24, 1970, ibid.; **"considered as a supplement,"** Professor Crowley to Father Walsh, April 10, 1970, box 6, folder Law School Self-Study, ibid.

97. **"the Law School would,"** Father Walsh to Professor Crowley, April 30, 1970, box 6, folder Law School Self-Study, ibid.; **"first be cleared," "uniquely concerned," "otherwise expressed,"** Professor Crowley to Father Walsh, April 10, 1970, ibid.

98. **Quotations** are in Professor Crowley to Father Walsh, April 10, 1970, ibid.

99. Professor Crowley to Father Walsh, April 10, 1970, ibid.

100. Mulligan to Father Walsh, November 30, 1970, box 6, folder Law School Dean—-1970, Walsh Papers, FU. One thousand dollars in 1970 is approximately $5,520 in present-day dollars. Fordham Law School's median salary of $18,500 in 1970 is approximately $102,000 in present-day dollars; $250 in 1970 is approximately $1,380 in present-day dollars; $18,000 in 1970 dollars is approximately $99,400 in present-day dollars; $500 in 1970 is approximately $2,760 in present-day dollars (see CPI, http://www.measuringworth.com/uscompare).

101. Father Walsh to Dean Mulligan, December 4, 1970, box 6, folder Law School Dean—1970, Walsh Papers, FU.

102. Joseph R. Cammarosano to Brother James M. Kenny, S.J., March 23, 1970, ibid.; see Table 6-1 Law Schools, Students, Faculty, Tuition, and Student Aid. **For the 1971 financial statement,** see School of Law Comparison of Operating Income and Expenditures: 1968–69 and 1969–70, box 26, folder Law School, Finlay Papers, FU. The student aid of $21,187 given in 1970 is approximately $117,000 in present-day dollars (see CPI, http://www.measuringworth.com/uscompare).

103. **Quotations** are in Cammarosano to Brother Kenny, March 23, 1970, box 6, folder Law School Dean—1970, Walsh Papers, FU; **for the income and expense statements,** see School of Law Comparison of Operating Income and Expenditures: 1968–69 and 1969–70, box 26, folder Law School, Finlay Papers, FU. The University's charge of $192,000 in 1970 is approximately $1,060,000 in present-day dollars (see CPI, http://www.measuringworth.com/uscompare).

104. **"shortly expend," "more than pay[s]," "primarily a 'gate-receipt' operation," "whether the [Law] School,"** ABA Inspection Report, April 28–29, 1958, 5–6, folder 13, box 1, FLS, FU; **"does point up the problem,"** William Hughes Mulligan to Reverend Laurence J. McGinley, October 9, 1958, box 5, folder 5, ibid.

105. **"tooth and nail,"** Professor Joseph Sweeney, interview by the author, September 14, 2010, FLSA; see also email from Professor Hugh Hansen to Robert Kaczorowski, September 20, 2010, ibid. The substance of this paragraph is based on my interview of Professor Sweeney and my interviews of Professor Barry Hawk, September 8, 2010, ibid.; Professor Joseph Perillo, September 9, 2010, ibid.; Professor Thomas Quinn, September 10, 2010, ibid.; Professor Gail Hollister, September 22, 2010, ibid.; letter from Professor Robert M. Byrn to the author, September 3, 2010, ibid.; and emails from Professor Hugh Hanson to the author, September 18 and 20, 2010. The other law school faculty that unionized at this time was that of the Rutgers School of Law—Camden.

106. **"with a great deal,"** Father Walsh to Mulligan, June 19, 1970, box 6, folder Law School Dean—1970, Walsh Papers, FU; Dean Mulligan tendered his resignation in Mulligan to Reverend Walsh, June 15, 1970, ibid.

107. McLaughlin interview, 22–23.

CHAPTER SEVEN: STRUGGLE FOR AUTONOMY

1. Dean Mulligan to Father Walsh, June 15, 1970, box 26, folder Law School, James C. Finlay Papers (hereafter after cited as Finlay Papers), Walsh Library, Fordham University (hereafter cited as FU).

2. The Honorable Joseph McLaughlin, interview by Robert Reilly, April 9, 1990, Transcript No. 107, Book 3, 24, Oral History Project (hereafter cited as OHP), Fordham Law School Archives (hereafter cited as FLSA). The faculty selected as their representatives Professors John Calamari, who chaired the committee, Robert Byrn, Richard Denzer, and Charles Whalen, S.J. Denis Klejna, president of the Student Bar Association, and Dennis McInerney, president of the Law School Alumni Association, represented the students and alumni respectively. Mulligan to Father Walsh, June 25, 1970, box 26, folder Law School, Finlay Papers, FU. Regarding the scope of the search, see John D. Calamari to Father Walsh, February 2, 1971, box 6, folder Search Committee for New Dean of Law School, Michael P. Walsh Papers, Walsh Library, Fordham University (hereafter cited Walsh Papers, FU); Exhibit A, Responses from Deans, n.d.,

attached to ibid.; Exhibit B, Alumni Response to Letter of August 17, 1970 re Search Committee, ibid.; Exhibit C, Responses from Fordham Law School Faculty, ibid.; Prof. Calamari to Members of Search Committee, n.d., Exhibit D, ibid. Professor Calamari incorporated the student nominations in the body of his letter to Father Walsh. See also Paul J. Reiss to Father Walsh, January 27, 1971, box 26, folder Law School, Finlay Papers, FU.

3. **"move the faculty,"** Byrn to Father Walsh, April 5, 1971, box 6, folder Search Committee for New Dean of Law School, Walsh Papers, FU; **"written extensively,"** **"There has been," "We need,"** Charles M. Whalen to Father Walsh, April 7, 1971, ibid.; **"simply qualified," "outstanding demonstrated," "far, far superior," "written extensively,"** Martin Fogelman to Father Walsh, n.d., ibid.

4. Denis McInerney to Father Walsh, April 8, 1971, box 6, folder Search Committee for New Dean of Law School, Walsh Papers, FU.

5. Reiss to Father Walsh, April 8, 1971, ibid.

6. Ibid.

7. McLaughlin interview, 25. The Judge's recollection was inaccurate. Among the "McLaughlin eight" were two Fordham Law School graduates, Lucille Buell and Thomas Fitzpatrick, both of whom graduated first in their graduating classes. Dean's Annual Report to the Alumni, 1971–72, 6–7, box 24, folder Dean's Reports 1971–89, Fordham Law School Papers, Walsh Library (hereafter cited as FLS, FU).

8. McLaughlin interview, 27.

9. **"we had Father Walsh,"** ibid.; **"a good way,"** ibid., 29; see also Father Walsh to McLaughlin, May 19, 1971, box 6, folder Law School Dean 1971–72, Walsh Papers, FU.

10. Self-interview of Reverend James C. Finlay, S.J., on January 29 and February 4, 1989, Transcript No. 39, Book 2, 28–29, OHP, FLSA.

11. McLaughlin interview, 50–51.

12. **Quotations** are in Denis McInerney to Dear Alumnus, December 8, 1971, box 6, folder Law School Dean 1971–72, Walsh Papers, FU; Robert M. Byrn to Rev. Michael P. Walsh, November 29, 1971, box 6, folder Law School Dean 1971–72, Walsh Papers, FU; Annual Report of the Dean to the Alumni, 1971–72, 1, box 24, folder Dean's Reports 1971–89, FLS, FU. The Law School committee consisted of two representatives of the Alumni, Dennis McInerney and Matt Mone, two faculty members, Robert M. Byrn and Barry Hawk, and one student representative, SBA President Tony Siano, and it worked out the logistics with the university development office.

13. Father Walsh to Bryn, December 6, 1971, box 6, folder Law School Dean 1971–72, Walsh Papers, FU.

14. Byrn to Father Walsh, March 22, 1972, box 6, folder Law School Dean – 1971–72, Walsh Papers, FU; this letter must be read in conjunction with the terms set forth in Byrn to Father Walsh, February 8, 1972, which expressed the Law School's views. The

University President expressed his approval of the final terms in Father Walsh to Byrn, March 24, 1972. For the university's development office perspectives on these issues, see Donald A. Miltner to Father Walsh, March 3, 1972, and Father Walsh to Brother Kenny, March 24, 1972. All cited correspondence is in box 6, folder Law School Dean – 1971–72, Walsh Papers, FU.

15. **Quotations** are in Dennis McInerney, Esq., interview by Robert Cooper Jr., May 1, 1989, Transcript No. 51, Book 2, 32–4, OHP, FLSA.

16. McLaughlin interview, 43–44.

17. Dean's Annual Report to Alumni, 1974–75, 1, box 24, folder Dean's Rerports, 1971–89, FLS, FU; contributions are reported in ibid., 10; **"this, we feel," "We have always,"** ibid.; see also Dean's Annual Report to Alumni, 1975–76, 1, inside cover, 9–10, box 24, folder Dean's Reports 1971–89, FLS, FU. Contributions of $105,000 in 1975 are approximately $418,000 in present-day dollars; contributions of $150,000 in 1976 are approximately $565,000 in present-day dollars (see CPI, http://www.measuringworth .com/uscompare).

18. Louis Stein, interview by Robert Cooper Jr., October 25, 1990, Transcript No. 139, Book 3, 7–9, OHP, FLSA. Stein believed that ethics were central to any activity or subject. He used his philanthropy to induce business schools, religious organizations, and universities "to understand that ethics must be taught alongside any subject that is being promoted in a given situation. We can't escape the ethical aspect," Stein emphasized. Ibid., 9.

19. Dean's Annual Report to Alumni, 1975–76, 1, inside cover, 9–10, box 24, folder Dean's Reports 1971–89, FLS, FU; Minutes of Faculty Meeting of August 20, 1976, folder Faculty Minutes 1976–77, FLSA; Minutes of Faculty Meeting of October 29, 1979, folder Faculty Minutes 1979–80, FLSA. Contibutions of $124,000 in 1976 are approximately $467,000 in present-day dollars; $6,000 in 1976 approximately $22,600 in present-day dollars; the university chair requirement of $1,000,000 and $700,000 the Law School raised in 1979 are approximately $2,960,000 and $2,070,000 in present-day dollars (see CPI, http://www.measuringworth.com/uscompare).

20. **"your gift reduces,"** Dean's Annual Report to Alumni, 1976–77, np, box 24, folder Dean's Reports 1971–89, FLS, FU; **"other law schools," "unless we can,"** Dean's Annual Report to Alumni, 1977–78, 10, box 24, folder Dean's Reports 1971–89, FLS, FU. See also "Long-Range Plan of the Fordham University School of Law," 75, ABA Profiles & Questionnaires 1988–96, box 6, loose, Law School Storage; Dean's Annual Report to Alumni, 1981–82, 10, box 24, folder Dean's Reports 1971–89, FLS, FU.

21. Report of the Student Five Year Plan Commission, November 1971, 1, box 30, folder 1, FLS, FU (hereafter cited as Student Plan, 1971). The student's five-year plan was essentially the work of a commission composed of thirteen law student leaders recruited from the Student Bar Association, the *Fordham Law Review*, and the *Fordham Journal of Urban Law*. The student commission's chair was SBA President

Anthony J. Siano and its members included Mary C. Daly, who later joined the Fordham Law School faculty and then became dean of St. John's Law School, and Loretta A. Preska, who serves as US District Court Judge in the Southern District of New York. Other commission members were: Joseph Abinanti, David J. Ciminesi, Hugh D. Fyfe, Peter Goldman, Robert Hegman, Donald Kennedy, Robert Minyard, Dennis Phillips, Samuel Sansone, and David Zoffer. Anthony J. Siano to Dean McLaughlin, November 1, 1971, included in Student Plan, 1971.

22. Email from Robert Reilly to Robert Kaczorowski, September 16, 2010, FLSA. See also letter from Professor Robert M. Byrn to Professor Robert M. [sic] Kaczorowski, September 3, 2010, FLSA; note from Professor Gail Hollister to Robert Kaczorowski, September 15, 2010, FLSA. **For graduates' success in job placement**, see infra notes 40–51 and accompanying text.

23. Letter from Professor Robert M. Byrn to Professor Robert M. [sic] Kaczorowski, September 3, 2010; note from Professor Gail Hollister to Robert Kaczorowski, September 15, 2010.

24. Student Plan 1971, 10.

25. Ibid., 12–15.

26. Ibid., 25.

27. Ibid., 25–26. Students corresponded with representatives of eighteen law schools concerning their programs. The law schools are Brooklyn, Boston University, Columbia, Duke, Georgetown, George Washington, Harvard, New York University, Northwestern, St. John's, Stanford, University of California at Berkeley, University of Chicago, University of Michigan, University of Pennsylvania, University of Virginia, and Yale University.

28. **Quotations** from Five Year Plan of the Fordham University School of Law, January 11, 1972, 1, box 30, folder 1, FLS, FU (hereafter cited as Five Year Plan 1972) (emphasis added).

29. After his appointment to the US Court of Appeals for the Second Circuit, Dean Mulligan continued to insist that the purpose of a law school " 'was to prepare students for the bar exam and the rest was baloney.' He was militant about it," Professor Hugh Hansen related. Email from Professor Hugh Hansen to the author, September 19, 2010. Judge Mulligan made this statement to Professor Hansen in a discussion they were having in which Hansen had asserted that the purpose of law schools "was [sic] train students to think in certain ways and to explore what law should be as well as what it is" ibid., 2–3.

30. Five Year Plan 1972, 3, 4–12.

31. Ibid., 14.

32. Ibid., 15.

33. Ibid., 19–20.

34. Student Plan 1971, 2–3, 28–29.

35. **Quotations** are in Student Plan 1971, 3–4; see also Five Year Plan 1972, 16–17, 21–22.

36. **Quotations** are in Five Year Plan 1972, 16–17, 21–22; see also Student Plan 1971, 3–4. A faculty research fund of $24,000 in 1971 is approximately $127,000 in present-day dollars; $4 in 1971 is approximately $21.20 in present-day dollars (see CPI, http://www.measuringworth.com/uscompare).

37. Student Plan 1971, 31–23.

38. **Biographical information about Simon Gourdine** is at http://www.answers.com/topic/simon-gourdine. Barry Hawk recounted Crowley's and Gourdine's efforts to recruit black students and the reasons for their failure in an interview with the author, August 31, 2010, FLSA; for data relating to minority student enrollments and student aid in the late 1980s and beyond, see infra chapter 8, Tables 8-1, 8-2, and 8-3.

39. Student Plan 1971, 31–32, 33–34, 34–35. Student aid of $110,000 in 1972 is approximately $564,000 in present-day dollars (see CPI, http://www.measuringworth.com/uscompare).

40. McLaughlin niterview, 36; John D. Feerick, interview by Robert Reilly, September 20, 1991, Transcript No. 148, Book No. 2, 21–22, OHP, FLSA.

41. McLaughlin interview, 36.

42. Robert Reilly, interview by Robert Cooper Jr., December 9, 1991, Transcript No. 98, Book 3, 25, OHP, FLSA. Law firm starting salaries of $21,000 in 1975, $25,000 in 1976, $30,000 in 1977, and $35,000 in 1978 are approximately $83,700, $94,200, $106,000, and $115,000 in present-day dollars (see CPI, http://www.measuringworth.com/uscompare).

43. Reilly interview, 26.

44. Minutes of Faculty Meeting of May 26, 1977, folder Faculty Minutes 1976–77, FLSA; Minutes of Faculty Meeting of August 25, 1977, folder Faculty Minutes 1977–78, FLSA.

45. Dean's Annual Report to Alumni, 1974–75, 8–9, box 24, folder Dean's Reports 1971–89, FLS, FU. All of these statistics were listed in Dean's Annual Report to Alumni, 1977–78, 1, ibid. The cover of the Dean's Report for 1977–78 had quotes from Shakespearean plays, including, "for to be pretentious 'bout our virtues would be to gild refined gold, to paint the lily, to throw perfume on the violet" (King John, IV, 1) "and we do neither gild nor paint, but here and there do perfume the proceedings a bit" (Romeo and Juliet, II, 1).

46. Minutes of Faculty Meeting of May 26, 1976, folder Faculty Minutes 1975–76, FLSA; Minutes of Faculty Meeting of May 26, 1977, folder Faculty Minutes 1976–77, FLSA; Minutes of Faculty Meeting of May 25, 1978, folder Faculty Minutes 1977–78, FLSA; Dean's Annual Report to Alumni, 1976–77, n.p., box 24, folder Dean's Reports 1971–89, FLS, FU.

47. Dean's Annual Report to Alumni, 1977–78, 3, box 24, folder Dean's Reports 1971–89, FLS, FU.

48. Minutes of Faculty Meeting of May 25, 1979, folder Faculty Minutes 1978–79, FLSA; Minutes of Faculty Meeting of February 24, 1981, Minutes of Faculty Meeting of April 7, 1981, folder Faculty Minutes 1980–81, FLSA. A report on Placement is attached to Minutes of Faculty Meeting of April 7, 1981. McLaughlin included the placement information in his Dean's Annual Report to the Alumni 1978–79, 5, box 24, folder Dean's Reports 1971–89, FLS, FU; and Dean's Annual Report to the Alumni 1979–80, 7, box 24, folder Dean's Reports 1971–89, FLS, FU.

49. **Quotations** are in Dean's Annual Report to the Alumni 1979–80, 8, box 24, folder Dean's Reports 1971–89, FLS, FU.

50. **"notable success," "pointed out,"** Father Finlay to Reiss and Dr. Joseph F. X. McCarthy, October 1, 1979, box 12, folder ABA 1979–83, Finlay Papers, FU; Report of the State Education Department Observer on An ABA-AALS Inspection at Fordham University Law School September 26–29, 1979, attached to Donald Y. Nutter to Father Finlay, November 2, 1979 and Father Finlay to Nutter, November 5, 1979, box 12, folder ABA 1979–83, Finlay Papers, FU. Dean McLaughlin announced the *Harvard Business Review* finding in Dean's Annual Report to the Alumni 1979–80, 1, box 24, folder Dean's Reports 1971–89, FLS, FU.

51. Minutes of Faculty Meeting of February 24, 1981, folder Faculty Minutes 1980–81, FLSA; Minutes of Faculty Meeting of April 7, 1981, folder Faculty Minutes 1980–81, FLSA, Placement Report attached. Minutes of Faculty Meeting of May 22, 1981, folder Faculty Minutes 1980–81, FLSA.

52. Five Year Plan 1972, 23–26; Student Plan 1971, 23–24. The budget of $93,000 in 1973 is approximately $449,000 in present-day dollars (see CPI, http://www.measuringworth.com/uscompare).

53. **The committee** was chaired by Professor Michael M. Martin and included Professors Joseph M. Perillo and Michael R. Lanzarone. Professor Robert M. Byrn served as counsel. Report of Committee to Review the Five Year Plan, September 10, 1975, 2–5, FLSA (hereafter cited as Review Committee Report). Dean McLaughlin informed the alumni that the revised curriculum resulted from the five-year plan. Annual Report of the Dean to the Alumni, 1971–72, 2–5, box 24, folder Dean's Reports 1971–89, FLS, FU. Resource rankings were based on the number of students, student-to-faculty ratio, number of full-time faculty, average class hours per week taught by full-time faculty, and number of volumes in the library. See Annual Report of the Dean to the Alumni, 1971–72, 3, footnote *. Some of the law schools in Fordham's resource ranking group 3 were Cincinnati, Hastings, Indianapolis, Mississippi, Villanova, Western Reserve, Colorado, Kansas, New Mexico, St. Louis, and Wayne State. Columbia, New York University and Georgetown Law Schools were in group 1, St. Johns was in group 4.

54. Review Committee Report, 8, 10–11, 9–10, 12.

55. Ibid., 11. **Clinical courses** are also discussed in Annual Report of the Dean to the Alumni, 1971–72, 3, box 24, FLS, FU.

56. Review Committee Report, 23–25, 26–27.

57. Ibid, 28.

58. Ibid., 29–30. The book budget increase of $65,000 in 1971 to $100,000 in 1975 is approximately $344,000 to $398,000 in present-day dollars; the supplements of $5,000 to $7,000 in 1975 dollars are approximately $19,900 to $27,900 in present-day dollars (see CPI, http://www.measuringworth.com/uscompare).

59. Ibid., 32–33. The proposed library expenditures of $22,000 and $15,000 in 1972 are approximately $113,000 and $76,900 in present-day dollars; the required library budget of $600,000 in 1972 is approximately $3,080,000 in present-day dollars (see CPI, http://www.measuringworth.com/uscompare).

60. Joseph R. Cammarosano to Constantine Katsoris, June 15, 1972, box 6, folder Law School Dean 1971–72, Walsh Papers; Cammarosano and Paul J. Reiss to Law School Faculty Bargaining Committee, June 15, 1972; Father Walsh to Cammarosano, May 31, 1972; Cammarosano to Father Walsh, May 25, 1972; Joseph R. Crowley, to Cammarosano, May 16, 1972; Reiss to Father Walsh, September 8, 1971; Reiss to Father Walsh, August 3, 1971; Perillo to Father Walsh, July 7, 1971; Father Walsh to Perillo, July 1, 1971; Perillo to Father Walsh, June 17, 1971; Walsh to Perillo, May 6, 1971; Perillo to Father Walsh, April 30, 1971. All cited correspondence are in box 6, folder Law School Dean 1971–72, Walsh Papers, FU.

61. McLaughlin to Father Finlay, November 19, 1971, box 26, folder Law School, Finlay Papers, FU. A faculty salary of $21,000 in 1971 is approximately $111,000 in present-day dollars (see CPI, http://www.measuringworth.com/uscompare).

62. Reiss to McLaughlin, February 23, 1972, box 26, folder Law School, Finlay Papers, FU. The *Fordham Urban Law Journal* began publication in the summer of 1971, just as Mulligan ended his tenure as dean and Dean McLaughlin began his. It was originally funded by Louis Stein to enable students who were very interested in "the real estate field, as to what direction urban development should take" to build a better urban community. See Stein interview, 5. Father Finlay was unmoved by a barrage of petitions to fund the *ULJ*. See Father Finlay to Judge William Hughes Mulligan, December 21, 1972, box 26, folder Law School, Finlay Papers, FU; Judge Mulligan to Father Finlay, December 15, 1972; Father Finlay to John D. Feerick, December 14, 1972; Feerick to Father Finlay, December 8, 1972; Joyce P. Davis to Father Finlay, December 15, 1972; Father Finlay to Theodore H. Latty, December 14, 1972; Latty to Father Finlay, December 7, 1972; Father Finlay to Louis J. Lefkowitz, December 12, 1972; Lefkowitz to Father Finlay, December 8, 1972; Father Finlay to Manuel A. Cuadrado, December 12, 1972; Cuadrado to Father Finlay, December 7, 1972; Michael Lanzarone to Paul J. Reiss,

December 11, 1972; Reiss to Dean McLaughlin, December 1, 1972; all cited correspondence are in box 26, folder Law School, Finlay Papers, FU. See also Minutes of Faculty Meeting, December 12, 1972; Annual Report of the Dean to the Alumni, 1972–73, 5, box 24, FLSA, FU; Annual Report of the Dean to the Alumni, 1973–74, n.p., box 24. A budget increase of $57,000 in 1973 is approximately $275,000 in present-day dollars (see CPI, http://www.measuringworth.com/uscompare).

63. All of the information in this paragraph was provided by Dean James P. White in a telephone interview conducted by author on June 23, 2008.

64. Ibid.

65. Ibid.; **"the idea of independent,"** Father Finlay to Cammarosano and Reiss, May 29, 1973, box 12, folder ABA 1973–75, Finlay Papers, FU; **"it is ironic,"** Cammarosano to Reiss, May 29, 1973, box 12, folder ABA 1973–75, Finlay Papers; **"take a hard look,"** Reiss to McLaughlin, June 4, 1973, box 12, folder ABA 1973–75, Finlay Papers, FU; for the **ABA's standards and policies,** see Millard H. Rudd to Dean McLaughlin, May 21, 1973, box 12, folder ABA 1973–75, Finlay Papers; McLaughlin to Rudd, May 24, 1973, box 12, folder ABA 1973–75, Finlay Papers, FU.

66. **Quotations** are in Report of the Joint Visitation Team of the Association of American Law Schools and the Council on Legal Education of the American Bar Association on the Fordham Law School December 1973, (hereafter cited as 1973 ABA Report), "Overview," and 29, box 12, folder ABA 1973–75, Finlay Papers, FU. Copies of this Report are also in box 26, folder Law School, Finlay Papers, FU; and box 18, folder 1 Accreditation 1974, FLS, FU.

67. Ibid., 7–8, 11–15, 15–19; See Table 1, Comparison of Rate of Expansion of the Book Collection at Fordham and at Eight Comparable Law School Libraries, ibid., 18. The median faculty salary of $23,600 in 1973 dollars is approximately $114,000 in present-day dollars; the book budget of $94,000 in 1973 is approximately $454,000 in present-day dollars, and the required book budget increase of $25,000 in 1973 is approximately $121,000 in present-day dollars (see CPI, http://www.measuringworth.com/uscompare).

68. Dennis McInerney to Dear Alumnus, December 8, 1971, box 6, folder Law School Dean 1971–72, Walsh Papers, FU; Robert M. Byrn to Rev. Michael P. Walsh, November 29, 1971, box 6, folder Law School Dean 1971–72, Walsh Papers, FU; Annual Report of the Dean to the Alumni, 1971–72, box 24, FLS, FU.

69. Byrn to Father Walsh, March 22, 1972, box 6, folder Law School Dean 1971–72, Walsh Papers, FU; this letter must be read in conjunction with the terms set forth in Byrn to Father Walsh, February 8, 1972, which expressed the Law School's views. The university president expressed his approval of the final terms in Father Walsh to Byrn, March 24, 1972. **For the university's development office perspectives on these issues**, see Donald A. Miltner to Father Walsh, March 3, 1972, and Father Walsh to Brother

Kenny, March 24, 1972. The cited correspondence are in box 6, folder Law School Dean 1971–72, Walsh Papers, FU.

70. **Quotations** are in 1973 ABA Report, 6.

71. **Quotations** are in ABA Report, "Overview," box 12, folder ABA 1973–75, Finlay Papers, FU; copies of this Report are also in box 26, folder Law School, Finlay Papers, FU; and box 18, folder 1, Accreditation 1974, FLS, FU.

72. James C. Finlay to Dean John B. Neibel, March 5, 1974, box 26, folder Law School, Finlay Papers, FU.

73. Ibid.

74. Paul J. Reiss to Father Finlay, March 7, 1974, box 12, folder ABA 1973–75, Finlay Papers, FU.

75. Ibid.

76. **All of Father Finlay's statements** are in Father Finlay to Neibel, March 12, 1974, box 12, folder ABA 1973–75, Finlay Papers, FU and Finlay to Millard H. Ruud, March 15, 1974, ibid.; Ruud's reply is in Millard H. Ruud to Father Finlay, March 20, 1974, ibid.

77. Neibel to Father Finlay, March 27, 1974, box 12, folder ABA 1973–75, Finlay Papers, FU.

78. James P. White to Father Finlay and Dean McLaughlin, August 8, 1974, box 12, folder ABA 1973–75, Finlay Papers, FU.

79. Ibid.

80. **Quotations** are in ibid.; **for faculty salaries**, see Median Salaries for Academic Year 1974–75 of Full-time Teachers at Approved Law Schools, attached to James P. White to Deans of Approved Law Schools, December 6, 1974, box 12, folder ABA 1973–75, Finlay Papers, FU.

81. Father Finlay to James P. White, January 14, 1975, box 12, folder ABA 1973–75, Finlay Papers, FU.

82. Ibid.; Report to American Bar Association, attached to ibid.

83. Salaries – Fordham University School of Law 1970–71 Through 1974–75, Table included in ibid.; Report to American Bar Association, attached to Father Finlay to James P. White, January 14, 1975, box 12, folder ABA 1973–75, Finlay Papers, FU; Interview of John D. Feerick by Robert Reilly on September 20, 1991, Transcript No. 148, Book No. 2, 25, OHP, FLSA. The increase in faculty salaries from $403,270 in 1971 to $729,800 in 1975 is approximately $2,140,000 to $2,910,000 in present-day dollars, and the total increase of $326,530 is $1,300,000 in present-day dollars; the $7,600 increase in the median salary in 1975 is approximately $30,300 in present-day dollars; the rise in the median salary of $18,400 in 1971 to $26,000 in 1975 is an increase of approximately $97,400 to $104,000 in present-day dollars; the increase in the book budget of $7,000 in 1973 is approximately $33,800 in present-day dollars; the Law school request

for an increase of $16,000 in 1973 is approximately $77,200 in present-day dollars, and the ABA estimate of $25,000 to bring the book collection up to where it should be in 1973 is approximately $121,000 in present-day dollars (see CPI, http://www.measuringworth.com/uscompare). The increases in faculty salaries occurred at the time that the law faculty organized itself into a union. Some faculty believe that the increases in faculty salaries were attributable to the faculty union. See, for example, letter from Prof. Robert M. Byrn to Prof. Robert J. Kaczorowski, September 3, 2010, FLSA; interview with Professor Joseph Perillo by author, September 9, 2010, FLSA; interview with Professor Professor Thomas Quinn by author, September 10, 2010, FLSA; interview with Professor Joseph Sweeney by the author, September 14, 2010, FLSA. The union may have been responsible for some of the increase in faculty salaries, but the union would not have been responsible for the increases in the library budget. It would appear that pressure from the ABA Council and Accreditation Committee were also responsible for these budgetary increases.

84. James P. White to Father Finlay and Dean McLaughlin, February 14, 1975, box 12, folder ABA 1973–75, Finlay Papers, FU.

85. Ibid.

86. Father Finlay to White, March 20, 1975, box 12, folder ABA 1973–75, Finlay Papers, FU; A Chronological Summary of the Reaccreditation Process for the School of Law Conducted by the Section of Legal Education and Admission to the Bar of the American Bar Association, attached to John B. Neibel to Father Finlay, February 27, 1974, box 12, folder ABA 1973–75, Finlay Papers, FU; Notes from a meeting held on Friday, April 25, 1975, May 12, 1975, box 12, folder ABA 1973–75, Finlay Papers, FU. White specified the kinds of problems these law schools were having that cast doubt on the quality of their programs: "the problems of non-retention of non-tenured faculty (too frequent turnovers in faculty); inadequacies of libraries so far as books or staffing were concerned; inadequate buildings; a breakdown of communications between the Dean and the President of the University such that the Dean couldn't see the President; a judgment concerning what the school is as compared with what it should or might be; should a school be aiming at national pre-eminence or pre-eminence with a state or region." Notes from a meeting held on Friday, April 25, 1975, May 12, 1975, box 12, folder ABA 1973–75, Finlay Papers, FU.

87. Notes from a meeting held on Friday, April 25, 1975, May 12, 1975, box 12, folder ABA 1973–75, Finlay Papers, FU.

88. Cammarosano to Father Finlay, April 28, 1975, box 12, folder ABA 1973–75, Finlay Papers, FU.

89. Father Finlay to Dr. Lloyd Elliott, April 7, 1975, box 12, folder ABA 1973–75, Finlay Papers, FU.

90. Ibid.

91. Elliott to Father Finlay, April 11, 1975, box 12, folder ABA 1973–75, Finlay Papers, FU; Father Finlay's handwritten notes in ibid.

92. R. W. Nahstoll to Father Finlay, May 13, 1975, box 12, folder ABA 1973–75, Finlay Papers, FU.

93. John A. Fitterer, S.J., to Father Finlay, May 19, 1975, box 12, folder ABA 1973–75, Finlay Papers, FU.

94. Ibid.

95. Ibid.

96. Father Finlay to Nahstoll, June 5, 1975, box 12, folder ABA 1973–75, Finlay Papers, FU.

97. R. W. Nahstoll to Very Rev. James C. Finlay, S.J., June 20, 1975, box 12, folder ABA 1973–75, Finlay Papers, FU.

98. Father Finlay to Professor White, July 2, 1975, box 26, folder Law School, Finlay Papers, FU. The surplus of $155,672 and total revenues of $2,310,103 in 1973 are approximately $751,000 and $11,100,000 in present-day dollars; the surplus of $176,983 and total revenues of $2,504,246 in 1974 are approximately $770,000 and $10,900,000 in present-day dollars (see CPI, http://www.measuringworth.com/uscompare).

99. Father Finlay to Professor White, July 2, 1975, box 26, folder Law School, Finlay Papers, FU. The physical plant expense of $362,271 in 1973 and $404,868 in 1974 are approximately $1,750,000 and $1,760,000 in present-day dollars (see CPI, http://www .measuringworth.com/uscompare).

100. Amount and Disposition of Surplus resulting from the Operations of the School of Law, attached to Father Finlay to Professor White, July 2, 1975, box 26, folder Law School, Finlay Papers, FU; Fordham University School of Law Revenues and Expenditures, attached to ibid. Father Finlay did not explain that the University used different ratios to determine the FTE value for part-time law students and the FTE value for part-time students in the other departments of the university. It counted each part-time law student as three-quarters of a full-time student, but it counted each part-time student in all of the other schools and departments of the university as only one-third of a full-time student. This resulted in a larger FTE for the Law School student population than for the rest of the university. The disparity in these ratios had a significant effect on cost allocation. For example, in 1971–72, the Law School's enrollment was 851, of whom 502 were full-time students and 349 part-time students. The rest of the university had a total enrollment of 12,591, consisting of 7,695 full-time and 4,896 part-time students. The number of Law School FTE students, 764, was 89.8 percent of the Law School's total enrollment of 851 students. The FTE for the rest of Fordham University, 9311, was only 73.9 percent of the total student enrollment of 12,591. For the 1970–71 academic year, applying the university's calculus to general administration expenditures of $738,794 and general expenditures of $1,621,738 resulted in a Law School allocation of $60,581 ($321,000 in present-day dollars) and $132,983 ($704,000 in present-day dollars) respectively. If the university used the one-third calculus for Law School FTEs as it did for the other university FTEs, the Law

School would have been charged only $49,499 ($262,000 in present-day dollars) and $108,656 ($575,000 in present-day dollars), or $24,327 ($128,000 in present-day dollars) less. Office of Management and Budget Review, Fordham University, Memorandum, May 22, 1972, box 26, folder Law School, Finlay Papers, FU. The indirect expenses of $253,016 in 1973 and $280,099 in 1974 are approximately $1,220,000 and $1,220,000 in present-day dollars; the physical plant and indirect expenses of $615,287 in 1973 are approximately $2,970,000 in present-day dollars; the Law School's total expenses of $2,154,431 in 1973 are approximately $10,400,000 in present-day dollars; these figures of $654,967 and $2,327,263 in 1974 are approximately $2,850,000 and $10,100,000 in present-day dollars respectively; annual plant replacement cost of $200,000 in 1974 is approximately $870,000 in present-day dollars; total payment to Fordham University of $815,287 in 1973 is approximately $3,930,000 in present-day dollars; total payment to Fordham University of $884,967 in 1974 is approximately $3,850,000 in present-day dollars; the Law School's surplus of $155,672 in 1973 is approximately $751,000 in present-day dollars and increased the total payments to the university to $970,959 in 1973, approximately $4,690,000 in present-day dollars, out of its total revenue for 1973 of $2,310,103, which is approximately $11,100,000 in present-day dollars; for 1974, the Law School's surplus of $176,983 is approximately $854,000 in present-day dollars; its total payment to Fordham University of $1,061,950 is approximately $5,130,000 in present-day dollars; $738,794 in 1971 dollars is approximately $3,910,000 in present-day dollars; $1,621,738 in 1971 dollars is approximately $8,590,000 in present-day dollars (see CPI, http://www.measuringworth.com/uscompare).

101. Father Finlay to Professor White, November 26, 1975, box 18, folder Accreditation 1974, FLS, FU. The different understandings are illustrated in Vice President Reiss's attempted justification of the Law School's contribution to the plant fund, which included charges to retire the debt on the Lowenstein Building and Lincoln Center Plaza even though the Law School building was debt free. Acknowledging that the amount that should be charged to the Law School was "not obvious to me," and conceding that one could reasonably argue that none of the debt service should be charged to the Law School, Reiss countered that "at least $2,500,000 of the $3,500,000 cost of the [Law School] building was derived from this Plant Fund," and, therefore, one could argue that the fact that the Law School building "was actually paid for in greater measure from existing University plant funds and the other building by incurring debt should not [excuse] the Law School from participating in the retirement of the campus debt." Reiss thought this was "a good example of the difficulty of disentangling financially one school from a University which conducts its fiscal affairs as one unit." Reiss to Dean Lewis M. Collens, October 10, 1979, box 12, folder ABA 1979–87, Finlay Papers, FU.

102. Professor White to Father Finlay, September 12, 1975, box 18, folder Accreditation 1974, FLS, FU; Father Finlay to Professor White, November 26, 1975, ibid. Fordham University also defended other ABA challenges to its accounting policies, such as

the method the university used to calculate the amount it charged to the Law School for indirect expenses. Father Finlay explained that the university applied the three-quarter formula to part-time law students to calculate FTE students for Indirect Expenses because they finished the program in four rather than three years. However, he failed to explain why the part-time students in all of the University's other schools were counted as only one-half FTE. Nor did he explain that the one-half FTE for non-law students represented an increase from the one-third ratio the university used prior to 1973. It is reasonable to infer that the university increased this calculation to give the appearance of greater equity in expense allocations as suggested by Father Fitterer. Father Finlay also defended against the ABA's claim that the amount of indirect expenses charged to the Law School was not justified because the Law School did not derive equivalent benefits from the university due to "its physical location separate from the main campus, and the extent to which it utilizes the services available from central administration." Father Finlay claimed that the Law School used a number of university facilities and services in the Lincoln Center Campus for lectures, conferences, receptions and meetings for alumni and guests. He also claimed that law students used "the athletic facilities provided on that campus," and the law faculty used the faculty dining facilities. The Law School's commencement exercises were held on the Robert Moses Plaza, "an integral part of the campus at Lincoln Center." Father Finlay noted that, although the Law School used the university development office staff and facilities "to a considerably higher degree than do other schools," the university did not assess a "charge or discount to the funds received through these activities to offset the costs to the University in raising the funds. Rather [sic] the entire amount of funds raised . . . is allocated for direct use by the Law School." Father Finlay did not mention that the university administration demanded that the Law School do its fund raising through the university's development office, which enabled the university administration to maintain control over the Law School's fund-raising revenues and to divert donations from the Law School to the university whenever the donor failed to state explicitly that his donations was intended for the Law School. White to Father Finlay, September 12, 1975, box 18, folder Accreditation 1974, FLS, FU; Father Finlay to Professor White, November 26, 1975, box 18, folder Accreditation 1974, FLS, FU. Bundy Aid of $2,631,000 in 1975 is approximately $10,500,000 in present-day dollars; the $600 in 1975 for each graduate is approximately $2,390 in present-day dollars; Bundy Aid for Law School graduates of $199,800 in 1975 is approximately $796,000 in present-day dollars; plant replacement of $200,000 charged to the Law School in 1975 is approximately $797,000 in present-day dollars (see CPI, http://www.measuringworth.com/uscompare).

103. Professor White to Father Finlay and Dean McLaughlin, January 21, 1976, box 18, folder Accreditation 1974, FLS, FU.

104. Professor White to Father Finlay and Dean McLaughlin, April 22, 1976, box 18, folder Accreditation 1974, FLS, FU.

105. Professor White to Father Finlay and Dean McLaughlin, October 12, 1976, box 18, folder Accreditation 1974, FLS, FU.

106. Fordham Law School Accreditation, Memorandum of Leo A. Larkin to F. E. Larkin, November 3, 1976, box 12, folder ABA 1976–79, Finlay Papers, FU.

107. **Quotations** are in Fordham Law School Accreditation, Memorandum of Leo A. Larkin to F. E. Larkin, November 3, 1976, 11, box 12, folder ABA 1976–79, Finlay Papers, FU.

108. Ibid., 12.

109. Ibid., 13.

110. **"contest in court," "with espousing a selective,"** ibid., 14; **"for impairment of," "to the risk,"** ibid., 24

111. **"real basic hangup," "relationship between," "one half of the tuition,"** Fordham University Secretary Michael J. Sheehan's Notes of Meeting of November 20, 1976, 2, box 12, folder ABA 1976–79, Finlay Papers, FU; **"The average in private,"** ibid., 6; **"sufficiently excessive," "for you people," "ripping off the Law School,"** ibid., 16.

112. **"necessary data," "Prior attempts to obtain," "well within,"** Self-Study Report of the Faculty of the Fordham University School of Law, March 30, 1979, 4, box 18, folder Accreditation 1974–88, FLS, FU; **"it is simply," "almost as though," "view university administration,"** Memorandum from Joseph F. X. McCarthy to Dean McLaughlin, May 22, 1979, box 18, folder Accreditation 1974–88, FLS, FU.

113. **Quotations** are in Memorandum from Joseph F. X. McCarthy to Dean McLaughlin, May 22, 1979, box 18, folder Accreditation 1974–88, FLS, FU.

114. Sheehan's Notes of Meeting of November 20, 1976, 15, box 12, folder ABA 1976–79, Finlay Papers, FU.

115. **Quotations** are in Father Finlay to Professor White, January 6, 1977, box 18, folder Accreditation 1974–88, FLS, FU. Unfortunately, the file does not contain the financial information transmitted to the ABA.

116. **Quotations** are in Professor White to Father Finlay and Dean McLaughlin, June 1, 1977, box 18, folder Accreditation 1974, FLS, FU; see also White to Father Finlay and Dean John D. Feerick, December 16, 1982, box 18, folder Accreditation 1974–88, FLS, FU; White to Father Finlay and Dean Feerick, April 28, 1983, box 18, folder Accreditation 1974–88, FLS, FU; White to Father Finlay and Dean Feerick, November 16, 1983, box 18, folder Accreditation 1974–88, FLS, FU.

117. **"serious deficiency," "unreasonably low," "adequate training,"** James P. White to Father Finlay and Dean Feerick, November 16, 1983, box 12, folder ABA 1979–83, Finlay Papers, FU. **"a severe communication problem," "thought the**

library," Father Finlay to Reiss and Dr. Joseph F.X. McCarthy, October 1, 1979, box 12, folder ABA 1979–83, Finlay Papers, FU. **Enrollment numbers** are in Report of the State Education Department Observer on An ABA-AALS Inspection at Fordham University Law School September 26–29, 1979, (hereafter cited as 1979 Reinspection Report) attached to Donald Y. Nutter to Father Finlay, November 2, 1979 and Father Finlay to Nutter, November 5, 1979, box 12, folder ABA 1979–83, Finlay Papers, FU. The 1979 Reinspection Report is attached to Lewis M. Collens to Father Finlay and Dean McLaughlin, January 23, 1980, and to Millard H. Ruud to Father Finlay and Dean McLaughlin, February 27, 1980, box 12, folder ABA 1979–83, Finlay Papers, FU. See tables attached to Conrad P. Rutkowski to Father Finlay, September 5, 1979, folder ABA 1979–83, box 12, Finlay Papers, FU. It is worth noting that the ABA did not fault Fordham for inadequate faculty salaries. As of December 1978, Fordham ranked nineteenth among all law schools in the faculty's median salaries and fringe benefits, five ranks below number fourteen Georgetown, and fifteenth in average faculty salaries and fringe benefits, just behind number fourteen Georgetown. However, Fordham Law School's full-time faculty numbered only twenty-six, whereas Georgetown's numbered forty-nine. The Law School's Library ranked fortieth in total volumes and volume equivalent of microforms. Georgetown ranked twenty-ninth.

118. 1979 Reinspection Report, 6.

119. Self-Study Report of the Faculty of the Fordham University School of Law, March 30, 1979, 2, box 18, folder Accreditation 1974–88, FLS, FU. Professor Kelso's study was published in *Learning and the Law* 2 (1975): 51.

120. **Quotations** are in Self-Study Report of the Faculty of the Fordham University School of Law, March 30, 1979, 2, box 18, folder Accreditation 1974–88, FLS, FU. The citations are: *National Law Journal* (September 18, 1978): 6; *Juris Doctor*, (August/ September 1978): 27; *New York Law Journal* (February 25, 1976): 1; *ABA Journal* 61 (January 1975): 99.

121. **"particularly threatening,"** Report of the Ad Hoc Committee [of the Board of Trustees] on the School of Law, June 1980, 5, box 13, folder Trustees – Law School, Finlay Papers, FU; **"major complaint,"** ibid., 7; **"good faith," "should certainly,"** ibid., 13. Father Finlay's statement is in Father Finlay to Dr. Theodore J. St. Antonine [*sic*], June 3, 1980, box 13, folder Trustees – Law School, Finlay Papers, FU. A copy of the Report of the Ad Hoc Committee on the School of Law is in box 18, folder Accreditation 1974–88, FLS, FU.

122. Report of the Ad Hoc Committee [of the Board of Trustees] on the School of Law, June, 1980, 13–14, box 13, folder Trustees – Law School, Finlay Papers, FU.

123. **"a serious deficiency," "when used,"** White to Father Finlay and Acting Dean Joseph M. Perillo, November 24, 1981, box 18, folder Accreditation 1974–88,FLS, FU; **"that the membership,"** John A. Bauman to Father Finlay and Dean McLaughlin,

November 18, 1980, box 12, folder ABA 1979–83, Finlay Papers, FU. See also Ruud to Father Finlay and Dean McLaughlin, June 23, 1980, box 12, folder ABA 1979–83, Finlay Papers, FU; Father Finlay's response is attached to Father Finlay to Ruud, October 1, 1980, box 12, folder ABA 1979–83, Finlay Papers, FU. A concise outline of the actions and reactions and the correspondence that flowed between the ABA and Fordham University from September 1979 to November 1983 is attached to the letter from White to Finlay and Feerick, November 16, 1983 box 12, folder ABA 1979–83, Finlay Papers, FU. A copy of this document is in box 18, Accreditation 1974–88, FLS, FU. The $8,000,000 building addition in 1984 is approximately $16,500,000 in present-day dollars (see CPI, http://www.measuringworth.com/uscompare).

124. **Quotations** are in White to Father Finlay and Acting Dean Perillo, November 24, 1981, box 18, folder Accreditation 1974–88, FLS, FU.

125. Minutes of Faculty Meeting of April 7, 1981, folder Faculty Minutes 1980–81, FLSA; Minutes of Faculty Meeting of May 22, 1981, box 18, folder Accreditation 1974–88, FLS, FU. **Expenditure per FTE student data** are in White to Deans of ABA Approved Law Schools, April 26, 1982, attached to Acting Dean Perillo to Dr. Paul Reiss, May 10, 1982, box 18, folder Accreditation 1974–88, FLS, FU. Other law schools in New York reported the following amounts: New York University ($13,311); Columbia ($10,052); Cornell ($8,080); Albany ($6,103); Brooklyn ($5,760); Syracuse ($5,634); New York Law School ($4,787); Yeshiva ($4,308); Hofstra ($4,026); SUNY Buffalo ($3,896). Some of the other Catholic law schools reported much higher expenditures than Fordham's: Georgetown ($7,331); Notre Dame ($6,416); Boston College ($4,630); Loyola–Los Angeles ($4,523); Villanova ($4,510); San Diego ($4,165); Marquette ($4,132); Santa Clara ($3,983); Catholic University ($3,950); Loyola-New Orleans ($3,939); St. Mary's ($3,939); San Francisco ($3,895); DePaul ($3,824); St. Louis ($3,697); Creighton ($3,502); Detroit University ($3,462); Dayton ($3,325). $3,277 in 1982 is approximately $7,290 in present-day dollars; $3,138 in 1982 is approximately $6,980 in present-day dollars; $3,267 in 1982 is approximately $7,260 in present-day dollars; $3,183 in 1982 is approximately $7,080 in present-day dollars; $2,839 in 1982 is approximately $6,310 in present-day dollars (see CPI, http://www.measuringworth .com/uscompare).

126. McLaughlin interview, 56.

CHAPTER EIGHT: RESURGENCE OF FORDHAM LAW SCHOOL

1. **All quotations** are in Dean's Annual Report to Alumni, 1981–82, 2, box 24, folder Dean's Reports 1971–89, Fordham Law School Papers, Walsh Library (hereinafter cited as FLS, FU).

2. **"half jokingly," "one of the best," "trustee liaison,"** Self-interview of Reverend James C. Finlay, S.J., on January 29 and February 4, 1989, Transcript No. 39, Book 2, 60, Oral History Project (hereafter cited as OHP), Fordham Law School Archives

(hereafter cited as FLSA); **"the guiding genius," "shadow dean,"** Dean's Annual Report to Alumni, 1976–77, n.p., box 24, folder Dean's Reports 1971–89, FLS, FU.

3. "Comments to Kaczorowski," attached to email from Joseph Perillo to Robert Kaczorowski, September 9, 2010, FLSA; Interview of Professor Joseph Sweeney by the author on September 14, 2010, FLSA. Professor Sweeney chaired the dean's search committee.

4. "Comments to Kaczorowski," attached to email from Joseph Perillo to Robert Kaczorowski, September 9, 2010, FLSA; interview of Professor Joseph Sweeney by the author on September 14, 2010, FLSA.

5. **Quotations** are in John D. Feerick, interview by Robert Reilly on September 20, 1991, Transcript No. 148, Book No. 2, 27, OHP, FLSA.

6. **Quotations** are in Feerick interview, 31–35; see also Interview of Frances M. Blake by Robert Reilly on October 18, 1988, Transcript No. 23, Book 1, 13, OHP, FLSA.

7. Quotations are in John D. Feerick to Dean White, September 30, 1983, box 12, folder ABA 1979–83, James C. Finlay Papers, Walsh Library (hereafter cited as Finlay Papers, FU); **for the square footage per FTE student,** see White to Deans of ABA-Approved Law Schools, "Total Net Square Footage per FTE Student," April 25, 1983, box 18, folder Accreditation 1974–88, FLS, FU.

8. Report on Fordham University School of Law, March 6–9, 1994, 61, box 4, folder 1994/1995 Correspondence and Responses to the 1993/1994 Site Evaluation, Law School Storage (hereinafter cited LSS); 1993–94 Dean's Report to Reverend Joseph A. O'Hare, S.J., from John D. Feerick, September 1, 1994, 3, box 4, loose, ABA Site Evaluation 1994/1992, Self Study 1986/1994, LSS.

9. **Quotations** are in Report on Fordham University School of Law, March 6–9, 1994, 64, box 4, folder 1994/1995 Correspondence and Responses to the 1993/1994 Site Evaluation, LSS. Dean Feerick concurred in the ABA Report. See 1993–94 Dean's Report to Reverend Joseph A. O'Hare, S.J., from John D. Feerick, September 1, 1994, 4, box 4, loose, ABA Site Evaluation 1994/1992, Self Study 1986/1994, LSS.

10. Report on Fordham University School of Law, February 28 to March 3, 2001, May 22, 2002 (follow-up visit), 45, enclosed in John A. Sebert to Very Reverend Joseph A. O'Hare, S.J., and Dean William Michael Treanor, November 22, 2002, FLSA

11. James P. White to Deans of ABA Approved Law Schools, April 26, 1982, box 18, folder Accreditation 1974–1988, FLS, FU. The Total Law School Expenditures Per FTE Student in 1982 in approximate present-day dollars are as follows: $3,277 is $7,290; $3,138 is $6,980; $13,311 is $29,600; $10,052 is $22,300; $8,080 is $18,000; $5,760 is $12,800; $5,634 is $12,500; $4,787 is $10,600; $4,308 is $9,580; $4,026 is $8,950; $3,896 is $8,660; $7,331 is $16,300; $6,416 is $14,300; $4,630 is $10,300; $4,510 is $10,000; $3,696 is $8,220 (see CPI, http://www.measuringworth.com/uscompare).

12. Dean James P. White, telephone interview conducted by the author on June 23, 2008.

13. White to Finlay and Feerick, November 16, 1983, box 18, folder Accreditation 1974–88, FLS, FU. See also the correspondence between the ABA and Fordham University from 1979 to 1983 in box 18, folder Accreditation 1974–88, FLS, FU.

14. Except as otherwise noted, the **quotations** are in White interview; Dean Feerick's views are in Report on Fordham University School of Law, February 28–March 3, 2001, May 22, 2002 (follow-up Visit), 43, enclosed in John A. Sebert to Very Reverend Joseph A. O'Hare, S.J., and Dean William Michael Treanor, November 22, 2002, FLSA; **"cordial, mutually supportive,"** Report of the Site Inspection Team, Fordham University School of Law, November 2–5, 1986, 37, box 4, ABA Site Evaluation 1994–95, Self-Study 1986/94, loose, LSS.

15. White interview.

16. Cammarosano to Reverend Joseph A. O'Hare, December 9, 1987, box 18, folder Accreditation 1974–88, FLS, FU. That the Law School repaid its debt to the university for the 1984 building expansion is mentioned in James P. White to Reverend Joseph A. O'Hare, S.J., and John D. Feerick, May 10, 1995, 1–2, box 4, folder 1994/1995 Correspondence and Responses to the 1993/94 Site Evaluation, LSS.

17. **"many conversations,"** email from Joseph Perillo to Robert Kaczorowski, September 9, 2010, FLSA; **"that the only person,"** email from Judge Joseph M. McLaughlin to Robert Kaczorowski, October 15, 2010, FLSA; Professor Joseph Sweeney, interview by the author, September 14, 2010, FLSA; conversation between Dean John Feerick and the author, October 21, 2010.

18. **Quotations** are in Report of the Site Inspection Team, Fordham University School of Law, November 2–5, 1986, 3, box 4, ABA Site Evaluation 1994–95, Self-Study 1986/94, loose, LSS.

19. **Quotations** are in Cammarosano to Reverend Joseph A. O'Hare, December 9, 1987, box 18, folder Accreditation 1974–88, FLS, FU. **The data on tuition** are in Report on Fordham University School of Law, March 6–9, 1994, 57, box 4, folder 1994/1995 Correspondence and Responses to the 1993/1994 Site Evaluation, LSS. Tuition of $10,360 in 1987 and $17,900 in 1993 are approximately $19,600 and $26,600 in present-day dollars; the increase of $7,540 in 1993 is approximately $11,200 in present-day dollars (see CPI, http://www.measuringworth.com/uscompare).

20. **Quotations** are in Cammarosano to Reverend Joseph A. O'Hare, December 9, 1987, box 18, folder Accreditation 1974–88, FLS, FU. The 1987 Overhead costs and calculations in present-day dollars are as follows: $4,017,318 is approximately $7,590,000; $11,478,053 is approximately $21,700,000; $838,588 is approximately $1,580,000 in present-day dollars (see CPI, http://www.measuringworth.com/uscompare).

21. Report on Fordham University School of Law, March 6–9, 1994, 4–5, box 4, folder 1994/1995 Correspondence and Responses to the 1993/1994 Site Evaluation, LSS.

John A. Fitterer, S.J., to Father Finlay, May 19, 1975, box 12, folder ABA 1973–75, Finlay Papers, FU. For Father Fitterer's advice, see *infra* chapter 7n93–95 and accompanying discussion.

22. **Quotations** are in Report on Fordham University School of Law, March 6–9, 1994, 64–65, box 4, folder 1994/1995 Correspondence and Responses to the 93/94 Site Evaluation, LSS. See also Report on Fordham University School of Law, November 2–5, 1986, 2, enclosed in James P. White to Very Reverend Joseph A. O'Hare, S.J., and Dean John D. Feerick, December 10, 1986, box 4, loose, ABA Site Evaluation 1994/95 Self-Study 1986–94, LSS. The $750,000 assessments in 1994 dollars are approximately $1,090,000 in present-day dollars; the $1,000,000 surplus in 1994 is approximately $1,450,000 in present-day dollars; the $4,000,000 loan in 1994 is approximately $5,790,000 in present-day dollars (see CPI, http://www.measuringworth.com/uscompare).

23. James P. White to Reverend Joseph A. O'Hare, S.J., and John D. Feerick, May 10, 1995, 1–2, box 4, folder 1994/1995 Correspondence & Responses to the 93/94 Site Evaluation, LSS. As described in this communication, the Law School and Fordham University were in discussions regarding an 80 percent to 20 percent split on overheard expenses. However, the Law School's 2001 self-study characterized the discussions as involving indirect expenses. Inasmuch as the Law School and the university administration had agreed to limit overhead expenses chargeable to the Law School to 20 percent, it appears that the 2001 self-study is the more accurate description of the 1995 discussions. See Self-Study 2001, Fordham University School of Law, January 10, 2001, 97, FLSA.

24. Report on Fordham University School of Law, February 28–March 3, 2001, May 22, 2002 (follow-up visit), 2, 43, enclosed in John A. Sebert to Very Reverend Joseph A. O'Hare, S.J., and Dean William Michael Treanor, November 22, 2002, FLSA; Self-Study 2001, Fordham University School of Law, January 10, 2001, 9–10, 95–97, FLSA.

25. **Quotations** are in Self-Study 2001, Fordham University School of Law, January 10, 2001, 9, FLSA; Report on Fordham University School of Law, February 28–March 3, 2001, May 22, 2002 (follow-up visit), 45, enclosed in John A. Sebert to Very Reverend Joseph A. O'Hare, S.J., and Dean William Michael Treanor, November 22, 2002, FLSA. The $1,000,000 shifted to the University in 1998, 1999, 2000, and 2001 are approximately $1,320,000, $1,290,000, $1,250,000, and $1,210,000 in present-day dollars (see CPI, http://www.measuringworth.com/uscompare).

26. **Quotations** are in Self-Study 2001, Fordham University School of Law, January 10, 2001, 96–97 and 100, FLSA; Report on Fordham University School of Law, February 28–March 3, 2001, May 22, 2002 (follow-up visit), 43–44, enclosed in John A. Sebert to Very Reverend Joseph A. O'Hare, S.J., and Dean William Michael Treanor, November 22, 2002, FLSA. **The percentages of the budget financed by fund raising** are in Self-Study 2008, Fordham University School of Law, October 6, 2008, 89, FLSA.

27. **"needs and aspirations," "high quality students," "quiet phase,"** Self-Study 2001, Fordham University School of Law, January 10, 2001, 96–97,FLSA; **"a major endowment," "the academic programs," "preeminent law schools,"** John D. Feerick, interview by Robert Reilly, September 20, 1991, Transcript No. 148, Book No. 2, 37, OHP, FLSA. The $10,000,000 endowment in 2001 is approximately $12,100,000 in present-day dollars (see CPI, http://www.measuringworth.com/uscompare).

28. **Quotations** are in John D. Feerick, interview by Robert Reilly, September 20, 1991, Transcript No. 148, Book No. 2, 31–35, OHP, FLSA; see also Interview of Frances M. Blake by Robert Reilly on October 18, 1988, Transcript No. 23, Book 1, 13, OHP, FLSA; Dean's Annual Report to the Alumni 1982–83, 2, 3, box 24, folder Dean's Reports 1971–89, FLS,FU; Dean's Annual Report to the Alumni 1983–84, 1–2, box 24, folder Dean's Reports 1971–89, FLS,FU. The bequest of $2,600,000 and donation of $1,000,000 in 1984 are approximately $5,370,000 and $2,060,000 in present-day dollars (see CPI, http://www.measuringworth.com/uscompare).

29. Dennis McInerney, Esq., interview by Robert Cooper Jr., May 1, 1989, Transcript No. 51, Book 2, 14, OHP, FLSA.

30. **"ultimately the product,"** Self-Study 2001, Fordham University School of Law, January 10, 2001, 99, FLSA; Dean's Annual Report to the Alumni 1983–84, 12, box 24, folder Dean's Reports 1971–89, FLS, FU; Dean's Annual Report to the Alumni 1985–86, 13, ibid.; Dean's Annual Report to the Alumni 1987–88, 13, ibid.; Dean's Annual Report to the Alumni 1992–93, 23, Kissam Law Library; Dean's Annual Report to the Alumni 1994–95, 30, 3, ibid.; Dean's Annual Report to the Alumni 1998–99, 5, 25, ibid.; **$11 million in gifts and pledges,** Dean's Annual Report to the Alumni 2000–2001, 25, ibid. I based the endowment of about $50 million in 2002, Dean Feerick's last year as dean, on the 2008 Self-Study, which reported that the endowment total in 2003 was $56 million. Self-Study 2008, Fordham University School of Law, October 6, 2009, 89, FLSA. Contributions to the Law School in present-day dollars are as follows: $288,000 in 1984 is approximately $595,000 in present-day dollars; $653,000 in 1986 is approximately $1,280,000 in present-day dollars; $1,000,000 in 1988 is approximately $1,810,000 in present-day dollars; $2,248,000 in 1993 is approximately $3,340,000 in present-day dollars; $13,200,000 in 1993 is approximately $19,600,000 in present-day dollars; $4,000,000 in 1995 is approximately $5,630,000 in present-day dollars; $1,100,000 in 1995 is approximately $1,550,000 in present-day dollars; $7,300,000 in 1999 is approximately $9,400,000 in present-day dollars; $33,000,000 in 1998 is approximately $43,400,000 in present-day dollars; $8,000,000 in 1998 is approximately $10,500,000 in present-day dollars; $50,000,000 in 2002 is approximately $59,600,000 in present-day dollars; $11,000,000 in 2002 is approximately $13,100,000 in present-day dollars (see CPI, http://www.measuringworth.com/uscompare).

31. See, for example, Dean's Annual Report to the Alumni 1986–87, 12, box 24, folder Dean's Reports 1971–89, FLS, FU; Dean's Annual Report to the Alumni 1987–88,

13, ibid.; Dean's Annual Report to the Alumni 1988–89, 13, ibid. **Regarding the percentage of the annual budget financed by contributions**, see supra note 26 and accompanying text. **Fordham University's small endowment** is stated in Report on Fordham University School of Law, November 2–5, 1986, 2, enclosed in James P. White to the Very Reverend Joseph A. O'Hare, S.J., and Dean John D. Feerick, December 10, 1986, box 4, loose, ABA Site Evaluation 1994/95 Self-Study 1986/94, LSS.

32. Self-Study 2001, Fordham University School of Law, January 10, 2001, 99–100, FLSA. Total contributions of $27,000,000 in 2000 dollars are approximately $33,600,000 in present-day dollars (see CPI, http://www.measuringworth.com/uscompare).

33. Report of the Site Inspection Team, Fordham University School of Law, November 2–5, 1986, 37, box 4, loose, ABA Site Evaluation 1994–95, Self-Study 1986/94, LSS.

34. Ibid., 5; **"define its mission,"** ibid., 37.

35. Dean Feerick reported a full-time faculty of thirty-eight in his first dean's report. Dean's Annual Report to the Alumni 1981–82, 2, box 24, folder Dean's Reports 1971–89, FLS, FU. Although the Law School reported to the ABA in 1986 a faculty of 39, the ABA discounted the Associate Dean, Robert M. Byrn, and John M. Olin Professor of Law and Jurisprudence, Ernest van den Haag, and numbered it at 37. **Quotations** are in Report on Fordham University School of Law, November 2–5, 1986, 7, enclosed in James P. White to Very Reverend Joseph A. O'Hare, S.J., and Dean John D. Feerick, December 10, 1986, box 4, loose, ABA Site Evaluation 1994/95 Self-Study 1986/94, LSS. **The student-faculty ratio** is in ibid. **The six women** were Mary Daly, Helen Hadjiyannakis, Gail Hollister, Maria Marcus, Georgene Vairo, and Deborah Batts. **The two minorities** were Professors Batts and Frank Chiang.

36. **"a steady stream," "appears to do,"** *"do not advance"* (emphasis added), **"seems to address," "contribute heavily," "activity is healthy," "when done to,"** Report on Fordham University School of Law, November 2–5, 1986, 8, enclosed in James P. White to Very Reverend Joseph A. O'Hare, S.J., and Dean John D. Feerick, December 10, 1986, box 4, loose, ABA Site Evaluation 1994/95 Self-Study 1986/94, loose, LSS; **"faculty publication,"** ibid., 5.

37. **"to favor publication," "the best indication," "enhance a law school's," "to the extent," "appears to have consigned,"** ibid., 9; **"was told,"** email from Hugh Hansen to Robert Kaczorowski, September 18, 2010, FLSA.

38. John D. Calamari and Joseph M. Perillo, *The Law of Contracts* (St. Paul, Minn.: West Publishing, 1970); *Calamari and Perillo on Contracts* (St. Paul, Minn.: West Group, 5th ed., 2003); *Calamari and Perillo on Contracts* (St. Paul, Minn.: Thomson Reuters, 6th ed., 2009). **For Professors Calamari's and Perillo's casebook,** see *Cases and Problems on Contracts* (St. Paul, Minn.: West Publishing, 1978). The fourth and

most recent edition was published in 2004 with Professor Helen H. Bender as the third author. **For the ABA's assessment of Professor Teclaff,** see supra, chapter 7, note 67 and accompanying text.

39. **On summer research grants,** see "Long-Range Plan of the Fordham University School of Law, 1986," 35, box 6, loose, ABA Profiles & Questionnaires 1988–96, LSS; **all quotations** are in Report on Fordham University School of Law, November 2–5, 1986, 9, enclosed in James P. White to Very Reverend Joseph A. O'Hare, S.J., and Dean John D. Feerick, December 10, 1986, box 4, loose, ABA Site Evaluation 1994/95 Self-Study 1986/94, LSS.

40. **"failure of the school," "continued use,"** Report of the Site Inspection Team, Fordham University School of Law, November 2–5, 1986, 38, box 4, loose, ABA Site Evaluation 1994–95, Self-Study 1986/94, LSS; **"time-to-time interests," "uncertain whether,"** ibid., 25; **"tended to allow,"** ibid., 5.

41. **"may not be,"** James P. White to Very Reverend Joseph A. O'Hare, S.J., and Dean John D. Feerick, May 4, 1987, 10, box 4, loose, ABA Site Evaluation 1994–95, Self-Study 1986/94, LSS; **"little more," "school-sponsored,"** ibid., 9. **On simulation courses and appointments of Directors of Legal Writing and Clinical Programs,** see Report of the Site Inspection Team, Fordham University School of Law, November 2–5, 1986, 24.

42. **All quotations** are in Report on Fordham University School of Law, March 6–9, 1994, 1, box 4, folder 1994/1995 Correspondence and Responses to the 93/94 Site Evaluation, LSS.

43. **Quotations** are in Self-Study Fordham University School of Law, Janunary 24, 1994, 4–5, box 4, loose, ABA Site Evaluation 1994/1992 Self-Study 1986/1994, LSS.

44. **Quotations** are in ibid.

45. **Quotations** are in ibid.

46. **Quotations** are in Report on Fordham University School of Law, March 6–9, 1994, 15, box 4, folder 1994/1995 Correspondence and Responses to the 93/94 Site Evaluation, LSS. The 1994 self-study claimed there were fifty-one members of the tenured and tenure-track faculty, but the ABA inspectors concluded from its review of workload statistics that the full-time faculty was forty-nine. See ibid., 17. The backgrounds of the faculty appointments can be found in specific issues of the Dean's Annual Report to the Alumni from 1981 to 1996.

47. **Quotations** are in Report on Fordham University School of Law, March 6–9, 1994, 18–19, box 4, folder 1994/1995 Correspondence and Responses to the 93/94 Site Evaluation, LSS. Whereas Professor Hugh Hansen "was told in no uncertain terms by the senior faculty that [he] should only publish in the Fordham Law Review" when he was hired in the late 1970s, by the mid-1980s, senior faculty no longer insisted that new faculty publish only in Fordham law journals. **The quote** is in email from Professor Hugh Hansen to Robert Kaczorowski, September 18, 2010, FLSA.

48. Fordham University School of Law Self-Study January 24, 1994, 68, Box 4, loose, ABA Site Evaluation 1994/1992 Self-Study 1996–94, LSS. See also, Report on Fordham University School of Law, March 6–9, 1994, 19, box 4, folder 1994/1995 Correspondence and Responses to the 93/94 Site Evaluation, LSS.

49. Report on Fordham University School of Law, March 6–9, 1994, 19, box 4, folder 1994/1995 Correspondence and Responses to the 93/94 Site Evaluation, LSS. **Legal History faculty ranking:** http://tinyurl.com/lh-ranking; **Constitutional Law faculty ranking:** http://tinyurl.com/conlaw-ranking.

50. Report on Fordham University School of Law, February 28–March 3, 2001, May 22, 2002 (follow-up visit), 25–26, enclosed in John A. Sebert to Very Reverend Joseph A. O'Hare, S.J., and Dean William Michael Treanor, November 22, 2002, FLSA; Fordham University School of Law Self-Study 2001, January 10, 2001, 49–50, FLSA. **The study of academic distinction** is recounted in ibid., 2. The study is cited, Brian Leiter, "Measuring the Academic Distinction of Law Faculties," *Journal of Legal Studies* 29 (2000): 451, 482.

51. **Quotations** are in Feerick interview, 40.

52. Report on Fordham University School of Law, November 2–5, 1986, 8, enclosed in James P. White to Very Reverend Joseph A. O'Hare, S.J., and Dean John D. Feerick, December 10, 1986, box 4, ABA Site Evaluation 1994/95 Self-Study 1986/94, loose, LSS.

53. Report on Fordham University School of Law, March 6–9, 1994, 17–18, box 4, folder 1994/1995 Correspondence and Responses to the 93/94 Site Evaluation, LSS.

54. Report on Fordham University School of Law, February 28–March 3, 2001, May 22, 2002 (follow-up visit), 20–23, enclosed in John A. Sebert to Very Reverend Joseph A. O'Hare, S.J., and Dean William Michael Treanor, November 22, 2002,FLSA.

55. Fordham University School of Law Self-Study 2001, January 10, 2001, 43, 46–47, FLSA; Report on Fordham University School of Law, February 28–March 3, 2001, May 22, 2002 (follow-up visit), 21–23, enclosed in John A. Sebert to Very Reverend Joseph A. O'Hare, S.J., and Dean William Michael Treanor, November 22, 2002, FLSA.

56. Report on Fordham University School of Law, February 28–March 3, 2001, May 22, 2002 (follow-up visit), 21, enclosed in John A. Sebert to Very Reverend Joseph A. O'Hare, S.J., and Dean William Michael Treanor, November 22, 2002, FLSA.

57. AALS Report on Fordham University School of Law, March 6–9, 1994, 44, box 4, folder 1994/1995 Correspondence and Responses to the 93/94 Site Evaluation, ABA Site Evaluation 1994/1992 Self-Study 1986–94, LSS; Self-Study Fordham University School of Law, January 24, 1994, 11, box 4, loose, ABA Site Evaluation 1994/1992 Self-Study 1996–94, LSS; Report on Fordham University School of Law February 28–March 3, 2001, May 22, 2002 (follow-up visit), 9–11, FLSA.

58. AALS Report on Fordham University School of Law, March 6–9, 1994, 44, box 4, folder 1994/1995 Correspondence and Responses to the 93/94 Site Evaluation, ABA

Site Evaluation 1994/1992 Self-Study 1986–94, LSS; Self-Study Fordham University School of Law, January 24, 1994, 11, box 4, loose, ABA Site Evaluation 1994/1992 Self-Study 1996–94, LSS.

59. Report on Fordham University School of Law February 28–March 3, 2001, May 22, 2002 (follow-up visit), 9, FLSA; **Securities Arbtitration Clinic,** Dean's Annual Report to the Alumni 1997–98, 8, Law School Library; **"tremendous progress,"** **"enhance the image,"** ibid., 48; **seventeenth in the nation,** Dean's Report to the Alumni, 2001/2002, November 2002, 3, Law School Library.

60. **"is nationally recognized,"** Report on Fordham University School of Law February 28–March 3, 2001, May 22, 2002 (follow-up visit), 48, FLSA; **"skill set required,"** **"have a command,"** **"selected students,"** Self-Study 2001 Fordham University School of Law, January 10, 2001, 23, FLSA; **"entire law school community,"** ibid., 24; **"Law School thus gives,"** ibid., 13. **The courses were:** Professional Responsibility; Corporate and International Practice, and Corporate Counsel. The seminars were: Criminal Advocacy; Public Interest Law; Regulatory, Tax and International Practice; Lawyering for Individuals; Advanced Seminar in Public Interest Law, ibid., 23n22.

61. **Quotations** are in Self-Study 2001 Fordham University School of Law, January 10, 2001, 23, FLSA.

62. **"the quality of,"** **"supervised analytic writing,"** Report on Fordham University School of Law February 28–March 3, 2001, May 22, 2002 (follow-up visit), 8, FLSA; **"impressive in its scale,"** ibid., 48; see also Self-Study 2001 Fordham University School of Law, January 10, 2001, 15, FLSA.

63. Report on Fordham University School of Law February 28–March 3, 2001, May 22, 2002 (follow-up visit), 8, FLSA.

64. Self-Study 2001 Fordham University School of Law, January 10, 2001, 30, FLSA.

65. Ibid., 31–32.

66. Ibid., 32–33.

67. Ibid., 35.

68. **"the foremost international,"** ibid., 36–38; Fordham University School of Law Self-Study January 24, 1994, 23, Box 4, loose, ABA Site Evaluation 1994/1992 Self-Study 1996–94, LSS; see also, ibid., 24–26. **Top twenty programs** reported in Dean's Report to the Alumni, 2001/2002, November 2002, 13, Law School Library.

69. Self-Study 2001 Fordham University School of Law, January 10, 2001, 36–39, FLSA; Report on Fordham University School of Law February 28–March 3, 2001, May 22, 2002 (follow-up visit), 16–17, FLSA.

70. **Quotations** are in Self-Study 2001 Fordham University School of Law, January 10, 2001, 76, FLSA.

71. **"the primary source,"** Self-Study 2001 Fordham University School of Law, January 10, 2001, 77, FLSA. Typical placements include: the Legal Aid Society; Harlem

Legal Services; Gay Men's Health Crisis; Lambda Legal Defense and education Fund; the Center for Reproductive Law and Policy; the NYC Family Court Mediation Project; local, state, and federal prosecutors' offices; the United Nations; NYC's International Human Rights Rescue Committee, ibid., 79.

72. Dean's Report to Reverend Joseph A. O'Hare, S.J., from John D. Feerick, September 1, 1994, 12, box 4, loose, ABA Site Evaluation 1994/1992, Self Study 1986/1994, LSS; Report on Fordham University School of Law, February 28–March 3, 2001, May 22, 2002 (follow-up visit), 11, 34–35, enclosed in John A. Sebert to Very Reverend Joseph A. O'Hare, S.J., and Dean William Michael Treanor, November 22, 2002, FLSA; Dean's Annual Report to the Alumni 1997–98, 6–7, Law School Library.

73. "the curricular," "to improve relative," "rationalize development," "the financial resources," Action of the Accreditation Committee, October/November 2002, 7, attached to John A. Sebert to Very Reverend Joseph A. O'Hare, S.J., and Dean William Michael Treanor, November 22, 2002, FLSA; "one of the best," Feerick interview, 40. The endowment of $57,800,143 in 2002 is approximately $68,900,000 in present-day dollars (see CPI, http://www.measuringworth.com/uscompare).

74. "nearly half the total," Long-Range Plan of the Fordham University School of Law, 1986, 37, box 6, loose, ABA Profiles & Questionnaires 1988–96, LSS; "library facility," Action of the Accreditation Committee, October/November 2002, 8, attached to John A. Sebert to Very Reverend Joseph A. O'Hare, S.J., and Dean William Michael Treanor, November 22, 2002, FLSA.

75. "identified as one," "built carefully," "title count," Long-Range Plan of the Fordham University School of Law, 1986, 39, box 6, loose, ABA Profiles & Questionnaires 1988–96, LSS; see also James P. White to Very Reverend Joseph A. O'Hare, S.J., and Dean John D. Feerick, May 4, 1987, 9, box 4, loose, ABA Site Evaluation 1994–95, Self-Study 1986/94, LSS. The gift of $330,000 in 1981 is approximately $779,000 in present-day dollars (see CPI, http://www.measuringworth.com/uscompare).

76. "full time to law library," "inconsistent with ABA Standard 205," "under which she may," Report of the Site Inspection Team, Fordham University School of Law, November 2–5, 1986, 12, box 4, loose, ABA Site Evaluation 1994–95, Self-Study 1986/94, LSS; "not on the law faculty," ibid., 11. On Dr. Teclaff's resignation, see Dean's Annual Report to the Alumni 1985–86, 6, box 24, folder Dean's Reports 1971–89, FLS, FU.

77. "apparent that," "should be considering steps," Report of the Site Inspection Team, Fordham University School of Law, November 2–5, 1986, 12, box 4, loose, ABA Site Evaluation 1994–95, Self-Study 1986/94, LSS; "tend[ed] to cause," ibid., 39; "little opportunity," "rise considerably," ibid., 13; "still [earned] salaries below," James P. White to Very Reverend Joseph A. O'Hare, S.J., and Dean John D. Feerick, May 4, 1987, 9, box 4, loose, ABA Site Evaluation 1994–95, Self-Study 1986/94, LSS; "increased

significantly," Action of the Accreditation Committee, October/November 2002, 7, attached to John A. Sebert to Very Reverend Joseph A. O'Hare, S.J., and Dean William Michael Treanor, November 22, 2002, FLSA. The 1986 ABA report (15–23) has a concise summary of its overall evaluation of the Law Library in the context of the trends in modern law librarianship and information management and technology.

78. **Quotations** are in Report on Fordham University School of Law, March 6–9, 1994, 63, box 4, folder 1994/1995 Correspondence and Responses to the 93/94 Site Evaluation, LSS; enrollment statistics are in Dean's Report to Reverend Joseph A. O'Hare, S.J., from John D. Feerick, September 1, 1994, 8, box 4, loose, ABA Site Evaluation 1994/1992, Self Study 1986/1994, LSS. The 1986 minority percent is in Report on Fordham University School of Law, November 2–5, 1986, 9, enclosed in James P. White to Very Reverend Joseph A. O'Hare, S.J., and Dean John D. Feerick, December 10, 1986, 8, box 4, loose, ABA Site Evaluation 1994/95 Self-Study 1986/94, LSS.

79. **"first-of-its-kind auction,"** Dean's Annual Report to the Alumni 1998–99, 23, Law School Library; **700 students**, Dean's Annual Report to the Alumni 1994–95, 28, Law School Library; **"for its outstanding growth,"** Dean's Report to Reverend Joseph A. O'Hare, S.J., from John D. Feerick, September 1, 1994, 12, box 4, loose, ABA Site Evaluation 1994/1992, Self Study 1986/1994, LSS; **$175,000** reported in Dean's Annual Report to the Alumni 1995–96, 3, Law School Library. The Student Sponsored Fellowship of $175,000 in 1996 is approximately $239,000 in present-day dollars (see CPI, http://www.measuringworth.com/uscompare); **"significantly increased," "to serve as leaders,"** Dean's Annual Report to the Alumni 1997–98, 6–7, Law School Library; see also, Report on Fordham University School of Law, February 28–March 3, 2001, May 22, 2002 (follow-up visit), 11, 34–35, enclosed in John A. Sebert to Very Reverend Joseph A. O'Hare, S.J., and Dean William Michael Treanor, November 22, 2002, FLSA.

80. Report on Fordham University School of Law, March 6–9, 1994, 54–55, box 4, folder 1994/1995 Correspondence and Responses to the 93/94 Site Evaluation, LSS; Self-Study 2001, Fordham University School of Law, January 10, 2001, 69, FLSA. The other student organizations are: Amsterdam Houses Children's Law Project; American Bar Association/Law Student Division; Amnesty International; Asian/Pacific American Law Students Association; Black Law Students Association; Catholic Law Students Association; Central, Southern and Eastern European Law Association; Clan Na Gael; Death Penalty Defense Project; Family Court Mediation Project; Fordham Federalist Society, Fordham Law Community Service Project; Fordham Law School Democrats; Fordham Law Follies; Fordham Law Women; Fordham Republican Law Students and Alumni Association; Fordham Student Sponsored Fellowship; Gavel and Shield Association; Gay and Lesbian Law Association; Habitat for Humanity; Hellenic Law Students Association (superceded); Housing Advocacy Project; Immigration Advocacy Program; International Law Society; Irish Law Students Association (superceded);

Italian-American Law Students Association; Jewish Law Students Association; Latin American Law Students Association; National Lawyers Guild; Older and Wiser Law Students; Phi Alpha Delta Law Fraternity; Police Misconduct Action Network; Sports Law Society; Society of the Ethical Treatment of Animals (defunct in 2000); Student Loan Repayment Group; Unemployment Action Center; Workfare Action Center; Yearbook; ACCESS (inactive in 2000); THE ADVOCATE.

81. **"the first word," "from the very," "a self-confessed skeptic,"** Thomas H. Martinson, *The Best Law Schools* (Lawrenceville, N.J.: Arco Books, 1993), attached as Appendix D in 1993–94 Dean's Report to Reverend Joseph A. O'Hare, S.J., from John D. Feerick, September 1, 1994, box 4, loose, ABA Site Evaluation 1994/1992, Self-Study 1986/1994, LSS **"students appear quite,"** quoted in Self-Study 2001, Fordham University School of Law, January 10, 2001, 3, FLSA; **"accessible, available," "Fordham is obviously,"** Report on Fordham University School of Law, March 6–9, 1994, 56, box 4, folder 1994/1995 Correspondence and Responses to the 93/94 Site Evaluation, LSS.

82. **"can be proud," "dramatic results,"** Report on Fordham University School of Law, March 6–9, 1994, 53, box 4, folder 1994/1995 Correspondence and Responses to the 93/94 Site Evaluation, LSS; see also 1986 Long-Range Plan of the Fordham University School of Law, 6, box 6, loose, ABA Profiles and Questionnaires 1988–96, LSS; Aid to minority students of $255,800 in 1989 and $777,925 in 1993 are approximately $443,000 and $1,150,000 in present-day dollars, respectively; minority grants and loans of $134,650 in 1989 and $446,520 in 1993 are approximately $233,000 and $663,000 in present-day dollars, respectively; total aid to minority students of $390,450 in 1989 and $1,224,445 in 1993 is approximately $676,000 and $1,820,000 in present-day dollars, respectively (see CPI, http://www.measuringworth.com/uscompare).

83. Report on Fordham University School of Law, February 28–March 3, 2001, May 22, 2002 (follow-up visit), 33–34, enclosed in John A. Sebert to Very Reverend Joseph A. O'Hare, S.J., and Dean William Michael Treanor, November 22, 2002, FLSA. **Report of surveys** is in Self-Study 2001 Fordham University School of Law, January 10, 2001, 60–62, FLSA. See also, ibid., 61.

84. Self-Study 2001 Fordham University School of Law, January 10, 2001, 61, FLSA.

85. Feerick interview, 35–36; Self-Study 2001 Fordham University School of Law, January 10, 2001, 61, FLSA.

86. **All quotations** from Feerick interview, 38–39.

87. "Long-Range Plan of the Fordham University School of Law, 1986," 55, box 6, loose, ABA Profiles & Questionnaires 1988–96, LSS.

88. Ibid., 56, 59.

89. **"substantially better,"** James P. White to Very Reverend Joseph A. O'Hare, S.J., and Dean John D. Feerick, May 4, 1987, 7, box 4, loose, ABA Site Evaluation 1994–95, Self-Study 1986/94, LSS; **all other quotes** are in Report of the Site Inspection

Team, Fordham University School of Law, November 2–5, 1986, 30, box 4, loose, ABA Site Evaluation 1994–95, Self-Study 1986/94, LSS.

90. "Long-Range Plan of the Fordham University School of Law, 1986," 63, box 6, loose, ABA Profiles & Questionnaires 1988–96, LSS.

91. Ibid., 60, 66.

92. Ibid., 67.

93. **"family responsibilities,"** ibid., 69; **"markedly higher salaries,"** ibid., 70. Salaries of $52,000 and $27,000 in 1986 and $65,000 in 1987 are approximately $102,000, $52,900, and $123,000 in present-day dollars, respectively (see CPI, http://www.measuringworth.com/uscompare).

94. Self-Study 2001 Fordham University School of Law, January 10, 2001, 71, FLSA.

95. Ibid., 72.

96. Ibid., 66.

97. **"providing high quality,"** Action of the Accreditation Committee, October/November 2002, 8, attached to John A. Sebert to Very Reverend Joseph A. O'Hare, S.J., and Dean William Michael Treanor, November 22, 2002, FLSA; Dean's Annual Report to Alumni 2000–1, 4–5, 20–21, Law School Library.

98. Dean's Annual Report to Alumni 2000–2001, 4–5, 20–23, Law School Library.

99. **"in all of the top,"** ibid., 7. **On the study of academic distinction and Fordham Law School's rank of twentieth,** see Brian Leiter, "Mearsuring the Academic Distinction of Law Faculties," *Journal of Legal Studies* XXIX (January 2000): 482.

100. Dean's Annual Report to Alumni 2000–1, 11–13, 17, 23, Law School Library.

101. Dean's Annual Report to Alumni, 2001–2, 2, Law School Library.

102. **"single biggest administrative," "nearly every aspect," "Still to be ironed out,"** Report on Fordham University School of Law, February 28–March 3, 2001, May 22, 2002 (follow-up visit), 49, enclosed in John A. Sebert to Very Reverend Joseph A. O'Hare, S.J., and Dean William Michael Treanor, November 22, 2002, FLSA; **"consider carefully,"** Action of the Accreditation Committee, October/November 2002, 9, attached to John A. Sebert to Very Reverend Joseph A. O'Hare, S.J., and Dean William Michael Treanor, November 22, 2002, FLSA.

INDEX